1995-96 Guide to Small Group Resources

Judy Hamlin, PhD.

VICTOR BOOKS
A DIVISION OF SCRIPTURE PRESS PUBLICATIONS INC.
USA CANADA ENGLAND

Editor: Newton Hamlin, Pamela T. Campbell
Cover Design: Scott Rattray
Cover Illustration: Jimmy Holdern

Recommended Dewey Decimal Classification: 016
Suggested Subject Heading: DIRECTORY OF SMALL GROUP MATERIALS

ISBN: 1-56476-496-6

1 2 3 4 5 6 7 8 9 10 Printing / Year 99 98 97 96 95

VICTOR BOOKS
A Division of SP Publications, Inc.
1825 College Avenue
Wheaton, Illinois 60187

To Newt Hamlin,
my editor, friend, and husband:
and to my son, Andrew.
Both are truly gifts from God.

CONTENTS

DEAR USER

In the four years since the first edition of this guide was published with NavPress, the small group market has changed dramatically. Over 300 books, Bible studies, videos, and other works have gone out of print, while over 650 new curricula have entered the market.

Publishers have added features that facilitate group interaction and enhance leaders' abilities. Particularly impressive are some new video materials, including David C. Cook', *PEP Groups for Moms: Building Relationships with Your Children* and other PEP titles, and Word's updated *No! Is The Positive Answer* and *How to Help Your Kids Get Along.* Video packages are an especially nice break for groups that continue to meet for more than two years, or for leaders who "need a break."

This reference tool is designed to make your selection of materials both efficient and effective. So many curricula and small-group products exist that without such a tool it is virtually impossible to tap the wealth of available resources.

Forty-six publishers are represented here, offering more than 1,500 small group books and other materials. As with the first resource guide, my prayer continues to be that this issue will promote knowledge and appreciation of those publishers' past, present, and future efforts. God has been good to provide so many authors and publishers.

I commend Victor Books for accepting the challenge of publishing this work, and for that company's impressive statement in the small group marketplace, offering over 300 books and materials. At a time when most resources are going up in price Victor has made this tool affordable not only for coordinators of groups, libraries, and bookstores, but also for small group leaders.

My special thanks to my friend and editor Pam Campbell, who has endured my schedule and championed the value of this resource.

Finally, as you can see from the new title this guide will now be updated every other year. Tell others about its existence, so it can be used more fully, and so other publishers will add to the wealth of resources. And if you are impressed with the ultimate impact of any material, I encourage you to drop a note to the publisher's marketing department. We all like to get good news.

—Judy Hamlin, Ph.D.
President, Small Group Services

INTRODUCTION

PURPOSE

This directory will help laypeople, coordinators of small groups, ministers of education, bookstore personnel, and librarians become familiar with publishers of small group curricula. They can then use that curricula to the best advantage in building community, studying God's Word, and reaching out to others with the good news of Jesus Christ. The available software stands alone and provides a more interactive source of materials.

SCOPE

Since no directory can possibly cover a whole field and meet everyone's needs, only curricula on the open market are covered, including junior high, senior high, young adult, and adult materials. No attempt was made to gather denominational materials. No attempt was made to censor any information.

You will find books and materials listed from 46 publishers. Of those 46 publishers, 10 have only 1–2 books included. Of the remaining 36, 12 have 3–12 entries, 12 have 14–29 entries, 9 have 59–91 entries, two have 124–137, and the last has 299. Over 1,550 entries are included.

PRICE

Prices are noted for all curricula. When an accompanying leader's guide is indicated, the price is not given. Prices for student material are given, since budgetary considerations sometimes are equally as important as selection.

ACQUISITION OF MATERIALS

Materials were acquired from each publisher, along with catalogs, promotional materials, and current price sheets. In all but approximately 100 cases, the actual resource was used for the evaluation. The other resources are not yet on the market, and were evaluated based on promotional materials and with the assistance of the publishers.

If you publish or distribute curricula or materials you wish to include in an update of this directory, send them to:

Judy Hamlin, President
Small Group Services
5702 Sam Houston Circle
Austin, TX 78731
(512) 795-9967

HOW TO USE THIS REFERENCE TOOL

1. Before examining the curricula, describe the target user group, including:

   a. Age
   b. Stage in life
   c. Stage in spiritual walk
   d. Time available for group meeting
   e. Number of weeks willing to commit
   f. Felt needs and/or areas of interest

2. Decide which index will be most helpful in finding the type of curriculum you are interested in. For example, if you want something that deals with grace, turn to the subject index and look under "Grace." Each entry in the subject index includes the name of the publisher, which may help you narrow your choice of possible resources. Each entry also includes a location number at the end that directs you to the corresponding main entry, which includes detailed information about the resources in which you are interested.

3. Examine the following information in the main entry as you look for a match:

   a. Scope of curriculum as indicated in title
   b. Author's name
   c. Author's previous materials
   d. Series
   e. Publisher
   f. Date of publication. If you are dealing with a certain segment of the population (i.e., baby boomers) more recent, contemporary curricula might be desirable.

4. Scan the basic information:

   a. Number of lessons in a study. To gain a first-time commitment, a 6–8 week study is best.
   b. Time parameters. Time spent in actual group setting.
   c. Number of pages in the study.
   d. Average number of questions.
   e. Audience (see paragraph on page 13).
   f. Format. A workbook format may be more desirable than one requiring an additional notebook, especially in an evangelistic study.
   g. Type of study. For an evangelistic group, a topical study may be preferable to a book.

5. Examine the features.

   a. Thirty-six features are possible for each entry. For a new leader, leader's notes may be important. Many recent curricula include prayer helps.
   b. Personal application (see paragraph on pages 13-14).
   c. Relationship building (see paragraph on page 14).
   d. Preparation time. Refers to student "out of class" time; no attempt is made to evaluate leader preparation time.
   e. Leader's guide availability (separate book). Many books now have leader's notes within the study.
   f. ISBN
   g. Size

6. Familiarize yourself with the subjects listed in the subject index on page 29. This can help trigger thoughts on access points for material.

7. Read the "comment" section to assure a study meets the needs of a given group, or to clarify that the title describes the content.

8. Maintain records on curricula used. This can help later when you want to recommend successful materials. The following reproducible "Curricula Tracking Form" can facilitate this process. Have each leader complete and file the form for reference.

CURRICULA TRACKING FORM

SMALL GROUP PROFILE

Name____________________________ Leader/Host/Hostess

Address of Group Meeting (Host/Hostess)

____

City, State, Zip____________________________

Phone (Host/Hostess) ________________ Home________________Work

Phone (Leader) ________________ Home________________Work

Day of Meeting________________ Time of Meeting________________

Group Type

☐ Married/Young Children ☐ Married/Teens ☐ Men's Group

☐ Single Parent/Young Children ☐ Single/Teens ☐ Senior Adults

☐ Business Persons ☐ Empty Nesters ☐ Recovery Group

☐ Newly Married ☐ Homemakers ☐ Discipleship Group

☐ Other________________

CURRICULUM TITLE: ____________________________

Author________________ Date of Publication ________________

Publisher________________ Series Title ________________

Outside Study Time ________________ In Group Time ________________

Number of Pages__________ Number of Lessons __________ ISBN__________

Average Number of Questions per Lesson ________________ Price________________

Level of Difficulty ☐ Low ☐ Moderate ☐ High

I Would Recommend This Study ☐ Yes ☐ No

Why, or why not?

EXPLANATION OF INFORMATION

This largest section of this guide is the list of main entries, which details the features of each curriculum item. (A sample entry appears below.) These main entries are listed alphabetically by *the author's last name.* Entries in which no author is named are alphabetized by *title* and are listed at the beginning of the main entry section.

In addition, each entry is listed in indexes sorted by title, publisher, series, subject, and book of the Bible. The heads in the first four indexes are alphabetical. The Old and New Testament index is in the order of books in the Bible. The entries in the title index are also in alphabetical order. The entries in the subject index, the Old and New Testament index, the publisher index, and the series index are in order based on the location number.

Author: Brestin, Dee **178**
Series: A Bible Study for Women
Title: *Joy of Women's Friendship, The: Sharing the Gift of Intimacy*
Publisher: Victor Books, 1993 ISBN: 1-56476-052-9

Num. Sess.	Group Time	Num. Pgs.	Avg. Qst.	Price	Audience	Format	Bible Study
9	75–90	104	15	$4.99	New Christian	Workbk	Topical

Features: Intro to Leading a Study, Intro to Study, Prayer Helps, Scrpt Memory Helps, Follow Up, Ldr's Notes
★★★★ Personal Application Preparation Time: Med
★★ Relationship Building Ldr. Guide: No Size: 6.0 x 9.0
Subjects: Friendships, Women's Issues
Comments: This guide explores early relationships, such as those with mothers, siblings, and childhood friends. Models like Miriam and Jochebed, Rachel and Leah, and the young women friends in the Song of Songs provide fascinating insights. As friendships mature, many women experience the joy of ministry partners, mentors, and soul-mates. This guide helps them make these friendships the best they can be. The study is arranged so that participants can study daily assignments.

AUTHOR
Name of author(s) is given. When an entry has more than two authors, an et al. designation is given after the listing of first author. In a few entries, an author's name may not appear exactly as it appears in the book. For cataloging purposes a single form for any given author is used. (Example: Chuck or Charles R. Swindoll will always appear Charles R. Swindoll.)

SERIES
The publisher series title is abbreviated when necessary.

TITLE
The title of the entry is listed. Entries beginning with "A" or "The" are listed according to the first important word. Subtitles are given, space permitting.

PUBLISHER
Name of the publisher, or in some cases the distributor, is listed, followed by the publication date.

NUMBER OF SESSIONS-Num Sess.
The number of sessions in the curriculum is indicated. When entry is for Bible Study Resources or a book, total number of chapters is given.

GROUP TIME
A time range—from minimum to maximum number of minutes, depending on time spent in fellowship and prayer—is provided.

NUMBER OF PAGES—Num Pgs.
The last numbered page in the item is indicated. When blank pages at the end are counted by the publishers, the catalog publisher count is given. When a book exceeds 180 pages the number is rounded off to the closest 10th. On books over 750 pages no number is provided.

AVERAGE NUMBER OF QUESTIONS—Avg Qst.
An average number of questions per chapter is given. When the range is too great to provide a meaningful average number, a "vry" designation has been given. When there are no questions a not applicable "N/A" designation is given.

PRICE
Current (1995) catalog prices are always subject to change.

AUDIENCE
Three categories are possible: beginner, new Christian, and mature Christian. A "beginner" audience is anyone who is open to Christian study (a commitment to Christ is not assumed). "Beginner" does not necessarily imply that mature believers would not enjoy or benefit from the study. A "new Christian" audience has exceeded beginner level and assumed a commitment to Christ. A "mature Christian" audience is asked to commit itself to homework and a longer period of time. At this level, personal application and relationship building are not primary features but byproducts; a designation of mature Christian with a 1 rating in Personal Application and a 1 rating in Relationship Building is common. It does not in any way reflect a poor study. On the contrary, this is probably desirable.

FORMAT
Options include book, workbook, video, and audio. "Book" is designated when the entry is in a book format and no questions are provided, or they're provided at the end of a chapter. The designation also applies to Bible studies in book format but with no space for response to questions. "Workbook" is the designation for studies that provide room for response to questions. "Video" is used when the entry is a video kit. "Audio" means the entry is an audio kit. This category is not used often. Usually audio tapes may be ordered to supplement a printed Bible study. For example, for a Chuck Swindoll entry, audio is indicated as a feature.

BIBLE STUDY
Options are topical, book, character, and no. A topical study treats a subject from a scriptural basis (*Divorce, Recovery*). A book study deals with a book of the Bible (*Letters to Timothy*). A character study deals with a Bible book character (*Nehemiah, Succeeding by Serving*). "No" indicates the study is not a Bible study, but includes Bible study resources (*The Small Group Leaders' Training Course*).

FEATURES
A list of enhancements is mentioned for each entry. Possible features include the following: introduction to leading a study, introduction to the study, objectives, bibliography, prayer helps, Scripture memory, worship helps, study overview, no group questions, prediscussion questions, digging deeper questions, follow-up, summary, Scripture printed leader's notes, drawings, cartoons, photos, handouts, personal study questions, charts, transparency masters, glossary, maps, agenda, index, cross-references, topical index, appendix, cassettes available, exam, word study, publicity ideas, book inc., video study guide, book available. Only the features of the book to be studied are listed. If a curriculum is evaluated and an accompanying leader's guide includes additional features, they are not listed under "Features." If space permits, those features are given in the comments section.

PERSONAL APPLICATION
This rating is based on the inclusion of personal application questions and the presence of certain

features such as introduction, follow-up, summary, personal study questions, drawings, cartoons, photos, prayer helps, and format of the entry. The subject and how it is treated by the author is taken into consideration, as is, in some cases, the amount of Scripture used to support the study.

RELATIONSHIP BUILDING

This rating is based on the inclusion of the following: features like an introduction, agenda, prayer helps, and worship helps; the presence of a warm-up or icebreaker section; and in some cases contemporary treatment when it is important. A low rating in this category does not imply that a group won't build strong relationships while using the given entry. Any leader or group members can build relationships if they choose. A low rating simply means that the printed or taped material does not include much overt help in building relationships. Such a product leaves relationship building up to the leader and members.

PREPARATION TIME

None—no homework required; Low—up to one hour; Med—from one to three hours; High—over three hours.

LEADER'S GUIDE—Ldr. Guide

(apart from the study)

"Yes" indicates a leader's guide is available; "No" indicates not available. Look under "Features" for an indication that leader's notes are included in the study book.

ISBN

The International Standard Book Number (ISBN) assigned to each entry by the Library of Congress is listed; for video kits the number from the video kit is given. The breaks in the ISBN number may not always be correct (Example: 1-56399-001-6 may appear 1-56399-001-6)

SIZE

The size of each entry from left to right then top to bottom is listed. This information is useful for library shelf placement and for group leaders who have a particular size in mind. For example, one might want a study that fits inside a Bible.

SUBJECTS

See page 29 for a complete listing. At least one subject is given for each entry.

COMMENTS

A brief overview of each entry outlines the contents and benefits of that particular study.

LOCATION NUMBER

Entries are numbered consecutively from 1 to 1553. Each entry in the indexes includes a location number so that you can quickly find the resource in the main entry list.

PUBLISHER PHILOSOPHY STATEMENTS

The philosophy statements presented here will help acquaint you with the publishers of small group curriculum.

AGLOW PUBLICATIONS

Aglow Publications is a ministry of Women's Aglow Fellowship, International. Women all over the world are finding support in the pages of Aglow Publications. A dedicated team of writers, editors, and artists create quality materials to equip women for the challenges of today and the opportunities of tomorrow. Through books, Bible studies, evangelistic literature, and the bimonthly Aglow magazine, Aglow Publications has been equipping women for over twenty years.

Women Aglow Fellowship is an international, interdenominational organization of renewed Christian women. In 1967, four women in Seattle, Washington, began to pray for a way Spirit-filled women might fellowship together. From an initial luncheon meeting, Women's Aglow Fellowship has grown into an international organization of over 2,500 fellowships in 103 nations on six contents.

Women's Aglow Fellowship provides support, education, training, and ministry opportunities to help women worldwide discover their true identity in Jesus Christ through the power of the Holy Spirit. We believe that:

- All women and men are created equal in the image of God, each with dignity and value.
- God has a unique purpose for each of us, and equips us for that purpose.
- We can reach our full potential only after finding identity and restoration in Jesus Christ.

AUGSBURG FORTRESS PUBLISHERS

Augsburg Fortress Publishers produce resources to help proclaim God's saving Gospel of justification by grace for Christ's sake through faith alone, according to the apostolic witness in the Holy Scripture, preserving and transmitting the Gospel faithfully to future generations.

- Confess the Triune God, Father, Son, and Holy Spirit.
- Confess Jesus Christ as Lord and Saviour and the Gospel as the power of God for the salvation of all who believe.
- Accept the canonical Scriptures of the Old and New Testaments as the inspired Word of God and the authoritative source and norm of faith and life.

BETHANY HOUSE PUBLISHERS

Bethany House Publishers' most significant curriculum effort is the Building Books Young Adult Curriculum. This series of eight student books and teacher's guides provides young adults with a strongly biblically-oriented lesson that can be used for Bible classes, small group studies, or individual devotional study.

Each book presents thirty-four lessons essential for Christian growth and covers the practical themes of developing Bible study skills, Christian character, commitment, confidence, discipline, relationships, values, and defending the Gospel against cults. These books meet a need for groups looking for a straight biblical study without denominational affiliation.

Bethany also offers curriculum related either to best-selling books or audio tape series from best-selling authors for which a study guide was designed. In both cases the curriculum was designed to accompany and enhance the message of the original product.

CHURCH DEVELOPMENT RESOURCES
Church Development Resources, which provides the Men's Life and women's Coffee Break programs and materials, is a service organization committed to helping churches be vital and growing. Our aim is to provide attractive, up-to-date Bible study materials that are biblically sound, strategically accurate, and culturally relevant. Leadership training, consultation, and support services are also available through a network of regional personnel.

GOSPEL LIGHT PUBLICATIONS/REGAL BOOKS
The mission of Gospel Light is to know Christ and make Him known; to provide His church with effective Bible teaching and learning resources for use in making disciples, empowering them for godly living, equipping them for ministry and the evangelization of the world.

Gospel Light affirms: We believe the Bible to be the divinely inspired and authoritative Word of God, the only infallible rule of faith and practice.

We believe in one God, creator and sustainer of the universe, who eternally exists in three persons: Father, Son, and Holy Spirit.

We believe in the Lord Jesus Christ, who being fully God became fully man, was born of a virgin, lived a sinless life, died on a cross, was raised bodily, is exalted to God's right hand, and will personally come again.

We believe that all have sinned and are guilty before God, and, as a result, all, both individually and corporately, suffer the consequences of the fall and are under condemnation.

We believe that because of His love God sent His Son, Jesus Christ, who inaugurated His kingdom, provided an atonement for sin, conquered the principalities and powers, is reconciling the world to Himself, and will consummate His kingdom in righteousness, power, and glory.

We believe that all those who repent and believe in Christ are delivered from the judgment of God and are born again into life eternal, and are called to be instruments of God's righteousness and reconciliation in human society.

We believe in the Holy Spirit who glorified Jesus Christ, works in all peoples to bring them to faith and obedience, and dwells in believers equipping and empowering them for lives of holiness and fruitful service.

We believe that the Church, the Body of Christ, consists of all believers and exists to fulfill Christ's mission, making disciples of all nations and bringing healing and justice to human society, all to the glory of God.

We believe in the resurrection of the body, the everlasting punishment of unbelievers and the everlasting blessedness of believers in the presence of Christ.

GROUP PUBLISHING, INC.
Group's mission statement: To encourage Christian growth in children, youth, and those who nurture them.

Doctrinal statement: We believe the Bible is the inspired, authoritative Word of God. We believe there is one God, eternally existent in three persons: Father, Son, and Holy Spirit. We believe in the deity of Jesus Christ, in His virgin birth, in His sinless life, in His shed blood, in His bodily resurrection, in His ascension to the right hand of the Father, and in His personal return.

Group's active (experiential) learning philosophy: All Group curricula and teaching resources are based on active learning. Where young people learn by doing—through experiences. With active learning, young people will grow in wisdom, maturity, and faith. Active learning is a discovery process that helps learning stick. It's the opposite of passive learning where a teacher tells students what to think and believe. The active (experiential) learning process involves: *Action*—when students do something. It can be a direct experience, game simulation or role play. *Reflection*—when students talk about how they felt about the experience. Everyone shares. *Interpretation*—when students discover a message from the experience. Here's when teenagers discover the relevancy of the Bible—to their own lives today. *Application*—helps apply the teaching to each young person's everyday life—with a commitment to change. These active learning experiences can be applied to groups of any size—from small to large.

Group is: *Interdenominational*—our products and services are used by people of all Christian denominations. Group is is no way connected with nor subject to any particular denominational body, but rather serves them all. *Innovative*—Group stays on the cutting edge of youth and children's ministry by providing the largest single collection of youth and family ministry resources in the world. *Independent*—Group is a privately held Colorado corporation and is not connected with any other company or organization.

INTERVARSITY PRESS
The goals and purpose of InterVarsity Press are to serve the university, the church, and the world by creating quality products and services that communicate the lordship of Christ over all of life. As the publishing arm of InterVarsity Christian Fellowship, our books are consistent with the IVCF statement of faith.

In all of our publishing we believe that it crucial to communicate effectively to the intended audience through books that exhibit high standards of quality and have integrity. We also want to publish books that develop people in Christlikeness and are responsibly biblical.

IVCF small groups include four basic components: inductive study, prayer and worship, community, and outreach. InterVarsity Press small group books and Bible study guides explore these aspects of small group life from a variety of perspectives.

LAY ACTION MINISTRY PROGRAM, INC.
The Mission of LAMP is to provide the resources necessary to produce healthier and more effective churches. Thus each local church will develop into the ministry and equipping center God intends it to be. Our mission is encapsulated in our operational maxim: *"Assisting Churches to Develop Mobilized Disciples."*

Developing small group ministries, fostering one-to-one discipleship and assisting churches in assessing their own strengths, weaknesses, and needs is integral to our ministry. But we are not "just another publisher." We care about the life and ministry of each pastor, Sunday School teacher, discipler, motivated layman, and those that want to be. Personalized service that focuses heavily on you the person is what we do the best. We realize that you don't just need resources; you need someone with experience in ministry who can relate to your frustrations, joys, hurdles and triumphs. You want someone who is knowledgeable about what will best help you and your church reach your goals and your community for Christ. Someone that will even pray with you about your ministry. The staff of LAMP enjoys serving Christ by serving His Church. That's what makes LAMP unique.

MOODY PRESS
The mission of Moody Press is to educate and edify the Christian and to evangelize the nonChristian by ethically publishing conservative, evangelical Christian literature and other media for all ages, around the world. Moody Press has earned a reputation for publishing books that draw solid solutions from Scripture. Answers that really work in the world. To help you delve more deeply in Scripture on your own. To help you reach your own conclusions about the issues you face. So you can engage your culture, and change it for Christ.

NAVPRESS
We believe that people exist to know and glorify God, and that we are in the world in order to draw the lost to know Christ. We also believe that spiritual growth is primarily a relationship with Christ and with others; that prayer, Scripture study, etc., are means toward the end of knowing Christ; and that believers will draw the lost to Christ to the extent that they incarnate the Gospel. That is, the Word of God needs to become flesh in believer's lives, and those believers need to dwell among the lost.

Small groups, we think, are integral to this growth in incarnating the Gospel. Therefore, NavPress small group materials will support the church in equipping ordinary people in this process. They will help group members, leaders, and coordinators deal with the complex issues of contemporary society in the light of who Christ is. They will serve believers from a range of traditions and a variety of group types. They will foster fun and productive group relationships, be rooted in biblical truth, and be culturally relevant.

NEWLIFE PUBLICATIONS
NewLife Publications is a publishing division of Campus Crusade for Christ. Headquartered in Orlando, Florida, the ministry publishes Campus Crusade Basic Materials; a variety of books, booklets, pamphlets and study guides; and videos and audio cassettes which complement the book line.

The mission of NewLife Publications is to produce, market and distribute up-to-date tools for evangelism and discipleship to help ministering Christians win and disciple others for Christ. NewLife Publications seeks to publish books which are biblically rooted, life related, and culturally relevant.

ROPER PRESS
We at Roper Press are committed to the Word of God. We know its impact on the hearts and lives of

people and, by God's grace, will continue to produce Bible study materials that are true to the Word of God, that honor and glorify the Lord Jesus Christ, and that minister to the needs of believers.

Roper Press is known for its rich heritage and commitment to evangelical Bible study. Our materials are widely used and respected wherever Bible teaching has priority. Whether for Sunday School, Vacation Bible School, Christian school, youth conference, or home Bible study, we are committed to focusing on God's Word as the answer for the twentieth-century man.

We realize that commitment, character, and credentials, while essential, are not sufficient apart from the ministry of the Holy Spirit in individual lives. Author, editor, teacher, and student alike must come before God with an attitude of submissiveness and expectancy, knowing that personal response to the Word of God is absolutely essential. God can and will bring about changes in our lives that will honor and glorify the Lord Jesus Christ. This is our ultimate goal.

SERENDIPITY HOUSE

Serendipity is a philosophy of ministry that includes small groups at the heart and center of the church; it is a movement of many like-minded people who have a passion for seeing the church renewed; it is an institution that trains pastors and church leaders in this philosophy of ministry and to be used by those that have been trained.

Serendipity did not grow up in the academic world but instead came out of the trenches of daily contact with nonchurched and counter-cultural ministry, our concepts for small groups, "which we call strategies," are quite different from any other ministry organization that employs small groups. For instance, we believe that every church must have at least five different models: (1) discipleship groups, (2) covenant groups, (3) support groups, (4) recovery groups, and (5) task/mission groups. A church that is only one of these models is by definition limiting the scope of its small group program.

The preceding strategies are the reasons why we feel it is important that groups follow a progressive, ever-deepening approach to Bible study. In the first seven weeks, when the group should focus on group building, we strongly recommend Bible stories that allow you to share your own personal story through the stories in the Bible. In the second phase, when the need is a spiritual formation, we recommend a deeper form of Bible study often called inductive Bible study, in which the emphasis is upon cognitive material.

Serendipity has a very clear statement of purpose. Our objective is to see an effective small group ministry in every church in the United States by the year 2000. We are intentional about this objective with training for pastors, church leaders, and small group leaders. Our curricula are essential to this training, but are never intended to stand alone.

SERVANT PUBLICATIONS

Since Servant Publications opened its doors in 1972, our aim has never been to build the biggest, the brightest, or the most successful Christian publishing company. Instead, we have tried in a small way to publish books that will introduce men and women to the Gospel, strengthen Christians in their life with God, and help people sort out light from darkness in an age of confusion.

We believe that God is asking us to build bridges among all our brothers and sisters in Christ. So, for most of our history, we've made it our mission to publish for Protestant and Catholic readers. Such a strategy doesn't always make sense in the marketplace, but it works out pretty well in the kingdom of God, where Jesus prays for our unity.

HAROLD SHAW PUBLISHERS

God's people need each other as they live out their faith in this world. Small groups provide ideal settings for outreach and growth as people discover God's Word for themselves and encourage one another to put it into practice. Being in a small group of caring people opens up a whole new dimension of growing that can't take place individually or in large groups.

Shaw Publishers is committed to providing materials that will promote spiritual growth as people study and apply God's Word together. Inductive questions lead to responsible interpretation of Scripture. In the interactive, personal environment of a small group, Scripture, and prayer interact with the Bible in life-changing ways. They challenge seekers and Christians from a diverse range of backgrounds to investigate Scripture and live out its truth.

SHEPHERD MINISTRIES

We believe America's teenagers are facing greater struggles and possess fewer biblical values than at any time in the history of our nation. Therefore our mission is defined to be:

- Creating opportunities to present biblical values and spiritual solutions to both churched and unchurched teenagers through conferences, crusades, and media.
- Arranging for these teenagers to receive spiritual counseling and appropriate resource materials.
- Motivating, mobilizing, and training youth workers and parents to understand and become involved in the rescue, nurture, and discipleship of America's teenagers.

STANDARD PUBLISHING

Our philosophy: To teach God's Word with excitement. To study the whole Bible systematically. To build each lesson upon specific learning objectives. To use a variety of the most effective teaching methods. To involve students actively in the learning process. To ensure that lessons change students' lives. To give special emphasis to such basic Bible doctrines as the creation of the world and man by direct act of God; the deity of Jesus Christ, His virgin birth, His miracles, His atoning death, His bodily resurrection, and His return.

TYNDALE HOUSE PUBLISHERS

Our corporate purpose is to minister to the spiritual needs of people, primarily through literature consistent with biblical principles.

VICTOR BOOKS

Victor Books seeks to equip learners and educators for ministries in and outside the church. Our corporate mission statement reflects their goals: "Called by God and committed to produce excellent, Bible-based, life-related curriculum, books, and Christian education products that will be used to reach and teach people for Christ.

As Bible study moves beyond Sunday School into weekday slots, Victor Books realizes that one product or format will not meet all the needs of those involved in various types of small groups. Therefore, Victor Books is committed to developing a complete line of quality books for use in a variety of settings. Our intention is to provide small group members and their leaders with solid biblical principles, relevancy, and flexibility in methods and topics.

Leader's Guides appear in many of our trade books as tools for discussion. For those who prefer a classroom format of teaching along with ideas for group interaction and response, we recommend our trade books which have separate leader's guides.

More and more church leaders are stressing a strong relationship emphasis in small groups to help meet the isolation and interpersonal needs of people within our large, often impersonal society who are feeling the need to belong to an intimate community. If a small group is looking for something other than the traditional teacher/student format, we recommend GroupBuilder Resources, a line specifically geared to help Baby Boomers (1) build relationships by sharing their lives and experiences, (2) find direction in God's Word, and (3) practice the truths they learn in the context of their small group. This line includes small group studies aimed at special needs as well as resources and training materials for small group leaders.

TruthSeed presents a wide range of topics and biblical books in an inductive discussion format. Designed for small groups or personal study, this series has benefited from extensive field testing and offers assistance to small group leaders with group dynamics, brief commentary notes, and a bibliography for further reading. For groups that want help planning their whole time together, TruthSeed provides related activities in worship, relationship building, prayer, and creative projects.

Victor has particularly focused on meeting the special needs of women through the Jill Briscoe Series, Women's Inductive Series, Tapestry Collection, and Dee Brestin Series. Written by experts in the field of Bible study, these books provide women with encouragement, guidance, and spiritual nourishment.

For children and youth, we provide SonPower High School Small Group Studies, High School and Junior High Electives, as well as Inductive and Discipleship studies.

WORD, INC.

Small groups are a vital part of the growth and vitality of the local church. It is in these non-threatening, fellowship laboratories of learning that most Christians find their greatest source of spiritual growth. Love, acceptance, and security are combined with the power of prayer, Scripture study, and worship to provide a fertile ground for the Holy Spirit's work of sanctification.

Word is committed to providing the most effective resources for these small groups. Our programs offer a wide variety of designs, formats, and approaches. Audio, video, and print are often combined to meet a stated goal. Each program is unique. Target age groups play a vital part in design as well as the gifts and talents of the speaker or writer.

Theologically, Word's small group resource can be trusted to uphold the highest view of spiritual authority and maintain a thoroughly evangelical perspective. Men and women of integrity share their insight from a variety of denominational backgrounds but with the one goal of glorifying Christ and equipping the believer for the work of the kingdom.

ZONDERVAN PUBLISHING HOUSE

Zondervan small group materials are written with one goal in mind, to allow the Spirit of God to use the Word of God to strengthen us in Christ. To accomplish that goal, all of Zondervan's newer study guides have several key features:

- The questions help you discover what the Bible says rather than simply telling you the answers.

This teaches people how to feed themselves from Scripture rather than always relying on the insights of "experts."

- The questions are open ended, encouraging more than one answer. This makes your group discussions more lively and allows people to hear several perspectives.

- The studies are personal, helping you to apply the passage to your everyday situations. We believe this is the ultimate goal of Bible study.
- Most studies focus on only one or two passages. This allows you to see Scripture in its context, avoiding the temptation of prooftexting and the frustration of "Bible hopscotch" (jumping from verse to verse).
- Every study guide contains leader's notes. These provide additional insights into the questions, given tips on group dynamics, and provide helpful background information about the passage. With these notes, almost anyone can lead an effective study.

Whether used by small groups, Sunday School classes, neighborhood Bible studies, or by individuals in their quiet times, all Zondervan Bible studies are designed to allow the Scriptures to renew our minds so that we can be transformed by the Spirit of God.

PUBLISHER ADDRESSES AND PHONE NUMBERS

Abingdon Press
PO Box 801
Nashville, TN 37202
Customer Service 1-800-251-3320
Fax 1-615-749-6577

Aglow Publications
PO Box 1548
Lynnwood, WA 98046-1558
Customer Service 1-800-755-2456
Office 1-206-775-7282
Fax 1-206-778-9615

Augsburg Fortress Publishers
426 South Fifth Street
Box 1209
Minneapolis, MN 55440-1209
Customer Service 1-800-328-4648
Office 1-612-330-3300
Fax 612-330-3215

Baker Book House
PO Box 6287
Grand Rapids, MI 49516-6287
Customer Service 1-800-877-2665
Office 1-616-676-9185
Fax 616-676-9573

Bethany House Publishers
11300 Hampshire Avenue S.
Minneapolis, MN 55438
Customer Service 1-800-328-6109
Office 1-612-829-2500
Fax 1-612-829-2503

Bridge Publishing, Inc.
2500 Hamilton Boulevard
South Plainfield, NJ 07080
Customer Service 1-800-631-5802

Broadman Press
127 Ninth Avenue, North
Nashville, TN 37234
Customer Service 1-800-251-3225
Fax 1-615-251-3870

Chrism (Gospel Publishing House)
Division of General Counsel of the Assemblies of God
1445 Booneville Ave.
Springfield, MO 65802-1894
Office 1-417-831-8000
Customer Service 1-800-641-4310
Order Fax 1-800-328-0294

Christian Literature Crusade
PO Box 1449
Fort Washington, PA 19034
Customer Service 1-800-659-1240
Office 1-215-542-1242

Church Development Resources
2850 Kalamazoo Avenue
Grand Rapids, MI 49560
Customer Service 1-800-333-8300 (U.S.)
Customer Service 1-800-263-4252 (Canada)
Office 1-616-251-3870

Church Growth, Inc.
PO Box 541
Monrovia, CA 91017
Customer Service 1-800-423-4844
Office 1-818-305-1280
Fax 1-818-305-1286

Cokesbury
Box 801
Nashville, TN 37202
Customer Service 1-800-672-1789
Office 1-615-749-6113
Fax 1-800-445-8189

David C. Cook Church Ministries
850 North Grove Avenue
Elgin, IL 60120-2892
Customer Service 1-800-323-7543
Office 1-708-741-2400
Fax 1-708-741-1522

Faith at Work
150 S. Washington Street
Suite 204
Falls Church, VA 22046
Office 1-703-237-3426
Fax 1-703-237-0157

Gospel Films, Inc.
PO Box 455
Muskegon, MI 49443-0455
Customer Service 1-800-253-0413
Office 1-616-773-3361
Fax 1-616-777-1847

Gospel Light Publications
2300 Knoll Drive
Ventura, CA 93003
Customer Service 1-800-446-7735
Office 1-805-644-9721
Fax 1-805-644-4729
Fax 1-805-650-8713

Graded Press
(See The United Methodist Publishing House)

Group Publishing, Inc.
2890 N. Monroe Avenue
Box 481
Loveland, CO 80539-9935
Customer Service 1-800-447-1070
Bookstores 1-800-541-5200
Office 1-303-669-3836
Fax 1-303-669-3269

Harvest House Publishers
1075 Arrowsmith
Eugene, Oregon 97402
Office 1-503-343-0123
Customer Service 1-800-547-8979

Holt, Rinehart, Winston, Inc.
6277 Sea Harbor Drive
Orlando, FL 32821
Customer Service 1-800-782-4479

InterVarsity Press
PO Box 1400
Downers Grove, IL 60515
Customer Service 1-800-843-9487
Office 1-708-964-5700
Fax 1-708-964-1251

Lay Action Ministry Program, Inc.
2000 W. Littleton Blvd.
Littleton, CO 80120
Customer Service 1-800-707-LAMP (5267)
Office 1-303-730-8340

Maranatha Publications, Inc.
PO Box 1799
Gainesville, FL 32602
Customer Service 1-904-375-6000
Fax 1-904-375-6000

Moody Press
820 North LaSalle Drive
Chicago, IL 60610
Customer Service 1-800-621-7105

NavPress Order Department
PO Box 9099
Oxnard, CA 93091
Customer Service 1-800-366-7788

New Hope
(See Woman's Missionary Union — WMU)

NewLife Publications
A Ministry of Campus Crusade For Christ
PO Box 593684
Orlando, FL 32859-3684
Customer Service 1-800-235-7255
Office 1-407-826-2145
Fax 1-407-826-2149

Prentice-Hall, Inc.
200 Old Tappan Road
Old Tappan, NJ 07675
Customer Service 1-800-922-0579

Questar Publishers, Inc.
305 West Adams Street
PO Box 1720
Sisters, OR 97759
1-503-549-1144
Fax 1-503-549-2044

Recovery Publications, Inc.
1201 Knoxville Street
San Diego, CA 92110
Customer Service 1-800-873-8384

Regal Books, Division of Gospel Light
2300 Knoll Drive
Ventura, CA 93003
Customer Service 1-800-446-7735

Roper Press, Inc.
4737-A Gretna
Dallas, TX 75207
Customer Service 1-214-630-4808

Serendipity House, Inc.
PO Box 1012
Littleton, CO 80160
Customer Service 1-800-525-9563

Servant Publications
840 Airport Boulevard
PO Box 8617
Ann Arbor, MI 48107
Customer Service 1-313-761-8505

Harold Shaw Publishers
388 Gundersen Drive
PO Box 567
Wheaton, IL 60189
Customer Service 1-800-742-9782
Office 1-708-665-6700
Fax 1-708-665-6793

Shepherd Ministries
2845 West Airport Freeway, Suite 137
Irving, TX 75062
Customer Service 1-214-570-7599

Standard Publishing
8121 Hamilton Avenue
Cincinnati, OH 45231
Customer Service 1-800-543-1301
Office 1-513-931-4050
Fax 1-513-931-0904

Stephen Ministries
8016 Dale
St. Louis, MO 63117-1449
Customer Service 1-314-645-5511
Fax 1-314-645-9133

Tebunah Ministries
7053 Lindell Blvd.
St. Louis, MO 63130
1-314-725-1450

Tyndale House Publishers
351 Executive Drive
Box 80
Wheaton, IL 60189-0080
Customer Service 1-800-323-9400
Office 1-708-668-8300

The United Methodist Publishing House
201 Eighth Avenue South
P.O. Box 801
Nashville, TN 37202

Victor Books
1825 College Avenue
Wheaton, IL 60187
Customer Service 1-800-323-9409
Office 1-708-668-6000
Fax 1-708-668-3806

Warner Press
1200 East Fifth Street
PO Box 2499
Anderson, IN 46018
Customer Service 1-800-347-6468

The Westminster Press
100 Witherspoon Street
Louisville, KY 40202-1396
Customer Service 1-800-523-1631

WMU (Woman's Missionary Union)
Customer Service or New Hope Customer Service
PO Box 830711
Birmingham, AL 35283-0711
Customer Service 1-800-968-7301
Office 1-205-991-8100
Fax 1-205-991-4990

Word, Inc.
1501 LBJ Freeway, Suite 650
Dallas, TX 75234
Customer Service 1-800-945-3932
Office 1-214-488-9673

Word Ministry Resources
PO Box 2518
Waco, TX 76702-2518
Customer Service 1-800-933-9673, Ext. 2037

Zondervan Publishing House
5300 Patterson Avenue, S.E.
Grand Rapids, MI 49530
Customer Service 1-800-727-3480
Office 1-616-698-6900
Fax 1-616-698-3293

INDEXES

SUBJECT HEADINGS

Abortion
Accountability
Addictions
Aging
Angels
Anger
Apocalyptic
Apologetics
Baptism
Beliefs
Bible Personalities
Bible Study
Caring
Charismatic Interest
Christian Life
Christian Living
Church Life
Commitments
Communication
Conflict
Counseling
Cults
Decision Making
Devotionals
Discipleship
Divorce
Emotions
Eschatology
Ethics
Evangelism
Failure
Faith
False Teachers
Family
Fasting
Forgiveness
Friendships
Fruit of the Spirit
God
God's Promises
Gospels
Grace
Grief
Guilt
Heaven/Hell
Holiness
Holy Spirit
Holy Week
Homosexuality
Hope
Integrity
Jesus: Life/Teaching
Joy
Leader's Guide
Leadership
Loneliness
Love
Marriage
Materialism
Medical Issues
Men's Issues
Mercy
Miracles
Missions
Money
Morals
New Age
New Testament
Obedience
Occult
Old Testament
Parables
Parenting
Pastoral Epistles
Prayer
Prison Epistles
Prophecy
Psychology
Reconciliation
Relationships
Renewal
Repentance
Satan
Self-esteem
Self-help
Senior Adults
Sermon on the Mount
Service

Sexual Issues
Singles' Issues
Small Group Resource
Social Issues
Spiritual Gifts
Spiritual Warfare
Stewardship
Stress
Success
Suffering
Support
Teens: Apologetics
Teens: Bible/Personalities
Teens: Bible Study
Teens: Christian Living
Teens: Communication
Teens: Cults
Teens: Decisions
Teens: Devotionals
Teens: Discipleship
Teens: Drugs/Drinking
Teens: Emotions
Teens: Ethics
Teens: Evangelism
Teens: Family
Teens: Friends
Teens: God
Teens: Heaven/Hell
Teens: Holy Spirit
Teens: Jesus Life
Teens: Junior High
Teens: Leadership
Teens: Materialism
Teens: Media
Teens: Miracles
Teens: Missions
Teens: Music
Teens: New Testament
Teens: Occult
Teens: Old Testament
Teens: Peer Pressure
Teens: Prayer
Teens: Psychology
Teens: Relationships
Teens: Resources
Teens: Self-esteem
Teens: Self-image
Teens: Senior High
Teens: Sexuality
Teens: Spiritual Gift
Teens: Theology
Teens: Values
Teens: Youth Life
Ten Commandments
Theology
Time
Victorious Living
Weight Control
Wholeness
Wisdom
Women's Issues
Work
Worship
Young Marrieds
Youth Life

SUBJECT INDEX

Bible Study

Caring

Charismatic Interest

Christian Life

Christian Living

Church Life

Commitments

Discipleship

Evangelism

Failure

Faith

Friendships

Fruit of the Spirit

God's Promises

Gospels

Grace

Joy

Loneliness

Love

Marriage

Materialism

Medical Issues

Men's Issues

Morals

New Age

New Testament

Obedience

Parenting

Pastoral Epistles

Prayer

Prison Epistles

Prophecy

Psychology

Reconciliation

Relationships

Renewal

Repentance

Satan

Self-esteem

Self-help

Sexual Issues

Singles' Issues

Small Group Resource

Social Issues

Spiritual Gifts

Spiritual Warfare

Stewardship

Stress

Teens: Apologetics

Teens: Bible/Pers.

Teens: Bible Study

Teens: Devotionals

Teens: Discipleship

Teens: Drugs/Drinking

Teens: Emotions

Teens: Ethics

Teens: Evangelism

Teens: Family

Teens: Friends

Teens: God

Teens: Heaven/Hell

Teens: Holy Spirit

Teens: Jesus Life

Teens: Junior High

Teens: Occult

Teens: Old Testament

Teens: Peer Pressure

Teens: Prayer

Teens: Psychology

Teens: Relationships

Teens: Resources

Teens: Self-esteem

Teens: Self-image

Teens: Senior High

Victorious Living

Work

Worship

Young Marrieds

Youth Life

OLD AND NEW TESTAMENT HEADINGS

Genesis
Exodus
Leviticus
Numbers/Deuteronomy
Joshua
Judges
Ruth
1 & 2 Samuel
Kings/Chronicles
Ezra/Nehemiah
Esther
Job
Psalms
Proverbs
Ecclesiastes
Song of Solomon
Major Prophets
Isaiah/Jeremiah
Lamentations
Ezekiel
Daniel
Jonah
Minor Prophets

Matthew
Mark
Luke
John
Acts
Romans
1 Corinthians
2 Corinthians
Galatians
Ephesians
Philippians
Colossians/Philemon
1 & 2 Thessalonians
1 & 2 Timothy/Titus
Hebrews
James
1 & 2 Peter
1, 2, & 3 John/Jude
Revelation

OLD AND NEW TESTAMENT INDEX

Judges

Ruth

1 & 2 Samuel

Kings/Chronicles

Ezra/Nehemiah

Esther

Job

Psalms

Proverbs

Ecclesiastes

Hebrews

James

1 & 2 Peter

1, 2, & 3 John/Jude

Revelation

TITLE INDEX

E

G

H

I

J

M

R

S

U

V

W

PUBLISHER INDEX

$14.95, ***1079***
Giving the Body a Lift by Using Your Spiritual Gift, $14.95, ***1080***
Growing in Faith When Challenged by Change, $14.95, ***1081***
Staying on Fire in a Wet-Blanket World, $14.95, ***1082***
Walking With God When You Have Feet of Clay, $14.95, ***1103***
Making Two Halves a Whole: Studies for Parents in Blended Families, $19.95, ***1109***
Just Me & the Kids: Building Healthy Single-Parent Families, $299.00, ***1225***
Gospel On the Go, $9.95, ***1226***
Home Remedies, $19.95, ***1286***
First Family Tree, $9.95, ***1324***
Stress Fractures, $19.95, ***1381***
Strike the Original Match, $19.95, ***1382***
Strong Family, The, $19.95, ***1383***
Living the Toughest Teachings of Jesus, $14.95, ***1397***
Names of Jesus, The: Group Study Guide, $10.95, ***1402***
Names of Jesus, The, $7.95, ***1403***
Bringing the New Testament to Life, $19.95, ***1409***
Finding God's Way in Your World Today, $14.95, ***1419***
Parenting Alone: Studies for Single Parents, $19.95, ***1434***
Enjoying Life With Little Ones: Studies for Parents of Young Children, $19.95, ***1436***
Bringing the Christian Faith to Life, $19.95, ***1493***
Fanning the Flames of Light, $5.49, ***1509***
Living Life to the Fullest, $5.49, ***1510***
Loving God in a Hostile World, $5.49, ***1511***
Revealing the Heart of a Servant: A Study of Mark, $5.49, ***1512***
Thriving in the Midst of Chaos, $5.49, ***1513***

Faith at Work, Inc.
With Tongues of Fire: Five Women From the Book of Acts, $33.00, ***121***
Faith as Vision and Venture, $3.00, ***162***
Making Peace with the Pieces of My Life, $2.50, ***163***
Great Biblical Themes, $2.50, ***699***
Group Encounters with the Bible, $2.50, ***700***
Journeying in the Spirit, $2.50, ***701***
Lessons in the Life of Faith, $2.50, ***702***

Gospel Films, Inc.
A.D., $99.95, ***423***
Divorce Recovery Workshop: Rebuilding the Castle That Has Come Down, $59.95, ***558***
How Should We Then Live? $99.95, ***1221***
Whatever Happened to the Human Race? $99.95, ***1222***
Religious Apartheid, $49.95, ***1223***
Family Fears: Overcoming the Worries That Threaten Our Families, $79.95, ***1231***
Creative Grandparenting: How to Love and Nurture a New Generation, $39.95, ***1232***
Winning Your Kids Back From the Media, $49.95, ***1239***
One Is a Whole Number, $59.95, ***1288***
Ultimate Issues: Right Answers to Wrong Thinking, $19.95, ***1299***

Gospel Light Publications
Christ B.C., $6.99, ***9***
Christian Basics, $16.99, ***10***
Christian Relationships, $16.99, ***11***
Faith in Action, $16.99, ***18***
Great Old Testament Leaders, $16.99, ***21***
Great Truths From Ephesians, $16.99, ***22***
Great Words From God's Word, $16.99, ***23***
Jesus in the Book of Mark, $16.99, ***34***
Lifestyles of the Not-So-Famous from the Bible, $16.99, ***39***
Parables of Jesus, The, $16.99, ***46***
Power of God, The, $16.99, ***50***
Trial and Testimony of the Early Church, $99.95, ***57***
Life Choices for a Lasting Marriage, $9.99, ***147***
So What's A Christian Anyway, $2.99, ***270***
Yo! I'm A Christian Now What? $2.99, ***271***
Word on Prayer and the Devotional Life, The, $16.99, ***273***
Word on Sex, Drugs & Rock "N" Roll, $16.99, ***274***
Word on the Basics of Christianity, The, $16.99, ***275***
Resolving Conflict in Your Marriage,

Graded Press (See The United Methodist Publishing House)

Group Publishing, Inc.

Alive! God in Intimate Relationship with You, $5.00, ***832***
Changed! Reflecting Your Love for God, $5.00, ***833***
Fulfilled! Enjoying God's Purpose for You, $5.00, ***834***
Jesus! God in You Made Possible, $5.00, ***835***
Powerful! God Enabling You, $5.00, ***836***
Rich! God Meeting Your Deepest Needs, $5.00, ***837***
Leader's Guide: God In You Series, $7.00, ***838***
Exploring the Essentials, $5.00, ***871***
Who's in Control? $5.00, ***872***
How to Build a Small Group Ministry, $20.00, ***952***
How to Lead Small Groups, $6.00, ***953***
Hunger for Healing, A, $129.00, ***994***
Self-Image, $5.00, ***1001***
Exodus, $6.00, ***1028***
1 Samuel, $6.00, ***1029***
Daughters of Eve: Study Guide, $5.00, ***1057***
Learning to Love God, $6.00, ***1070***
Learning to Love Ourselves, $6.00, ***1071***
Learning to Love Others, $6.00, ***1072***
What God Does When Men Pray, $5.00, ***1075***
Hope Has Its Reasons, $79.00, ***1093***
Anger, $5.00, ***1117***
Hebrews, $6.00, ***1134***
Proverbs, $6.00, ***1135***
Colossians & Philemon, $6.00, ***1242***
To Run and Not Grow Tired, $5.00, ***1250***
To Walk and Not Grow Weary, $5.00, ***1251***
Your Work Matters to God, $6.00, ***1274***
Stress, $5.00, ***1276***
Blessing, The: A Study Guide for Small Groups, $6.00, ***1285***
Celebrating Life: Catching the Thieves That Steal Your Joy, $6.00, ***1386***
When the Squeeze Is On: Growing Through Pressure, $5.00, ***1393***
Hiding from Love, $6.00, ***1405***
Loneliness, $5.00, ***1412***
Strategies for a Successful Marriage, $6.00, ***1420***
Friends & Friendship: The Secrets of Drawing Closer, $9.00, ***1445***
Spiritual Disciplines for the Christian Life, $6.00, ***1450***

New Hope

Ideas for Hospital Ministries, $4.95, ***82***
Holy Spirit! Our Redemptive Force, $21.95, ***130***
Uniquely Gifted: Discovering Your Spiritual Gifts, $7.95, ***287***
Father, The! His Redemptive Plan, $21.95, ***325***
My Place In God's Purpose, $6.95, ***366***
Relationship Skills, $5.95, ***453***
Sharing God's Greatest Gift, $4.95, ***455***
Heart's Cry: Principles of Prayer, $6.95, ***456***
Praying Life, The: Living Beyond Your Limits, $7.95, ***457***
Group Building Skills, $5.95, ***634***
Communication Skills, $5.95, ***647***
Time Management, $5.95, ***896***
Ideas for Homebound Ministries, $4.95, ***933***
Meeting Needs Through Support Groups, $5.95, ***935***
Son, The! His Redemptive Sacrifice, $21.95, ***954***
Conflict Management, $5.95, ***1228***
Meeting The World: Ministering Cross-Culturally, $3.95, ***1296***

NewLife Publications

Christian Adventure, The — Step 1, $4.99, ***193***
Christian and Giving, The — Step 8, $4.99, ***194***
Christian and Witnessing, The — Step 7, $4.99, ***195***
Christian and the Bible, The — Step 5, $4.99, ***196***
Christian and Prayer, The — Step 4, $4.99, ***197***
Christian and the Abundant Life, The — Step 2, $4.99, ***198***
Christian and the Holy Spirit, The — Step 3, $4.99, ***199***
Christian and Obedience, The — Step 6, $4.99, ***200***
Exploring the New Testament, $4.99, ***201***
Exploring the Old Testament, $4.99, ***202***
Five Steps of Christian Growth, $2.25, ***203***
Handbook for Christian Maturity, A, $14.99, ***204***
How You Can Be A Fruitful Witness, $1.99, ***205***
How You Can Be Filled with the Holy Spirit, $1.99, ***206***
How You Can Be Sure You Are a Christian,

Elijah: Obedience in a Threatening World, $4.99, ***322***
King David: Trusting God for a Lifetime, $4.99, ***323***
Peter: Fisherman to Follower, $4.99, ***324***
Acts 1–12: God Moves in the Early Church, $4.99, ***330***
James: Faith in Action, $4.99, ***331***
Mark: God in Action, $4.99, ***332***
Paul: Thirteenth Apostle, $4.99, ***333***
Women Who Achieved for God, $4.99, ***334***
Women Who Believed God, $4.99, ***335***
Wholly Single, $4.99, ***498***
Personal Integrity, $4.99, ***517***
Redeeming Time, $4.99, ***518***
Genesis: Walking with God (Revised Edition), $4.99, ***567***
Jonah, Habakkuk & Malachi: Living Responsibly, $4.99, ***568***
Letters to the Thessalonians, $4.99, ***569***
Letters to Timothy: Discipleship in Action, $4.99, ***570***
Men Like Us: Ordinary Men, Extraordinary God, $4.99, ***667***
1 Corinthians: Problems & Solutions in a Growing Church, $4.99, ***713***
Hebrews: Foundations for Faith, $4.99, ***716***
Parables of Jesus, $4.99, ***717***
Relationships, $4.99, ***718***
Revelation: The Lamb Who Is the Lion, $4.99, ***719***
Sermon on the Mount, $4.99, ***720***
You Can Start A Bible Study Group: Making Friends, Changing Lives, $4.99, ***722***
Encouraging Others: Biblical Models for Caring, $4.99, ***792***
Prayer: Discovering What Scripture Says, $4.99, ***799***
Luke: Following Jesus, $4.99, ***818***
Job: Trusting Through Trials, $4.99, ***824***
Philippians: God's Guide to Joy, $4.99, ***825***
Psalms: A Guide to Prayer & Praise, $4.99, ***826***
Galatians, Titus & Philemon, $4.99, ***849***
John: The Living Word, $4.99, ***850***
Managing Money, $4.99, ***856***
Moneywise: Biblical Spending, Saving, Sharing, $4.99, ***858***
One Body, One Spirit, $4.99, ***859***
Tending Creation, $4.99, ***861***
Great Passages of the Bible, $4.99, ***1094***
Great People of the Bible, $4.99, ***1095***
Great Prayers of the Bible, $4.99, ***1096***
Pilgrims in Progress, $8.99, ***1099***
Strengthened to Serve: 2 Corinthians, $4.99, ***1101***
Parenting Alone, $4.99, ***1102***
Discipleship: The Growing Christian's Lifestyle, $4.99, ***1119***
Growing Through Life's Challenges, $4.99, ***1122***
Romans: The Christian Story, $4.99, ***1125***
Senior Saints: Growing Older in God's Family, $4.99, ***1126***
When Servants Suffer: Finding Purpose in Pain, $4.99, ***1136***
Friendship Evangelism, $4.99, ***1147***
Servant Leadership, $4.99, ***1227***
Colossians: Focus on Christ, $4.99, ***1267***
Matthew: People of the Kingdom, $4.99, ***1277***
Spiritual Disciplines, $4.99, ***1278***
Worship: Discovering What Scripture Says, $4.99, ***1279***
Guidance & God's Will, $4.99, ***1301***
Satisfying Work: Christian Living from Nine to Five, $4.99, ***1318***
Fulfilling Work, $4.99, ***1321***
Marriage: Learning from Couples in Scripture, $4.99, ***1322***
Ruth & Daniel: God's People in an Alien Society, $4.99, ***1325***
Who Is Jesus? In His Own Words, $4.99, ***1411***
Holy Ambition, $4.99, ***1414***
Lifestyle Priorities, $4.99, ***1447***
Angels and Other Spiritual Beings, $4.99, ***1540***
Doing Justice, Showing Mercy, $4.99, ***1541***
Prophets, The: God's Truth Tellers, $4.99, ***1542***
Proverbs: Wisdom That Works, $4.99, ***1543***

Shepherd Ministries

Discussion Manual for Student Relationships — Volume 2, $8.95, ***939***
Discussion Manual for Student Relationships — Volume 1, $8.95, ***940***
Discussion Manual for Student

The United Methodist Publishing House

Victor Books

Contagious Christianity: A Study of First Thessalonians, $4.99, ***1349***
Daniel: God's Pattern For The Future, $4.99, ***1350***
David: A Man After God's Own Heart, $4.99, ***1351***
Esther: A Woman for Such a Time as This, $4.99, ***1352***
Faith That Endures In Times Like These, $4.99, ***1353***
Following Christ the Man of God: A Study of John 6–14, $4.99, ***1354***
Galatians: Letter of Liberation, $4.99, ***1355***
Great Stories From Old Testament Lives, $4.99, ***1356***
Growing Pains, $4.99, ***1357***
Growth of An Expanding Mission, The: A Study of Acts 10:1–18:18, $4.99, ***1358***
He Gave Gifts, $4.99, ***1359***
Improving Your Serve: The Art of Unselfish Living, $4.99, ***1360***
Issues and Answers in Jesus' Day, $4.99, ***1361***
Jesus, Our Lord, $4.99, ***1362***
John the Baptizer, $4.99, ***1363***
Joseph: From Pit to Pinnacle, $4.99, ***1364***
Laugh Again: Experience Outrageous Joy, $4.99, ***1365***
Living Above The Level of Mediocrity: A Commitment to Excellence, $4.99, ***1366***
Living on the Ragged Edge: Coming to Terms with Reality, $4.99, ***1367***
Look at the Book, A: A Bible Survey, $4.99, ***1368***
Memorable Scenes From Old Testament Homes, $4.99, ***1369***
Minister Everyone Would Respect, A: A Study of 2 Corinthians 8–13, $4.99, ***1370***
Ministry Anyone Could Trust, A: A Study of 2 Corinthians 1–7, $4.99, ***1371***
Moses: God's Man For a Crisis, $4.99, ***1372***
New Testament Postcards, $3.99, ***1373***
Practical Helps for a Hurting Church: A Study of 1 Corinthians, $4.99, ***1374***
Practical Life of Faith, The: A Study of Hebrews 11–13, $4.99, ***1375***
Preeminent Person of Christ, The: A Study of Hebrews 1–10, $4.99, ***1376***
Simple Faith, $4.99, ***1377***
Steadfast Christianity: A Study of Second Thessalonians, $4.99, ***1378***
Stones of Remembrance, $4.99, ***1379***
Strengthening Your Grip: Essentials in an Aimless World, $4.99, ***1380***
Strong Reproofs for a Scandalous Church: A Study of 1 Corinthians, $4.99, ***1384***
What It Takes To Win, $4.99, ***1385***
Maximum Marriage, $159.99, ***1400***
How to Help Your Kids Get Along, $59.99, ***1408***

Zondervan

Behold Your God: Studies on the Attributes of God, $5.99, ***76***
Loving & Obeying God: Studies on 1 Samuel, $6.99, 77
Our Perfect Example: Following God's Ways, $4.99, ***133***
Our Wise Counselor: Seeking God's Guidance, $4.99, ***134***
Beloved Unbeliever: Loving Your Husband into the Faith, $8.99, ***137***
Growing Godly: Studies on Bible Women, $4.99, ***141***
Mourning: The Prelude to Laughter, $4.99, ***265***
Heart Trouble: Studies on Christian Character, $5.99, ***277***
Mastering Motherhood, $6.99, ***278***
Building Your Church: Using Your Gifts, Time and Resources, $4.99, ***426***
Discovering the Church: Becoming Part of God's New Community, $4.99, ***427***
"Follow Me!" Walking with Jesus in Everyday Life, $4.99, ***428***
Friendship with God: Developing Intimacy with God, $4.99, ***429***
Impacting Your World: Becoming a Person of Influence, $4.99, ***430***
Incomparable Jesus, The: Experiencing the Power of Christ, $4.99, ***431***
Leader's Guide 1: Friendship With God, The Incomparable Jesus, $15.99, ***432***
Leader's Guide 2: Discovering the Church, Building Your Church, $19.99, ***433***
Faithfulness: The Foundation of True Friendship, $4.99, ***534***

SERIES INDEX

MAIN ENTRIES BY AUTHOR

Author: 1
Series: Discover Life
Title: *Be a Winner*
Publisher: Church Development Resources, 1986

Num. Sess.	Group Time	Num. Pgs.	Avg. Qst.	Price	Audience	Format	Bible Study
7	45-60	16	6	$2.70	Beginner	Workbk	Topical

Features: Intro to Study, Follow Up, Full Scrpt Printed
★★★ Personal Application   Preparation Time: None
★★ Relationship Building   Ldr. Guide: Yes   Size: 8.50 x 11.0
Subjects: Emotions, Evangelism, Men's Issues, Self-esteem
Comments: This seven-week study explores winning over worry, discouragement, anger, guilt, low self-esteem, busyness, and temptation. Old and New Testament Scriptures are included. Accompanying materials are designed for non-Christians and the non-churched, and homework is not required. Lessons are distributed prior to each study. Bible passages are printed, eliminating student embarrassment over inability to find passages or bringing a Bible to a public place.

Author: 2
Series: Studies in Christian Living
Title: *Beginning a New Life—Book 2*
Publisher: NavPress, 1964   ISBN: 0-89109-078-9

Num. Sess.	Group Time	Num. Pgs.	Avg. Qst.	Price	Audience	Format	Bible Study
4	45-60	27	Vary	$3.00	New Christian	Workbk	Topical

Features: Intro to Study
★★ Personal Application   Preparation Time: Low
★★ Relationship Building   Ldr. Guide: No   Size: 5.50 x 8.50
Subjects: Discipleship, Teens: Devotionals, Teens: Discipleship, Teens: Jesus Life
Comments: This study for new believers (age 15 and up) is used by many churches for basic discipleship follow up. Book 2 includes these topics: "New Life," "The Lordship of Christ," "The Devotional Life," and "Witnessing for Christ." This series helps new Christians establish personal Bible study and practice the essentials of Christian life. Could be used as a small group study aid for new believers.

Author: 3
Series:
Title: *Bible Visual, The: Resource Book*
Publisher: Regal Books, 1989   ISBN: 0-83071-368-9

Num. Sess.	Group Time	Num. Pgs.	Avg. Qst.	Price	Audience	Format	Bible Study
15	—	290	N/A	$19.99		Book	No

Features: Intro to Study, Drawings, Charts, Maps
Personal Application   Preparation Time:
Relationship Building   Ldr. Guide: Size: 8.50 x 11.25
Subjects: Bible Study, Small Group Resource
Comments: This book provides a wide variety of reproducible resources for individual or group Bible study. Visual aids include: maps, to place Scriptural events; charts and graphs, to explain Bible facts; outlines to simplify; key verses; timelines; and perforated pages for easy removal for copying. These resources make it easier to study or teach God's Word at any level.

Author: 4
Series:
Title: *Caring Evangelism: Participants Manual*
Publisher: Stephen Ministries, 1992

Num. Sess.	Group Time	Num. Pgs.	Avg. Qst.	Price	Audience	Format	Bible Study
16	60-75	172	Vary	$9.95	New Christian	Workbk	Topical

Features: Intro to Study, Objectives, Prayer Helps
★★★★ Personal Application   Preparation Time: Low
★★★★ Relationship Building   Ldr. Guide: Yes   Size: 8.50 x 11.0
Subjects: Evangelism
Comments: For each of 16 modules, this book furnishes complete outlines of lectures, discussions, and exercises with room for personal notes. "Focus Notes" provide examples of what to say and what not to say; "Closing" has participants select one activity to pursue during the week. Readings at the end of the manual provide practical ideas and daily resources such as responding to difficult questions, biblical stories and promises, ways of talking about God's love and prayer.

Author: 5
Series:
Title: *Caring Evangelism: Administrative Handbook*
Publisher: Stephen Ministries, 1992

Num. Sess.	Group Time	Num. Pgs.	Avg. Qst.	Price	Audience	Format	Bible Study
	—	79	N/A	$5.95		Book	Topical

Features: Intro to Study, Study Overview
Personal Application   Preparation Time:
Relationship Building   Ldr. Guide: Size: 8.50 x 11.0
Subjects: Evangelism
Comments: This handbook addresses major challenges leaders face as they organize and publicize "Caring Evangelism" to their congregations. It includes details of setting up the course, explaining scheduling options, and a general introduction to the material. Also included are ready-to-use publicity resources that overcome fears and hesitance to get involved, how to conduct the course, get feedback from participants, and teaching tips, as well as information on vision casting.

Author: 6
Series:
Title: *Catholic Serendipity New Testament for Groups*
Publisher: Serendipity House, 1990   ISBN: 1-88341-918-2

Num. Sess.	Group Time	Num. Pgs.	Avg. Qst.	Price	Audience	Format	Bible Study
68	60-90	510	Vary	$7.95	Beginner	Book	Book

Features: Intro to Leading a Study, Intro to Study, Digging Deeper Quest, Full Scrpt Printed, Charts, Index
★★ Personal Application   Preparation Time: None
★★ Relationship Building   Ldr. Guide: No   Size: 6.50 x 9.25
Subjects: New Testament
Comments: This book includes 5,000 "flow" questions in margins beside biblical text; 48 ready-made studies on favorite Bible stories; 20 complete Bible study courses on popular themes; special introductions for each book in the New Testament; and a subject index of important words, people, and places. There are three levels of discussion questions, icebreakers, digging deeper, and reflections.

Author: 7
Series: Video Curriculum Resource
Title: *Champions*
Publisher: Word, 1988 ISBN: 8-01960-079-5

Num. Sess.	Group Time	Num. Pgs.	Avg. Qst.	Price	Audience	Format	Bible Study
4	60-90	N/A	Vary	$159.99	Mature Christian	Video	Topical

Features: Intro to Study
★★★★ Personal Application Preparation Time: None
★★★ Relationship Building Ldr. Guide: Yes Size: 10.25 x 13.0
Subjects: Teens: Emotions, Teens: Friends, Teens: Peer Pressure
Comments: This four-session video study helps youth deal with peer pressure, excellence, disappointment, and relationships. Professional and Olympic athletes host 4 30″ sessions: former Cardinals' quarterback Neil Loma; Los Angeles Dodger Orel Hershiser; three-time Grand Prix motorcyle racing champion Freddie Spencer; and Olympic women's basketball gold medalist Cheryl Miller. Each segment is enhanced by Christian music.

Author: 8
Series: Design for Discipleship
Title: *Character of the Christian, The—Book 4*
Publisher: NavPress, 1973 ISBN: 0-89109-039-8

Num. Sess.	Group Time	Num. Pgs.	Avg. Qst.	Price	Audience	Format	Bible Study
5	60-75	48	20	$3.00	New Christian	Workbk	Topical

Features: Intro to Study, Summary, Charts
★★ Personal Application Preparation Time: Med
★★ Relationship Building Ldr. Guide: Yes Size: 5.50 x 8.50
Subjects: Christian Living, Discipleship, Integrity, Teens: Discipleship
Comments: This is book 4 in a comprehensive study on basic biblical principles and standards for following Christ. Since God's desire for believers involves inner qualities as well as outward behavior, it is imperative to learn what Scripture says about the Christian character. The five areas to be studied are: "The Call to Fruitful Living," "Genuine Love in Action," "Purity of Life," "Integrity in Living," and "Character in Action."

Author: 9
Series:
Title: *Christ B.C.*
Publisher: Gospel Light Publications, 1990 ISBN: 0-83071-448-0

Num. Sess.	Group Time	Num. Pgs.	Avg. Qst.	Price	Audience	Format	Bible Study
13	60-75	154	N/A	$6.99	Beginner	Book	Charctr

Features: Intro to Leading a Study, Intro to Study, Objectives, Prayer Helps, Study Overview, Follow Up, Ldr's Notes, Handouts
★★★ Personal Application Preparation Time: Low
★★★ Relationship Building Ldr. Guide: Yes Size: 5.0 x 8.0
Subjects: Jesus: Life/Teaching, Old Testament, Prophecy
Comments: This teacher's manual helps participants explore and understand Christ as revealed in the Old Testament. The study describes Old Testament events, personalities, symbols, and prophecies that teach about Jesus. Included are Bible commentary notes, Bible background, life application, session plans, handouts, and leader's lesson guide sheets. A daily devotional is available.

Author: 10
Series: Jr. High Builders
Title: *Christian Basics*
Publisher: Gospel Light Publications, 1987

Num. Sess.	Group Time	Num. Pgs.	Avg. Qst.	Price	Audience	Format	Bible Study
13	30-60	190	Vary	$16.99	Beginner	Workbk	Topical

Features: Intro to Leading a Study, Intro to Study, Objectives, Prayer Helps, Scripture Memory Helps, Follow Up, Drawings, Cartoons, Handouts, Publicity Ideas
★★★★ Personal Application Preparation Time: Low
★★★★ Relationship Building Ldr. Guide: No Size: 11.0 x 8.50
Subjects: Teens: Bible Study, Teens: Christian Living, Teens: Discipleship, Teens: Friends, Teens: Junior High, Teens: Prayer
Comments: This 13-week study covers the basics of Christianity. It begins with a definition of "belief," then examines the benefits of being a Christian, the cost of discipleship, Bible study, prayer, the Church, the Christlike lifestyle, love, friendship, and the world's influences.

Author: 11
Series: Jr. High Builders
Title: *Christian Relationships*
Publisher: Gospel Light Publications, 1988 ISBN: 0-83071-701-3

Num. Sess.	Group Time	Num. Pgs.	Avg. Qst.	Price	Audience	Format	Bible Study
13	30-60	180	Vary	$16.99	Beginner	Workbk	Topical

Features: Intro to Leading a Study, Intro to Study, Objectives, Prayer Helps, Scrpt Memory Helps, Follow Up, Drawings, Cartoons, Handouts, Publicity Ideas
★★★★ Personal Application Preparation Time: Low
★★★★ Relationship Building Ldr. Guide: No Size: 11.0 x 8.50
Subjects: Teens: Junior High, Teens: Relationships
Comments: This 13-week study contains everything necessary for teaching junior highers about Christians' relationships with God, themselves, and others. The resource contains session plans for the leader, reproducible worksheets, and take-home sheets. Includes lecture-oriented Bible study outlines, action games, and clip art illustrations.

Author: 12
Series: Discover Life
Title: *Climbing Higher*
Publisher: Church Development Resources, 1989

Num. Sess.	Group Time	Num. Pgs.	Avg. Qst.	Price	Audience	Format	Bible Study
7	45-60	16	6	$2.70	Beginner	Workbk	Topical

Features: Intro to Study, Follow Up, Full Scrpt Printed
★★★ Personal Application Preparation Time: None
★★ Relationship Building Ldr. Guide: Yes Size: 8.50 x 11.0
Subjects: Christian Living, Commitments, Evangelism, Faith, Obedience, Prayer
Comments: This study challenges participants to climb higher spiritually, using the disciplines of prayer, Scripture reading, commitment, faith, obedience, witnessing, and love. Explores how discipline molds a walk of faith. Homework is not required. Lessons are distributed prior to each study. Bible passages are printed, eliminating embarrassment over trying to find a passage or bringing a Bible to a public place.

Author: 13
Series:
Title: *Coffee Break Evangelism Manual*
Publisher: Church Development Resources, 1986

Num. Sess.	Group Time	Num. Pgs.	Avg. Qst.	Price	Audience	Format	Bible Study
7	—	66	N/A	$5.55		Book	No

Features:
Personal Application — Preparation Time:
Relationship Building — Ldr. Guide: — Size: 5.50 x 8.50
Subjects: Evangelism, Small Group Resource
Comments: This book shows how to organize an evangelistic Bible study in a church that will reach neighbors and help new Christians grow and mature. Specifically it shows how to start "Coffee Break Evangelism" groups, providing the program's principles, methods of study, and material and leadership training. It also promotes a complementary children's outreach program called "Story Hour." Also available in Korean.

Author: 14
Series: Cross Signs
Title: *Cross Signs Series Planning Guide*
Publisher: Augsburg Fortress Publishers, 1992

Num. Sess.	Group Time	Num. Pgs.	Avg. Qst.	Price	Audience	Format	Bible Study
	—	24	N/A	$5.50	New Christian	Book	Topical

Features: Intro to Study
Personal Application — Preparation Time:
Relationship Building — Ldr. Guide: — Size: 11.0 x 8.50
Subjects:
Comments: This guide offers an overview and step-by-step planning for implementing the Cross Signs Series in small groups. It includes logos, clip art, and bulletin inserts.

Author: 15
Series: Discover Life
Title: *David: The Making of a Man of God*
Publisher: Church Development Resources, 1988

Num. Sess.	Group Time	Num. Pgs.	Avg. Qst.	Price	Audience	Format	Bible Study
7	45-60	16	6	$2.70	Beginner	Workbk	Charctr

Features: Intro to Study, Follow Up, Full Scrpt Printed
★★★ Personal Application — Preparation Time: None
★★ Relationship Building — Ldr. Guide: Yes — Size: 8.50 x 11.0
Subjects: Bible Personalities, Faith, Psalms, Success, 1 & 2 Samuel
Comments: This study on David is from 1 and 2 Samuel and Psalms. It makes it easy to identify with David's challenges, temptations, and successes, and see how crucial faith is to life. Accompanying materials are designed for non-Christians and the non-churched, and homework is not required. Lessons are distributed prior to each study. Bible passages are printed, thus eliminating embarrassment over students being unable to find a passage or bringing a Bible to a public place.

Author: 16
Series: Studies in Christian Living
Title: *Developing Your Faith—Book 5*
Publisher: NavPress, 1964 — ISBN: 0-89109-081-9

Num. Sess.	Group Time	Num. Pgs.	Avg. Qst.	Price	Audience	Format	Bible Study
5	45-60	30	Vary	$3.00	New Christian	Workbk	Topical

Features: Intro to Study
★★ Personal Application — Preparation Time: Low
★★ Relationship Building — Ldr. Guide: No — Size: 5.50 x 8.50
Subjects: Discipleship, God, Holy Spirit, Teens: Discipleship
Comments: This five-lesson study for new believers ages fifteen and older is used by many churches for basic discipleship follow up. Book five investigates these topics: "Who Is God?" "The Holy Spirit," "Know Your Enemy," "Our Conflict with Sin," and "The Return of Christ." This series of six studies helps new Christians establish personal Bible study and learn and practice the essentials of Christian life. This series could be used as a small-group study aid for new believers.

Author: 17
Series: Discover Life
Title: *Encounters with Christ*
Publisher: Church Development Resources, 1986

Num. Sess.	Group Time	Num. Pgs.	Avg. Qst.	Price	Audience	Format	Bible Study
7	45-60	16	6	$2.70	Beginner	Workbk	Charctr

Features: Intro to Study, Follow Up, Full Scrpt Printed
★★★ Personal Application — Preparation Time: None
★★ Relationship Building — Ldr. Guide: Yes — Size: 8.50 x 11.0
Subjects: Evangelism, Grace, Jesus: Life/Teaching, Men's Issues
Comments: This study focuses on seven scenarios from Jesus' life, in which He encounters sinners, hypocrites, skeptics, and common, rich, and fearful people. It shows that God's forgiving grace is available to all through Christ. Accompanying materials are designed for non-Christians and the non-churched. Lessons are distributed prior to each study. Bible passages are printed in the study, thus eliminating embarrassment over students' inability to find a passage or bring a Bible.

Author: 18
Series: Jr. High Builders
Title: *Faith in Action*
Publisher: Gospel Light Publications, 1989

Num. Sess.	Group Time	Num. Pgs.	Avg. Qst.	Price	Audience	Format	Bible Study
13	30-60	190	Vary	$16.99	Beginner	Workbk	Topical

Features: Intro to Leading a Study, Intro to Study, Objectives, Prayer Helps, Scrpt Memory Helps, Follow Up, Drawings, Cartoons, Handouts, Publicity Ideas
★★★★ Personal Application — Preparation Time: Low
★★★★ Relationship Building — Ldr. Guide: No — Size: 11.0 x 8.50
Subjects: Teens: Christian Liv, Teens: Junior High
Comments: This 13-week study contains everything necessary for teaching junior highers practical ways to demonstrate their faith, and about character qualities to set as their goals. The resource contains session plans for the leader, reproducible worksheets, and take-home sheets. Action games and clip art illustrations enhance the study.

Author: 19
Series: Design for Discipleship
Title: *Foundations for Faith—Book 5*
Publisher: NavPress, 1973 ISBN: 0-89109-040-1

Num. Sess.	Group Time	Num. Pgs.	Avg. Qst.	Price	Audience	Format	Bible Study
5	60-75	45	21	$3.00	New Christian	Workbk	Topical

Features: Intro to Study, Summary
★★ Personal Application Preparation Time: Med
★★ Relationship Building Ldr. Guide: Yes Size: 5.50 x 8.50
Subjects: Discipleship, Faith, God, Holy Spirit, Teens: Discipleship
Comments: This is book five in a comprehensive study series on basic biblical principles and standards for following Christ. Five foundations covered include: "Who Is God?" "The Authority of God's Word," "The Holy Spirit," "Spiritual Warfare," and "The Return of Christ." As participants better understand biblical truth, they will begin seeing more things from God's point of view.

Author: 20
Series:
Title: *Good Things Come in Small Groups*
Publisher: InterVarsity, 1985 ISBN: 0-87784-917-X

Num. Sess.	Group Time	Num. Pgs.	Avg. Qst.	Price	Audience	Format	Bible Study
17	—	190	N/A	$9.99		Book	No

Features: Bibliography, Index
Personal Application Preparation Time:
Relationship Building Ldr. Guide: Size: 5.50 x 8.25
Subjects: Small Group Resource
Comments: This book, on the dynamics of good group life, was actually written by a small group. It is a complete guidebook of the "ins and outs," the "ups and downs" of the life of a successful group. It discusses every facet from how to start a group to creating a churchwide strategy for growth. It explores nurture, worship, community, mission, leadership, group dynamics, and the stages of change in groups. The book includes many ideas, tips, and group activities.

Author: 21
Series: Jr. High Builders
Title: *Great Old Testament Leaders*
Publisher: Gospel Light Publications, 1989

Num. Sess.	Group Time	Num. Pgs.	Avg. Qst.	Price	Audience	Format	Bible Study
13	30-60	190	Vary	$16.99	Beginner	Workbk	Topical

Features: Intro to Leading a Study, Intro to Study, Objectives, Prayer Helps, Scrpt Memory Helps, Follow Up, Drawings, Cartoons, Handouts, Publicity Ideas
★★★★ Personal Application Preparation Time: Low
★★★★ Relationship Building Ldr. Guide: No Size: 11.0 x 8.50
Subjects: Teens: Bible/Pers., Teens: Junior High, Teens: Old Testament
Comments: This 13-week study contains everything necessary for honing junior highers' leadership abilities, and teaching a sensitivity to God as displayed by Abraham, Moses, David, and Daniel. The resource contains session plans for the leader, reproducible classroom worksheets, and take-home sheets.

Author: 22
Series: Jr. High Builders
Title: *Great Truths From Ephesians*
Publisher: Gospel Light Publications, 1989

Num. Sess.	Group Time	Num. Pgs.	Avg. Qst.	Price	Audience	Format	Bible Study
13	30-60	190	Vary	$16.99	Beginner	Workbk	Topical

Features: Intro to Leading a Study, Intro to Study, Objectives, Prayer Helps, Scrpt Memory Helps, Follow Up, Drawings, Cartoons, Handouts, Publicity Ideas
★★★★ Personal Application Preparation Time: Low
★★★★ Relationship Building Ldr. Guide: No Size: 1.0 x 8.50
Subjects: Teens: Discipleship, Teens: Junior High, Teens: New Testament
Comments: This 13-week study covers important truths from Ephesians. Topics include spiritual blessings, wisdom, inner strength, unity, maturity, armor, and more. The resource contains session plans for the leader, reproducible worksheets, and take-home sheets.

Author: 23
Series: Jr. High Builders
Title: *Great Words From God's Word*
Publisher: Gospel Light Publications, 1989

Num. Sess.	Group Time	Num. Pgs.	Avg. Qst.	Price	Audience	Format	Bible Study
13	30-60	190	Vary	$16.99	Beginner	Workbk	Topical

Features: Intro to Leading a Study, Intro to Study, Objectives, Prayer Helps, Scrpt Memory Helps, Follow Up, Drawings, Cartoons, Handouts, Publicity Ideas
★★★★ Personal Application Preparation Time: Low
★★★★ Relationship Building Ldr. Guide: No Size: 11.0 x 8.50
Subjects: Teens: Discipleship, Teens: Junior High, Teens: Theology
Comments: This 13-week study contains everything necessary for teaching junior highers theological concepts: "God," "Grace," "Peace," "Love," "Sin," "Faith," "Worship," "Stewardship," and more. The resource contains session plans for the leader, reproducible classroom worksheets, and take-home sheets.

Author: 24
Series:
Title: *Group's Best Junior High Meetings—Volume 2*
Publisher: Group Publishing, 1989 ISBN: 1-55945-009-6

Num. Sess.	Group Time	Num. Pgs.	Avg. Qst.	Price	Audience	Format	Bible Study
35	60-90	250	Vary	$16.99	New Christian	Book	Topical

Features: Intro to Leading a Study, Objectives, Prayer Helps, Ldr's Notes, Handouts, Charts
★★★★ Personal Application Preparation Time: None
★★★★ Relationship Building Ldr. Guide: No Size: 8.25 x 11.0
Subjects: Teens: Family, Teens: Junior High, Teens: Peer Pressure Teens: Relationships
Comments: This, the second volume of a two-part series, provides 35 complete meeting plans that focus on topics important to junior high students, such as coping with peer pressure, getting along better with parents, making room for God, building self-confidence, and exploring tough issues. Easy-to-use plans and guidelines are provided.

Author: 25
Series:
Title: *Group's Best Junior High Meetings—Volume 1*
Publisher: Group Publishing, 1987 ISBN: 0-93152-958-1

Num. Sess.	Group Time	Num. Pgs.	Avg. Qst.	Price	Audience	Format	Bible Study
58	60-90	320	Vary	$19.99	New Christian	Book	Topical

Features: Intro to Leading a Study, Objectives, Prayer Helps, Ldr's Notes, Drawings, Handouts
★★★★ Personal Application Preparation Time: None
★★★★ Relationship Building Ldr. Guide: No Size: 8.25 x 11.0
Subjects: Teens: Christian Living, Teens: Decisions, Teens: Ethics, Teens: Family, Teens: Friends, Teens: Junior High
Comments: Volume 1 of a two-part series provides 58 ready-to-use meeting schedules to help junior high students with self-image, friendship, family, faith, values, decisions, life issues, service, and seasonal and special events. Easy-to-use plans and guidelines are provided, as well as activities, games, and Bible studies.

Author: 26
Series: Studies in Christian Living
Title: *Growing as a Christian—Book 4*
Publisher: NavPress, 1964 ISBN: 0-89109-080-0

Num. Sess.	Group Time	Num. Pgs.	Avg. Qst.	Price	Audience	Format	Bible Study
5	45-60	30	Vary	$3.00	New Christian	Workbk	Topical

Features: Intro to Study
★★ Personal Application Preparation Time: None
★★ Relationship Building Ldr. Guide: No Size: 5.50 x 8.50
Subjects: Discipleship, Integrity, Obedience, Teens: Discipleship
Comments: This five-lesson study for new believers ages 15 and older is used by many churches for basic discipleship follow up. Book 4 explores Christian character in five chapters: "Maturing in Christ," "Demonstrating Christ," "Developing Integrity," "Growing in Discipleship," and "Obedience and Blessing." This series of six studies helps new Christians establish personal Bible study and learn and practice the essentials of Christian life.

Author: 27
Series: Growing in Christ
Title: *Growing in Christ*
Publisher: NavPress, 1957 ISBN: 0-89109-157-2

Num. Sess.	Group Time	Num. Pgs.	Avg. Qst.	Price	Audience	Format	Bible Study
13	45-60	80	Vary	$5.00	New Christian	Workbk	Topical

Features: Intro to Study, Prayer Helps, Scrpt Memory Helps, Drawings
★★ Personal Application Preparation Time: Low
★★ Relationship Building Ldr. Guide: No Size: 5.50 x 8.50
Subjects: Christian Living, Discipleship, Forgiveness, Prayer
Comments: This unabridged combination of "Lessons on Assurance" and "Lessons on Christian Living" is a 13-week follow up course for new Christians. Questions and exercises are keyed to memory verses, and a special section includes memory verse cards that correspond to each chapter. Topics include: "Assurance of Salvation," "Answered Prayer," "Victory over Sin," "Forgiveness," "Guidance," "Putting Christ First in Your Life," "Relying on the Lord's Strength."

Author: 28
Series: Design for Discipleship
Title: *Growing in Discipleship—Book 6*
Publisher: NavPress, 1973 ISBN: 0-89109-041-X

Num. Sess.	Group Time	Num. Pgs.	Avg. Qst.	Price	Audience	Format	Bible Study
5	60-75	46	18	$3.00	New Christian	Workbk	Topical

Features: Intro to Study, Summary, Charts, Maps
★★ Personal Application Preparation Time: Med
★★ Relationship Building Ldr. Guide: Yes Size: 5.50 x 8.50
Subjects: Discipleship, Evangelism, Stewardship, Teens: Discipleship
Comments: This is book six in a comprehensive study series on basic biblical principles and standards for following Christ. The following lessons reinforce that Christians should share the blessings they receive from the Lord: "What Is a Disciple?" "The Responsible Steward," "Helping Others Find Christ," "Follow-up," and "World Vision." The series is designed to help participants establish personal Bible study, examine Bible truths, and learn and practice essentials of discipleship.

Author: 29
Series:
Title: *"Highly Recommended: Coffee Break"*
Publisher: Church Development Resources, 1991

Num. Sess.	Group Time	Num. Pgs.	Avg. Qst.	Price	Audience	Format	Bible Study
	—	N/A	N/A	$14.95		Video	

Features:
Personal Application Preparation Time:
Relationship Building Ldr. Guide: Size: 4.50 x 8.50
Subjects: Evangelism, Small Group Resource
Comments: This 23" video opens with a testimony of a young girl finding Jesus. It presents a visual picture of the activities and results of a Coffee Break Evangelistic Bible study program, which can be implemented in any church. It provides both a history of Coffee Break and statistics on its growth. The program is specifically designed to be nonthreatening, and no prior Bible knowledge is required. Takes an inductive approach. Story Hour for children is available.

Author: 30
Series:
Title: *How to Organize and Conduct Men's Life*
Publisher: Church Development Resources, 1992

Num. Sess.	Group Time	Num. Pgs.	Avg. Qst.	Price	Audience	Format	Bible Study
	—	36	N/A	$3.50			

Features: Intro to Study
Personal Application Preparation Time:
Relationship Building Ldr. Guide: Size: 6.0 x 9.0
Subjects: Small Group Resource
Comments: This book describes overall strategies and specific elements of successful Bible study programs for men called "Men's Life." It discusses "how" and "why" the programs are tailored for men, focusing on team leadership, the nuts and bolts of planning, inviting friends, leading lessons, and troubleshooting. A listing of all "Men's Life" study materials is included.

Author: 31
Series:
Title: *Husbands and Wives: God's Design for the Family*
Publisher: NavPress, 1980 ISBN: 0-89109-028-2

Num. Sess.	Group Time	Num. Pgs.	Avg. Qst.	Price	Audience	Format	Bible Study
6	60-90	95	23	$5.00	New Christian	Workbk	Topical

Features: Bibliography, Study Overview, Summary, Ldr's Notes, Charts
★★★ Personal Application Preparation Time: Med
★★★ Relationship Building Ldr. Guide: No Size: 5.50 x 8.50
Subjects: Family, Love, Marriage, Relationships, Sexual Issues, Singles' Issues
Comments: This study for engaged, married, or single men and women describes what the Scriptures say about values, roles, expectations, and conflicts in marriage. Specific biblical teaching, important for both marriage partners, is explored. Includes self-image, communication, love, conflicts, the sexual relationship, and the responsibilities of husbands and wives.

Author: 32
Series:
Title: *Inside Inspirit: An Introductory Manual*
Publisher: Church Development Resources, 1994

Num. Sess.	Group Time	Num. Pgs.	Avg. Qst.	Price	Audience	Format	Bible Study
	—	31	N/A	$5.50			

Features: Intro to Study, Appendix
Personal Application Preparation Time:
Relationship Building Ldr. Guide: Size: 5.50 x 8.50
Subjects: Small Group Resource
Comments: "Inspirit" is a small group strategy for reaching busy people who aren't in churches, and showing them the Bible's relevance in their lives. It's a workplace model for the unchurched, suspicious of the organized church, but spiritually curious. This book outlines meetings and formats and profiles potentially successful teaching/leading styles. It concludes with additional resources and available training and curricula.

Author: 33
Series: Discover Life
Title: *James: Faith at Work*
Publisher: Church Development Resources, 1988

Num. Sess.	Group Time	Num. Pgs.	Avg. Qst.	Price	Audience	Format	Bible Study
7	45-60	16	6	$2.70	Beginner	Workbk	Book

Features: Intro to Study, Follow Up, Full Scrpt Printed
★★★ Personal Application Preparation Time: None
★★ Relationship Building Ldr. Guide: Yes Size: 8.50 x 11.0
Subjects: Evangelism, Faith, James, Men's Issues
Comments: This verse-by-verse study of James helps participants understand what faith means in everyday life. Areas covered include "Trials and Temptations," "Listening and Doing," "Faith and Deeds," and "Taming the Tongue." Accompanying materials are designed for non-Christians and the non-churched, and homework is not required. Lessons are distributed prior to each study. Bible passages are printed, thus eliminating potential embarrassment over finding a passage.

Author: 34
Series: Jr. High Builders
Title: *Jesus in the Book of Mark*
Publisher: Gospel Light Publications, 1987

Num. Sess.	Group Time	Num. Pgs.	Avg. Qst.	Price	Audience	Format	Bible Study
12	30-60	190	Vary	$16.99	Beginner	Workbk	Topical

Features: Intro to Leading a Study, Intro to Study, Objectives, Prayer Helps, Scrpt Memory Helps, Follow Up, Drawings, Cartoons, Handouts, Publicity Ideas
★★★★ Personal Application Preparation Time: Low
★★★★ Relationship Building Ldr. Guide: No Size: 11.0 x 8.50
Subjects: Teens: Jesus Life, Teens: Junior High, Teens: New Testament
Comments: This 12-week study, based on Mark's Gospel, contains everything necessary for teaching junior high students about Christ. It reveals Christ's identity, His power, and how He handled temptation. Other lessons cover the Parable of the Sower, self-denial, the humble servant, Christ's predictions of our future, giving one's life to God.

Author: 35
Series: Studies in Christian Living
Title: *Knowing Jesus Christ—Book 1*
Publisher: NavPress, 1964 ISBN: 0-89109-077-0

Num. Sess.	Group Time	Num. Pgs.	Avg. Qst.	Price	Audience	Format	Bible Study
3	45-60	29	Vary	$3.00	New Christian	Workbk	Topical

Features: Intro to Study, Full Scrpt Printed
★★ Personal Application Preparation Time: Low
★★ Relationship Building Ldr. Guide: No Size: 5.50 x 8.50
Subjects: Discipleship, Teens: Discipleship, Teens: Jesus Life
Comments: This three-lesson study for new believers ages 15 and older is used by many churches for basic discipleship follow up. Book 1 includes: "Who Is Jesus Christ?" "The Work of Jesus Christ," and "Eternal Life in Christ." This series of six studies helps new Christians establish personal Bible study and learn and practice the essentials of Christian life. This series could be used as a small-group study aid for new believers.

Author: 36
Series: Design for Discipleship
Title: *Leader's Guide: Design for Discipleship*
Publisher: NavPress, 1980 ISBN: 0-89109-043-6

Num. Sess.	Group Time	Num. Pgs.	Avg. Qst.	Price	Audience	Format	Bible Study
7	—	80	N/A	$4.00		Workbk	

Features:
Personal Application Preparation Time:
Relationship Building Ldr. Guide: Size: 5.50 x 8.50
Subjects: Bible Study, Leader's Guide
Comments: This series features seven step-by-step Bible studies, from laying a foundation in Christ to ensuring unfading hope. Each five-chapter book offers practical, verse-by-verse Bible study that encourages personal response to God's Word. The leader's guide includes basic components for group study and leader preparation. Each chapter has a stated objective, and leaders can design their own discussion questions or use questions provided. A summary thought is also presented.

Author: 37
Series: Growing in Christ
Title: *Lessons on Assurance*
Publisher: NavPress, 1957 ISBN: 0-89109-160-2

Num. Sess.	Group Time	Num. Pgs.	Avg. Qst.	Price	Audience	Format	Bible Study
5	45-60	32	8	$3.00	New Christian	Workbk	Topical

Features: Intro to Study, Scrpt Memory Helps, Full Scrpt Printed, Drawings
★★★ Personal Application Preparation Time: Low
★★ Relationship Building Ldr. Guide: No Size: 5.50 x 8.50
Subjects: Christian Living, Discipleship, God's Promises, Prayer
Comments: This study for new Christians presents short Bible studies on five basic promises God gives believers: assurance of salvation, answered prayer, victory over sin, forgiveness, and guidance. Each study concentrates on a Bible passage that presents one of God's promises, and participants are encouraged to memorize it. These lessons are particularly useful in groups or classes for beginners.

Author: 38
Series: Growing in Christ
Title: *Lessons on Christian Living*
Publisher: NavPress, 1957 ISBN: 0-89109-162-9

Num. Sess.	Group Time	Num. Pgs.	Avg. Qst.	Price	Audience	Format	Bible Study
8	45-60	46	12	$3.00	New Christian	Workbk	Topical

Features: Intro to Study, Prayer Helps, Scrpt Memory Helps
★★ Personal Application Preparation Time: Low
★★ Relationship Building Ldr. Guide: No Size: 5.50 x 8.50
Subjects: Christian Living, Church Life, Discipleship, Money, Stewardship
Comments: In this study participants will learn eight principles and promises God gives His children, and their corresponding responsibilities and privileges. The eight principles include: putting Christ first, relying on the Lord's strength, the importance of the Bible, love, giving, the church, good works, and witnessing. For each principle there is a memory verse.

Author: 39
Series: Jr. High Builders
Title: *Lifestyles of the Not-So-Famous from the Bible*
Publisher: Gospel Light Publications, 1990

Num. Sess.	Group Time	Num. Pgs.	Avg. Qst.	Price	Audience	Format	Bible Study
13	30-60	210	Vary	$16.99	Beginner	Workbk	Charctr

Features: Intro to Leading a Study, Intro to Study, Objectives, Prayer Helps, Scrpt Memory Helps, Follow Up, Drawings, Cartoons, Handouts, Publicity Ideas
★★★★ Personal Application Preparation Time: Low
★★★★ Relationship Building Ldr. Guide: No Size: 11.0 x 8.50
Subjects: Teens: Bible/Pers., Teens: New Testament, Teens: Old Testament
Comments: This 13-week study contains everything necessary for teaching junior high students about several wonderful but often overlooked Bible characters. Those discussed include Ehud, Deborah, Gideon, Hannah, the widow of Zaraphath, Naaman, Josiah.

Author: 40
Series:
Title: *Living Proof*
Publisher: NavPress, 1990 ISBN: 9-90073-982-5

Num. Sess.	Group Time	Num. Pgs.	Avg. Qst.	Price	Audience	Format	Bible Study
12	75-90	96	Vary	$119.00	New Christian	Video	Topical

Features: Intro to Study, Bibliography, Prayer Helps, Digging Deeper, Quest, Follow Up, Drawings, Photos, Book Incl, Video Study Guide
★★★★ Personal Application Preparation Time: Low
★★★★ Relationship Building Ldr. Guide: Yes Size: 10.50 x 11.50
Subjects: Evangelism, Small Group Resource
Comments: This 12-lesson video study on lifestyle evangelism includes memorable characters, humor, and scenes that may startle participants, who learn to share the Gospel with their friends, neighbors, and coworkers. Participants learn how to develop relationships with unbelievers, model the Christian message in their lives, and eventually present the Bible's claims in a nonthreatening manner.

Author: 41
Series: Discover Life
Title: *Man and His World, A*
Publisher: Church Development Resources, 1988

Num. Sess.	Group Time	Num. Pgs.	Avg. Qst.	Price	Audience	Format	Bible Study
7	45-60	16	6	$2.70	Beginner	Workbk	Topical

Features: Follow Up, Full Scrpt Printed
★★★ Personal Application Preparation Time: None
★★ Relationship Building Ldr. Guide: Yes Size: 8.50 x 11.0
Subjects: Christian Living, Evangelism, Friendships, Marriage, Men's Issues, Money, Relationships, Work
Comments: This seven-week study focuses on humanity's outer world, discussing topics such as work, friends, children, money, goals, marriage, and spirituality. Accompanying materials are designed for non-Christians and the non-churched, and homework is not required. Lessons are distributed prior to each study. The leader's guide provides additional questions.

Author: 42
Series:
Title: *Men's Life Training Workshop*
Publisher: Church Development Resources, 1990

Num. Sess.	Group Time	Num. Pgs.	Avg. Qst.	Price	Audience	Format	Bible Study
6	—	N/A	Vary	$113.90	New Christian	Video	No

Features: Intro to Study, Study Overview, Video Study Guide
Personal Application Preparation Time: None
Relationship Building Ldr. Guide: Yes Size: 10.25 x 12.50
Subjects: Evangelism, Small Group Resource
Comments: This training kit includes: two interactive video tapes (four and a half hours) which train men as if they were at a live workshop; "Man Alive," a 20″ video on Men's Life; complete leader's guide, notes, and helps; a student manual; "How to Organize and Conduct Men's Life," a practical outline; and complete organizational materials. The training is designed to reach and motivate men to know and follow Christ.

Author: 43
Series:
Title: *Navigator Bible Studies Handbook, The*
Publisher: NavPress, 1994 ISBN: 0-89109-075-4

Num. Sess.	Group Time	Num. Pgs.	Avg. Qst.	Price	Audience	Format	Bible Study
12	—	140	N/A	$7.00			

Features: Appendix
Personal Application Preparation Time:
Relationship Building Ldr. Guide: Size: 5.50 x 8.50
Subjects: Bible Study, Small Group Resource
Comments: This resource is divided into two units: the basics of Bible study, which gives background information on all methods of Bible study, and types of Bible studies which teach the time-tested method the Navigators have used in past decades. Unit one covers: "Knowing Your Goal," "Your Approach," and "Steps for Changing Your Life." Unit two covers: "Bible Study for a Lifetime," "Questions and Answers Bible Studies," and "How to Do" seven specific types of studies.

Author: 44
Series: Discover Life
Title: *Nehemiah, Succeeding by Serving*
Publisher: Church Development Resources, 1988

Num. Sess.	Group Time	Num. Pgs.	Avg. Qst.	Price	Audience	Format	Bible Study
7	45-60	16	6	$2.70	Beginner	Workbk	Book

Features: Follow Up, Full Scrpt Printed
★★★ Personal Application Preparation Time: None
★★ Relationship Building Ldr. Guide: Yes Size: 8.50 x 11.0
Subjects: Evangelism, Ezra/Nehemiah, Joy, Obedience, Service
Comments: This verse-by-verse study of Nehemiah shows how to succeed against great odds and accomplish something important to God. Nehemiah prayed, trusted God, faced fear, and led others to discover joy. Accompanying materials are designed for non-Christians and the non-churched, and homework is not required. Printed Bible passages eliminate possible embarrassment over being unable to find a passage or over bringing a Bible to a public place.

Author: 45
Series: Design for Discipleship
Title: *Our Hope in Christ—Book 7*
Publisher: NavPress, 1980 ISBN: 0-89109-042-8

Num. Sess.	Group Time	Num. Pgs.	Avg. Qst.	Price	Audience	Format	Bible Study
7	60-75	43	Vary	$3.00	New Christian	Workbk	Topical

Features: Intro to Study, Summary, Cross Ref
★★ Personal Application Preparation Time: Med
★★ Relationship Building Ldr. Guide: Yes Size: 5.50 x 8.50
Subjects: Discipleship, Hope, Teens: Discipleship, Teens: New Testament
Comments: This is book 7 in a comprehensive study on basic biblical principles and standards for following Christ. Participants will learn how to study New Testament books chapter by chapter—in this case, 1 Thessalonians—a method called "comprehensive book analysis." It includes three steps: a survey of the entire book, a chapter-by-chapter analysis, and a summary.

Author: 46
Series: Jr. High Builders
Title: *Parables of Jesus, The*
Publisher: Gospel Light Publications, 1988

Num. Sess.	Group Time	Num. Pgs.	Avg. Qst.	Price	Audience	Format	Bible Study
13	30-60	165	Vary	$16.99	Beginner	Workbk	Topical

Features: Intro to Leading a Study, Intro to Study, Objectives, Prayer Helps, Scrpt Memory Helps, Follow Up, Drawings, Cartoons, Handouts, Publicity Ideas
★★★★ Personal Application Preparation Time: Low
★★★★ Relationship Building Ldr. Guide: No Size: 11.0 x 8.50
Subjects: Teens: Christian Liv, Teens: Decisions, Teens: Junior High, Teens: New Testament, Teens: Relationships
Comments: This 13-week study contains everything necessary for teaching important lessons learned from Christ's parables. Lessons include "Making Choices," "Building One's Life on Christ," "Being Obedient," "A Believer's Attitude."

Author: 47
Series:
Title: *Parents & Children: God's Design for the Family*
Publisher: NavPress, 1980 ISBN: 0-89109-029-0

Num. Sess.	Group Time	Num. Pgs.	Avg. Qst.	Price	Audience	Format	Bible Study
6	60-90	95	18	$5.00	New Christian	Workbk	Topical

Features: Intro to Study, Bibliography, Study Overview, Follow Up, Ldr's Notes, Charts
★★★ Personal Application Preparation Time: Med
★★★ Relationship Building Ldr. Guide: No Size: 5.50 x 8.50
Subjects: Family, Parenting, Relationships, Singles' Issues
Comments: In this study for engaged, married, or single men and women with children or anticipating them, participants learn how to use biblical principles in rearing children. Thought-provoking lessons cover goals for parents, instruction for children, qualities for right relationships, teaching responsibility, and training and planning for the future. Family projects are encouraged.

Author: 48
Series: Discover Life
Title: *Peter: The Making of a Disciple*
Publisher: Church Development Resources, 1988

Num. Sess.	Group Time	Num. Pgs.	Avg. Qst.	Price	Audience	Format	Bible Study
7	45-60	16	6	$2.70	Beginner	Workbk	Topical

Features: Intro to Study, Follow Up, Full Scrpt Printed
★★★ Personal Application Preparation Time: None
★★ Relationship Building Ldr. Guide: Yes Size: 8.50 x 11.0
Subjects: Bible Personalities, Evangelism, God, Men's Issues
Comments: This study of Peter covers passages from Matthew, Luke, John, and Acts. Lessons include: "Meet the Master," "He Walked on Water," "How to Be a Rock," and more. God changed Peter from a shaking reed to solid rock. Accompanying materials are designed for non-Christians and the non-churched, and homework is not required. Lessons are distributed prior to each study. Bible passages are printed.

Author: 49
Series:
Title: *Pick & Choose: Program Ideas for Youth Ministry*
Publisher: Group Publishing, 1994 ISBN: 1-55945-199-8

Num. Sess.	Group Time	Num. Pgs.	Avg. Qst.	Price	Audience	Format	Bible Study
	—	N/A	N/A	$19.99			

Features:
Personal Application Preparation Time:
Relationship Building Ldr. Guide: Size:
Subjects: Teens: Resources
Comments: This resource provides 200 creative ideas to help youth leaders avoid last-minute meeting planning pressures. In a card format each one lists a title or theme, appropriate group size, activity length, and necessary supplies for handy reference. Each card has space to document when ideas have been used. Included are: crowdbreakers and games, group builders and affirmations, quick devotions, active discussion starters, outreach projects.

Author: 50
Series: Jr. High Builders
Title: *Power of God, The*
Publisher: Gospel Light Publications, 1988

Num. Sess.	Group Time	Num. Pgs.	Avg. Qst.	Price	Audience	Format	Bible Study
13	30-60	180	Vary	$16.99	Beginner	Workbk	Topical

Features: Intro to Leading a Study, Intro to Study, Objectives, Prayer Helps, Scrpt Memory Helps, Follow Up, Drawings, Cartoons, Handouts, Publicity Ideas
★★★★ Personal Application Preparation Time: Low
★★★★ Relationship Building Ldr. Guide: No Size: 11.0 x 8.50
Subjects: Teens: Christian Liv, Teens: Junior High
Comments: This 13-week study contains everything necessary for teaching junior high students about God's power, as demonstrated in the early days of the church. Examples include the power to forgive, share, change, and reach out. Includes lecture-oriented Bible study outlines. Action games and clip art illustrations enhance the study.

Author: 51
Series: Discover Life
Title: *Proverbs: Wisdom for Living*
Publisher: Church Development Resources, 1988

Num. Sess.	Group Time	Num. Pgs.	Avg. Qst.	Price	Audience	Format	Bible Study
8	45-60	20	7	$3.50	Beginner	Workbk	Book

Features: Intro to Study, Follow Up, Full Scrpt Printed
★★★ Personal Application Preparation Time: None
★★ Relationship Building Ldr Guide: Yes Size: 8.50 x 11.0
Subjects: Evangelism, Proverbs, Wisdom
Comments: This study of Proverbs concerns wisdom, living, work, wealth, words, marriage, relationships, character, and religion. Accompanying materials are designed for non-Christians and the non-churched, and homework is not required. Lessons are distributed prior to each study. Bible passages are printed, which eliminates potential embarrassment over being unable to find a passage or over bringing a Bible to a public place. The leader's guide provides additional questions.

Author: 52
Series:
Title: *Serendipity Bible for Groups*
Publisher: Serendipity House, 1988

Num. Sess.	Group Time	Num. Pgs.	Avg. Qst.	Price	Audience	Format	Bible Study
	60-90	N/A	Vary	$17.95	Beginner	Book	Book

Features: Intro to Leading a Study, Intro to Study, Digging Deeper Quest, Full Scrpt Printed, Index
★★★ Personal Application Preparation Time: None
★★★ Relationship Building Ldr Guide: No Size: 6.50 x 9.25
Subjects: New Testament, Old Testament
Comments: This Bible for groups includes the following: the complete NIV text; thousands of "open," "dig," and "reflect" questions; 36 ready-made study courses; 96 ready-made studies on favorite Bible stories; 66 specialized book studies; 20 pages of subject indexes; and 13 full-color maps. Appropriate for beginning or advanced groups. Adding a notebook for recording responses will be helpful.

Author: 53
Series:
Title: *Serendipity New Testament for Groups*
Publisher: Serendipity House, 1986 ISBN: 1-88341-919-0

Num. Sess.	Group Time	Num. Pgs.	Avg. Qst.	Price	Audience	Format	Bible Study
68	60-90	510	Vary	$7.95	Beginner	Book	Book

Features: Intro to Leading a Study, Intro to Study, Digging Deeper Quest, Full Scrpt Printed, Index
★★★ Personal Application Preparation Time: None
★★★ Relationship Building Ldr Guide: No Size: 6.50 x 9.25
Subjects: New Testament
Comments: The Serendipity New Testament for Groups includes 5,000 "flow" questions in the margin beside the biblical text; 48 ready-made studies on favorite Bible stories; 20 complete Bible study courses on popular themes; special introductions for each book in the New Testament; and a subject index of important words, people, and places. Appropriate for beginning or advanced groups. A notebook is needed.

Author: 54
Series: Studies in Christian Living
Title: *Serving Others—Book 6*
Publisher: NavPress, 1964 ISBN: 0-89109-082-7

Num. Sess.	Group Time	Num. Pgs.	Avg. Qst.	Price	Audience	Format	Bible Study
5	45-60	28	Vary	$3.00	New Christian	Workbk	Topical

Features: Intro to Study, Maps
★★ Personal Application Preparation Time: Low
★★ Relationship Building Ldr Guide: No Size: 5.50 x 8.50
Subjects: Discipleship, Service, Teens: Discipleship, Teens: Prayer
Comments: This five-lesson study for new believers ages 15 and older is used by many churches for basic discipleship follow up. Book 6 deals with these topics: "Helping Others Find Christ," "Follow-up," "Power in Prayer," "Scriptural Giving," and "World Vision." This series of six studies helps new Christians establish personal Bible study and learn and practice the essentials of Christian life. This series could be used as a small-group aid for new believers.

Author: 55
Series: Design for Discipleship
Title: *Spirit-filled Christian, The—Book 2*
Publisher: NavPress, 1973 ISBN: 0-89109-037-1

Num. Sess.	Group Time	Num. Pgs.	Avg. Qst.	Price	Audience	Format	Bible Study
5	60-75	47	17	$3.00	New Christian	Workbk	Topical

Features: Intro to Study, Summary, Charts
★★ Personal Application Preparation Time: Med
★★ Relationship Building Ldr Guide: Yes Size: 5.50 x 8.50
Subjects: Discipleship, Evangelism, Holy Spirit, Obedience, Prayer, Teens: Discipleship
Comments: This is a comprehensive study series on basic biblical principles for following Christ. Topics include the way to live a Spirit-filled, Christ-centered life and include: "The Obedient Christian," "God's Word in Your Life," "Conversing with God," "Fellowship with Christians," and "Witnessing for Christ." Designed to help participants establish personal Bible study.

Author: 56
Series: Studies in Christian Living
Title: *Talking with Christ—Book 3*
Publisher: NavPress, 1964 ISBN: 0-89109-079-7

Num. Sess.	Group Time	Num. Pgs.	Avg. Qst.	Price	Audience	Format	Bible Study
4	45-60	30	Vary	$3.00	New Christian	Workbk	Topical

Features: Intro to Study
★★ Personal Application Preparation Time: Low
★★ Relationship Building Ldr Guide: No Size: 5.50 x 8.50
Subjects: Discipleship, Teens: Discipleship, Teens: Prayer
Comments: This four-lesson study for new believers ages 15 and older is used by many churches for basic discipleship follow up. Book 3 includes these topics: "The Church," "What Is the Bible?" "God's Word in Your Life," and "Principles of Prayer." This series of six studies helps new Christians establish personal Bible study and learn and practice the essentials of Christian life. This series could be used as a small-group study aid for new believers.

Author: 57
Series:
Title: *Trial and Testimony of the Early Church*
Publisher: Gospel Light Publications, 1991

Num. Sess.	Group Time	Num. Pgs.	Avg. Qst.	Price	Audience	Format	Bible Study
6	45-60	N/A	12	$99.95	New Christian	Video	Topical

Features: Intro to Leading a Study, Intro to Study, Objectives, Follow Up, Book Incl
★★★★ Personal Application Preparation Time: None
★★★★ Relationship Building Ldr Guide: Yes Size: 11.50 x 9.0
Subjects: Church Life, Jesus: Life/Teaching, Theology
Comments: This video package includes six half-hour video programs, curricula for 6 or 12 sessions, full-color companion book, full issue of *Christian History* magazine, reproducible student activity sheets, and bulletin inserts for each program. Goes to actual early church locations to discover how early believers were able to spread across the whole Roman Empire in spite of terrible persecution.

Author: 58
Series:
Title: *Twelve Steps for Christians*
Publisher: Recovery Publications, 1994 ISBN: 0-94140-557-5

Num. Sess.	Group Time	Num. Pgs.	Avg. Qst.	Price	Audience	Format	Bible Study
12	—	240	N/A	$9.95		Book	Topical

Features: Intro to Study, Appendix
Personal Application Preparation Time:
Relationship Building Ldr Guide: Size: 5.50 x 8.50
Subjects: Self-help, Support
Comments: This resource merges the practical wisdom of the Twelve Steps with spiritual truths of the Bible. A combination of recovery and spirituality, it offers Christians effective ways to work a traditional Twelve-Step program while naming Jesus Christ as their Higher Power. This material is primarily for adults whose childhoods were negatively affected by a less than nurturing environment. Enables participants to reexamine their relationships with God.

Author: 59
Series: Design for Discipleship
Title: *Walking with Christ—Book 3*
Publisher: NavPress, 1973 ISBN: 0-89109-038-X

Num. Sess.	Group Time	Num. Pgs.	Avg. Qst.	Price	Audience	Format	Bible Study
5	60-75	44	19	$3.00	New Christian	Workbk	Topical

Features: Intro to Study, Summary, Cartoons, Charts
★★ Personal Application Preparation Time: Med
★★ Relationship Building Ldr Guide: Yes Size: 5.50 x 8.50
Subjects: Discipleship, Faith, God's Promises, Service, Teens: Discipleship
Comments: This is a comprehensive study series on basic biblical principles and standards for following Christ. Participants will study five important aspects of their life with Him: "Maturing in Christ," "The Lordship of Christ," "Faith and Promises of God," "Knowing God's Will," and "Walking as a Servant." The series is designed to help participants establish personal Bible study.

Author: 60
Series: Discover Life
Title: *Woman and Her World, A*
Publisher: Church Development Resources, 1989

Num. Sess.	Group Time	Num. Pgs.	Avg. Qst.	Price	Audience	Format	Bible Study
7	45-60	16	5	$2.70	Beginner	Workbk	Topical

Features: Intro to Study, Follow Up, Full Scrpt Printed
★★★ Personal Application Preparation Time: None
★★ Relationship Building Ldr Guide: Yes Size: 8.50 x 11.0
Subjects: Christian Living, Evangelism, Friendships, Marriage, Money, Relationships, Women's Issues, Work
Comments: Old and New Testament passages help participants explore women's unique needs and perspectives. Seven lessons review important areas of a woman's life: work, friends, children, money, goals, marriage, and spirituality. Accompanying materials are designed for non-Christians and the non-churched, and homework is not required. Lessons are distributed prior to each study.

Author: 61
Series: Discover Life
Title: *Women Who Found A Way: Leader's Guide*
Publisher: Church Development Resources, 1990

Num. Sess.	Group Time	Num. Pgs.	Avg. Qst.	Price	Audience	Format	Bible Study
8	45-60	34	6	$5.00	Beginner	Book	Topical

Features: Intro to Leading a Study, Follow Up, Summary, Full Scrpt Printed
★★★★ Personal Application Preparation Time: None
★★ Relationship Building Ldr Guide: Yes Size: 8.50 x 11.0
Subjects: Bible Personalities, Faith
Comments: This study examines biblical characters—prominent and not-so-prominent women—who found a way to be the persons God called them to be. Studied are: "Hannah: Prayers and Promises"; "Abigail: Unfading Beauty"; "The Shunammite Woman: Faith in Action"; "Mary: Chosen for a Special Task"; "Mary and Martha"; and "Two Women Who Found Jesus."

Author: 62
Series: Discover Life
Title: *Women Who Found A Way*
Publisher: Church Development Resources, 1990

Num. Sess.	Group Time	Num. Pgs.	Avg. Qst.	Price	Audience	Format	Bible Study
8	45-60	34	6	$5.00	Beginner	Book	Topical

Features: Intro to Leading a Study, Follow Up, Summary, Full Scrpt Printed
★★★★ Personal Application Preparation Time: None
★★ Relationship Building Ldr Guide: Yes Size: 8.50 x 11.0
Subjects: Bible Personalities, Faith
Comments: This study examines biblical characters—prominent and not-so-prominent women—who found a way to be the women God called them to be. Studied are: "Hannah: Prayers and Promises"; "Abigail: Unfading Beauty"; "The Shunammite Woman: Faith in Action"; "Mary: Chosen for a Special Task"; "Mary and Martha"; and "Two Women Who Found Jesus."

Author: 63
Series: Design for Discipleship
Title: *Your Life in Christ—Book 1*
Publisher: NavPress, 1973 ISBN: 0-89109-036-3

Num. Sess.	Group Time	Num. Pgs.	Avg. Qst.	Price	Audience	Format	Bible Study
4	60-75	30	16	$3.00	New Christian	Workbk	Topical

Features: Intro to Leading a Study, Summary, Charts
★★ Personal Application Preparation Time: Med
★★ Relationship Building Ldr Guide: Yes Size: 5.50 x 8.50
Subjects: Discipleship, Holy Spirit, Teens: Discipleship
Comments: This is book one in a comprehensive study series on basic biblical principles and standards for following Christ. Lessons include: "God Cares for You," "The Person of Jesus Christ," "The Work of Christ," and "The Spirit Within You." The series is designed to help participants establish personal Bible study, examine Bible truths, and learn and practice essentials of discipleship. Homework is suggested.

Author: Reginald Johnson 64
Series:
Title: *Your Personality and the Spiritual Life*
Publisher: Victor Books, 1995 ISBN: 1-56476-385-4

Num. Sess.	Group Time	Num. Pgs.	Avg. Qst.	Price	Audience	Format	Bible Study
		180	3	$8.99		Book	Topical

Features:
★★★★ Personal Application Preparation Time: Low
Relationship Building Ldr Guide: No Size: 5.50 x 8.50
Subjects: Spiritual Gifts
Comments: Understanding who you are can deepen your relationship with God. Using the widely accepted Myers-Briggs Type Theory, the author analyzes the various personality types with actual case studies from Scripture. Then he offers biblically based guidelines to manage personality vulnerability and affirm spiritual gifts and strengths.

Author: Aaseng, Rolf E. 65
Series: Small Group Bible Studies
Title: *Justice for a Troubled World*
Publisher: Augsburg Fortress Publishers, 1975

Num. Sess.	Group Time	Num. Pgs.	Avg. Qst.	Price	Audience	Format	Bible Study
4	60-75	16	32	$1.15	New Christian	Book	Book

Features: Intro to Study, Prayer Helps, Digging Deeper Quest
★★ Personal Application Preparation Time: None
★★ Relationship Building Ldr Guide: No Size: 8.50 x 5.50
Subjects: Bible Personalities, Minor Prophets
Comments: In this short, six-session study on the book of Amos, the concern is not to interpret every detail and historical reference of the book. Rather, the study notes similarities to the present day and discovers what the Word of God has to say to Christians. A key passage in the book is 5:21-24, which is a cry for justice and righteousness.

Author: Aaseng, Rolf E. 66
Series: Small Group Bible Studies
Title: *Turning the World Upside Down*
Publisher: Augsburg Fortress Publishers, 1975

Num. Sess.	Group Time	Num. Pgs.	Avg. Qst.	Price	Audience	Format	Bible Study
8	60-75	32	34	$1.45	New Christian	Book	Book

Features: Intro to Study, Prayer Helps
★★★ Personal Application Preparation Time: None
★★★ Relationship Building Ldr Guide: No Size: 8.50 x 5.50
Subjects: Acts, Church Life, Parables
Comments: This small pamphlet includes eight chapter-by-chapter sessions on Acts. It is a complete look at the book. The study is important because it provides information about Jesus not found in the Gospels, especially certain parables and information on the post-resurrection days. It answers the question: How did the Christian Church begin? The two central figures in the book are Peter and Paul. Questions marked with a star are especially intended for group discussion.

Author: Abercrombie, Katie 67
Series: Group's Active Bible Curriculum
Title: *Dealing With Life's Pressures*
Publisher: Group Publishing, 1993 ISBN: 1-55945-232-3

Num. Sess.	Group Time	Num. Pgs.	Avg. Qst.	Price	Audience	Format	Bible Study
4	35-60	43	Vary	$9.99	Beginner	Workbk	Topical

Features: Intro to Leading a Study, Intro to Study, Objectives, Study Overview, Ldr's Notes, Handouts, Agenda, Publicity Ideas
★★★★ Personal Application Preparation Time: None
★★★★ Relationship Building Ldr Guide: No Size: 8.50 x 11.0
Subjects: Teens: Christian Liv, Teens: Emotions, Teens: Family, Teens: Senior High
Comments: This course teaches teenagers to rely on God during stressful times, explore society's expectations for them, see failure as an opportunity for growth, and discover how to cope with family pressures. Participants are reminded that God is always with them and that God's expectations matter most.

Author: Adair, James R. and Harry Verploegh 68
Series:
Title: *101 Days In The Gospels With Oswald Chambers*
Publisher: Victor Books, 1992 ISBN: 0-89693-120-X

Num. Sess.	Group Time	Num. Pgs.	Avg. Qst.	Price	Audience	Format	Bible Study
	10-20	380	N/A	$14.99	New Christian	Book	Book

Features: Intro to Study, Full Scrpt Printed
★★★★ Personal Application Preparation Time: None
★ Relationship Building Ldr Guide: No Size: 6.25 x 9.25
Subjects: Devotionals
Comments: This outstanding devotional book provides 101 days of reading from the Gospels, followed by related insights from Oswald Chambers' classic "My Utmost for His Highest" and 30 of his other works. Included are accounts from Jesus' birth to His ascension, many of them blending details from two or more of the Gospels. This devotional will nurture readers and help them climb to new levels in their walks with Jesus Christ.

Author: Adams, David 69
Series: Group's Active Bible Curriculum
Title: *Gospel of John, The: Jesus' Teachings*
Publisher: Group Publishing, 1990 ISBN: 1-55945-208-0

Num. Sess.	Group Time	Num. Pgs.	Avg. Qst.	Price	Audience	Format	Bible Study
4	35-60	47	Vary	$9.99	Beginner	Workbk	Book

Features: Intro to Leading a Study, Intro to Study, Objectives, Study Overview, Ldr's Notes, Drawings, Handouts, Agenda, Publicity Ideas
★★★★ Personal Application Preparation Time: None
★★★★ Relationship Building Ldr Guide: No Size: 8.50 x 11.0
Subjects: Teens: Jesus Life, Teens: New Testament, Teens: Senior High
Comments: This four-lesson study helps senior high students discover the meaning of Jesus' message. Students will learn what it means to have new life in Christ, discover ways to live out their faith, rely on Him for direction in life, uncover the excitement of following Him daily, and gain insight into Jesus' message for contemporary times. Instructions are easy to follow and provide multiple options for teachers.

Author: Adams, David 70
Series: Group's Active Bible Curriculum
Title: *Life After High School*
Publisher: Group Publishing, 1991 ISBN: 1-55945-220-X

Num. Sess.	Group Time	Num. Pgs.	Avg. Qst.	Price	Audience	Format	Bible Study
4	35-60	48	Vary	$9.99	Beginner	Workbk	Topical

Features: Intro to Leading a Study, Intro to Study, Objectives, Study Overview, Ldr's Notes, Handouts, Agenda, Publicity Ideas
★★★★ Personal Application Preparation Time: None
★★★★ Relationship Building Ldr Guide: No Size: 8.50 x 11.0
Subjects: Teens: Christian Liv, Teens: Decisions, Teens: Family, Teens: Senior High, Teens: Youth Life
Comments: This course teaches senior highers the keys to independence. Participants work to understand how parents feel when their teens move away, explore the value of keeping in touch with friends and family, understand the positive and negative issues of leaving home, and examine biblical accounts of independence.

Author: Adams, Jay E. 71
Series:
Title: *Thirst for Wholeness, A*
Publisher: Victor Books, 1988 ISBN: 0-89693-455-1

Num. Sess.	Group Time	Num. Pgs.	Avg. Qst.	Price	Audience	Format	Bible Study
13	60-90	143	N/A	$8.99	New Christian	Book	Topical

Features: Prayer Helps
★★★★ Personal Application Preparation Time: Med
★★★ Relationship Building Ldr Guide: Yes Size: 5.50 x 8.0
Subjects: Christian Life, Failure, James, Obedience, Prayer, Wholeness
Comments: This book offers solutions to people whose spiritual integrity is in question. Taken from James, it concentrates on how a person can become a complete Christian from the inside out. Lessons discuss the following: resisting temptation, conquering doubt, praying effectively, having good motives, overcoming anger, being genuine, remaining faithful, and more. The closing lesson, "What All This Means to You," discusses the implications of this study on the individual.

Author: Adler, Ronald B. 72
Series:
Title: *Looking Out, Looking In*
Publisher: Holt, 1990 ISBN: 0-03030-834-8

Num. Sess.	Group Time	Num. Pgs.	Avg. Qst.	Price	Audience	Format	Bible Study
9	—	370	N/A	$33.25		Book	No

Features: Cartoons, Photos, Charts, Index
Personal Application Preparation Time:
Relationship Building Ldr Guide: Size: 8.25 x 10.25
Subjects: Small Group Resource
Comments: This book, designed to help leaders become better communicators, is presented in textbook form, with emphasis on experiential learning through exercises and other activities. Ideas are developed through a variety of readings. Chapter topics include "getting started," self-concept and communication, perception, words and meanings, nonverbal communication, listening as opposed to hearing, emotions, positive relationships, and resolving conflict.

Author: Aeschliman, Gordon 73
Series: Global Issues
Title: *Leadership in the 21st Century*
Publisher: InterVarsity, 1990 ISBN: 0-83084-902-5

Num. Sess.	Group Time	Num. Pgs.	Avg. Qst.	Price	Audience	Format	Bible Study
6	45-60	48	12	$4.99	Beginner	Workbk	Topical

Features: Intro to Leading a Study, Intro to Study, Bibliography
★★★★ Personal Application Preparation Time: Low
★★★★ Relationship Building Ldr Guide: No Size: 5.50 x 8.25
Subjects: Caring, Ethics, Leadership, Service
Comments: This six-week study considers what it will mean to be a Christian leader in the next century, including specific requirements, and how gifts can best be used to serve Christ. It addresses vital issues such as courage, service, personal ethics, compassion for the world, ability to communicate love, and a leader's relationship with God. It helps participants understand what their roles might be as the church faces this challenge.

Author: Albers, Robert H. 74
Series: Youth Talk
Title: *Real Difficulties*
Publisher: Augsburg Fortress Publishers, 1994

Num. Sess.	Group Time	Num. Pgs.	Avg. Qst.	Price	Audience	Format	Bible Study
5	45-60	46	N/A	$4.95	Beginner	Book	Topical

Features: Prayer Helps, Worship Helps, Photos
★★★★ Personal Application Preparation Time: Low
★★★★ Relationship Building Ldr Guide: Yes Size: 8.0 x 11.0
Subjects: Teens: Decisions, Teens: Junior High, Teens: Youth Life
Comments: An alternative to the "textbook approach," these studies are energetic, contemporary, and modeled after popular teen magazines. Advice columns, fiction, poetry, and other features are mostly written by youth. Statistics show a growing inability among youth to cope with life's difficulties. This course offers youth a base of strength, love, and security centered on God's promises. From this base, students will find courage to face personal difficulties in positive ways.

Author: Albers, Robert H. and Kent Johnson 75
Series: Cross Signs
Title: *Why Do People Suffer? Responding to Evil and Suffering: Unit 8*
Publisher: Augsburg Fortress Publishers, 1993

Num. Sess.	Group Time	Num. Pgs.	Avg. Qst.	Price	Audience	Format	Bible Study
7	90-105	48	5	$3.75	New Christian	Book	Topical

Features: Intro to Study, Prayer Helps, Worship Helps
★★★ Personal Application Preparation Time: Low
★★ Relationship Building Ldr Guide: Yes Size: 5.50 x 8.50
Subjects: Suffering
Comments: Cross Signs, a Bible study series for adult small groups, features nine units of study which focus on key faith questions. This study of selected biblical texts provides insights into human suffering, reasons for it, and God's steadfast presence in the midst of it.

Author: Alexander, Myrna 76
Series: Woman's Workshop Series
Title: *Behold Your God: Studies on the Attributes of God*
Publisher: Zondervan, 1978 ISBN: 0-31037-131-7

Num. Sess.	Group Time	Num. Pgs.	Avg. Qst.	Price	Audience	Format	Bible Study
13	90-120	124	18	$5.99	New Christian	Workbk	Charctr

Features: Intro to Leading a Study, Intro to Study, Scrpt Memory Helps
★★ Personal Application Preparation Time: Med
★★ Relationship Building Ldr Guide: No Size: 5.25 x 8.0
Subjects: God, Theology, Women's Issues
Comments: In this study of God's character and person, each lesson covers a truth about God's character: loving, supreme and sovereign, all-powerful, good, omniscient, all-wise, omnipresent, immutable, faithful, holy, just, and worthy to be praised. It prepares participants "to consistently lean on God," and "to know Him"; it also encourages practical application of this knowledge to daily living.

Author: Alexander, Myrna 77
Series: Woman's Workshop Series
Title: *Loving & Obeying God: Studies on 1 Samuel*
Publisher: Zondervan, 1982 ISBN: 0-31037-141-4

Num. Sess.	Group Time	Num. Pgs.	Avg. Qst.	Price	Audience	Format	Bible Study
13	60-90	139	16	$6.99	Beginner	Workbk	Book

Features: Intro to Leading a Study, Intro to Study, Overview, Maps
★★ Personal Application Preparation Time: Med
★★ Relationship Building Ldr Guide: No Size: 5.25 x 8.0
Subjects: God, Obedience, Women's Issues, 1 & 2 Samuel
Comments: This historical narrative on Samuel describes the obedience and disobedience of key individuals who professsed love for God. It concerns men who became "living definitions of what it is to be after God's heart," in particular, Samuel and David. Participants see real people grappling with godly principles. The study includes generous background information on the history, culture, and attitudes of the Israelites and their neighbors.

Author: Allender, Dr. Dan B. 78
Series:
Title: *Bold Love*
Publisher: NavPress, 1993 ISBN: 8-90073-322-2

Num. Sess.	Group Time	Num. Pgs.	Avg. Qst.	Price	Audience	Format	Bible Study
7	60-90	N/A	8	$119.00	Beginner	Video	Topical

Features: Intro to Leading a Study, Intro to Study, Prayer Helps, Ldr's Notes, Book Incl, Video Study Guide
★★★★ Personal Application Preparation Time: None
★★★★ Relationship Building Ldr Guide: No Size: 10.50 x 13.50
Subjects: Communication, Love, Relationships
Comments: This seven-lesson video study presents dramatic vignettes of dysfunctional families to help viewers learn to better relate to others. Participants discover: the surprising goals of biblical love; what it really means to "turn the other cheek"; what it means to "honor" a wicked parent; and more. Each session includes: warm up questions; video segment (15″–20″); discussion questions (30″).

Author: Allen, Dr. David 79
Series:
Title: *Shattering the Gods Within*
Publisher: Moody Press, 1994 ISBN: 0-80248-249-X

Num. Sess.	Group Time	Num. Pgs.	Avg. Qst.	Price	Audience	Format	Bible Study
13	60-90	190	N/A	$15.99	New Christian	Book	Topical

Features: Intro to Study, No Grp Discussion Quest
★★★★ Personal Application Preparation Time: Low
★★ Relationship Building Ldr Guide: No Size: 6.25 x 9.50
Subjects: Christian Life, God
Comments: Modern people have developed many substitutes for the one true God of the Bible, including addictions, self-absorption, materialism, substances, entertainment, pleasures, problems, patterns of living, careers, and empty religions. Many Christians give in to the tugs of these would-be idols, often not even realizing the compromises they make. The author shows readers how to identify their own "inner-idols" and offers ways out. No questions are provided.

Author: Allen, Loyd 80
Series: Spiritual Development Work
Title: *Gift Quest: A Search For Spiritual Gifts*
Publisher: Woman's Missionary Union, 1993 ISBN: 1-56309-099-6

Num. Sess.	Group Time	Num. Pgs.	Avg. Qst.	Price	Audience	Format	Bible Study
	—	38	N/A	$4.95		Workbk	Topical

Features: Intro to Leading a Study, Bibliography, Ldr's Notes
Personal Application Preparation Time:
Relationship Building Ldr Guide: No Size: 8.50 x 11.0
Subjects: Teens: Discipleship, Teens: Spiritual Gifts
Comments: This guide helps teenagers discover their spiritual gifts, and begin learning how to use these blessings in the work of God's church. This workout provides personal inventory warm-up activities, as well as endurance drills to discover the source, biblical basis, character, and purpose of the spiritual gifts that best fit. Final instructions are provided to continue this workout and a challenge to use the gifts in God's service.

Author: Anderson, J. Kerby 81
Series:
Title: *Signs of Warning, Signs of Hope*
Publisher: Moody Press, 1994 ISBN: 0-80247-835-2

Num. Sess.	Group Time	Num. Pgs.	Avg. Qst.	Price	Audience	Format	Bible Study
10	60-75	240	N/A	$17.99	Beginner	Book	Topical

Features: Intro to Study, Charts
★★★★ Personal Application Preparation Time: Low
★ Relationship Building Ldr Guide: No Size: 6.25 x 9.25
Subjects: Social Issues
Comments: This book is an attempt by a leading social critic to warn readers of impending turbulence. The author states that baby boomers (people born between 1946 and 1964) are on a collision course with seven crises: purpose, disillusionment, priorities, relationships, loneliness, security, and spirituality. This book helps baby boomers prepare to heed the signs of these crises and live better lives. A trained leader will be required.

Author: Anderson, Monnie 82
Series:
Title: *Ideas for Hospital Ministries*
Publisher: New Hope, 1992 ISBN: 1-56309-023-6

Num. Sess.	Group Time	Num. Pgs.	Avg. Qst.	Price	Audience	Format	Bible Study
	—	39	N/A	$4.95		Book	

Features: Intro to Study, Drawings
Personal Application Preparation Time:
Relationship Building Ldr Guide: Size: 8.50 x 11.0
Subjects: Missions, Small Group Resource, Support
Comments: For those afraid of hospital visitation this resource can help overcome fears and result in successful hospital ministries. The author spells out the right way to begin either group or individual ministries. Ideas and advice for ministering to special types of patients are outlined in the book and prepare caregivers to reach out to maternity patients, the elderly, patients with AIDS, and many others. A good resource for small group mission projects.

Author: Anderson, Neil T. 83
Series:
Title: *Victory Over The Darkness: Study Guide*
Publisher: Regal Books, 1994 ISBN: 0-83071-669-6

Num. Sess.	Group Time	Num. Pgs.	Avg. Qst.	Price	Audience	Format	Bible Study
13	60-90	144	Vary	$8.99	New Christian	Workbk	Topical

Features: Book Avail
★★★★ Personal Application Preparation Time: Med
★★ Relationship Building Ldr Guide: Size: 5.50 x 8.50
Subjects: Spiritual Warfare
Comments: This study helps participants understand and live by important truths from Scripture, which make it possible to recognize and ward off Satan's attacks. It should be used in conjuction with the book of the same title ($9.99). Includes thought-provoking personal reflection questions and applications for each chapter. Chapter titles include: "Winning the Battle for Your Mind"; "You Must Be Real in Order To Be Right"; and "Healing Emotional Wounds From Your Past."

Author: Anderson, Paul 84
Series: Building Books
Title: *Building Christian Character*
Publisher: Bethany House, 1980 ISBN: 0-87123-436-X

Num. Sess.	Group Time	Num. Pgs.	Avg. Qst.	Price	Audience	Format	Bible Study
34	45-60	48	Vary	$6.99	New Christian	Workbk	Topical

Features: Intro to Study, Scrpt Memory Helps
★★ Personal Application Preparation Time: Low
★★ Relationship Building Ldr Guide: Yes Size: 8.50 x 11.0
Subjects: Teens: Christian Liv, Teens: Discipleship
Comments: This in-depth study for young adults uses 34 Bible examples to give the true meaning of Christian character traits. The examples show practical ways each trait can be applied in a Christian's life today and propose appropriate memory Scriptures to reinforce the truth. Character traits include perseverance, forgiveness, self-control, gentleness, confidence, wisdom, fairness, enthusiasm, and more.

Author: Anthony, Michelle 85
Series: Group's Active Bible Curriculum
Title: *Doing Your Best*
Publisher: Group Publishing, 1993 ISBN: 1-55945-142-4

Num. Sess.	Group Time	Num. Pgs.	Avg. Qst.	Price	Audience	Format	Bible Study
4	35-60	45	Vary	$9.99	Beginner	Workbk	Topical

Features: Intro to Leading a Study, Intro to Study, Objectives, Study Overview, Ldr's Notes, Handouts, Agenda, Publicity Ideas
★★★★ Personal Application Preparation Time: None
★★★★ Relationship Building Ldr Guide: No Size: 8.50 x 11.0
Subjects: Teens: Christian Liv, Teens: Junior High, Teens: Relationships, Teens: Values
Comments: This course lends a hand to junior highers as they strive for excellence. It shows them what God expects from them, and how He is there to help them do their best. Participants explore how to have excellent relationships with God, how to make their school lives reflect their spiritual lives, how to choose values according to His Word.

Author: Anthony, Michelle 86
Series: Group's Active Bible Curriculum
Title: *Today's Faith Heroes*
Publisher: Group Publishing, 1994 ISBN: 1-55945-141-6

Num. Sess.	Group Time	Num. Pgs.	Avg. Qst.	Price	Audience	Format	Bible Study
4	35-60	47	Vary	$9.99	Beginner	Workbk	Topical

Features: Intro to Leading a Study, Intro to Study, Objectives, Study Overview, Ldr's Notes, Handouts, Agenda, Publicity Ideas
★★★★ Personal Application Preparation Time: None
★★★★ Relationship Building Ldr Guide: No Size: 8.50 x 11.0
Subjects: Teens: Christian Liv, Teens: Junior High, Teens: Missions
Comments: This course offers junior highers positive Christian role models to follow, including Madeline Manning Mims, Michael W. Smith, Mother Teresa, and Bruce Olson. Participants explore how to remain faithful during tough times, understand the importance of living to glorify God, and see the value of serving others. It can be adapted for a Bible class or youth meeting. Activity sheets are reproducible.

Author: Arn, Charles 87
Series:
Title: *Growing in Love*
Publisher: Church Growth, 1984

Num. Sess.	Group Time	Num. Pgs.	Avg. Qst.	Price	Audience	Format	Bible Study
13	60-75	112	Vary	$156.00	Beginner	Video	Topical

Features: Study Overview, Ldr's Notes, Transpcy Masters, Agenda, Book Incl, Video Study Guide
★★★ Personal Application Preparation Time: None
★★★ Relationship Building Ldr Guide: No Size: 11.25 x 11.50
Subjects: Caring, Church Life, Love, Marriage, Relationships
Comments: This 13-week study helps participants learn how to express and practice Christian love. They learn that love is not just attitude, but action. The kit includes complete leader's notes; instructional video; masters for overhead transparencies; and sample participant pack, including text, workbook, application guide, and personal "love quotient" inventory.

Author: Arndt, Elise 88
Series:
Title: *Mother's Time, A*
Publisher: Victor Books, 1987 ISBN: 0-89693-338-5

Num. Sess.	Group Time	Num. Pgs.	Avg. Qst.	Price	Audience	Format	Bible Study
13	60-90	156	N/A	$8.99	Beginner	Book	Topical

Features:
★★★★ Personal Application Preparation Time: Med
★★★★ Relationship Building Ldr Guide: Yes Size: 5.50 x 8.0
Subjects: Parenting, Time, Women's Issues
Comments: This study presents practical advice for modern Christian mothers, whose days are filled with diapers and teething babies, car pools, and Little League, and whose time demands exceed the supply. Participants learn that one solution to mothers' time crunch is doing God's will. Mothers can learn to deal with time pressures and take time to learn each day.

Author: Arndt, Elise 89
Series:
Title: *Mother's Touch, A*
Publisher: Victor Books, 1983 ISBN: 0-88207-101-7

Num. Sess.	Group Time	Num. Pgs.	Avg. Qst.	Price	Audience	Format	Bible Study
13	60-75	151	N/A	$8.99	Beginner	Book	Topical

Features:
★★★ Personal Application Preparation Time: Low
★★★ Relationship Building Ldr Guide: Yes Size: 5.50 x 8.0
Subjects: Family, Parenting, Women's Issues
Comments: This 13-week study of mothers' roles in the lives of children covers such topics as: balancing a child's dependence; working outside the home; making each child feel special; integrating Christian principles into everyday life; and realizing the obligation to bring one's child to the Lord. One lesson, "New in the Nest," looks at pregnancy in an "older" woman. A leader's guide includes transparency masters.

Author: Arnold, Jeffrey 90
Series:
Title: *Big Book on Small Groups, The*
Publisher: InterVarsity, 1992 ISBN: 0-83081-377-2

Num. Sess.	Group Time	Num. Pgs.	Avg. Qst.	Price	Audience	Format	Bible Study
13	—	260	10	$10.99			

Features:
Personal Application Preparation Time:
Relationship Building Ldr Guide: Size: 6.0 x 9.0
Subjects: Small Group Resource
Comments: This book offers information on the basics of group life: leadership, inductive Bible study, worship, caring, praying, evangelizing, and mission. Instructions and outlines are included for use in training small group leaders. The first four chapters (or four training sessions) provide basics for getting started. The remainder of the book provides support and nurture necessary to take a group to maturity. At the end of each chapter are questions for individual or group use.

Author: Arnold, Jeffrey 91
Series: LifeGuide Bible Study
Title: *Discovering the Bible for Yourself*
Publisher: InterVarsity, 1993 ISBN: 0-83081-387-X

Num. Sess.	Group Time	Num. Pgs.	Avg. Qst.	Price	Audience	Format	Bible Study
10	60-75	151	3	$8.99	Beginner	Book	Topical

Features: Intro to Study, Ldr's Notes, Persnl Study Quest, Appendix
★★★★ Personal Application Preparation Time: Low
★★★ Relationship Building Ldr Guide: No Size: 5.50 x 8.25
Subjects: Bible Study, Small Group Resource
Comments: This ten-week study introduces inductive Bible study, outlining a step-by-step approach which follows a simple pattern of observation, interpretation, and application. Chapters 2 and 3 address the "big picture," showing how to gain a basic overview of a Bible book before digging deeper. Chapters 4–10 demonstrate how to apply the principles of inductive study to individual passages. This book is suitable for individuals, small groups, or Sunday School classes.

Author: Arnold, Jeffrey 92
Series: LifeGuide Bible Study
Title: *Small Group Starter Kit*
Publisher: InterVarsity, 1995 ISBN: 0-83081-073-0

Num. Sess.	Group Time	Num. Pgs.	Avg. Qst.	Price	Audience	Format	Bible Study
6	45-60	64	12	$4.99	New Christian	Workbk	Book

Features: Intro to Leading a Study, Intro to Study, Ldr's Notes
★★★ Personal Application Preparation Time: Low
★★★★ Relationship Building Ldr Guide: No Size: 5.50 x 8.25
Subjects: Bible Study, Small Group Resource
Comments: This study allows a new small group to build significant relationships, grow in their knowledge and understanding of Scripture, and learn how to reach out to others. It is easy to use and provides everything needed for the first meetings of a small group, including getting acquainted exercises, a plan for setting expectations, and studying Scripture.

Author: Arp, Claudia 93
Series: Parents Encouraging Parent
Title: *PEP Groups for MOMS: Building Relationships with Your Children*
Publisher: David C. Cook Publishing Co., 1994 ISBN: 6-12506-890-0

Num. Sess.	Group Time	Num. Pgs.	Avg. Qst.	Price	Audience	Format	Bible Study
5	90-120	N/A	Vary	$299.00	Beginner	Video	Topical

Features: Intro to Study, Objectives
★★★★ Personal Application Preparation Time: Low
★★★★ Relationship Building Ldr Guide: Yes Size: 8.50 x 11.0
Subjects: Family, Parenting, Relationships
Comments: PEP Groups, a complete program for mothers of children of all ages, is ideal for community outreach and "mother's day out" programs. A kit includes four videos, promotional brochures and posters, director's handbook, leader's guide, six study books, and additional programming ideas, and may be used year after year. This program equips moms with biblical principles for effective parenting.

Author: Arp, Dave and Claudia 94
Series: Parents Encouraging Parents
Title: *PEP Groups for Parents of Teens*
Publisher: David C. Cook Publishing Co., 1994 ISBN: 6-12506-783-1

Num. Sess.	Group Time	Num. Pgs.	Avg. Qst.	Price	Audience	Format	Bible Study
8	60-90	N/A	N/A	$299.00	Beginner	Video	Topical

Features: Intro to Study, Objectives, Cartoons, Publicity Ideas
★★★★ Personal Application Preparation Time: Low
★★★★ Relationship Building Ldr Guide: Yes Size: 8.50 x 11.0
Subjects: Family, Parenting, Relationships
Comments: PEP Groups, a complete program for parents of children of all ages, is ideal for community outreach. The kit includes four videos, promotional brochures and posters, director's handbook and leader's guide, six study books, and additional programming ideas. It has a long shelf life, enabling single or married parents to strengthen their marriages, build supportive friendships with other parents.

Author: Arthur, Kay 95
Series:
Title: *Call to Follow Jesus, The*
Publisher: Harvest House Publishers, 1994 ISBN: 1-56507-221-9

Num. Sess.	Group Time	Num. Pgs.	Avg. Qst.	Price	Audience	Format	Bible Study
13	45-60	76	6	$4.99	New Christian	Book	Book

Features: Intro to Study, Scrpt Memory Helps, Follow Up, Drawings, Charts, Maps
★★★★ Personal Application Preparation Time: Med
★★ Relationship Building Ldr Guide: No Size: 5.25 x 8.0
Subjects: Luke
Comments: This study is designed to totally involve readers for 15″ daily. Instructions are given for interpreting Bible text by asking "5 'Ws and H" (what, who, where, why, and how), and how to implement the author's tried and true methods of marking and highlighting key elements of Scripture. This study enables readers to deny themselves, take up the cross, and follow Jesus.

Author: Arthur, Kay 96
Series:
Title: *Free From Bondage God's Way*
Publisher: Harvest House Publishers, 1994 ISBN: 1-56507-205-7

Num. Sess.	Group Time	Num. Pgs.	Avg. Qst.	Price	Audience	Format	Bible Study
13	45-60	87	6	$4.99	New Christian	Book	Book

Features: Intro to Study, Scrpt Memory Helps, Follow Up, Drawings, Charts, Maps
★★★★ Personal Application Preparation Time: Med
★★ Relationship Building Ldr Guide: No Size: 5.25 x 8.0
Subjects: Ephesians, Galatians
Comments: This study is designed to totally involve readers for 15″ daily. Instructions regard how to interpret Bible text by asking "5 'Ws and H" (what, who, where, why, and how), and how to implement the author's tried and true methods of marking and highlighting key elements of Scripture. In this study participants discover matchless freedom found in Christ, and see God's grace in action.

Author: Arthur, Kay **97**
Series:
Title: *Lord Teach Me To Pray*
Publisher: Harvest House Publishers, 1994 ISBN: 1-56507-252-9

Num. Sess.	Group Time	Num. Pgs.	Avg. Qst.	Price	Audience	Format	Bible Study
4	45-60	159	10	$7.99	New Christian	Book	Topical

Features: Cassette Avail
★★★★ Personal Application Preparation Time: Med
★★ Relationship Building Ldr Guide: No Size: 5.25 x 8.0
Subjects: Prayer
Comments: This 28-day study, based on the Lord's Prayer, provides practical insights that help participants know "how to pray," "what to pray," and "what to expect" when praying. It can be used in small group settings, prayer groups, Sunday school classes, as discipleship material, or simply by itself.

Author: Arthur, Kay **98**
Series:
Title: *Teach Me Your Ways*
Publisher: Harvest House Publishers, 1994 ISBN: 1-56507-204-9

Num. Sess.	Group Time	Num. Pgs.	Avg. Qst.	Price	Audience	Format	Bible Study
13	45-60	160	5	$6.99	New Christian	Book	Book

Features: Intro to Study, Scrpt Memory Helps, Follow Up, Drawings, Charts, Maps
★★★★ Personal Application Preparation Time: Med
★★ Relationship Building Ldr Guide: No Size: 5.25 x 8.0
Subjects: Genesis, Exodus, Leviticus, Numbers, Deuteronomy
Comments: This study is designed to totally involve readers for 15″ daily. Instructions regard how to interpret Bible text by asking "5'Ws and an H" (what, who, when, where, why, and how), and how to implement the author's tried and true methods of marking and highlighting key elements of Scripture. In this study participants can learn about creation, man, marriage, sin, and civilization.

Author: Ashker, Helene **99**
Series:
Title: *Jesus Cares for Women*
Publisher: NavPress, 1987 ISBN: 0-89109-190-4

Num. Sess.	Group Time	Num. Pgs.	Avg. Qst.	Price	Audience	Format	Bible Study
5	45-60	68	7	$7.00	New Christian	Workbk	Topical

Features: Intro to Study, Ldr's Notes
★★★★ Personal Application Preparation Time: None
★★★★ Relationship Building Ldr Guide: No Size: 5.50 x 8.50
Subjects: Singles' Issues, Small Group Resource, Women's Issues
Comments: This study was written for women who, like its author, have known fear and hesitancy about sharing their faith. Participants can learn to overcome inhibitions and experience the joy of confidently sharing God's Good News through this women's Bible study. The leader's guide takes a step-by-step approach to each lesson. The 22-page reproducible study explores how Jesus interacted with five special women in the Bible.

Author: Atchison, Liam & Precious **100**
Series: IBC Discussion Guide
Title: *Grief*
Publisher: NavPress, 1993 ISBN: 0-89109-743-0

Num. Sess.	Group Time	Num. Pgs.	Avg. Qst.	Price	Audience	Format	Bible Study
6	60-90	80	6	$5.00	Beginner	Workbk	Topical

Features: Intro to Leading a Study, Intro to Study, Prayer Helps, Follow Up, Ldr's Notes
★★★★ Personal Application Preparation Time: None
★★★★ Relationship Building Ldr Guide: No Size: 5.25 x 8.25
Subjects: Counseling, Grief, Support
Comments: "Grief" is one of six studies that identify how life struggles affect the way participants relate to themselves, others, and God. Helps participants cope with some form of grief to gain the courage to face tragedy as bad, not natural. Rather than forcing participants into feeling more "Christian" by passing their losses off as "all for the best," this study steers them into healthy grieving and healing processes.

Author: Atkins, Tim, et al. **101**
Series: SonPower Youth Sources
Title: *Love, Sex, and Dating Series, The: Leader's Guide*
Publisher: Victor Books, 1993 ISBN: 1-56476-237-8

Num. Sess.	Group Time	Num. Pgs.	Avg. Qst.	Price	Audience	Format	Bible Study
	—	95	N/A	$5.99	New Christian	Book	Topical

Features: Intro to Leading a Study, Intro to Study, Objectives
★★★★ Personal Application Preparation Time: Med
★★★ Relationship Building Ldr Guide: Yes Size: 6.0 x 9.0
Subjects: Leader's Guide, Teens: Resources, Teens: Sexuality
Comments: This is the leaders guide for "Love: Making It Last"; "Dating: Going Out in Style"; and "Sex: Desiring the Best." There is an overview lesson for teaching the study in 1 session or in 4 lessons, each corresponding to 3 chapters in the book. The lessons build on ideas that are discussed in previous lessons, but they can also stand alone. Each lesson includes fun activities, solid biblical teaching, and exercises that challenge participants to apply what they read.

Author: Backus, William & Steven Wiese **102**
Series:
Title: *Finding the Freedom of Self-Control*
Publisher: Bethany House, 1988 ISBN: 1-55661-004-1

Num. Sess.	Group Time	Num. Pgs.	Avg. Qst.	Price	Audience	Format	Bible Study
13	60-75	95	Vary	$4.99	New Christian	Workbk	Topical

Features: Intro to Study, Prayer Helps, Summary
★★★ Personal Application Preparation Time: Med
★★ Relationship Building Ldr Guide: No Size: 5.0 x 8.0
Subjects: Accountability, Addictions, Christian Living, Self-help, Support
Comments: This study addresses the problem of self-control, whether the cause is procrastination or bondage to an addiction. Among the study's goals: to identify personal self-control problems and misbelief; to challenge participants to apply Scripture truths to life situations; to involve them in growth and initiative through specific assignments; and to break the pattern of old habits and build new habits of self-control. This study guide is designed to accompany the book by the same title.

Author: Backus, William & Marie Chapian **103**
Series:
Title: *Telling Yourself the Truth: A Study Guide*
Publisher: Bethany House, 1981 ISBN: 0-87123-567-6

Num. Sess.	Group Time	Num. Pgs.	Avg. Qst.	Price	Audience	Format	Bible Study
14	45-60	41	11	$3.99	New Christian	Workbk	Topical

Features: Intro to Study, Cassette Avail
★★★ Personal Application Preparation Time: Med
★★ Relationship Building Ldr Guide: Yes Size: 5.0 x 8.0
Subjects: Counseling, Emotions, Psychology, Self-help
Comments: This study, a companion to the book and tape by the same title, helps participants understand that most of what happens in life can be attributed to the way people think. The life-changing message, called "misbelief therapy," can help people deal with common problems in the home and in their circumstances, environment, and thinking. It is based on the Bible, not on psychological speculations. Understanding truth can help people locate and remove misbeliefs.

Author: Backus, William & Candace **104**
Series:
Title: *Untwisting Twisted Relationships*
Publisher: Bethany House, 1989 ISBN: 1-55661-089-0

Num. Sess.	Group Time	Num. Pgs.	Avg. Qst.	Price	Audience	Format	Bible Study
11	60-75	63	17	$4.99	New Christian	Workbk	Topical

Features: Prayer Helps
★★★★ Personal Application Preparation Time: Med
★★★ Relationship Building Ldr Guide: Yes Size: 5.0 x 8.0
Subjects: Christian Living, Family, Holy Spirit, Psychology, Relationships, Support
Comments: This study, to be used in conjunction with the book of the same title, helps restore close ties with family and friends. It identifies twists that prevent close personal relationships; challenges individuals to honestly apply God's truth to these situations; and encourages people to allow the Holy Spirit to get involved in the restoration process.

Author: Bacon, Dr. Daniel W. **105**
Series: Lay Action Ministry
Title: *Equipping for Missions: A Guide to Making Career Decisions*
Publisher: Lay Action Ministry Program, 1992

Num. Sess.	Group Time	Num. Pgs.	Avg. Qst.	Price	Audience	Format	Bible Study
12	60-75	159	Vary	$6.95	New Christian	Workbk	Topical

Features:
★★★ Personal Application Preparation Time: Low
★★★ Relationship Building Ldr. Guide: Yes Size: 5.50 x 8.50
Subjects: Missions
Comments: This LAMP lay training publication includes step-by-step instructions which can help serious Christians understand how an individual life can make a significant contribution to God's global purpose. Dr. Bacon provides information, counsel, suggestions, checklists, and resources to guide seekers through the crucial steps of decision-making, guidance, preparation, and training. It is designed for either group or individual study. Homework is required.

Author: Bajema, Edith L. **106**
Series: Discover Your Bible
Title: *Discover Genesis: The Patriarchs*
Publisher: Church Development Resources, 1991

Num. Sess.	Group Time	Num. Pgs.	Avg. Qst.	Price	Audience	Format	Bible Study
13	45-60	47	7	$2.10	Beginner	Workbk	Book

Features: Intro to Study, Glossary
★★★ Personal Application Preparation Time: None
★★ Relationship Building Ldr. Guide: Yes Size: 5.50 x 8.50
Subjects: Bible Personalities, Faith, Genesis, God
Comments: This third study in a three-part series on Genesis continues the story of Abraham's family, tracing the history of his son Isaac, his grandson Jacob, and his great-grandson Joseph. It exposes a family involved in deceit, favoritism, violence, and jealousy, but also a magnificent faith in God. This series is intended for small group Bible study; however, it can be used profitably for personal study.

Author: Bajema, Edith L. **107**
Series: Discover Your Bible
Title: *Discover Jesus In John—The Lives He Touched*
Publisher: Church Development Resources, 1992

Num. Sess.	Group Time	Num. Pgs.	Avg. Qst.	Price	Audience	Format	Bible Study
9	60-75	80	8	$1.75	Beginner	Workbk	Book

Features: Intro to Study, Glossary
★★★ Personal Application Preparation Time: None
★★ Relationship Building Ldr. Guide: Yes Size: 5.50 x 8.50
Subjects: John
Comments: This continuation of the study of John introduces participants to biblical personalities, including rough fishermen from Galilee, a searching Pharisee, prostitutes, and more. One thing all these had in common was that Jesus touched their lives. Participants are exhorted to be prepared to meet a Savior who rejects the stern religion of legalism, and a Teacher who condemns hypocrisy and self-righteousness.

Author: Bajema, Edith L. **108**
Series: Inspirit
Title: *Does God Want to Spoil My Fun?*
Publisher: Church Development Resources, 1994

Num. Sess.	Group Time	Num. Pgs.	Avg. Qst.	Price	Audience	Format	Bible Study
6	30-90	176	5	$12.00	Beginner	Book	Topical

Features: Intro to Leading a Study, Prayer Helps, Follow Up, Full Scrpt Printed
★★★★ Personal Application Preparation Time: None
★★★ Relationship Building Ldr. Guide: Yes Size: 8.50 x 11.0
Subjects: Addictions, Materialism, Sexual Issues
Comments: This six-lesson study responds to the idea that people think life's no fun when God's around. Participants will explore biblical guidelines and see how some people push the limits. Lessons include such topics as substance abuse, materialism, self-centeredness, revenge, sexuality, and control. This book includes a leader's guide and ten discussion handouts (participants sheets).

Author: Bajema, Edith L. 109
Series: Inspirit
Title: *Holding Together When It's Falling Apart*
Publisher: Church Development Resources, 1994

Num. Sess.	Group Time	Num. Pgs.	Avg. Qst.	Price	Audience	Format	Bible Study
6	30-90	190	5	$12.00	Beginner	Book	Topical

Features: Intro to Leading a Study, Prayer Helps, Follow Up, Full Scrpt Printed
★★★★ Personal Application Preparation Time: None
★★★ Relationship Building Ldr. Guide: Yes Size: 8.50 x 11.0
Subjects: Relationships, Self-esteem, Time
Comments: This six-lesson study addresses issues of everyday life, relationships, self-concepts, and helps participants find ways to hold life together when it seems to be falling apart. Lesson titles include: "I Am Too Busy"; "I Don't Like Who I Am"; "I Can't Seem to Improve Myself"; "My Relationships Are Shallow"; "My Relationships Aren't Working"; and "I Can't Do This On My Own."

Author: Bajema, Edith L. 110
Series: Core Values Series
Title: *Priority of Prayer, The*
Publisher: Church Development Resources, 1993

Num. Sess.	Group Time	Num. Pgs.	Avg. Qst.	Price	Audience	Format	Bible Study
	—	31	N/A	$1.35			

Features:
Personal Application Preparation Time:
Relationship Building Ldr. Guide: Size: 5.0 x 7.0
Subjects: Prayer, Small Group Resource
Comments: This resource reinforces the principles and practices necessary for Coffee Break leaders to experience the fruit of the Spirit and joy of the harvest. It begins with a testimony of a group life changed as a result of prayer. It discusses the "why" of prayer, what prayer can do, ways to make prayer part of the Coffee Break program, and what makes prayer effective.

Author: Baker, Donald 111
Series: LifeGuide Bible Study
Title: *Joshua: The Power of God's Promises*
Publisher: InterVarsity, 1988 ISBN: 0-83081-024-2

Num. Sess.	Group Time	Num. Pgs.	Avg. Qst.	Price	Audience	Format	Bible Study
12	45-60	61	12	$4.99	New Christian	Workbk	Book

Features: Intro to Leading a Study, Intro to Study, Ldr's Notes
★ Personal Application Preparation Time: Low
★ Relationship Building Ldr. Guide: No Size: 5.50 x 8.25
Subjects: Bible Personalities, God's Promises, Joshua, Obedience
Comments: Joshua is a book for people whose prayers seem to go unanswered, who wonder if God is really alive and active, and who desire fresh assurance of God's dependability. Practical truths describe how Christians can enjoy God's promises fulfilled in Joshua's life, as he led the Israelites through the Jordan River to conquer the Promised Land. The study reveals how Christians today can rely on God's promises when they obey His commands.

Author: Baker, Donald 112
Series: LifeGuide Bible Study
Title: *Philippians: Jesus Our Joy*
Publisher: InterVarsity, 1985 ISBN: 0-83081-013-7

Num. Sess.	Group Time	Num. Pgs.	Avg. Qst.	Price	Audience	Format	Bible Study
9	45-60	58	11	$4.99	New Christian	Workbk	Book

Features: Intro to Leading a Study, Intro to Study, Ldr's Notes
★ Personal Application Preparation Time: Low
★ Relationship Building Ldr. Guide: No Size: 5.50 x 8.25
Subjects: Joy, Philippians, Prison Epistles, Suffering
Comments: Paul, writing to the Philippians from prison, said, "Rejoice in the Lord always." Paul experienced a joy not dependent on circumstances, a contentment difficulties could not suppress. This study teaches how to live joyfully in the midst of troubles by focusing attention on the One who is over every situation. The final lesson is a thematic overview which highlights the most important points for application.

Author: Baldwin, Stanley C. 113
Series:
Title: *What Did Jesus Say About That?*
Publisher: Victor Books, 1975 ISBN: 0-88207-718-X

Num. Sess.	Group Time	Num. Pgs.	Avg. Qst.	Price	Audience	Format	Bible Study
13	60-75	178	N/A	$8.99	New Christian	Book	Topical

Features: Intro to Study
★★★★ Personal Application Preparation Time: Low
★★★ Relationship Building Ldr. Guide: Yes Size: 5.50 x 8.0
Subjects: Divorce, Eschatology, Faith, Jesus: Life/Teaching, Marriage, Money, Obedience, Prayer, Relationships
Comments: In this 13-week study of Christ's major teachings, participants will learn what Jesus said about the following: God, faith, the Word, Himself, prayer, following Him, sin, life after death, freedom and obedience, money, relating to others, marriage and divorce, and His return. The leader's guide offers many helps and reproducible response sheets.

Author: Ball-Kilbourne, Dr. Gary L. 114
Series:
Title: *Get Acquainted With Your Bible*
Publisher: Abingdon Press, 1993 ISBN: 0-68714-046-3

Num. Sess.	Group Time	Num. Pgs.	Avg. Qst.	Price	Audience	Format	Bible Study
8	60-105	72	N/A	$4.00	Beginner	Book	Topical

Features: Intro to Study, Worship Helps, Drawings, Photos
★★★ Personal Application Preparation Time: Low
★★★ Relationship Building Ldr. Guide: Yes Size: 7.0 x 10.0
Subjects: Bible Study, Youth Life
Comments: This basic introduction to the Bible, easy to use and easy to understand, is ideal for newly organized church groups or classes, new church members, and adults with little or no Bible background. Designed for group study, the eight sessions also can be used as a self-directed study.

Author: Ball-Kilbourne, Dr. Gary L. 115
Series:
Title: *Get Acquainted With Your Bible: Leader's Guide*
Publisher: Abingdon Press, 1993 ISBN: 0-68714-047-1

Num. Sess.	Group Time	Num. Pgs.	Avg. Qst.	Price	Audience	Format	Bible Study
8	60-105	48	N/A	$4.50	Beginner	Book	Topical

Features: Intro to Leading a Study, Intro to Study, Prayer Helps, Worship Helps, Photos
★★★ Personal Application Preparation Time:
★★★ Relationship Building Ldr. Guide: Size: 8.50 x 11.0
Subjects: Bible Study, Youth Life
Comments: This leader's guide contains complete plans for eight study sessions and is easily adaptable to many types of settings. Each session includes a basic outline with several learning ideas, including activities such as reading, working on projects, imaginative play, and artistic expression. Leaders can choose ideas that best suit their class and their teaching skills.

Author: Ball-Kilbourne, Debra 116
Series:
Title: *Journey Through The Bible: Genesis, Leader's Guide*
Publisher: Cokesbury, 1994

Num. Sess.	Group Time	Num. Pgs.	Avg. Qst.	Price	Audience	Format	Bible Study
13	30-60	72	4	$4.95	New Christian	Book	Book

Features: Intro to Leading a Study, Maps
Personal Application Preparation Time:
Relationship Building Ldr. Guide: Size: 8.50 x 11.0
Subjects: Leader's Guide
Comments: This leader's guide provides answers to questions in the student book, as well as additional Bible helps. A section on "How to Create Excitement for Bible Study" is also helpful. A chart provides a timeline for events in Genesis and beyond.

Author: Ball-Kilbourne, Debra 117
Series:
Title: *Journey Through The Bible: Genesis*
Publisher: Cokesbury, 1994

Num. Sess.	Group Time	Num. Pgs.	Avg. Qst.	Price	Audience	Format	Bible Study
13	30-60	112	4	$2.95	New Christian	Book	Book

Features: Intro to Study, Maps
★★★ Personal Application Preparation Time: Med
★★★ Relationship Building Ldr. Guide: Yes Size: 5.50 x 8.50
Subjects: Genesis
Comments: This resource can help adults gain basic Bbile literacy through an organized, book-by-book approach. Each session covers a major passage of Scripture. Sessions on Genesis include: "Creation"; "Sin"; "Flood"; "Pride and Confusion"; "Covenant and Sojourn"; "Willfulness and Grace"; "Hospitality and Laughter"; "Sodom and Gomorrah"; "Sacrifice"; "Esau and Jacob"; "Jacob and God"; "Dreams"; and "Restoration."

Author: Ball-Kilbourne, Dr. Gary L. 118
Series:
Title: Who Is Jesus? 13 Answers That Can Change Your Life: Teacher Book
Publisher: Cokesbury, 1994 ISBN: 0-68778-214-7

Num. Sess.	Group Time	Num. Pgs.	Avg. Qst.	Price	Audience	Format	Bible Study
13	75-90	48	N/A	$9.95	New Christian	Book	Charctr

Features: Prayer Helps, Full Scrpt Printed
★★★★ Personal Application Preparation Time:
★★★★ Relationship Building Ldr. Guide: Size: 8.25 x 11.0
Subjects: Jesus: Life/Teaching
Comments: For adults who want to clarify their understanding of Jesus and His call on their lives. The teacher book contains complete plans for 13 study sessions and adapts easily to many types of settings. Teachers are provided with each session's stated purpose, Bible background, a step-by-step teaching plan, and instructions on how to use the audio tape included in the teacher kit.

Author: Ball-Kilbourne, Dr. Gary L. 119
Series:
Title: *Who Is Jesus? 13 Answers That Can Change Your Life*
Publisher: Cokesbury, 1994 ISBN: 0-68778-205-8

Num. Sess.	Group Time	Num. Pgs.	Avg. Qst.	Price	Audience	Format	Bible Study
13	75-90	64	7	$5.00	New Christian	Workbk	Charctr

Features: Intro to Study, Full Scrpt Printed, Cassette Avail
★★★★ Personal Application Preparation Time: None
★★★★ Relationship Building Ldr. Guide: Yes Size: 7.25 x 10.0
Subjects: Jesus: Life/Teaching
Comments: The story of Jesus is presented through 13 biblical titles, using images from early disciples to confess His impact on their lives. Included are Son of David, Liberator, Messiah, Teacher/Rabbi, Son of God, Son of Man, Servant, Judge, Light of the World, Lamb of God, Lord, Savior and Good Shepherd. Can be used in a new believers' class. It brings adults face-to-face with Christ in their personal lives, community, and world.

Author: Balswick, Jack, et. al. 120
Series: GroupBuilder Resources
Title: *Gift of Gender, The*
Publisher: Victor Books, 1991 ISBN: 0-89693-882-4

Num. Sess.	Group Time	Num. Pgs.	Avg. Qst.	Price	Audience	Format	Bible Study
8	75-90	144	Vary	$5.99	New Christian	Workbk	Topical

Features: Intro to Leading a Study, Objectives, Digging Deeper Quest, Follow Up, Scrpt Printed, Ldr's Notes, Cartoons, Personal Quest
★★★★ Personal Application Preparation Time: Low
★★★ Relationship Building Ldr. Guide: No Size: 6.0 x 9.0
Subjects: Leadership, Marriage, Men's Issues, Parenting, Sexual Issues, Women's Issues, Work
Comments: Examines 8 aspects of gender roles and embraces a biblical model for manhood and womanhood. Topics include traditional roles, power, control, dependence, sexuality and spirituality, fathering and mothering, friendship, gender in the workplace, and gender in leadership. Includes optional activities and hints for leaders.

Author: Bankson, Marjory Zoet **121**
Series:
Title: *With Tongues of Fire: Five Women From the Book of Acts*
Publisher: Faith at Work, 1990

Num. Sess.	Group Time	Num. Pgs.	Avg. Qst.	Price	Audience	Format	Bible Study
5	60-75	N/A	4	$33.00	Beginner	Video	Charctr

Features: Intro to Study, Video Study Guide
★★★ Personal Application Preparation Time: None
★★★ Relationship Building Ldr. Guide: No Size: 0.0 x 0.0
Subjects: Bible Personalities
Comments: In this video series, Marjory Zoet Bankson acts out the roles of five biblical women: Mary, the Mother of Jesus (17″); Sapphira (12 1/2″); Rhoda (8″); Lydia (12″); and Priscilla (11″). A discussion guide which accompanies the video is for small group use and includes Scripture passages to be read, a getting acquainted exercise, and video instructions. Following the video are discussion questions. Participants are encouraged to apply the lessons to their own lives.

Author: Banks, Robert & Gordon Preece **122**
Series: GroupBuilder Resources
Title: *Getting the Job Done Right*
Publisher: Victor Books, 1992 ISBN: 0-89693-957-X

Num. Sess.	Group Time	Num. Pgs.	Avg. Qst.	Price	Audience	Format	Bible Study
8	75-90	143	Vary	$5.99	New Christian	Workbk	Topical

Features: Intro to Leading a Study, Intro to Study, Objectives, Prayer Helps, Full Scrpt Printed, Ldr's Notes, Drawings, Persnl Study Quest
★★★★ Personal Application Preparation Time: Med
★★★★ Relationship Building Ldr. Guide: No Size: 6.0 x 9.0
Subjects: Work
Comments: This 8-lesson study concerns work, its significance beyond putting in hours and picking up a paycheck. Participants see how adopting a biblical view of work can adjust attitudes on and off the job. Lessons cover God's wider view of work, when God goes to work, work's love/hate relationship, God's employees, juggling callings, worthy work, balancing work and leisure, and the Sunday-Monday connection.

Author: Barna, George **123**
Series:
Title: *Baby Busters: The Disillusioned Generation*
Publisher: Moody Press, 1992 ISBN: 1-88127-319-9

Num. Sess.	Group Time	Num. Pgs.	Avg. Qst.	Price	Audience	Format	Bible Study
10	60-75	158	N/A	$9.99	Beginner	Book	Topical

Features: Charts, Appendix
★★★★ Personal Application Preparation Time: Low
★★ Relationship Building Ldr. Guide: No Size: 6.0 x 9.0
Subjects: Social Issues
Comments: This book sheds light on the rising generation—11 to 29-year-olds—who will soon be leaders and molders of this nation. The author provides a comprehensive examination of this generation coming of age. Among topics explored are the demographics of Baby Busters, how they differ from previous generations, expectations, values, morals, and perspectives that shape their lives, their lifestyles and personal relationships, and views on family and work.

Author: Barna, George **124**
Series:
Title: *If Things Are So Good, Why Do I Feel So Bad?*
Publisher: Moody Press, 1994 ISBN: 0-80249-244-4

Num. Sess.	Group Time	Num. Pgs.	Avg. Qst.	Price	Audience	Format	Bible Study
13	60-90	260	5	$16.99	New Christian	Book	Topical

Features: Bibliography, Follow Up, Appendix
★★★★ Personal Application Preparation Time: Med
★★ Relationship Building Ldr. Guide: No Size: 6.50 x 9.25
Subjects: Leadership, Relationships, Success
Comments: This book reveals Americans' attitudes about family, relationships, career, leisure, and the media. The author exposes the dichotomy of internal attitudes and external advantages. He uncovers root causes of troubles in America and answers a logical question: What can we do, as a nation and church, to escape poverty of values, purpose, and joy?

Author: Barton, R. Ruth **125**
Series: Fisherman Bible Studyguide
Title: *Becoming Women of Purpose*
Publisher: Shaw, 1992 ISBN: 0-87788-061-1

Num. Sess.	Group Time	Num. Pgs.	Avg. Qst.	Price	Audience	Format	Bible Study
13	45-60	77	10	$4.99	Beginner	Workbk	Topical

Features: Intro to Leading a Study, Intro to Study, Follow Up, Ldr's Notes
★★★★ Personal Application Preparation Time: Low
★★★ Relationship Building Ldr. Guide: No Size: 5.25 x 8.25
Subjects: Bible Personalities, Women's Issues
Comments: This 13-week study begins with the story of Esther, who was transformed from a frightened and somewhat passive woman into one of strength, courage, and action. Participants can identify themselves as women of purpose as they explore God's purpose in their creation, salvation, giftedness, and preparation. Three elements of purposeful living are explored.

Author: Barton, R. Ruth **126**
Series: Fisherman Bible Studyguide
Title: *Women Like Us: Wisdom for Today's Issues*
Publisher: Shaw, 1989 ISBN: 0-87788-943-0

Num. Sess.	Group Time	Num. Pgs.	Avg. Qst.	Price	Audience	Format	Bible Study
13	45-60	94	12	$4.99	Mature Christian	Workbk	Topical

Features: Intro to Leading a Study, Intro to Study, Bibliography, Prayer Helps, Ldr's Notes
★★★ Personal Application Preparation Time: None
★★ Relationship Building Ldr. Guide: No Size: 5.0 x 8.25
Subjects: Bible Personalities, Marriage, Medical Issues, Singles' Issues, Social Issues, Wisdom, Women's Issues
Comments: This study deals with contemporary female issues: singleness, sanctity of life, infertility, caring for aging parents, materialism, and the role of women in marriage and ministry. Each lesson begins with a study of a real woman whose life portrays contemporary issues: the Samaritan woman, Mary, Martha, Sarah, Abigail, Hannah, Ruth.

Author: Baylis, Robert **127**
Series: Fisherman Bible Studyguide
Title: *Ephesians: Living in God's Household*
Publisher: Shaw, 1976 ISBN: 0-87788-223-1

Num. Sess.	Group Time	Num. Pgs.	Avg. Qst.	Price	Audience	Format	Bible Study
11	45-60	64	10	$4.99	Mature Christian	Workbk	Book

Features: Intro to Leading a Study, Intro to Study, Prayer Helps
★★ Personal Application Preparation Time: Low
★★ Relationship Building Ldr. Guide: No Size: 5.0 x 8.25
Subjects: Church Life, Ephesians, Family, Marriage
Comments: This study is divided into two parts and is concluded with a reinforcement study. Paul wrote a letter about unity. In the study, Jew and Gentile, slave and free—all are to live as family members. The roles are defined for husband and wife, brother and sister, parent and child in regard to conduct which draws people closer together, living as members of God's household. Ephesians distills the deepest of Paul's teachings about Jesus Christ and His church.

Author: Bechtle, Michael A. & Jay Kesler **128**
Series: Christian Lifestyle Series
Title: *Sharpening Your Everyday Ethics*
Publisher: David C. Cook Publishing Co., 1991 ISBN: 1-55513-378-9

Num. Sess.	Group Time	Num. Pgs.	Avg. Qst.	Price	Audience	Format	Bible Study
7	45-60	88	Vary	$14.95	New Christian	Workbk	Topical

Features: Intro to Study, Prayer Helps, Drawings, Handouts, Persnl Study Quest
★★★ Personal Application Preparation Time: None
★★★ Relationship Building Ldr. Guide: Yes Size: 8.50 x 11.0
Subjects: Ethics
Comments: This study helps adults of all ages, especially Boomers and younger, answer such questions as: How much time can I spend on fun when God has so much work for me to do? When does "sharing" become gossip? Is it really cheating when I cut corners or let a half-truth slip by? How much attention should I pay to the way I look? Appropriate for singles, marrieds, new, or mature Christians.

Author: Becker, Calvin W. **129**
Series: Teach Yourself the Bible
Title: *First and Second Timothy and Titus: Letters to Two Young Men*
Publisher: Moody Press, 1964 ISBN: 0-80242-646-8

Num. Sess.	Group Time	Num. Pgs.	Avg. Qst.	Price	Audience	Format	Bible Study
8	60-75	64	37	$4.50	New Christian	Workbk	Book

Features: Intro to Leading a Study, Exam
★★ Personal Application Preparation Time: Low
★★ Relationship Building Ldr. Guide: No Size: 5.50 x 8.50
Subjects: Christian Living, Pastoral Epistles, 1 & 2 Timothy/Titus
Comments: This study of 1 and 2 Timothy and Titus—part of a 25-book series—covers the Pastoral Epistles, which best reflect Paul's love. In fact, his advice to these men encourages contemporary Christians, both in their ministries and personal lives. The format includes a series of fill-in-the-blank questions, and checkups to test participants' grasp of Scriptural truths. The series, although designed for self-study, also includes suggestions for group study.

Author: Beck, Rosalie, et al. **130**
Series: The Contact Series
Title: *Holy Spirit! Our Redemptive Force*
Publisher: New Hope, 1993 ISBN: 1-56309-064-3

Num. Sess.	Group Time	Num. Pgs.	Avg. Qst.	Price	Audience	Format	Bible Study
12	60-75	220	Vary	$21.95	New Christian	Book	Charctr

Features: Intro to Study, Objectives, Prayer Helps, Scrpt Memory Helps, Cassette Avail
★★★ Personal Application Preparation Time: High
★★★ Relationship Building Ldr. Guide: Yes Size: 10.25 x 11.75
Subjects: Holy Spirit, Missions
Comments: Contact is a 12-week experience in Bible study, prayer, and personal reflection. Each week, participants spend five days in personal learning, using a learner's notebook that contains 60 daily sessions. At the end of each week's study a two-page small group plan is provided. Helps participants understand the Holy Spirit. A facilitator's guide and cassette tape are $8.95.

Author: Beltz, Dr. Bob **131**
Series: Promise Keepers
Title: *Daily Disciplines for the Christian Man*
Publisher: NavPress, 1993 ISBN: 0-89109-765-1

Num. Sess.	Group Time	Num. Pgs.	Avg. Qst.	Price	Audience	Format	Bible Study
8	45-60	155	3	$8.00	New Christian	Book	Topical

Features: Intro to Study, Charts, Appendix
★★★ Personal Application Preparation Time: Low
★★ Relationship Building Ldr. Guide: No Size: 5.50 x 8.50
Subjects: Christian Living, Men's Issues
Comments: Part of the Promise Keepers series, this study inspired by the author's personal need, presents seven clear and simple steps that enable men to live one day at a time with Christ, empowered by the Holy Spirit. The 12-step program inspired this study, which transforms the most foundational operating principles of walking with Christ into a daily program for spiritual vitality. The steps include: "Acknowledging Our Need"; "Affirming God's Power"; "Tapping Into the Power."

Author: Beman, Larry F., et al. **132**
Series:
Title: *More Faith Matters for Young Adults*
Publisher: Cokesbury, 1994 ISBN: 0-68778-005-5

Num. Sess.	Group Time	Num. Pgs.	Avg. Qst.	Price	Audience	Format	Bible Study
26	30-90	128	Vary	$12.95	Beginner	Book	Topical

Features: Intro to Leading a Study, Intro to Study, Prayer Helps, Handouts
★★★★ Personal Application Preparation Time: Low
★★★ Relationship Building Ldr. Guide: No Size: 10.0 x 7.0
Subjects: Prayer, Youth Life
Comments: This study is geared for use with young adults ages 18–30. Lessons cover issues of morality, faith, biblical understanding, and contemporary concerns, all deeply rooted in United Methodist principles. Each session includes one page that can be photocopied and distributed to class members. Topics include: How can Christians handle stress? Why should I pray? How can I forgive?

Author: Bennett, Phyllis 133
Series: The Knowing God Series
Title: *Our Perfect Example: Following God's Ways*
Publisher: Zondervan, 1994 ISBN: 0-31048-331-X

Num. Sess.	Group Time	Num. Pgs.	Avg. Qst.	Price	Audience	Format	Bible Study
6	45-60	64	12	$4.99	Beginner	Workbk	Topical

Features: Intro to Leading a Study, Intro to Study, Objectives, Prayer Helps, Scrpt Memory Helps, Ldr's Notes, Charts
★★★★ Personal Application Preparation Time: Low
★★★ Relationship Building Ldr. Guide: No Size: 5.50 x 8.50
Subjects: God, Jesus: Life/Teaching
Comments: One of eight in a series, this guide looks at why God is the ultimate example of moral and spiritual perfection. It shows how people can be transformed through following His ways. As normal lifestyles begin to lose vitality, old habits will be replaced by new ones, and self-centered relationships will be transformed into Christ-centered friendships.

Author: Bennett, Phyllis 134
Series: The Knowing God Series
Title: *Our Wise Counselor: Seeking God's Guidance*
Publisher: Zondervan, 1994 ISBN: 0-31048-311-5

Num. Sess.	Group Time	Num. Pgs.	Avg. Qst.	Price	Audience	Format	Bible Study
6	45-60	64	12	$4.99	Beginner	Workbk	Topical

Features: Intro to Leading a Study, Intro to Study, Objectives, Scrpt Memory Helps, Follow Up, Ldr's Notes
★★★★ Personal Application Preparation Time: Low
★★★ Relationship Building Ldr. Guide: No Size: 5.50 x 8.50
Subjects: Decision Making, God, Wisdom
Comments: One of eight in the series, this guide shows participants why they should seek God's wisdom and guidance in every decision they face. It deals with making right decisions and receiving God's guidance for choices. The study reveals why wisdom is one of God's greatest gifts to His children. It shows how to grow in godly wisdom, and how to become more sensitive to the Spirit's leading.

Author: Benson, Dennis C. 135
Series:
Title: *Dennis Benson's Creative Bible Studies: Matthew–Acts*
Publisher: Group Publishing, 1985 ISBN: 0-93152-901-8

Num. Sess.	Group Time	Num. Pgs.	Avg. Qst.	Price	Audience	Format	Bible Study
	30-60	660	Vary	$21.99	Beginner	Workbk	Book

Features: Intro to Leading a Study, Intro to Study, Prayer Helps, Ldr's Notes, Drawings, Cross Ref
★★★ Personal Application Preparation Time: Low
★★ Relationship Building Ldr. Guide: No Size: 6.0 x 9.0
Subjects: Teens: Bible Study, Teens: New Testament
Comments: This study, covering from Matthew through Acts, provides 401 complete, easy-to-prepare Bible studies, each including a "how-to-use" introduction, insight into Scriptural meaning, and an extensive index. Each study is designed to get teenagers totally involved in experiencing the Scriptures. The studies are designed for use in a Bible class, youth meeting, or retreat setting.

Author: Benson, Dennis C. 136
Series:
Title: *Dennis Benson's Creative Bible Studies: Romans–Revelation*
Publisher: Group Publishing, 1988 ISBN: 0-93152-952-2

Num. Sess.	Group Time	Num. Pgs.	Avg. Qst.	Price	Audience	Format	Bible Study
	30-60	280	Vary	$16.99	Beginner	Workbk	Book

Features: Intro to Leading a Study, Intro to Study, Prayer Helps, Ldr's Notes, Drawings, Charts, Cross Ref, Topical Index
★★★ Personal Application Preparation Time: Low
★★ Relationship Building Ldr. Guide: No Size: 6.0 x 9.0
Subjects: Teens: Bible Study, Teens: New Testament
Comments: This study, which includes 146 studies of the biblical books from Romans to Revelation, is a companion to Benson's book on the Gospels and Acts. Each easy-to-prepare study features a "how-to-use" introduction, insights into Scriptural meaning, and an extensive index. Methods include using inexpensive objects such as bread, banners, construction paper, salt, boxes, rocks, and old clothing.

Author: Berry, Jo 137
Series:
Title: *Beloved Unbeliever: Loving Your Husband into the Faith*
Publisher: Zondervan, 1981 ISBN: 0-31042-621-9

Num. Sess.	Group Time	Num. Pgs.	Avg. Qst.	Price	Audience	Format	Bible Study
10	60-90	169	Vary	$8.99	New Christian	Workbk	Topical

Features: Intro to Study, Charts
★★★★ Personal Application Preparation Time: Med
★★★ Relationship Building Ldr. Guide: No Size: 5.25 x 8.0
Subjects: Evangelism, Faith, Love, Marriage, Women's Issues
Comments: This study gives hope to unequally yoked wives. Using a Scriptural framework of love, it shows how a wife can love her spouse into the Kingdom without compromising her faith. Realizing that she has been placed in the unique position of representing God to the man she loves should be an encouragement. While admitting there are no simple answers, guidance and useful suggestions are offered. Information and personal stories precede each Scriptural lesson.

Author: Bertolini, Dewey M. 138
Series: SonPower Youth Sources
Title: *Back To The Heart of Youth Work*
Publisher: Victor Books, 1995 ISBN: 1-56476-396-X

Num. Sess.	Group Time	Num. Pgs.	Avg. Qst.	Price	Audience	Format	Bible Study
	—	220	N/A	$9.99		Book	

Features:
Personal Application Preparation Time:
Relationship Building Ldr. Guide: Size: 6.0 x 9.0
Subjects: Teens: Resources
Comments: This book is written for volunteer and professional youth workers who feel battered, bruised, and bloody. Because effective youth ministry must begin in the heart, the author has written the book to rekindle a flickering passion for youth work, fanning it into blazing fires in the hearts of readers. He shows how to develop proven character, a biblical philosophy of ministry, and practical methodology.

Author: Bickel, Kurt **139**
Series: Group's Active Bible Curriculum
Title: *Getting Along with Parents*
Publisher: Group Publishing, 1990 ISBN: 1-55945-202-1

Num. Sess.	Group Time	Num. Pgs.	Avg. Qst.	Price	Audience	Format	Bible Study
4	35-60	44	Vary	$9.99	Beginner	Workbk	Topical

Features: Intro to Leading a Study, Intro to Study, Objectives, Study Overview, Ldr's Notes, Handouts, Agenda, Publicity Ideas
★★★ Personal Application Preparation Time: None
★★★ Relationship Building Ldr. Guide: No Size: 8.50 x 11.0
Subjects: Teens: Family, Teens: Senior High
Comments: This study helps Christian teenagers build quality relationships with their parents. Senior highers will learn about basic communication, parental expectations, trust and love, and honor. It can be adapted for a Bible class or youth meeting, and activities and Bible studies are included as separate sheets that can be reproduced. The instructions are easy to follow and offer multiple options for teachers.

Author: Blankley, Ron **140**
Series: LifeGuide Bible Study
Title: *John's Letters: Discovering Genuine Christianity*
Publisher: InterVarsity, 1990 ISBN: 0-83081-020-X

Num. Sess.	Group Time	Num. Pgs.	Avg. Qst.	Price	Audience	Format	Bible Study
13	45-60	63	11	$4.99	New Christian	Workbk	Topical

Features: Intro to Leading a Study, Intro to Study, Ldr's Notes
★★★ Personal Application Preparation Time: Low
★★★ Relationship Building Ldr. Guide: No Size: 5.50 x 8.25
Subjects: Faith, 1, 2 & 3 John/Jude
Comments: This study of John's letters describes the difference between genuine Christians and those who merely profess to know Christ. John writes to expose the false claims of those whose conduct contradicts their claims. He also provides strong assurance to those whose lifestyle is consistent with their Christian faith. With power and simplicity, John helps Christians focus their attention on what really matters—both now and for eternity.

Author: Bloem, Diane Brummel **141**
Series: Woman's Workshop Series
Title: *Growing Godly: Studies on Bible Women*
Publisher: Zondervan, 1983 ISBN: 0-31023-151-5

Num. Sess.	Group Time	Num. Pgs.	Avg. Qst.	Price	Audience	Format	Bible Study
13	60-90	77	18	$4.99	Beginner	Workbk	Charctr

Features: Intro to Study
★★ Personal Application Preparation Time: Low
★★ Relationship Building Ldr. Guide: No Size: 5.25 x 8.0
Subjects: Bible Personalities, Christian Living, Women's Issues
Comments: This is a study of 17 women in the Bible, their environments, circumstances that shaped them, sins that blighted them, and their stages of growth. Participants will see how God worked in each life and recognize stages of growth as well as blights and beauties; they will become aware of and appreciate the beauty of others, and become understanding of others' circumstances. Women discussed include Dinah, Miriam, Rahab, Naomi, Ruth, Lydia.

Author: Bloomfield, Arthur E. **142**
Series:
Title: *All Things New: The Prophecies of Revelation Explained*
Publisher: Bethany House, 1960 ISBN: 0-87123-520-X

Num. Sess.	Group Time	Num. Pgs.	Avg. Qst.	Price	Audience	Format	Bible Study
22	60-90	32	Vary	$1.99	Mature Christian	Book	Book

Features: No Grp Discussion Quest, Charts
★ Personal Application Preparation Time: High
★ Relationship Building Ldr. Guide: No Size: 5.0 x 8.0
Subjects: Eschatology, Prophecy, Revelation
Comments: This study, to be used in conjunction with the book by the same title, presents the Book of Revelation scene by scene. The study guide questions for each lesson are not review questions, but form outlines of the chapters. The many charts included are necessary for following the text. The study helps participants understand the nature, purpose, and method of presentation, or structure, of Revelation, a prophecy of the church and future of the saints.

Author: Boa, Kenneth & Larry Moody **143**
Series:
Title: *I'm Glad You Asked*
Publisher: Victor Books, 1982 ISBN: 0-88207-354-0

Num. Sess.	Group Time	Num. Pgs.	Avg. Qst.	Price	Audience	Format	Bible Study
13	60-75	230	N/A	$9.99	Beginner	Book	Topical

Features: Intro to Study, Bibliography, Charts
★★★★ Personal Application Preparation Time: Low
★★ Relationship Building Ldr. Guide: Yes Size: 5.50 x 8.0
Subjects: Apologetics, Evangelism, Theology
Comments: This 13-lesson study helps participants become able defenders of the Christian perspective. It uncovers alternatives to the Christian worldview, then demonstrates why that worldview is valid. The text provides answers to basic questions people ask, and guides participants logically through them, using a helpful flow chart. It shows how each objection is really an opportunity to present the Gospel. This study is highly illustrative and informative, and good for seekers.

Author: Board, Stephen **144**
Series: Fisherman Bible Studyguide
Title: *Great Doctrines of the Bible*
Publisher: Shaw, 1992 ISBN: 0-87788-356-4

Num. Sess.	Group Time	Num. Pgs.	Avg. Qst.	Price	Audience	Format	Bible Study
10	60-75	78	13	$4.99	New Christian	Workbk	Topical

Features: Intro to Leading a Study, Intro to Study, Follow Up, Ldr's Notes
★★★ Personal Application Preparation Time: Low
★★ Relationship Building Ldr. Guide: No Size: 5.25 x 8.25
Subjects: Theology
Comments: This 10-week study shows participants how key Bible passages have become the foundation of key Christian "doctrines," or beliefs. It helps reinforce fundamental beliefs by reviewing those passages and tying them to doctrines such as salvation, Christ the God-man, church mission and message, ethics, the Trinity, and end times. The guide gives suggestions for both leaders and members.

Author: Bock, Betty 145
Series:
Title: *You Can Make a Difference*
Publisher: Woman's Missionary Union, 1992 ISBN: 1-56309-060-0

Num. Sess.	Group Time	Num. Pgs.	Avg. Qst.	Price	Audience	Format	Bible Study
	—	116	N/A	$6.95		Book	

Features: Bibliography
Personal Application Preparation Time:
Relationship Building Ldr. Guide: No Size: 5.50 x 8.50
Subjects: Small Group Resource, Women's Issues
Comments: This book provides guidelines for advocacy of people such as the aging, those with disabilities and AIDS, divorced individuals, abuse and rape survivors, the homeless, and the poor. It describes hurtful situations that keep others from experiencing wholeness in life, and shows how those situations can change. The first chapter serves as an overview of advocacy, and includes Scriptural insights, a definition of an advocate, and other clarifying details.

Author: Bockelman, Wilfred 146
Series: Small Group Bible Studies
Title: *Blowing in the Wind*
Publisher: Augsburg Fortress Publishers, 1975

Num. Sess.	Group Time	Num. Pgs.	Avg. Qst.	Price	Audience	Format	Bible Study
6	60-75	24	7	$1.35	New Christian	Book	Charctr

Features: Intro to Study, Prayer Helps
★★★ Personal Application Preparation Time: None
★★★ Relationship Building Ldr. Guide: No Size: 8.50 x 5.50
Subjects: Holy Spirit
Comments: This small pamphlet includes six sessions on the Holy Spirit. It does not promise to cover the topic completely but rather to provide insights and the opportunity to grow spiritually. The six sessions are titled: "The New Birth"; "The Promise of the Spirit"; "The Coming of the Spirit"; "Sanctification"; "Gifts of the Spirit"; and "The Spirit Speaks."

Author: Boehi, David 147
Series: HomeBuilders Couples
Title: *Life Choices for a Lasting Marriage*
Publisher: Gospel Light Publications, 1993 ISBN: 0-83071-627-0

Num. Sess.	Group Time	Num. Pgs.	Avg. Qst.	Price	Audience	Format	Bible Study
6	60-90	150	Vary	$9.99	Beginner	Workbk	Topical

Features: Intro to Study, Appendix
★★★★ Personal Application Preparation Time: Low
★★★★ Relationship Building Ldr. Guide: Yes Size: 5.75 x 8.50
Subjects: Family, Marriage
Comments: This study deals with choices that couples make that shape their lives and marriages. Couples learn that good choices depend on having God at the center of their marriage, ways to transform their marriage and build a solid foundation, how materialism and busyness can drive a wedge between a couple, what to do when tempted to compromise one's marriage, how to fight to keep a strong marriage. Homework assignments enhance application of the study.

Author: Boice, James Montgomery 148
Series:
Title: *Ordinary Men Called by God: Abraham, Moses & David*
Publisher: Victor Books, 1982 ISBN: 0-89693-047-5

Num. Sess.	Group Time	Num. Pgs.	Avg. Qst.	Price	Audience	Format	Bible Study
13	60-90	142	N/A	$8.99	New Christian	Book	Charctr

Features: Intro to Study
★★★★ Personal Application Preparation Time: Low
★★★ Relationship Building Ldr. Guide: Yes Size: 5.50 x 8.0
Subjects: Bible Personalities, Church Life, Faith, Family, Service, Work
Comments: This study of Abraham, Moses, and David concerns God's call to these ordinary Old Testament men, who became extraordinary men of faith and accomplishment. Their examples of courage, faithfulness, and humility offer practical lessons in Christian living and service to God. The leader's guide provides goals for each lesson and reproducible transparency masters.

Author: Bolton, Joy 149
Series:
Title: *Ideas for Community Ministries*
Publisher: Woman's Missionary Union, 1993 ISBN: 1-56309-075-9

Num. Sess.	Group Time	Num. Pgs.	Avg. Qst.	Price	Audience	Format	Bible Study
	—	75	N/A	$5.95		Book	

Features: Intro to Study, Bibliography, Ldr's Notes, Index
Personal Application Preparation Time:
Relationship Building Ldr. Guide: Size: 8.50 x 11.0
Subjects: Missions, Small Group Resource
Comments: This idea-packed book for community ministry projects defines community ministry, explains how to get others involved, and provides ideas for selecting projects. Projects and resources include: addiction ministry, AIDS ministry, Baptist centers and church weekday ministries, bereavement care ministry, children and youth, crisis pregnancy/unwed mothers, families in crisis, homelessness, hospice, hospitals, housing, hunger, internationals, literacy.

Author: Boomsma, Sylvia 150
Series: Discover Your Bible
Title: *Discover: Comfort*
Publisher: Church Development Resources, 1988

Num. Sess.	Group Time	Num. Pgs.	Avg. Qst.	Price	Audience	Format	Bible Study
11	60-75	39	7	$2.10	Beginner	Workbk	Book

Features: Intro to Study, Summary, Glossary
★★★ Personal Application Preparation Time: None
★★ Relationship Building Ldr. Guide: Yes Size: 5.50 x 8.50
Subjects: Emotions, God, Marriage, Suffering, Wisdom
Comments: This inductive study on comfort concerns Scripture that speaks of the human struggle with suffering and evil. It also examines passages that speak of God's love, wisdom, and tender care for His children. This is an honest study of hard questions believers face when they experience pain or hardship. There are no pat answers, but participants will draw closer to the Father of compassion and God of all comfort.

Author: Boomsma, Sylvia **151**
Series: Discover Your Bible
Title: *Discover: Esther*
Publisher: Church Development Resources, 1991

Num. Sess.	Group Time	Num. Pgs.	Avg. Qst.	Price	Audience	Format	Bible Study
6	60-75	47	6	$2.30	Beginner	Workbk	Book

Features: Intro to Study, Glossary
★★★ Personal Application Preparation Time: None
★★ Relationship Building Ldr. Guide: Yes Size: 5.50 x 8.50
Subjects: Esther
Comments: The story of Esther shows that someone does indeed work "behind the scenes" in the circumstances of life. That someone is God. Though not mentioned even once, God's directing of Esther's twists and turns is undeniable. Characters as colorful as any daytime drama make Esther's story rich with valor, envy, love, and greed. Through it all God has always been at work, lovingly "orchestrating" circumstances for the good of those He loves.

Author: Boomsma, Sylvia **152**
Series: Discover Your Bible
Title: *Discover Jesus In John—Who He Is*
Publisher: Church Development Resources, 1992

Num. Sess.	Group Time	Num. Pgs.	Avg. Qst.	Price	Audience	Format	Bible Study
13	60-75	90	7	$2.45	Beginner	Workbk	Book

Features: Intro to Study, Glossary
★★★ Personal Application Preparation Time: None
★★ Relationship Building Ldr. Guide: Yes Size: 5.50 x 8.50
Subjects: John
Comments: In this first of three studies in the Gospel of John, participants will learn the true identity of Jesus Christ and consider a fundamental question: Is Jesus the Savior? John's answer is clear. He writes "that you may believe that Jesus is the Christ, the Son of God, and that by believing you may have life in His name" (John 20:31). As participants review selected passages from the Gospel of John, they can discover the meaning of the words Jesus used to describe Himself.

Author: Boomsma, Sylvia **153**
Series: Discover Your Bible
Title: *Discover Jesus In John—Why He Came*
Publisher: Church Development Resources, 1993

Num. Sess.	Group Time	Num. Pgs.	Avg. Qst.	Price	Audience	Format	Bible Study
12	60-75	96	6	$2.10	Beginner	Workbk	Book

Features: Glossary
★★★ Personal Application Preparation Time: None
★★ Relationship Building Ldr. Guide: Yes Size: 5.50 x 8.50
Subjects: John
Comments: In this study of John's Gospel, participants can walk with Jesus through the darkest days of His life, and witness the acts of love He shared with His disciples. They can feel His pain as He died a criminal's death for people He came to save. Each person who studies this account of Jesus must ask why He came, is He really the Savior, and could He be their personal Savior?

Author: Boomsma, Sylvia **154**
Series: Discover Your Bible
Title: *Discover: Ruth*
Publisher: Church Development Resources, 1991

Num. Sess.	Group Time	Num. Pgs.	Avg. Qst.	Price	Audience	Format	Bible Study
4	45-60	20	6	$1.00	Beginner	Workbk	Book

Features: Intro to Study, Glossary
★★★ Personal Application Preparation Time: None
★★ Relationship Building Ldr. Guide: Yes Size: 5.50 x 8.50
Subjects: Bible Personalities, Faith, Obedience, Ruth
Comments: This inductive study of Ruth deals with a God of details. It shows participants that He really knows their needs and cares about how they're met. It also reveals how ordinary people in ordinary times—Ruth and Naomi—through faith and willingness to obey God caused extraordinary things to happen. Contemporary Christians see that God often does His greatest work during the hardest times in life. The study is intended for small groups, but is ideal for personal study.

Author: Booth, Michelle **155**
Series: Tapestry Collection
Title: *Gold in the Ashes*
Publisher: Victor Books, 1993 ISBN: 1-56476-050-2

Num. Sess.	Group Time	Num. Pgs.	Avg. Qst.	Price	Audience	Format	Bible Study
8	60-90	94	16	$5.99	New Christian	Workbk	Book

Features: Intro to Leading a Study, Intro to Study, Objectives, Prayer Helps, Follow Up, Ldr's Notes, Charts
★★★★ Personal Application Preparation Time: Low
★★★★ Relationship Building Ldr. Guide: No Size: 6.0 x 9.0
Subjects: Job, Wisdom
Comments: This study of the ancient Book of Job helps participants find the gold in their own ashes. In it, they can explore the relationship between despair and reason, find ways to salvage faith in the midst of suffering, think through ways to serve friends who are stranded in the ash pit, and who, like Job, learn to survive.

Author: Booth, Michelle **156**
Series: Tapestry Collection
Title: *Steadfast Faith In Times of Turmoil*
Publisher: Victor Books, 1995 ISBN: 1-56476-326-9

Num. Sess.	Group Time	Num. Pgs.	Avg. Qst.	Price	Audience	Format	Bible Study
8	60-90	96	Vary	$5.99	New Christian	Workbk	Topical

Features: Intro to Leading a Study, Intro to Study, Prayer Helps, Digging Deeper Quest, Follow Up, Persnl Study Quest, Charts
★★★★ Personal Application Preparation Time: Low
★★★ Relationship Building Ldr. Guide: No Size: 6.0 x 9.0
Subjects: Faith, Old Testament
Comments: This book was written for women who feel their lives are simply merry-go-rounds of children's music lessons, soccer practices, and the preparation of endless lunches and dinners. It's also written for those who struggle with more serious turmoil, such as divorce, unemployment, illness, and death. For these women, the book offers biblical guidance to anchor their faith.

Author: Borchers, Deena 157
Series: Group's Active Bible Curriculum
Title: *Changing the World*
Publisher: Group Publishing, 1992 ISBN: 1-55945-236-6

Num. Sess.	Group Time	Num. Pgs.	Avg. Qst.	Price	Audience	Format	Bible Study
4	35-60	40	Vary	$9.99	Beginner	Workbk	Topical

Features: Intro to Leading a Study, Intro to Study, Objectives, Study Overview, Ldr's Notes, Handouts, Agenda, Publicity Ideas
★★★★ Personal Application Preparation Time: None
★★★★ Relationship Building Ldr. Guide: No Size: 8.50 x 11.0
Subjects: Teens: Christian Liv, Teens: Missions, Teens: Senior High
Comments: The lessons in this book help senior highers make a difference in the world. Participants discover how as individuals they can impact the world and learn practical ways to live out their faith at home. Senior high youth see how they can spread their influence around the world. Adaptable for Bible classes or youth meetings. Activity sheets are reproducible. Student books are not required.

Author: Borchers, Deena 158
Series: Group's Active Bible Curriculum
Title: *Communicating With Friends*
Publisher: Group Publishing, 1992 ISBN: 1-55945-228-5

Num. Sess.	Group Time	Num. Pgs.	Avg. Qst.	Price	Audience	Format	Bible Study
4	35-60	41	Vary	$9.99	Beginner	Workbk	Topical

Features: Intro to Leading a Study, Intro to Study, Objectives, Study Overview, Ldr's Notes, Handouts, Agenda, Publicity Ideas
★★★★ Personal Application Preparation Time: None
★★★★ Relationship Building Ldr. Guide: No Size: 8.50 x 11.0
Subjects: Teens: Communication, Teens: Friends, Teens: Senior High
Comments: Four sessions explore the importance of effective communication in all aspects of life. Teen participants understand the importance of clear and effective communication, learn how to be better listeners, discover why communication breaks down, learn methods to mend broken communication, and explore examples of both effective and ineffective communication in the Bible.

Author: Borgstadt, Chip, et al. 159
Series:
Title: *Group Tube-a-loon Book*
Publisher: Group Publishing, 1994 ISBN: 1-55945-798-8

Num. Sess.	Group Time	Num. Pgs.	Avg. Qst.	Price	Audience	Format	Bible Study
	—	72	N/A	$10.99			

Features: Intro to Study
Personal Application Preparation Time:
Relationship Building Ldr. Guide: Size: 5.50 x 8.50
Subjects: Teens: Junior High, Teens: Resources
Comments: This is a fun-packed resource book for kids of all ages. "Tube-a-loon" is a 7′ long, air-filled tube that can be tons of fun. Outdoor, indoor, and relay games are included. The games, activities, team-builders, Bible applications, and races will put smiles on faces in all kinds of places. It comes complete with five "Tube-a-loons" in a variety of colors.

Author: Borthwick, Paul 160
Series:
Title: *101 Ways to Simplify Your Life*
Publisher: Victor Books, 1992 ISBN: 0-89693-058-0

Num. Sess.	Group Time	Num. Pgs.	Avg. Qst.	Price	Audience	Format	Bible Study
7	60-75	139	N/A	$8.99	Beginner	Book	Topical

Features: Intro to Study, Bibliography
★★★★ Personal Application Preparation Time: Low
★★★ Relationship Building Ldr. Guide: No Size: 5.50 x 8.50
Subjects: Psychology, Stress, Time
Comments: This book challenges readers to take the first steps toward more tranquil, balanced lifestyles. The author believes people must unclutter their hectic lives to realize God's full potential. Each chapter includes practical tips to cut back, trade down, and establish new priorities and realistic expectations. The book helps readers regain control, relieve stress, and avoid burn-out. For a small group that's ready, it can serve as a "fun" break. Leaders must develop questions.

Author: Bowe, Julie Henriksen 161
Series: Youth Talk
Title: *Self-esteem*
Publisher: Augsburg Fortress Publishers, 1993

Num. Sess.	Group Time	Num. Pgs.	Avg. Qst.	Price	Audience	Format	Bible Study
5	45-60	46	N/A	$4.95	Beginner	Book	Topical

Features: Prayer Helps, Worship Helps, Photos
★★★★ Personal Application Preparation Time: Low
★★★★ Relationship Building Ldr. Guide: Yes Size: 8.0 x 11.0
Subjects: Teens: Junior High, Teens: Self-esteem, Teens: Values
Comments: An alternative to the "textbook approach," these studies are energetic, contemporary, and modeled after popular teen magazines. Advice columns, fiction, poetry, and other features are mostly written by youth. God wants us to love ourselves. Helps youth answer the question "Who am I?" positively, recognizing not only who they are, but who they can become. Topics: "Under cover," "Shopping for values," "When mistakes add up," "The lonely number 1."

Author: Boyle, Nancy 162
Series:
Title: *Faith as Vision and Venture*
Publisher: Faith at Work, 1992

Num. Sess.	Group Time	Num. Pgs.	Avg. Qst.	Price	Audience	Format	Bible Study
6	45-60	34	Vary	$3.00	Beginner	Workbk	Topical

Features: Intro to Study, Bibliography
★★★ Personal Application Preparation Time: None
★★★★ Relationship Building Ldr. Guide: No Size: 5.50 x 8.50
Subjects: Faith
Comments: This 6-lesson study is an introduction to relational Bible study. The 6 passages studied each tell a story, and each is divided into 4 parts. Part 1 describes the scene where the study takes place. Parts 2 and 3 allow students to identify with one of the characters, as participant or spectator. Part 4 helps participants find the Good News for themselves in the story. Finally, participants give each story a name. Can be studied in a weekend retreat.

Author: Boyle, Nancy & Richard C. Meyer **163**
Series:
Title: *Making Peace with the Pieces of My Life*
Publisher: Faith at Work, 1988

Num. Sess.	Group Time	Num. Pgs.	Avg. Qst.	Price	Audience	Format	Bible Study
6	45-60	28	Vary	$2.50	New Christian	Book	Topical

Features: No Grp Discussion Quest
★★ Personal Application Preparation Time: Low
★★ Relationship Building Ldr. Guide: No Size: 5.50 x 8.50
Subjects: Christian Living, Friendships, Reconciliation, Relationships, Wholeness
Comments: This six-lesson study, derived from a series of articles reprinted from *Faith at Work* magazine, covers six aspects of "making peace." It helps participants understand peace from a biblical perspective and apply it in their own lives; with family, friends, and enemies; at work; and in general, with the earth. Assumes that the peace of Christ is a lifetime process of searching.

Author: Bradburn, Dave, et al. **164**
Series: Discovery Series
Title: *Families In Flux*
Publisher: David C. Cook Publishing Co., 1994 ISBN: 0-78145-169-8

Num. Sess.	Group Time	Num. Pgs.	Avg. Qst.	Price	Audience	Format	Bible Study
15	60-90	144	15	$9.95	Beginner	Workbk	Topical

Features: Intro to Study, Prayer Helps, Worship Helps, Study Overview, Pre-discussion Quest, Full Scrpt Printed, Ldr's Notes, Cartoons, Persnl Study Quest
★★★★ Personal Application Preparation Time: Med
★★★★ Relationship Building Ldr. Guide: Yes Size: 7.25 x 9.25
Subjects: Teens: Family, Teens: Senior High
Comments: Includes 15 studies to be used over a 3-week period. Participants complete 5 studies during the week prior to their small group meeting. Lessons respond to questions like: Why don't my parents treat me like an adult? Why don't they trust me? How can I cope with the problems in my family? What if I don't get married?

Author: Bradley, John & Jay Carty **165**
Series:
Title: *Unlocking Your Sixth Suitcase*
Publisher: NavPress, 1991 ISBN: 8-90073-175-0

Num. Sess.	Group Time	Num. Pgs.	Avg. Qst.	Price	Audience	Format	Bible Study
10	75-90	N/A	2	$59.00	Beginner	Video	Topical

Features: Intro to Leading a Study, Intro to Study, Bibliography, Book Incl, Video Study Guide
★★★★ Personal Application Preparation Time: Med
★★★★ Relationship Building Ldr. Guide: Yes Size: 10.0 x 12.25
Subjects: Communication, Relationships, Success
Comments: This 10-sesson video helps participants discover and put their natural God-given abilities to work in every area of their lives: relationships, job, church work, hobbies, community responsibilities, and ministry contributions. Each session includes a 10″ introduction by John Bradley and Jay Carty. Sessions include: "Discovering Your Talents"; "You and Your Relationships."

Author: Brandt, Jack **166**
Series: The Lifechange Series
Title: *Galatians*
Publisher: NavPress, 1989 ISBN: 0-89109-562-4

Num. Sess.	Group Time	Num. Pgs.	Avg. Qst.	Price	Audience	Format	Bible Study
12	60-90	137	17	$6.00	New Christian	Workbk	Book

Features: Intro to Leading a Study, Intro to Study, Bibliography, Prayer Helps, Worship Helps, Study Overview, Digging Deeper Quest, Summary, Charts, Maps, Cross Ref, Word Study
★★★ Personal Application Preparation Time: Med
★★★ Relationship Building Ldr. Guide: No Size: 5.50 x 8.50
Subjects: False Teachers, Galatians
Comments: This verse-by-verse study of Galatians concerns Paul's sternest defense against false teachings. Certain people were saying, "In order to keep His favor, you have to maintain His standards by your own efforts." Paul reaffirms that Christians can only live right with God by faith in Him. Participants will gain a firm foundation of Galatians.

Author: Brase, Lee & Henry Helsabeck **167**
Series:
Title: *Praying from God's Heart*
Publisher: NavPress, 1993 ISBN: 0-89109-792-9

Num. Sess.	Group Time	Num. Pgs.	Avg. Qst.	Price	Audience	Format	Bible Study
9	60-90	95	14	$6.00	New Christian	Workbk	Topical

Features: Intro to Leading a Study, Prayer Helps, Follow Up
★★★★ Personal Application Preparation Time: Med
★★★★ Relationship Building Ldr. Guide: No Size: 5.50 x 8.50
Subjects: Prayer
Comments: Designed specifically for small group studies, this workbook guides participants to a deeper understanding of God as they learn to focus on His attributes rather than their own desires. It shows people who talk to God regularly but worry that their prayers are superficial, unscriptural, or ineffective; how to pray Scripturally and deeply, with a God-focused heart. Participants will experience practicing prayer, praying Scripturally, the power of group prayer, praising God.

Author: Breckenridge, Marilyn Saure **168**
Series: Small Group Bible Studies
Title: *Epistles of Joy*
Publisher: Augsburg Fortress Publishers, 1980

Num. Sess.	Group Time	Num. Pgs.	Avg. Qst.	Price	Audience	Format	Bible Study
4	60-75	16	14	$1.15	New Christian	Book	Book

Features: Intro to Study, Prayer Helps
★★★ Personal Application Preparation Time: None
★★★ Relationship Building Ldr. Guide: No Size: 8.50 x 5.50
Subjects: Faith, Joy, Philippians, Prison Epistles, Relationships, Victorious Living
Comments: This small pamphlet uses a chapter-by-chapter approach to Philippians. Session 1 is "Christ: The Source"; session 2, "Christ: The Ideal"; session 3, "Christ: The Goal"; and session 4, "Christ: The Provider." Paul's letter contains 4 truths: the centrality of Christ in a life of faith, the need for unity in a Christian community, salvation through faith in Jesus, and the joy of being a Christian.

Author: Breese, Dave 169
Series:
Title: *Know the Marks of Cults*
Publisher: Victor Books, 1975 ISBN: 0-89693-236-2

Num. Sess.	Group Time	Num. Pgs.	Avg. Qst.	Price	Audience	Format	Bible Study
13	60-90	119	N/A	$8.99	Beginner	Book	Topical

Features: Intro to Study
★★★★ Personal Application Preparation Time: Med
★★ Relationship Building Ldr. Guide: Yes Size: 5.50 x 8.0
Subjects: Cults
Comments: This book describes both characteristics and errors of modern cults, and tells how to avoid them. It is not a study of specific cults, but a vehicle to develop the spiritual facility for instantly recognizing marks of the cults. Recognizing cultic characteristics, coupled with early correction, can prevent future spiritual tragedy. Suggested methods for teaching and leading discussions are available in the leader's guide.

Author: Brestin, Dee 170
Series:
Title: *And Then We Were Women*
Publisher: Victor Books, 1994 ISBN: 1-56476-343-9

Num. Sess.	Group Time	Num. Pgs.	Avg. Qst.	Price	Audience	Format	Bible Study
13	60-90	175	N/A	$8.99	Beginner	Book	Topical

Features: Cartoons, Photos
★★★★ Personal Application Preparation Time: Low
★★★ Relationship Building Ldr. Guide: Yes Size: 5.50 x 8.0
Subjects: Family, Friendships, Parenting, Psychology, Women's Issues
Comments: This study explores the impact of women's friendships on marriage and mothering. It describes how to be a supportive friend, sister, and mother, and responds to whether an ex-wife and new wife can get along. An outline for individual or group study follows each chapter. A leader's guide is available, providing session goals, lesson plans, application and prayer suggestions, and reproducible handouts.

Author: Brestin, Dee 171
Series: Fisherman Bible Studyguide
Title: *Ecclesiastes: God's Wisdom for Evangelism*
Publisher: Shaw, 1980 ISBN: 0-87788-212-6

Num. Sess.	Group Time	Num. Pgs.	Avg. Qst.	Price	Audience	Format	Bible Study
13	60-75	93	16	$4.99	Mature Christian	Workbk	Book

Features: Intro to Leading a Study, Intro to Study, Bibliography, Prayer Helps
★★ Personal Application Preparation Time: None
★★ Relationship Building Ldr. Guide: No Size: 5.0 x 8.25
Subjects: Ecclesiastes, Wisdom
Comments: Deals with applying God's answers to humanity's deepest questions. Three thousand years ago the writer of Ecclesiastes asked, "What is the meaning of life?" People have been struggling for the answer ever since. His conclusion is that neither wisdom, material possessions, sensual pleasure, power, nor prestige can satisfy our needs and give meaning to life.

Author: Brestin, Dee 172
Series: Fisherman Bible Studyguide
Title: *Examining the Claims of Jesus*
Publisher: Shaw, 1985 ISBN: 0-87788-246-0

Num. Sess.	Group Time	Num. Pgs.	Avg. Qst.	Price	Audience	Format	Bible Study
7	45-60	64	14	$4.99	Beginner	Workbk	Topical

Features: Intro to Leading a Study, Intro to Study, Prayer Helps, Full Scrpt Printed
★★★ Personal Application Preparation Time: Low
★★ Relationship Building Ldr. Guide: No Size: 5.0 x 8.25
Subjects: Evangelism, Jesus: Life/Teaching
Comments: This guide, based on the first 5 chapters of John with Scripture included, examines who Christ is and what He has promised every believer. Following the first 5 lessons, 2 optional studies deal with "Who Is a Christian (Romans)?" and "The Christian's Identity and Purpose (1 Peter)." These 2 studies clarify the Gospel, and give participants time to plan the next study.

Author: Brestin, Dee 173
Series:
Title: *Friendships of Women, The*
Publisher: Victor Books, 1988 ISBN: 0-89693-432-2

Num. Sess.	Group Time	Num. Pgs.	Avg. Qst.	Price	Audience	Format	Bible Study
13	60-90	180	N/A	$8.99	Beginner	Book	Topical

Features:
★★★ Personal Application Preparation Time: Med
★★★ Relationship Building Ldr. Guide: Yes Size: 5.50 x 8.0
Subjects: Bible Personalities, Friendships, Relationships, Women's Issues
Comments: This study examines the biblical friendship of Ruth and Naomi, revealing a pattern for friendship that can help women discover and focus their gifts for intimacy. Specific lessons concern why women are friendlier than men, the mentoring relationship, and reflections of Christ. A leader's guide with transparency masters is available.

Author: Brestin, Dee 174
Series:
Title: *Friendships of Women Workbook, The*
Publisher: Victor Books, 1995 ISBN: 1-56476-407-9

Num. Sess.	Group Time	Num. Pgs.	Avg. Qst.	Price	Audience	Format	Bible Study
	—	240	N/A	$15.99		Book	

Features: Bibliography, Prayer Helps
Personal Application Preparation Time:
Relationship Building Ldr. Guide: Size: 7.50 x 9.75
Subjects: Bible Personalities, Friendships, Relationships, Women's Issues
Comments: This helpful workbook takes an insightful look at power and pain in female relationships. Includes the entire text of the bestselling *The Friendships of Women,* Scriptural references, the author's personal reflections, prayer and journaling exercises, and suggestions for small group use.

Author: Brestin, Dee **175**
Series: Fisherman Bible Studyguide
Title: *How Should a Christian Live? 1, 2 & 3 John*
Publisher: Shaw, 1985 ISBN: 0-87788-351-3

Num. Sess.	Group Time	Num. Pgs.	Avg. Qst.	Price	Audience	Format	Bible Study
12	45-60	80	13	$4.99	New Christian	Workbk	Book

Features: Intro to Leading a Study, Intro to Study, Prayer Helps, Scrpt Memory Helps
★★★ Personal Application Preparation Time: Low
★★ Relationship Building Ldr. Guide: No Size: 5.0 x 8.25
Subjects: Christian Living, God, Obedience, 1, 2 & 3 John/Jude
Comments: The study encourages new believers to live lives of Christ-like compassion and obedience. Practical questions addressed in this study include: How can I experience more of the daily presence of God? What qualities should characterize my life as a child of God? What is the difference between immature and mature love? How can I be sure that I am going to Heaven?

Author: Brestin, Dee and Peggy Johnston **176**
Series:
Title: *Joy of Eating Right, The: Spiritual and Nutritional Principles*
Publisher: Victor Books, 1993 ISBN: 0-89693-879-4

Num. Sess.	Group Time	Num. Pgs.	Avg. Qst.	Price	Audience	Format	Bible Study
10	75-90	111	12	$4.99	Beginner	Workbk	Topical

Features: Intro to Leading a Study, Intro to Study, Bibliography, Prayer Helps, Scrpt Memory Helps, Follow Up, Ldr's Notes, Charts, Appendix
★★★★ Personal Application Preparation Time: Med
★★★ Relationship Building Ldr. Guide: No Size: 6.0 x 9.0
Subjects: Weight Control, Women's Issues
Comments: Diets seldom produce long-term results, but changing eating habits will. Healthy eating habits can contribute enormously to a woman's spiritual, emotional, and physical health. Weight graphs, habit graphs, suggested food programs, and group support all help women develop lifelong habits of eating right. The study is structured for daily assignments.

Author: Brestin, Dee **177**
Series:
Title: *Joy of Hospitality, The: Recovering a Lost Art*
Publisher: Victor Books, 1993 ISBN: 1-56476-033-2

Num. Sess.	Group Time	Num. Pgs.	Avg. Qst.	Price	Audience	Format	Bible Study
8	75-90	96	16	$4.99	New Christian	Workbk	Topical

Features: Intro to Leading a Study, Intro to Study, Prayer Helps, Scrpt Memory Helps, Follow Up, Ldr's Notes
★★★★ Personal Application Preparation Time: Med
★★ Relationship Building Ldr. Guide: No Size: 6.0 x 9.0
Subjects: Christian Living, Women's Issues
Comments: Author Brestin knows that women want to make their homes havens from the storms of life, whether those homes are dorm rooms, apartments, or mansions. This guide helps them do that for their own families, extended families, friends, and those in their paths who have spiritual, emotional, or physical needs. A special section on hospitality and the holidays can be reprinted for groups.

Author: Brestin, Dee **178**
Series:
Title: *Joy of Women's Friendship, The: Sharing the Gift of Intimacy*
Publisher: Victor Books, 1993 ISBN: 1-56476-052-9

Num. Sess.	Group Time	Num. Pgs.	Avg. Qst.	Price	Audience	Format	Bible Study
9	75-90	104	15	$4.99	New Christian	Workbk	Topical

Features: Intro to Leading a Study, Intro to Study, Prayer Helps, Scrpt Memory Helps, Follow Up, Ldr's Notes
★★★★ Personal Application Preparation Time: Med
★★★ Relationship Building Ldr. Guide: No Size: 6.0 x 9.0
Subjects: Friendships, Women's Issues
Comments: This guide explores early relationships, such as those with mothers, siblings, and childhood friends. Models like Miriam and Jochebed, Rachel and Leah, and the young women friends in the Song of Songs provide fascinating insights. As friendships mature, many women experience the joy of ministry partners, mentors, and soul-mates. This guide helps them make friendships the best they can be.

Author: Brestin, Dee **179**
Series:
Title: *Lifestyles of Christian Women, The*
Publisher: Victor Books, 1991 ISBN: 0-89693-911-1

Num. Sess.	Group Time	Num. Pgs.	Avg. Qst.	Price	Audience	Format	Bible Study
	—	180	N/A	$7.99			

Features:
★★★★ Personal Application Preparation Time: Low
★★★ Relationship Building Ldr. Guide: Yes Size: 5.50 x 8.0
Subjects: Small Group Resource, Women's Issues
Comments: Do Christian lifestyles really differ from those of women who don't know Christ? This study takes an honest, thorough look at this question, aiming to help participants examine and possibly reshape their own lifestyles. Fifty questions are posed to thousands of Christian women including: which would you say most closely describes your marriage, egalitarian or hierarchal? Have you engaged in premarital sex, infidelity, or abortion? and many more.

Author: Brestin, Dee **180**
Series: Fisherman Bible Studyguide
Title: *Proverbs & Parables: God's Wisdom for Living*
Publisher: Shaw, 1975 ISBN: 0-87788-694-6

Num. Sess.	Group Time	Num. Pgs.	Avg. Qst.	Price	Audience	Format	Bible Study
16	60-75	96	12	$4.99	Beginner	Workbk	Book

Features: Intro to Leading a Study, Intro to Study, Prayer Helps
★★ Personal Application Preparation Time: None
★★ Relationship Building Ldr. Guide: No Size: 5.0 x 8.25
Subjects: Parables, Proverbs, Wisdom
Comments: Each chapter in this study matches the truth of an Old Testament proverb with a New Testament parable, and applies them to twentieth-century life. Both the proverbs and parables reveal the constant wisdom of God. From Solomon, participants learn to seek God's wisdom "like silver and search for it as for hidden treasures." They will also learn that "in Christ are hidden all the treasures of wisdom and knowledge" (Colossians 2:3).

Author: Brestin, Dee **181**
Series:
Title: *Woman of Insight, A*
Publisher: Victor Books, 1995 ISBN: 1-56476-456-7

Num. Sess.	Group Time	Num. Pgs.	Avg. Qst.	Price	Audience	Format	Bible Study
8	60-90	96	Vary	$4.99	New Christian	Workbk	Topical

Features: Intro to Leading a Study, Intro to Study, Prayer Helps, Follow Up, Ldr's Notes
★★★★ Personal Application Preparation Time: Med
★★★★ Relationship Building Ldr. Guide: No Size: 6.0 x 9.0
Subjects: Ecclesiastes, Wisdom
Comments: This study includes 8 studies from Ecclesiastes that focus on seeking wisdom in regard to mentoring, worldly pursuits, choices, sovereignty of God, relationships, justice, character, simplicity, faith, and maturity in age. Brestin sheds light on this challenging book and offers models like Amy Carmichael and Ethel Waters who applied the principles found in Ecclesiastes. Includes songs and hymns.

Author: Brestin, Dee **182**
Series:
Title: *Woman of Joy, A*
Publisher: Victor Books, 1995 ISBN: 1-56476-454-0

Num. Sess.	Group Time	Num. Pgs.	Avg. Qst.	Price	Audience	Format	Bible Study
8	60-90	96	Vary	$4.99	New Christian	Workbk	Topical

Features: Intro to Leading a Study, Intro to Study, Prayer Helps, Follow Up, Ldr's Notes
★★★★ Personal Application Preparation Time: Med
★★★★ Relationship Building Ldr. Guide: No Size: 6.0 x 9.0
Subjects: 1, 2 & 3 John/Jude
Comments: This study leads women through 1, 2, and 3 John, showing them how to live joyous lives of love and victory. Includes songs and hymns appropriate for worship in small groups. Shows how the letters of John can help women know more of the presence, love, and joy of God.

Author: Brestin, Dee **183**
Series:
Title: *Woman of Value, A*
Publisher: Victor Books, 1995 ISBN: 1-56476-455-9

Num. Sess.	Group Time	Num. Pgs.	Avg. Qst.	Price	Audience	Format	Bible Study
10	60-90	96	Vary	$4.99	New Christian	Workbk	Topical

Features: Intro to Leading a Study, Intro to Study, Prayer Helps, Follow Up, Ldr's Notes
★★★★ Personal Application Preparation Time: Med
★★★★ Relationship Building Ldr. Guide: No Size: 6.0 x 9.0
Subjects: Proverbs
Comments: This study, based on the Book of Proverbs, explores 10 characteristics of honorable character, including awe of God, discretion, trust, faithfulness, and honesty. Each lesson takes a quality that God values in a woman, examines the Proverbs about it, and then brings it to life by contrasting a woman who possessed the quality with one who lacked the quality.

Author: Brestin, Steve & Dee **184**
Series: Fisherman Bible Studyguide
Title: *Building Your House on the Lord: Marriage & Parenthood*
Publisher: Shaw, 1976 ISBN: 0-87788-099-9

Num. Sess.	Group Time	Num. Pgs.	Avg. Qst.	Price	Audience	Format	Bible Study
13	60-90	96	13	$4.99	New Christian	Workbk	Topical

Features: Intro to Leading a Study, Intro to Study, Prayer Helps
★★ Personal Application Preparation Time: None
★★ Relationship Building Ldr. Guide: No Size: 5.0 x 8.25
Subjects: Family, Marriage, Parenting
Comments: This study focuses on families and marriages built on the foundation of Jesus Christ, which stands in spite of outside pressure. It objectively presents two divergent perspectives on Christian marriage: the traditional perspective—the "hierarchical" model—and the "egalitarian" model. Are wives to be submissive? Or should there be mutual submission under God for both man and woman? The text lends itself to both interpretations and both are explained.

Author: Brestin, Steve & Dee **185**
Series: Fisherman Bible Studyguide
Title: *Friendship: Portraits in God's Family Album*
Publisher: Shaw, 1986 ISBN: 0-87788-287-8

Num. Sess.	Group Time	Num. Pgs.	Avg. Qst.	Price	Audience	Format	Bible Study
11	45-60	80	12	$4.99	Beginner	Workbk	Topical

Features: Intro to Leading a Study, Intro to Study, Prayer Helps
★★★ Personal Application Preparation Time: None
★★★ Relationship Building Ldr. Guide: No Size: 5.0 x 8.25
Subjects: Bible Personalities, Christian Living, Friendships, Relationships
Comments: This study offers insights for better, more meaningful friendships by examining historical models, including Abraham, Ruth, David and Jonathan, Mary and Elizabeth, Jesus, and Barnabas. The characteristics of commitment, unfailing kindness, and open sharing are repeated. Jesus is reflected in the faces of historical models, the One who models each of these characteristics perfectly.

Author: Brestin, Steve & Dee **186**
Series: Fisherman Bible Studyguide
Title: *Higher Ground: Steps Toward Christian Maturity*
Publisher: Shaw, 1978 ISBN: 0-87788-345-9

Num. Sess.	Group Time	Num. Pgs.	Avg. Qst.	Price	Audience	Format	Bible Study
14	45-60	91	14	$4.99	New Christian	Workbk	Topical

Features: Intro to Leading a Study, Intro to Study, Prayer Helps, Worship Helps
★★★ Personal Application Preparation Time: None
★★★ Relationship Building Ldr. Guide: No Size: 5.0 x 8.25
Subjects: Discipleship, Faith, Holy Spirit, Joy, Victorious Living
Comments: Spiritual maturity can be attained, and the Scriptures show the way. This study can help every believer achieve a victorious life. Subject matter includes: the joy of salvation, the power of the Spirit-controlled life, living by faith, overcoming the valleys, effectual prayer and praise. Jesus said, "Blessed are those who hunger and thirst for righteousness, for they shall be satisfied." This study can satisfy.

Author: Brestin, Steve & Dee 187
Series: Fisherman Bible Studyguide
Title: *1 & 2 Peter, Jude: Called for a Purpose*
Publisher: Shaw, 1987 ISBN: 0-87788-703-9

Num. Sess.	Group Time	Num. Pgs.	Avg. Qst.	Price	Audience	Format	Bible Study
13	45-60	78	12	$4.99	New Christian	Workbk	Book

Features: Intro to Leading a Study, Intro to Study, Prayer Helps, Scrpt Memory Helps, Worship Helps
★★★ Personal Application Preparation Time: Low
★★ Relationship Building Ldr. Guide: No Size: 5.0 x 8.25
Subjects: Faith, False Teachers, Holiness, Hope, 1 & 2 Peter, 1, 2 & 3 John/Jude
Comments: Theme "called" is followed in each lesson—"called" for a purpose, to be hopeful, to be holy, to a new identity, to submission in the world, to complete devotion to Christ, to live for God, to eternal glory, to rely on God's provision, to combat false teaching, to prepare for the Lord's return, to persevere in faith, and more.

Author: Bridges, Jerry 188
Series:
Title: *Practice of Godliness, The*
Publisher: NavPress, 1983 ISBN: 0-89109-498-9

Num. Sess.	Group Time	Num. Pgs.	Avg. Qst.	Price	Audience	Format	Bible Study
12	60-90	70	11	$5.00	New Christian	Workbk	Topical

Features: Intro to Leading a Study
★★★ Personal Application Preparation Time: Med
★★ Relationship Building Ldr. Guide: No Size: 5.50 x 8.50
Subjects: Christian Living, Fruit of the Spirit, God
Comments: This study, designed to be used in conjunction with the book of the same name, leads participants to growth in fear of, love for, and devotion to God—the three basic elements essential to godly living. The lessons are designed to allow the Holy Spirit to cultivate humility, contentment, thankfulness, joy, holiness, self-control, faithfulness, peace, patience and gentleness, kindness and goodness, and love.

Author: Bridges, Jerry 189
Series:
Title: *Pursuit of Holiness, The*
Publisher: NavPress, 1978 ISBN: 0-89109-025-8

Num. Sess.	Group Time	Num. Pgs.	Avg. Qst.	Price	Audience	Format	Bible Study
12	45-60	55	7	$4.00	New Christian	Workbk	Topical

Features: Intro to Study
★★★★ Personal Application Preparation Time: Med
★ Relationship Building Ldr. Guide: Yes Size: 5.50 x 8.50
Subjects: Discipleship, Holiness
Comments: This study, which accompanies the book of the same name, guides participants toward the joy of living a life pleasing to God. The book reveals undiluted truth about sin and how to overcome it, about temptation and how to say no. The lessons bear titles like "Responsibility for Holiness," "A Holy Standing in Christ," "The Continuing Struggle with Sin," "Holiness in Body and Spirit," "Discipline," and "Holiness in an Unholy World."

Author: Bridges, Jerry 190
Series:
Title: *Transforming Grace*
Publisher: NavPress, 1991 ISBN: 0-89109-644-2

Num. Sess.	Group Time	Num. Pgs.	Avg. Qst.	Price	Audience	Format	Bible Study
8	60-90	96	12	$6.00	New Christian	Workbk	Topical

Features: Intro to Leading a Study, Prayer Helps, Scrpt Memory Helps, Pre-discussion Quest, Digging Deeper Quest, Follow Up, Ldr's Notes, Persnl Study Quest, Book Avail
★★★★ Personal Application Preparation Time: Low
★★★ Relationship Building Ldr. Guide: No Size: 5.25 x 8.25
Subjects: Christian Living, Grace
Comments: This companion guide to Bridges' book by the same name can be used without reading the book. Each session includes an excerpt from the book as well as Scripture references for discussion. Sessions help users understand what grace is and how one can live by it (as opposed to by performance or license) in practical, everyday ways.

Author: Bridges, Jerry 191
Series:
Title: *Trusting God: Even When Life Hurts*
Publisher: NavPress, 1989 ISBN: 0-89109-241-2

Num. Sess.	Group Time	Num. Pgs.	Avg. Qst.	Price	Audience	Format	Bible Study
12	60-90	112	13	$6.00	New Christian	Workbk	Topical

Features: Intro to Leading a Study, Prayer Helps, Scrpt Memory Helps
★★★★ Personal Application Preparation Time: Med
★★★ Relationship Building Ldr. Guide: No Size: 5.50 x 8.50
Subjects: Christian Living, God
Comments: This study guide serves as a companion to the book *Trusting God*, which concerns God's sovereignty. The guide expounds on the fundamental principles of the book, the three essential truths about God: God is completely sovereign; God is infinite in wisdom; and God is perfect in love. The book is optional for completion of the study.

Author: Bridges, Steve 192
Series: Group's Active Bible Curriculum
Title: *Today's Media: Choosing Wisely*
Publisher: Group Publishing, 1993 ISBN: 1-55945-144-0

Num. Sess.	Group Time	Num. Pgs.	Avg. Qst.	Price	Audience	Format	Bible Study
4	35-60	47	Vary	$9.99	Beginner	Workbk	Topical

Features: Intro to Leading a Study, Intro to Study, Objectives, Study Overview, Ldr's Notes, Handouts, Agenda, Publicity Ideas
★★★★ Personal Application Preparation Time: None
★★★★ Relationship Building Ldr. Guide: No Size: 8.50 x 11.0
Subjects: Teens: Christian Liv, Teens: Junior High, Teens: Media, Teens: Music
Comments: This course guides junior highers as they sort through media messages and gives them tools to evaluate the impact these worldly messages have on their lives. Participants compare Scriptural values with media values, discover humor in the Bible and how it relates to them, and examine the lyrics of popular musicians.

Author: Bright, Bill **193**
Series: Ten Basic Steps
Title: *Christian Adventure, The—Step 1*
Publisher: NewLife Publications, 1994 ISBN: 1-56399-030-X

Num. Sess.	Group Time	Num. Pgs.	Avg. Qst.	Price	Audience	Format	Bible Study
7	60-75	80	Vary	$4.99	New Christian	Workbk	Topical

Features: Intro to Leading a Study, Intro to Study, Objectives, Bibliography, Scrpt Memory Helps, Charts
★★★★ Personal Application Preparation Time: Med
★★ Relationship Building Ldr. Guide: Yes Size: 5.25 x 8.25
Subjects: Christian Life, Devotionals, Discipleship, Jesus: Life/Teaching
Comments: This overall study is designed to help participants experience the adventure of a full, abundant, purposeful, and fruitful life in Christ. Step 1 in the 10-part series explores the key to the indwelling life of Christ, what it means to follow Him as Lord and Master, how to develop a more consistent walk with God, how to apply principles of spiritual growth to daily life, and how to have a powerful, ministry.

Author: Bright, Bill **194**
Series: Ten Basic Steps
Title: *Christian and Giving, The—Step 8*
Publisher: NewLife Publications, 1968 ISBN: 1-56399-037-7

Num. Sess.	Group Time	Num. Pgs.	Avg. Qst.	Price	Audience	Format	Bible Study
8	60-75	80	Vary	$4.99	New Christian	Workbk	Topical

Features: Intro to Leading a Study, Intro to Study, Objectives, Bibliography, Scrpt Memory Helps, Charts
★★★★ Personal Application Preparation Time: Med
★★★ Relationship Building Ldr. Guide: Yes Size: 5.25 x 8.25
Subjects: Accountability, Christian Life, Devotionals, Discipleship, Stewardship
Comments: This study covers Step 8 in a 10-part series designed to lead participants toward Christian maturity. It features eight lessons on stewardship, including God's ownership, stewardship of time, bodies, gifts, and possessions, and the final accounting to the Master. The final lesson is a review.

Author: Bright, Bill **195**
Series: Ten Basic Steps
Title: *Christian and Witnessing, The—Step 7*
Publisher: NewLife Publications, 1968 ISBN: 1-56399-036-9

Num. Sess.	Group Time	Num. Pgs.	Avg. Qst.	Price	Audience	Format	Bible Study
7	60-75	80	Vary	$4.99	New Christian	Workbk	Topical

Features: Intro to Leading a Study, Intro to Study, Objectives, Bibliography, Scrpt Memory Helps
★★★★ Personal Application Preparation Time: Med
★★ Relationship Building Ldr. Guide: Yes Size: 5.25 x 8.25
Subjects: Christian Life, Devotionals, Discipleship, Evangelism, Holy Spirit, Prayer
Comments: This study covers Step 7 in a 10-part series designed to lead participants toward Christian maturity. It features seven lessons on witnessing, including: why we should witness, how to witness, and others dealing with the qualifications and biblical authority of witnessing, prayer, and the Holy Spirit's activity in witnessing.

Author: Bright, Bill **196**
Series: Ten Basic Steps
Title: *Christian and the Bible, The—Step 5*
Publisher: NewLife Publications, 1968 ISBN: 1-56399-034-2

Num. Sess.	Group Time	Num. Pgs.	Avg. Qst.	Price	Audience	Format	Bible Study
8	60-75	80	Vary	$4.99	New Christian	Workbk	Topical

Features: Intro to Leading a Study, Intro to Study, Objectives, Bibliography, Scrpt Memory Helps, Charts
★★★★ Personal Application Preparation Time: Med
★★ Relationship Building Ldr. Guide: Yes Size: 5.25 x 8.25
Subjects: Bible Study, Christian Life, Devotionals, Discipleship
Comments: This study covers Step 5 in a 10-part series designed to lead participants toward Christian maturity. In the study participants learn why the Bible is God's unique, inspired Word to man, gain confidence in the trustworthiness of God's Work, discover the promise that can be claimed by believers, learn how to study the Bible more effectively, and discover the supernatural power of God's Word.

Author: Bright, Bill **197**
Series: Ten Basic Steps
Title: *Christian and Prayer, The—Step 4*
Publisher: NewLife Publications, 1968 ISBN: 1-56399-033-4

Num. Sess.	Group Time	Num. Pgs.	Avg. Qst.	Price	Audience	Format	Bible Study
7	60-75	64	Vary	$4.99	New Christian	Workbk	Topical

Features: Intro to Leading a Study, Intro to Study, Objectives, Bibliography, Scrpt Memory Helps, Charts
★★★★ Personal Application Preparation Time: Med
★★★ Relationship Building Ldr. Guide: Yes Size: 5.25 x 8.25
Subjects: Christian Life, Devotionals, Discipleship, Prayer
Comments: This study, Step 4 in a 10-part series, is designed to teach participants how to tap into the power of prayer. They learn the true purpose of prayer, how the Father, Son, and Holy Spirit answer prayer, how to use the great power of prayer effectively. "Planning Your Daily Devotional Time," provides specific guidlines on establishing time, place, goals, and content for prayer life.

Author: Bright, Bill **198**
Series: Ten Basic Steps
Title: *Christian and the Abundant Life, The—Step 2*
Publisher: NewLife Publications, 1968 ISBN: 1-56399-031-8

Num. Sess.	Group Time	Num. Pgs.	Avg. Qst.	Price	Audience	Format	Bible Study
8	60-75	64	Vary	$4.99	New Christian	Workbk	Topical

Features: Intro to Leading a Study, Intro to Study, Objectives, Bibliography, Scrpt Memory Helps, Charts
★★★★ Personal Application Preparation Time: Med
★★ Relationship Building Ldr. Guide: Yes Size: 5.25 x 8.25
Subjects: Christian Life, Devotionals, Discipleship, Jesus: Life/Teaching
Comments: This study covers Step 2 in a 10-part series designed to lead participants toward Christian maturity. It discusses the problem of sin and temptation and the spiritual warfare of life. The study helps participants gain a better understanding of abundant life, experience God's power to change lives, focus on new priorities, and become more radiant witnesses for Christ.

Author: Bright, Bill **199**
Series: Ten Basic Steps
Title: *Christian and the Holy Spirit, The—Step 3*
Publisher: NewLife Publications, 1968 ISBN: 1-56399-032-6

Num. Sess.	Group Time	Num. Pgs.	Avg. Qst.	Price	Audience	Format	Bible Study
7	60-75	80	Vary	$4.99	New Christian	Workbk	Topical

Features: Intro to Leading a Study, Intro to Study, Objectives, Bibliography, Scrpt Memory Helps
★★★★ Personal Application Preparation Time: Med
★★ Relationship Building Ldr. Guide: Yes Size: 5.25 x 8.25
Subjects: Christian Life, Devotionals, Discipleship, Holy Spirit, Jesus: Life/Teaching
Comments: This study, Step 3 in a 10-part series, is designed to lead participants toward Christian maturity and show them how to make the Spirit-filled life a moment-by-moment reality. Participants discover who the Holy Spirit is and why He came, how to empowered by the Holy Spirit, how to overcome discouragement and live joyfully.

Author: Bright, Bill **200**
Series: Ten Basic Steps
Title: *Christian and Obedience, The—Step 6*
Publisher: NewLife Publications, 1968 ISBN: 1-56399-035-0

Num. Sess.	Group Time	Num. Pgs.	Avg. Qst.	Price	Audience	Format	Bible Study
7	60-75	80	Vary	$4.99	New Christian	Workbk	Topical

Features: Intro to Leading a Study, Intro to Study, Objectives, Bibliography, Scrpt Memory Helps
★★★★ Personal Application Preparation Time: Med
★★ Relationship Building Ldr. Guide: Yes Size: 5.25 x 8.25
Subjects: Christian Life, Devotionals, Discipleship, Obedience
Comments: This study covers Step 6 in a 10-part series designed to lead participants toward Christian maturity. In the study participants discover why it is so important to obey God, how to obey God from the heart, how to be secure in fellowship with God, how to live daily in God's grace, and why Christians need not fear what others think of them. The final lesson is a review.

Author: Bright, Bill **201**
Series: Ten Basic Steps
Title: *Exploring the New Testament*
Publisher: NewLife Publications, 1994 ISBN: 1-56399-039-3

Num. Sess.	Group Time	Num. Pgs.	Avg. Qst.	Price	Audience	Format	Bible Study
10	60-75	80	Vary	$4.99	New Christian	Workbk	Topical

Features: Intro to Leading a Study, Intro to Study, Scrpt Index
★★★★ Personal Application Preparation Time: Med
★★ Relationship Building Ldr. Guide: Yes Size: 5.25 x 8.25
Subjects: Devotionals, Discipleship, Gospels, New Testament
Comments: This study is Step 10 in a 10-part series designed to lead participants toward Christian maturity. It highlights the New Testament through ten lessons, including ones on Matthew, Mark, Luke, John, and Acts; the letters to the Romans, Corinthians, Galatians, prison Epistles, pastoral Epistles, general Epistles, Revelation, and a recap. The final lesson is a review.

Author: Bright, Bill **202**
Series: Ten Basic Steps
Title: *Exploring the Old Testament*
Publisher: NewLife Publications, 1994 ISBN: 1-56399-038-5

Num. Sess.	Group Time	Num. Pgs.	Avg. Qst.	Price	Audience	Format	Bible Study
9	60-75	80	Vary	$4.99	New Christian	Workbk	Topical

Features: Intro to Leading a Study, Intro to Study, Scrpt Memory Helps, Summary
★★★★ Personal Application Preparation Time: Med
★★ Relationship Building Ldr. Guide: Yes Size: 5.25 x 8.25
Subjects: Bible Personalities, Devotionals, Discipleship
Comments: This study covers Step 9 in a 10-part series designed to lead participants toward Christian maturity. It highlights the Old Testament through 9 lessons, on the promised Messiah, Moses, the Passover, Exodus, law and grace, deliverance and forgiveness, Elijah, and Jeremiah. The final lesson is a review.

Author: Bright, Bill **203**
Series:
Title: *Five Steps of Christian Growth*
Publisher: NewLife Publications, 1994 ISBN: 1-56399-021-0

Num. Sess.	Group Time	Num. Pgs.	Avg. Qst.	Price	Audience	Format	Bible Study
5	60-75	48	Vary	$2.25	New Christian	Workbk	Topical

Features: Scrpt Memory Helps, Follow Up, Charts
★★★★ Personal Application Preparation Time: Low
★★★ Relationship Building Ldr. Guide: Yes Size: 5.25 x 8.25
Subjects: Discipleship, Holy Spirit, Teens: Discipleship
Comments: This 5-lesson study outlines 5 steps of Christian growth. Lesson titles include: "How to Be Sure You Are a Christian," "How you can Grow as a Christian," "How you can Be Filled with the Holy Spirit," and "How you can Walk in the Spirit." Participants can gain a better understanding of their own journeys as Christians, and how to better counsel others. Each lesson closes with an action point or points, which serve as follow ups to the lesson for personal application.

Author: Bright, Bill **204**
Series: Ten Basic Steps
Title: *Handbook for Christian Maturity, A*
Publisher: NewLife Publications, 1994 ISBN: 1-56399-040-7

Num. Sess.	Group Time	Num. Pgs.	Avg. Qst.	Price	Audience	Format	Bible Study
10	60-75	450	Vary	$14.99	New Christian	Workbk	Topical

Features: Intro to Study, Objectives, Bibliography, Scrpt Memory Helps, Charts
★★★★ Personal Application Preparation Time: Med
★★★ Relationship Building Ldr. Guide: Yes Size: 5.25 x 8.25
Subjects: Devotionals, Discipleship, Holy Spirit, Obedience, Prayer
Comments: This handbook is a compilation of an 11-segment series designed to lead Christians toward maturity. It begins with the "Uniqueness of Jesus," then covers the following topics: the Christian adventure, abundant life, the Holy Spirit, prayer, the Bible, obedience, witnessing, the Christian and giving, and Old and New Testament highlights. Practical and easy to follow, it is ideal for daily devotions.

Author: Bright, Bill 205
Series: Transferable Concepts
Title: *How You Can Be A Fruitful Witness*
Publisher: NewLife Publications, 1991 ISBN: 1-56399-004-0

Num. Sess.	Group Time	Num. Pgs.	Avg. Qst.	Price	Audience	Format	Bible Study
1	45-60	64	9	$1.99	New Christian	Book	Topical

Features: Intro to Study, Persnl Study Quest, Cassette Avail
★★★★ Personal Application Preparation Time: Low
★ Relationship Building Ldr. Guide: No Size: 3.50 x 5.25
Subjects: Singles' Issues
Comments: This study guide explores how Christian participants can be sure of their faith, then continue to grow and become fruitful witnesses for Christ. It spells out spiritual preparation and practical skills needed to introduce others to Christ. Chapter titles include: "The Adventure of Witnessing"; "Steps for Personal Preparation"; "Taking the Initiative"; and "Success in Witnessing."

Author: Bright, Bill 206
Series: Transferable Concepts
Title: *How You Can Be Filled with the Holy Spirit*
Publisher: NewLife Publications, 1991 ISBN: 1-56399-002-4

Num. Sess.	Group Time	Num. Pgs.	Avg. Qst.	Price	Audience	Format	Bible Study
1	45-60	64	8	$1.99	New Christian	Book	Topical

Features: Intro to Study, Persnl Study Quest
★★★★ Personal Application Preparation Time: Med
★★ Relationship Building Ldr. Guide: No Size: 3.50 x 5.25
Subjects: Discipleship, Holy Spirit
Comments: This study, 1 of a 10-part series, shows participants how to become filled with the Spirit. It cuts through all the confusion surrounding the controversial subject of the Holy Spirit and gives answers clearly and simply. Participants will learn the "who," "what," and "why" of the Spirit and "how" to appropriate His fullness. The "Transferable Concepts" series presents practical ideas/truths, to be communicated without distortion.

Author: Bright, Bill 207
Series: Transferable Concepts
Title: *How You Can Be Sure You Are a Christian*
Publisher: NewLife Publications, 1991 ISBN: 1-56399-000-8

Num. Sess.	Group Time	Num. Pgs.	Avg. Qst.	Price	Audience	Format	Bible Study
1	45-60	64	7	$1.99	New Christian	Book	Topical

Features: Intro to Study, Persnl Study Quest
★★★★ Personal Application Preparation Time: Med
★★ Relationship Building Ldr. Guide: No Size: 3.50 x 5.25
Subjects: Commitments, Discipleship, Evangelism, Faith
Comments: This study, 1 of a 10-part series, shows participants how to be sure of their salvation. Well-suited for group lessons, the study deals with three types of commitment—intellectual, emotional, and volitional—involved in the most important decision in a person's life. Participants will not only solidify their faith, they will learn truths to pass on to others.

Author: Bright, Bill 208
Series: Transferable Concepts
Title: *How You Can Experience God's Love and Forgiveness*
Publisher: NewLife Publications, 1991 ISBN: 1-56399-001-6

Num. Sess.	Group Time	Num. Pgs.	Avg. Qst.	Price	Audience	Format	Bible Study
1	45-60	64	7	$1.99	New Christian	Book	Topical

Features: Intro to Study
★★★★ Personal Application Preparation Time: Med
★★★ Relationship Building Ldr. Guide: No Size: 3.50 x 5.25
Subjects: Discipleship, Forgiveness, God
Comments: This study, 1 of a 10-part series, shows participants how to experience God's love and forgiveness. Once salvation is experienced and initial joy enjoyed, Christians of all eras are faced with the challenge of living in a morally decadent world. The study outlines all the problems and challenges posed by the world, then outlines and discusses God's solution. This study is part of a series called "Transferable Concepts."

Author: Bright, Bill 209
Series: Transferable Concepts
Title: *How You Can Experience the Adventure of Giving*
Publisher: NewLife Publications, 1991 ISBN: 1-56399-009-1

Num. Sess.	Group Time	Num. Pgs.	Avg. Qst.	Price	Audience	Format	Bible Study
1	45-60	88	5	$1.99	New Christian	Book	Topical

Features: Intro to Study, Persnl Study Quest
★★★ Personal Application Preparation Time: Low
★ Relationship Building Ldr. Guide: No Size: 3.50 x 5.25
Subjects: Stewardship
Comments: This study provides proof that sacrificial giving can become a thrilling and rewarding element in the life of every Christian. This brief booklet encourages Christians to prayerfully evaluate the ultimate destinations of their gifts. Chapter titles include: "Preparing for the Adventure"; "Enjoying God's Abundant Blessings"; "God Wants You to Be Financially Free"; "How to Trust God for Your Finances"; "Recognizing God's Priority for Missions"; and "Experiencing the Adventure."

Author: Bright, Bill 210
Series: Transferable Concepts
Title: *How You Can Help Fulfill the Great Commission*
Publisher: NewLife Publications, 1991 ISBN: 1-56399-006-7

Num. Sess.	Group Time	Num. Pgs.	Avg. Qst.	Price	Audience	Format	Bible Study
1	45-60	64	8	$1.99	New Christian	Book	Topical

Features: Intro to Study, Persnl Study Quest
★★★ Personal Application Preparation Time: Low
★ Relationship Building Ldr. Guide: No Size: 3.50 x 5.25
Subjects: Singles' Issues
Comments: This study examines Jesus' command to evangelize and disciple the world, the greatest command of all time given by the greatest person who ever lived. Christians today face the unprecedented opportunity of fulfilling the Great Commission in this generation. Chapter titles include: "The Greatest Challenge Ever Given"; "A Vision for the World"; "A Global Strategy"; "Your 'Personal Strategy'"; and "You Can Help Change the World."

Author: Bright, Bill **211**
Series: Transferable Concepts
Title: *How You Can Introduce Others to Christ*
Publisher: NewLife Publications, 1991 ISBN: 1-56399-005-9

Num. Sess.	Group Time	Num. Pgs.	Avg. Qst.	Price	Audience	Format	Bible Study
1	45-60	64	7	$1.99	New Christian	Book	Topical

Features: Intro to Study, Persnl Study Quest
★★★ Personal Application Preparation Time: Low
★ Relationship Building Ldr. Guide: No Size: 3.50 x 5.25
Subjects: Singles' Issues
Comments: This study teaches participants how to use the Four Spiritual Laws to present the Gospel to friends, neighbors, and loved ones, in the power of the Holy Spirit. Chapter titles include: "You Can Change Your World"; "Eight Reasons Jesus Wants You to Witness"; "How You Can Witness Effectively"; "Leading the New Christian to Full Assurance"; and "Thirty-Day Experiment."

Author: Bright, Bill **212**
Series: Transferable Concepts
Title: *How You Can Love By Faith*
Publisher: NewLife Publications, 1991 ISBN: 1-56399-007-5

Num. Sess.	Group Time	Num. Pgs.	Avg. Qst.	Price	Audience	Format	Bible Study
1	45-60	64	8	$1.99	New Christian	Book	Topical

Features: Intro to Study, Persnl Study Quest
★★★ Personal Application Preparation Time: Low
★ Relationship Building Ldr. Guide: No Size: 3.50 x 5.25
Subjects: Discipleship, Faith
Comments: This study illustrates how Christians can possess and demonstrate in their daily lives the supernatural agape love of Christ by faith. This radical love changed the first-century world and continues to be the driving force that draws unbelievers to Christ. This brief booklet demonstrates how agape love can reconcile enemies and break down barriers of class, color, and race.

Author: Bright, Bill **213**
Series: Transferable Concepts
Title: *How You Can Pray with Confidence*
Publisher: NewLife Publications, 1991 ISBN: 1-56399-008-3

Num. Sess.	Group Time	Num. Pgs.	Avg. Qst.	Price	Audience	Format	Bible Study
1	40-50	64	6	$1.99	Beginner	Book	Topical

Features: Intro to Study, Persnl Study Quest
★★★★ Personal Application Preparation Time: Low
★★ Relationship Building Ldr. Guide: No Size: 3.50 x 5.25
Subjects: Prayer
Comments: This study guide explores how prayer can be a transferable concept; i.e., a truth which can be transferred (communicated) person to person, spiritual generation to generation, without distortion or dilution of its original meaning. In this case, the transferable concept is the power of prayer. The author answers vital questions: who can pray, why pray, to whom do we pray, when to pray, what to pray for, and how to pray with confidence.

Author: Bright, Bill **214**
Series: Transferable Concepts
Title: *How You Can Walk in the Spirit*
Publisher: NewLife Publications, 1991 ISBN: 1-56399-003-2

Num. Sess.	Group Time	Num. Pgs.	Avg. Qst.	Price	Audience	Format	Bible Study
1	45-60	64	6	$1.99	New Christian	Book	Topical

Features: Intro to Study, Persnl Study Quest
★★★★ Personal Application Preparation Time: Med
★★ Relationship Building Ldr. Guide: No Size: 3.50 x 5.25
Subjects: Discipleship, Faith, Holy Spirit
Comments: This study, one of a ten-part series, shows participants how to walk in the Spirit. It moves Christians from simply having the power and presence of God's indwelling Spirit to a conscious recognition and application of His Spirit. This study is part of a series called "Transferable Concepts," practical ideas/truths to be communicated without distortion or dilution.

Author: Bright, Bill **215**
Series: Ten Basic Steps
Title: *Introduction: The Uniqueness of Jesus*
Publisher: NewLife Publications, 1994 ISBN: 1-56399-029-6

Num. Sess.	Group Time	Num. Pgs.	Avg. Qst.	Price	Audience	Format	Bible Study
7	60-75	80	Vary	$4.99	New Christian	Workbk	Charctr

Features: Intro to Leading a Study, Intro to Study
★★★★ Personal Application Preparation Time: Med
★★★ Relationship Building Ldr. Guide: Yes Size: 5.25 x 8.25
Subjects: Faith, Jesus: Life/Teaching, Singles' Issues
Comments: This is the introduction to "Ten Basic Steps Toward Christian Maturity," a series designed to provide participants with a foundation for their faith, and to help them share their faith with others. It includes: Why Jesus was truly "a man without equal"; how He changed the way we live and think today; what it means to let Christ live His life in you; and the secret of His power to turn you into a victorious, fruitful Christian.

Author: Bright, Bill **216**
Series:
Title: *Leader's Guide: Five Steps of Christian Growth*
Publisher: NewLife Publications, 1994 ISBN: 1-56399-022-9

Num. Sess.	Group Time	Num. Pgs.	Avg. Qst.	Price	Audience	Format	Bible Study
5	60-75	112	N/A	$5.99	New Christian		

Features: Intro to Leading a Study, Objectives, Bibliography, Prayer Helps, Follow Up, Charts
★★★★ Personal Application Preparation Time: High
★★ Relationship Building Ldr. Guide: Yes Size: 5.25 x 8.25
Subjects: Discipleship, Holy Spirit, Leader's Guide, Teens: Discipleship
Comments: This informative leader's guide includes comprehensive instructions. Special helps reduce preparation time. It gives first time small group leaders confidence by covering even the smallest details, such as room preparation, welcoming newcomers, helping others feel comfortable, getting a discussion started, keeping your group focused, and making the study applicable. A video is available.

Author: Bright, Bill **217**
Series:
Title: *Leader's Guide: 10 Basic Steps Toward Christian Maturity*
Publisher: NewLife Publications, 1994 ISBN: 1-56399-028-8

Num. Sess.	Group Time	Num. Pgs.	Avg. Qst.	Price	Audience	Format	Bible Study
10	—	550	N/A	$14.99	New Christian		

Features: Intro to Leading a Study, Objectives, Bibliography, Prayer Helps
★★★★ Personal Application Preparation Time:
★★★★ Relationship Building Ldr. Guide: Size: 5.25 x 8.25
Subjects: Devotionals, Discipleship, Holy Spirit, Leader's Guide, Obedience, Prayer, Singles' Issues
Comments: This is the leader's guide for the book by the same title. It provides: leader's objectives, leader's resources, opening prayers, discussion starters, lesson development, life applications, closing prayers, and additional background material. This time-tested study series is designed to provide participants with a sure foundation for their faith.

Author: Bright, Bill **218**
Series:
Title: *Life Without Equal*
Publisher: NewLife Publications, 1992 ISBN: 1-56399-011-3

Num. Sess.	Group Time	Num. Pgs.	Avg. Qst.	Price	Audience	Format	Bible Study
9	30-45	128	7	$4.99	Beginner	Book	Topical

Features: Bibliography, Persnl Study Quest, Appendix
★★★★ Personal Application Preparation Time: Low
★★ Relationship Building Ldr. Guide: No Size: 4.25 x 7.0
Subjects: Christian Life, Repentance, Singles' Issues
Comments: Dr. Bright explains how any person can receive a dynamic new life through faith in Jesus Christ. He shows readers how to release Christ's resurrection power in their own lives and join other Christians to help change the world. Participants can discover the pardon, purpose, peace, and power that results from living Christian lives. A self-study guide provides 20 questions, while a group discussion guide provides seven questions.

Author: Bright, Bill **219**
Series:
Title: *Man Without Equal, A*
Publisher: NewLife 2000 Publications, 1992 ISBN: 1-56399-012-1

Num. Sess.	Group Time	Num. Pgs.	Avg. Qst.	Price	Audience	Format	Bible Study
8	30-45	128	6	$4.99	Beginner	Book	Charctr

Features: Bibliography, Persnl Study Quest, Charts, Appendix
★★★★ Personal Application Preparation Time: Low
★★ Relationship Building Ldr. Guide: No Size: 4.25 x 7.0
Subjects: Jesus: Life/Teaching, Singles' Issues
Comments: Bill Bright explores why Jesus was history's greatest revolutionary. Drawing upon more than 45 years of research, the author shows the impact Jesus has made on society and how He continues to change the way people live and think today. A book for anyone who wants to take a fresh look at the Man who truly was—and is—without equal. Available in Spanish. A 30″ dramatic video is available for $14.99 (1-56399-014-8).

Author: Bright, Bill **220**
Series:
Title: *Man Without Equal, A*
Publisher: NewLife 2000 Publications, 1991 ISBN: 1-56399-014-8

Num. Sess.	Group Time	Num. Pgs.	Avg. Qst.	Price	Audience	Format	Bible Study
1	60-75	N/A	6	$14.99	Beginner	Video	Charctr

Features: Persnl Study Quest, Book Avail
★★★★ Personal Application Preparation Time: None
★★★★ Relationship Building Ldr. Guide: No Size: 4.25 x 7.50
Subjects: Evangelism, Jesus: Life/Teaching
Comments: On this 30″ video the life of Jesus unfolds through dramatic recreations and breathtaking portraits from the great masters. It is a compelling video for anyone who wants to take a fresh look at the Man who truly was, and is, without equal. A card insert with the video gives six questions for reflection and discussion. Dr. Bill Bright explores the unique birth, earthly life, teaching, death, and resurrection of Jesus Christ. Available in Spanish.

Author: Bright, Bill **221**
Series:
Title: *Reaching Your World Through Witnessing Without Fear*
Publisher: NewLife Publications, 1994 ISBN: 1-56399-061-X

Num. Sess.	Group Time	Num. Pgs.	Avg. Qst.	Price	Audience	Format	Bible Study
6	60-75	64	Vary	$29.99	New Christian	Video	Charctr

Features: Intro to Study, Bibliography, Follow Up, Persnl Study Quest, Video Study Guide
★★★★ Personal Application Preparation Time: Low
★★★★ Relationship Building Ldr. Guide: No Size: 4.25 x 7.25
Subjects: Evangelism, Jesus: Life/Teaching
Comments: This package includes a self-study workbook, sample tracts and two videos containing all six sessions. Each video segment begins with a dramatic vignette. Key truths communicated include: "Discovering Your World"; "Becoming Usable"; "Finding Common Ground"; "Sharing With Confidence"; "Overcoming Objections"; and "Beginning a New Life." Book only $9.99.

Author: Briscoe, Jill **222**
Series: Jill Briscoe Bible Study
Title: *Before You Say "Amen"*
Publisher: Victor Books, 1989 ISBN: 0-89693-637-6

Num. Sess.	Group Time	Num. Pgs.	Avg. Qst.	Price	Audience	Format	Bible Study
8	60-90	105	18	$6.99	New Christian	Workbk	Topical

Features: Intro to Leading a Study, Intro to Study, Prayer Helps, Digging Deeper Quest, Follow Up
★★★★ Personal Application Preparation Time: Med
★★★★ Relationship Building Ldr. Guide: No Size: 6.0 x 9.0
Subjects: Devotionals, Prayer, Women's Issues
Comments: This study on prayer encourages participants to improve their devotional lives by practicing personal and corporate prayer. Subjects covered include: beginning to pray, praising, model prayers, conditions of prayer, and praying for others and ourselves. Each lesson provides a devotional narrative, suggestions for group discussion and prayer, and a Bible study for more advanced study.

Author: Briscoe, Jill **223**
Series: Jill Briscoe Bible Study
Title: *Body Language*
Publisher: Victor Books, 1987 ISBN: 0-89693-319-9

Num. Sess.	Group Time	Num. Pgs.	Avg. Qst.	Price	Audience	Format	Bible Study
8	60-90	108	19	$6.99	New Christian	Workbk	Topical

Features: Intro to Leading a Study, Bibliography, Prayer Helps, Digging Deeper Quest, Follow Up, Agenda
★★★ Personal Application Preparation Time: Med
★★★ Relationship Building Ldr. Guide: No Size: 6.0 x 9.0
Subjects: Caring, Christian Living, Women's Issues
Comments: In this study on body language, when actions speak louder than words, participants are challenged to consider how the world is affected by what they say and do. Lessons address subjects like: the body as a physical entity; transforming minds; changing hearts; taming tongues; helping hands; seeing eyes; and listening ears. Participants are reminded that there are many ways to communicate.

Author: Briscoe, Jill **224**
Series: Jill Briscoe Bible Study
Title: *Evergrowing, Evergreen*
Publisher: Victor Books, 1986 ISBN: 0-89693-255-9

Num. Sess.	Group Time	Num. Pgs.	Avg. Qst.	Price	Audience	Format	Bible Study
7	60-90	96	18	$6.99	New Christian	Workbk	Book

Features: Intro to Leading a Study, Bibliography, Prayer Helps, Digging Deeper Quest, Follow Up, Full Scrpt Printed
★★★ Personal Application Preparation Time: Med
★★★ Relationship Building Ldr. Guide: No Size: 6.0 x 9.0
Subjects: Bible Personalities, God, Psalms, Women's Issues, Worship
Comments: This study of 7 selected psalms can help participants get to know God, themselves, and their world better. Psalms 1, 18, 23, 27, 51, 119, and 137 are included. David wrote many of the psalms; others are attributed to Solomon, Asaph, the sons of Korah, and Moses. Psalms are used for public as well as private worship.

Author: Briscoe, Jill **225**
Series: Jill Briscoe Bible Study
Title: *Faith Enough to Finish*
Publisher: Victor Books, 1987 ISBN: 0-89693-238-9

Num. Sess.	Group Time	Num. Pgs.	Avg. Qst.	Price	Audience	Format	Bible Study
8	60-90	108	20	$6.99	New Christian	Workbk	Book

Features: Intro to Leading a Study, Bibliography, Prayer Helps, Digging Deeper Quest, Follow Up, Agenda
★★★ Personal Application Preparation Time: Med
★★★ Relationship Building Ldr. Guide: No Size: 6.0 x 9.0
Subjects: Faith, Hebrews, Women's Issues
Comments: In this eight-lesson study of Hebrews, participants will discover what it means to endure. First-century believers who, because of increasing hostility, were in danger of "drifting away" from the faith, were told to draw near and hold fast—the eternal Son of God is supreme and sufficient. The study uses discussions like one on Christ, "the author and finisher of our faith," to provide that steadfastness.

Author: Briscoe, Jill **226**
Series: Jill Briscoe Bible Study
Title: *God's Name, God's Nature*
Publisher: Victor Books, 1988 ISBN: 0-89693-584-1

Num. Sess.	Group Time	Num. Pgs.	Avg. Qst.	Price	Audience	Format	Bible Study
9	60-90	108	17	$6.99	New Christian	Workbk	Topical

Features: Intro to Leading a Study, Bibliography, Prayer Helps, Digging Deeper Quest, Follow Up, Agenda
★★★ Personal Application Preparation Time: Med
★★★ Relationship Building Ldr. Guide: No Size: 6.0 x 9.0
Subjects: God, Old Testament, Women's Issues
Comments: This study is designed to teach participants more about God through His Old Testament names, such as Elohim, Adonai, Jehovah-Jireh, Jehovah-Rophe, Jehovah-Nissi, and Jehovah-Shalom. God's names unlock the mystery of His nature; reveal His heart, mind, and soul; capture the imagination; and bring believers to His feet in wonder, love, and praise.

Author: Briscoe, Jill **227**
Series: Jill Briscoe Bible Study
Title: *Grace to Go On*
Publisher: Victor Books, 1989 ISBN: 0-89693-762-3

Num. Sess.	Group Time	Num. Pgs.	Avg. Qst.	Price	Audience	Format	Bible Study
8	60-90	103	15	$6.99	New Christian	Workbk	Topical

Features: Intro to Leading a Study, Intro to Study, Bibliography, Prayer Helps, Digging Deeper Quest, Follow Up, Charts, Agenda
★★★ Personal Application Preparation Time: Med
★★★ Relationship Building Ldr. Guide: No Size: 6.0 x 9.0
Subjects: Charismatic Interest, Grace, Holy Spirit, Spiritual Gifts, Women's Issues
Comments: This study explores symbols of the Holy Spirit that abound in Scripture, including: the "fire" that ignites, the "wind" of change, the "oil" of gladness, the "water" of life, the abused "dove," the Spirit's "gifts," the "fruit" that blossoms, and the "cloud" of glory. Participants will experience a Holy Spirit that can enrich their souls.

Author: Briscoe, Jill **228**
Series: Jill Briscoe Bible Study
Title: *Heartbeat of Jesus, The*
Publisher: Victor Books, 1993 ISBN: 1-56476-102-9

Num. Sess.	Group Time	Num. Pgs.	Avg. Qst.	Price	Audience	Format	Bible Study
8	60-90	93	3	$6.99	New Christian	Workbk	Charctr

Features: Intro to Leading a Study, Bibliography, Prayer Helps, Scrpt Memory Helps, Digging Deeper Quest, Follow Up, Persnl Study Quest, Agenda
★★★ Personal Application Preparation Time: Med
★★★ Relationship Building Ldr. Guide: No Size: 6.0 x 9.0
Subjects: Jesus: Life/Teaching, Women's Issues
Comments: This eight week study examines the life of Jesus. It looks at the early years, His time with John the Baptist, His temptations, ministry, time in Gethsemane, crucifixion, resurrection, and promises. Participants can discover what motivated Jesus to "be about His Father's business" and then motivate Christians to do the same.

Author: Briscoe, Jill **229**
Series:
Title: *"Here Am I—Send Aaron!"*
Publisher: Victor Books, 1978 ISBN: 0-88207-767-8

Num. Sess.	Group Time	Num. Pgs.	Avg. Qst.	Price	Audience	Format	Bible Study
13	60-90	142	Vary	$7.99	New Christian	Book	Book

Features: Prayer Helps
★★★ Personal Application Preparation Time: Med
★★★ Relationship Building Ldr. Guide: Yes Size: 5.50 x 8.0
Subjects: Bible Personalities, Exodus, God
Comments: The study of Exodus shows how God directed the children of Israel through a reluctant leader, Moses. During the "desert" years, God miraculously transformed this insignificant saint into a persuasive communicator, sensitive to the Lord's call. Through the wilderness wanderings of Moses and his people, participants can identify their own spiritual strayings and redirect and enrich their daily lives. A leader's guide with reproducible student response sheets is available.

Author: Briscoe, Jill **230**
Series: Jill Briscoe Bible Study
Title: *Shelter From the Wind, A*
Publisher: Victor Books, 1991 ISBN: 0-89693-883-2

Num. Sess.	Group Time	Num. Pgs.	Avg. Qst.	Price	Audience	Format	Bible Study
8	75-120	96	20	$6.99	New Christian	Workbk	Book

Features: Intro to Study, Bibliography, Prayer Helps, Digging Deeper Quest
★★★ Personal Application Preparation Time: Med
★★★ Relationship Building Ldr. Guide: No Size: 6.0 x 9.0
Subjects: Isaiah/Jeremiah, Women's Issues
Comments: In this eight-lesson study of Isaiah, participants learn more about a God who regenerates, renews, and rewards. Being a prophet didn't exempt Isaiah from conflict. Being a Christian exempts no one either. Isaiah had to learn to live, love, and labor for God in the middle of some dangerous storms. Isaiah's example shows participants how to seek God as a shelter from wind and refuge from storms.

Author: Briscoe, Jill **231**
Series: Jill Briscoe Bible Study
Title: *Solid Ground*
Publisher: Victor Books, 1992 ISBN: 0-89693-884-0

Num. Sess.	Group Time	Num. Pgs.	Avg. Qst.	Price	Audience	Format	Bible Study
8	60-90	94	3	$6.99	New Christian	Workbk	Topical

Features: Intro to Leading a Study, Bibliography, Prayer Helps, Scrpt Memory Helps, Digging Deeper Quest, Follow Up, Persnl Study Quest, Agenda
★★★ Personal Application Preparation Time: Med
★★★ Relationship Building Ldr. Guide: No Size: 6.0 x 9.0
Subjects: Matthew, Sermon on the Mount, Women's Issues
Comments: Jesus taught people to build lives on His solid principles, in order to withstand life's storms. Shows participants how those principles are delineated in the Sermon on the Mount. Only by putting His Word into action can people know real happiness, for "blessed are those who are not only hearers of the Word but doers of it.

Author: Briscoe, Jill **232**
Series:
Title: *Wings*
Publisher: Victor Books, 1984 ISBN: 0-89693-574-4

Num. Sess.	Group Time	Num. Pgs.	Avg. Qst.	Price	Audience	Format	Bible Study
	10-20	370	N/A	$9.99	New Christian	Book	Topical

Features: Full Scrpt Printed
★★★★ Personal Application Preparation Time: None
★ Relationship Building Ldr. Guide: No Size: 5.50 x 8.50
Subjects: Devotionals
Comments: In this daily devotional book, Jill Briscoe shares her thoughts on a brief Scripture passage for each day, then offers her insights. Comments are down-to-earth and life related, and her meditations will challenge and encourage readers throughout the year.

Author: Briscoe, Jill **233**
Series: Jill Briscoe Bible Study
Title: *Woman of Substance, A*
Publisher: Victor Books, 1988 ISBN: 1-56476-267-X

Num. Sess.	Group Time	Num. Pgs.	Avg. Qst.	Price	Audience	Format	Bible Study
8	60-90	108	Vary	$6.99	New Christian	Workbk	Charctr

Features: Intro to Leading a Study, Prayer Helps, Scrpt Memory Helps, Digging Deeper Quest,Follow Up, Persnl Study Quest, Agenda
★★★ Personal Application Preparation Time: Med
★★★ Relationship Building Ldr. Guide: No Size: 6.0 x 9.0
Subjects: Bible Personalities, Esther, Women's Issues
Comments: This study of Esther, a woman in an unbelieving environment, shows how God can reach out of peoples' lives into the lives of others. It is a story of kings, queens, and commonplace ordinary people, who teach among other things that kings' palaces are not necessarily the only places where royalty can be found. It's designed for groups or individuals at different levels of spiritual maturity.

Author: Briscoe, Jill **234**
Series: Jill Briscoe Bible Study
Title: *Women in the Life of Jesus*
Publisher: Victor Books, 1986 ISBN: 0-89693-254-0

Num. Sess.	Group Time	Num. Pgs.	Avg. Qst.	Price	Audience	Format	Bible Study
8	60-90	96	17	$6.99	New Christian	Workbk	Topical

Features: Intro to Leading a Study, Bibliography, Prayer Helps, Digging Deeper Quest, Agenda
★★★ Personal Application Preparation Time: Med
★★★ Relationship Building Ldr. Guide: No Size: 6.0 x 9.0
Subjects: Bible Personalities, Jesus: Life/Teaching, Relationships, Singles' Issues, Women's Issues
Comments: This study deals with women who had an impact on Jesus' earthly ministry, including sorrowing, sick, sexual, sinful, single, spiritual, successful, and scheming women. By studying the lives of Mary of Nazareth, Mary of Bethany, Rahab, Jezebel, and many others, participants will deepen their relationship with Christ.

Author: Briscoe, Jill **235**
Series: Jill Briscoe Bible Study
Title: *Women Who Changed Their World*
Publisher: Victor Books, 1991 ISBN: 0-89693-001-7

Num. Sess.	Group Time	Num. Pgs.	Avg. Qst.	Price	Audience	Format	Bible Study
8	60-90	95	18	$6.99	New Christian	Workbk	Topical

Features: Intro to Leading a Study, Intro to Study, Prayer Helps, Scrpt Memory Helps, Digging Deeper Quest, Follow Up
★★★ Personal Application Preparation Time: Med
★★★ Relationship Building Ldr. Guide: No Size: 6.0 x 9.0
Subjects: Bible Personalities, Faith, Forgiveness, Friendships, Relationships, Women's Issues
Comments: This study helps participants learn more about qualities that allow women to make a difference. Women like Eve, Sarah, and Rahab took advantage of opportunities to influence their families, friends, or masters. Topics include: changing the world through sin, meekness, gifts, faith, strength, love, faithfulness, and forgiveness.

Author: Briscoe, Stuart **236**
Series:
Title: *David: A Heart for God*
Publisher: Victor Books, 1984 ISBN: 0-89693-466-7

Num. Sess.	Group Time	Num. Pgs.	Avg. Qst.	Price	Audience	Format	Bible Study
13	60-75	170	N/A	$7.99	New Christian	Book	Charctr

Features:
★★★★ Personal Application Preparation Time: Low
★★★ Relationship Building Ldr. Guide: Yes Size: 5.50 x 8.0
Subjects: Bible Personalities, Repentance, Senior Adults, Service, 1 & 2 Samuel
Comments: This 13-week study of David's triumphs, trials, and sins offers participants hope for becoming people after God's own heart. It leads them from a preoccupation with self to a new heart-attitude. The study concludes with a discussion of retirement, and how people will or won't serve the Lord. It compares retirees with David, who continued to serve God until the end of his life.

Author: Briscoe, Stuart **237**
Series:
Title: *Enjoying The Good Life*
Publisher: Victor Books, 1992 ISBN: 0-89693-960-X

Num. Sess.	Group Time	Num. Pgs.	Avg. Qst.	Price	Audience	Format	Bible Study
12	60-90	173	N/A	$7.99	New Christian	Book	Book

Features:
★★★ Personal Application Preparation Time: Low
★★ Relationship Building Ldr. Guide: Yes Size: 5.50 x 8.0
Subjects: Numbers/Deuteronomy
Comments: This study from the Book of Deuteronomy details God's instructions to His people, the Israelites, as they were about to enter the promised land He had given them. Participants learn about important principles, such as loving God for who He is, living a godly lifestyle in a godless world, passing spiritual values on to children, avoiding tendencies toward self-righteousness, making worship and celebration more vital and meaningful, and much more.

Author: Briscoe, Stuart **238**
Series: Fisherman Bible Studyguide
Title: *Fruit of the Spirit, The*
Publisher: Shaw, 1994 ISBN: 0-87788-258-4

Num. Sess.	Group Time	Num. Pgs.	Avg. Qst.	Price	Audience	Format	Bible Study
10	45-60	62	13	$4.99	New Christian	Workbk	Topical

Features: Intro to Leading a Study, Intro to Study, Prayer Helps, Ldr's Notes
★★★★ Personal Application Preparation Time: Low
★★★ Relationship Building Ldr. Guide: No Size: 5.25 x 8.25
Subjects: Fruit of the Spirit, Holy Spirit
Comments: In this 10-week study participants will learn their part and God's part in developing the nine spiritual qualities of the fruit of the Spirit. The 9 are love, joy, peace, patience, kindness, goodness, faithfulness, meekness, and self-control. The study explains that when it comes to living by the Spirit, Christians don't have the freedom to pick and choose which fruit should be exhibited.

Author: Briscoe, Stuart **239**
Series:
Title: *Hearing God's Voice Above The Noise*
Publisher: Victor Books, 1991 ISBN: 0-89693-002-5

Num. Sess.	Group Time	Num. Pgs.	Avg. Qst.	Price	Audience	Format	Bible Study
12	60-75	190	N/A	$7.99	New Christian	Book	Book

Features: Intro to Study
★★★ Personal Application Preparation Time: Low
★ Relationship Building Ldr. Guide: Yes Size: 5.50 x 8.0
Subjects: Minor Prophets
Comments: The minor prophets have much relevance to Christians today. They are called "minor" not because they are of minor significance, but because of their brevity. They were talking to the people of Judah and Israel who were failing dramatically to be the people they were called to be. Yet God was gracious. Prophets covered include Hosea, Joel, Amos, Obadiah, Jonah, Micah, Nahum, Habakkuk, Zephaniah, Haggai, Zechariah, and Malachi.

Author: Briscoe, Stuart & Jill **240**
Series:
Title: *Life, Liberty and the Pursuit of Holiness*
Publisher: Victor Books, 1993 ISBN: 1-56476-064-2

Num. Sess.	Group Time	Num. Pgs.	Avg. Qst.	Price	Audience	Format	Bible Study
10	60-75	190	Vary	$8.99	New Christian	Book	Topical

Features: Intro to Study, Prayer Helps, Ldr's Notes
★★★★ Personal Application Preparation Time: Low
★★ Relationship Building Ldr. Guide: No Size: 5.50 x 8.50
Subjects: Holiness
Comments: This study was written to clarify the order of preference to being healthy, holy, and happy. The author, as a child, rated them happy, healthy, and then holy, thinking that one must give up any hope of happiness if God is placed first. Through the study, participants discover that there is no conflict with being thoroughly happy, truly healthy, and practically holy. They can also learn what God means when He says, "Be holy, because I am holy."

Author: Briscoe, Stuart 241
Series: Fisherman Bible Studyguide
Title: *Ten Commandments, The: God's Rules for Living*
Publisher: Shaw, 1995 ISBN: 0-87788-803-5

Num. Sess.	Group Time	Num. Pgs.	Avg. Qst.	Price	Audience	Format	Bible Study
10	45-60	64	12	$4.99	New Christian	Workbk	Topical

Features: Intro to Leading a Study, Intro to Study, Ldr's Notes
★★★ Personal Application Preparation Time: None
★★★ Relationship Building Ldr. Guide: No Size: 5.0 x 8.25
Subjects: Ten Commandments
Comments: This study explores each commandment with a view to applying it to the modern relativistic, "anything goes" society. Participants learn that rather than just being a repressive list of "thou shalt nots," these commandments can be effective guidelines that restrain people from hurtful actions, serve as mirrors for our sin, and truly free Christians to love God and others.

Author: Briscoe, Stuart 242
Series:
Title: *What Works When Life Doesn't*
Publisher: Victor Books, 1976 ISBN: 0-88207-725-2

Num. Sess.	Group Time	Num. Pgs.	Avg. Qst.	Price	Audience	Format	Bible Study
13	60-75	168	N/A	$8.99	New Christian	Book	Topical

Features: Intro to Study
★★★★ Personal Application Preparation Time: Low
★★★ Relationship Building Ldr. Guide: Yes Size: 5.50 x 8.0
Subjects: Emotions, Psalms, Stress
Comments: This 13-week study of selected psalms shows how they not only describe the human predicament, but also prescribe principles for overcoming such life problems as discouragement, depression, fear, and stress. Lessons propose solutions to other perplexing problems and demonstrate how studying psalms can offer peace. A leader's guide includes reproducible transparency masters.

Author: Brooks, Keith L. 243
Series: Teach Yourself the Bible
Title: *Acts: Adventures of the Early Church*
Publisher: Moody Press, 1963 ISBN: 0-80240-125-2

Num. Sess.	Group Time	Num. Pgs.	Avg. Qst.	Price	Audience	Format	Bible Study
12	60-90	96	48	$4.50	New Christian	Workbk	Book

Features: Intro to Leading a Study, Intro to Study, Exam
★★ Personal Application Preparation Time: Low
★★ Relationship Building Ldr. Guide: No Size: 5.50 x 8.50
Subjects: Acts
Comments: The book of Acts outlines the work of the Holy Spirit in the early Church. It is a record of His advent, activity, and power at the beginning of the Church. The format for this study—1 of 25 in this series—includes fill-in-the-blank questions and checkups to test participants' grasp of Scriptural truths. The series is designed for self-study, but suggestions for group study and a four-year plan for using the series are also included.

Author: Brooks, Keith L. 244
Series: Teach Yourself the Bible
Title: *Basic Bible Study: For New Christians*
Publisher: Moody Press, 1961 ISBN: 0-80240-478-2

Num. Sess.	Group Time	Num. Pgs.	Avg. Qst.	Price	Audience	Format	Bible Study
8	45-60	48	22	$4.50	New Christian	Workbk	Topical

Features: Intro to Leading a Study, Exam
★★ Personal Application Preparation Time: Low
★★ Relationship Building Ldr. Guide: No Size: 5.50 x 8.50
Subjects: Discipleship, Prayer
Comments: This Bible study covers the basics for new Christians. Topics include: God's way of salvation, our blessings in Christ, the consecrated life, how to meet temptation, how to pray, and more. The format includes a series of fill-in-the-blank questions and checkups test participants' grasp of Scriptural truths. This 25-book series is designed for self-study; however, suggestions for group study, and a 4-year plan for using the series, are included.

Author: Brooks, Keith L. 245
Series: Teach Yourself the Bible
Title: *Christian Character Course*
Publisher: Moody Press, 1961 ISBN: 0-80241-301-3

Num. Sess.	Group Time	Num. Pgs.	Avg. Qst.	Price	Audience	Format	Bible Study
8	45-60	48	31	$4.50	New Christian	Workbk	Topical

Features: Intro to Leading a Study, Exam
★★ Personal Application Preparation Time: Low
★★ Relationship Building Ldr. Guide: No Size: 5.50 x 8.50
Subjects: Discipleship, Ethics, Fruit of the Spirit, Service
Comments: This study examines eight characteristics of a true believer, including humility, love, purity, integrity, generosity, and steadfastness. Participants will learn about Christian ethics and practical Christian service. The format includes a series of fill-in-the-blank questions, and checkups to test participants' grasp of Scriptural truths. This 25-book series is designed for self-study; however, suggestions for group study are included.

Author: Brooks, Keith L. 246
Series: Teach Yourself the Bible
Title: *Colossians and Philemon: The Epistles of Truth and Love*
Publisher: Moody Press, 1964 ISBN: 0-80241-525-3

Num. Sess.	Group Time	Num. Pgs.	Avg. Qst.	Price	Audience	Format	Bible Study
8	45-60	48	22	$4.50	New Christian	Workbk	Book

Features: Intro to Leading a Study, Exam
★★ Personal Application Preparation Time: Low
★★ Relationship Building Ldr. Guide: No Size: 5.50 x 8.50
Subjects: Church Life, Colossians/Philemon, False Teachers, Forgiveness, Hope, Leadership, Prison Epistles, Service, Suffering
Comments: This study—part of a 25-book series—deals with letters the Apostle Paul sent to the Colossians and Philemon. The former was sent to Colossae to warn against errors of doctrine and practice; the latter was a private letter to a Colossian Christian. The format for this study includes a series of fill-in-the-blank questions and checkups to test participants' grasp of Scriptural truths.

Author: Brooks, Keith L. 247
Series: Teach Yourself the Bible
Title: *Ephesians: The Epistle of Christian Maturity*
Publisher: Moody Press, 1964 ISBN: 0-80242-333-7

Num. Sess.	Group Time	Num. Pgs.	Avg. Qst.	Price	Audience	Format	Bible Study
8	60-75	64	40	$4.50	New Christian	Workbk	Book

Features: Intro to Leading a Study, Exam
★★ Personal Application Preparation Time: Low
★★ Relationship Building Ldr. Guide: No Size: 5.50 x 8.50
Subjects: Discipleship, Ephesians, Theology
Comments: This study of Ephesians—part of a 25-book series—concerns a timeless letter for God's Church. The practical and doctrinal sides of this epistle deal with a believer's place in Christ and Christ's place in a believer. The format includes a series of fill-in-the- blank questions and checkups to test participants' grasp of Scriptural truths. The series is designed for self-study; however, suggestions for group study, and a 4-year plan for using the series, are included.

Author: Brooks, Keith L. 248
Series: Teach Yourself the Bible
Title: *First and Second Thessalonians: Jesus Is Coming Again!*
Publisher: Moody Press, 1964 ISBN: 0-80242-645-X

Num. Sess.	Group Time	Num. Pgs.	Avg. Qst.	Price	Audience	Format	Bible Study
8	45-60	48	23	$4.50	New Christian	Workbk	Book

Features: Intro to Leading a Study, Exam
★★ Personal Application Preparation Time: Low
★★ Relationship Building Ldr. Guide: No Size: 5.50 x 8.50
Subjects: Eschatology, 1 & 2 Thessalonians
Comments: This study outlines the 4 reasons Paul wrote 1 and 2 Thessalonians: to confirm young believers, to encourage them in the face of persecution, to correct doctrinal errors, and to teach them what God has revealed about the Lord's return. The format includes a series of fill-in-the-blank questions and checkups to test participants' grasp of Scriptural truths. This 25-book series is designed for self-study, but also includes group study helps.

Author: Brooks, Keith L. 249
Series: Teach Yourself the Bible
Title: *First Corinthians: Order in the Church*
Publisher: Moody Press, 1964 ISBN: 0-80242-649-2

Num. Sess.	Group Time	Num. Pgs.	Avg. Qst.	Price	Audience	Format	Bible Study
12	45-60	64	24	$4.50	New Christian	Workbk	Book

Features: Intro to Leading a Study, Intro to Study, Exam
★★ Personal Application Preparation Time: Low
★★ Relationship Building Ldr. Guide: No Size: 5.50 x 8.50
Subjects: Church Life, 1 Corinthians
Comments: Paul wrote 1 Corinthians in response to issues concerning paganism. He appealed to predominantly Gentile church members to remember their high positions in Christ, and the reality of their union with Him. The format of this study—1 of 25 in this series—includes a series of fill-in-the-blank questions and checkups to test participants' grasp of Scriptural truths. The series is designed for self-study; however, suggestions for group study are included.

Author: Brooks, Keith L. 250
Series: Teach Yourself the Bible
Title: *Galatians: The Epistle of Christian Liberty*
Publisher: Moody Press, 1963 ISBN: 0-80242-925-4

Num. Sess.	Group Time	Num. Pgs.	Avg. Qst.	Price	Audience	Format	Bible Study
8	45-60	48	22	$4.50	New Christian	Workbk	Book

Features: Intro to Leading a Study, Exam
★★ Personal Application Preparation Time: Low
★★ Relationship Building Ldr. Guide: No Size: 5.50 x 8.50
Subjects: Galatians, Victorious Living
Comments: This study of Galatians—part of a 25-book series—is about Paul's letter calling believers back to the pure Gospel of Jesus Christ. Lessons cover the origin, maintenance, experience, superiority, effects, and practice of Christian liberty. The format includes a series of fill-in-the-blank questions; checkups test participants' grasp of Scriptural truths. The series is designed for self-study; however, suggestions for group study are included.

Author: Brooks, Keith L. 251
Series: Teach Yourself the Bible
Title: *Great Prophetic Themes*
Publisher: Moody Press, 1962 ISBN: 0-80243-320-0

Num. Sess.	Group Time	Num. Pgs.	Avg. Qst.	Price	Audience	Format	Bible Study
12	45-60	64	21	$4.50	New Christian	Workbk	Topical

Features: Intro to Leading a Study, Exam
★★ Personal Application Preparation Time: Low
★★ Relationship Building Ldr. Guide: No Size: 5.50 x 8.50
Subjects: Eschatology, Prophecy
Comments: This study of great prophetic themes—part of a 25-book series—covers much of the Old and New Testaments. For example, the Lord's Second Coming is mentioned 318 times in the 27 books of the New Testament, and numerous times in the Old Testament. The format includes a series of fill-in-the-blank questions, and checkups to test participants' grasp of Scriptural truths. Designed for self-study; however, suggestions for group study are included.

Author: Brooks, Keith L. 252
Series: Teach Yourself the Bible
Title: *Hebrews: The Beauty of Christ Unveiled*
Publisher: Moody Press, 1963 ISBN: 0-80243-507-6

Num. Sess.	Group Time	Num. Pgs.	Avg. Qst.	Price	Audience	Format	Bible Study
13	45-60	64	22	$4.50	New Christian	Workbk	Book

Features: Intro to Leading a Study, Exam
★★ Personal Application Preparation Time: Low
★★ Relationship Building Ldr. Guide: No Size: 5.50 x 8.50
Subjects: Faith, Hebrews, Obedience
Comments: This study of Hebrews—part of a 25-book series—concerns a book obviously inspired by God. Participants will learn of the superiority of Christ and the need for complete faith in Him and will be exhorted to obey Him in attitude and deed. The format includes a series of fill-in-the-blank questions, and checkups to test participants' grasp of Scriptural truths. The series is designed for self-study; however, suggestions for group study are included.

Author: Brooks, Keith L. 253
Series: Teach Yourself the Bible
Title: *James: Belief in Action*
Publisher: Moody Press, 1962 ISBN: 0-80244-227-7

Num. Sess.	Group Time	Num. Pgs.	Avg. Qst.	Price	Audience	Format	Bible Study
8	45-60	48	29	$4.50	New Christian	Workbk	Topical

Features: Intro to Leading a Study, Exam
★★ Personal Application Preparation Time: Low
★★ Relationship Building Ldr. Guide: No Size: 5.50 x 8.50
Subjects: Beliefs, Faith, James
Comments: This study of James emphasizes works as the fruit of faith and evidence of justification. It is based entirely on the new birth and a living salvation through Jesus Christ. The format includes a series of fill-in-the-blank questions; checkups test participants' grasp of Scriptural truths. This 25-book series is designed for self-study; however, suggestions for group study, and a 4-year plan for using the series, are included.

Author: Brooks, Keith L. 254
Series: Teach Yourself the Bible
Title: *Luke: The Gospel of God's Man*
Publisher: Moody Press, 1964 ISBN: 0-80245-047-4

Num. Sess.	Group Time	Num. Pgs.	Avg. Qst.	Price	Audience	Format	Bible Study
12	60-90	96	57	$4.50	New Christian	Workbk	Book

Features: Intro to Leading a Study, Charts, Exam
★★ Personal Application Preparation Time: Low
★★ Relationship Building Ldr. Guide: No Size: 5.50 x 8.50
Subjects: Jesus: Life/Teaching, Luke
Comments: This study concerns Luke's account of the man who was completely God, and God who became completely man. It covers Christ's life from birth to ascension. A chart listing distinctive features of the Gospels is beneficial. The format includes a series of fill-in-the-blank questions; checkups are included to test participants' grasp of Scriptural truths. This 25-book series is designed for self-study; however, suggestions for group study are included.

Author: Brooks, Keith L. 255
Series: Teach Yourself the Bible
Title: *Mark: The Gospel of God's Servant*
Publisher: Moody Press, 1964 ISBN: 0-80245-200-0

Num. Sess.	Group Time	Num. Pgs.	Avg. Qst.	Price	Audience	Format	Bible Study
12	60-90	77	35	$4.50	New Christian	Workbk	Book

Features: Intro to Leading a Study, Exam
★★ Personal Application Preparation Time: Low
★★ Relationship Building Ldr. Guide: No Size: 5.50 x 8.50
Subjects: Jesus: Life/Teaching, Mark, Service
Comments: This study of Mark is part of a 25-book series. Mark is a Gospel of service, presenting Jesus Christ as Servant, obedient even to death. Written primarily for Gentiles, it shows participants how to become servants of Christ. The format includes a series of fill-in-the-blank questions and checkups to test partipants' grasp of Scriptural truths. The series is designed for self-study; however, suggestions for group study, and a 4-year plan for using the series, are included.

Author: Brooks, Keith L. 256
Series: Teach Yourself the Bible
Title: *Matthew: The Gospel of God's King*
Publisher: Moody Press, 1963 ISBN: 0-80245-212-4

Num. Sess.	Group Time	Num. Pgs.	Avg. Qst.	Price	Audience	Format	Bible Study
12	60-90	96	48	$4.50	New Christian	Workbk	Book

Features: Intro to Leading a Study, Exam
★★ Personal Application Preparation Time: Low
★★ Relationship Building Ldr. Guide: No Size: 5.50 x 8.50
Subjects: Jesus: Life/Teaching, Matthew
Comments: The Gospel of Matthew serves as a bridge between Judaism and Christianity. Christ is presented as Mediator of a New Covenant, which began when His blood was shed. The format for this study includes fill-in-the-blank questions and checkups to test participants' grasp of Scriptural truths. This 25-book series is designed for self-study; however, suggestions for group study, and a 4-year plan for using the series, are included.

Author: Brooks, Keith L. 257
Series: Teach Yourself the Bible
Title: *Philippians: The Epistle of Christian Joy*
Publisher: Moody Press, 1963 ISBN: 0-80246-506-4

Num. Sess.	Group Time	Num. Pgs.	Avg. Qst.	Price	Audience	Format	Bible Study
8	45-60	48	24	$4.50	New Christian	Workbk	Book

Features: Intro to Leading a Study, Exam
★★ Personal Application Preparation Time: Low
★★ Relationship Building Ldr. Guide: No Size: 5.50 x 8.50
Subjects: Church Life, Joy, Philippians, Prison Epistles, Service, Suffering, Victorious Living
Comments: This study of Philippians—part of a 25-book series—reflects Paul's affection for the first church he established. Participants will benefit from studying the problems Philippian believers encountered as their congregation grew. The format includes a series of fill-in-the-blank questions and checkups to test participants' grasp of Scriptural truths. Suggestions for group study are included.

Author: Brooks, Keith L. 258
Series: Teach Yourself the Bible
Title: *Practical Bible Doctrine*
Publisher: Moody Press, 1962 ISBN: 0-80246-733-4

Num. Sess.	Group Time	Num. Pgs.	Avg. Qst.	Price	Audience	Format	Bible Study
12	60-75	80	33	$4.50	New Christian	Workbk	Topical

Features: Intro to Leading a Study, Exam
★★ Personal Application Preparation Time: Low
★★ Relationship Building Ldr. Guide: No Size: 5.50 x 8.50
Subjects: Apologetics, Eschatology, Holy Spirit, Satan
Comments: This study of practical Bible doctrine—part of a 25-book series—was written for new believers. Subjects include the inspiration of Scripture, Christ's incarnation and second coming, the Holy Spirit, and Satan. The format includes a series of fill-in-the-blank questions and checkups to test participants' grasp of Scriptural truths. The series is designed for self-study; however, suggestions for group study, and a four-year plan for using the series, are included.

Author: Brooks, Keith L. 259
Series: Teach Yourself the Bible
Title: *Revelation: The Future Foretold*
Publisher: Moody Press, 1962 ISBN: 0-80247-308-3

Num. Sess.	Group Time	Num. Pgs.	Avg. Qst.	Price	Audience	Format	Bible Study
12	45-60	80	23	$4.50	New Christian	Workbk	Book

Features: Intro to Leading a Study, Exam
★★ Personal Application Preparation Time: Low
★★ Relationship Building Ldr. Guide: No Size: 5.50 x 8.50
Subjects: Revelation
Comments: This study of Revelation—part of a 25-book series—clarifies a believer's God-given future. Christ's return should encourage participants to serve Him through holy lives until that time. The format includes a series of fill-in-the-blank questions, and checkups to test participants' grasp of Scriptural truths. The series is designed for self-study; however, suggestions for group study, and a four-year plan for using the series, are included.

Author: Brooks, Keith L. 260
Series: Teach Yourself the Bible
Title: *Romans: The Gospel for All*
Publisher: Moody Press, 1962 ISBN: 0-80247-372-5

Num. Sess.	Group Time	Num. Pgs.	Avg. Qst.	Price	Audience	Format	Bible Study
12	60-90	80	40	$4.50	New Christian	Workbk	Book

Features: Intro to Leading a Study, Intro to Study, Exam
★★ Personal Application Preparation Time: Low
★★ Relationship Building Ldr. Guide: No Size: 5.50 x 8.50
Subjects: Faith, Grace, Romans, Theology
Comments: Paul prepared the way for his visit to a predominantly Gentile church in Rome with a letter. This letter, called Romans, systematically sets forth the doctrine of justification by faith. The format for this study—1 of 25 in this series—includes fill-in-the-blank questions and checkups to test participants' grasp of Scriptural truths. The series is designed for self-study; however, suggestions for group study, and a 4-year plan of study, are included.

Author: Brown, Carol Breeden 261
Series: Bible Alive Studies
Title: *Bringing the Old Testament to Life*
Publisher: David C. Cook Publishing Co., 1993 ISBN: 0-78145-018-7

Num. Sess.	Group Time	Num. Pgs.	Avg. Qst.	Price	Audience	Format	Bible Study
13	45-60	144	Vary	$19.95	Beginner	Workbk	Book

Features: Intro to Study, Bibliography, Prayer Helps, Drawings, Handouts, Persnl Study Quest, Charts
★★★★ Personal Application Preparation Time: None
★★ Relationship Building Ldr. Guide: Yes Size: 8.50 x 11.0
Subjects: God, Old Testament
Comments: Provides an overview of the Old Testament for adults of all ages. It deals with questions such as: "What does the Old Testament have to do with me?" "Did God create evil?" "Does God speak to people today like He did in Old Testament times?" "What's the Old Testament all about?" and "Is God still involved in everyday life? No student book is required, and reproducible handouts are included.

Author: Brown, David 262
Series: Serendipity Support Group
Title: *Engagement: Are You Fit to be Tied?*
Publisher: Serendipity House, 1992 ISBN: 1-88341-963-8

Num. Sess.	Group Time	Num. Pgs.	Avg. Qst.	Price	Audience	Format	Bible Study
7	60-90	96	12	$5.45	Beginner	Workbk	Topical

Features: Intro to Leading a Study, Objectives, Bibliography, Prayer Helps, Full Scrpt Printed, Ldr's Notes, Cartoons, Agenda
★★★★ Personal Application Preparation Time:
★★★★ Relationship Building Ldr. Guide: No Size: 6.50 x 9.0
Subjects: Divorce, Marriage, Relationships
Comments: This study deals with issues common to couples who are engaged or are thinking about becoming engaged. Lessons are entitled: "High Hurdles"; "Love is— "; "Communication"; "How Close Can We Get?"; "Resolving Conflict"; "Money"; and "Sexual Intimacy." The format includes icebreakers, Bible study and prayer, and timelines are provided. It can be adapted for a 7 or 14 week study.

Author: Brown, David 263
Series: Serendipity Support Group
Title: *Newly Married: How to Have a Great First Year*
Publisher: Serendipity House, 1990 ISBN: 1-88341-957-3

Num. Sess.	Group Time	Num. Pgs.	Avg. Qst.	Price	Audience	Format	Bible Study
14	60-90	96	12	$5.45	Beginner	Workbk	Topical

Features: Intro to Leading a Study, Objectives, Bibliography, Prayer Helps, Full Scrpt Printed, Ldr's Notes, Cartoons, Agenda
★★★★ Personal Application Preparation Time: None
★★★★ Relationship Building Ldr. Guide: No Size: 6.50 x 9.0
Subjects: Marriage, Young Marrieds
Comments: This study deals with issues common to couples in their first year of marriage. It shows how to make the year one of growth and not just painful adjustment. It deals with questions such as, "What happens when the wedding bells stop tolling, or when friends and family visit, or when you have to get down to the business of being married?" and, "How do you get to know each other?"

Author: Brown, Pam 264
Series: Spiritual Development Work
Title: *Lean On Me: How to Help a Friend With a Problem*
Publisher: Woman's Missionary Union, 1993 ISBN: 1-56309-068-6

Num. Sess.	Group Time	Num. Pgs.	Avg. Qst.	Price	Audience	Format	Bible Study
	—	25	Vary	$4.95		Workbk	

Features:
Personal Application Preparation Time:
Relationship Building Ldr. Guide: Size: 8.50 x 11.0
Subjects: Teens: Discipleship, Teens: Friends, Teens: Relationships, Teens: Resources
Comments: This resource, which helps youths stretch Spiritual development through involvement in peer ministry, provides techniques and practice involved in learning how to care about and help others. The SDW series is 3 workbooks containing Bible study material that will strengthen youth's prayer life, stretch their involvement in peer ministry, and exercise their personal witnessing skills.

Author: Bruno, Bonnie **265**
Series: The Beatitude Series
Title: *Mourning: The Prelude to Laughter*
Publisher: Zondervan, 1993 ISBN: 0-31059-613-0

Num. Sess.	Group Time	Num. Pgs.	Avg. Qst.	Price	Audience	Format	Bible Study
6	45-60	60	13	$4.99	New Christian	Workbk	Topical

Features: Intro to Leading a Study, Intro to Study, Objectives, Prayer Helps, Scrpt Memory Helps, Follow Up, Ldr's Notes
★★★★ Personal Application Preparation Time: Low
★★ Relationship Building Ldr. Guide: No Size: 5.50 x 8.25
Subjects: Grief, Sermon on the Mount
Comments: This is one of 8 guides in The Beatitude Series. This study looks at Bible characters whose journeys through sorrow and grief have been recorded to help participants weather personal storms. It shows how God guides one safely through the low points of life. Lesson titles include: "A Time to Mourn"; "Good Grief"; "Hope For the Troubled"; "A Time to Dance"; "No More Tears"; and "Everlasting Joy."

Author: Bubna, Donald & Sarah Ricketts **266**
Series: Living Studies
Title: *Building People Through a Caring, Sharing Fellowship*
Publisher: Tyndale House, 1978 ISBN: 0-84230-187-9

Num. Sess.	Group Time	Num. Pgs.	Avg. Qst.	Price	Audience	Format	Bible Study
12	60-90	153	N/A	$7.99	New Christian	Book	Topical

Features: No Grp Discussion Quest
★★ Personal Application Preparation Time: Low
★★ Relationship Building Ldr. Guide: No Size: 5.0 x 8.0
Subjects: Leadership, Small Group Resource
Comments: This book responds to the question, "What are we supposed to be doing, anyway?" and explores practical steps a church can take to become a caring, sharing fellowship. Chapter titles include: "Let's Eat Together!" "Talking Together," "Come Cry with Me," and "The Witnessing Church."

Author: Budzowski, Bonnie **267**
Series: Shaw Contemporary Issues
Title: *Building Character*
Publisher: Shaw, 1994 ISBN: 0-87788-096-4

Num. Sess.	Group Time	Num. Pgs.	Avg. Qst.	Price	Audience	Format	Bible Study
8	30-45	48	10	$4.99	New Christian	Workbk	Topical

Features: Intro to Leading a Study, Intro to Study, Objectives, Bibliography, Follow Up, Ldr's Notes
★★★★ Personal Application Preparation Time: Low
★★★ Relationship Building Ldr. Guide: No Size: 5.25 x 8.25
Subjects: Christian Living, Joy, Obedience, Service, Victorious Living
Comments: Eight brief lessons help participants gain a perspective on Christian character. Bible passages help guide readers through subjects like life choices, a pilgrim's perspective, purity of heart, humility, justice, service, joy, and the fruit of the Spirit. This study isn't written to make people feel guilty or burdened, but to help them explore the ways God can transform people's lives. The author suggests journaling.

Author: Budzowski, Bonnie **268**
Series: Shaw Contemporary Issues
Title: *Enriching Relationships*
Publisher: Shaw, 1993 ISBN: 0-87788-214-2

Num. Sess.	Group Time	Num. Pgs.	Avg. Qst.	Price	Audience	Format	Bible Study
8	30-45	48	8	$4.99	Beginner	Workbk	Topical

Features: Intro to Leading a Study, Intro to Study, Objectives, Bibliography, Follow Up, Ldr's Notes
★★★★ Personal Application Preparation Time: Low
★★★ Relationship Building Ldr. Guide: No Size: 5.25 x 8.25
Subjects: Forgiveness, Relationships
Comments: This eight-week study guide develops Scriptural guidelines for relating to others. It deals with such diverse issues as managing conflict and cultivating healthy, long-lasting friendships through direct teachings and real-life Bible examples. Lessons include: "Living in God's Light"; "Living to Please God"; "Balancing Truth and Love"; "Sinless Anger"; "Tamed Tonques"; "Foundations of Forgiveness."

Author: Bulthuis, Charlene and Barbara Brouwer **269**
Series: Discover Your Bible
Title: *Discover: Hebrews*
Publisher: Church Development Resources, 1992

Num. Sess.	Group Time	Num. Pgs.	Avg. Qst.	Price	Audience	Format	Bible Study
17	60-75	104	6	$3.50	Beginner	Workbk	Book

Features: Intro to Study, Glossary
★★★ Personal Application Preparation Time: None
★★ Relationship Building Ldr. Guide: Yes Size: 5.50 x 8.50
Subjects: Hebrews
Comments: This inductive study of Hebrews helps participants understand a letter written to Christians who had been converted from the Jewish religion. Because of persecution, these people were being tempted to either go back to the Jewish religion or at least combine the Gospel with their former traditions. The writer of Hebrew reminds readers of the absolute superiority of Jesus Christ as the best expression of God's grace to mankind.

Author: Bundschuh, Rick & Tom Finley **270**
Series:
Title: *So What's A Christian Anyway?*
Publisher: Gospel Light Publications, 1989 ISBN: 0-83071-397-2

Num. Sess.	Group Time	Num. Pgs.	Avg. Qst.	Price	Audience	Format	Bible Study
14	45-60	31	Vary	$2.99	Beginner	Workbk	Topical

Features: Intro to Study, Cartoons, Charts
★★★★ Personal Application Preparation Time: Low
★★★★ Relationship Building Ldr. Guide: No Size: 7.0 x 10.75
Subjects: Teens: Discipleship, Teens: Evangelism
Comments: This 31-page comic-sized evangelism tool provides a fun and simple way to explain the basics of Christianity to youth. The first few pages briefly explain how to become a Christian. The remainder of the book deals with subjects of Christian growth and maturity, including: "How to Become a Christian"; "Belief"; "Benefits"; "Commitment"; "Ingredients for Growth"; "Bible Study"; "Bible Study Tools"; "Prayer"; "The Church"; "Love"; "Friends"; "Influenced by the World."

Author: Bundschuh, Rick & Tom Finley **271**
Series:
Title: *Yo! I'm A Christian Now What?*
Publisher: Gospel Light Publications, 1994 ISBN: 0-83071-466-9

Num. Sess.	Group Time	Num. Pgs.	Avg. Qst.	Price	Audience	Format	Bible Study
10	45-60	32	Vary	$2.99	Beginner	Workbk	Topical

Features: Intro to Study, Drawings, Cartoons
★★★★ Personal Application Preparation Time: Low
★★★★ Relationship Building Ldr. Guide: No Size: 7.0 x 10.75
Subjects: Teens: Discipleship
Comments: This fun resource, designed to help young Christians learn how to put faith into action, is cleverly disguised as a comic book. It features games, puzzles, and mazes interwoven with daily Scripture reading and rock-solid teaching to help kids ages 10–15 build a mature relationship with Christ. Contents include: "Faith in Action"; "Alien on Earth"; "What About Problems"; "Handling Problems"; "Temptation"; "Doing Good"; "Putting God First"; "Integrity and Character."

Author: Burkett, Larry **272**
Series:
Title: *Coming Economic Earthquake, The*
Publisher: Moody Press, 1991 ISBN: 0-80241-539-3

Num. Sess.	Group Time	Num. Pgs.	Avg. Qst.	Price	Audience	Format	Bible Study
19	60-75	270	N/A	$10.99	Beginner	Book	Topical

Features: Intro to Study, Charts, Appendix, Cassette Avail
★★★★ Personal Application Preparation Time: Low
★★ Relationship Building Ldr. Guide: No Size: 6.0 x 9.0
Subjects: Money, Social Issues
Comments: This book, revised and updated, confronts the Clinton budget, NAFTA, health care reform, and other critical issues that affect the nation's economic future. The author issues new warnings and new suggestions for securing financial stability. A trained leader will be required to formulate group discussion questions.

Author: Burns, Jim **273**
Series: YouthBuilders Group Bible
Title: *Word on Prayer and the Devotional Life, The*
Publisher: Gospel Light Publications, 1994 ISBN: 0-83071-643-2

Num. Sess.	Group Time	Num. Pgs.	Avg. Qst.	Price	Audience	Format	Bible Study
12	60-90	220	Vary	$16.99	Beginner	Workbk	Topical

Features: Intro to Leading a Study, Ldr's Notes
★★★★ Personal Application Preparation Time: Low
★★★★ Relationship Building Ldr. Guide: No Size: 8.50 x 11.0
Subjects: Teens: Devotionals, Teens: Prayer
Comments: Here's a way youth leaders can help young people learn how to spend time talking and listening to God. This curriculum helps youth learn how to communicate with God, develop disciplined devotional lives, and identify and practice the elements of prayer. It includes: reproducible student pages, 3 4-week modules, a flexible format, a section to involve parents, and "cheat sheets" study information on a single page.

Author: Burns, Jim **274**
Series: YouthBuilders Group Bible
Title: *Word on Sex, Drugs & Rock "N" Roll, The*
Publisher: Gospel Light Publications, 1994 ISBN: 0-83071-642-4

Num. Sess.	Group Time	Num. Pgs.	Avg. Qst.	Price	Audience	Format	Bible Study
12	60-90	190	Vary	$16.99	Beginner	Workbk	Topical

Features: Intro to Leading a Study, Ldr's Notes
★★★★ Personal Application Preparation Time: Low
★★★★ Relationship Building Ldr. Guide: No Size: 8.50 x 11.0
Subjects: Teens: Drugs/Drinking, Teens: Music, Teens: Sexuality
Comments: Every day young people are faced with critical and dangerous choices. For adults trying to talk to them, their input is generally ignored. It seems as if kids only want to listen to one another. This study helps youth discuss crucial issues with one another and gives them action-packed exercises to find answers in God's Word. It includes: reproducible student pages, 3 4-week modules, a flexible format, a section to involve parents.

Author: Burns, Jim **275**
Series: YouthBuilders Group Bible
Title: *Word on the Basics of Christianity, The*
Publisher: Gospel Light Publications, 1994 ISBN: 0-83071-644-0

Num. Sess.	Group Time	Num. Pgs.	Avg. Qst.	Price	Audience	Format	Bible Study
12	60-90	250	Vary	$16.99	Beginner	Workbk	Topical

Features:
★★★★ Personal Application Preparation Time: Low
★★★★ Relationship Building Ldr. Guide: No Size: 8.50 x 11.0
Subjects: Teens: Cults, Teens: Discipleship, Teens: Theology
Comments: Many young people are confused about God. A growing number of teens have no Christian background at all, and those who've grown up in the church sometimes roll God, Jesus, angels, and New Age thinking all into some kind of big cosmic lump. It can be a tricky situation, helping young people sort out misguided but passionately held ideas. This study can help young people come together on the solid ground of God's Word.

Author: Burns, Ridge and Pam Campbell **276**
Series: SonPower Youth Sources
Title: *No Youth Worker Is An Island*
Publisher: Victor Books, 1992 ISBN: 0-89693-735-6

Num. Sess.	Group Time	Num. Pgs.	Avg. Qst.	Price	Audience	Format	Bible Study
	—	210	N/A	$10.99			

Features: Intro to Study, Bibliography, Scrpt Memory Helps, Index
Personal Application Preparation Time:
Relationship Building Ldr. Guide: Size: 6.0 x 9.0
Subjects: Teens: Resources
Comments: Chapters summarize research the authors conducted on 100 youth workers as they shared challenges, frustrations, and dreams. In each chapter, readers find a statistical summary of the survey, stories from Ridge's ministry experience, Small Church Spotlight from Pam's perspective, and a Scripture meditation. The authors offer time-tested advice in key areas: reaching their communities, working effectively with their churches and staffs, ministering to parents.

Author: Bush, Barbara 277
Series: Woman's Workshop Series
Title: *Heart Trouble: Studies on Christian Character*
Publisher: Zondervan, 1985 ISBN: 0-31029-431-2

Num. Sess.	Group Time	Num. Pgs.	Avg. Qst.	Price	Audience	Format	Bible Study
11	90-120	140	12	$5.99	Beginner	Workbk	Topical

Features: Intro to Leading a Study, Digging Deeper Quest, Drawings
★★ Personal Application Preparation Time: Low
★★ Relationship Building Ldr. Guide: No Size: 5.25 x 8.0
Subjects: Christian Living, Emotions, Women's Issues
Comments: This study on Christian character—specifically the heart attitude—seeks biblical answers to questions about the heart. It probes and reveals: "What our habits reveal about us"; "If our actions speak of Christ in our lives"; "If our words expose heart disease such as envy or self-centeredness"; and "What the hidden intents of our hearts are." Participants will identify the kind of heart God intends for His children.

Author: Bush, Barbara 278
Series: Woman's Workshop Series
Title: *Mastering Motherhood*
Publisher: Zondervan, 1981 ISBN: 0-31043-031-3

Num. Sess.	Group Time	Num. Pgs.	Avg. Qst.	Price	Audience	Format	Bible Study
14	60-90	165	9	$6.99	Beginner	Workbk	Topical

Features: Intro to Leading a Study
★★ Personal Application Preparation Time: Med
★★ Relationship Building Ldr. Guide: No Size: 5.25 x 8.0
Subjects: Family, Parenting, Self-esteem, Women's Issues
Comments: This study on "mastering motherhood" investigates biblical patterns of parenting, and the roles and responsibilities of mothers in contemporary society. It will reassure mothers of their vital place in society, and renew their vision of motherhood as a strategic part of God's plan for the family. Chapter titles include: "Fighting the Current," "Preventive Discipline," and "Building Self-esteem in Children." A section titled "Before You Read On" is not recommended for group use.

Author: Bushnell, Trent 279
Series: SonPower Youth Sources
Title: *Dating, Identity & Bible Study*
Publisher: Victor Books, 1992 ISBN: 1-56476-022-7

Num. Sess.	Group Time	Num. Pgs.	Avg. Qst.	Price	Audience	Format	Bible Study
12	45-65	124	Vary	$13.99	Beginner	Workbk	Topical

Features: Intro to Leading a Study, Objectives, Drawings
★★★★ Personal Application Preparation Time: None
★★★★ Relationship Building Ldr. Guide: Size: 8.50 x 11.0
Subjects: Teens: Bible Study, Teens: Junior High, Teens: Senior High
Comments: These flexible sessions for junior and senior high schoolers offer three topics of four sessions each—one "hot" topic (dating), one topic on a particular aspect of spiritual life (identify), and one topic on a tough issue (Bible study). Each offers optional activities, additional resources, and clip art. These flex sessions allow veteran youth workers to give insights into their own youth. Participants should work straight through the 12 sessions, then use the units independently.

Author: Bushnell, Trent, et al. 280
Series: SonPower Youth Sources
Title: *Friendship, Tough Times, & God's Will*
Publisher: Victor Books, 1992 ISBN: 0-89693-099-8

Num. Sess.	Group Time	Num. Pgs.	Avg. Qst.	Price	Audience	Format	Bible Study
12	45-65	124	Vary	$13.99	Beginner	Workbk	Topical

Features: Intro to Leading a Study, Objectives, Drawings
★★★★ Personal Application Preparation Time: None
★★★★ Relationship Building Ldr. Guide: Size: 8.50 x 11.0
Subjects: Teens: Friends, Teens: Junior High, Teens: Resources, Teens: Senior High
Comments: These flexible sessions for junior and senior high schoolers offer three topics of four sessions each—one "hot" topic (friendship), one topic on a particular aspect of spiritual life (God's will), and one topic on a tough issue (tough times). Each offers optional activities, additional resources, and clip art. These flex sessions allow veteran youth workers to use insights into their youth.

Author: Bushnell, Trent 281
Series: SonPower Youth Sources
Title: *Sex, The Future & Prayer*
Publisher: Victor Books, 1992 ISBN: 1-56476-021-9

Num. Sess.	Group Time	Num. Pgs.	Avg. Qst.	Price	Audience	Format	Bible Study
12	45-65	126	Vary	$13.99	Beginner	Workbk	Topical

Features: Intro to Leading a Study, Objectives, Drawings
★★★★ Personal Application Preparation Time: None
★★★★ Relationship Building Ldr. Guide: Size: 8.50 x 11.0
Subjects: Teens: Junior High, Teens: Prayer, Teens: Senior High, Teens: Sexuality
Comments: These flexible sessions for junior and senior high schoolers offer three topics of four sessions each—one "hot" topic (sex), one topic on a particular aspect of spiritual life (the future), and one topic on a tough issue (prayer). Each offers optional activities, additional resources, and clip art. These flex sessions allow veteran youth workers to give insights into their own youth.

Author: Buswell, Sara 282
Series: Challenge Bible Study
Title: *Believers or Beguilers*
Publisher: Baker Book House, 1993 ISBN: 0-80101-046-2

Num. Sess.	Group Time	Num. Pgs.	Avg. Qst.	Price	Audience	Format	Bible Study
7	60-75	96	Vary	$4.99	New Christian	Workbk	Charctr

Features: Intro to Leading a Study, Intro to Study
★★★ Personal Application Preparation Time: Med
★★★ Relationship Building Ldr. Guide: No Size: 5.50 x 8.50
Subjects: Bible Personalities, Old Testament
Comments: This seven-lesson study of Old Testament women gives participants an opportunity to apply principles of God's character and design to their own personalities and circumstances. Lessons examine the choices, experiences, and reactions of the widow of Zarephath, Deborah, Keturah, Abishag, Rahab, Jochebed, Delilah, Potiphar's Wife, and Bathsheba. Includes questions prior to each lesson, Scripture passages, commentary, and directions for using the questions.

Author: Buswell, Sara 283
Series: Challenge Bible Study
Title: *Courageous Overcomers*
Publisher: Baker Book House, 1993 ISBN: 0-80101-047-0

Num. Sess.	Group Time	Num. Pgs.	Avg. Qst.	Price	Audience	Format	Bible Study
7	60-75	96	Vary	$4.99	New Christian	Workbk	Charctr

Features: Intro to Leading a Study, Intro to Study
★★★ Personal Application Preparation Time: Med
★★★ Relationship Building Ldr. Guide: No Size: 5.50 x 8.50
Subjects: Bible Personalities, Old Testament
Comments: This seven-lesson study invites participants to meet women of the Old Testament, and shows them how to apply principles of God's character and design as seen in those godly women to their own personalities and circumstances. Women studied include: Naaman's Maid, Naomi, Ruth, Sarah, Esther, Hannah, and the Shunammite Woman. The study plan includes questions prior to each lesson, Scripture passages, commentary, and directions for using the questions.

Author: Buswell, Sara 284
Series: Challenge Bible Study
Title: *Responding to God's Call*
Publisher: Baker Book House, 1993 ISBN: 0-80101-044-6

Num. Sess.	Group Time	Num. Pgs.	Avg. Qst.	Price	Audience	Format	Bible Study
7	60-75	112	Vary	$4.99	New Christian	Workbk	Charctr

Features: Intro to Leading a Study, Intro to Study
★★★ Personal Application Preparation Time: Med
★★★ Relationship Building Ldr. Guide: No Size: 5.50 x 8.50
Subjects: Bible Personalities
Comments: These 7 studies probe lessons learned by those who humbly yet positively answer God's call to service. Reviewing the lives of Adam, Abraham, Isaac, Jacob, Joseph, Moses, Samuel, David, Isaiah, and Ananias, it can help participants become more aware of God's character as caller, to men in the Old Testament and today. The study plan includes questions prior to each lesson, Scripture passages, commentary, and directions for using the questions.

Author: Buswell, Sara 285
Series: Challenge Bible Study
Title: *Selfless or Selfish*
Publisher: Baker Book House, 1993 ISBN: 0-80101-049-7

Num. Sess.	Group Time	Num. Pgs.	Avg. Qst.	Price	Audience	Format	Bible Study
6	60-75	72	Vary	$4.99	New Christian	Workbk	Charctr

Features: Intro to Leading a Study, Intro to Study
★★★ Personal Application Preparation Time: Med
★★★ Relationship Building Ldr. Guide: No Size: 5.50 x 8.50
Subjects: Bible Personalities, Old Testament
Comments: This 7-lesson study invites participants to meet women of the Old Testament, and shows them how to apply principles of God's character and design as seen in those godly women to their own personalities and circumstances. Women studied include: Zipporah, Hagar, Job's Wife, Leah, Lot's Wife, and Eve. The study plan includes questions prior to each lesson, Scripture passages, commentary, and directions for using the questions.

Author: Buswell, Sara 286
Series: Challenge Bible Study
Title: *Vain or Visionary*
Publisher: Baker Book House, 1993 ISBN: 0-80101-048-9

Num. Sess.	Group Time	Num. Pgs.	Avg. Qst.	Price	Audience	Format	Bible Study
6	60-75	84	Vary	$4.99	New Christian	Workbk	Charctr

Features: Intro to Leading a Study, Intro to Study
★★★ Personal Application Preparation Time: Med
★★★ Relationship Building Ldr. Guide: No Size: 5.50 x 8.50
Subjects: Bible Personalities, Old Testament
Comments: This six-lesson study of Old Testament women gives participants an opportunity to apply principles of God's character and design as seen in those godly women to their own personalities and circumstances. Leadership strength and foresight are the character traits explored through the lives of Rebekah, Rachel, Deborah, Huldah, Miriam, and Abigail. Includes questions prior to each lesson, Scripture passages, commentary, and directions for using the questions.

Author: Calvert, Stuart 287
Series:
Title: *Uniquely Gifted: Discovering Your Spiritual Gifts*
Publisher: New Hope, 1993 ISBN: 1-56309-061-9

Num. Sess.	Group Time	Num. Pgs.	Avg. Qst.	Price	Audience	Format	Bible Study
13	30-45	140	N/A	$7.95	New Christian	Book	Topical

Features: Intro to Study
★★★ Personal Application Preparation Time: Low
★★ Relationship Building Ldr. Guide: No Size: 5.50 x 8.50
Subjects: Church Life, Holy Spirit, Spiritual Gifts
Comments: This book provides readers with a biblical study of spiritual gifts, offering insights and instruction on the varied gifts God granted in biblical days, the gifts from the Spirit and how to use them in service. Intended for a 2½-hour course, it can be used for a women's retreat, or adapted by a leader for a 12-week, 30″–45″ home or office study.

Author: Campbell, Dr. Ross 288
Series:
Title: *How to Really Love Your Teenager*
Publisher: Victor Books, 1993 ISBN: 0-89693-067-X

Num. Sess.	Group Time	Num. Pgs.	Avg. Qst.	Price	Audience	Format	Bible Study
12	60-90	141	N/A	$9.99	Beginner	Book	Topical

Features:
★★★★ Personal Application Preparation Time: Low
★★ Relationship Building Ldr. Guide: No Size: 5.50 x 8.50
Subjects: Family, Parenting, Teens: Psychology
Comments: This book of commonsense guidelines shows how parents can do more than simply coexist with teenagers. The author offers ideas to help parents create solid, balanced approaches for relating to their teenagers. The skills they learn will help them communicate unconditional love, handle teenage anger as well as their own, deal with adolescent depression, and help their teenagers grow spiritually and intellectually.

Author: Campbell, Dr. Ross 289
Series:
Title: *How to Really Love Your Child*
Publisher: Victor Books, 1977 ISBN: 0-88207-751-1

Num. Sess.	Group Time	Num. Pgs.	Avg. Qst.	Price	Audience	Format	Bible Study
13	60-75	132	N/A	$9.99	New Christian	Book	Topical

Features: Intro to Study
★★★★ Personal Application Preparation Time: Low
★★★★ Relationship Building Ldr. Guide: Yes Size: 5.50 x 8.50
Subjects: Parenting, Wholeness
Comments: This 13-week study provides perspectives on parent-child relationships. Lessons detail three practical things that will help children feel loved and find emotional wholeness: the necessity of physical touch, positive eye contact, and how to give focused attention. The study is practical and immediately applicable. A leader's guide provides many helpful charts.

Author: Campbell, Pam & Stan 290
Series: BibleLog for Adults
Title: *Good News to Go—Book 2*
Publisher: Victor Books, 1991 ISBN: 0-89693-868-9

Num. Sess.	Group Time	Num. Pgs.	Avg. Qst.	Price	Audience	Format	Bible Study
13	60-75	180	Vary	$6.99	New Christian	Workbk	Book

Features: Intro to Leading a Study, Prayer Helps, Scrpt Memory Helps, Pre-discussion Quest, Digging Deeper Quest, Summary, Ldr's Notes, Cartoons, Persnl Study Quest, Charts
★★★★ Personal Application Preparation Time: Med
★★★ Relationship Building Ldr. Guide: No Size: 6.0 x 9.0
Subjects: Bible Personalities, Church Life, New Testament, Prayer, Worship
Comments: Book 2 in this 4-book series that propels adults through the New Testament in 1 year—covers Acts through 1 Corinthians. Leader's notes include icebreakers, study questions, suggestions for prayer, optional ideas, and assignments.

Author: Campbell, Pam & Stan 291
Series: BibleLog for Adults
Title: *Home at Last—Book 4*
Publisher: Victor Books, 1991 ISBN: 0-89693-870-0

Num. Sess.	Group Time	Num. Pgs.	Avg. Qst.	Price	Audience	Format	Bible Study
13	60-75	180	Vary	$6.99	New Christian	Workbk	Book

Features: Intro to Leading a Study, Prayer Helps, Scrpt Memory Helps, Pre-discussion Quest,Digging Deeper Quest, Summary, Ldr's Notes, Cartoons, Persnl Study Quest, Charts
★★★★ Personal Application Preparation Time: Med
★★★ Relationship Building Ldr. Guide: No Size: 6.0 x 9.0
Subjects: Faith, Heaven/Hell, New Testament
Comments: Book 4 in this 4-book series that propels adults through the New Testament in 1 year—covers Hebrews through Revelation. Leader's notes include icebreakers, study questions, suggestions for prayer, optional ideas, and assignments. The BibleLog series entertains while challenging adults to discover and apply Bible truths for themselves.

Author: Campbell, Pam & Stan 292
Series: BibleLog for Adults
Title: *Let There Be Life—Book 1*
Publisher: Victor Books, 1992 ISBN: 0-89693-871-9

Num. Sess.	Group Time	Num. Pgs.	Avg. Qst.	Price	Audience	Format	Bible Study
12	60-75	179	Vary	$6.99	New Christian	Workbk	Book

Features: Intro to Leading a Study, Intro to Study, Prayer Helps, Study Overview, Digging Deeper Quest, Follow Up, Ldr's Notes, Drawings, Charts, Maps
★★★★ Personal Application Preparation Time: Med
★★★ Relationship Building Ldr. Guide: No Size: 6.0 x 9.0
Subjects: Exodus, Genesis, Joshua, Judges, Leviticus, Numbers/ Deuteronomy, Old Testament, Ruth
Comments: Book 1 in this 4-book series covers Genesis through Ruth. Addresses establishing stronger family relationships, dealing with stress, and making the most of opportunities. Leader's notes include icebreakers, study questions, suggestions for prayer, and optional ideas.

Author: Campbell, Pam & Stan 293
Series: BibleLog for Adults
Title: *Priority Mail—Book 3*
Publisher: Victor Books, 1991 ISBN: 0-89693-869-7

Num. Sess.	Group Time	Num. Pgs.	Avg. Qst.	Price	Audience	Format	Bible Study
13	60-75	180	Vary	$6.99	New Christian	Workbk	Book

Features: Intro to Leading a Study, Prayer Helps, Scrpt Memory Helps, Pre-discussion Quest,Digging Deeper Quest, Summary, Ldr's Notes, Cartoons, Persnl Study Quest, Charts
★★★★ Personal Application Preparation Time: Med
★★★ Relationship Building Ldr. Guide: No Size: 6.0 x 9.0
Subjects: God's Promises, New Testament
Comments: The third in a 4-book series that propels adults through the New Testament in 1 year, this study covers 2 Corinthians through Philemon. Leader's notes include icebreakers, study questions, suggestions for prayer, optional ideas, and assignments. Participants examine Paul's letters for practical advice, deep truths, and incredible promises.

Author: Campbell, Pam & Stan 294
Series: BibleLog for Adults
Title: *Tunes, Tales, & Truths—Book 3*
Publisher: Victor Books, 1992 ISBN: 0-89693-873-5

Num. Sess.	Group Time	Num. Pgs.	Avg. Qst.	Price	Audience	Format	Bible Study
13	60-75	179	4	$6.99	New Christian	Workbk	Book

Features: Intro to Leading a Study, Prayer Helps, Scrpt Memory Helps, Digging Deeper Quest, Ldr's Notes, Cartoons, Persnl Study Quest
★★★★ Personal Application Preparation Time: Med
★★★★ Relationship Building Ldr. Guide: No Size: 6.0 x 9.0
Subjects: Ecclesiastes, Esther, Ezra/Nehemiah, Job, Old Testament, Proverbs, Psalms, Song of Solomon
Comments: This BibleLog series is designed to take participants through the Old Testament in a single year, by completing 1 session per week. This book goes from Ezra through Song of Songs. Current issues include dealing with failure, handling criticism, and understanding suffering.

Author: Campbell, Pam & Stan **295**
Series: BibleLog for Adults
Title: *Watchmen Who Wouldn't Quit—Book 4*
Publisher: Victor Books, 1992 ISBN: 0-89693-874-3

Num. Sess.	Group Time	Num. Pgs.	Avg. Qst.	Price	Audience	Format	Bible Study
13	60-75	179	4	$6.99	New Christian	Workbk	Book

Features: Intro to Leading a Study, Prayer Helps, Scrpt Memory Helps, Digging Deeper Quest, Ldr's Notes, Cartoons, Persnl Study Quest
★★★★ Personal Application Preparation Time: Med
★★★★ Relationship Building Ldr. Guide: No Size: 6.0 x 9.0
Subjects: Daniel, Ezekiel, Isaiah/Jeremiah, Jonah, Lamentations, Minor Prophets, Old Testament
Comments: Book 4 goes from Isaiah through Malachi, acquainting participants with watchmen who can provide them with solid help in the areas of confidence, loneliness, handling crises, and accountability. Leader's notes provide session topics, icebreakers, discussion questions, prayer suggestions, optional activities, and follow up.

Author: Campbell, Pam & Stan **296**
Series: BibleLog for Adults
Title: *When God Left Footprints—Book 1*
Publisher: Victor Books, 1991 ISBN: 0-89693-867-0

Num. Sess.	Group Time	Num. Pgs.	Avg. Qst.	Price	Audience	Format	Bible Study
13	60-75	180	Vary	$6.99	New Christian	Workbk	Book

Features: Intro to Leading a Study, Objectives, Prayer Helps, Scrpt Memory Helps, Pre-discussion Quest, Digging Deeper Quest, Summary, Ldr's Notes, Cartoons, Persnl Study Quest, Charts
★★★★ Personal Application Preparation Time: Med
★★★ Relationship Building Ldr. Guide: No Size: 6.0 x 9.0
Subjects: Gospels, Jesus: Life/Teaching, New Testament, Relationships
Comments: This study—Book 1 in a 4-book series that propels adults through the New Testament in 1 year—covers Matthew through John. Leader's notes include icebreakers, study questions, suggestions for prayer, and assignments. Participants get a comparison of Matthew, Mark, Luke, and John's pictures of the unique character of Jesus.

Author: Campbell, Pam & Stan **297**
Series: BibleLog for Adults
Title: *Who's Running This Kingdom?—Book 2*
Publisher: Victor Books, 1992 ISBN: 0-89693-872-7

Num. Sess.	Group Time	Num. Pgs.	Avg. Qst.	Price	Audience	Format	Bible Study
13	60-75	179	4	$6.99	New Christian	Workbk	Book

Features: Intro to Leading a Study, Prayer Helps, Scrpt Memory Helps, Digging Deeper Quest,Ldr's Notes, Cartoons, Persnl Study Quest
★★★★ Personal Application Preparation Time: Med
★★★★ Relationship Building Ldr. Guide: No Size: 6.0 x 9.0
Subjects: Kings/Chronicles, Old Testament, 1 & 2 Samuel
Comments: This BibleLog series is designed to take participants through the Old Testament in a single year, by completing 1 session per week. This book takes participants through the books of 1 & 2 Samuel, 1 & 2 Kings, and 1 & 2 Chronicles, through which they can witness the rise and fall of the kingdom of Israel. Addresses issues such as judgmentalism, success, dealing with worry and anxiety.

Author: Campbell, Roger **298**
Series:
Title: *Staying Positive in a Negative World*
Publisher: Victor Books, 1984 ISBN: 0-89693-377-6

Num. Sess.	Group Time	Num. Pgs.	Avg. Qst.	Price	Audience	Format	Bible Study
13	60-75	129	N/A	$8.99	New Christian	Book	Topical

Features: Intro to Study
★★★★ Personal Application Preparation Time: Low
★★★ Relationship Building Ldr. Guide: Yes Size: 5.50 x 8.0
Subjects: Emotions, Joy, Relationships
Comments: This 13-week study helps participants struggling with negative attitudes replace them with healthy, God-honoring positive attitudes. It addresses attitudes which, if allowed to continue, can devastate people emotionally and physically and affect their relationships with others, their churches, and other institutions. The final lessons challenge participants to a changed life full of adventure and joy. A leader's guide includes transparency masters.

Author: Campbell, Stan **299**
Series: BibleLog Series
Title: *Fighters & Writers—Book 3*
Publisher: Victor Books, 1988 ISBN: 0-89693-863-8

Num. Sess.	Group Time	Num. Pgs.	Avg. Qst.	Price	Audience	Format	Bible Study
13	60-75	142	Vary	$5.99	Beginner	Workbk	Book

Features: Intro to Study, Cartoons
★★★ Personal Application Preparation Time: Med
★★★ Relationship Building Ldr. Guide: Yes Size: 5.50 x 8.0
Subjects: Teens: Bible/Pers., Teens: Old Testament, Teens: Sexuality
Comments: This study—part of an eight-book Old and New Testament series for youth—covers Ezra to Song of Songs. Each session includes three steps: focus—on the topic; discovering—interactive Bible study; and response—application. Through Ezra, Nehemiah, Esther, and Job participants come face to face with pain, joy, sex, death, and hope. Written like a travelog, this series entertains while providing students with indelible Bible stories and truth.

Author: Campbell, Stan **300**
Series: BibleLog Series
Title: *From the Desk of the Apostle Paul—Book 7*
Publisher: Victor Books, 1989 ISBN: 0-89693-386-5

Num. Sess.	Group Time	Num. Pgs.	Avg. Qst.	Price	Audience	Format	Bible Study
13	60-75	154	Vary	$5.99	Beginner	Workbk	Book

Features: Intro to Study, Cartoons
★★★ Personal Application Preparation Time: Med
★★★ Relationship Building Ldr. Guide: Yes Size: 5.50 x 8.0
Subjects: Teens: Bible/Pers., Teens: New Testament
Comments: This study—part of an 8-book Old and New Testament series for youth—covers 2 Corinthians through Philemon. Each session includes 3 steps: focus—on the topic; discovering—interactive Bible study; and response—application. Participants see Paul's ancient letters with their modern applicability, still full of hope and incredible promise. Written like a travelog, this series entertains while providing students indelible Bible stories and truth.

Author: Campbell, Stan 301
Series: BibleLog Series
Title: *Growing Pains: The Church Hits the Road—Book 6*
Publisher: Victor Books, 1989 ISBN: 0-89693-384-9

Num. Sess.	Group Time	Num. Pgs.	Avg. Qst.	Price	Audience	Format	Bible Study
13	60-75	154	Vary	$5.99	Beginner	Workbk	Book

Features: Intro to Study, Cartoons
★★★ Personal Application Preparation Time: Med
★★★ Relationship Building Ldr. Guide: Yes Size: 5.50 x 8.0
Subjects: Teens: Bible/Pers., Teens: New Testament
Comments: This study—part of an 8-book Old and New Testament series for youth—covers Acts through 1 Corinthians. Each session includes 3 steps: focus—on the topic; discovering—interactive Bible study; and response—application. Participants go "on the road" with Peter and Paul, to see how the Church was started, and find out why they are entitled to many privileges as Christians. This series entertains while providing students with indelible Bible stories and truth.

Author: Campbell, Stan 302
Series: Young Teen Feedback
Title: *Higher Love—Leader's Book*
Publisher: Victor Books, 1991 ISBN: 0-89693-789-5

Num. Sess.	Group Time	Num. Pgs.	Avg. Qst.	Price	Audience	Format	Bible Study
12	60-90	128	Vary	$13.99	New Christian	Workbk	Topical

Features: Intro to Leading a Study, Objectives, Pre-discussion Quest, Digging Deeper Quest, Follow Up, Summary, Ldr's Notes, Handouts
★★★★ Personal Application Preparation Time: Med
★★★★ Relationship Building Ldr. Guide: Yes Size: 8.50 x 11.0
Subjects: Teens: Junior High, Teens: Relationships
Comments: This Young Teen Feedback Elective begins with the question "What is love?" It examines commonly held opinions of love and contrasts those with the biblical definition of love. This leader's book offers 3 4-week studies and includes reproducible student sheets.

Author: Campbell, Stan 303
Series: BibleLog Series
Title: *Jesus: God Undercover—Book 5*
Publisher: Victor Books, 1989 ISBN: 0-89693-382-2

Num. Sess.	Group Time	Num. Pgs.	Avg. Qst.	Price	Audience	Format	Bible Study
13	60-75	154	Vary	$5.99	Beginner	Workbk	Book

Features: Intro to Study, Cartoons, Charts
★★★ Personal Application Preparation Time: Med
★★★ Relationship Building Ldr. Guide: Yes Size: 5.50 x 8.0
Subjects: Teens: Jesus' Life, Teens: New Testament
Comments: This study—part of an 8-book Old and New Testament series for youth—covers Matthew through John. Each session includes 3 steps: focus—on the topic; discovering—interactive Bible study; and response—application. Participants get a behind-the-scenes comparison of Matthew, Mark, Luke, and John's picture of the unique character of Jesus. Written like a travelog, this series entertains while providing students with indelible Bible stories and truth.

Author: Campbell, Stan 304
Series: Young Teen Feedback
Title: *Nobody Like Me—Leader's Book*
Publisher: Victor Books, 1986 ISBN: 0-89693-188-9

Num. Sess.	Group Time	Num. Pgs.	Avg. Qst.	Price	Audience	Format	Bible Study
12	30-45	86	Vary	$13.99	New Christian	Book	Topical

Features: Intro to Study, Handouts
★★★★ Personal Application Preparation Time: None
★★★★ Relationship Building Ldr. Guide: Yes Size: 8.50 x 11.0
Subjects: Teens: Bible/Pers., Teens: Old Testament, Teens: Relationships, Teens: Self-image
Comments: This study helps young teens discover God's answers to their self-image questions. Deals with day-to-day problems like failure (based on Judges), image distorters (based on Bible characters), and popularity (based on Psalms). The format offers 3 4-week studies with reproducible student sheets or used consecutively as a 12-week elective. A student book is available.

Author: Campbell, Stan 305
Series: BibleLog Series
Title: *Saga Begins, The—Book 1*
Publisher: Victor Books, 1988 ISBN: 0-89693-656-2

Num. Sess.	Group Time	Num. Pgs.	Avg. Qst.	Price	Audience	Format	Bible Study
13	60-75	154	Vary	$5.99	Beginner	Workbk	Book

Features: Intro to Study, Cartoons, Charts, Maps
★★★ Personal Application Preparation Time: Med
★★★ Relationship Building Ldr. Guide: Yes Size: 5.50 x 8.0
Subjects: Teens: Family, Teens: Old Testament, Teens: Relationships
Comments: This study—part of an eight-book Old and New Testament series for youth—covers Genesis through Ruth. Each session includes three steps: focus—on the topic; discovering—interactive Bible study; and response—application. Participants will study betrayal, homosexuality, rape, family problems, and other evils. Positive biblical examples will challenge them to handle pressures, take risks based on God's promises, identify opportunities, and develop loving relationships.

Author: Campbell, Stan 306
Series: BibleLog Series
Title: *Saga Never Ends, The—Book 8*
Publisher: Victor Books, 1989 ISBN: 0-89693-388-1

Num. Sess.	Group Time	Num. Pgs.	Avg. Qst.	Price	Audience	Format	Bible Study
13	60-75	154	Vary	$5.99	Beginner	Workbk	Book

Features: Intro to Study, Cartoons
★★★ Personal Application Preparation Time: Med
★★★ Relationship Building Ldr. Guide: Yes Size: 5.50 x 8.0
Subjects: Teens: New Testament
Comments: This study—part of an eight-book Old and New Testament series for youth—covers Hebrews through Revelation. Each session includes three steps: focus—on the topic; discovering—interactive Bible study; and response—application. Participants move through the last nine books of the Bible, collecting valuable insights into the past, good advice for the present, and great expectations for the future.

Author: Campbell, Stan 307
Series: BibleLog Series
Title: *That's the Way the Kingdom Crumbles—Book 2*
Publisher: Victor Books, 1988 ISBN: 0-89693-658-9

Num. Sess.	Group Time	Num. Pgs.	Avg. Qst.	Price	Audience	Format	Bible Study
13	60-75	154	Vary	$5.99	Beginner	Workbk	Book

Features: Intro to Study, Cartoons
★★★ Personal Application Preparation Time: Med
★★★ Relationship Building Ldr. Guide: Yes Size: 5.50 x 8.0
Subjects: Teens: Christian Liv, Teens: Old Testament
Comments: This study—part of an 8-book Old and New Testament series for youth—covers 1 Samuel through 2 Chronicles. Each session includes 3 steps: focus—on the topic; discovering—interactive Bible study; and response—application. Positive examples of people of faith who refused to crumble challenge participants to depend on God rather than themselves, learn to overcome failures, and face the future with courage.

Author: Campbell, Stan 308
Series: BibleLog Series
Title: *What's This World Coming To?—Book 4*
Publisher: Victor Books, 1988 ISBN: 0-89693-865-4

Num. Sess.	Group Time	Num. Pgs.	Avg. Qst.	Price	Audience	Format	Bible Study
13	60-72	154	Vary	$5.99	Beginner	Workbk	Book

Features: Intro to Study, Cartoons
★★★ Personal Application Preparation Time: Med
★★★ Relationship Building Ldr. Guide: Yes Size: 5.50 x 8.0
Subjects: Teens: Old Testament
Comments: This study—part of an 8-book Old and New Testament series for youth—covers Isaiah through Malachi. Each session includes 3 steps: focus—on the topic; discovering—interactive Bible study; and response—application. Old Testament prophets foretell doom and destruction, as well as promises of God's provision and salvation. Participants learn about the relevance of those messages in contemporary society.

Author: Campolo, Anthony, Jr. 309
Series:
Title: *Power Delusion, The: A Serious Call to Consider Jesus'* Approach to Power
Publisher: Victor Books, 1983 ISBN: 0-88207-292-7

Num. Sess.	Group Time	Num. Pgs.	Avg. Qst.	Price	Audience	Format	Bible Study
13	60-75	165	N/A	$8.99	New Christian	Book	Topical

Features:
★★★★ Personal Application Preparation Time: Med
★★★★ Relationship Building Ldr. Guide: Yes Size: 5.50 x 8.0
Subjects: Relationships, Success, Wholeness
Comments: This study explores Christian attitudes concerning power. As participants struggle in a world that worships power—in the family, at school, in the office, at church, on the corporate level, or on the social scene—they will see that the worship of power is inherently wrong. They will be confronted by Christ, who emptied Himself of power and chose to triumph from a position of weakness—the Cross.

Author: Campolo, Anthony, Jr. 310
Series:
Title: *Success Fantasy, The*
Publisher: Victor Books, 1980 ISBN: 0-88207-796-1

Num. Sess.	Group Time	Num. Pgs.	Avg. Qst.	Price	Audience	Format	Bible Study
13	60-75	144	N/A	$9.99	New Christian	Book	Topical

Features:
★★★★ Personal Application Preparation Time: Low
★★★ Relationship Building Ldr. Guide: Yes Size: 5.50 x 8.0
Subjects: Cults, Ethics, Singles' Issues, Success
Comments: This study concerns success and how it is measured in contemporary culture. Chapter titles range from "School Daze" to "Symptoms of Mid-Life Males (and the Mid-Life Woman)" to "Single People" and finally "Throwaway People." Questions answered in the lessons include: Is success the birthright of the good? the blessing of God? the doctrine of a cult? or the way to wealth, power, and prestige? The leader's guide includes reproducible transparency masters.

Author: Campolo, Tony 311
Series:
Title: *Carpe Diem*
Publisher: Word, 1994 ISBN: 0-84998-076-3

Num. Sess.	Group Time	Num. Pgs.	Avg. Qst.	Price	Audience	Format	Bible Study
4	75-90	N/A	10	$129.99	Beginner	Video	Topical

Features: Intro to Leading a Study, Objectives, Follow Up, Handouts, Book Incl
★★★★ Personal Application Preparation Time: None
★★ Relationship Building Ldr. Guide: Yes Size: 11.0 x 13.0
Subjects: Faith, Family, Materialism, Victorious Living
Comments: In this 4-session video series, Tony Campolo helps us get in touch with unspoken needs, release passionate faith, and transform the world around them through their willingness to seize the moment and live life to its fullest. The kit includes two 48" videos, a leader's guide with reproducible handouts for viewers, and *Carpe Diem* hardcover book.

Author: Canales, Isaac 312
Series: Global Issues
Title: *Multi-Ethnicity*
Publisher: InterVarsity, 1990 ISBN: 0-83084-905-X

Num. Sess.	Group Time	Num. Pgs.	Avg. Qst.	Price	Audience	Format	Bible Study
6	45-60	48	13	$4.99	Beginner	Workbk	Topical

Features: Intro to Leading a Study, Intro to Study, Bibliography, Prayer Helps, Follow Up
★ Personal Application Preparation Time: Low
★ Relationship Building Ldr. Guide: No Size: 5.50 x 8.25
Subjects: Social Issues
Comments: This 6-week study helps participants explore ethnic diversity. The introduction defines God's "theology of welcome" and suggests that Christians continue to reject it; it proposes that God's way for servants of His Kingdom is one in which all ethnicities live together as His people. Leaders should read first, to determine its appropriateness for their group.

Author: Cannon, Ann **313**
Series: Group's Active Bible Curriculum
Title: *Peer Pressure*
Publisher: Group Publishing, 1990 ISBN: 1-55945-103-3

Num. Sess.	Group Time	Num. Pgs.	Avg. Qst.	Price	Audience	Format	Bible Study
4	35-60	48	Vary	$9.99	Beginner	Workbk	Topical

Features: Intro to Leading a Study, Intro to Study, Objectives, Study Overview, Ldr's Notes, Handouts, Agenda, Publicity Ideas
★★★ Personal Application Preparation Time: None
★★★ Relationship Building Ldr. Guide: No Size: 8.50 x 11.0
Subjects: Teens: Decisions, Teens: Friends, Teens: Junior High, Teens: Peer Pressure
Comments: This study equips young people to deal positively with peer pressure and helps them discover specific ways to stand up to friends' negative influences. Including lessons like "From Bad News to Good News," and "Keeping Friends While Making Good Decisions," it can be adapted for a Bible class or youth meeting.

Author: Cannon, Ann B. **314**
Series:
Title: *Somethin's Cookin': 50 Easy-To-Do Youth Programs*
Publisher: Abingdon Press, 1994 ISBN: 0-68739-076-1

Num. Sess.	Group Time	Num. Pgs.	Avg. Qst.	Price	Audience	Format	Bible Study
	—	126	N/A	$11.95		Book	Topical

Features: Intro to Study
Personal Application Preparation Time:
Relationship Building Ldr. Guide: Size: 8.50 x 11.0
Subjects: Teens: Resources
Comments: This youth program "cookbook" is filled with recipes for faith. With these ingredients, youth workers can add spiritual truth to their youth fellowship events, service projects, lock-ins, and weekly meetings, as well as milestones like finals, graduation, and getting a driver's license. Participants cook up good times and deep thoughts with these ingredients, and follow the recipes for meaningful devotional programs. Includes reproducible handouts.

Author: Capehart, Jody **315**
Series:
Title: *Becoming a Treasured Teacher*
Publisher: Victor Books, 1992 ISBN: 0-89693-979-0

Num. Sess.	Group Time	Num. Pgs.	Avg. Qst.	Price	Audience	Format	Bible Study
	—	179	N/A	$7.99		Book	

Features: Bibliography, Drawings, Appendix
Personal Application Preparation Time:
Relationship Building Ldr. Guide: Size: 5.50 x 8.50
Subjects: Leadership
Comments: In this book the author explores the essentials of teaching and illustrates practical pointers with touching and humorous stories drawn from a teaching career. It gives readers confidence and the skills to minister effectively and joyfully as teachers in their local churches.

Author: Carlson, E. Roald **316**
Series: Small Group Bible Studies
Title: *One Week*
Publisher: Augsburg Fortress Publishers, 1978

Num. Sess.	Group Time	Num. Pgs.	Avg. Qst.	Price	Audience	Format	Bible Study
6	60-75	24	20	$1.35	New Christian	Book	Topical

Features: Intro to Study, Prayer Helps
★★★ Personal Application Preparation Time: None
★★★ Relationship Building Ldr. Guide: No Size: 8.50 x 5.50
Subjects: Holy Week, Jesus: Life/Teaching
Comments: This short, six-session study of Holy Week is taken from Mark and will aid in understanding Jesus' life by clearly showing Mark's record of the events of Holy Week. Participants get a closeup of what Jesus said and did—and what was done to Him. The purpose is to provide a better understanding of "the Gospel of Jesus Christ, the Son of God" (1:1). Session topics include: confrontation, signs of the end, devotion and desertion, the Crucifixion, and the Resurrection.

Author: Carlson, Paula J. and Peter S. Hawkins **317**
Series:
Title: *Listening for God: Contemporary Literature and the Life of Faith*
Publisher: Augsburg Fortress Publishers, 1994 ISBN: 0-80662-715-8

Num. Sess.	Group Time	Num. Pgs.	Avg. Qst.	Price	Audience	Format	Bible Study
8	60-75	151	5	$9.99	New Christian	Book	Topical

Features: Intro to Study
★★★ Personal Application Preparation Time: Low
★★ Relationship Building Ldr. Guide: Yes Size: 5.50 x 8.50
Subjects: Christian Life, Faith
Comments: This reader includes 10 selections, brief author profiles, and reflection questions arranged in 8 chapters. Each chapter is supplemented by a video segment (eight 10″–12″ interviews), which introduces a featured author. The video and leader's guide is $49.99. This resource is designed to help readers investigate how life and faith can merge in surprising ways and places.

Author: Carney, Glandion **318**
Series: Global Issues
Title: *Urbanization*
Publisher: InterVarsity, 1990 ISBN: 0-83084-904-1

Num. Sess.	Group Time	Num. Pgs.	Avg. Qst.	Price	Audience	Format	Bible Study
6	45-60	48	12	$4.99	Beginner	Workbk	Topical

Features: Intro to Leading a Study, Intro to Study, Bibliography, Follow Up
★★ Personal Application Preparation Time: Low
★★ Relationship Building Ldr. Guide: No Size: 5.50 x 8.25
Subjects: Social Issues
Comments: This six-week study helps participants explore the pitfalls and possibilities of life in the city and the urban church's mission. It discusses cities' complex makeup—all types of religious, ethnic, educational, and economic backgrounds—which can confuse rural newcomers and others who move there because there's no place else to go.

Author: Cassady, David **319**
Series: Group's Active Bible Curriculum
Title: *Dating Decisions*
Publisher: Group Publishing, 1991 ISBN: 1-55945-215-3

Num. Sess.	Group Time	Num. Pgs.	Avg. Qst.	Price	Audience	Format	Bible Study
4	35-60	48	Vary	$9.99	Beginner	Workbk	Topical

Features: Intro to Leading a Study, Intro to Study, Objectives, Study Overview, Ldr's Notes, Handouts, Agenda, Publicity Ideas
★★★★ Personal Application Preparation Time: None
★★★★ Relationship Building Ldr. Guide: No Size: 8.50 x 11.0
Subject: Teens: Christian Liv, Teens: Relationships, Teens: Senior High, Teens: Sexuality
Comments: Four sessions show senior highers a Christian perspective on dating, and positive ways to get to know the opposite sex. Participants discover the keys to positive dating relationships, learn what the Bible says about "true" love, explore ways to avoid sexual temptation in dating, and discover healthy ways to handle "breaking up.

Author: Cassady, David **320**
Series: Group's Active Bible Curriculum
Title: *Faith for Tough Times*
Publisher: Group Publishing, 1991 ISBN: 1-55945-216-1

Num. Sess.	Group Time	Num. Pgs.	Avg. Qst.	Price	Audience	Format	Bible Study
4	35-60	48	Vary	$9.99	New Christian	Workbk	Topical

Features: Intro to Leading a Study, Intro to Study, Objectives, Study Overview, Ldr's Notes, Drawings, Handouts, Agenda, Publicity Ideas
★★★★ Personal Application Preparation Time: None
★★★★ Relationship Building Ldr. Guide: No Size: 8.50 x 11.0
Subject: Teens: Christian Liv, Teens: Emotions, Teens: Senior High
Comments: This study helps senior high students learn how faith can help when life throws a curve. In the four-lesson study, youth will discover how faith can help them deal with tragedies or disasters, learn how to respond to people who ridicule their faith, explore ways to overcome sadness and depression, and grow closer to God as they learn how to develop their faith. No student books are required.

Author: Castleman, Robbie **321**
Series: Fisherman Bible Studyguide
Title: *David: Man After God's Own Heart*
Publisher: Shaw, 1981 ISBN: 0-87788-164-2

Num. Sess.	Group Time	Num. Pgs.	Avg. Qst.	Price	Audience	Format	Bible Study
12	45-60	77	10	$4.99	New Christian	Workbk	Charctr

Features: Intro to Leading a Study, Intro to Study, Prayer Helps, Maps
★★ Personal Application Preparation Time: None
★★ Relationship Building Ldr. Guide: No Size: 5.0 x 8.25
Subject: Bible Personalities, God, Loneliness, Obedience, Success, 1 & 2 Samuel
Comments: This is the first of a 2-volume study of the life of David. Continuing through 2 Samuel 5, with an optional study on Psalm 40, it is for people who are lonely, depressed, afraid, joyful, sorrowful, pressured, discouraged, successful, faithless, obedient, or disobedient. At least 20 years passed between David's anointing and his coronation; he learned to deal with the pressure of uncertainty.

Author: Castleman, Robbie **322**
Series: Fisherman Bible Studyguide
Title: *Elijah: Obedience in a Threatening World*
Publisher: Shaw, 1986 ISBN: 0-87788-218-5

Num. Sess.	Group Time	Num. Pgs.	Avg. Qst.	Price	Audience	Format	Bible Study
10	45-60	77	10	$4.99	New Christian	Workbk	Charctr

Features: Intro to Leading a Study, Intro to Study, Prayer Helps, Maps
★★ Personal Application Preparation Time: Low
★★ Relationship Building Ldr. Guide: No Size: 5.0 x 8.25
Subject: Bible Personalities, Christian Living, Emotions, Faith, Obedience, Prayer
Comments: Examining Elijah's life as he experienced God's faithfulness and provision, this study will challenge Christians to be obedient to God, even in the midst of an unsympathetic culture. Elijah was human, a "man of like passion." He gave in to fear and depression and felt outnumbered, misunderstood, and insecure. But he found power in obedience and prayer.

Author: Castleman, Robbie **323**
Series: Fisherman Bible Studyguide
Title: *King David: Trusting God for a Lifetime*
Publisher: Shaw, 1981 ISBN: 0-87788-165-0

Num. Sess.	Group Time	Num. Pgs.	Avg. Qst.	Price	Audience	Format	Bible Study
12	45-60	80	11	$4.99	New Christian	Workbk	Charctr

Features: Intro to Leading a Study, Intro to Study, Maps
★★ Personal Application Preparation Time: Low
★★ Relationship Building Ldr. Guide: No Size: 5.0 x 8.25
Subject: Bible Personalities, Forgiveness, God, Integrity, Success, 1 & 2 Samuel
Comments: This second of a two-part study on David picks up in 2 Samuel 6 and concludes with 1 Kings 2, with an optional study on Psalm 139. It shows how David the king learned to handle the pressures of success through guidance, rebuke, patience, forgiveness, and discipline. Participants can learn with David how to maintain personal integrity while coping with conflict and depression.

Author: Castleman, Robbie **324**
Series: Fisherman Bible Studyguide
Title: *Peter: Fisherman to Follower*
Publisher: Shaw, 1989 ISBN: 0-87788-679-2

Num. Sess.	Group Time	Num. Pgs.	Avg. Qst.	Price	Audience	Format	Bible Study
12	45-60	74	11	$4.99	Beginner	Workbk	Charctr

Features: Intro to Leading a Study, Intro to Study, Ldr's Notes, Maps
★★★★ Personal Application Preparation Time: None
★★ Relationship Building Ldr. Guide: No Size: 5.25 x 8.25
Subject: Bible Personalities, Christian Life
Comments: This 12-week study of Peter illustrates God's promise in Philippians 1:6—God "who began a good work in you will carry it on to completion until the day of Christ Jesus." Simon Peter's life serves as proof that God's good work is neither without pain, risk, and hard lessons, nor is it without great joy. Lessons, which all begin with "Learning to . . ." cover obedience, choice, trust, belief, following, service, love, perseverance, starting again, change, and learning.

Author: Causey, Carol **325**
Series: The Contact Series
Title: *Father, The, His Redemptive Plan*
Publisher: New Hope, 1990 ISBN: 0-93662-597-X

Num. Sess.	Group Time	Num. Pgs.	Avg. Qst.	Price	Audience	Format	Bible Study
12	60-75	220	Vary	$21.95	New Christian	Book	Topical

Features: Intro to Study, Objectives, Prayer Helps, Scrpt Memory Helps, Cassette Avail
★★★ Personal Application Preparation Time: High
★★★ Relationship Building Ldr. Guide: Yes Size: 10.25 x 11.75
Subjects: Missions
Comments: Contact is a 12-week experience in Bible study, prayer, and personal reflection. Each week, participants spend 5 days in personal learning, using a learner's notebook that contains 60 daily sessions. At the end of each week's study a 2-page small group plan is provided. This study is an exploration of the world from God the Father's perspective.A facilitator's guide and cassette tape are $8.95.

Author: Ceckowski, Karen **326**
Series: Group's Active Bible Curriculum
Title: *Joy of Serving, The*
Publisher: Group Publishing, 1991 ISBN: 1-55945-210-2

Num. Sess.	Group Time	Num. Pgs.	Avg. Qst.	Price	Audience	Format	Bible Study
4	35-60	46	Vary	$9.99	New Christian	Workbk	Topical

Features: Intro to Leading a Study, Intro to Study, Objectives, Study Overview, Ldr's Notes, Drawings, Handouts, Agenda, Publicity Ideas
★★★★ Personal Application Preparation Time: None
★★★★ Relationship Building Ldr. Guide: No Size: 8.50 x 11.0
Subjects: Teens: Christian Liv, Teens: Senior High
Comments: This 4-lesson study helps senior high students discover the excitement of serving others. Students will build self-worth as they discover the satisfaction of serving others, learn to serve with enthusiasm, explore Jesus' life of servanthood, and build confidence by accepting the challenge of helping others. Instructions are easy to follow and provide multiple options for teachers. No student books are required.

Author: Chapin, Shelley **327**
Series: Equipped For Ministry
Title: *Counselors, Comforters, & Friends*
Publisher: Victor Books, 1992 ISBN: 0-89693-910-3

Num. Sess.	Group Time	Num. Pgs.	Avg. Qst.	Price	Audience	Format	Bible Study
	—	162	N/A	$9.99			

Features: Appendix
Personal Application Preparation Time:
Relationship Building Ldr. Guide: Size: 6.0 x 9.0
Subjects: Grief, Small Group Resource, Suffering, Support
Comments: This book explores both the biblical foundation and practical concerns of establishing a caregiving ministry in a church. Subjects discussed include Jesus' ministry of comfort, qualification for caregiving, setting up and maintaining a caregiving program, the ongoing role of the minister, and creating support groups. Features a complete appendix, supportive ministries/networks in the community and the church, helpful books, tapes, and videos.

Author: Chase, Betty N. **328**
Series: Family Growth Electives
Title: *Discipline Them, Love Them: Practical Projects for Parents*
Publisher: David C. Cook Publishing Co., 1982 ISBN: 0-89191-359-9

Num. Sess.	Group Time	Num. Pgs.	Avg. Qst.	Price	Audience	Format	Bible Study
	—	112	N/A	$15.95	New Christian	Workbk	Topical

Features: Intro to Leading a Study, Intro to Study, Bibliography, Drawings, Charts
Personal Application Preparation Time: Med
Relationship Building Ldr. Guide: No Size: 8.50 x 11.0
Subjects: Family, Parenting, Relationships, Self-esteem, Self-help
Comments: This self-help study book contains 26 "do-it-yourself" projects that help parents discover biblical principles for child rearing, develop skills and methods of effective discipline, and practice specific, practical ways to build self-esteem in their children. It offers suggestions for weekly share times with friends or small groups of friends who are also doing the project.

Author: Cho, Dr. Paul Yonggi & Harold Hostetler **329**
Series:
Title: *Successful Home Cell Groups*
Publisher: Bridge Publishing, 1981 ISBN: 0-88270-513-X

Num. Sess.	Group Time	Num. Pgs.	Avg. Qst.	Price	Audience	Format	Bible Study
15	—	176	N/A	$6.95		Book	No

Features:
Personal Application Preparation Time:
Relationship Building Ldr. Guide: Size: 5.50 x 8.0
Subjects: Small Group Resource
Comments: This book describes how Dr. Cho was led to his dynamic principle of growth, and details everything necessary to make home cell groups work. Chapter titles include: "Personal Ambition: Key to Disaster"; "Selling the Program to the Church"; "Satan's Counterattack: The Seven Obstacles"; "Home Cell Groups"; "Motivating Lay Leadership"; and "Preaching to a Growing Church."

Author: Christensen, Chuck & Winnie **330**
Series: Fisherman Bible Studyguide
Title: *Acts 1–12: God Moves in the Early Church*
Publisher: Shaw, 1979 ISBN: 0-87788-007-7

Num. Sess.	Group Time	Num. Pgs.	Avg. Qst.	Price	Audience	Format	Bible Study
15	45-60	94	9	$4.99	New Christian	Workbk	Book

Features: Intro to Leading a Study, Intro to Study, Prayer Helps, Maps
★★ Personal Application Preparation Time: None
★★ Relationship Building Ldr. Guide: No Size: 5.0 x 8.25
Subjects: Acts, Church Life, Holy Spirit, Joy, Service
Comments: In this study of Acts, groups will discuss the successes and failures of the New Testament church and will encourage the same power in today's local church. In the chapter-by-chapter study Luke lays down the pattern for local church life: a community of joyful believers; empowered by the Spirit; serving the Lord and one another; actively enlarging their circle of fellowship; tasting both persecution and God's protection; and participating in His supernatural work.

Author: Christensen, Chuck & Winnie **331**
Series: Fisherman Bible Studyguide
Title: *James: Faith in Action*
Publisher: Shaw, 1975 ISBN: 0-87788-421-8

Num. Sess.	Group Time	Num. Pgs.	Avg. Qst.	Price	Audience	Format	Bible Study
10	45-60	55	7	$4.99	New Christian	Workbk	Book

Features: Intro to Leading a Study, Intro to Study, Prayer Helps, Follow Up
★★ Personal Application Preparation Time: Low
★★ Relationship Building Ldr. Guide: No Size: 5.0 x 8.25
Subjects: Faith, James
Comments: This study of James centers on important goals for a mature Christian. Each chapter includes an introduction; goals—spiritual maturity and the victor's crown, and how the goals are achieved—dealing with hindrances, then calling faith into action. The "Putting It to Work" section provides an opportunity to apply lessons in a world of instability, Christian infighting, materialism, and words without actions.

Author: Christensen, Chuck & Winnie **332**
Series: Fisherman Bible Studyguide
Title: *Mark: God in Action*
Publisher: Shaw, 1972 ISBN: 0-87788-309-2

Num. Sess.	Group Time	Num. Pgs.	Avg. Qst.	Price	Audience	Format	Bible Study
18	60-75	94	10	$4.99	New Christian	Workbk	Book

Features: Intro to Leading a Study, Intro to Study, Prayer Helps, Maps
★★ Personal Application Preparation Time: None
★★ Relationship Building Ldr. Guide: No Size: 5.0 x 8.25
Subjects: Jesus: Life/Teaching, Mark
Comments: This chapter-by-chapter study is fast paced and effective in describing the person of Jesus—His teaching, healing, feeding the hungry, defeating the Devil, and training disciples to carry on His life-giving activities in their personal lives, church, and community. It reveals the spiritual principles underlying the Savior's teaching. Jesus is portrayed as a total man through daily events, energy, strain, strength, compassion, and full dependency upon God the Father.

Author: Christensen, Chuck & Winnie **333**
Series: Fisherman Bible Studyguide
Title: *Paul: Thirteenth Apostle*
Publisher: Shaw, 1986 ISBN: 0-87788-652-0

Num. Sess.	Group Time	Num. Pgs.	Avg. Qst.	Price	Audience	Format	Bible Study
15	45-60	96	10	$4.99	New Christian	Workbk	Charctr

Features: Intro to Leading a Study, Intro to Study, Prayer Helps, Maps
★★ Personal Application Preparation Time: None
★★ Relationship Building Ldr. Guide: No Size: 5.0 x 8.25
Subjects: Acts, Bible Personalities, Obedience
Comments: A chapter-by-chapter study of Acts 13–28 describes Paul as he is miraculously converted, then begins to minister, preach, and write. Paul emerges as a dynamic leader used by God to spearhead Christian outreach to Gentiles. Paul faced many difficulties, from prison to shipwreck, but he learned to trust God for help and wisdom. Paul serves as a role model for God's call for steadfastness under pressure in contemporary crises.

Author: Christensen, Winnie **334**
Series: Fisherman Bible Studyguide
Title: *Women Who Achieved for God*
Publisher: Shaw, 1984 ISBN: 0-87788-937-6

Num. Sess.	Group Time	Num. Pgs.	Avg. Qst.	Price	Audience	Format	Bible Study
12	45-60	94	11	$4.99	Beginner	Workbk	Charctr

Features: Intro to Leading a Study, Intro to Study, Prayer Helps
★★ Personal Application Preparation Time: None
★★ Relationship Building Ldr. Guide: No Size: 5.0 x 8.25
Subjects: Bible Personalities, God, Obedience, Women's Issues
Comments: This study gives insights into lives of women of faith whose willingness to act upon God's leading make them achievers for Him. Some of the achievers are little-known women, such as Zelophehad's daughters. Others, such as Deborah and Esther, are well-known role models for Christian women today. This five-part study issues a challenge to participants to respond to God with the same obedience and courage as shown by these great women.

Author: Christensen, Winnie **335**
Series: Fisherman Bible Studyguide
Title: *Women Who Believed God*
Publisher: Shaw, 1983 ISBN: 0-87788-936-8

Num. Sess.	Group Time	Num. Pgs.	Avg. Qst.	Price	Audience	Format	Bible Study
12	45-60	94	12	$4.99	Beginner	Workbk	Charctr

Features: Intro to Leading a Study, Intro to Study, Prayer Helps
★★ Personal Application Preparation Time: None
★★ Relationship Building Ldr. Guide: No Size: 5.0 x 8.25
Subjects: Bible Personalities, God, Prayer, Relationships, Women's Issues
Comments: This study includes: an introduction, followed by lessons on women who overcame their past, prayed, worshiped, developed positive family relationships, and never stopped growing. Each Bible character shares the following characteristics: a knowledge of the past, balanced perspective on the present, hope for the future, determination in spite of mistakes, and a personal relationship with God.

Author: Christenson, Evelyn **336**
Series:
Title: *Battling the Prince of Darkness*
Publisher: Victor Books, 1990 ISBN: 0-89693-251-6

Num. Sess.	Group Time	Num. Pgs.	Avg. Qst.	Price	Audience	Format	Bible Study
13	90-120	190	N/A	$8.99	New Christian	Book	Topical

Features:
★★★★ Personal Application Preparation Time: Low
★★ Relationship Building Ldr. Guide: Yes Size: 5.50 x 8.0
Subjects: Evangelism, Satan
Comments: This book serves as call to arms that encourages believers everywhere to join the battle, take the offensive, and help win people to Jesus Christ. Participants can discover the truth about the lost doctrine, the Prince of the Kingdom of Darkness, the Ruler of the Kingdom of Light, God's armor on for victory, Satan's armor off for the battle, spiritual warfare, praying for the lost, how to pray against Satan and pray for each other, and how to mobilize for action.

Author: Christenson, Evelyn 337
Series:
Title: *Gaining Through Losing*
Publisher: Victor Books, 1980 ISBN: 0-88207-344-3

Num. Sess.	Group Time	Num. Pgs.	Avg. Qst.	Price	Audience	Format	Bible Study
13	90-120	180	N/A	$8.99	New Christian	Workbk	Topical

Features: Intro to Study, Transpcy Masters, Cassette Avail
★★★★ Personal Application Preparation Time: Low
★★★★ Relationship Building Ldr. Guide: Yes Size: 5.50 x 8.0
Subjects: Christian Life, Divorce, Emotions, Failure, Faith, Grief, Money, Suffering, Women's Issues
Comments: This study shows how God can take life's disappointments and tragedies and turn them into unbelievable gains. Participants discover how such setbacks as death, separation, divorce, sickness, suffering, and financial loss can be used by God to make people spiritually richer. The study's gains through-losing experiences are reinforced by biblical precepts.

Author: Christenson, Evelyn 338
Series:
Title: *"Lord, Change Me!"*
Publisher: Victor Books, 1977 ISBN: 0-88207-756-2

Num. Sess.	Group Time	Num. Pgs.	Avg. Qst.	Price	Audience	Format	Bible Study
12	60-90	190	N/A	$8.99	New Christian	Book	Topical

Features: Intro to Study, Prayer Helps
★★★★ Personal Application Preparation Time: Med
★★★ Relationship Building Ldr. Guide: Yes Size: 5.50 x 8.0
Subjects: Christian Living, God, Satan, Wisdom, Women's Issues
Comments: This study was developed out of 14 months of life-changing personal experience with God. It outlines 7 methods God uses to perfect His change, and how He provides direction and means for changing lives. It points out how either subconscious or deliberate ways of thinking can be influenced by other people, sensual selves, demons, or by God. Participants can identify their sources of instruction by wisdom produced in their lives—by how they are changed.

Author: Christenson, Evelyn 339
Series:
Title: *What Happens When Women Pray*
Publisher: Victor Books, 1975 ISBN: 0-88207-715-5

Num. Sess.	Group Time	Num. Pgs.	Avg. Qst.	Price	Audience	Format	Bible Study
13	60-90	144	N/A	$9.99	New Christian	Book	Topical

Features: Intro to Study
★★★★ Personal Application Preparation Time: Med
★★★★ Relationship Building Ldr. Guide: Yes Size: 5.50 x 8.0
Subjects: Prayer, Women's Issues
Comments: This study presents practical, yet thoroughly biblical lessons on prayer. It is based on experiences at prayer seminars that resulted in thousands of women learning to pray. Participants will learn what happens when prayer becomes a real dynamic in their lives and their churches. A leader's guide with transparency masters is available.

Author: Christenson, Evelyn 340
Series:
Title: *What Happens When God Answers Prayer*
Publisher: Victor Books, 1994 ISBN: 1-56476-243-2

Num. Sess.	Group Time	Num. Pgs.	Avg. Qst.	Price	Audience	Format	Bible Study
12	60-90	200	N/A	$9.99	New Christian	Book	Topical

Features:
★★★★ Personal Application Preparation Time: Med
★★★★ Relationship Building Ldr. Guide: Yes Size: 5.50 x 8.0
Subjects: Prayer
Comments: This study looks at God's perspective on what He expects to happen as a result of His answers to prayer, and what happens to and through individuals after He answers. The author reminds readers that answers to prayer are not ends in themselves, but rather are God's ways of opening the next door of their lives and ushering them into the next era. A leader's guide with transparency masters is available.

Author: Christenson, Evelyn 341
Series:
Title: *What Happens When We Pray for Our Families*
Publisher: Victor Books, 1992 ISBN: 0-89693-541-8

Num. Sess.	Group Time	Num. Pgs.	Avg. Qst.	Price	Audience	Format	Bible Study
13	60-90	200	N/A	$9.99	Beginner	Book	Topical

Features:
★★★★ Personal Application Preparation Time: Med
★★★★ Relationship Building Ldr. Guide: Yes Size: 5.50 x 8.0
Subjects: Family, Prayer, Women's Issues
Comments: This book teaches how to hang on to faith when family members hurt, and when God doesn't seem to hear. It shows how to pray to restore family relationships when problems and misunderstandings arise, and how to pray for a baby before birth. It covers prayer to use when Satan attacks children in a myriad of ways (through peers, New Age teaching, TV, and videos), and how to pray when a loved one doesn't know Christ.

Author: Christenson, Larry 342
Series: Trinity Bible Series
Title: *Christ & His Church*
Publisher: Bethany House, 1973

Num. Sess.	Group Time	Num. Pgs.	Avg. Qst.	Price	Audience	Format	Bible Study
61	60-75	146	Vary	$5.99	Beginner	Workbk	Book

Features: Intro to Leading a Study, Intro to Study, Scrpt Memory Helps, Exam
★★ Personal Application Preparation Time: Med
★★ Relationship Building Ldr. Guide: Yes Size: 8.50 x 11.0
Subjects: Teens: New Testament
Comments: This study, at two lessons per week, leads youth through the entire New Testament in approximately one year. It's part of a three-study series that covers the entire Bible in three years. Each lesson includes reading for enjoyment; summarization of the main story line; answering fill-in-the-blank questions; noting, footnoting, and underlining important truths and teachings; and memorizing passages.

Author: Christenson, Larry & Nordis 343
Series:
Title: *Christian Couple, The: A Study Guide*
Publisher: Bethany House, 1979 ISBN: 0-87123-046-1

Num. Sess.	Group Time	Num. Pgs.	Avg. Qst.	Price	Audience	Format	Bible Study
8	45-60	44	2	$1.50	New Christian	Workbk	Topical

Features: Intro to Study, Persnl Study Quest
★★★ Personal Application Preparation Time: Med
★★ Relationship Building Ldr. Guide: Yes Size: 5.0 x 8.0
Subjects: Commitments, Hope, Marriage, Sexual Issues
Comments: This study, prepared for use with the book by the same title, examines some important dynamics of husband-wife relationships. Lessons concern hope and difficulty, commitment, sexual relationship, love needing a boost, roles, unity, going on, and more. Both men and women are challenged to succeed as husbands and wives. Each lesson has a stated purpose, an introduction, personal assignment, and group discussion questions.

Author: Christenson, Larry 344
Series:
Title: *Christian Family, The*
Publisher: Bethany House, 1972 ISBN: 0-87123-071-2

Num. Sess.	Group Time	Num. Pgs.	Avg. Qst.	Price	Audience	Format	Bible Study
9	60-90	63	Vary	$2.99	New Christian	Workbk	Topical

Features: Intro to Study, Prayer Helps, Ldr's Notes, Appendix, Cassette Avail
★★★ Personal Application Preparation Time: Med
★★★ Relationship Building Ldr. Guide: Yes Size: 5.0 x 8.0
Subjects: Family, Relationships
Comments: This study, companion to the book by the same title, features 2 parts. The first consists of establishing "Divine Order" in the home, and has to do with the relationship of order and authority between the various members in a family. The second part is "Practicing the Presence of Jesus." The lessons lead participants through the 2 parts simultaneously. A guide for using companion cassettes is included.

Author: Christenson, Larry 345
Series: Trinity Bible Series
Title: *Covenant, The*
Publisher: Bethany House, 1973

Num. Sess.	Group Time	Num. Pgs.	Avg. Qst.	Price	Audience	Format	Bible Study
58	60-75	144	Vary	$5.99	Beginner	Workbk	Book

Features: Intro to Leading a Study, Intro to Study, Scrpt Memory Helps, Exam
★★ Personal Application Preparation Time: Med
★★ Relationship Building Ldr. Guide: Yes Size: 8.50 x 11.0
Subjects: Teens: Old Testament
Comments: This study, at 2 lessons per week, leads youth through the first half the Old Testament approximately in 1 year. It's part of a 3-study series that covers the entire Bible in 3 years. Each lesson includes reading for enjoyment; summarization of the main story line; answering fill-in-the-blank questions; noting, footnoting, and underlining important truths and teachings; and memorizing passages.

Author: Christenson, Larry 346
Series: Trinity Bible Series
Title: *Kingdom, The*
Publisher: Bethany House, 1972

Num. Sess.	Group Time	Num. Pgs.	Avg. Qst.	Price	Audience	Format	Bible Study
59	60-75	136	Vary	$5.99	Beginner	Workbk	Book

Features: Intro to Leading a Study, Intro to Study, Scrpt Memory Helps, Exam
★★ Personal Application Preparation Time: Med
★★ Relationship Building Ldr. Guide: Yes Size: 8.50 x 11.0
Subjects: Teens: Old Testament
Comments: This study, at 2 lessons per week, leads youth through the second half the Old Testament in approximately 1 year. It's part of a 3-study series that covers the entire Bible in 3 years. Each lesson includes reading for enjoyment; summarization of the main story line; answering fill-in-the-blank questions; noting, footnoting, and underlining important truths and teachings; and memorizing passages.

Author: Christian, Aleeta Paulk 347
Series: LifeSearch
Title: *Juggling Demands*
Publisher: Abingdon Press, 1994 ISBN: 0-68777-867-0

Num. Sess.	Group Time	Num. Pgs.	Avg. Qst.	Price	Audience	Format	Bible Study
6	60-90	62	Vary	$4.95	Beginner	Workbk	Topical

Features: Intro to Leading a Study, Intro to Study, Prayer Helps, Worship Helps, Ldr's Notes
★★★★ Personal Application Preparation Time: None
★★★★ Relationship Building Ldr. Guide: No Size: 7.0 x 10.0
Subjects: Time
Comments: This 6-week study helps adults evaluate life's priorities, make decisions about juggling conflicting demands on their commitment, time, resources, and energy, and find help and develop skills for coping with these demands. Participants are encouraged to view topics, not only from personal concern, but also from a communal/congregational concern. The book contains leader aids and marginal notes.

Author: Chromey, Rick 348
Series: Group's Active Bible Curriculum
Title: *Christians in a Non-Christian World*
Publisher: Group Publishing, 1992 ISBN: 1-55945-224-2

Num. Sess.	Group Time	Num. Pgs.	Avg. Qst.	Price	Audience	Format	Bible Study
4	35-60	48	Vary	$9.99	Beginner	Workbk	Book

Features: Intro to Leading a Study, Intro to Study, Objectives, Study Overview, Ldr's Notes, Handouts, Agenda, Publicity Ideas
★★★★ Personal Application Preparation Time: None
★★★★ Relationship Building Ldr. Guide: No Size: 8.50 x 11.0
Subjects: Teens: New Testament, Teens: Senior High
Comments: This study shows senior highers how to live out their faith in everyday life. Participants experience how life's difficulties can make them stronger, explore the importance of acting on their Christian faith, discover the danger of uncontrolled words and develop strategies for taming their tongues, and learn how continual sin can reap eternal consequences. Activity sheets are reproducible.

Author: Chromey, Rick 349
Series: Group's Active Bible Curriculum
Title: *Money: A Christian Perspective*
Publisher: Group Publishing, 1991 ISBN: 1-55945-212-9

Num. Sess.	Group Time	Num. Pgs.	Avg. Qst.	Price	Audience	Format	Bible Study
4	35-60	48	Vary	$9.99	New Christian	Workbk	Topical

Features: Intro to Leading a Study, Intro to Study, Objectives, Study Overview, Ldr's Notes, Drawings, Handouts, Agenda, Publicity Ideas
★★★★ Personal Application Preparation Time: None
★★★★ Relationship Building Ldr. Guide: No Size: 8.50 x 11.0
Subjects: Teens: Christian Liv, Teens: Senior High
Comments: This study helps senior high students learn to use money wisely. Its four lessons portray the dangers of materialism and greed, uncover students' feelings about money and wealth, explore how to become "rich" in God's eyes, and learn practical ways to manage personal spending. Instructions are easy to follow and provide multiple options for teachers. No student books are required.

Author: Chromey, Rick 350
Series: Group's Active Bible Curriculum
Title: *Revelation*
Publisher: Group Publishing, 1992 ISBN: 1-55945-229-3

Num. Sess.	Group Time	Num. Pgs.	Avg. Qst.	Price	Audience	Format	Bible Study
4	35-60	40	Vary	$9.99	Beginner	Workbk	Book

Features: Intro to Leading a Study, Intro to Study, Objectives, Study Overview, Ldr's Notes, Handouts, Agenda, Publicity Ideas
★★★★ Personal Application Preparation Time: None
★★★★ Relationship Building Ldr. Guide: No Size: 8.50 x 11.0
Subjects: Teens: Bible Study, Teens: Christian Liv, Teens: New Testament, Teens: Senior High
Comments: This course helps answer teen questions about the Book of Revelation. Senior high participants learn about the Last Days and how the Book of Revelation applies to their daily lives. Plus, they'll become familiar with signs that mark the return of Jesus Christ. Can be adapted for a Bible class or youth meeting.

Author: Chromey, Rick 351
Series: Group's Active Bible Curriculum
Title: *Turning Depression Upside Down*
Publisher: Group Publishing, 1992 ISBN: 1-55945-135-1

Num. Sess.	Group Time	Num. Pgs.	Avg. Qst.	Price	Audience	Format	Bible Study
4	35-60	44	Vary	$9.99	Beginner	Workbk	Topical

Features: Intro to Leading a Study, Intro to Study, Objectives, Study Overview, Ldr's Notes, Handouts, Agenda, Publicity Ideas
★★★★ Personal Application Preparation Time: None
★★★★ Relationship Building Ldr. Guide: No Size: 8.50 x 11.0
Subjects: Teens: Christian Liv, Teens: Emotions, Teens: Senior High
Comments: This course teaches teenagers to trust God to bring joy in tough situations. Participants examine things that can cause depression, and explore how God can help them get beyond difficult times. They'll discover they're uniquely created and loved by God, appreciate and learn from the past to help face future challenges, recognize practical ways to celebrate daily life, and discover God's will for their lives.

Author: Church Discipleship Ministries 352
Series: The 2:7 Series
Title: *Growing Strong in God's Family*
Publisher: NavPress, 1974 ISBN: 0-89109-165-3

Num. Sess.	Group Time	Num. Pgs.	Avg. Qst.	Price	Audience	Format	Bible Study
10	90-120	146	Vary	$8.99	New Christian	Workbk	Topical

Features: Intro to Study, Scrpt Memory Helps, Follow Up, Summary, Ldr's Notes, Charts
★★★★ Personal Application Preparation Time: Med
★★★★ Relationship Building Ldr. Guide: No Size: 8.50 x 11.50
Subjects: Discipleship, Evangelism, Prayer, Relationships
Comments: This initial study of The 2:7 Series gives an introduction to the basics of Bible study, prayer, Scripture memory, and devotional time. It covers memorization of verses, effective quiet time, development of an evangelistic prayer list, conversational prayer techniques, and more. Benefits include a closer relationship with God, a keener sense of priorities, renewed concern for non-Christian friends.

Author: Church Discipleship Ministries 353
Series: The 2:7 Series
Title: *2:7 Series Course 3, The: The Ministering Disciple*
Publisher: NavPress, 1979 ISBN: 0-89109-168-8

Num. Sess.	Group Time	Num. Pgs.	Avg. Qst.	Price	Audience	Format	Bible Study
11	90-120	148	Vary	$10.00	Mature Christian	Workbk	Topical

Features: Scrpt Memory Helps, Summary, Charts, Maps
★★★★ Personal Application Preparation Time: Med
★★★★ Relationship Building Ldr. Guide: Yes Size: 8.50 x 11.50
Subjects: Discipleship, Evangelism
Comments: This is the third book in a five-book study that emphasizes Bible study, prayer, Scripture memory, and devotional time. This course focuses on fine-tuning witnessing skills, learning to effectively lead an evangelistic Bible study, building friendships with non-Christians, and world vision. It includes practical ways to stay involved with "the harvest"; Scripture cards and forms are included. Leadership training for instructors is required. Not available in bookstores.

Author: Church Discipleship Ministries 354
Series: The 2:7 Series
Title: *2:7 Series Course 4, The: The Ministering Disciple*
Publisher: NavPress, 1979 ISBN: 0-89109-169-6

Num. Sess.	Group Time	Num. Pgs.	Avg. Qst.	Price	Audience	Format	Bible Study
11	90-120	390	Vary	$10.00	Mature Christian	Workbk	Book

Features: Scrpt Memory Helps, Summary, Charts
★★★★ Personal Application Preparation Time: Med
★★★★ Relationship Building Ldr. Guide: Yes Size: 8.50 x 11.50
Subjects: Bible Study, Discipleship
Comments: The 4th in a 5-book study that emphasizes Bible study, prayer, Scripture memory, and devotional time, this course focuses on how to minister in triads, how to minister one-on-one, how to follow up effectively, and how to study inductively. Scripture cards and forms are included. Leadership training for instructors is required. Not available in bookstores.

Author: Church Discipleship Ministries **355**
Series: The 2:7 Series
Title: *2:7 Series Course 5, The: The Ministering Disciple*
Publisher: NavPress, 1979 ISBN: 0-89109-170-X

Num. Sess.	Group Time	Num. Pgs.	Avg. Qst.	Price	Audience	Format	Bible Study
11	90-120	220	Vary	$10.00	Mature Christian	Workbk	Book

Features: Scrpt Memory Helps, Summary
★★★★ Personal Application Preparation Time: Med
★★★★ Relationship Building Ldr. Guide: Yes Size: 8.50 x 11.50
Subjects: Discipleship, 1 & 2 Thessalonians
Comments: This final study in this series that emphasizes Bible study, prayer, Scripture memory, and devotional time, surveys the book of 1 Thessalonians while teaching inductive Bible study and provides for extended prayer time. An evaluation of The 2:7 Series concludes the study. Scripture cards and forms are included. Leadership training for instructors is required. Not available in bookstores.

Author: Church Discipleship Ministries **356**
Series: The 2:7 Series
Title: *2:7 Series Course 1, The: The Growing Disciple*
Publisher: NavPress, 1979 ISBN: 0-89109-166-1

Num. Sess.	Group Time	Num. Pgs.	Avg. Qst.	Price	Audience	Format	Bible Study
11	90-120	116	Vary	$8.99	Mature Christian	Workbk	Topical

Features: Intro to Study, Prayer Helps, Scrpt Memory Helps, Summary, Drawings, Cartoons
★★★★ Personal Application Preparation Time: Med
★★★★ Relationship Building Ldr. Guide: Yes Size: 8.50 x 11.50
Subjects: Discipleship, Prayer
Comments: This is the first of a 5-book study that emphasizes Bible study, prayer, Scripture memory, and devotional time. This course focuses on maturing in Christ, spiritual warfare, knowing God's will, preparing a personal testimony, prayer, and more. Completion of "Growing Strong in God's Family," the initial study in The 2:7 Series, is a prerequisite to the course. Not available in bookstores.

Author: Church Discipleship Ministries **357**
Series: The 2:7 Series
Title: *2:7 Series Course 2, The: The Growing Disciple*
Publisher: NavPress, 1979 ISBN: 0-89109-167-X

Num. Sess.	Group Time	Num. Pgs.	Avg. Qst.	Price	Audience	Format	Bible Study
11	90-120	100	Vary	$8.99	Mature Christian	Workbk	Topical

Features: Intro to Study, Scrpt Memory Helps, Summary, Charts
★★★★ Personal Application Preparation Time: Med
★★★★ Relationship Building Ldr. Guide: Yes Size: 8.50 x 11.50
Subjects: Discipleship, Fruit of the Spirit, Integrity
Comments: This is the second book in a 5-book study that emphasizes Bible study, prayer, Scripture memory, and devotional time. This course focuses on the call to fruitful living, friendship evangelism, love in action, purity of life, integrity in living, and more. Completion of courses 1 and 2 will give participants stronger foundations in Christian life, basic ministry skills and presenting the Gospel. Leadership training for instructors is required. Not available in bookstores.

Author: Churches Alive **358**
Series: Love One Another
Title: *Communicating: Conveying Truth With Love*
Publisher: NavPress, 1993 ISBN: 0-89109-785-6

Num. Sess.	Group Time	Num. Pgs.	Avg. Qst.	Price	Audience	Format	Bible Study
9	60-75	52	10	$5.00	New Christian	Workbk	Topical

Features: Cartoons, Charts
★★★ Personal Application Preparation Time: None
★★★ Relationship Building Ldr. Guide: Yes Size: 5.50 x 8.50
Subjects: Communication, Relationships
Comments: This study, 1 of 7 in the Love One Another series, helps participants apply God's commandment (to love the Lord their God with all their hearts, souls, minds, and strength) to daily life. On communication, it helps participants learn the ins and outs of effective communication, as they begin to realize that it can't be done alone. Only through the grace of God can people experience the kind of communication that draws them close together as a body.

Author: Churches Alive **359**
Series: Love One Another
Title: *Contributing: Helping Others Fulfill Their Potential*
Publisher: NavPress, 1993 ISBN: 0-89109-784-8

Num. Sess.	Group Time	Num. Pgs.	Avg. Qst.	Price	Audience	Format	Bible Study
8	60-75	46	9	$5.00	New Christian	Workbk	Topical

Features: Cartoons, Charts
★★★ Personal Application Preparation Time: None
★★★ Relationship Building Ldr. Guide: Yes Size: 5.50 x 8.50
Subjects: Relationships, Spiritual Gifts
Comments: This study, 1 of 7 in the Love One Another series, helps participants apply God's commandment (to love the Lord their God with all their hearts, souls, minds, and strength) to daily life. In this segment, participants begin to see how their gifts and resources can be used to help others, improve relationships, and express love. Eight lessons look at having and using spiritual gifts, contributing with good works, with comfort and encouragement, and more.

Author: Churches Alive **360**
Series: Love One Another
Title: *Developing Unity: Upholding the Oneness God Gives Me With Others*
Publisher: NavPress, 1993 ISBN: 0-89109-780-5

Num. Sess.	Group Time	Num. Pgs.	Avg. Qst.	Price	Audience	Format	Bible Study
9	60-75	46	9	$5.00	New Christian	Workbk	Topical

Features: Cartoons, Charts
★★★ Personal Application Preparation Time: None
★★★ Relationship Building Ldr. Guide: Yes Size: 5.50 x 8.50
Subjects: Family, Marriage, Relationships
Comments: This study helps participants apply God's commandment (to love the Lord their God with all their hearts, souls, minds, and strength) to daily life. This segment concerns the five levels of human relationship, from the most intimate, marriage, to the broadest, humankind. Nine lessons include: "Two Become One"; "Family Foundations"; and "Dynamic Fellowship."

Author: Churches Alive 361
Series: Love One Another
Title: *Forgiving: Pursuing Restoration in Relationships*
Publisher: NavPress, 1993 ISBN: 0-89109-778-3

Num. Sess.	Group Time	Num. Pgs.	Avg. Qst.	Price	Audience	Format	Bible Study
9	60-75	50	10	$5.00	New Christian	Workbk	Topical

Features: Cartoons, Charts
★★★ Personal Application Preparation Time: None
★★★ Relationship Building Ldr. Guide: Yes Size: 5.50 x 8.50
Subjects: Forgiveness, Relationships
Comments: This study, 1 of 7 in the Love One Another series, helps participants apply God's commandment (to love the Lord their God with all their hearts, souls, minds, and strength) to daily life. Nine lessons on forgiveness look at: "God's Forgiveness"; "Why God Forgives"; "Forgiving Others"; "Results of Forgiving"; "Perspective on Injustice"; "Reacting to Injustice"; "Results of an Unforgiving Spirit"; "Offending Others"; and "Being Offended."

Author: Churches Alive 362
Series: Love One Another
Title: *Honoring: Holding Others in High Regard*
Publisher: NavPress, 1993 ISBN: 0-89109-782-1

Num. Sess.	Group Time	Num. Pgs.	Avg. Qst.	Price	Audience	Format	Bible Study
9	60-75	50	10	$5.00	New Christian	Workbk	Topical

Features: Cartoons, Charts
★★★ Personal Application Preparation Time: None
★★★ Relationship Building Ldr. Guide: Yes Size: 5.50 x 8.50
Subjects: Relationships, Service
Comments: This study, 1 of 7 in the Love One Another series, helps participants apply God's commandment (to love the Lord their God with all their hearts, souls, minds, and strength) to daily life. Nine lessons include: "Seeing Value in Others"; "Honoring Leaders"; "Honoring Family Members"; "Deferring to Others"; "Serving Others"; "Humility Before God"; "Humility Before Others"; "Learning from Others"; and "Accepting Correction.

Author: Churches Alive 363
Series: Love One Another
Title: *Leader's Guide: Lead Your Group to Closer Personal* Relationships
Publisher: NavPress, 1993 ISBN: 0-89109-779-1

Num. Sess.	Group Time	Num. Pgs.	Avg. Qst.	Price	Audience	Format	Bible Study
	—	125	N/A	$5.00			

Features: Drawings, Charts
Personal Application Preparation Time:
Relationship Building Ldr. Guide: Size: 5.50 x 8.50
Subjects: Leader's Guide, Relationships
Comments: This leader's guide is for use with the Love One Another Bible study series. Seven studies include: "Forgiving"; "Understanding"; "Honoring"; "Submitting"; "Contributing"; "Communicating"; and "Developing Unity." Key concepts, goals, background information, and teaching ideas are provided for each chapter in each study. Also helpful are discussion starters, presentation ideas, and illustrations.

Author: Churches Alive 364
Series: Love One Another
Title: *Submitting: Letting God Use Others to Lead Me*
Publisher: NavPress, 1993 ISBN: 0-89109-786-4

Num. Sess.	Group Time	Num. Pgs.	Avg. Qst.	Price	Audience	Format	Bible Study
8	60-75	47	10	$5.00	New Christian	Workbk	Topical

Features: Cartoons, Charts
★★★ Personal Application Preparation Time: None
★★★ Relationship Building Ldr. Guide: Yes Size: 5.50 x 8.50
Subjects: Leadership, Relationships
Comments: This study, 1 of 7 in the Love One Another series, helps participants apply God's commandment (to love the Lord their God with all their hearts, souls, minds, and strength) to daily life. Eight lessons on submission look at: "The Sovereignty of God"; "The Nature of Submission"; "Good Leadership"; "The Responsibility of Leaders"; "Submitting at Work"; "Submission in the Family"; and "Submitting to Spiritual Leaders.

Author: Churches Alive 365
Series: Love One Another
Title: *Understanding: Approaching Things from Another's Point of View*
Publisher: NavPress, 1993 ISBN: 0-89109-781-3

Num. Sess.	Group Time	Num. Pgs.	Avg. Qst.	Price	Audience	Format	Bible Study
9	60-75	53	10	$5.00	New Christian	Workbk	Topical

Features: Cartoons, Charts
★★★ Personal Application Preparation Time: None
★★★ Relationship Building Ldr. Guide: Yes Size: 5.50 x 8.50
Subjects: Relationships
Comments: This study, 1 of 7 in the Love One Another series, helps participants apply God's commandment (to love the Lord their God with all their hearts, souls, minds, and strength) to daily life. Nine lessons on understanding include: "Keys to Understanding"; "Empathy"; "Recognizing Differences"; "Accepting Differences"; "Accommodating Others"; "Being Critical"; "Discernment"; "Understanding Other's Convictions"; and "Sensitivity to Other's Convictions."

Author: Clendinning, Monte M. 366
Series:
Title: *My Place In God's Purpose*
Publisher: New Hope, 1993 ISBN: 1-56309-100-3

Num. Sess.	Group Time	Num. Pgs.	Avg. Qst.	Price	Audience	Format	Bible Study
12	—	112	5	$6.95	New Christian	Book	Book

Features: Intro to Study, Scrpt Memory Helps, Persnl Study Quest, Maps
★★★ Personal Application Preparation Time: Low
★ Relationship Building Ldr. Guide: No Size: 5.50 x 8.50
Subjects: Ephesians, Galatians, Missions, Women's Issues
Comments: This commentary for women on Galatians and Ephesians encourages inductive Bible study with the use of reflection questions. It motivates women to action and involvement in ministry and missions. Using "Free to Be Me" as the study's theme, chapters address true freedom and call for spiritual growth, priorities, faith that doesn't depend upon law, taking a stand, and bringing liberation.

Author: Clowney, Edmund **367**
Series: The Bible Speaks Today
Title: *Message of 1 Peter, The*
Publisher: InterVarsity, 1989 ISBN: 0-83081-227-X

Num. Sess.	Group Time	Num. Pgs.	Avg. Qst.	Price	Audience	Format	Bible Study
12	60-120	250	Vary	$12.99	New Christian	Book	Book

Features: Appendix
★★★ Personal Application Preparation Time: Med
★★ Relationship Building Ldr. Guide: No Size: 5.50 x 8.25
Subjects: New Testament, 1 & 2 Peter
Comments: This series of Old and New Testament expositions are characterized by 3 goals: to expound the biblical text with accuracy, relate it to contemporary life, and be readable. Edmund Clowney believes that no true Christian can escape at least a measure of suffering for Christ's sake. Out of his firsthand knowledge as an apostle of Christ, Peter shows us what the story of Jesus' life means for us as we take up our cross and follow Him.

Author: Coddington, Dean & Donald Orvis **368**
Series: Lay Action Ministry
Title: *Christianity in the Workplace: Your Faith on the Job*
Publisher: Lay Action Ministry Program, 1989 ISBN: 0-89191-485-4

Num. Sess.	Group Time	Num. Pgs.	Avg. Qst.	Price	Audience	Format	Bible Study
12	60-90	128	Vary	$6.95	New Christian	Workbk	Topical

Features: Ldr's Notes
★★★ Personal Application Preparation Time: Low
★★★ Relationship Building Ldr. Guide: Yes Size: 5.25 x 8.25
Subjects: Decision Making, Ethics, Faith, Relationships, Work
Comments: This practical study helps Christians relate their faith to tough career issues. Topics included are: biblical principles applied to job priorities and decision making; working spouses; relationships on the job; dealing with Christians in business; unemployment; ethical questions; changing careers; and more. This series helps equip and involve laypeople in ministry. Homework is recommended.

Author: Coleman, Lyman, et al. **369**
Series: Serendipity Kick off
Title: *All Aboard: Six Sessions for Kicking Off a Group*
Publisher: Serendipity House, 1993 ISBN: 1-88341-900-X

Num. Sess.	Group Time	Num. Pgs.	Avg. Qst.	Price	Audience	Format	Bible Study
6	60-90	32	Vary	$1.95	Beginner	Workbk	Topical

Features: Intro to Leading a Study, Objectives, Prayer Helps, Full Scrpt Printed, Drawings, Agenda
★★★★ Personal Application Preparation Time: None
★★★★ Relationship Building Ldr. Guide: No Size: 6.50 x 8.25
Subjects: Bible Study, Small Group Resource
Comments: This study teaches 6 ways for people to get acquainted and begin a small group. It begins with starting up and deciding on a covenant. The next 4 chapters deal with participants' spiritual condition—past, present, future—and needs. The closing chapter helps evaluate where the group goes as it progresses. The format includes time for icebreakers, Bible study, and prayer.

Author: Coleman, Lyman **370**
Series: Serendipity Focus Group
Title: *Basics: Confirming What I Believe*
Publisher: Serendipity House, 1994 ISBN: 1-88341-989-1

Num. Sess.	Group Time	Num. Pgs.	Avg. Qst.	Price	Audience	Format	Bible Study
7	60-80	64	Vary	$3.95	Beginner	Workbk	Topical

Features: Intro to Leading a Study, Intro to Study, Bibliography, Digging Deeper Quest, Summary, Full Scrpt Printed
★★★★ Personal Application Preparation Time: None
★★★★ Relationship Building Ldr. Guide: No Size: 6.50 x 9.25
Subjects: Christian Living, Faith, Stress
Comments: This study on the basics of the Christian faith confirms what Christians should believe. Each lesson examines a basic tenet of faith by looking at God the Father, Jesus Christ, the Holy Spirit, the church universal, forgiveness of sins, and life everlasting. Only major themes are covered.

Author: Coleman, Lyman & Denny Rydberg **371**
Series: Serendipity Youth
Title: *Beginnings: Taking a Leap*
Publisher: Serendipity House, 1989 ISBN: 1-88341-949-2

Num. Sess.	Group Time	Num. Pgs.	Avg. Qst.	Price	Audience	Format	Bible Study
7	60-80	48	Vary	$2.50	Beginner	Workbk	Topical

Features: Digging Deeper Quest, Full Scrpt Printed, Drawings, Photos
★★★★ Personal Application Preparation Time: None
★★★★ Relationship Building Ldr. Guide: No Size: 6.50 x 9.25
Subjects: Teens: Christian Liv, Teens: Junior High
Comments: This study considers seven stages of commitments: beginnings, turning points, growing pains, struggles, life together, hanging in there, and next steps. After a group-building introductory exercise, participants can choose a Basic Bible Study, which includes case studies followed by questions and selected Scripture followed by questions, or a Deeper Bible Study, a more in-depth study of applicable Scripture concluding with personal application questions.

Author: Coleman, Lyman **372**
Series: Serendipity Youth
Title: *Challenge: Climbing Higher*
Publisher: Serendipity House, 1994 ISBN: 1-88341-953-0

Num. Sess.	Group Time	Num. Pgs.	Avg. Qst.	Price	Audience	Format	Bible Study
7	60-80	48	Vary	$2.50	Beginner	Workbk	Topical

Features: Digging Deeper Quest, Full Scrpt Printed, Ldr's Notes, Photos
★★★★ Personal Application Preparation Time: None
★★★★ Relationship Building Ldr. Guide: No Size: 6.50 x 9.25
Subjects: Teens: Discipleship, Teens: Junior High, Teens: Senior High
Comments: This study includes 7 lessons: "Go for Broke"; "Mountain Training"; "Pot Holes"; "Rebounding"; "Spreading the News"; "Old Habits"; and "Community." After a group-building introductory exercise, participants may opt for case studies followed by questions and selected Scripture followed by questions, or a more in-depth study of Scripture with personal application questions.

Author: Coleman, Lyman 373
Series: Serendipity Youth
Title: *Choices: Dare to Be Different*
Publisher: Serendipity House, 1994 ISBN: 1-88341-946-8

Num. Sess.	Group Time	Num. Pgs.	Avg. Qst.	Price	Audience	Format	Bible Study
9	60-80	48	Vary	$2.50	Beginner	Workbk	Topical

Features: Digging Deeper Quest, Full Scrpt Printed, Ldr's Notes, Photos
★★★★ Personal Application Preparation Time: None
★★★★ Relationship Building Ldr. Guide: No Size: 6.50 x 9.25
Subjects: Teens: Christian Liv, Teens: Decisions, Teens: Ethics, Teens: Junior High, Teens: Sexuality
Comments: This study includes seven lessons about choices on moral issues titled: "Holy Grail"; "Possessions"; "Using Your Abilities"; "Concerns/Causes"; "Sex"; "Spiritual Calling"; and "Bottom Line." After a group-building introductory exercise, leaders can opt for case studies followed by questions or a more in-depth study.

Author: Coleman, Lyman 374
Series: Serendipity Youth
Title: *Confirmation: The Apostles' Creed*
Publisher: Serendipity House, 1994 ISBN: 1-88341-954-9

Num. Sess.	Group Time	Num. Pgs.	Avg. Qst.	Price	Audience	Format	Bible Study
7	60-80	48	Vary	$2.50	Beginner	Workbk	Topical

Features: Digging Deeper Quest, Full Scrpt Printed
★★★★ Personal Application Preparation Time: None
★★★★ Relationship Building Ldr. Guide: No Size: 6.50 x 9.25
Subjects: Teens: Discipleship
Comments: This 7-lesson study on Christian basics covers God the Father, the creation story; Jesus Christ, the birth story; Holy Spirit, pentecost foretold; church universal, early church life; forgiveness of sins, crucifixion; resurrection of the body, the resurrection story; and life everlasting. Every session has a coaching plan for the youth leader and step-by-step instructions. Each session has a 4-step plan for interactive learning with crowdbreakers, warm ups, and Bible study.

Author: Coleman, Lyman, et al. 375
Series: Serendipity Focus Group
Title: *Core Values: Changing From the Inside Out*
Publisher: Serendipity House, 1994 ISBN: 1-88341-987-5

Num. Sess.	Group Time	Num. Pgs.	Avg. Qst.	Price	Audience	Format	Bible Study
7	60-80	64	Vary	$3.95	Beginner	Workbk	Topical

Features: Intro to Leading a Study, Intro to Study, Bibliography, Digging Deeper Quest, Summary, Full Scrpt Printed
★★★★ Personal Application Preparation Time: None
★★★★ Relationship Building Ldr. Guide: No Size: 6.50 x 9.25
Subjects: Christian Living, Morals, Relationships
Comments: This study is about discovering core values which can help participants change from the inside out, starting with clarification of how the world is viewed, and how people function and respond in the world. Lessons look at some of the ways Scripture challenges perspectives and thinking. Two study options: the Sermon on the Mount or the writings of Paul, Timothy and James.

Author: Coleman, Lyman, et al. 376
Series: Serendipity Kick off
Title: *Couples: Six Sessions for Starting a Couple's Group*
Publisher: Serendipity House, 1993 ISBN: 1-88341-905-0

Num. Sess.	Group Time	Num. Pgs.	Avg. Qst.	Price	Audience	Format	Bible Study
6	60-90	32	Vary	$1.95	Beginner	Workbk	Topical

Features: Intro to Leading a Study, Objectives, Prayer Helps, Full Scrpt Printed, Drawings,Agenda
★★★★ Personal Application Preparation Time: None
★★★★ Relationship Building Ldr. Guide: No Size: 6.50 x 8.25
Subjects: Marriage
Comments: This 6-week course, designed for couples who want to start small groups, is highly interactive. The study sessions include: "Our Wedding: A Funny Thing Happened"; "Our Courtship: How It All Began"; "Our Honeymoon: When Was It Over?" "Our Humble Beginnings: How Did We Ever Make It?" "Our Love Life: Time for a Check Up"; "Our Tomorrow: Getting On With Life Together.

Author: Coleman, Lyman, et al. 377
Series: Serendipity Kick Off
Title: *Emerge: Six Sessions for Spiritual Beginners*
Publisher: Serendipity House, 1993 ISBN: 1-88341-902-6

Num. Sess.	Group Time	Num. Pgs.	Avg. Qst.	Price	Audience	Format	Bible Study
6	60-90	32	Vary	$1.95	Beginner	Workbk	Topical

Features: Intro to Leading a Study, Objectives, Prayer Helps, Full Scrpt Printed, Drawings,Agenda
★★★★ Personal Application Preparation Time: None
★★★★ Relationship Building Ldr. Guide: No Size: 6.50 x 8.25
Subjects: Evangelism
Comments: This 6-session study is designed for spiritual beginners. It is highly interactive. The study sessions include: "Turning Point: My Spiritual Beginnings"; "Growing Pains: My Spiritual Journey"; "Spiritual Fitness: My Spiritual Appetite"; "Honest Doubts: Where Is God When It Hurts?" "Healing: Do You Want to be Healed?" "Life Together: Sharing Our Story." Includes icebreakers, Bible study, and prayer.

Author: Coleman, Lyman & Richard Peace 378
Series: Mastering the Basics
Title: *Ephesians*
Publisher: Serendipity House, 1988 ISBN: 1-88341-930-1

Num. Sess.	Group Time	Num. Pgs.	Avg. Qst.	Price	Audience	Format	Bible Study
7	60-75	64	Vary	$4.95	Beginner	Workbk	Book

Features: Intro to Leading a Study, Intro to Study, Digging Deeper Quest, Summary, Full Scrpt Printed, Photos, Maps, Agenda
★★★ Personal Application Preparation Time: Low
★★★ Relationship Building Ldr. Guide: Yes Size: 9.50 x 8.0
Subjects: Ephesians, Grace, Prison Epistles
Comments: This is a verse-by-verse, 7- or 13-week study of Ephesians, 1 of 4 letters known as the Prison Epistles. Paul, while in prison, wrote to churches in the Roman province of Asia. "Mastering the Basics," a comprehensive, integrated program for personal or small group study, is expository teaching with a master teacher. Evangelism is demonstrated through the "empty chair" concept.

Author: Coleman, Lyman, et al. **379**
Series: Serendipity Focus Group
Title: *Gifts & Calling: Targeting Your Passion*
Publisher: Serendipity House, 1994 ISBN: 1-88341-988-3

Num. Sess.	Group Time	Num. Pgs.	Avg. Qst.	Price	Audience	Format	Bible Study
7	60-80	64	Vary	$3.95	Beginner	Workbk	Topical

Features: Intro to Leading a Study, Intro to Study, Bibliography, Digging Deeper Quest, Summary, Full Scrpt Printed
★★★★ Personal Application Preparation Time: None
★★★★ Relationship Building Ldr. Guide: No Size: 6.50 x 9.25
Subjects: Christian Living, Spiritual Gifts
Comments: This 7-week study helps participants search for their calling, and how they can use the gifts the Spirit has given them in that calling. Lessons include: "Hearing God's Call"; "Finding Your Gift"; "Taking the Risk"; "The Role of Money"; "Our Attitude Toward Work"; and "The Servant Mind." It features 2 tracks: Track 1 runs approximately 60″. Track 2 takes the study deeper (90-120″ are required).

Author: Coleman, Lyman, et al. **380**
Series: Serendipity Group
Title: *Gospel of Mark: Exploring the Life of Jesus*
Publisher: Serendipity House, 1989 ISBN: 1-88341-917-4

Num. Sess.	Group Time	Num. Pgs.	Avg. Qst.	Price	Audience	Format	Bible Study
13	60-90	96	Vary	$3.95	Beginner	Workbk	Book

Features: Intro to Study, Full Scrpt Printed
★★★ Personal Application Preparation Time: None
★★★ Relationship Building Ldr. Guide: No Size: 6.50 x 9.0
Subjects: Jesus: Life/Teaching, Mark, Wholeness
Comments: This verse-by-verse, 13- or 26-week study of Mark discusses biblical viewpoints on the identity of Jesus, radical lifestyles, values, conflict with "religious" people, wholeness, and why Jesus died. Three levels of discussion include "icebreakers," "digging deeper," and "reflection." Notes and commentary help participants with difficult words or passages. "Seven Common Small Group Ailments and How to Overcome Them"—provides direction for new groups.

Author: Coleman, Lyman **381**
Series: Serendipity Youth
Title: *Hangin' Together*
Publisher: Serendipity House, 1994 ISBN: 1-88341-948-4

Num. Sess.	Group Time	Num. Pgs.	Avg. Qst.	Price	Audience	Format	Bible Study
7	60-80	48	Vary	$2.50	Beginner	Workbk	Topical

Features: Digging Deeper Quest, Full Scrpt Printed, Ldr's Notes, Photos
★★★★ Personal Application Preparation Time: None
★★★★ Relationship Building Ldr. Guide: No Size: 6.50 x 9.25
Subjects: Teens: Friends, Teens: Junior High, Teens: Relationships, Teens: Senior High
Comments: This study includes 7 lessons: "Friendship"; "Being Real"; "He's Not Heavy, He's My Brother"; "I Appreciate You"; "Tough Love"; "Going the Distance"; "Happiness Is." After a group-building introductory exercise there are 2 options for study: case studies followed by questions and a more in-depth study of Scripture.

Author: Coleman, Lyman **382**
Series: Serendipity Youth
Title: *Hassles: Problems That Hit Home*
Publisher: Serendipity House, 1994 ISBN: 1-88341-952-2

Num. Sess.	Group Time	Num. Pgs.	Avg. Qst.	Price	Audience	Format	Bible Study
7	60-80	48	Vary	$2.50	Beginner	Workbk	Topical

Features: Digging Deeper Quest, Full Scrpt Printed, Photos
★★★★ Personal Application Preparation Time: None
★★★★ Relationship Building Ldr. Guide: No Size: 6.50 x 9.25
Subjects: Teens: Relationships, Teens: Senior High, Teens: Youth Life
Comments: This study considers 7 areas of relationships: life's headaches, family flare-ups, killer cliques, breakups, power plays, "why me, Lord?" and breaking free. After a group-building introductory exercise, participants are given two options for study: "Basic Bible Study," which includes case studies followed by questions and selected Scripture followed by questions; and "Deeper Bible Study," a more in-depth study of applicable Scripture with personal application questions.

Author: Coleman, Lyman **383**
Series: Serendipity Youth
Title: *Hot Issues: Hard Core*
Publisher: Serendipity House, 1994 ISBN: 1-88341-947-6

Num. Sess.	Group Time	Num. Pgs.	Avg. Qst.	Price	Audience	Format	Bible Study
7	60-80	48	Vary	$2.50	Beginner	Workbk	Topical

Features: Prayer Helps, Digging Deeper Quest, Full Scrpt Printed, Cartoons, Photos
★★★★ Personal Application Preparation Time: None
★★★★ Relationship Building Ldr. Guide: No Size: 6.50 x 9.25
Subjects: Teens: Christian Liv, Teens: Cults, Teens: Drugs/Drinking, Teens: Emotions, Teens: Senior High
Comments: This study considers current tough issues facing teens such as: drugs/alcohol, lust, suicide, violence, and the occult. After a group-building introductory exercise, there are two options for study: case studies followed by questions or a more in-depth study of applicable Scripture.

Author: Coleman, Lyman & Richard Peace **384**
Series: Mastering the Basics
Title: *James*
Publisher: Serendipity House, 1986 ISBN: 1-88341-933-6

Num. Sess.	Group Time	Num. Pgs.	Avg. Qst.	Price	Audience	Format	Bible Study
7	60-75	64	Vary	$4.95	Beginner	Workbk	Book

Features: Intro to Leading a Study, Intro to Study, Digging Deeper Quest, Summary, Full Scrpt Printed, Photos, Maps, Agenda
★★★ Personal Application Preparation Time: Low
★★★ Relationship Building Ldr. Guide: Yes Size: 9.50 x 8.0
Subjects: Ethics, Faith, James
Comments: This verse-by-verse, 7- or 13-week study on James reveals his ethical concerns regarding how Christian faith is to be lived daily. "Mastering the Basics," a comprehensive, integrated program for personal or small group study, is expository teaching with a master teacher. Evangelism is demonstrated through the "empty chair" concept.

Author: Coleman, Lyman, et al. **385**
Series: Serendipity Focus Group
Title: *Jesus: Up Front and Personal*
Publisher: Serendipity House, 1994 ISBN: 1-88341-990-5

Num. Sess.	Group Time	Num. Pgs.	Avg. Qst.	Price	Audience	Format	Bible Study
7	60-80	64	Vary	$3.95	Beginner	Workbk	Topical

Features: Intro to Leading a Study, Intro to Study, Bibliography, Digging Deeper Quest, Summary, Full Scrpt Printed
★★★★ Personal Application Preparation Time: None
★★★★ Relationship Building Ldr. Guide: No Size: 6.50 x 9.25
Subjects: Christian Living, Jesus: Life/Teaching
Comments: This seven-week study on the life of Christ looks at Jesus as teacher, healer, a person who was tempted, revolutionary, redeemer, and reconciler. The purpose of the study is not to serve as a chronology of Jesus' life, but rather to serve as snapshots in a photograph album. Two tracks allow the study to run either 60″ or 90″–120″. The first of the seven lessons is dedicated to getting acquainted.

Author: Coleman, Lyman, et al. **386**
Series: Serendipity Focus Group
Title: *Man to Man: Beyond Football and the Weather*
Publisher: Serendipity House, 1994 ISBN: 1-88341-995-6

Num. Sess.	Group Time	Num. Pgs.	Avg. Qst.	Price	Audience	Format	Bible Study
7	60-80	64	Vary	$3.95	Beginner	Workbk	Topical

Features: Intro to Leading a Study, Intro to Study, Bibliography, Digging Deeper Quest, Summary, Full Scrpt Printed
★★★★ Personal Application Preparation Time: None
★★★★ Relationship Building Ldr. Guide: No Size: 6.50 x 9.25
Subjects: Men's Issues
Comments: This study addresses 7 things men are afraid to talk about. Men explore and discuss their feelings, fears, relationships, doubts, and their "dark sides." It redefines manhood, based on a de-emphasis of physical courage and prowess, and an emphasis on spiritual courage. This new-found courage allows men to face spiritual and emotional issues of the past.

Author: Coleman, Lyman, et al. **387**
Series: Serendipity Focus Group
Title: *Marketplace: Surviving In the Real World*
Publisher: Serendipity House, 1994 ISBN: 1-88341-992-1

Num. Sess.	Group Time	Num. Pgs.	Avg. Qst.	Price	Audience	Format	Bible Study
7	60-80	64	Vary	$3.95	Beginner	Workbk	Topical

Features: Intro to Leading a Study, Intro to Study, Bibliography, Digging Deeper Quest, Summary, Full Scrpt Printed
★★★★ Personal Application Preparation Time: None
★★★★ Relationship Building Ldr. Guide: No Size: 6.50 x 9.25
Subjects: Ethics, Materialism, Work
Comments: In this 7-week study participants look at the dilemmas of running their own business, including ethical dilemmas. They consider honesty as a policy, how to treat employees, responsibility to government, necessity of risk-taking, money management, and the value of service to customers or clients. Participants seek to determine how Christ's Lordship can be reflected in their business.

Author: Coleman, Lyman, et al. **388**
Series: Serendipity Kick off
Title: *Men: Six Sessions for Starting a Men's Group*
Publisher: Serendipity House, 1993 ISBN: 1-88341-907-7

Num. Sess.	Group Time	Num. Pgs.	Avg. Qst.	Price	Audience	Format	Bible Study
6	60-90	32	Vary	$1.95	Beginner	Workbk	Topical

Features: Intro to Leading a Study, Objectives, Prayer Helps, Full Scrpt Printed, Drawings,Agenda
★★★★ Personal Application Preparation Time: None
★★★★ Relationship Building Ldr. Guide: No Size: 6.50 x 8.25
Subjects: Bible Study, Men's Issues
Comments: This six-session study is designed for men who want to start small groups. The study sessions include: male bonding, role models, parental expectations, testing, and fourth and goal. The format includes time for icebreakers, Bible study, and prayer. Timelines are provided for in each lesson.

Author: Coleman, Lyman, et al. **389**
Series: Mastering the Basics
Title: *Parables*
Publisher: Serendipity House, 1991 ISBN: 1-88341-936-0

Num. Sess.	Group Time	Num. Pgs.	Avg. Qst.	Price	Audience	Format	Bible Study
13	60-75	64	Vary	$4.95	Beginner	Workbk	Book

Features: Intro to Leading a Study, Intro to Study, Digging Deeper Quest, Summary, Full Scrpt Printed, Photos
★★★★ Personal Application Preparation Time: Med
★★ Relationship Building Ldr. Guide: No Size: 9.50 x 8.0
Subjects: Parables
Comments: The parables are used in the Gospels to compare aspects of common, everyday life with reality about the kingdom of God. This verse-by-berse study on each of the parables is a comprehensive, integrated program. It can be used either in self study, with a small intimate group, or a church-wide group, led by a pastor or gifted teacher.

Author: Coleman, Lyman, et al. **390**
Series: Serendipity Focus Group
Title: *Parenting: Not Just a Stroll in the Park*
Publisher: Serendipity House, 1994 ISBN: 1-88341-996-4

Num. Sess.	Group Time	Num. Pgs.	Avg. Qst.	Price	Audience	Format	Bible Study
7	60-90	64	Vary	$3.95	Beginner	Workbk	Topical

Features: Intro to Leading a Study, Intro to Study, Bibliography, Digging Deeper Quest, Summary, Full Scrpt Printed
★★★★ Personal Application Preparation Time: None
★★★★ Relationship Building Ldr. Guide: No Size: 6.50 x 9.25
Subjects: Parenting
Comments: This 7-week study addresses 7 stages of family life, beginning with "It's a Boy!," and continuing with "Diaper Days," "He Got That From You," "Parents in Pain," "Parental Expectations," and ending with "Family of God." Jesus' birth and life help parents come to a greater understanding of parenting. Track 1 allows the study to run approximately 60″. Track 2 takes 90″–120″.

Author: Coleman, Lyman & Richard Peace **391**
Series: Mastering the Basics
Title: *Philippians*
Publisher: Serendipity House, 1988 ISBN: 1-88341-977-8

Num. Sess.	Group Time	Num. Pgs.	Avg. Qst.	Price	Audience	Format	Bible Study
7	60-75	64	Vary	$4.95	Beginner	Workbk	Book

Features: Intro to Leading a Study, Intro to Study, Digging Deeper Quest, Summary, Full Scrpt Printed, Photos, Maps, Agenda
★★★ Personal Application Preparation Time: Low
★★★ Relationship Building Ldr. Guide: Yes Size: 9.50 x 8.0
Subjects: Joy, Philippians, Prison Epistles, Suffering, Victorious Living
Comments: This verse-by-verse, 7- or 13-week study is about Philippians, a book Paul wrote from prison to a church confronted with many problems. He helps them find joy in the midst of a hard situation, and also helps twentieth-century seekers put joy in perspective. Joy is not always equal to satisfaction. "Mastering the Basics" is expository teaching with a master teacher.

Author: Coleman, Lyman, et al. **392**
Series: Serendipity Group
Title: *Philippians/Ephesians: Becoming a Caring Community*
Publisher: Serendipity House, 1989 ISBN: 1-88341-926-3

Num. Sess.	Group Time	Num. Pgs.	Avg. Qst.	Price	Audience	Format	Bible Study
16	60-90	64	Vary	$3.95	Beginner	Workbk	Book

Features: Intro to Study, Full Scrpt Printed
★★★ Personal Application Preparation Time: None
★★★ Relationship Building Ldr. Guide: No Size: 6.50 x 9.0
Subjects: Caring, Ephesians, Joy, Philippians, Prison Epistles, Relationships, Stress
Comments: This verse-by-verse, 8- or 10-week study of Philippians and 8- or 11-week study of Ephesians discusses biblical viewpoints on thriving in the midst of chaos, anxiety, stress management, discouragement, living with limits, honest relationships, and conflict resolution. Three levels of discussion include "icebreakers," "digging deeper," and "reflection."

Author: Coleman, Lyman, et al. **393**
Series: Serendipity Kick off
Title: *Plunge: Six Sessions for Getting Involved In Your Church*
Publisher: Serendipity House, 1993 ISBN: 1-88341-901-8

Num. Sess.	Group Time	Num. Pgs.	Avg. Qst.	Price	Audience	Format	Bible Study
6	60-90	32	Vary	$1.95	Beginner	Workbk	Topical

Features: Intro to Leading a Study, Objectives, Prayer Helps, Full Scrpt Printed, Drawings,Agenda
★★★★ Personal Application Preparation Time: None
★★★★ Relationship Building Ldr. Guide: No Size: 6.50 x 8.25
Subjects: Bible Study, Church Life
Comments: This 6-session study, designed to get participants involved in their churches, is highly interactive. The study sessions include: "P = Personality: Getting to Know You"; "L = Life: Sharing Your Story"; "U = Urge: Sharing Your Passion"; "N = Needs: God's Calling for You"; "G = Gifts: Putting Your Gifts to Work"; and "E = Enlistment: Signing on the Dotted Line." Includes icebreakers, Bible study, and prayer.

Author: Coleman, Lyman & Denny Rydberg **394**
Series: Serendipity Youth
Title: *Pressures: Finding The Balance*
Publisher: Serendipity House, 1994 ISBN: 1-88341-950-6

Num. Sess.	Group Time	Num. Pgs.	Avg. Qst.	Price	Audience	Format	Bible Study
7	60-80	48	Vary	$2.50	Beginner	Workbk	Topical

Features: Prayer Helps, Digging Deeper Quest, Full Scrpt Printed, Drawings, Photos, Charts
★★★★ Personal Application Preparation Time: None
★★★★ Relationship Building Ldr. Guide: No Size: 6.50 x 9.25
Subjects: Teens: Christian Liv, Teens: Junior High, Teens: Peer Pressure, Teens: Senior High
Comments: This study includes 7 lessons: "Stress"; "Parental Expectations"; "Peer Pressure"; "Moral Issues"; "Sexual Desires"; "Spiritual Struggles"; and "Decisions, Decisions." After a group-building introductory exercise, there are two options for study: case studies followed by questions and a more in-depth study of applicable Scripture.

Author: Coleman, Lyman, et al. **395**
Series: Serendipity Group
Title: *Revelation: Looking at the End of Time*
Publisher: Serendipity House, 1989 ISBN: 1-88341-923-9

Num. Sess.	Group Time	Num. Pgs.	Avg. Qst.	Price	Audience	Format	Bible Study
13	60-90	96	Vary	$3.95	Beginner	Workbk	Book

Features: Intro to Study, Full Scrpt Printed
★★★ Personal Application Preparation Time: None
★★★ Relationship Building Ldr. Guide: No Size: 6.50 x 9.0
Subjects: Apocalyptic, Eschatology, Heaven/Hell, Revelation
Comments: This verse-by-verse, 13- or 26-week study of Revelation discusses biblical viewpoints on Heaven, hell, wars and persecution, terror, tears, Final Judgment, Paradise found, and what difference they make. Three levels of discussion questions include "icebreakers," "digging deeper," and "reflection. An insert—"Seven Common Small Group Ailments and How to Overcome Them"—is fun and provides direction for new groups.

Author: Coleman, Lyman & Richard Peace **396**
Series: Mastering the Basics
Title: *Romans*
Publisher: Serendipity House, 1988 ISBN: 1-88341-927-1

Num. Sess.	Group Time	Num. Pgs.	Avg. Qst.	Price	Audience	Format	Bible Study
13	60-75	128	Vary	$4.95	Beginner	Workbk	Book

Features: Intro to Leading a Study, Intro to Study, Digging Deeper Quest, Summary, Full Scrpt Printed, Photos, Maps, Agenda
★★★ Personal Application Preparation Time: Low
★★★ Relationship Building Ldr. Guide: Yes Size: 9.50 x 8.0
Subjects: Hope, Romans, Victorious Living
Comments: This verse-by-verse, 13- or 28-week study of Romans discusses how God will judge each person on the Final Day. Both justification and salvation are explored. Mastering the Basics, a comprehensive, integrated program for personal or small group study, is expository teaching with a master teacher. Evangelism is demonstrated through the "empty chair" concept.

Author: Coleman, Lyman, et al. **397**
Series: Serendipity Group
Title: *Romans: Discovering God's Plan for the World*
Publisher: Serendipity House, 1989 ISBN: 1-88341-925-5

Num. Sess.	Group Time	Num. Pgs.	Avg. Qst.	Price	Audience	Format	Bible Study
15	60-90	80	Vary	$3.95	Beginner	Workbk	Book

Features: Intro to Study, Full Scrpt Printed
★★★ Personal Application Preparation Time: None
★★★ Relationship Building Ldr. Guide: No Size: 6.50 x 9.0
Subjects: Failure, Hope, Morals, Romans, Victorious Living
Comments: This verse-by-verse, 15- or 27-week study of Romans discusses biblical viewpoints on our responsibility to God's creation, moral failure, shame, inner conflict, hope, serenity, transformation, inner strength, and ultimate triumph. Three levels of discussion questions include "icebreakers," "digging deeper," and "reflection." Notes and commentary help participants with difficult words or passages.

Author: Coleman, Lyman, et al. **398**
Series: Serendipity Focus Group
Title: *Self Portrait: Taking Inventory of Yourself*
Publisher: Serendipity House, 1994 ISBN: 1-88341-994-8

Num. Sess.	Group Time	Num. Pgs.	Avg. Qst.	Price	Audience	Format	Bible Study
7	60-80	64	Vary	$3.95	Beginner	Workbk	Topical

Features: Intro to Leading a Study, Intro to Study, Bibliography, Digging Deeper Quest, Summary, Full Scrpt Printed
★★★★ Personal Application Preparation Time: None
★★★★ Relationship Building Ldr. Guide: No Size: 6.50 x 9.25
Subjects: Leadership, Psychology, Relationships
Comments: In this study on self-awareness, participants can take personal inventories to find answers to the question, "Who am I?" Responses to the question include how they view themselves and how others view them. Participants review their own self-images, values, personalities, and hang-ups, to discover what they believe, fear, and hope for in their lives.

Author: Coleman, Lyman, et al. **399**
Series:
Title: *Serendipity Starter Kit*
Publisher: Serendipity House, 1994

Num. Sess.	Group Time	Num. Pgs.	Avg. Qst.	Price	Audience	Format	Bible Study
	—	N/A	N/A	$99.00			

Features:
Personal Application Preparation Time:
Relationship Building Ldr. Guide: Size: 0.0 x 0.0
Subjects: Small Group Resource
Comments: In this kit are tools for starting a small group program in a church. It includes an 11″ video designed to "sell" church committees, director's manual with material for launching small groups, a group leader's manual that is a guidebook for rookie leaders, samples of all Serendipity materials, a *Serendipity Bible for Groups,* and a volume of the *Family Fun Bible* all organized in a handy carrying album.

Author: Coleman, Lyman **400**
Series: Serendipity Youth
Title: *Serendipity Youth Bible Study Series: Coach's Book*
Publisher: Serendipity House, 1994 ISBN: 1-88341-916-6

Num. Sess.	Group Time	Num. Pgs.	Avg. Qst.	Price	Audience	Format	Bible Study
56	60-80	79	Vary	$2.50	Beginner	Workbk	Topical

Features: Ldr's Notes, Agenda
★★★★ Personal Application Preparation Time: None
★★★★ Relationship Building Ldr. Guide: No Size: 6.50 x 9.25
Subjects: Teens: Resources
Comments: This book is the coaching plan for each course in the Serendipity Youth series. Each session has a 4-step plan for interactive learning, with crowd breakers, warm ups, Bible study, and caring. Three categories and levels of intensity make up the nine courses. They are: Category 1—"Relationships"; Up Close, Belonging, and Hassles. Category 2—"On Morality"; Choices, Pressures, and Hot Issues. Category 3—"On Spirituality"; Beginnings, Confirmation, and Challenge.

Author: Coleman, Lyman, et al. **401**
Series: Mastering the Basics
Title: *Sermon on the Mount*
Publisher: Serendipity House, 1991 ISBN: 1-88341-937-9

Num. Sess.	Group Time	Num. Pgs.	Avg. Qst.	Price	Audience	Format	Bible Study
13	60-75	64	244	$4.95	Beginner	Workbk	Book

Features: Intro to Study, Digging Deeper Quest, Full Scrpt Printed
★★★★ Personal Application Preparation Time: Med
★★ Relationship Building Ldr. Guide: No Size: 9.50 x 8.0
Subjects: Matthew, Sermon on the Mount
Comments: The Sermon on the Mount is a picture of what the inner character of a follower of Jesus in any age is meant to be like. This text covers the Beatitudes, the Lord's Prayer, the admonition to "consider the lilies of the field," and the parable of two men who built their houses on sand and rock. This Mastering the Basics study can be used either in self-study, with a small intimate group, or a church-wide group, led by a pastor or gifted teacher.

Author: Coleman, Lyman, et al. **402**
Series: Serendipity Focus Group
Title: *Singles: The Secret Behind the Smile*
Publisher: Serendipity House, 1994 ISBN: 1-88341-998-0

Num. Sess.	Group Time	Num. Pgs.	Avg. Qst.	Price	Audience	Format	Bible Study
7	60-80	64	Vary	$3.95	Beginner	Workbk	Topical

Features: Intro to Leading a Study, Intro to Study, Bibliography, Digging Deeper Quest, Summary, Full Scrpt Printed
★★★★ Personal Application Preparation Time: None
★★★★ Relationship Building Ldr. Guide: No Size: 6.50 x 9.25
Subjects: Christian Living, Loneliness, Sexual Issues, Singles' Issues
Comments: In this study participants explore issues that affect single adults by following the lives of 2 single adults: Jesus (track 1 studies) and the Apostle Paul (track 2 studies). Their words and teachings are used to explore such issues as friendship, choices, loneliness, feelings of rejection, and sexuality. Track 1 the study takes 60″. Track 2 takes 90″–120″.

Author: Coleman, Lyman, et al. **403**
Series: Serendipity Focus Group
Title: *Stressed Out: Hot, Dry and About to Crumble*
Publisher: Serendipity House, 1994 ISBN: 1-88341-999-9

Num. Sess.	Group Time	Num. Pgs.	Avg. Qst.	Price	Audience	Format	Bible Study
7	60-90	64	Vary	$3.95	Beginner	Workbk	Topical

Features: Intro to Leading a Study, Intro to Study, Bibliography, Digging Deeper Quest, Summary, Full Scrpt Printed
★★★★ Personal Application Preparation Time: None
★★★★ Relationship Building Ldr. Guide: No Size: 6.50 x 9.25
Subjects: Stress, Work
Comments: This 7-week study deals with stress, from worry, work, failure, conflict, loss, and overload. These 7 lessons serve as prescriptions for the emotionally drained. It features 2 tracks: Using track 1 allows the study to run approximately 60″. Track 2 takes the study deeper, to cover track 1 and 2 in the same lesson (90″–120″ are required). Brief leader notes are in the margin.

Author: Coleman, Lyman **404**
Series: Serendipity Youth
Title: *Up Close: Who Am I?*
Publisher: Serendipity House, 1994 ISBN: 1-88341-951-4

Num. Sess.	Group Time	Num. Pgs.	Avg. Qst.	Price	Audience	Format	Bible Study
7	60-80	48	Vary	$2.50	Beginner	Workbk	Topical

Features: Digging Deeper Quest, Full Scrpt Printed, Photos
★★★★ Personal Application Preparation Time: None
★★★★ Relationship Building Ldr. Guide: No Size: 6.50 x 9.25
Subjects: Teens: Christian Liv, Teens: Junior High, Teens: Psychology, Teens: Self-image
Comments: This study considers 7 areas teens face when evaluating their identities: their uniqueness, personality, abilities, problems, values, faith, and future. After a group-building introductory exercise, participants may choose a basic Bible study, which includes case studies followed by questions and selected Scripture followed by questions, or a more in-depth study of applicable Scripture.

Author: Coleman, Lyman **405**
Series:
Title: *Video Training Kit for Leaders*
Publisher: Serendipity House, 1993 ISBN: 1-88341-904-2

Num. Sess.	Group Time	Num. Pgs.	Avg. Qst.	Price	Audience	Format	Bible Study
6	75-90	64	Vary	$99.00	Beginner	Video	Topical

Features:
Personal Application Preparation Time:
Relationship Building Ldr. Guide: Size: 0.0 x 0.0
Subjects: Small Group Resource
Comments: This 6-session study includes the following topics: "Small Groups"; "Fundamentals"; "Lifecycle of a Group"; "Principles of Bible Study"; "Problems"; and "The Next Step." Each session has four components: "Roll Call" (getting to know each other), "Instruction" (watching the video), "Interaction" (group leaders use the "All Aboard" book for practice), and "Wrap Up" (leaders motivate people and encourage them to believe in God's plan for their churches).

Author: Coleman, Lyman, et al. **406**
Series: Serendipity Focus Group
Title: *Warfare: Overcoming the Dragon*
Publisher: Serendipity House, 1994 ISBN: 1-88341-991-3

Num. Sess.	Group Time	Num. Pgs.	Avg. Qst.	Price	Audience	Format	Bible Study
7	60-80	64	Vary	$3.95	Beginner	Workbk	Topical

Features: Intro to Leading a Study, Intro to Study, Bibliography, Digging Deeper Quest, Summary, Full Scrpt Printed
★★★★ Personal Application Preparation Time: None
★★★★ Relationship Building Ldr. Guide: No Size: 6.50 x 9.25
Subjects: Christian Living, Spiritual Warfare
Comments: This study explores spiritual warfare as a multilevel conflict between good and evil. It begins by looking at humankind's first encounter with evil, in the Garden of Eden. It examines the players involved, their battle preparation, weapons, daily battles, major battles, and their ultimate victory in Christ. It features two tracks: Track 1 runs approximately 60″. Track 2 takes 90″–120″.

Author: Coleman, Lyman, et al. **407**
Series: Serendipity Focus Group
Title: *Whol-i-ness: Holy, Wholly, Holey*
Publisher: Serendipity House, 1994 ISBN: 1-88341-997-2

Num. Sess.	Group Time	Num. Pgs.	Avg. Qst.	Price	Audience	Format	Bible Study
7	60-90	64	Vary	$3.95	Beginner	Workbk	Topical

Features: Intro to Leading a Study, Intro to Study, Bibliography, Digging Deeper Quest, Summary, Full Scrpt Printed
★★★★ Personal Application Preparation Time: None
★★★★ Relationship Building Ldr. Guide: No Size: 6.50 x 9.25
Subjects: Christian Living, Wholeness
Comments: Each session examines a different dimension: spiritual, physical, vocational, emotional, relational, and volitional. It suggests that Jesus offers wholeness for the body, mind, and spirit. In a world that is frail, fractured, and frazzled, it serves as good news. It features 2 tracks: Using track 1 allows the study to run approximately 60″. Track 2, 90″–120″.

Author: Coleman, Lyman, et al. **408**
Series: Serendipity Kick Off
Title: *Women: Six Sessions for Starting a Women's Group*
Publisher: Serendipity House, 1993 ISBN: 1-88341-906-9

Num. Sess.	Group Time	Num. Pgs.	Avg. Qst.	Price	Audience	Format	Bible Study
6	60-90	32	Vary	$1.95	Beginner	Workbk	Topical

Features: Intro to Leading a Study, Objectives, Prayer Helps, Full Scrpt Printed, Drawings,Agenda
★★★★ Personal Application Preparation Time: None
★★★★ Relationship Building Ldr. Guide: No Size: 6.50 x 8.25
Subjects: Bible Study, Women's Issues
Comments: This 6-session study is designed for people starting women's groups. The study sessions include: "Ready . . . Set . . . Go . . ."; Stressed For Success"; "Face Value"; "U-Turn Permitted"; "Maxed Out"; and "Now What." The format includes time for icebreakers, Bible study, and prayer. Timelines are provided for in each lesson.

Author: Coleman, Lyman 409
Series:
Title: *Youth Ministry Encyclopedia*
Publisher: Serendipity House, 1985 ISBN: 0-00619-822-8

Num. Sess.	Group Time	Num. Pgs.	Avg. Qst.	Price	Audience	Format	Bible Study
48	35-60	240	Vary	$15.95	Beginner	Book	No

Features: Digging Deeper Quest, Cartoons, Photos, Agenda
★★★★ Personal Application Preparation Time: None
★★★★ Relationship Building Ldr. Guide: No Size: 8.50 x 9.50
Subjects: Small Group Resource, Teens: Bible Study
Comments: The Youth Ministry Encyclopedia contains 200 group-building exercises for youth ministry leaders, which have been gathered over a 20-year period. Included are: 101 group games for starting youth meetings; 55 communication exercises for getting acquainted; 48 Bible studies for small group discussions; schedules for staff training, retreats, week-long camps; and a 6-session program for building a youth ministry team.

Author: Coleman, Lyman & Richard Peace 410
Series: Mastering the Basics
Title: *1 Corinthians*
Publisher: Serendipity House, 1988 ISBN: 1-88341-929-8

Num. Sess.	Group Time	Num. Pgs.	Avg. Qst.	Price	Audience	Format	Bible Study
13	60-75	120	Vary	$4.95	Beginner	Workbk	Book

Features: Intro to Leading a Study, Intro to Study, Digging Deeper Quest, Summary, Full Scrpt Printed, Photos, Maps, Agenda
★★★ Personal Application Preparation Time: Low
★★★ Relationship Building Ldr. Guide: Yes Size: 9.50 x 8.0
Subjects: Christian Living, 1 Corinthians
Comments: This is a verse-by-verse, 13- or 27-week study of 1 Corinthians, a practical, issue-oriented letter in which Paul tells his readers what they ought and ought not do. Mastering the Basics, a comprehensive, integrated series for personal or small group study, features expository teaching with a master teacher. Evangelism is demonstrated through the "empty chair" concept.

Author: Coleman, Lyman, et al. 411
Series: Serendipity Bible Study
Title: *1 Corinthians: Taking On the Tough Issues*
Publisher: Serendipity House, 1989 ISBN: 1-88341-920-4

Num. Sess.	Group Time	Num. Pgs.	Avg. Qst.	Price	Audience	Format	Bible Study
13	60-90	64	Vary	$3.95	Beginner	Workbk	Book

Features: Intro to Study, Full Scrpt Printed
★★★ Personal Application Preparation Time: None
★★★ Relationship Building Ldr. Guide: No Size: 6.50 x 9.0
Subjects: Addictions, Decision Making, Relationships, Sexual Issues, Spiritual Gifts, 1 Corinthians
Comments: This verse-by-verse, 13- or 24-week study of 1 Corinthians discusses biblical viewpoints on sexual addiction, alcohol abuse, making choices, spiritual gifts, personal conflicts, legal battles, divided loyalty, death, and resurrection. Three levels of discussion questions include "icebreakers," "digging deeper," and "reflection." Notes and commentary help participants with difficult words or passages.

Author: Coleman, Lyman, et al. 412
Series: Serendipity Bible Study
Title: *1 John/Galatians: Exposing Religious Counterfeits*
Publisher: Serendipity House, 1989 ISBN: 1-88341-922-0

Num. Sess.	Group Time	Num. Pgs.	Avg. Qst.	Price	Audience	Format	Bible Study
12	60-90	64	Vary	$3.95	Beginner	Workbk	Book

Features: Intro to Study, Full Scrpt Printed
★★★ Personal Application Preparation Time: None
★★★ Relationship Building Ldr. Guide: No Size: 6.50 x 9.0
Subjects: Cults, Faith, False Teachers, Fruit of the Spirit, Galatians, Occult, 1, 2 & 3 John/Jude
Comments: This verse-by-verse, 5- or 8-week study of 1 John and 7- or 13-week study of Galatians discusses biblical viewpoints on the New Age movement, cults, legalism, false teaching, what real community looks like, fruit of the Spirit, and perfect love. Three levels of discussion include "icebreakers," "digging deeper," and "reflection." Notes and commentary help with difficult words or passages.

Author: Coleman, Lyman & Richard Peace 413
Series: Mastering the Basics
Title: *1 Peter*
Publisher: Serendipity House, 1988 ISBN: 1-88341-934-4

Num. Sess.	Group Time	Num. Pgs.	Avg. Qst.	Price	Audience	Format	Bible Study
7	60-75	64	Vary	$4.95	Beginner	Workbk	Book

Features: Intro to Leading a Study, Intro to Study, Digging Deeper Quest, Summary, Full Scrpt Printed, Photos, Maps, Agenda
★★★ Personal Application Preparation Time: Low
★★★ Relationship Building Ldr. Guide: Yes Size: 9.50 x 8.0
Subjects: Hope, Suffering, 1 & 2 Peter
Comments: Peter wrote his first letter to comfort and encourage Christians in the midst of "painful trials." Peter exhorts Christians to rejoice because of their great "hope." This verse-by-verse, 7- or 10-week study is a part of Mastering the Basics, a comprehensive, integrated series for personal or small group study. Evangelism is demonstrated through the "empty chair" concept.

Author: Coleman, Lyman, et al. 414
Series: Serendipity Bible Study
Title: *1 Peter/James: Living Through Difficult Times*
Publisher: Serendipity House, 1989 ISBN: 1-88341-924-7

Num. Sess.	Group Time	Num. Pgs.	Avg. Qst.	Price	Audience	Format	Bible Study
16	60-90	62	Vary	$3.95	Beginner	Workbk	Book

Features: Intro to Study, Full Scrpt Printed
★★★ Personal Application Preparation Time: None
★★★ Relationship Building Ldr. Guide: No Size: 6.50 x 9.0
Subjects: Caring, Ethics, Failure, Hope, James, Suffering, Work, 1 & 2 Peter
Comments: This verse-by-verse, 8- or 10-week study of 1 Peter and 8- or 12-week study of James discusses biblical viewpoints on coping when the world is against you, suffering abuse, embarrassment, failure, social ethics, faith at work, hope, caring for one another, and healing. Three levels of discussion include "icebreakers," "digging deeper," and "reflection.

Author: Coleman, Lyman & Richard Peace **415**
Series: Mastering the Basics
Title: *1 & 2 Timothy*
Publisher: Serendipity House, 1988 ISBN: 1-88341-932-8

Num. Sess.	Group Time	Num. Pgs.	Avg. Qst.	Price	Audience	Format	Bible Study
7	60-75	64	Vary	$4.95	Beginner	Workbk	Book

Features: Intro to Leading a Study, Intro to Study, Digging Deeper Quest, Summary, Full Scrpt Printed, Photos, Maps, Agenda
★★★ Personal Application Preparation Time: Low
★★★ Relationship Building Ldr. Guide: Yes Size: 9.50 x 8.0
Subjects: False Teachers, Obedience, Pastoral Epistles, Service, 1 & 2 Timothy/Titus
Comments: First Timothy gives instructions on how to cope with false teachers; 2 Timothy was written when Paul was in prison, lonely, and emploring Timothy to come to his side and accept the torch of his ministry. This verse-by-verse, 7- or 13-week study is part of Mastering the Basics.

Author: Coleman, Lyman, et al. **416**
Series: Serendipity Bible Study
Title: *1 & 2 Timothy & Titus: Learning to Thrive in a Hostile World*
Publisher: Serendipity House, 1989 ISBN: 1-88341-921-2

Num. Sess.	Group Time	Num. Pgs.	Avg. Qst.	Price	Audience	Format	Bible Study
16	60-90	64	Vary	$3.95	Beginner	Workbk	Book

Features: Intro to Study, Full Scrpt Printed
★★★ Personal Application Preparation Time: None
★★★ Relationship Building Ldr. Guide: No Size: 6.50 x 9.0
Subjects: Leadership, Money, Pastoral Epistles, Sexual Issues, Stress, 1 & 2 Timothy/Titus
Comments: This verse-by-verse, 6- or 9-week study of 1 Timothy, 6-week study of 2 Timothy, and 4-week study of Titus discusses biblical viewpoints on money, the opposite sex, pressure, leadership, excellence, spiritual disciplines, and staying on course. Three levels of discussion questions include "icebreakers," "digging deeper," and "reflection." Notes help participants with difficult words or passages.

Author: Coleman, William **417**
Series: SonPower Youth Sources
Title: *Being a Christian at School*
Publisher: Victor Books, 1994 ISBN: 1-56476-291-2

Num. Sess.	Group Time	Num. Pgs.	Avg. Qst.	Price	Audience	Format	Bible Study
6	60-75	67	Vary	$2.99	New Christian	Workbk	Topical

Features:
★★★★ Personal Application Preparation Time: None
★★★★ Relationship Building Ldr. Guide: Yes Size: 5.50 x 8.50
Subjects: Teens: Evangelism, Teens: Senior High
Comments: This study explores how youth can maintain a Christian witness and reach friends for Christ. Lessons deal with being lonely; being natural, up front, and standing up for beliefs; choosing between arrogance and pride or confidence and kindness; choosing the right friends without acting better than others, being obnoxious, condemning, and turning others off; and preparing solid foundations before being faced with temptation. Leader's guide, $4.99.

Author: Connelly, Douglas **418**
Series: LifeGuide Bible Study
Title: *Daniel: Spiritual Living in a Secular World*
Publisher: InterVarsity, 1986 ISBN: 0-83081-031-5

Num. Sess.	Group Time	Num. Pgs.	Avg. Qst.	Price	Audience	Format	Bible Study
12	45-60	63	11	$4.99	New Christian	Workbk	Book

Features: Intro to Leading a Study, Intro to Study, Ldr's Notes
★ Personal Application Preparation Time: Low
★ Relationship Building Ldr. Guide: No Size: 5.50 x 8.25
Subjects: Bible Personalities, Daniel, God, Major Prophets
Comments: This study is divided into 2 parts: Daniel 1–6 focuses on the life and character of Daniel as a "man" of God; Daniel 7–12 focuses on him as the "messenger" of God, and includes a series of visions given to Daniel for the Gentile nations and Israel. The study does not defend one particular prophetic system; rather, it uses Daniel to expand our understanding of God's program for the future of the world, and to promote trust in a Sovereign God for "our" future.

Author: Connelly, Douglas **419**
Series: LifeGuide Bible Study
Title: *John: The Way to True Life*
Publisher: InterVarsity, 1990 ISBN: 0-83081-006-4

Num. Sess.	Group Time	Num. Pgs.	Avg. Qst.	Price	Audience	Format	Bible Study
26	45-60	112	12	$4.99	Beginner	Workbk	Topical

Features: Intro to Leading a Study, Intro to Study, Ldr's Notes
★★★ Personal Application Preparation Time: Low
★★★ Relationship Building Ldr. Guide: No Size: 5.50 x 8.25
Subjects: Gospels, Jesus: Life/Teaching, John
Comments: This chapter-by-chapter study of John is divided into 2 parts: Jesus, the living Word of God; and Jesus, the living Way to God. John encourages a fresh look at Jesus. Leaders are motivated to introduce their groups to John's Gospel by comparing the 4 Gospels in regard to authorship, audience, purpose, and message. In this way, emphasis can be placed on John's unique contribution to an understanding of Jesus Christ.

Author: Connelly, Douglas **420**
Series: LifeGuide Bible Study
Title: *Meeting the Spirit*
Publisher: InterVarsity, 1993 ISBN: 0-83081-068-4

Num. Sess.	Group Time	Num. Pgs.	Avg. Qst.	Price	Audience	Format	Bible Study
12	45-60	61	12	$4.99	New Christian	Workbk	Topical

Features: Intro to Leading a Study, Intro to Study, Ldr's Notes
★★★ Personal Application Preparation Time: Low
★★ Relationship Building Ldr. Guide: No Size: 5.50 x 8.25
Subjects: Holy Spirit, Spiritual Gifts
Comments: This 12-week study examines critical questions such as: Who is the Holy Spirit? How does He change our lives? How does He work in the world? Key passages of Scripture teach participants the truths about the Spirit of God and what He is anxious to do in people's lives. Lessons include: meeting the Holy Spirit, the Spirit invades, speaks, renews, empowers, comforts, guides, liberates, equips, transforms, influences, and unifies.

Author: Consiglio, Dr. William **421**
Series:
Title: *Homosexual No More*
Publisher: Victor Books, 1991 ISBN: 0-89693-935-9

Num. Sess.	Group Time	Num. Pgs.	Avg. Qst.	Price	Audience	Format	Bible Study
11	90-105	200	N/A	$8.99	New Christian	Book	Topical

Features: Intro to Study, Bibliography, No Grp Discussion Quest, Glossary
★★ Personal Application Preparation Time: Med
★★ Relationship Building Ldr. Guide: No Size: 5.50 x 8.50
Subjects: Homosexuality, Self-help, Support, Men's Issues
Comments: This is a book for overcomers and for those who want to help them. Consiglio ministry to hundreds of Christian men struggling with homosexual thoughts, desires, or behavior is thoroughly biblical and follows an approach he calls "reorientation therapy." Through this program, overcomers deal with the blocked emotional development that diverted them from God's design.

Author: Cooper, Darien B. **422**
Series:
Title: *You Can Be the Wife of a Happy Husband*
Publisher: Victor Books, 1974 ISBN: 0-88207-711-2

Num. Sess.	Group Time	Num. Pgs.	Avg. Qst.	Price	Audience	Format	Bible Study
13	60-75	156	N/A	$8.99	New Christian	Book	Topical

Features: Intro to Study, Cassette Avail
★★★★ Personal Application Preparation Time: Low
★★★★ Relationship Building Ldr. Guide: Yes Size: 5.50 x 8.0
Subjects: Joy, Marriage, Women's Issues
Comments: This 13-week study reviews biblical principles for a lasting, happy marriage, and promotes a clear understanding of a wife's responsibility. Lesson titles include: "Accepting Your Husband as He Is"; "Helping Your Husband Love Himself"; and "How to Handle Problems and Trials." The joy of marriage can last "till death do us part."

Author: Cooper, Stuart **423**
Series:
Title: *A.D.*
Publisher: Gospel Films, 1985 ISBN: 1-55568-098-4

Num. Sess.	Group Time	Num. Pgs.	Avg. Qst.	Price	Audience	Format	Bible Study
12	60-75	N/A	Vary	$99.95	Beginner	Audio	Book

Features: Intro to Study, Appendix, Video Study Guide
★★★★ Personal Application Preparation Time: None
★★★★ Relationship Building Ldr. Guide: Yes Size: 0.0 x 0.0
Subjects: Acts, Bible Personalities, Bible Study, Evangelism, New Testament
Comments: The events of Acts come alive in this authentic epic covering the years A.D. 30–69. It's a good resource for churches or home groups wishing to study the New Testament times and the Book of Acts. It includes a 52-page study guide to a 12-week study. Filmed on location in Palestine, it stars Ben Vereen, Colleen Dewhurst, Ava Gardner, Susan Sarandon, Richard Roundtree, and Anthony Andrews.

Author: Cosgrove, Francis M., Jr. **424**
Series:
Title: *Essentials of Discipleship*
Publisher: Roper Press, 1989 ISBN: 0-86606-257-2

Num. Sess.	Group Time	Num. Pgs.	Avg. Qst.	Price	Audience	Format	Bible Study
12	60-90	96	22	$6.95	New Christian	Workbk	Topical

Features: Intro to Leading a Study, Prayer Helps, Scrpt Memory Helps
★★★★ Personal Application Preparation Time: Med
★★★★ Relationship Building Ldr. Guide: No Size: 5.25 x 8.50
Subjects: Discipleship
Comments: This study of the book by the same title helps participants experience the great adventure of living for Christ and realize the honor of being called His disciples. It provides practical projects and methods for achieving the goal. It explains how to experience Christ's Lordship, study the Bible, choose a church, enjoy true fellowship, memorize Scripture, and more.

Author: Cosgrove, Francis M., Jr. **425**
Series:
Title: *Essentials of New Life: What a New Christian Needs to Know*
Publisher: Roper Press, 1988 ISBN: 0-86606-258-0

Num. Sess.	Group Time	Num. Pgs.	Avg. Qst.	Price	Audience	Format	Bible Study
8	60-75	180	N/A	$6.95	New Christian	Book	Topical

Features: No Grp Discussion Quest, Charts, Index
★★★★ Personal Application Preparation Time: Low
★★ Relationship Building Ldr. Guide: Yes Size: 5.50 x 8.0
Subjects: Christian Life, Discipleship
Comments: This book was written as a resource for pastors and churches, to help them follow up with new converts, and support their growth in Christ. The necessities for this group study include: "Knowing You Have Eternal Life"; "The Importance of the Bible in Daily Life"; "How to Go About Learning Bible Truths"; and more. It can be most effectively used for a new Christian class with a closed format. New students should go from lesson 1 to 8 without interruptions.

Author: Cousins, Don & Judson Poling **426**
Series: Walking With God Series
Title: *Building Your Church: Using Your Gifts, Time and Resources*
Publisher: Zondervan, 1992 ISBN: 0-31059-183-X

Num. Sess.	Group Time	Num. Pgs.	Avg. Qst.	Price	Audience	Format	Bible Study
13	75-90	92	Vary	$4.99	New Christian	Workbk	Topical

Features: Intro to Study, Objectives, Prayer Helps, Scrpt Memory Helps, Follow Up
★★★★ Personal Application Preparation Time: Low
★★★★ Relationship Building Ldr. Guide: Yes Size: 6.25 x 9.25
Subjects: Church Life, Money, Service, Spiritual Gifts
Comments: Willow Creek Community Church developed this 6-book series to correspond to 4 aspects of a mature Christian who must walk with God, live the Word, contribute to the work, and impact the world. This fifth study in the series looks at the biblical view of a healthy church. It describes how to build up the body of Christ through serving and giving, with special attention given to spiritual gifts.

Author: Cousins, Don & Judson Poling 427
Series: Walking With God Series
Title: *Discovering the Church*
Publisher: Zondervan, 1992 ISBN: 0-31059-173-2

Num. Sess.	Group Time	Num. Pgs.	Avg. Qst.	Price	Audience	Format	Bible Study
12	75-90	63	Vary	$4.99	New Christian	Workbk	Topical

Features: Intro to Study, Objectives, Prayer Helps, Scrpt Memory Helps, Follow Up
★★★★ Personal Application Preparation Time: Low
★★★★ Relationship Building Ldr. Guide: Yes Size: 6.25 x 9.25
Subjects: Church Life, Service
Comments: Willow Creek Community Church developed this 6-book series to correspond to 4 aspects of a mature Christian who must walk with God, live the Word, contribute to the work, and impact the world. Fourth in the series, this combined with the fifth book reveals the biblical view of a healthy church. Participants learn how the church can impact their lives in profound ways.

Author: Cousins, Don & Judson Poling 428
Series: Walking With God Series
Title: *"Follow Me!" Walking with Jesus in Everyday Life*
Publisher: Zondervan, 1992 ISBN: 0-31059-163-5

Num. Sess.	Group Time	Num. Pgs.	Avg. Qst.	Price	Audience	Format	Bible Study
13	75-90	74	Vary	$4.99	New Christian	Workbk	Topical

Features: Intro to Study, Objectives, Prayer Helps, Scrpt Memory Helps, Follow Up
★★★★ Personal Application Preparation Time: Low
★★★★ Relationship Building Ldr. Guide: Yes Size: 6.25 x 9.25
Subjects: Jesus: Life/Teaching, Miracles, Parables, Prophecy
Comments: Willow Creek Community Church developed this 6-book series. Third in the series, this book completes a study of Christ that focuses on His Lordship, and closely examines His betrayal, death, and Resurrection. This contemporary approach responds to the questions: How does someone follow Jesus today? How does He affect our relationship, work, and finances?

Author: Cousins, Don & Judson Poling 429
Series: Walking With God Series
Title: *Friendship with God: Developing Intimacy with God*
Publisher: Zondervan, 1992 ISBN: 0-31059-143-0

Num. Sess.	Group Time	Num. Pgs.	Avg. Qst.	Price	Audience	Format	Bible Study
13	75-90	81	Vary	$4.99	New Christian	Workbk	Topical

Features: Intro to Study, Objectives, Prayer Helps, Scrpt Memory Helps, Follow Up
★★★★ Personal Application Preparation Time: Low
★★★★ Relationship Building Ldr. Guide: Yes Size: 6.25 x 9.25
Subjects: Holy Spirit, Prayer
Comments: Willow Creek Community Church developed this 6-book series to correspond to 4 aspects of a mature Christian who must walk with God, live the Word, contribute to the work, and impact the world. This study is the foundation for all other lessons in the series. Participants can discover the God who loves them in a fresh way, see how He has sought them out, and that He really desires to know them.

Author: Cousins, Don & Judson Poling 430
Series: Walking With God Series
Title: *Impacting Your World: Becoming a Person of Influence*
Publisher: Zondervan, 1992 ISBN: 0-31059-193-7

Num. Sess.	Group Time	Num. Pgs.	Avg. Qst.	Price	Audience	Format	Bible Study
12	75-90	85	Vary	$4.99	New Christian	Workbk	Topical

Features: Intro to Study, Objectives, Prayer Helps, Scrpt Memory Helps, Follow Up
★★★★ Personal Application Preparation Time: Low
★★★★ Relationship Building Ldr. Guide: Yes Size: 6.25 x 9.25
Subjects: Singles' Issues
Comments: Willow Creek Comunity Church developed this 6-book series to correspond to 4 aspects of a mature Christian who must walk with God, live the Word, contribute to the work, and impact the world. This book completes the series and provides practical helps for believers to share their stories of faith in Christ. Evangelism, put in perspective, becomes the natural result of a disciple's lifestyle.

Author: Cousins, Don & Judson Poling 431
Series: Walking With God Series
Title: *Incomparable Jesus, The: Experiencing the Power of Christ*
Publisher: Zondervan, 1992 ISBN: 0-31059-153-8

Num. Sess.	Group Time	Num. Pgs.	Avg. Qst.	Price	Audience	Format	Bible Study
13	75-90	79	Vary	$4.99	New Christian	Workbk	Topical

Features: Intro to Study, Objectives, Prayer Helps, Scrpt Memory Helps, Follow Up
★★★★ Personal Application Preparation Time: Low
★★★★ Relationship Building Ldr. Guide: Yes Size: 6.25 x 9.25
Subjects: Jesus: Life/Teaching, Miracles, Parables, Prophecy
Comments: Willow Creek Community Church developed this 6-book series. Second in the series, this lesson can be used with the next, *Follow Me!* as a 2-part study on the life of Christ. Through an inductive study of Matthew 1–15 and other material, participants can discover the wonder and majesty as well as the tenderness and compassion of Jesus.

Author: Cousins, Don & Judson Poling 432
Series: Walking With God Series
Title: *Leader's Guide 1: Friendship With God*
Publisher: Zondervan, 1992 ISBN: 0-31059-203-8

Num. Sess.	Group Time	Num. Pgs.	Avg. Qst.	Price	Audience	Format	Bible Study
39	—	330	N/A	$15.99		Book	

Features: Intro to Leading a Study, Intro to Study, Prayer Helps, Scrpt Memory Helps
Personal Application Preparation Time:
Relationship Building Ldr. Guide: Size: 6.25 x 9.25
Subjects: Leader's Guide
Comments: This leader's manual covers the first 3 guides in the Series: "Friendship With God"; "The Incomparable Jesus"; and "Follow Me!" The material in the student guides is reproduced in full, and leaders are also given additional background material, suggestions for building relationships, insights into group dynamics, and additional questions and projects that can add interest to the discussion.

Author: Cousins, Don & Judson Poling 433
Series: Walking With God Series
Title: *Leader's Guide 2: Discovering the Church*
Publisher: Zondervan, 1992 ISBN: 0-31059-213-5

Num. Sess.	Group Time	Num. Pgs.	Avg. Qst.	Price	Audience	Format	Bible Study
	—	300	N/A	$19.99			

Features:
Personal Application Preparation Time:
Relationship Building Ldr. Guide: Size: 6.25 x 9.25
Subjects: Leader's Guide
Comments: This leader's manual covers the second 3 guides in the Willow Creek series: *Discovering the Church, Building Your Church,* and *Impacting Your World.* The material in the students' guides is reproduced in full. But the leader is also given additional background material, suggestions for building relationships, insights into group dynamics, and additional questions and projects that can add interest to the discussion.

Author: Coyle, Neva 434
Series: Free to Be Thin
Title: *Abiding: Honesty in Relationship*
Publisher: Bethany House, 1980 ISBN: 0-87123-411-4

Num. Sess.	Group Time	Num. Pgs.	Avg. Qst.	Price	Audience	Format	Bible Study
8	60-90	48	Vary	$3.99	New Christian	Workbk	Topical

Features: Intro to Study, No Grp Discussion Quest, Cassette Avail
★★★ Personal Application Preparation Time: Med
★ Relationship Building Ldr. Guide: No Size: 5.50 x 8.50
Subjects: Self-help, Support, Victorious Living
Comments: Study number 3 in this series, dealing with the scriptural concept of "abiding," helps participants come to a new understanding of the unique relationship God offers His children. The lessons cover affliction and oppression, crying unto the Lord, truth, relationships, and victory. The study sequence of basic journal sheets—a guide for your daily quiet time, Bible lesson, and tape—allows the fullest understanding.

Author: Coyle, Neva 435
Series: Free to Be Thin
Title: *Diligence: Temples Under Construction*
Publisher: Bethany House, 1982 ISBN: 0-87123-408-4

Num. Sess.	Group Time	Num. Pgs.	Avg. Qst.	Price	Audience	Format	Bible Study
8	60-90	38	Vary	$3.99	New Christian	Workbk	Topical

Features: No Grp Discussion Quest, Cassette Avail
★★★ Personal Application Preparation Time: Med
★ Relationship Building Ldr. Guide: No Size: 5.50 x 8.50
Subjects: Self-help, Support, Victorious Living
Comments: Study number 5 in this series is designed to reinforce participants' effort; this is not the time to quit, it's the time to be diligent. A review of previous principles helps users evaluate current progress and chart future steps. The study sequence for this lesson is reversed, with tape first, then the study and assignments. Key Scriptures are Ezra 6:3 ("Let the temple be rebuilt") and Ezra 6:12 ("Let it be carried out with diligence").

Author: Coyle, Neva 436
Series: Free to Be Thin
Title: *Freedom: Escape from the Ordinary*
Publisher: Bethany House, 1980 ISBN: 0-87123-410-6

Num. Sess.	Group Time	Num. Pgs.	Avg. Qst.	Price	Audience	Format	Bible Study
6	60-90	47	Vary	$3.99	New Christian	Workbk	Topical

Features: Intro to Study, No Grp Discussion Quest, Cassette Avail
★★★ Personal Application Preparation Time: Med
★ Relationship Building Ldr. Guide: No Size: 5.50 x 8.50
Subjects: Self-help, Support, Victorious Living
Comments: Study number 4 in this series helps participants understand how to deal with temptation, and even be strengthened by it. It examines 1 Corinthians 10:13 from several perspectives. A study sequence of basic journal sheets—guides for daily quiet time, Bible lesson, and tape—allows fullest understanding. A calorie account sheet is also included.

Author: Coyle, Neva 437
Series: Free to Be Thin
Title: *Free to Be Thin—Study Guide No. 2—Discipline*
Publisher: Bethany House, 1980 ISBN: 0-87123-169-7

Num. Sess.	Group Time	Num. Pgs.	Avg. Qst.	Price	Audience	Format	Bible Study
5	60-90	31	Vary	$3.99	New Christian	Workbk	Topical

Features: No Grp Discussion Quest, Follow Up, Cassette Avail
★★★ Personal Application Preparation Time: Med
★ Relationship Building Ldr. Guide: No Size: 5.50 x 8.50
Subjects: Addictions, Self-help, Support, Victorious Living
Comments: This study, second in a series of eight, concerns leading disciplined lives and accomplishing God's work. This lesson covers spiritual exercise, God's provision for endurance, discipline, and correction, and includes ten principles to help achieve the goal. A sample calorie account sheet is also included.

Author: Coyle, Neva 438
Series: Free to Be Thin
Title: *Free to Be Thin—Study Guide No. 1—Getting Started*
Publisher: Bethany House, 1980 ISBN: 0-87123-163-8

Num. Sess.	Group Time	Num. Pgs.	Avg. Qst.	Price	Audience	Format	Bible Study
7	60-90	61	Vary	$4.99	New Christian	Workbk	Topical

Features: Intro to Study, Objectives, No Grp Discussion Quest, Follow Up, Cassette Avail
★★★ Personal Application Preparation Time: Med
★ Relationship Building Ldr. Guide: No Size: 5.50 x 8.50
Subjects: Addictions, Self-help, Support, Victorious Living
Comments: This study, a weight-loss plan that links how to eat with how to live, can be used with the book *Free to Be Thin* and/or with the tape series of the same name. The lessons include basic journal sheets with a Scripture for the day, a brief Bible study, and tape. Establishing discipline is a goal of this first study, which includes recommended diet guidelines and food facts.

Author: Coyle, Neva 439
Series: Free to Be Thin
Title: *Obedience: Developing a Listening Heart*
Publisher: Bethany House, 1980 ISBN: 0-87123-409-2

Num. Sess.	Group Time	Num. Pgs.	Avg. Qst.	Price	Audience	Format	Bible Study
7	60-90	59	Vary	$3.99	New Christian	Workbk	Topical

Features: Prayer Helps, No Grp Discussion Quest, Cassette Avail
★★★ Personal Application Preparation Time: Med
★ Relationship Building Ldr. Guide: No Size: 5.50 x 8.50
Subjects: Obedience, Self-help, Support, Victorious Living
Comments: Study 6 in this series helps participants develop a listening heart. It issues a call for obedience, which allows complete freedom from lists, guidelines, and fear, and requires listening intently to the Lord. Two principal lessons cover "The Covenant Relationship" and "Fasting." The study sequence is basic journal sheets, then Bible study and a tape.

Author: Coyle, Neva 440
Series: Free to Be Thin
Title: *Perseverance: For People Under Pressure*
Publisher: Bethany House, 1986 ISBN: 0-87123-888-8

Num. Sess.	Group Time	Num. Pgs.	Avg. Qst.	Price	Audience	Format	Bible Study
6	60-90	57	Vary	$3.99	New Christian	Workbk	Topical

Features: Intro to Study, No Grp Discussion Quest, Cassette Avail
★★★ Personal Application Preparation Time: Med
★ Relationship Building Ldr. Guide: No Size: 5.50 x 8.50
Subjects: Self-help, Stress, Support, Victorious Living
Comments: Study 8 from this series is designed for those who are tempted to quit, who simply are tired of resisting the enemy, overcoming temptation, and disciplining their bodies and minds. Lessons reflect the author's personal trials and pressures and candidly reveal how God uses them to shape a believer's life. "Formula for Crisis," "The Fall," "This Is Only a Test," "Perseverance," "The Perfect Me," and "Wanting Nothing" are lesson titles.

Author: Coyle, Neva 441
Series: Free to Be Thin
Title: *Restoration: Discovering What Takes Place Between Return and Restore*
Publisher: Bethany House, 1985 ISBN: 0-87123-851-9

Num. Sess.	Group Time	Num. Pgs.	Avg. Qst.	Price	Audience	Format	Bible Study
6	60-90	61	Vary	$3.99	New Christian	Workbk	Topical

Features: Intro to Study, Scrpt Memory Helps, No Grp Discussion Quest, Cassette Avail
★★★ Personal Application Preparation Time: Med
★ Relationship Building Ldr. Guide: No Size: 5.50 x 8.50
Subjects: Renewal, Self-help, Support, Victorious Living
Comments: Study 7 in this series is designed to help participants who may have faltered in their spiritual life or commitment get back on track. Lessons cover return, readiness, relief, rest, renewal, and restoration. A restoration goal planner is included. The study sequence follows basic journal sheets, then Bible study and includes a tape.

Author: Crabb, Dr. Larry 442
Series:
Title: *Inside Out Video*
Publisher: NavPress, 1987 ISBN: 9-90073-592-7

Num. Sess.	Group Time	Num. Pgs.	Avg. Qst.	Price	Audience	Format	Bible Study
4	60-75	N/A	N/A	$79.00	Beginner	Video	Topical

Features: Video Study Guide
★★★★ Personal Application Preparation Time: Low
★★ Relationship Building Ldr. Guide: No Size: 10.50 x 12.50
Subjects: Counseling, Emotions, Psychology, Relationships
Comments: This 4-part lecture video series helps participants experience real change, by exploring what it takes to live life with deeper honesty, humility, and freedom. Each video contains one approximately 45" session. Video titles are: "Don't Look Inside Me, I'm Not Sure I Like What's There"; and "I Don't Want to Admit It, but I Know Something's Wrong." The take-home guide is simply a tool to help participants reflect on the video series; it's not a study guide.

Author: Crabb, Dr. Larry 443
Series:
Title: *Inside Out*
Publisher: NavPress, 1988 ISBN: 0-89109-281-1

Num. Sess.	Group Time	Num. Pgs.	Avg. Qst.	Price	Audience	Format	Bible Study
12	60-90	107	17	$6.00	New Christian	Workbk	Topical

Features: Intro to Leading a Study, Digging Deeper Quest, Charts
★★★★ Personal Application Preparation Time: Med
★★ Relationship Building Ldr. Guide: No Size: 5.50 x 8.50
Subjects: Counseling, Emotions, Psychology, Relationships
Comments: This study, a companion to the book *Inside Out,* will help participants move toward a relationship with Christ and others that will bring the richest life possible. Each lesson is divided into five sections: an excerpt from the book that highlights the major point; "Looking Inside," a reflection on the excerpt; "Identifying the Problem," a deeper look at the point; "Exploring Relationships"; and "Moving Toward Change," the wrap-up.

Author: Crabb, Dr. Larry 444
Series: IBC Discussion Guide
Title: *Who We Are & How We Relate*
Publisher: NavPress, 1992 ISBN: 0-89109-694-9

Num. Sess.	Group Time	Num. Pgs.	Avg. Qst.	Price	Audience	Format	Bible Study
6	—	87	N/A	$7.00			No

Features:
Personal Application Preparation Time:
Relationship Building Ldr. Guide: Size: 5.25 x 8.25
Subjects: Counseling, Relationships, Small Group Resource, Support
Comments: This book is written for use with the Institute of Biblical Counseling series. Each seeks to identify how the "struggle" affects the way participants relate to themselves, others, and God. Topics covered in this title are: "People are Relational, Not Mechanical"; "People are Passionate, Not Merely Dutiful"; "People are Thoughtful, Not Driven"; "People are Purposeful Not Reactive"; and "People are Selfish Not Giving."

Author: Crabtree, Jack 445
Series:
Title: *Play It Safe: Keeping Your Kids and Youth Ministry Alive*
Publisher: Victor Books, 1993 ISBN: 1-56476-110-X

Num. Sess.	Group Time	Num. Pgs.	Avg. Qst.	Price	Audience	Format	Bible Study
	—	220	N/A	$9.99			

Features: Intro to Leading a Study
Personal Application Preparation Time:
Relationship Building Ldr. Guide: Size: 6.0 x 9.0
Subjects: Teens: Resources
Comments: This book dispenses timely and sensible advice for youth leaders who want to avoid mishaps caused by haphazard planning and poor judgment. It covers a wide range of subjects, including insurance coverage, screening and training potential counselors, vehicle safety, camping and water sports, "high risk" events like rock climbing and biking, and what to do when the worst does happen.

Author: Curtis, Brent 446
Series: IBC Discussion Guide
Title: *Guilt*
Publisher: NavPress, 1992 ISBN: 0-89109-692-2

Num. Sess.	Group Time	Num. Pgs.	Avg. Qst.	Price	Audience	Format	Bible Study
6	60-90	70	9	$5.00	Beginner	Workbk	Topical

Features: Intro to Leading a Study, Intro to Study, Prayer Helps, Follow Up, Ldr's Notes
★★★★ Personal Application Preparation Time: None
★★★★ Relationship Building Ldr. Guide: No Size: 5.25 x 8.25
Subjects: Counseling, Guilt, Support
Comments: "Guilt" is 1 of 6 studies that identify how life struggles affect the way participants relate to themselves, others, and God. Six lessons explore how one can escape from performance-induced guilt, including: how to distinguish true guilt from false guilt, how guilt is related to shame, how guilt functions and shapes one's perceptions, and how to take steps that free one from false guilt.

Author: Cuthbertson, Dr. Duane 447
Series:
Title: *Raising Your Child, Not Your Voice*
Publisher: Victor Books, 1986 ISBN: 0-89693-342-3

Num. Sess.	Group Time	Num. Pgs.	Avg. Qst.	Price	Audience	Format	Bible Study
13	60-75	138	N/A	$8.99	New Christian	Book	Topical

Features: Intro to Study
★★★★ Personal Application Preparation Time: Low
★★★★ Relationship Building Ldr. Guide: Yes Size: 5.50 x 8.0
Subjects: Family, Parenting
Comments: This 13-week study introduces participants to assertive Scriptural parenting, offering ways to "train up" children without breaking their spirits or their parents' vocal cords. A temperament analysis test allows participants to discover their parenting style as well as their child's "bent." They will learn how to discipline in a way that fits both personalities. One lesson provides 8 steps to a changed heart, based on the fourth chapter of James.

Author: Cutler, William & Richard Peace 448
Series: Serendipity Support Group
Title: *Blended Families: Yours, Mine, Ours*
Publisher: Serendipity House, 1990 ISBN: 1-88341-956-5

Num. Sess.	Group Time	Num. Pgs.	Avg. Qst.	Price	Audience	Format	Bible Study
14	60-90	80	12	$5.45	Beginner	Workbk	Topical

Features: Intro to Leading a Study, Objectives, Bibliography, Prayer Helps, Full Scrpt Printed, Ldr's Notes, Cartoons, Agenda
★★★★ Personal Application Preparation Time: Low
★★★★ Relationship Building Ldr. Guide: No Size: 6.50 x 9.0
Subjects: Family, Marriage, Support
Comments: This study offers Old and New Testament insights on blended families. Lessons include "The Phenomenon Called Blended Families," "Stepfamilies vs. First Families," "The Children," "The 'Ex' Factor," "The Stretching, Straining Family Ties," "Nurturing the Marriage," and "Finding Inner Strength." Case studies, personal reflection, and biblical passages help participants deal with the stepparent issues.

Author: Cutler, William & Richard Peace 449
Series: Serendipity Support Group
Title: *Dealing with Grief & Loss: Hope in the Midst of Pain*
Publisher: Serendipity House, 1990 ISBN: 1-88341-958-1

Num. Sess.	Group Time	Num. Pgs.	Avg. Qst.	Price	Audience	Format	Bible Study
14	60-90	80	9	$5.45	Beginner	Workbk	Topical

Features: Intro to Leading a Study, Intro to Study, Objectives, Bibliography, Prayer Helps, Full Scrpt Printed, Ldr's Notes, Cartoons, Agenda
★★★★ Personal Application Preparation Time: None
★★★★ Relationship Building Ldr. Guide: No Size: 6.50 x 9.0
Subjects: Divorce, Emotions, Grief, Hope, Suffering, Support, Work
Comments: This study, which deals with grief and loss, is based on shared feelings. Death, divorce, unemployment, failed expectations, severe injury, and major illness are discussed as experiences that bring pain. The many sources of grief and loss vary from person to person, but the feelings experienced are similar: shock, denial, anger, depression, and bargaining.

Author: Cutler, William 450
Series: Serendipity Support Group
Title: *Golden Years: Riding the Crest*
Publisher: Serendipity House, 1990 ISBN: 1-88341-967-0

Num. Sess.	Group Time	Num. Pgs.	Avg. Qst.	Price	Audience	Format	Bible Study
7	60-90	128	12	$5.45	Beginner	Workbk	Topical

Features: Intro to Leading a Study, Objectives, Bibliography, Prayer Helps, Full Scrpt Printed, Ldr's Notes, Cartoons, Agenda
★★★★ Personal Application Preparation Time: None
★★★★ Relationship Building Ldr. Guide: No Size: 6.50 x 9.0
Subjects: Aging, Senior Adults
Comments: This study is for anyone who is retired or about to retire. It discusses opportunities for senior citizens, experiences of post-retirement, difficulties of aging, health, friends, faith in Christ, and the life to come. The format includes icebreakers, Bible study and prayer. Timelines are provided. It can be adapted for a 7 or 14 week study.

Author: Cutler, William & Richard Peace 451
Series: Serendipity Support Group
Title: *Parenting Adolescents: Easing the Way to Adulthood*
Publisher: Serendipity House, 1990 ISBN: 1-88341-959-X

Num. Sess.	Group Time	Num. Pgs.	Avg. Qst.	Price	Audience	Format	Bible Study
14	60-90	80	10	$5.45	Beginner	Workbk	Topical

Features: Intro to Leading a Study, Objectives, Bibliography, Prayer Helps, Full Scrpt Printed, Ldr's Notes, Cartoons, Agenda
★★★★ Personal Application Preparation Time: None
★★★★ Relationship Building Ldr. Guide: No Size: 6.50 x 9.0
Subjects: Faith, Parenting, Self-esteem, Support
Comments: This study uses New Testament Scriptures to address issues concerning teenagers, who are neither kids nor adults. Helpful lessons include communicating love, nurturing self-esteem, dealing with crises, and passing on the faith. Paul's ministry is examined as a model for parenting, as Paul was a "parent" to congregations he founded.

Author: Cutler, William 452
Series: Serendipity Support Group
Title: *Single Parents: Flying Solo*
Publisher: Serendipity House, 1991 ISBN: 1-88341-969-7

Num. Sess.	Group Time	Num. Pgs.	Avg. Qst.	Price	Audience	Format	Bible Study
7	60-90	96	Vary	$5.45	Beginner	Workbk	Topical

Features: Intro to Leading a Study, Objectives, Bibliography, Prayer Helps, Full Scrpt Printed, Ldr's Notes, Drawings, Cartoons, Agenda
★★★★ Personal Application Preparation Time: None
★★★★ Relationship Building Ldr. Guide: No Size: 6.50 x 9.25
Subjects: Parenting, Singles' Issues, Work
Comments: This study on single parenting is based on shared life experiences, which can be the foundation of a support group. Issues include the following: suddenly being single; being a single working parent; dealing with an ex-spouse; creating a healthy home; embracing singleness; and developing inner strength. Derived from Scriptures in Genesis and selected New Testament books.

Author: Damon, Roberta McBride 453
Series: Leadership Skills For Women
Title: *Relationship Skills*
Publisher: New Hope, 1993 ISBN: 1-56309-082-1

Num. Sess.	Group Time	Num. Pgs.	Avg. Qst.	Price	Audience	Format	Bible Study
5	45-60	68	Vary	$5.95	New Christian	Book	Topical

Features: Intro to Study
★★★★ Personal Application Preparation Time: Low
★★ Relationship Building Ldr. Guide: No Size: 5.50 x 8.50
Subjects: Leadership, Psychology, Relationships, Women's Issues
Comments: One of 5 books in the Leadership Skills for Women series, this book offers women an opportunity to look closely at relationships with themselves, family and friends, and with God. Lessons show participants characteristics of healthy relationships, the development of relationships, and what to expect from them. Participants discover how to profile themselves, evaluate current relationships, and take a look at Mary and Martha who provide lessons in teamwork.

Author: Davis, Lindsey 454
Series: Bible Study for Christian
Title: *2 Corinthians—Volumes 1 & 2*
Publisher: Cokesbury, 1989 ISBN: 0-68776-142-5

Num. Sess.	Group Time	Num. Pgs.	Avg. Qst.	Price	Audience	Format	Bible Study
6	45-60	N/A	Vary	$25.00	New Christian	Video	Book

Features: Intro to Leading a Study, Intro to Study, Video Study Guide
★★★ Personal Application Preparation Time: Low
★★★ Relationship Building Ldr. Guide: Yes Size: 4.75 x 8.0
Subjects: Accountability, Church Life, Hope, Integrity, Obedience, Repentance, Service, Suffering, 2 Corinthians
Comments: This 2-volume video lecture series includes 6 20″ lessons on Paul's second letter to the Corinthian Christians. The apostle, convinced he had been forthright and consistent in his dealings with them, made a final appeal for self-correction, for loyal submission to rightful authority, and for members of the divided church to work together for the common good.

Author: Davis, Tammy Fann 455
Series:
Title: *Sharing God's Greatest Gift*
Publisher: New Hope, 1992 ISBN: 1-56309-059-7

Num. Sess.	Group Time	Num. Pgs.	Avg. Qst.	Price	Audience	Format	Bible Study
4	45-60	50	5	$4.95	New Christian	Book	Topical

Features: Scrpt Memory Helps, Persnl Study Quest
★★★ Personal Application Preparation Time: Low
★★ Relationship Building Ldr. Guide: No Size: 5.50 x 8.50
Subjects: Relationships, Singles' Issues
Comments: This guide provides instructions on becoming a dynamic witness, and includes practical tips on topics such as having a healthy self-image, developing a personal testimony, creating a witnessing style, recognizing witnessing opportunities, building witness relationships, and guiding a witness encounter. Questions at the end of each chapter enhance the reading. A group study plan is included. It can be completed in 4 1-hour sessions; or taught in 12 segments.

Author: Dean, Jennifer Kennedy 456
Series:
Title: *Heart's Cry: Principles of Prayer*
Publisher: New Hope, 1992 ISBN: 1-56309-047-3

Num. Sess.	Group Time	Num. Pgs.	Avg. Qst.	Price	Audience	Format	Bible Study
12	30-45	116	Vary	$6.95	New Christian	Book	Topical

Features: Ldr's Notes
★★★ Personal Application Preparation Time: Low
★★ Relationship Building Ldr. Guide: No Size: 5.50 x 8.50
Subjects: Prayer
Comments: As participants explore such biblical imperatives as "Delight in the Lord"; "Pray without Ceasing"; "Pray in the Spirit"; "Stand in the Gap"; "Ask . . . Seek . . . Knock"; "Be Still and Know"; they'll discover new insights into the principles of confession, intercession, contemplation, praying Scripture, and thanksgiving. Written for a 2½-hour session this study can be adapted for 12 30″ home or office study sessions.

Author: Dean, Jennifer Kennedy 457
Series:
Title: *Praying Life, The: Living Beyond Your Limits*
Publisher: New Hope, 1993 ISBN: 1-56309-091-0

Num. Sess.	Group Time	Num. Pgs.	Avg. Qst.	Price	Audience	Format	Bible Study
4	75-90	96	8	$7.95	New Christian	Book	Topical

Features: Intro to Study, Prayer Helps, Drawings, Charts
★★★ Personal Application Preparation Time: Med
★ Relationship Building Ldr. Guide: No Size: 5.50 x 8.50
Subjects: Christian Life, Prayer
Comments: This book describes the author's quest to know how to pray, and positions prayer as the driving force of a Christian's life. Its 4 sections cover the purpose, process, promise, and practice of prayer. Specifics deal with its definition, necessity and author; and its requirements, results, times, and forms. Each section closes with a series of review questions. It's not written for a group Bible study, but can be adapted.

Author: DeBoar, Jeanlyn 458
Series: Bible Alive Studies
Title: *Bringing the Gospels to Life*
Publisher: David C. Cook Publishing Co., 1993 ISBN: 0-78145-019-5

Num. Sess.	Group Time	Num. Pgs.	Avg. Qst.	Price	Audience	Format	Bible Study
13	45-60	144	Vary	$19.95	Beginner	Workbk	Book

Features: Intro to Study, Bibliography, Prayer Helps, Drawings, Handouts, Persnl Study Quest, Charts
★★★★ Personal Application Preparation Time: None
★★ Relationship Building Ldr. Guide: Yes Size: 8.50 x 11.0
Subjects: God, Gospels, Jesus: Life/Teaching
Comments: This complete leader's guide provides an overview of the Gospels for adults of all ages. It answers questions such as: "How could Jesus be both God and human?" "Why do the Gospels differ?" "What's the point of parables?" "Is faith in Christ still relevant?" and "What difference does Christ's death make?" The format provides everything needed for 13 complete sessions. Reproducible handouts.

Author: Delffs, Dudley J. 459
Series: Thinking Through Disciple
Title: *How People Change*
Publisher: NavPress, 1993 ISBN: 0-89109-737-6

Num. Sess.	Group Time	Num. Pgs.	Avg. Qst.	Price	Audience	Format	Bible Study
8	60-75	80	13	$5.00	New Christian	Workbk	Topical

Features: Bibliography, Prayer Helps, Follow Up, Ldr's Notes
★★★★ Personal Application Preparation Time: None
★★★ Relationship Building Ldr. Guide: No Size: 5.50 x 8.50
Subjects: Relationships
Comments: This study, 1 of 4 in a series, provides a look at what it means to follow Christ in modern culture. Eight lessons explore factors that contribute to authentic inner change. Participants look at how their views of God are formed, God's love and acceptance, His desire for inner rather than outer change, the Holy Spirit's involvement in change, the role of the community of believers in true change, and their part in maintaining ongoing relationships with God.

Author: Delffs, Dudley J. 460
Series: Thinking Through Discipleship
Title: *Improving Your Relationships*
Publisher: NavPress, 1993 ISBN: 0-89109-738-4

Num. Sess.	Group Time	Num. Pgs.	Avg. Qst.	Price	Audience	Format	Bible Study
8	60-75	80	10	$5.00	New Christian	Workbk	Topical

Features: Prayer Helps, Scrpt Memory Helps, Follow Up, Ldr's Notes
★★★★ Personal Application Preparation Time: None
★★★ Relationship Building Ldr. Guide: No Size: 5.50 x 8.50
Subjects: Relationships
Comments: This study, 1 of 4 in a series, provides a look at what it means to follow Christ in modern culture. Eight lessons explore what makes risk possible, what honesty is and isn't, what it means to love both neighbors and enemies, what intimacy is and how it nourishes, and why examining the heart (rather than skill training) is essential for effective communication. Leader's notes are in the margin of this study.

Author: Dettoni, John M. 461
Series: GroupBuilder Resources
Title: *Down From the Ivory Tower*
Publisher: Victor Books, 1994 ISBN: 1-56476-323-4

Num. Sess.	Group Time	Num. Pgs.	Avg. Qst.	Price	Audience	Format	Bible Study
8	75-90	144	Vary	$5.99	New Christian	Workbk	Book

Features: Intro to Leading a Study, Intro to Study, Objectives, Prayer Helps, Digging Deeper Quest, Follow Up, Full Scrpt Printed, Ldr's Notes, Cartoons, Persnl Study Quest, Charts
★★★★ Personal Application Preparation Time: Low
★★★★ Relationship Building Ldr. Guide: No Size: 6.0 x 9.0
Subjects: Romans, Theology
Comments: Participants studying 8 sessions from Romans 1–8 can learn how to build a livable theology that answers "so what?" questions of life. Session titles include: "Living by Faith"; "First the Bad News"; "Guilty or Not Guilty"; "Model Students"; "Peace and Joy in Life's Ups and Downs"; "New Life"; and "Never Abandoned; and Always Loved."

Author: Dettoni, John M. 462
Series: GroupBuilder Resources
Title: *Open to Closeness*
Publisher: Victor Books, 1991 ISBN: 0-89693-881-6

Num. Sess.	Group Time	Num. Pgs.	Avg. Qst.	Price	Audience	Format	Bible Study
8	75-90	144	Vary	$5.99	New Christian	Workbk	Topical

Features: Intro to Leading a Study, Objectives, Digging Deeper Quest, Follow Up, Full Scrpt Printed, Ldr's Notes, Cartoons, Persnl Study Quest
★★★★ Personal Application Preparation Time: Low
★★★★ Relationship Building Ldr. Guide: No Size: 6.0 x 9.0
Subjects: Holiness, Joy, Philippians, Relationships, Victorious Living
Comments: This study helps small groups learn about and practice building close, warm relationships as they study eight aspects of biblical intimacy found in the Book of Philippians. Sessions deal with such topics as communicating affection, like-mindedness, Jesus' attitude of humility, mending relationships, holy thoughts and actions, and the gift of intimacy. Includes optional activities and hints for leaders.

Author: DeWindt, Joan **463**
Series: Discover Your Bible
Title: *Discover: Christmas*
Publisher: Church Development Resources, 1994

Num. Sess.	Group Time	Num. Pgs.	Avg. Qst.	Price	Audience	Format	Bible Study
4	60-75	46	5	$1.00	Beginner	Workbk	Topical

Features: Intro to Study, Glossary
★★★★ Personal Application Preparation Time: None
★★ Relationship Building Ldr. Guide: Yes Size: 5.50 x 8.50
Subjects: Jesus: Life/Teaching
Comments: In this study participants discover God's unfolding plan for Christmas over the centuries, and are challenged to decide what they believe Christmas is all about.

Author: Dickinson, Dr. Richard W. **464**
Series: The Recovery Bookshelf
Title: *Child In Each of Us Workbook, The*
Publisher: Victor Books, 1992 ISBN: 1-56476-026-X

Num. Sess.	Group Time	Num. Pgs.	Avg. Qst.	Price	Audience	Format	Bible Study
11	90-120	280	N/A	$15.99	Beginner	Workbk	Topical

Features: Intro to Study, Bibliography, Prayer Helps, Scrpt Memory Helps, Persnl Study Quest, Appendix, Book Incl
★★★★ Personal Application Preparation Time: Med
★★ Relationship Building Ldr. Guide: No Size: 7.50 x 9.50
Subjects: Self-esteem, Self-help, Support
Comments: Modern Christians struggle with feelings of loneliness, fear, insecurity, and shame. Often this unresolved pain manifests itself in "over-extended" patterns of living. They overwork, overeat, overcommit, overspend, over-spiritualize, and over-obsess about love and sex. This workbook is designed to help Christians regain a sense of balance. Includes the full text of the book and encourages journaling.

Author: Dickinson, Dr. Richard W. **465**
Series: The Recovery Bookshelf
Title: *Child In Each of Us, The*
Publisher: Victor Books, 1991 ISBN: 0-89693-937-5

Num. Sess.	Group Time	Num. Pgs.	Avg. Qst.	Price	Audience	Format	Bible Study
10	90-120	180	N/A	$8.99	Beginner	Book	Topical

Features: Intro to Study, Persnl Study Quest
★★★★ Personal Application Preparation Time: Med
★★ Relationship Building Ldr. Guide: Yes Size: 5.50 x 8.0
Subjects: Self-esteem, Self-help, Support
Comments: In this book, readers embark on a journey to: heal the wounds of childhood, break the cycle of negative thoughts and actions, recover a sense of self-esteem in Christ, change destructive patterns in parenting, feel a freedom and aliveness not felt in a long time. This study is for people seeking to improve their relationships with mates, families, friends, and even with God Himself. It's for an inner child that needs nurturing.

Author: Dieterich, Henry **466**
Series: Catholic Bible Study Guide
Title: *Faith: A Guide to Following God*
Publisher: Servant Publications, 1988 ISBN: 0-89283-356-4

Num. Sess.	Group Time	Num. Pgs.	Avg. Qst.	Price	Audience	Format	Bible Study
9	60-75	76	5	$5.99	Beginner	Workbk	Topical

Features: Intro to Study, Scrpt Memory Helps, Summary, Charts
★★★ Personal Application Preparation Time: Low
★ Relationship Building Ldr. Guide: No Size: 5.0 x 8.0
Subjects: Christian Living, Faith, God
Comments: This nine-part study discusses what the Bible says about faith: what it is, how it affects believers, and how to have more of it. This easy-to-use guide introduces a few pertinent questions, and provides a basis for beginning a life of faith or growing in faith. Its format includes Scripture texts, commentary, questions, exercises for in-depth study, and tips for Christian living.

Author: Dinnan, Anne, et al. **467**
Series: Discovery Series
Title: *Who Am I?*
Publisher: David C. Cook Publishing Co., 1994 ISBN: 0-78145-134-5

Num. Sess.	Group Time	Num. Pgs.	Avg. Qst.	Price	Audience	Format	Bible Study
15	60-90	144	15	$9.95	Beginner	Workbk	Topical

Features: Intro to Study, Prayer Helps, Worship Helps, Study Overview, Pre-discussion Quest, Full Scrpt Printed, Cartoons, Persnl Study Quest
★★★★ Personal Application Preparation Time: Med
★★★★ Relationship Building Ldr. Guide: Yes Size: 7.25 x 9.25
Subjects: Teens: Self-esteem, Teens: Senior High, Teens:Spiritual Gift
Comments: This study challenges youth to push their walk with God to the limit, seek His best, and be nothing but their best for Him. Youth will discover their personal worth by focusing on the following questions: What am I doing here? What's my purpose in life? Do I really matter? and Does anybody really care? The studies begin with an activity or story and include some Scripture.

Author: Dobson, Dr. James C. and Gary L. Bauer **468**
Series:
Title: *Children At Risk*
Publisher: Word, 1991 ISBN: 0-84998-030-5

Num. Sess.	Group Time	Num. Pgs.	Avg. Qst.	Price	Audience	Format	Bible Study
3	75-90	N/A	7	$129.95	Beginner	Video	Topical

Features: Intro to Leading a Study, Appendix, Publicity Ideas
★★★★ Personal Application Preparation Time: None
★★★★ Relationship Building Ldr. Guide: No Size: 11.0 x 12.50
Subjects: Parenting, Social Issues
Comments: In this video series, Dobson and Bauer spell the dangers of a secular humanistic worldview, as well as strategies for winning the battle for the hearts and minds of modern children. Areas discussed include the unraveling of culture, secular humanists' primary strategy of driving a wedge between parents and children, adolescent sexuality, issues of life or death (abortion, euthanasia, and infanticide), and a 4-point plan to rebuild America.

Author: Dobson, Dr. James C. 469
Series:
Title: *Life On The Edge: Preparing for the Challenges of Adulthood*
Publisher: Word, 1993 ISBN: 0-84998-037-2

Num. Sess.	Group Time	Num. Pgs.	Avg. Qst.	Price	Audience	Format	Bible Study
7	60-90	N/A	7	$139.99	New Christian	Video	Topical

Features: Intro to Leading a Study, Objectives, Prayer Helps, Handouts, Agenda, Book Incl
★★★★ Personal Application Preparation Time: None
★★★★ Relationship Building Ldr. Guide: No Size: 10.75 x 12.0
Subjects: Teens: Decisions, Teens: Peer Pressure, Teens: Relationships, Teens: Values, Youth Life
Comments: In this video, Dr. Dobson talks heart-to-heart with teens entering adulthood. He tackles misguided thinking about respect, love, safe sex, God's will, emotions, and lifestyle choices. Viewers learn how to develop lasting relationships, stand up against peer pressure, and discover God's desire for their lives.

Author: Dobson, Dr. James C. 470
Series: LifeTopics
Title: *Love for a LifeTime*
Publisher: David C. Cook Publishing Co., 1992 ISBN: 1-55513-572-2

Num. Sess.	Group Time	Num. Pgs.	Avg. Qst.	Price	Audience	Format	Bible Study
13	45-60	144	Vary	$19.95	Beginner	Workbk	Topical

Features: Intro to Leading a Study, Intro to Study, Objectives, Prayer Helps, Drawings, Handouts, Persnl Study Quest, Publicity Ideas
★★★ Personal Application Preparation Time: None
★★★ Relationship Building Ldr. Guide: Yes Size: 8.50 x 11.0
Subjects: Divorce, Marriage, Money
Comments: This self-contained leader's guide combines learning activities for small group interaction and practical application with excerpts and biblical teaching from Dobson's *Love for a LifeTime*. It helps couples of all ages set realistic marital expectations, handle money matters, celebrate their differences, and avoid common "marriage killers" that can lead to divorce. Student books are not required.

Author: Dobson, Dr. James C. 471
Series:
Title: *Preparing for Adolescence*
Publisher: Regal Books, 1978 ISBN: 0-83071-258-5

Num. Sess.	Group Time	Num. Pgs.	Avg. Qst.	Price	Audience	Format	Bible Study
	—	190	N/A	$8.99	Beginner	Book	Topical

Features: Intro to Study, Cassette Avail
Personal Application Preparation Time:
Relationship Building Ldr. Guide: Yes Size: 5.50 x 8.50
Subjects: Parenting, Teens: Christian Liv
Comments: This book prepares youth to handle the extreme pressures of maturing. Author Dobson communicates directly and sincerely to youth about inferiority, conformity, puberty, romantic love, and identity. Other Preparing for Adolescence resources include a workbook for students, teachers, and parents; 20 10″ sessions for parents and preteens; 6 tapes for parents and kids (2 for parents only); and a youth course for kids 9–14. Leader's notes and reproducible student pages.

Author: Dobson, Dr. James C. 472
Series:
Title: *Turn Your Heart Toward Home*
Publisher: Word, 1990 ISBN: 8-03007-179-5

Num. Sess.	Group Time	Num. Pgs.	Avg. Qst.	Price	Audience	Format	Bible Study
6	75-105	N/A	11	$129.95	Beginner	Video	Topical

Features: Intro to Study, Prayer Helps, Follow Up, Agenda, Publicity Ideas, Book Incl
★★★★ Personal Application Preparation Time: None
★★★★ Relationship Building Ldr. Guide: No Size: 11.0 x 12.0
Subjects: Family, Parenting
Comments: This 6-session video helps family members capture opportunities to build their lives together. It addresses problems facing modern families, including: prioritizing time for family; parenting young children or adolescents; attacks on family values, such as governmental interference, abortion, and pornography; overcoming painful childhoods and how to build heritages that strengthen homes.

Author: Dobson, Dr. James C. 473
Series:
Title: *When God Doesn't Make Sense*
Publisher: Tyndale House, 1993 ISBN: 0-84238-227-5

Num. Sess.	Group Time	Num. Pgs.	Avg. Qst.	Price	Audience	Format	Bible Study
11	—	250	N/A	$17.99	New Christian	Book	Topical

Features: Cassette Avail
Personal Application Preparation Time:
Relationship Building Ldr. Guide: Size: 6.25 x 9.25
Subjects: Christian Living, Suffering
Comments: This book is for people who are struggling with trials and heartaches they can't understand. Why do disease, divorce, rejection, death, or sorrow plague Christians who are trying to serve the Lord? It deals unflinchingly with life's most troubling question, "Why?" Drawing on his experience as a Christian counselor, Dobson brings hope to the discouraged. Helps believers avoid "the betrayal barrier," a sense that God is abandoning them amidst the storms of life.

Author: Dobson, Dr. James C. 474
Series:
Title: *When God Doesn't Make Sense: Study Guide*
Publisher: Tyndale House, 1994 ISBN: 0-84238-239-9

Num. Sess.	Group Time	Num. Pgs.	Avg. Qst.	Price	Audience	Format	Bible Study
11	60-90	69	11	$5.99	New Christian	Workbk	Topical

Features: Cassette Avail, Book Avail
★★★★ Personal Application Preparation Time: Med
★★★ Relationship Building Ldr. Guide: No Size: 6.0 x 9.0
Subjects: Christian Living, Suffering
Comments: This guide, for use with the book by the same title, helps participants go beyond just reading Dobson's book to thinking through life issues and events that lead to frustration with God. Arguing against disillusionment and despair, it helps Christians nurture their faith in the Lord. The questions in this guide assist participants discussing the most important stories, quotes, and Scriptures from the book, and allow group members to learn from one another's experiences.

Author: Dockrey, Karen 475
Series:
Title: *Are You There, God?*
Publisher: Victor Books, 1993 ISBN: 1-56476-090-1

Num. Sess.	Group Time	Num. Pgs.	Avg. Qst.	Price	Audience	Format	Bible Study
6	60-75	55	Vary	$2.99	New Christian	Workbk	Charctr

Features:
★★★★ Personal Application Preparation Time: None
★★★★ Relationship Building Ldr. Guide: Yes Size: 5.50 x 8.50
Subjects: Teens: Discipleship, Teens: God, Teens: Senior High
Comments: This study investigates God's character. Lessons deal with the following questions: How can I know if God is real? If I question or doubt, am I bad? Why do I have so many questions? If God exists, does He care about me? How does He show His care? How do I respond to His care? What is God really like? When bad things happen, does it mean God's mad? What is faith? What does it mean to be spiritual in everyday life? Why should I be faithful to God?

Author: Dockrey, Karen 476
Series:
Title: *From Frustration to Freedom*
Publisher: Victor Books, 1992 ISBN: 0-89693-233-8

Num. Sess.	Group Time	Num. Pgs.	Avg. Qst.	Price	Audience	Format	Bible Study
10	60-90	108	12	$5.99	New Christian	Workbk	Book

Features: Intro to Leading a Study, Intro to Study, Objectives, Scrpt Memory Helps, Digging Deeper Quest, Follow Up, Ldr's Notes
★★★★ Personal Application Preparation Time: Med
★★★ Relationship Building Ldr. Guide: No Size: 6.0 x 9.0
Subjects: Emotions, Ethics, Failure, God, Grace, Romans, Women's Issues
Comments: This study reveals how God can equip us to find freedom in Christ. Shows how to find freedom from destructive habits and human expectations, freedom to live God's type of love and fulfill His expectations. Excellent for resolving struggles such as hypocrisy, pride, suffering, bad habits, sin, sadness, anger, loneliness, and feeling useless.

Author: Dockrey, Karen, et al. 477
Series: Ready for Life
Title: *How to Be a Good Friend: Book 1*
Publisher: Victor Books, 1994 ISBN: 1-56476-283-1

Num. Sess.	Group Time	Num. Pgs.	Avg. Qst.	Price	Audience	Format	Bible Study
6	45-60	69	N/A	$5.99	Beginner	Workbk	Topical

Features: Intro to Study, Objectives, Digging Deeper Quest, Follow Up, Agenda
★★★★ Personal Application Preparation Time: None
★★★★ Relationship Building Ldr. Guide: No Size: 7.0 x 10.0
Subjects: Teens: Friends, Teens: Junior High
Comments: This 6-book series is designed to help youth workers teach biblically based life skills during the critical junior high years. Each book contains six meetings that focus on specific life skills. Lesson titles on choosing friends and keeping friendships strong, include "Friends Forever"; "A Good Investment"; "Shhh! It's A Secret"; "Lend Me Your Ears"; "Staying Close"; and "Steering Right."

Author: Dockrey, Karen, et al. 478
Series: Ready for Life
Title: *How to Explain What You Believe: Book 6*
Publisher: Victor Books, 1994 ISBN: 1-56476-288-2

Num. Sess.	Group Time	Num. Pgs.	Avg. Qst.	Price	Audience	Format	Bible Study
6	45-60	77	N/A	$5.99	Beginner	Workbk	Topical

Features: Intro to Study, Objectives, Digging Deeper Quest, Follow Up, Agenda
★★★★ Personal Application Preparation Time: None
★★★★ Relationship Building Ldr. Guide: No Size: 7.0 x 10.0
Subjects: Teens: Evangelism, Teens: Junior High
Comments: This 6-book series is designed to help youth workers teach biblically based life skills during the critical junior high years. This book teaches young people biblical principles for sharing faith with other people. Lessons include: "Lost and Found"; "True Love"; "Rejected, Accepted"; "Who Died, Why"; "Come to the Party"; and "On the Spot."

Author: Dockrey, Karen, et al. 479
Series: Ready for Life
Title: *How to Get Along With The Opposite Sex: Book 2*
Publisher: Victor Books, 1994 ISBN: 1-56476-284-X

Num. Sess.	Group Time	Num. Pgs.	Avg. Qst.	Price	Audience	Format	Bible Study
6	45-60	67	N/A	$5.99	Beginner	Workbk	Topical

Features: Intro to Study, Objectives, Digging Deeper Quest, Follow Up, Agenda
★★★★ Personal Application Preparation Time: None
★★★★ Relationship Building Ldr. Guide: No Size: 7.0 x 10.0
Subjects: Teens: Junior High, Teens: Sexuality
Comments: This 6-book series is designed to help youth workers teach biblically based life skills during the critical junior high years. This book teaches young people biblical principles for respecting, treating, and behaving around other young men and women. Lessons include "Getting Along"; "Respect"; "Get Real"; "Friendzy"; "Smile"; and "The Birds and the Bees."

Author: Dockrey, Karen, et al. 480
Series: Ready for Life
Title: *How to Know What God Wants: Book 5*
Publisher: Victor Books, 1994 ISBN: 1-56476-287-4

Num. Sess.	Group Time	Num. Pgs.	Avg. Qst.	Price	Audience	Format	Bible Study
6	45-60	67	N/A	$5.99	Beginner	Workbk	Topical

Features: Intro to Study, Objectives, Digging Deeper Quest, Follow Up, Agenda
★★★★ Personal Application Preparation Time: None
★★★★ Relationship Building Ldr. Guide: No Size: 7.0 x 10.0
Subjects: Teens: Christian Liv, Teens: Junior High
Comments: This 6-book series is designed to help youth workers teach biblically based life skills during the critical junior high years. Each book contains six meetings, focused on specific life skills. Lessons for youth on seeking and following God's will in daily life include: "Only the Best"; "Just Ask"; "Where There's a W.I.L.L., There's a Way"; "Good Advice"; "Check It Out"; and "Just Do It."

Author: Dockrey, Karen, et al. 481
Series: Ready for Life
Title: *How to Teach Your Parents: Book 3*
Publisher: Victor Books, 1994 ISBN: 1-56476-285-8

Num. Sess.	Group Time	Num. Pgs.	Avg. Qst.	Price	Audience	Format	Bible Study
6	45-60	79	N/A	$5.99	Beginner	Workbk	Topical

Features: Intro to Study, Objectives, Digging Deeper Quest, Follow Up, Agenda
★★★★ Personal Application Preparation Time: None
★★★★ Relationship Building Ldr. Guide: No Size: 7.0 x 10.0
Subjects: Teens: Family, Teens: Junior High
Comments: This 6-book series is designed to help youth workers teach biblically based life skills during the critical junior high years. Each book contains six meetings, focused on specific life skills. This book helps young people apply biblical principles for communicating and getting along with their parents. Lessons include: "Open Doors"; "Are You Positive"; "Help"; "Just Do It"; "Respect"; and "Unde-feeted."

Author: Dockrey, Karen, et al. 482
Series: Ready for Life
Title: *How to Win In Life: Book 4*
Publisher: Victor Books, 1994 ISBN: 1-56476-286-6

Num. Sess.	Group Time	Num. Pgs.	Avg. Qst.	Price	Audience	Format	Bible Study
6	45-60	78	N/A	$5.99	Beginner	Workbk	Topical

Features: Intro to Study, Objectives, Digging Deeper Quest, Follow Up, Agenda
★★★★ Personal Application Preparation Time: None
★★★★ Relationship Building Ldr. Guide: No Size: 7.0 x 10.0
Subjects: Teens: Junior High, Teens: Values, Teens: Youth Life
Comments: This 6-book series is designed to help youth workers teach bibllically based life skills during the critical junior high years. Each book contains six meetings, focused on specific life skills. This book teaches biblical principles for making goals and finding success, as defined by the Bible. Lessons include: "Success"; "Winning"; "Goal to Go"; "Step by Step"; "Accountability"; and "Winners and Losers."

Author: Dockrey, Karen 483
Series: SonPower Youth Sources
Title: *I Thought You Were My Friend!*
Publisher: Victor Books, 1994 ISBN: 1-56476-290-4

Num. Sess.	Group Time	Num. Pgs.	Avg. Qst.	Price	Audience	Format	Bible Study
73	60-75	73	Vary	$2.99	New Christian	Workbk	Topical

Features:
★★★★ Personal Application Preparation Time: None
★★★★ Relationship Building Ldr. Guide: Yes Size: 5.50 x 8.50
Subjects: Teens: Friends, Teens: Senior High
Comments: This study explores friendship for youth and young adults. Lessons deal with friendship—it is something built, not found; discovering ways to get rid of "weedish" behavior and grow true joy in friendship; how clear communication can build joy through being together and sharing life; choosing to go through sad times with friends, even though it's not easy; rather than depending on labels, embracing God as the designer of friendships.

Author: Dockrey, Karen 484
Series: Tapestry Collection
Title: *Tuned-Up Parenting*
Publisher: Victor Books, 1994 ISBN: 1-56476-211-4

Num. Sess.	Group Time	Num. Pgs.	Avg. Qst.	Price	Audience	Format	Bible Study
8	90-120	95	11	$5.99	New Christian	Workbk	Topical

Features: Intro to Study, Objectives, Prayer Helps, Scrpt Memory Helps, Ldr's Notes, Charts
★★★★ Personal Application Preparation Time: Low
★★★★ Relationship Building Ldr. Guide: No Size: 6.0 x 9.0
Subjects: Family, Parenting
Comments: This study is for parents who want to bring wholesome balance to their homes. It teaches parents to pull the strings of discipline taut, but not taut enough to snap, to expect the best, but forgive the worst. Opposite, but equally important, ingredients pepper the entire job description: words balanced with example; structure balanced with freedom; and discipline balanced with approval.

Author: Dockrey, Karen 485
Series: SonPower Youth Sources
Title: *What's a Kid Like Me Doing in a Family Like This?: Leader's Edition*
Publisher: Victor Books, 1992 ISBN: 0-89693-113-7

Num. Sess.	Group Time	Num. Pgs.	Avg. Qst.	Price	Audience	Format	Bible Study
6	60-75	86	N/A	$4.99	New Christian	Book	Topical

Features: Intro to Study, Study Overview, Handouts
★★★★ Personal Application Preparation Time: Low
★★★★ Relationship Building Ldr. Guide: Size: 5.50 x 8.50
Subjects: Teens: Family, Teens: Resources
Comments: Six sessions on family relationships explores choices at home that can make families happier; working with parents on goals that can turn destructive pressure into creative pressure; and developing understanding skills for closeness with parents. It covers asking parents for what is needed and thanking them, unconditional acceptance, and spiritual growth.

Author: Dockrey, Karen 486
Series:
Title: *When a Hug Won't Fix the Hurt*
Publisher: Victor Books, 1993 ISBN: 1-56476-062-6

Num. Sess.	Group Time	Num. Pgs.	Avg. Qst.	Price	Audience	Format	Bible Study
10	75-90	175	N/A	$7.99	Beginner	Book	Topical

Features: Bibliography, No Grp Discussion Quest
★★★ Personal Application Preparation Time: Low
★ Relationship Building Ldr. Guide: No Size: 5.50 x 8.50
Subjects: Parenting, Psychology, Suffering, Support
Comments: This book helps parents with children in crises, who experience intense physical or emotional pain, maybe both. It responds to questions such as how to help a child cope with a life-threatening illness, chronic handicap, or the death of someone close. Features include ideas to help family and friends show that they care, bite-size insights into a child's feelings during crisis, chapter summaries that highlight "take-away" information, and suggested books for support.

Author: Doornenbal, Baukje & Tjitske Lemstra 487
Series:
Title: *Homemaking: A Bible Study for Women at Home*
Publisher: NavPress, 1981 ISBN: 0-89109-033-9

Num. Sess.	Group Time	Num. Pgs.	Avg. Qst.	Price	Audience	Format	Bible Study
12	45-60	72	7	$5.00	New Christian	Workbk	Topical

Features:
★★ Personal Application Preparation Time: Low
★★ Relationship Building Ldr. Guide: No Size: 5.50 x 8.50
Subjects: Parenting, Women's Issues
Comments: This study of homemaking is for women who want to be motivated and led by God's Word in their responsibilities at home. Topics include the clarification of expectations, defining one's divine task, identifying and using one's gifts, altering one's thinking about worldly things, and developing good habits for one's self and children. Homemaking is a calling.

Author: Downall, Donn C., et al. 488
Series:
Title: *Favorite Bible Passages: More Lessons From Familiar Text*
Publisher: Cokesbury, 1990

Num. Sess.	Group Time	Num. Pgs.	Avg. Qst.	Price	Audience	Format	Bible Study
26	45-60	112	N/A	$2.95	New Christian	Book	Book

Features:
★★★ Personal Application Preparation Time: Low
★★ Relationship Building Ldr. Guide: Yes Size: 5.50 x 8.50
Subjects: Decision Making
Comments: These lessons provide a biblical basis for facing life's decisions and encourages a deeper personal faith. Half the lessons come from the Old Testament, half from the New Testament. Each chapter includes: Words for Bible Times, Words for Our Time, and Words for My Life. Lessons include: Adam and Eve, Jacob's Ladder, Psalm 121, the Lord's Prayer, the Good Samaritan, the Day of Pentecost, and more.

Author: Downall, Donn C. 489
Series:
Title: *Favorite Bible Passages: Lessons from 26 Familiar Texts*
Publisher: Cokesbury, 1989

Num. Sess.	Group Time	Num. Pgs.	Avg. Qst.	Price	Audience	Format	Bible Study
26	—	112	N/A	$2.95		Book	Book

Features: Prayer Helps, No Grp Discussion Quest
Personal Application Preparation Time:
Relationship Building Ldr. Guide: Yes Size: 5.50 x 8.50
Subjects: New Testament, Old Testament
Comments: This book deals with passages of Scripture Christians have known for years and gives fresh insight that brings the response, "I never thought of it that way." Volume 1 lessons include Psalm 23, Ruth, Esther, the Great Commission, the Beatitudes, 1 Corinthians 13, and more.

Author: Downall, Donn C., et al. 490
Series:
Title: *Favorite Bible Passages: Vol. 2, Teacher Book*
Publisher: Cokesbury, 1990

Num. Sess.	Group Time	Num. Pgs.	Avg. Qst.	Price	Audience	Format	Bible Study
26	—	56	N/A	$4.95	New Christian	Book	Book

Features: Prayer Helps, Summary
Personal Application Preparation Time:
Relationship Building Ldr. Guide: Size: 8.50 x 11.0
Subjects: Decision Making
Comments: This leader's guide provides lessons with purpose statements, Bible background, how to begin, how to develop, and notes from words for Bible times, our time, and the teacher's life. A summary and written prayer are provided at the conclusion of each lesson.

Author: Drury, Keith 491
Series: Group's Active Bible Curriculum
Title: *Your Life as a Disciple*
Publisher: Group Publishing, 1990 ISBN: 1-55945-204-8

Num. Sess.	Group Time	Num. Pgs.	Avg. Qst.	Price	Audience	Format	Bible Study
4	35-60	45	Vary	$9.99	New Christian	Workbk	Topical

Features: Intro to Leading a Study, Intro to Study, Objectives, Study Overview, Ldr's Notes, Handouts, Agenda, Publicity Ideas
★★★ Personal Application Preparation Time: None
★★★ Relationship Building Ldr. Guide: No Size: 8.50 x 11.0
Subjects: Teens: Discipleship, Teens: Senior High
Comments: This study helps Christian teenagers develop a desire to serve God and build confidence to withstand attacks to their faith. Four lessons discuss the first disciples, qualifications for being a disciple, the "cost" of being a disciple, and how to accept the responsibility of being a disciple. The course could be adapted for use in a Bible class or youth meeting, and activities and Bible studies are included.

Author: Duckworth, John 492
Series: Young Teen Feedback
Title: *School Zone, The—Leader's Book*
Publisher: Victor Books, 1986 ISBN: 0-89693-198-6

Num. Sess.	Group Time	Num. Pgs.	Avg. Qst.	Price	Audience	Format	Bible Study
12	30-45	86	Vary	$13.99	New Christian	Book	Topical

Features: Intro to Study, Handouts
★★★★ Personal Application Preparation Time: None
★★★★ Relationship Building Ldr. Guide: Yes Size: 8.50 x 11.0
Subjects: Teens: Emotions, Teens: Peer Pressure, Teens: Relationships
Comments: This twelve-lesson study helps young teens learn to live their faith at school and cope with concerns about problems such as peer pressure, competition, relationships, and authority in a school setting. Each session is based on interviews with youth, including feedback on personal needs and concerns. This guide offers four-week studies with reproducible student sheets. A student book is available.

Author: Duckworth, Marion 493
Series: A Bible Study for Women
Title: *Celebrate Who You Are: 9 Studies on the Identity & Roles of Women*
Publisher: Victor Books, 1990 ISBN: 0-89693-816-6

Num. Sess.	Group Time	Num. Pgs.	Avg. Qst.	Price	Audience	Format	Bible Study
9	60-75	96	20	$5.99	New Christian	Workbk	Topical

Features: Intro to Leading a Study, Intro to Study, Scrpt Memory Helps, Follow Up, Ldr's Notes
★★★★ Personal Application Preparation Time: Med
★★★ Relationship Building Ldr. Guide: No Size: 6.0 x 9.0
Subjects: Genesis, God, Women's Issues
Comments: In this study, women will discover that their identity and role are not synonymous. The study guides participants through Genesis 1–5 and related Scripture, helping them discover a biblical view of themselves and celebrate who they are—gifted creatures called by God to use their abilities in constructive ways.

Author: Duckworth, Marion 494
Series:
Title: *Decisive Woman, The*
Publisher: Victor Books, 1993 ISBN: 1-56476-058-8

Num. Sess.	Group Time	Num. Pgs.	Avg. Qst.	Price	Audience	Format	Bible Study
12	60-90	143	6	$8.99	New Christian	Book	Topical

Features: No Grp Discussion Quest
★★★★ Personal Application Preparation Time: Low
★ Relationship Building Ldr. Guide: No Size: 5.50 x 8.50
Subjects: Decision Making, Morals, Women's Issues
Comments: This book presents 5 key principles for moral guidance that help readers focus their thoughts on God's character. In the process, women become more confident, decisive people God wants them to be. Being a decisive woman today involves more than just choosing a political party affiliation. Values once black and white have become gray, placing convictions in conflict. It means forming convictions to reflect the character of God.

Author: Duckworth, Marion 495
Series: Tapestry Collection
Title: *Pure Passion*
Publisher: Victor Books, 1994 ISBN: 1-56476-222-X

Num. Sess.	Group Time	Num. Pgs.	Avg. Qst.	Price	Audience	Format	Bible Study
8	90-120	111	26	$5.99	New Christian	Workbk	Book

Features: Intro to Leading a Study, Intro to Study, Objectives, Prayer Helps, Follow Up, Ldr's Notes, Persnl Study Quest, Charts
★★★★ Personal Application Preparation Time: Med
★★★★ Relationship Building Ldr. Guide: No Size: 6.0 x 9.0
Subjects: Marriage, Sexual Issues, Song of Solomon
Comments: This 8-week study for helping women explore their sexuality, deals with issues such as talking to a husband about sex, cultivating sexual and other intimacies, married passion ("the best"), romance and sexual love, breathing life into a numbed marriage, enjoying aging love, and discovering how God's gift of married love mirrors Himself. The study is designed for women with busy lives.

Author: Duckworth, Marion 496
Series: Tapestry Collection
Title: *Renewed on the Run*
Publisher: Victor Books, 1991 ISBN: 0-89693-878-6

Num. Sess.	Group Time	Num. Pgs.	Avg. Qst.	Price	Audience	Format	Bible Study
9	60-90	96	Vary	$5.99	New Christian	Workbk	Book

Features: Intro to Leading a Study, Intro to Study, Prayer Helps, Digging Deeper Quest, Follow Up, Ldr's Notes, Persnl Study Quest
★★★★ Personal Application Preparation Time: Low
★★★ Relationship Building Ldr. Guide: No Size: 6.0 x 9.0
Subjects: Renewal, Women's Issues, 1 & 2 Peter
Comments: This inductive Bible study for women on the move includes nine lessons on 1 Peter. This study helps busy contemporary women restore their purpose for living. The study includes a journaling exercise as well as prayer helps.

Author: Dugan, Richard 497
Series: Building Books
Title: *Building Christian Commitment*
Publisher: Bethany House, 1982 ISBN: 0-87123-831-4

Num. Sess.	Group Time	Num. Pgs.	Avg. Qst.	Price	Audience	Format	Bible Study
34	45-60	45	Vary	$6.99	New Christian	Workbk	Topical

Features: Scrpt Memory Helps, Persnl Study Quest
★★ Personal Application Preparation Time: Low
★★ Relationship Building Ldr. Guide: Yes Size: 8.50 x 11.0
Subjects: Teens: Bible/Pers., Teens: Christian Liv, Teens: Emotions
Comments: This 34-lesson study for young adults on Bible characters discusses what made them heroes, why they sometimes failed, and how they grew toward spiritual maturity. From "Joseph, the Lemonade Maker," to "Diotrephes, the Man Who Loved to Be First," these challenging studies help young people understand how to deal with discouragement, failure, obstacles, temptations, selfishness, and practical issues that face them every day.

Author: Duin, Julia 498
Series: Shaw Contemporary Issues
Title: *Wholly Single*
Publisher: Shaw, 1991 ISBN: 0-87788-945-7

Num. Sess.	Group Time	Num. Pgs.	Avg. Qst.	Price	Audience	Format	Bible Study
8	30-45	48	5	$4.99	Beginner	Workbk	Topical

Features: Intro to Leading a Study, Intro to Study, Bibliography, Follow Up, Ldr's Notes
★★★★ Personal Application Preparation Time: Low
★★★ Relationship Building Ldr. Guide: No Size: 5.25 x 8.25
Subjects: Loneliness, Relationships, Service, Sexual Issues, Singles' Issues
Comments: Eight short lessons help single adults tackle issues such as loneliness, celibacy, sexual purity, and intimacy from a biblical perspective. Challenging questions include: Are you allowing your singleness to make you more like Jesus? How do you react to the challenges of singleness? Does singleness enhance ministry or detract from it?

Author: Dunlap-Berg, Larry **499**
Series: LifeSearch
Title: *Environment, The*
Publisher: Abingdon Press, 1994 ISBN: 0-68777-878-6

Num. Sess.	Group Time	Num. Pgs.	Avg. Qst.	Price	Audience	Format	Bible Study
6	60-90	62	Vary	$4.95	Beginner	Workbk	Topical

Features: Intro to Leading a Study, Intro to Study, Prayer Helps, Worship Helps, Ldr's Notes
★★★★ Personal Application Preparation Time: None
★★★★ Relationship Building Ldr. Guide: No Size: 7.0 x 10.0
Subjects: Social Issues
Comments: The focus of this 6-week study is on ways participants affect and are affected by the environment. It helps maintain a balance between environment as public policy issues, and as issues of personal responsibility both are explored from individual and communal contexts. The book contains leader aids and marginal notes. How to lead with minimal preparation time is also included.

Author: Dunnam, Maxie **500**
Series:
Title: *Exodus — Volumes 1–3*
Publisher: Cokesbury, 1989 ISBN: 0-68776-134-4

Num. Sess.	Group Time	Num. Pgs.	Avg. Qst.	Price	Audience	Format	Bible Study
11	45-60	N/A	Vary	$40.00	New Christian	Video	Book

Features: Intro to Leading a Study, Intro to Study, Prayer Helps, Ldr's Notes, Video Study Guide
★★★ Personal Application Preparation Time: Low
★★★ Relationship Building Ldr. Guide: Yes Size: 4.75 x 8.0
Subjects: Exodus, God
Comments: This 3-volume video focuses on Exodus, an exciting book on God's delivering Israel out of Egyptian bondage, protecting and sustaining them through wilderness wandering, and bringing them to Canaan. To contemporary participants, it is a picture of a spiritual journey from the bondage of sin, to freedom and full inheritance in Christ.

Author: Dunnam, Maxie **501**
Series: Bible Study for Christian
Title: *Gospel of Mark, The — Volumes 1–3*
Publisher: Cokesbury, 1988 ISBN: 0-68776-006-2

Num. Sess.	Group Time	Num. Pgs.	Avg. Qst.	Price	Audience	Format	Bible Study
9	90-120	128	Vary	$40.00	New Christian	Audio	Book

Features: Intro to Leading a Study, Intro to Study, Prayer Helps, Video Study Guide
★★★★ Personal Application Preparation Time: Low
★★★ Relationship Building Ldr. Guide: Yes Size: 4.75 x 8.0
Subjects: Christian Living, Jesus: Life/Teaching, Mark
Comments: This 3-volume video study covers the Gospel of Mark, giving participants a picture of Christ having returned. It shows them that, in Christ, the limitless power of God is incarnated and available to all. It's valid, relevant subject matter for contemporary Christians. A leader's guide contains insights and questions for use in a group, and the study is effective for personal use.

Author: Dunnam, Maxie **502**
Series: Bible Study for Christian
Title: *More Than Conquerors — Volumes 1–3*
Publisher: Cokesbury, 1988 ISBN: 0-68776-014-3

Num. Sess.	Group Time	Num. Pgs.	Avg. Qst.	Price	Audience	Format	Bible Study
8	90-120	111	Vary	$40.00	New Christian	Video	Topical

Features: Intro to Leading a Study, Intro to Study, Prayer Helps, Video Study Guide
★★★★ Personal Application Preparation Time: Low
★★★ Relationship Building Ldr. Guide: Yes Size: 4.75 x 8.0
Subjects: Christian Living, Faith, New Testament, Victorious Living
Comments: This 3-volume video study shows participants the promise and glory of Christian life. It draws, from Paul's letters, major affirmations of Christian faith and is concentrated on the fact that Christ came to offer abundant life. A study book can be used with the videotapes, and correspondence course worksheets may be completed and returned for review by Cokesbury.

Author: Dunnam, Maxie **503**
Series: Bible Study for Christian
Title: *Twelve Parables of Jesus — Volumes 1–3*
Publisher: Cokesbury, 1988 ISBN: 0-68776-031-3

Num. Sess.	Group Time	Num. Pgs.	Avg. Qst.	Price	Audience	Format	Bible Study
11	90-120	119	Vary	$40.00	New Christian	Video	Topical

Features: Intro to Leading a Study, Intro to Study, Prayer Helps, Video Study Guide
★★★★ Personal Application Preparation Time: Low
★★★ Relationship Building Ldr. Guide: Yes Size: 4.75 x 8.0
Subjects: Christian Living, Parables
Comments: This 3-volume study teaches Bible truth through storytelling, or parables. Through them, participants see the world in which Christ lived, as well as His mind and spirit. The study portrays lessons for living in the Kingdom of God. It's valid, relevant subject matter for contemporary Christians. A leader's guide contains insights and questions for use in a group.

Author: Dunn, Dr. Van Bogard **504**
Series:
Title: *Journey Through The Bible: Matthew*
Publisher: Cokesbury, 1994

Num. Sess.	Group Time	Num. Pgs.	Avg. Qst.	Price	Audience	Format	Bible Study
13	30-60	112	4	$2.95	New Christian	Book	Book

Features: Intro to Study, Maps
★★★ Personal Application Preparation Time: Med
★★★ Relationship Building Ldr. Guide: Yes Size: 5.50 x 8.50
Subjects: Matthew
Comments: This book-by-book approach can help adults gain a basic literacy of the Bible. Sessions include: Jesus' birth, baptism, temptation, ministry of preaching, teaching, healing; Jesus' ministry accepted, rejected, affirmed, completed, and continued. A map of ancient Palestine is provided.

Author: Dunn, Dr. Van Bogard **505**
Series:
Title: *Journey Through The Bible: Matthew, Leader's Guide*
Publisher: Cokesbury, 1994

Num. Sess.	Group Time	Num. Pgs.	Avg. Qst.	Price	Audience	Format	Bible Study
13	30-60	72	N/A	$4.95	New Christian	Book	Book

Features: Intro to Leading a Study, Maps
Personal Application Preparation Time:
Relationship Building Ldr. Guide: Size: 8.50 x 11.0
Subjects: Leader's Guide
Comments: This leader's guide provides answers to questions in the student book, as well as additional Bible helps. A section on "How to create excitement for Bible study" is also helpful. An article on "Matthew and His Gospel" can add to a teacher's impact.

Author: Dunn, Richard **506**
Series: SonPower Youth Sources
Title: *Can't Fight the Feelings*
Publisher: Victor Books, 1990 ISBN: 0-89693-043-2

Num. Sess.	Group Time	Num. Pgs.	Avg. Qst.	Price	Audience	Format	Bible Study
6	60-75	40	Vary	$2.99	New Christian	Workbk	Topical

Features:
★★★★ Personal Application Preparation Time: None
★★★★ Relationship Building Ldr. Guide: Yes Size: 5.50 x 8.50
Subjects: Teens: Emotions, Teens: Senior High
Comments: This study explores emotions of high school students. Lessons deal with practical strategies for responding to youths' emotions without freezing them out, what to do when you don't feel like loving, and giving and receiving affirmation of who we are in Christ. Participants cover overcoming feelings of despair, learning to apply the biblical pattern of resolution, and making smart decisions despite emotional pressures. This study is interactive.

Author: Dunn, Richard **507**
Series: SonPower Youth Sources
Title: *Leading From the Back of the Line: Leader's Edition*
Publisher: Victor Books, 1992 ISBN: 1-56476-002-2

Num. Sess.	Group Time	Num. Pgs.	Avg. Qst.	Price	Audience	Format	Bible Study
6	60-75	80	N/A	$4.99	New Christian	Book	Topical

Features: Intro to Study, Prayer Helps, Study Overview
★★★★ Personal Application Preparation Time: Low
★★★★ Relationship Building Ldr. Guide: Yes Size: 5.50 x 8.50
Subjects: Teens: Bible Study, Teens: Leadership, Teens: Resources
Comments: Six sessions on servant leadership for youth and young adults explore Jesus' radical call to servant leadership, doubts and fears facing young leaders as they prepare to serve God, and God's faithfulness in empowering servant leaders to overcome enormous external obstacles. They cover application of specifics learned in areas of servant leadership, the expansion of vision, and a summary of the first 5 sessions.

Author: Dunn, Richard **508**
Series: Small Group Studies
Title: *Where Do You Think Sex Came From?*
Publisher: Victor Books, 1991 ISBN: 0-89693-195-1

Num. Sess.	Group Time	Num. Pgs.	Avg. Qst.	Price	Audience	Format	Bible Study
6	45-60	45	Vary	$4.99	Beginner	Workbk	Topical

Features: Prayer Helps, Follow Up
★★★★ Personal Application Preparation Time: None
★★★★ Relationship Building Ldr. Guide: Yes Size: 5.50 x 8.50
Subjects: Teens: Junior High, Teens: Peer Pressure, Teens: Senior High, Teens: Sexuality
Comments: This 6-session study for high school students helps create an environment of acceptance and challenge. Topics covered include looking at God's view of sex and sexuality, expressing God-given sexuality, setting standards for dating relationships, controlling sexual desire, dealing with peer pressure, and encouraging one another to keep commitments.

Author: Dunn, Richard **509**
Series: Small Group Studies
Title: *Why Not Love All of Me?*
Publisher: Victor Books, 1991 ISBN: 0-89693-183-8

Num. Sess.	Group Time	Num. Pgs.	Avg. Qst.	Price	Audience	Format	Bible Study
6	45-60	45	Vary	$4.99	Beginner	Workbk	Topical

Features: Prayer Helps, Follow Up
★★★★ Personal Application Preparation Time: None
★★★★ Relationship Building Ldr. Guide: Yes Size: 5.50 x 8.50
Subjects: Teens: Junior High, Teens: Relationships, Teens: Senior High
Comments: This 6-session study for high school students helps create an environment of acceptance and challenge and offers a supportive community to strengthen their personal and spiritual growth. Topics covered include a view of the whole person from God's perspective, loving God from the inside out, friendships with members of the opposite sex, Christian dating, and developing a "high view" of marriage as God intended.

Author: Eaton, Chris and Kim Hurst **510**
Series: Singles Ministry Resources
Title: *Vacations With a Purpose: Leader's Manual*
Publisher: David C. Cook Publishing Co., 1993 ISBN: 0-78145-042-X

Num. Sess.	Group Time	Num. Pgs.	Avg. Qst.	Price	Audience	Format	Bible Study
	—	220	N/A	$18.95			

Features: Bibliography, Appendix
Personal Application Preparation Time:
Relationship Building Ldr. Guide: Size: 7.0 x 10.0
Subjects: Commitments, Leader's Guide, Missions
Comments: This comprehensive planning guide covers all important aspects of a missions trip, including recruiting and training team members; selecting the mission site and project; maintaining good relationships among the team, with the nationals, and with missions agencies; debriefing, reflecting, and telling others after the trip is completed. It can help create opportunities for members of a church and community to broaden their perspectives as world Christians.

Author: Eaton, Chris and Kim Hurst **511**
Series: Singles Ministry Resources
Title: *Vacations With a Purpose*
Publisher: David C. Cook Publishing Co., 1994 ISBN: 0-78145-041-1

Num. Sess.	Group Time	Num. Pgs.	Avg. Qst.	Price	Audience	Format	Bible Study
5	—	120	N/A	$5.95	Mature Christian	Workbk	No

Features: Bibliography
Personal Application Preparation Time:
Relationship Building Ldr. Guide: Size: 5.50 x 8.50
Subjects: Commitments, Missions
Comments: This book covers everything from finances, language, on the field, debriefing, and back-at-home study material for a mission trip. This resource is adaptable to specific needs at every stage participants experience before (preparing the heart, suitcase, and expectations), during (for recording discoveries, thoughts, and feelings), and after the trip (to debrief, evaluate, and plan future trips).

Author: Eims, LeRoy **512**
Series:
Title: *Be a Motivational Leader*
Publisher: Victor Books, 1981 ISBN: 0-89693-008-4

Num. Sess.	Group Time	Num. Pgs.	Avg. Qst.	Price	Audience	Format	Bible Study
13	60-90	132	N/A	$8.99	Beginner	Book	Topical

Features:
★★★ Personal Application Preparation Time: Med
★★★ Relationship Building Ldr. Guide: Yes Size: 5.50 x 8.0
Subjects: Bible Personalities, Caring, Leadership
Comments: This study helps participants learn how to motivate and equip people to be and do their best for Christ. It outlines time-tested keys leaders need to unlock their greatest treasure—enthusiastic, involved people serving with them. Scriptural directories, especially the teaching of Solomon, and personal experiences are used in lessons on being a responsible, growing, exemplary, inspiring, efficient, caring, goal-oriented, decisive, and competent leader.

Author: Eims, LeRoy **513**
Series:
Title: *Be the Leader You Were Meant to Be*
Publisher: Victor Books, 1975 ISBN: 0-88207-723-6

Num. Sess.	Group Time	Num. Pgs.	Avg. Qst.	Price	Audience	Format	Bible Study
13	60-90	132	N/A	$8.99	New Christian	Book	Topical

Features:
★★ Personal Application Preparation Time: Med
★★ Relationship Building Ldr. Guide: Yes Size: 5.50 x 8.0
Subjects: Leadership
Comments: This study analyzes and applies biblical teaching on leadership. The current crisis in leadership makes this look at Old and New Testament truths and Christ's teachings, with their clear and understandable leadership principles, particularly relevant. The study uses illustrations of both biblical principles and personal experiences. A leader's guide with transparency masters is available.

Author: Elliot, Diane **514**
Series: SonPower Youth Sources
Title: *Breaking the Gender Barrier In Youth Ministry*
Publisher: Victor Books, 1995 ISBN: 1-56476-497-4

Num. Sess.	Group Time	Num. Pgs.	Avg. Qst.	Price	Audience	Format	Bible Study
	—	202	N/A	$9.99			

Features:
Personal Application Preparation Time:
Relationship Building Ldr. Guide: Size: 6.0 x 9.0
Subjects: Teens: Resources
Comments: This resource, which draws on the experiences of many youth workers to discuss gender-related issues in the field of youth ministry, is one of few books for women in youth ministry. Each contributor is an experienced youth worker with topical expertise, and the book is specifically written for women and the men who work with them. Topics addressed include roles of women in youth work, the importance of male-female teams, special ministries to girls.

Author: Ellis, Lee and Larry Burkett **515**
Series:
Title: *Finding the Career That Fits You*
Publisher: Moody Press, 1994 ISBN: 0-80241-668-3

Num. Sess.	Group Time	Num. Pgs.	Avg. Qst.	Price	Audience	Format	Bible Study
12	90-120	114	Vary	$19.99	Beginner	Workbk	Topical

Features: Intro to Study, Charts
★★★★ Personal Application Preparation Time: Med
★★ Relationship Building Ldr. Guide: No Size: 8.50 x 11.0
Subjects: Self-help, Support, Work
Comments: This workbook helps participants discover the person God made them to be, through insightful looks at their personalities, skills, life values, and vocational interests. The authors walk participants through the job-search process and give them the confidence they need to start or change their careers and lives. This resource can be helpful for a job search support group, but a trained leader is required.

Author: English, Donald **516**
Series: The Bible Speaks Today
Title: *Message of Mark, The*
Publisher: InterVarsity, 1992 ISBN: 0-83081-231-8

Num. Sess.	Group Time	Num. Pgs.	Avg. Qst.	Price	Audience	Format	Bible Study
7	60-120	250	10	$12.99	New Christian	Book	Book

Features: Intro to Study, Bibliography
★★★ Personal Application Preparation Time: Med
★★ Relationship Building Ldr. Guide: No Size: 5.50 x 8.25
Subjects: Mark, New Testament
Comments: This series of Old and New Testament expositions are characterized by 3 goals: to expound the biblical text with accuracy, relate it to contemporary life, and be readable. Mark's Gospel answers questions like: Who was Jesus? What does it mean that He was the Son of God? Where do we fit into God's redemptive plan? Fast-paced and to the point, a viewers' guide to the series helps participants appreciate the study and become involved.

Author: Engstrom Ted W. 517
Series: Shaw Contemporary Issues
Title: *Personal Integrity*
Publisher: Shaw, 1990 ISBN: 0-87788-671-7

Num. Sess.	Group Time	Num. Pgs.	Avg. Qst.	Price	Audience	Format	Bible Study
8	30-45	45	5	$4.99	Beginner	Workbk	Topical

Features: Intro to Leading a Study, Intro to Study, Follow Up, Ldr's Notes
★★★★ Personal Application Preparation Time: Low
★★★ Relationship Building Ldr. Guide: No Size: 5.25 x 8.25
Subjects: Accountability, Christian Living, Integrity, Money
Comments: This study will challenge Christians to place their lives under the scrutiny of Scripture regarding honesty and righteousness. Questions deal with participants' personal lives: Are people habitually truthful—even when alone with tax forms? When people fail, do they confess sins, or hide and cover up wrongs? Is integrity practiced at home as well as in the public eye?

Author: Engstrom Ted W. 518
Series: Shaw Contemporary Issues
Title: *Redeeming Time*
Publisher: Shaw, 1991 ISBN: 0-87788-718-7

Num. Sess.	Group Time	Num. Pgs.	Avg. Qst.	Price	Audience	Format	Bible Study
8	30-45	48	5	$4.99	Beginner	Workbk	Topical

Features: Intro to Leading a Study, Intro to Study, Bibliography, Follow Up, Ldr's Notes
★★★★ Personal Application Preparation Time: Low
★★★ Relationship Building Ldr. Guide: No Size: 5.25 x 8.25
Subjects: Stress, Time, Work
Comments: Eight short lessons help participants gain a biblical perspective on time. Questions discussed include: Who controls your time? Are you busier than ever, but accomplishing less? How can you make time for the important things in life as well as for the urgent? As participants understand the gift of time God gives them, they'll be better prepared to live according to purpose, rather than pressure.

Author: Erdahl, Lowell O. 519
Series: Small Group Bible Studies
Title: *Forgiveness*
Publisher: Augsburg Fortress Publishers, 1982

Num. Sess.	Group Time	Num. Pgs.	Avg. Qst.	Price	Audience	Format	Bible Study
6	60-75	24	16	$1.35	New Christian	Book	Topical

Features: Intro to Study, Prayer Helps
★★★ Personal Application Preparation Time: None
★★★ Relationship Building Ldr. Guide: No Size: 8.50 x 5.50
Subjects: Christian Living, Forgiveness, Relationships
Comments: This short, six-session study explores some of the many meanings of forgiveness in daily living. The goal is to gain a better understanding of the theological concept of forgiveness, and also to have a more vital experience of being both forgiven and forgiving.

Author: Erwin, Gayle D. 520
Series: Proven Word
Title: *Jesus Style, The*
Publisher: Word, 1983 ISBN: 0-84992-989-X

Num. Sess.	Group Time	Num. Pgs.	Avg. Qst.	Price	Audience	Format	Bible Study
30	45-60	210	4	$9.99	Mature Christian	Book	Charctr

Features: Intro to Leading a Study, Intro to Study, Ldr's Notes
★★ Personal Application Preparation Time: Low
★★ Relationship Building Ldr. Guide: No Size: 5.50 x 8.0
Subjects: Christian Living, Jesus: Life/Teaching, Service, Theology
Comments: The main theme of The Jesus Style is that Jesus is the full revelation of the Father and that the clearest definition of His nature is found in Jesus' teachings. The primary trait that flows through the study is servanthood. It is a condensed primer for becoming others-centered, calling participants to touch others with the spirit of servanthood. Written in short, unnumbered chapters, it is accompanied with study questions for a small group.

Author: Evans, Tony 521
Series:
Title: *Our God Is Awesome*
Publisher: Moody Press, 1994 ISBN: 0-80246-187-5

Num. Sess.	Group Time	Num. Pgs.	Avg. Qst.	Price	Audience	Format	Bible Study
20	90-120	380	4	$15.99	New Christian	Book	Charctr

Features: Index, Topical Index
★★★★ Personal Application Preparation Time: Med
★ Relationship Building Ldr. Guide: No Size: 6.0 x 8.75
Subjects: God, Worship
Comments: This study details fourteen key characteristics of God and examines how they can enhance and cultivate relationships with Him. Readers study the sufficiency, holiness, sovereignty, glory, omniscience, omnipresence, omnipotence, wisdom, word, goodness, wrath, love, grace, and incarnation of God. By studying these characteristics, Christians can sense changes in their spiritual attitudes. Questions are provided for personal application.

Author: Evenhouse, Neva 522
Series: Discover Your Bible
Title: *Discover: Acts—Part 1*
Publisher: Church Development Resources, 1988

Num. Sess.	Group Time	Num. Pgs.	Avg. Qst.	Price	Audience	Format	Bible Study
13	60-75	48	8	$2.45	Beginner	Workbk	Book

Features: Intro to Study, Summary, Charts, Glossary, Maps
★★★ Personal Application Preparation Time: None
★★ Relationship Building Ldr. Guide: Yes Size: 5.50 x 8.50
Subjects: Acts, Church Life, Holy Spirit
Comments: This inductive study of the book of Acts chapters 1–12 deals with the Christian church's birth and early years. It documents opposition the church faced from both Jews and Romans, and problems within the church itself. It bears witness to God's Holy Spirit, who guided and empowered the Gospel of salvation in Jesus. Participants will be inspired and challenged by the lives of God's people in the early church.

Author: Evenhouse, Neva **523**
Series: Discover Your Bible
Title: *Discover: Acts—Part 2*
Publisher: Church Development Resources, 1985

Num. Sess.	Group Time	Num. Pgs.	Avg. Qst.	Price	Audience	Format	Bible Study
15	60-75	56	9	$2.85	Beginner	Workbk	Book

Features: Intro to Study, Summary, Maps
★★★ Personal Application Preparation Time: None
★★ Relationship Building Ldr. Guide: Yes Size: 5.50 x 8.50
Subjects: Acts, Church Life, Holy Spirit
Comments: This inductive study of Acts 13–22 deals with the Christian church's birth and early years. It documents opposition the church faced from both Jews and Romans, and problems within the church itself. It bears witness to God's Holy Spirit, who guided and empowered the Gospel of salvation in Jesus. Participants will be inspired and challenged by the lives of God's people in the early church. Also available in Korean.

Author: Evenhouse, Neva **524**
Series: Discover Your Bible
Title: *Discover: Colossians*
Publisher: Church Development Resources, 1989

Num. Sess.	Group Time	Num. Pgs.	Avg. Qst.	Price	Audience	Format	Bible Study
6	60-75	23	7	$1.30	Beginner	Workbk	Book

Features: Intro to Leading a Study, Summary, Glossary
★★★ Personal Application Preparation Time: None
★★ Relationship Building Ldr. Guide: Yes Size: 5.50 x 8.50
Subjects: Church Life, Colossians/Philemon, Faith, False Teachers, Hope, Service, Suffering
Comments: Colossians, Paul's letter to the Christians at Colossae, communicates with all ages and cultures. He writes about knowing God, about who Jesus Christ is. His warning against false human philosophies and his practical advice on how to live out one's faith are as topical in modern churches as in ancient Colossae. Participants in this inductive study will find out more about who Jesus is.

Author: Evenhouse, Neva **525**
Series: Discover Your Bible
Title: *Discover: James*
Publisher: Church Development Resources, 1991

Num. Sess.	Group Time	Num. Pgs.	Avg. Qst.	Price	Audience	Format	Bible Study
6	60-75	49	6	$1.30	Beginner	Workbk	Book

Features: Intro to Study, Glossary
★★★ Personal Application Preparation Time: None
★★ Relationship Building Ldr. Guide: Yes Size: 5.50 x 8.50
Subjects: James
Comments: James, one of the first New Testament books written, is a practical, nuts-and-bolts letter that considers deep questions about Christian faith. Is faith enough? What role do good works play? James' repeated calls for deeds and good works to accompany faith make this book both practical and challenging. Though written to first-century Christians, modern readers can greatly benefit from James' straightforward wisdom.

Author: Evenhouse, Neva **526**
Series: Discover Your Bible
Title: *Discover: Philippians*
Publisher: Church Development Resources, 1990

Num. Sess.	Group Time	Num. Pgs.	Avg. Qst.	Price	Audience	Format	Bible Study
6	60-75	47	6	$1.30	Beginner	Workbk	Book

Features: Intro to Study, Glossary
★★★ Personal Application Preparation Time: None
★★ Relationship Building Ldr. Guide: Yes Size: 5.50 x 8.50
Subjects: Philippians
Comments: Through this letter Paul speaks to believers everywhere about the importance of standing firm in faith, deepening a personal relationship with Christ, living in humility and unity with other believers, and grasping the peace and joy each child of God can experience in Jesus Christ, regardless of circumstances. It teaches God's children how to be blameless and pure, shine like stars, hold out the Word of life, and light their corners of a dark world.

Author: Evenhouse, Neva **527**
Series: Discover Your Bible
Title: *Discover: Romans—Part 2*
Publisher: Church Development Resources, 1984

Num. Sess.	Group Time	Num. Pgs.	Avg. Qst.	Price	Audience	Format	Bible Study
10	60-75	40	7	$2.00	Beginner	Workbk	Book

Features: Intro to Study, Summary, Glossary
★★★ Personal Application Preparation Time: None
★★ Relationship Building Ldr. Guide: Yes Size: 5.50 x 8.50
Subjects: Faith, Grace, Romans
Comments: This inductive study of Romans chapters 9–16 emphasizes that all people need to be put right with God, which can happen only by faith. It points out that salvation cannot be earned and is undeserved; it is God's gift. Those entering new relationships with God by faith live in union with Christ and are enabled by the Spirit to live Christian lives. These chapters help participants deal with how Christians are to treat one another.

Author: Evenhouse, Neva **528**
Series: Discover Your Bible
Title: *Discover: Romans—Part 1*
Publisher: Church Development Resources, 1984

Num. Sess.	Group Time	Num. Pgs.	Avg. Qst.	Price	Audience	Format	Bible Study
16	60-75	56	6	$3.00	Beginner	Workbk	Book

Features: Intro to Study, Summary, Glossary
★★★ Personal Application Preparation Time: None
★★ Relationship Building Ldr. Guide: Yes Size: 5.50 x 8.50
Subjects: Faith, Grace, Romans
Comments: This inductive study of Romans chapters 1–8 emphasizes that all people need to be put right with God, which can happen only by faith. It points out that salvation cannot be earned and is undeserved; it is God's gift. Those entering new relationships with God by faith live in union with Christ and are enabled by the Spirit to live Christian lives. These chapters help participants deal with how Christians are to treat one another.

Author: Evenhouse, Neva 529
Series: Discover Your Bible
Title: *Discover: The Gospel of Mark—Part 2*
Publisher: Church Development Resources, 1985

Num. Sess.	Group Time	Num. Pgs.	Avg. Qst.	Price	Audience	Format	Bible Study
13	60-75	48	7	$2.45	Beginner	Workbk	Book

Features: Intro to Study, Summary, Maps
★★★ Personal Application Preparation Time: None
★★ Relationship Building Ldr. Guide: Yes Size: 5.50 x 8.50
Subjects: Jesus: Life/Teaching, Mark
Comments: This inductive study of Mark chapters 9–16 offers a vigorous, straightforward account of Jesus' public ministry—from His baptism to His death and resurrection. Mark wrote this account from information he received from Roman Christians, and he pictured Jesus as a man of action, the powerful Son of God, who "did not come to be served, but to serve, and to give His life as a ransom for many" (Mark 10:45). A comprehensive leader's guide is available.

Author: Evenhouse, Neva 530
Series: Discover Your Bible
Title: *Discover: The Gospel of Mark—Part 1*
Publisher: Church Development Resources, 1985

Num. Sess.	Group Time	Num. Pgs.	Avg. Qst.	Price	Audience	Format	Bible Study
13	60-75	45	7	$2.45	Beginner	Workbk	Book

Features: Intro to Study, Summary, Glossary
★★★ Personal Application Preparation Time: None
★★ Relationship Building Ldr. Guide: Yes Size: 5.50 x 8.50
Subjects: Jesus: Life/Teaching, Mark
Comments: This inductive study of Mark chapters 1–8 offers a vigorous, straightforward account of Jesus' public ministry—from His baptism to His death and resurrection. Mark wrote this account from information he received from Roman Christians, and he pictured Jesus as a man of action, the powerful Son of God, who "did not come to be served, but to serve, and to give His life as a ransom for many" (Mark 10:45). A comprehensive leader's guide is available.

Author: Evenhouse, Neva 531
Series: Discover Your Bible
Title: *Discover: 1 John*
Publisher: Church Development Resources, 1989

Num. Sess.	Group Time	Num. Pgs.	Avg. Qst.	Price	Audience	Format	Bible Study
6	60-75	21	6	$1.30	Beginner	Workbk	Book

Features: Intro to Study, Summary, Glossary
★★★ Personal Application Preparation Time: None
★★ Relationship Building Ldr. Guide: Yes Size: 5.50 x 8.50
Subjects: False Teachers, God, Marriage, 1, 2 & 3 John/Jude
Comments: This inductive study of 1 John helps participants learn what it means that God is "Light" and "Love." John's letter is full of imagery that helps students understand God. It also helps them better understand what it means to believe in God. The letter, written to counter false teachers, helps believers identify and resist false teachings. A comprehensive leader's guide is available. Also available in Korean.

Author: Evenhouse, Neva 532
Series: Discover Your Bible
Title: *Discover: 1 & 2 Thessalonians*
Publisher: Church Development Resources, 1990

Num. Sess.	Group Time	Num. Pgs.	Avg. Qst.	Price	Audience	Format	Bible Study
6	60-75	44	9	$1.30	Beginner	Workbk	Book

Features: Intro to Study, Glossary
★★★ Personal Application Preparation Time: None
★★ Relationship Building Ldr. Guide: Yes Size: 5.50 x 8.50
Subjects: 1 & 2 Thessalonians
Comments: Paul's letters to the Thessalonians have much to say to believers today, including how to live godly lives, what to believe about the return of Jesus Christ, and being ready for His return. Through these short but powerful books, group members can "discover" what it means to have faith, and how that faith can affect day-to-day living.

Author: Everson, A. Joseph and Carol Weiser 533
Series: Cross Signs
Title: *Who Is Our God? Portraits of God: Unit 3*
Publisher: Augsburg Fortress Publishers, 1992

Num. Sess.	Group Time	Num. Pgs.	Avg. Qst.	Price	Audience	Format	Bible Study
7	90-105	48	5	$3.75	New Christian	Book	Charctr

Features: Intro to Study, Prayer Helps, Worship Helps
★★★ Personal Application Preparation Time: Low
★★ Relationship Building Ldr. Guide: Yes Size: 5.50 x 8.50
Subjects: God
Comments: In this study, participants can learn more about God's nature and presence in their lives through Scripture, their own experiences, and the stories of others. The study reflects on various dimensions of biblical monotheism, or belief in one active God. According to the biblical record, the concept began with Sarah and Abraham.

Author: Eyre, Jacalyn 534
Series: Fruit of the Spirit
Title: *Faithfulness: The Foundation of True Friendship*
Publisher: Zondervan, 1991 ISBN: 0-31053-671-5

Num. Sess.	Group Time	Num. Pgs.	Avg. Qst.	Price	Audience	Format	Bible Study
6	45-60	48	12	$4.99	New Christian	Workbk	Topical

Features: Intro to Study, Ldr's Notes
★★★ Personal Application Preparation Time: None
★★ Relationship Building Ldr. Guide: No Size: 5.50 x 8.50
Subjects: Christian Living, Commitments, Forgiveness, Friendships, Fruit of the Spirit, Relationships
Comments: This 6-week study looks at essential qualities participants must acquire to become faithful friends; qualities that help lay a foundation for lasting relationships. Lessons include: "A Commitment to Be There"; "A Willingness to Forgive"; "A Promise of Support"; "Honoring Our Commitments"; "Fulfilling Our Responsibilities"; and "The Rewards of Faithfulness."

Author: Eyre, Stephen D. & Jacalyn Eyre **535**
Series: Spiritual Encounter Guides
Title: *Abiding in Christ's Love*
Publisher: InterVarsity, 1994 ISBN: 0-83081-183-4

Num. Sess.	Group Time	Num. Pgs.	Avg. Qst.	Price	Audience	Format	Bible Study
4	30-45	95	Vary	$4.99	New Christian	Workbk	Topical

Features: Intro to Study, Charts
★★★★ Personal Application Preparation Time: Med
★ Relationship Building Ldr. Guide: No Size: 5.50 x 8.25
Subjects: Devotionals, John
Comments: This 4-week personal study guide leads participants through John 13–17. Daily devotion and study times help them find intimacy with God. John 13–17 moves from Jesus' public ministry to His private ministry, and reveals His most intimate conversations with followers during His last days on earth. He told them how they could continue to live in His presence and how His Spirit would care for and work through them.

Author: Eyre, Stephen D. & Jacalyn Eyre **536**
Series: Spiritual Encounter Guides
Title: *Anticipating Christ's Return*
Publisher: InterVarsity, 1994 ISBN: 0-83081-182-6

Num. Sess.	Group Time	Num. Pgs.	Avg. Qst.	Price	Audience	Format	Bible Study
4	30-45	111	Vary	$4.99	New Christian	Workbk	Topical

Features: Intro to Study, Prayer Helps, Charts
★★★★ Personal Application Preparation Time: Med
★ Relationship Building Ldr. Guide: No Size: 5.50 x 8.25
Subjects: Devotionals, Revelation, Apocalyptic
Comments: This 4-week personal study guide leads participants through Revelation. From Revelation they see who Christ wants them to be, and what He wants His Church to be like as it waits His return. The study discusses the future of this world and how Christians should be prepared for its end. It helps participants live in hope today while awaiting the future. It could be used to supplement a small group study or as a 25-week office study.

Author: Eyre, Stephen D. **537**
Series: LifeGuide Bible Study
Title: *Christian Beliefs*
Publisher: InterVarsity, 1989 ISBN: 0-83081-061-7

Num. Sess.	Group Time	Num. Pgs.	Avg. Qst.	Price	Audience	Format	Bible Study
12	45-60	64	12	$4.99	Beginner	Workbk	Topical

Features: Intro to Leading a Study, Intro to Study, Ldr's Notes
★ Personal Application Preparation Time: Low
★ Relationship Building Ldr. Guide: No Size: 5.50 x 8.25
Subjects: Beliefs, Christian Living, God, Holy Spirit, Relationships, Theology
Comments: This discussion of Christian beliefs can provide the foundation for a healthy relationship with God and others. It begins with ways God reveals Himself and continues with strength and comfort in His power. It offers guidance for developing a relationship with the Holy Spirit, recognizing the effects of sin, renewing fellowship with God, and applying this knowledge in the church.

Author: Eyre, Stephen D. & Jacalyn Eyre **538**
Series: Spiritual Encounter Guides
Title: *Daring to Follow Jesus*
Publisher: InterVarsity, 1993 ISBN: 0-83081-179-6

Num. Sess.	Group Time	Num. Pgs.	Avg. Qst.	Price	Audience	Format	Bible Study
4	30-45	112	Vary	$4.99	New Christian	Workbk	Topical

Features: Intro to Study, Prayer Helps, Charts
★★★★ Personal Application Preparation Time: Med
★ Relationship Building Ldr. Guide: No Size: 5.50 x 8.25
Subjects: Devotionals, Jesus: Life/Teaching
Comments: This 4-week personal study guide investigates the 4 Gospels and the Epistles. Mark describes the beginnings of Jesus' ministry as He called the disciples. Matthew reveals what Jesus taught the disciples about how to live life in His kingdom. Luke uncovers the saving purpose of Jesus' ministry as He goes to Jerusalem to be crucified. John looks at Jesus' death on the cross and the events surrounding His resurrection.

Author: Eyre, Stephen D. & Jacalyn Eyre **539**
Series: Spiritual Encounter Guides
Title: *Enjoying Christ's Blessings*
Publisher: InterVarsity, 1994 ISBN: 0-83081-181-8

Num. Sess.	Group Time	Num. Pgs.	Avg. Qst.	Price	Audience	Format	Bible Study
4	30-45	109	Vary	$4.99	New Christian	Workbk	Topical

Features: Intro to Study, Prayer Helps, Charts
★★★★ Personal Application Preparation Time: Med
★ Relationship Building Ldr. Guide: No Size: 5.50 x 8.25
Subjects: Devotionals, Ephesians
Comments: This 4-week personal study guide leads participants through Ephesians. Daily devotions and study times help them find intimacy with God. Clarifies several points: the heavenly realms and the blessings and spiritual battles that take place there; the church is the arena in which heaven and earth meet and are blended to create a community of light and life; the power of God through history working to bring all people of the world together under Christ Lordship.

Author: Eyre, Stephen D. **540**
Series: Spiritual Encounter Guides
Title: *Entering God's Presence*
Publisher: InterVarsity, 1992 ISBN: 0-83081-176-1

Num. Sess.	Group Time	Num. Pgs.	Avg. Qst.	Price	Audience	Format	Bible Study
4	30-45	96	Vary	$4.99	New Christian	Workbk	Topical

Features: Intro to Study, Prayer Helps, Charts
★★★★ Personal Application Preparation Time: Med
★ Relationship Building Ldr. Guide: No Size: 5.50 x 8.25
Subjects: Devotionals, Prayer
Comments: This 4-week personal study guide leads participants through the basic components of the Christian life. Week 1— "Warming Up to God"; Week 2— "Studying and Meditating on Scripture"; Week 3— "Meditating on Life"; and Week 4— "Praying." A month-long series of guided quiet times has a two-fold purpose, to encourage fellowship with God and provide skills that will become lifelong disciplines.

Author: Eyre, Stephen D. & Jacalyn 541
Series: LifeGuide Bible Study
Title: *Matthew: Being Discipled by Jesus*
Publisher: InterVarsity, 1987 ISBN: 0-83081-003-X

Num. Sess.	Group Time	Num. Pgs.	Avg. Qst.	Price	Audience	Format	Bible Study
24	45-60	96	12	$4.99	New Christian	Workbk	Book

Features: Intro to Leading a Study, Intro to Study, Ldr's Notes
★ Personal Application Preparation Time: Low
★ Relationship Building Ldr. Guide: No Size: 5.50 x 8.25
Subjects: Grief, Jesus: Life/Teaching, Matthew, Suffering
Comments: This 2-part study of Matthew will help produce better disciples and disciplemakers. The first part, "Discovering the King," focuses on the identity and authority of Jesus; the second part, "The Rejection and Resurrection of the King," focuses on Jesus as He encounters opposition and persecution. Matthew, a tax collector, was most concerned with practical application: how to handle anger, envy, suffering, grief, and more.

Author: Eyre, Stephen D. 542
Series: The TruthSeed Series
Title: *Old Testament Prayer: Faith of Our Fathers*
Publisher: Victor Books, 1995 ISBN: 1-56476-368-4

Num. Sess.	Group Time	Num. Pgs.	Avg. Qst.	Price	Audience	Format	Bible Study
6	45-60	80	12	$4.99	Beginner	Workbk	Topical

Features: Intro to Leading a Study, Intro to Study, Bibliography, Prayer Helps, Scrpt Memory Helps, Ldr's Notes, Persnl Study Quest
★★★ Personal Application Preparation Time: None
★★★ Relationship Building Ldr. Guide: No Size: 6.0 x 9.0
Subjects: Old Testament, Prayer
Comments: This new series of inductive Bible studies enables men and women to experience community and develop godliness in either discussion group or personal settings. Questions are designed and field-tested for seekers, new believers, and mature Christians. Enrichment material for further study is provided along with a bibliography. Includes 6 sessions on how to pray the prayers of our ancestors in faith.

Author: Eyre, Stephen D. 543
Series: Fruit of the Spirit
Title: *Patience: The Benefits of Waiting*
Publisher: Zondervan, 1991 ISBN: 0-31053-681-2

Num. Sess.	Group Time	Num. Pgs.	Avg. Qst.	Price	Audience	Format	Bible Study
6	45-60	48	12	$4.99	New Christian	Workbk	Topical

Features: Intro to Study, Ldr's Notes
★★★ Personal Application Preparation Time: None
★★ Relationship Building Ldr. Guide: No Size: 5.50 x 8.50
Subjects: Christian Living, Forgiveness, Fruit of the Spirit, Obedience
Comments: This 6-week study, using passages from Proverbs and the New Testament, helps participants appreciate God's kindness so that they will be motivated to be kind to others. Lessons include: "The Benefits of Patience," "The Blessings of Perseverance," "The Virtue of Slowness," "Patience and Forgiveness," "Waiting for the Lord," and "Waiting Until the End."

Author: Eyre, Stephen D. 544
Series: Spiritual Encounter Guides
Title: *Sinking Your Roots in Christ*
Publisher: InterVarsity, 1992 ISBN: 0-83081-177-X

Num. Sess.	Group Time	Num. Pgs.	Avg. Qst.	Price	Audience	Format	Bible Study
4	30-45	96	Vary	$4.99	New Christian	Workbk	Topical

Features: Intro to Study, Prayer Helps, Charts
★★★★ Personal Application Preparation Time: Med
★ Relationship Building Ldr. Guide: No Size: 5.50 x 8.25
Subjects: Colossians/Philemon, Devotionals
Comments: This 4-week personal study guide leads participants through the Book of Colossians. The Apostle Paul wrote this letter to help the Colossians confront false teachers who somehow managed to combine elements of Jewish legalism with Gentile mystery religions. The author offers daily help to participants who want to approach God, meditate on Scripture, and pray. The study covers Paul's guidance to the Colossians concerning the dos and don'ts of believing.

Author: Eyre, Stephen D. & Jacalyn Eyre 545
Series: Spiritual Encounter Guides
Title: *Sitting at the Feet of Jesus*
Publisher: InterVarsity, 1993 ISBN: 0-83081-178-8

Num. Sess.	Group Time	Num. Pgs.	Avg. Qst.	Price	Audience	Format	Bible Study
4	30-45	95	Vary	$4.99	New Christian	Workbk	Topical

Features: Intro to Study, Prayer Helps
★★★★ Personal Application Preparation Time: Med
★ Relationship Building Ldr. Guide: No Size: 5.50 x 8.25
Subjects: Devotionals, Sermon on the Mount
Comments: This 4-week personal study guide leads participants through the Sermon on the Mount. Daily devotion and study times help readers find intimacy with God. Week 1— "Qualities of Discipleship"; Week 2—"Righteous Relationships"; Week 3—"Righteous Acts and Attitudes"; and Week 4—"Righteous Results." It could be used to supplement a small group study, or as a 26-week office study.

Author: Eyre, Stephen D. 546
Series: The Discipleship Series
Title: *Spiritual Disciplines*
Publisher: Zondervan, 1992 ISBN: 0-31054-751-2

Num. Sess.	Group Time	Num. Pgs.	Avg. Qst.	Price	Audience	Format	Bible Study
6	45-60	63	12	$4.99	New Christian	Workbk	Topical

Features: Intro to Leading a Study, Intro to Study, Objectives, Scrpt Memory Helps, Follow Up, Ldr's Notes
★★★★ Personal Application Preparation Time: Med
★★ Relationship Building Ldr. Guide: No Size: 5.50 x 8.50
Subjects: Discipleship, Prayer, Worship
Comments: This guide introduces us to 6 key disciplines that deepen our knowledge of God and guide us in paths of godly thinking and action. Lesson titles include: "Prayer: The Quiet Power"; "Meditation: The Window to Scripture"; "Fellowship: The Family Discipline"; "Worship: The Pathway to God"; "Fasting: Feasting on God"; and "Simplicity: Making God Number One."

Author: Eyre, Stephen D. & Jacalyn Eyre **547**
Series: Spiritual Encounter Guides
Title: *Waiting on the Lord*
Publisher: InterVarsity, 1994 ISBN: 0-83081-180-X

Num. Sess.	Group Time	Num. Pgs.	Avg. Qst.	Price	Audience	Format	Bible Study
4	30-45	96	Vary	$4.99	New Christian	Workbk	Topical

Features: Intro to Study, Prayer Helps, Charts
★★★★ Personal Application Preparation Time: Med
★ Relationship Building Ldr. Guide: No Size: 5.50 x 8.25
Subjects: Devotionals, Psalms
Comments: This 4-week personal study guide leads participants through a series of Psalms which is intended to make it easier to wait on the Lord. Divided into 11 parts, it covers: waiting for security, for the Lord's time, for direction, in hope, for deliverance, for protection, for the Lord's love, for the Lord, for vindication, for relief and patience. It could be used to supplement a small group study or as a 27-week office study.

Author: Fagerstrom, Douglas L. **548**
Series:
Title: *Single Adult Ministry: The Next Step*
Publisher: Victor Books, 1993 ISBN: 1-56476-066-9

Num. Sess.	Group Time	Num. Pgs.	Avg. Qst.	Price	Audience	Format	Bible Study
	—	270	N/A	$17.99		Book	

Features:
Personal Application Preparation Time:
Relationship Building Ldr. Guide: Size: 6.50 x 9.50
Subjects: Homosexuality, Singles' Issues, Small Group Resource
Comments: From the Network of Single Adult Leaders (NSL) readers get input on such topics as: developing volunteers, starting a weekday ministry, reaching out beyond your group, ministering to children of divorce, dealing with homosexuality, and revitalizing a stagnant ministry. Also included are three chapters on divorce recovery, as approached from individual counseling, small group, and workshop methods.

Author: Fairbairn, Don **549**
Series: Lay Action Ministry
Title: *Contending for the Faith: Apologetics in Action*
Publisher: Lay Action Ministry Program, 1992

Num. Sess.	Group Time	Num. Pgs.	Avg. Qst.	Price	Audience	Format	Bible Study
12	60-75	126	Vary	$6.95	New Christian	Workbk	Topical

Features: Intro to Study
★★★ Personal Application Preparation Time: Low
★★★ Relationship Building Ldr. Guide: Yes Size: 5.50 x 8.50
Subjects: Apologetics, Singles' Issues
Comments: This Lamp lay training publication can equip people to defend and share their faith, especially with intellectual unbelievers. The study is divided into three sections: an introduction to apologetics describing the "Why" and evaluating claims to truth; "The Defensive Task: Demonstrating the Truth of Christianity" which looks at the reliability of the Bible, the existence and nature of God, Jesus as God and man; and "The Offensive Task: Responding to Other World Views."

Author: Fennema, Deb **550**
Series: Discover Your Bible
Title: *Discover Jonah: Leader's Guide*
Publisher: Church Development Resources, 1994

Num. Sess.	Group Time	Num. Pgs.	Avg. Qst.	Price	Audience	Format	Bible Study
4	60-75	36	6	$1.85	Beginner	Workbk	Charctr

Features: Intro to Study
★★★ Personal Application Preparation Time: None
★★ Relationship Building Ldr. Guide: Yes Size: 5.50 x 8.50
Subjects: Bible Personalities
Comments: The story of Jonah is among the most familiar in the Bible. Some people recognize it as a wild fish tale told in an old Sunday School class. But it is undeniably an action-packed plot, filled with all the twists and turns of a modern-day thriller. Who was Jonah? How did he end up in the belly of a monstrous fish? And why? Jonah's story, recounted in 4 short chapters, answers these questions and more about God, obedience, and what it means to answer His call.

Author: Fennema, Deb **551**
Series: Discover Your Bible
Title: *Discover: 1 & 2 Peter*
Publisher: Church Development Resources, 1993

Num. Sess.	Group Time	Num. Pgs.	Avg. Qst.	Price	Audience	Format	Bible Study
10	60-75	70	6	$2.00	Beginner	Workbk	Book

Features: Intro to Study, Glossary
★★★ Personal Application Preparation Time: None
★★ Relationship Building Ldr. Guide: Yes Size: 5.50 x 8.50
Subjects: 1 & 2 Peter
Comments: In these 2 letters, Peter feeds Jesus' sheep, believers scattered throughout the region. He prepares them to face persecution, warns them of false teachers, and reminds them how they are to live as "a people belonging to God." As Peter wrote these letters, he was nearing the end of his life. Shortly after 2 Peter was written, he suffered a martyr's death at the hand of Nero, the Roman emperor.

Author: Ferguson, Dr. David, et al. **552**
Series: Intimate Life Series
Title: *Parenting With Intimacy*
Publisher: Victor Books, 1995 ISBN: 1-56476-522-9

Num. Sess.	Group Time	Num. Pgs.	Avg. Qst.	Price	Audience	Format	Bible Study
	—	244	N/A	$15.99			

Features:
Personal Application Preparation Time:
Relationship Building Ldr. Guide: Size: 6.0 x 9.0
Subjects: Family, Parenting
Comments: This book can help parents learn to develop styles of parenting based on biblical principles of intimacy. It should be used with a companion workbook, which promotes an integration of newly acquired knowledge with behavioral patterns. Family issues addressed include understanding the intimacy needs of each member of the family, the importance of adapting as your child changes, and the challenge of single parenthood and adopted children.

Author: Ferguson, Dr. David 553
Series: Intimate Life Series
Title: *Parenting With Intimacy Workbook*
Publisher: Victor Books, 1995 ISBN: 1-56476-523-7

Num. Sess.	Group Time	Num. Pgs.	Avg. Qst.	Price	Audience	Format	Bible Study
	—	274	N/A	$14.99			

Features:
Personal Application Preparation Time:
Relationship Building Ldr. Guide: Size: 7.50 x 9.25
Subjects: Family, Parenting
Comments: This workbook is companion to the book by the same title, and both can be used in individual and small group studies. Together they can help parents learn to develop styles of parenting based on biblical principles of intimacy. Family issues addressed include understanding the intimacy needs of each member of the family, the importance of adapting as a child changes, and the challenge of single parenthood and adopted children.

Author: Fields, Don 554
Series: LifeGuide Bible Study
Title: *Nehemiah: The Courage to Face Opposition*
Publisher: InterVarsity, 1994 ISBN: 0-83081-033-1

Num. Sess.	Group Time	Num. Pgs.	Avg. Qst.	Price	Audience	Format	Bible Study
13	45-60	64	11	$4.99	New Christian	Workbk	Book

Features: Intro to Leading a Study, Intro to Study, Ldr's Notes
★★ Personal Application Preparation Time: Low
★ Relationship Building Ldr. Guide: No Size: 5.50 x 8.25
Subjects: Ezra/Nehemiah
Comments: This study of Nehemiah shows a leader who faced opposition and difficulty from every side, even from his own people. Yet he stood against the enemy and trusted God. Participants who aren't confronted by enemies in war can still learn from Nehemiah's courage, faith, and follow through. His gifts in administration and perseverance enabled him to mold people into "people of God" even if it required him to be harsh at times.

Author: Finzel, Hans 555
Series: GroupBuilder Resources
Title: *Observe Interpret Apply: How to Study the Bible Inductively*
Publisher: Victor Books, 1994 ISBN: 1-56476-221-1

Num. Sess.	Group Time	Num. Pgs.	Avg. Qst.	Price	Audience	Format	Bible Study
9	75-90	240	10	$12.99	New Christian	Workbk	Topical

Features: Intro to Leading a Study, Objectives, Charts, Appendix
★★★★ Personal Application Preparation Time: Med
★★★ Relationship Building Ldr. Guide: No Size: 7.25 x 9.25
Subjects: Bible Study
Comments: This book provides tools necessary for participants to discover "refreshing mountain streams" of biblical truth. With "observation," participants search for answers to the who, what, when, and where. "Interpretation" examines passage structure by looking for comparison, parallels, contrast, and climax, as participants ask "how" and "why" questions. "Application" challenges participants to apply text to their lives. Provides examples, outlines, space, and encouragement.

Author: Fisher, Mary 556
Series: Global Issues
Title: *People and Technology*
Publisher: InterVarsity, 1990 ISBN: 0-83084-909-2

Num. Sess.	Group Time	Num. Pgs.	Avg. Qst.	Price	Audience	Format	Bible Study
6	45-60	47	13	$4.99	Beginner	Workbk	Topical

Features: Intro to Leading a Study, Intro to Study, Biblio., Follow Up
★★ Personal Application Preparation Time: Low
★★ Relationship Building Ldr. Guide: No Size: 5.50 x 8.25
Subjects: Faith, Morals, Social Issues
Comments: This 6-week study explores how faith and life intersect in an increasingly complex technological society. Questions addressed include: "Is technology leading us to think differently about ourselves?" and "Is it drawing us away from the mysteries of human relationships?" The introduction states that technology can't help produce an improved moral dimension of life and ministry; it sometimes has to be bypassed for the sake of moral living.

Author: Fishwick, Nina M. 557
Series:
Title: *Strength Not My Own, A: Leader's Guide*
Publisher: Standard Publishing, 1992 ISBN: 0-87403-745-X

Num. Sess.	Group Time	Num. Pgs.	Avg. Qst.	Price	Audience	Format	Bible Study
13	45-60	64	N/A	$3.99	New Christian	Book	Topical

Features: Objectives, No Grp Discussion Quest
★★★ Personal Application Preparation Time: None
★★ Relationship Building Ldr. Guide: Yes Size: 5.50 x 8.50
Subjects: Christian Life
Comments: This course is based on Lawson's book, *A Strength Not My Own.* Since it contains 13 lessons, it's optimal use is in a 3-month study with 13 weekly sessions. However, churches can use it as a summer vacation Bible school course or other short-term study. Lessons cover: "When I Am Little, Then I Am Big," "When I Am Poor, Then I Am Rich," "How to Walk by Faith," and "Everything I Need for Joy."

Author: Flanagan, Dr. Bill 558
Series:
Title: *Divorce Recovery Workshop*
Publisher: Gospel Films, 1990

Num. Sess.	Group Time	Num. Pgs.	Avg. Qst.	Price	Audience	Format	Bible Study
6	105-120	34	Vary	$59.95	Beginner	Video	Topical

Features: Intro to Study, Bibliography, Study Overview, Agenda, Appendix, Publicity Ideas, Video Study Guide
★★★★ Personal Application Preparation Time: Low
★★★★ Relationship Building Ldr. Guide: Yes Size: 14.0 x 9.0
Subjects: Divorce, Forgiveness, Relationships, Singles' Issues
Comments: This 3-tape, 6-part video workshop deals with divorce recovery. The information is based on Jim Smoke's *Growing Through Divorce*. The 6 sessions include: "Is This Really Happening to Me?," "Coping with Your Ex-spouse," "Assuming New Responsibilities," "Being a Single Parent," "Finding and Experiencing Forgiveness," and "Thinking About New Relationships.

Author: Flynn, Leslie B. 559
Series:
Title: *Twelve, The*
Publisher: Victor Books, 1982 ISBN: 0-88207-310-9

Num. Sess.	Group Time	Num. Pgs.	Avg. Qst.	Price	Audience	Format	Bible Study
13	60-75	141	N/A	$8.99	New Christian	Book	Charctr

Features:
★★★ Personal Application Preparation Time: Low
★★★ Relationship Building Ldr. Guide: Yes Size: 5.50 x 8.0
Subjects: Bible Personalities, Jesus: Life/Teaching
Comments: In this 13-week study, we learn about Jesus' disciples and ask questions, such as "Who were they?" "What were they like before they met Jesus?" and "How did He change them?" The disciples were ordinary men until Jesus touched their lives. The study examines their personalities and actions as recorded in Scripture. A leader's guide includes reproducible transparency masters.

Author: Flynn, Leslie B. 560
Series:
Title: *19 Gifts of the Spirit*
Publisher: Victor Books, 1994 ISBN: 1-56476-337-4

Num. Sess.	Group Time	Num. Pgs.	Avg. Qst.	Price	Audience	Format	Bible Study
21	60-75	230	N/A	$8.99	New Christian	Book	Topical

Features: No Grp Discussion Quest
★★★ Personal Application Preparation Time: Low
★★ Relationship Building Ldr. Guide: Size: 5.50 x 8.50
Subjects: Fruit of the Spirit, Spiritual Gifts, Theology
Comments: This book nondogmatically provides both enumeration and classification of gifts. The author understands that scholars have differences of opinion, revealing more or fewer gifts and arranging them in various categories. Nonetheless, he feels the listing and grouping in this volume have merit. He defines 19 gifts, discusses their value for today, states their purpose, and helps readers discover and use their gifts. Questions are not provided for group discussions.

Author: Ford, Leighton 561
Series: LifeGuide Bible Study
Title: *Meeting Jesus*
Publisher: InterVarsity, 1988 ISBN: 0-83081-060-9

Num. Sess.	Group Time	Num. Pgs.	Avg. Qst.	Price	Audience	Format	Bible Study
13	45-60	79	12	$4.99	Beginner	Workbk	Topical

Features: Intro to Leading a Study, Intro to Study, Ldr's Notes
★★ Personal Application Preparation Time: Low
★★ Relationship Building Ldr. Guide: No Size: 5.50 x 8.25
Subjects: Evangelism, Gospels, Jesus: Life/Teaching
Comments: A study for anyone who wants a fresh look at Jesus. The Gospels—Matthew, Mark, Luke, and John—although similar, have unique perspectives on the story of Jesus. This study guide selects 13 key facets of the story of Jesus that disclose His person, teaching, actions, and claims. Each study explores who Jesus was, and what He can be in our lives today.

Author: Foster, Harry 562
Series:
Title: *Normal Christian Life, The*
Publisher: Christian Literature Crusade, 1976 ISBN: 0-87508-418-4

Num. Sess.	Group Time	Num. Pgs.	Avg. Qst.	Price	Audience	Format	Bible Study
14	45-60	52	10	$2.95	Beginner	Book	Topical

Features: Intro to Study
★★★★ Personal Application Preparation Time: Low
★★ Relationship Building Ldr. Guide: No Size: 4.25 x 7.0
Subjects: Christian Life, Faith
Comments: This is a companion guide to the book by the same title. Each of 14 chapters draws attention to salient factors and suggests questions for thought and discussion. This classic study traces in practical terms the steps along the pathway of faith and presents God's eternal purpose in simple terms. Its central theme: "Christ, Our Life."

Author: Fretheim, Terence E. 563
Series: Search Weekly Bible
Title: *Unit 10/Ruth, 1 & 2 Samuel, 1 & 2 Kings*
Publisher: Augsburg Fortress Publishers, 1985

Num. Sess.	Group Time	Num. Pgs.	Avg. Qst.	Price	Audience	Format	Bible Study
8	90-105	64	Vary	$5.50	New Christian	Book	Book

Features: Intro to Study, Objectives, Prayer Helps, Worship Helps, Follow Up, Summary
★★ Personal Application Preparation Time: Med
★★ Relationship Building Ldr. Guide: Yes Size: 8.50 x 11.0
Subjects: Kings/Chronicles, Ruth, 1 & 2 Samuel
Comments: This 8-week study is devoted to selected passages from the Books of Ruth, 1 & 2 Samuel, and 1 & 2 Kings. The outline for Unit 10 is as follows: "A Time of Transition"; "The United Monarchy"; and "The Divided Monarchy." These sessions will lead participants through the history of Israel from the end of the period of the judges (about 1050 B.C.) to the fall of Jerusalem in 586 B.C.

Author: Fretheim, Terence E. 564
Series: Search Weekly Bible
Title: *Unit 9/Deuteronomy, Joshua, Judges*
Publisher: Augsburg Fortress Publishers, 1985

Num. Sess.	Group Time	Num. Pgs.	Avg. Qst.	Price	Audience	Format	Bible Study
8	90-105	64	Vary	$5.50	New Christian	Book	Book

Features: Intro to Study, Objectives, Prayer Helps, Worship Helps, Follow Up, Summary
★★ Personal Application Preparation Time: Med
★★ Relationship Building Ldr. Guide: Yes Size: 8.50 x 11.0
Subjects: Joshua, Judges, Numbers/Deuteronomy
Comments: This is a study of selected passages from Deuteronomy, Joshua, and Judges. The series is divided into 5 themes: Beginnings, Journey, Struggles, Experiences, and Hopes. The 3-part outline of this study includes: "The Book of the Covenant"; "The Basic Content of the Book of the Covenant"; and "Struggles for Life within the Covenant Relationship.

Author: Friedeman, Matt **565**
Series:
Title: *Accountability Connection*
Publisher: Victor Books, 1992 ISBN: 0-89693-052-1

Num. Sess.	Group Time	Num. Pgs.	Avg. Qst.	Price	Audience	Format	Bible Study
9	75-90	200	Vary	$8.99	New Christian	Book	Topical

Features: Intro to Leading a Study, Intro to Study, Bibliography, Follow Up, Ldr's Notes, Charts, Appendix
★★★★ Personal Application Preparation Time: Med
★★★★ Relationship Building Ldr. Guide: No Size: 5.50 x 8.50
Subjects: Accountability, Christian Life, Small Group Resource
Comments: Accountability groups, as Friedman explains, provide encouragement and strength in areas in which participants have failed. Having worked with many accountability groups, the author offers clear, simple steps for getting started. He addresses readers one-on-one, probing major life issues 1 chapter at a time, including topics such as money, devotional life, mission, sex, health, and family.

Author: Friends In Recovery **566**
Series:
Title: *Twelve Steps, The: A Spiritual Journey*
Publisher: Recovery Publications, 1988 ISBN: 0-94140-544-3

Num. Sess.	Group Time	Num. Pgs.	Avg. Qst.	Price	Audience	Format	Bible Study
30	105-120	270	Vary	$15.95	Beginner	Workbk	Topical

Features: Intro to Study, Bibliography, Appendix, Publicity Ideas
★★★★ Personal Application Preparation Time: Med
★★★★ Relationship Building Ldr. Guide: No Size: 8.50 x 11.0
Subjects: Counseling, Family, Psychology, Support
Comments: This study, for individuals reared in emotionally repressive and dysfunctional families, uses the "Twelve Steps" process in a Christian context. It is written by people reared in alcoholic and dysfunctional homes. Having felt no love and security as children, they were not able to mature into healthy, functional adults. This book contains explicit, detailed writing exercises for each step on the road to recovery; it reaffirms God's dominion and can lead a person to God.

Author: Fromer, Margaret **567**
Series: Fisherman Bible Studyguide
Title: *Genesis: Walking with God (Revised Edition)*
Publisher: Shaw, 1991 ISBN: 0-87788-359-9

Num. Sess.	Group Time	Num. Pgs.	Avg. Qst.	Price	Audience	Format	Bible Study
25	45-60	96	12	$4.99	Beginner	Workbk	Book

Features: Intro to Leading a Study, Intro to Study, Prayer Helps, Follow Up
★★★ Personal Application Preparation Time: None
★★ Relationship Building Ldr. Guide: No Size: 5.0 x 8.25
Subjects: Bible Personalities, Genesis, God
Comments: This study, which combines 2 former titles into 1 expanded edition, explores such fascinating Bible characters as Adam, Eve, Noah, Abraham, Sarah, Isaac, Jacob, and Joseph. In meeting some of God's first friends, and studying Bible passages in Genesis, participants learn to walk more intimately with Him.

Author: Fromer, Margaret & Sharrel Keyes **568**
Series: Fisherman Bible Studyguide
Title: *Jonah, Habakkuk & Malachi: Living Responsibly*
Publisher: Shaw, 1982 ISBN: 0-87788-432-3

Num. Sess.	Group Time	Num. Pgs.	Avg. Qst.	Price	Audience	Format	Bible Study
12	45-60	68	11	$4.99	Beginner	Workbk	Book

Features: Intro to Leading a Study, Intro to Study, Prayer Helps, Ldr's Notes
★★★ Personal Application Preparation Time: None
★★ Relationship Building Ldr. Guide: No Size: 5.0 x 8.25
Subjects: Bible Personalities, Holiness, Minor Prophets, Old Testament
Comments: This study of Jonah, Habakkuk, and Malachi shows how, then and now, God confronts individuals through His prophets, reminding them of His holiness, of His character, of the breadth of His perspective and love, and of the kind of responsible living He desires for all people. Each book demonstrates the prophet's change of heart toward God and His ways.

Author: Fromer, Margaret & Sharrel Keyes **569**
Series: Fisherman Bible Studyguide
Title: *Letters to the Thessalonians*
Publisher: Shaw, 1975 ISBN: 0-87788-489-7

Num. Sess.	Group Time	Num. Pgs.	Avg. Qst.	Price	Audience	Format	Bible Study
8	45-60	64	10	$4.99	New Christian	Workbk	Book

Features: Intro to Leading a Study, Intro to Study, Pre-discussion Quest, Ldr's Notes
★★ Personal Application Preparation Time: Low
★★ Relationship Building Ldr. Guide: No Size: 5.0 x 8.25
Subjects: False Teachers, Theology, 1 & 2 Thessalonians
Comments: This study is a response to the questions and problems new Christians were facing in Thessalonica. Paul's ministry there had been cut short, so his letters continued the discipleship course. Four things stand out: Paul's deep personal love for his readers; his concern that they stand for the truth about God and Jesus; his insistence that this right doctrine make a practical difference in their lives.

Author: Fromer, Margaret & Sharrel Keyes **570**
Series: Fisherman Bible Studyguide
Title: *Letters to Timothy: Discipleship in Action*
Publisher: Shaw, 1974 ISBN: 0-87788-490-0

Num. Sess.	Group Time	Num. Pgs.	Avg. Qst.	Price	Audience	Format	Bible Study
12	45-60	76	12	$4.99	New Christian	Workbk	Book

Features: Intro to Leading a Study, Intro to Study, Pre-discussion Quest, Ldr's Notes, Charts
★★ Personal Application Preparation Time: Low
★★ Relationship Building Ldr. Guide: No Size: 5.0 x 8.25
Subjects: Caring, Discipleship, Leadership, 1 & 2 Timothy/Titus
Comments: This chapter-by-chapter study of 1 & 2 Timothy is practical for those who struggle with a sense of inadequacy in the face of church problems and errant doctrine. Paul's letters to Timothy reflect Timothy's need for encouragement and confidence building. Paul's example of how to care and love, build up, and pray for others is one all can learn from.

Author: Fryling, Alice **571**
Series:
Title: *Disciple-Makers' Handbook*
Publisher: InterVarsity, 1989 ISBN: 0-83081-266-0

Num. Sess.	Group Time	Num. Pgs.	Avg. Qst.	Price	Audience	Format	Bible Study
13	—	210	N/A	$9.99	Mature Christian	Book	No

Features: Intro to Study, Bibliography, Appendix
Personal Application Preparation Time:
Relationship Building Ldr. Guide: Size: 5.50 x 8.25
Subjects: Caring, Discipleship, Faith, Friendships, Relationships, Small Group Resource
Comments: It describes how to begin a healthy discipling relationship. It offers practical help in the following: overcoming fears about discipling others, beginning a discipling relationship, learning to be a friend, learning how people change, modeling the Christian life, using Scripture in disciplemaking, helping a friend who hurts, and helping others share their faith. Includes time-tested resources.

Author: Fryling, Alice & Robert **572**
Series:
Title: *Handbook for Engaged Couples, A*
Publisher: InterVarsity, 1977 ISBN: 0-87784-363-5

Num. Sess.	Group Time	Num. Pgs.	Avg. Qst.	Price	Audience	Format	Bible Study
15	45-60	72	6	$5.99	Beginner	Workbk	Topical

Features: Intro to Study, Bibliography
★★★★ Personal Application Preparation Time: Low
★★★★ Relationship Building Ldr. Guide: No Size: 5.50 x 8.25
Subjects: Commitments, Marriage, Parenting, Relationships
Comments: This 15-week study is primarily for engaged couples who view engagement as a serious commitment that leads to the deepest and most permanent of human relationships. It encourages open, honest communication in the light of Scripture. It helps familiarize couples with each other's long-range ambitions, vacation preferences, and philosophy on child-rearing. It also helps them resolve differences. The study covers the time of engagement.

Author: Fryling, Alice & Robert **573**
Series:
Title: *Handbook for Married Couples, A*
Publisher: InterVarsity, 1984 ISBN: 0-87784-923-4

Num. Sess.	Group Time	Num. Pgs.	Avg. Qst.	Price	Audience	Format	Bible Study
13	45-60	92	5	$5.99	Beginner	Workbk	Topical

Features: Intro to Study, Bibliography
★★★ Personal Application Preparation Time: Low
★★★ Relationship Building Ldr. Guide: No Size: 5.50 x 8.25
Subjects: Decision Making, Failure, Joy, Marriage, Money, Sexual Issues
Comments: This 14-week study is designed for husbands and wives who want to stay out of marital trouble and focus on a course of growth and joy. The format features a manageable series of readings and exercises, and homework is recommended. Topics covered include communication, conflict resolution, decision making, money, spiritual growth, sexual fulfillment, failure, and setting goals.

Author: Fryling, Alice & Robert **574**
Series:
Title: *Handbook for Parents, A*
Publisher: InterVarsity, 1991 ISBN: 0-83081-742-5

Num. Sess.	Group Time	Num. Pgs.	Avg. Qst.	Price	Audience	Format	Bible Study
12	45-60	136	4	$6.99	Beginner	Workbk	Topical

Features: Intro to Study, Bibliography, Persnl Study Quest, Charts
★★★★ Personal Application Preparation Time: Low
★★★★ Relationship Building Ldr. Guide: No Size: 5.50 x 8.25
Subjects: Family, Parenting
Comments: This 12-week study is for parents who realize the challenge they face. Questions dealt with include: "What place should anger have in our family?" "Why does our child, whom we deeply love, feel unloved?" "Can we learn to build family members up rather than tearing them down in our daily interactions?" "In what ways are our family's needs changing?" "How can each of us as parents get our needs met in this family?" Includes personal reflection questions.

Author: Gaiser, Frederick J. **575**
Series: Search Weekly Bible
Title: *Unit 13/Psalms*
Publisher: Augsburg Fortress Publishers, 1986

Num. Sess.	Group Time	Num. Pgs.	Avg. Qst.	Price	Audience	Format	Bible Study
8	90-105	64	Vary	$5.50	New Christian	Book	Book

Features: Intro to Study, Objectives, Prayer Helps, Worship Helps, Follow Up, Summary
★★ Personal Application Preparation Time: Med
★★ Relationship Building Ldr. Guide: Yes Size: 8.50 x 11.0
Subjects: Psalms
Comments: This review of the book of Psalms is 1 of 20 units of a 5-year study titled "Search." This 8 session study looks at selected psalms beginning with a 2-session introduction, then moving from lament (3 sessions) to praise (3 sessions). It is divided into 3 parts: "Sweeter Than Honey!" "Out of the Depths"; and "Praise the Lord!" This study can lead participants to greater depths of praise.

Author: Galvin, Dr. James C., et al. **576**
Series: Life Application
Title: *Daniel*
Publisher: Tyndale House, 1989 ISBN: 0-84232-731-2

Num. Sess.	Group Time	Num. Pgs.	Avg. Qst.	Price	Audience	Format	Bible Study
13	60-90	84	12	$4.99	New Christian	Workbk	Book

Features: Intro to Leading a Study, Intro to Study, Study Overview, Digging Deeper Quest, Full Scrpt Printed, Drawings, Charts, Maps, Cross Ref
★★★ Personal Application Preparation Time: Med
★★★ Relationship Building Ldr. Guide: No Size: 6.50 x 9.0
Subjects: Caring, Daniel, Faith, God, Major Prophets
Comments: This study, which contains the complete text of Daniel, gives a historical account of the faithful Jews who lived in captivity and shows how God is in control of Heaven and earth, directing the nations and caring for His people. The study is divided into two main sections, Daniel's life (1:1–6:28) and Daniel's visions (7:1–12:13).

Author: Galvin, Dr. James C., et al. 577
Series: Life Application
Title: *Mark*
Publisher: Tyndale House, 1989 ISBN: 0-84232-715-0

Num. Sess.	Group Time	Num. Pgs.	Avg. Qst.	Price	Audience	Format	Bible Study
13	60-90	120	10	$4.99	New Christian	Workbk	Book

Features: Intro to Leading a Study, Intro to Study, Study Overview, Digging Deeper Quest, Full Scrpt Printed, Drawings, Charts, Maps, Cross Ref, Appendix
★★★ Personal Application Preparation Time: Med
★★★ Relationship Building Ldr. Guide: No Size: 6.50 x 9.0
Subjects: Jesus: Life/Teaching, Mark
Comments: This study presents the person, work, and teachings of Jesus. Mark was the first Gospel written, and the other Gospels quote all but 31 of its verses. Mark records more miracles than any other Gospel. The study has 3 main parts: Jesus' birth and preparation; Jesus' message and ministry; and Jesus' death and resurrection.

Author: Galvin, Dr. James C., et al. 578
Series: Life Application
Title: *1, 2 Timothy & Titus*
Publisher: Tyndale House, 1989 ISBN: 0-84232-734-7

Num. Sess.	Group Time	Num. Pgs.	Avg. Qst.	Price	Audience	Format	Bible Study
13	60-90	84	15	$4.99	New Christian	Workbk	Book

Features: Intro to Leading a Study, Intro to Study, Study Overview, Digging Deeper Quest, Full Scrpt Printed, Drawings, Charts, Maps, Cross Ref
★★★ Personal Application Preparation Time: Med
★★★ Relationship Building Ldr. Guide: No Size: 6.50 x 9.0
Subjects: Church Life, Faith, Leadership, Marriage, Obedience, Pastoral Epistles, Service, Theology, 1 & 2 Timothy/Titus
Comments: First Timothy offers instructions on right beliefs and instructions for the church and its leaders. Second Timothy reveals Paul's heart and his priorities: sound doctrine, steadfast faith, confident endurance, and enduring love. It offers foundations of Christian service.

Author: Gangel, Kenneth O. and Betty 579
Series: Accent On Truth
Title: *Defending Christian Liberty*
Publisher: David C. Cook Publishing Co., 1993 ISBN: 0-89636-299-X

Num. Sess.	Group Time	Num. Pgs.	Avg. Qst.	Price	Audience	Format	Bible Study
12	60-90	94	18	$5.49	New Christian	Workbk	Book

Features: Intro to Study, Digging Deeper Quest, Cartoons
★★★★ Personal Application Preparation Time: Med
★★ Relationship Building Ldr. Guide: No Size: 6.0 x 9.0
Subjects: Galatians
Comments: This practical treatment of Galatians demonstrates that it is as relevant today as in Paul's day. The Gospel condones neither legalism nor license. Paul challenges believers to return to basic salvation doctrine. Freedom and grace serve as central themes in Paul's defense of the Gospel. Dynamics of faith and significance of God's grace take Christians beyond the tentacles of the old nature and into a life of genuine liberty.

Author: Gangel, Kenneth O. and Betty 580
Series: Accent On Truth
Title: *Encountering the King: A Study of Matthew*
Publisher: David C. Cook Publishing Co., 1994 ISBN: 0-89636-307-4

Num. Sess.	Group Time	Num. Pgs.	Avg. Qst.	Price	Audience	Format	Bible Study
12	60-90	112	19	$5.49	New Christian	Workbk	Book

Features: Intro to Study, Digging Deeper Quest, Cartoons
★★★★ Personal Application Preparation Time: Med
★★ Relationship Building Ldr. Guide: No Size: 6.0 x 9.0
Subjects: Matthew
Comments: This study of Matthew reveals the dramatic history of Christ's life. Like the book of Genesis in the Old Testament, Matthew forms a foundation for understanding the New Testament, particularly the movement from presenting a Gospel of the King of Jews only, toward the universal appeal proclaimed by Paul and other members of his missionary team.

Author: Gangel, Kenneth O. 581
Series:
Title: *Feeding and Leading*
Publisher: Victor Books, 1989 ISBN: 0-89693-678-3

Num. Sess.	Group Time	Num. Pgs.	Avg. Qst.	Price	Audience	Format	Bible Study
20	—	330	N/A	$19.99		Book	

Features: Bibliography, Charts
Personal Application Preparation Time:
Relationship Building Ldr. Guide: Size: 6.50 x 9.50
Subjects: Leadership, Small Group Resource
Comments: This book focuses on a question: How well is a church's leadership or administrative team functioning? It begins with foundations of the administrative process, then focuses on the vocational Christian leader, pastor, president, principle, mission executive, and targeting issues such as spiritual leadership, leadership style, organization of work, goal setting, and long-range planning. It also covers the assessment of interests, needs of potential leaders, and much more.

Author: Gangel, Kenneth O. and Betty 582
Series: Accent On Truth
Title: *Growing in Grace and Godliness*
Publisher: David C. Cook Publishing Co., 1992 ISBN: 0-89636-291-4

Num. Sess.	Group Time	Num. Pgs.	Avg. Qst.	Price	Audience	Format	Bible Study
12	60-90	109	19	$5.49	New Christian	Workbk	Book

Features: Intro to Study, Digging Deeper Quest, Cartoons
★★★★ Personal Application Preparation Time: Med
★★ Relationship Building Ldr. Guide: No Size: 6.0 x 9.0
Subjects: 1 & 2 Timothy/Titus
Comments: These 3 books allow participants to eavesdrop on conversations among pastors. They expose Pastor Paul's heart for Timothy and his congregation, and his concern for Titus. In 1 Timothy, Paul focuses on doctrine and godliness, personal holiness, public worship, and church officers. Second Timothy teaches Christians to proclaim the faith, and Titus shows how to practice faith. Advice includes personal living, congregational teaching, and shepherding.

Author: Gangel, Kenneth O. and Betty **583**
Series: Accent On Truth
Title: *Learning to Be the Church*
Publisher: David C. Cook Publishing Co., 1992 ISBN: 0-89636-288-4

Num. Sess.	Group Time	Num. Pgs.	Avg. Qst.	Price	Audience	Format	Bible Study
12	60-90	108	18	$5.49	New Christian	Workbk	Book

Features: Intro to Study, Digging Deeper Quest, Cartoons, Maps
★★★★ Personal Application Preparation Time: Med
★★ Relationship Building Ldr. Guide: No Size: 6.0 x 9.0
Subjects: Acts
Comments: Twelve studies on Acts allow participants to discover first-hand how adventures, persecutions, successes, and failures of the early church can touch lives today. Subjects covered include five crucial truths to share with others about Christ, Peter's reason for focusing on Jesus' name before the Sanhedrin, responding to someone in the New Age or a satanic cult, and God's sovereignty.

Author: Gangel, Kenneth O. and Betty **584**
Series: Accent On Truth
Title: *Rejoicing in Faith and Freedom*
Publisher: David C. Cook Publishing Co., 1993 ISBN: 0-89636-292-2

Num. Sess.	Group Time	Num. Pgs.	Avg. Qst.	Price	Audience	Format	Bible Study
12	60-90	109	19	$5.49	New Christian	Workbk	Book

Features: Intro to Study, Digging Deeper Quest, Cartoons
★★★★ Personal Application Preparation Time: Med
★★ Relationship Building Ldr. Guide: No Size: 6.0 x 9.0
Subjects: Romans
Comments: This study of Romans concerns law and grace, faith and righteousness. For early Christians, faith meant intense, difficult, heart-wrenching decisions. Lions were real, and Rome's opposition unrelenting. Into this arena, Paul introduces the solid doctrinal foundation that Roman Christians needed. The message for modern Christians is that God expects them to know His truth, and declare with the same courage those who faced lions for their faith.

Author: Gangel, Kenneth O. **585**
Series:
Title: *Unwrap Your Spiritual Gifts: A Complete Coverage of God-Given Abilities*
Publisher: Victor Books, 1983 ISBN: 0-88207-102-5

Num. Sess.	Group Time	Num. Pgs.	Avg. Qst.	Price	Audience	Format	Bible Study
13	60-90	117	N/A	$8.99	New Christian	Book	Topical

Features:
★★★ Personal Application Preparation Time: Med
★★ Relationship Building Ldr. Guide: Yes Size: 5.50 x 8.0
Subjects: Christian Living, Church Life, New Testament, Spiritual Gifts
Comments: This study reviews abilities that help participants identify and use God-given spiritual gifts. By studying the New Testament, participants learn the difference between spiritual gifts and natural talents. Believers are encouraged to go beyond identifying their gifts to developing and using them for growing a local church and for building up all believers. A leader's guide with transparency masters is available.

Author: Gariepy, Henry **586**
Series:
Title: *Portraits of Perseverance*
Publisher: Victor Books, 1989 ISBN: 0-89693-149-8

Num. Sess.	Group Time	Num. Pgs.	Avg. Qst.	Price	Audience	Format	Bible Study
	10-20	220	N/A	$9.99	Beginner	Book	Book

Features: Intro to Study
Personal Application Preparation Time:
Relationship Building Ldr. Guide: Size: 5.50 x 8.50
Subjects: Devotionals, Job
Comments: This book of 100 meditations helps readers persevere through the struggles of their lives and emerge knowing that their Redeemer lives. It deals with such trials of life as divorce, depression, rebellious children, terminal cancer, unemployment, being out of money, soured friendship, and spiritual dryness. The meditations come from the Book of Job.

Author: Gariepy, Henry **587**
Series:
Title: *100 Portraits of Christ*
Publisher: Victor Books, 1987 ISBN: 1-56476-121-5

Num. Sess.	Group Time	Num. Pgs.	Avg. Qst.	Price	Audience	Format	Bible Study
	10-20	240	N/A	$10.99	New Christian	Book	Charctr

Features: Intro to Study, Index
★★★★ Personal Application Preparation Time: None
★★★★ Relationship Building Ldr. Guide: No Size: 5.50 x 8.0
Subjects: Devotionals, Jesus: Life/Teaching
Comments: This book is a biography of the person and ministry of Christ, as revealed by 100 names and titles ascribed to Him in Scripture. Each name and title is a revealing portrait of the Lord, providing readers with fresh insights and applications of their meaning for Christian living. The portraits are in four divisions: "Our Lord's Eternity"; "Our Lord's Earthly Life and Ministry"; "Our Lord's Abiding Ministry"; and "Our Lord's Self-Portraits ('I Am's')."

Author: Gates, Rebecca **588**
Series: A Bible Study for Women
Title: *Beauty of a Disciplined Life, The*
Publisher: Victor Books, 1987 ISBN: 0-89693-248-6

Num. Sess.	Group Time	Num. Pgs.	Avg. Qst.	Price	Audience	Format	Bible Study
10	60-90	96	9	$5.99	New Christian	Workbk	Book

Features: Intro to Leading a Study, Intro to Study, Objectives, Follow Up, Summary, Ldr's Notes
★★★ Personal Application Preparation Time: Med
★★ Relationship Building Ldr. Guide: No Size: 6.0 x 9.0
Subjects: Friendships, Marriage, Money, Proverbs, Relationships, Self-esteem, Stress, Wisdom, Women's Issues
Comments: These ten lessons from Proverbs help participants acquire and practice self-discipline that can help contemporary women resolve problems such as hectic schedules, financial burdens, marital stress, relational problems, and low self-esteem. Lessons cover the disciplines of wisdom, marital faithfulness, energy, quietness, speech, humility.

Author: Geisler, Norman & Thomas Howe 589
Series:
Title: *When Critics Ask*
Publisher: Victor Books, 1992 ISBN: 0-89693-698-8

Num. Sess.	Group Time	Num. Pgs.	Avg. Qst.	Price	Audience	Format	Bible Study
	—	600	N/A	$25.99		Book	

Features: Intro to Study, Bibliography, Index
Personal Application Preparation Time:
Relationship Building Ldr. Guide: Size: 6.25 x 9.25
Subjects: Small Group Resource
Comments: This comprehensive volume offers clear answers to major Bible controversies from Genesis to Revelation, and staunchly defends the authority and inspiration of Scripture. Written in a problem/solution format, the authors cover over 800 questions which critics and doubters raise about the Bible. Three extensive indices—topical, Scripture, and unorthodox doctrines—offer quick access to specific areas of interest. The book prepares readers to defend the hope found within.

Author: Geisler, Norman & Ron Brooks 590
Series:
Title: *When Skeptics Ask: A Handbook on Christian Evidences*
Publisher: Victor Books, 1990 ISBN: 0-89693-766-6

Num. Sess.	Group Time	Num. Pgs.	Avg. Qst.	Price	Audience	Format	Bible Study
	—	350	N/A	$23.99			

Features: Bibliography, Glossary, Index, Topical Index, Appendix
Personal Application Preparation Time:
Relationship Building Ldr. Guide: Size: 6.25 x 9.50
Subjects: Apologetics, Small Group Resource
Comments: This book gives a wide audience an orderly treatment of a wide variety of apologetic topics. It can be particularly useful to those who are evangelizing high school and college students, as well as thinking laypeople. It is easy to understand, covers most important areas, and answers many questions which regularly confront Christians. It can help all Christians defend their faith.

Author: Getz, Gene A. 591
Series: Biblical Renewal Series
Title: *Building Up One Another*
Publisher: Victor Books, 1976 ISBN: 0-88207-744-9

Num. Sess.	Group Time	Num. Pgs.	Avg. Qst.	Price	Audience	Format	Bible Study
13	60-75	120	N/A	$8.99	New Christian	Book	Topical

Features: Intro to Study
★★★★ Personal Application Preparation Time: Low
★★★ Relationship Building Ldr. Guide: Yes Size: 5.50 x 8.0
Subjects: Caring, Church Life, Relationships, Service
Comments: This study discusses 12 significant actions Christians must take toward one another to build up the Body of Christ. Each lesson includes a practical section, a series of steps for employing these actions. The 12 actions include, among others, honoring, accepting, greeting, serving, submitting, and encouraging one another.

Author: Getz, Gene A. 592
Series: Biblical Renewal Series
Title: *Encouraging One Another*
Publisher: Victor Books, 1981 ISBN: 0-88207-256-0

Num. Sess.	Group Time	Num. Pgs.	Avg. Qst.	Price	Audience	Format	Bible Study
13	60-75	143	N/A	$8.99	New Christian	Book	Topical

Features: Intro to Study, Maps
★★★★ Personal Application Preparation Time: Low
★★★ Relationship Building Ldr. Guide: Yes Size: 5.50 x 8.0
Subjects: Acts, Bible Personalities, Caring, Church Life, Relationships
Comments: This study stresses the need for Christians to encourage one another. A major portion follows the chronological and sequential development of Christianity in the Book of Acts. Barnabas, whose name means "son of encouragement," is an outstanding model. His "encouraging" lifestyle illustrates the process of mutual ministry for every member of the Body of Christ. Each chapter closes with a challenge, prayer, or "life response" segment.

Author: Getz, Gene A. 593
Series:
Title: *Joseph: Finding God's Strength in Times of Trial*
Publisher: Regal Books, 1983 ISBN: 0-83071-347-6

Num. Sess.	Group Time	Num. Pgs.	Avg. Qst.	Price	Audience	Format	Bible Study
13	60-75	168	Vary	$6.99	New Christian	Book	Topical

Features:
★★★★ Personal Application Preparation Time: Med
★★★★ Relationship Building Ldr. Guide: Yes Size: 5.0 x 8.0
Subjects: Bible Personalities, Parenting, Suffering
Comments: This study shows, through a look at Joseph's life, that God sometimes allows His children to suffer in order to accomplish His special purposes for their lives. Participants will find strength in God's arms when suffering, as did Joseph. This study looks at the effects of family background, what happens when parents show favoritism, and more. A separate leader's guide offers an 8- to 13-week study format. A reproducible lesson handout section is included.

Author: Getz, Gene A. 594
Series: Biblical Renewal Series
Title: *Loving One Another*
Publisher: Victor Books, 1979 ISBN: 0-88207-786-4

Num. Sess.	Group Time	Num. Pgs.	Avg. Qst.	Price	Audience	Format	Bible Study
13	60-75	143	N/A	$8.99	New Christian	Book	Topical

Features: Charts
★★★★ Personal Application Preparation Time: Low
★★★ Relationship Building Ldr. Guide: Yes Size: 5.50 x 8.0
Subjects: Caring, Church Life, Evangelism
Comments: This study offers a total New Testament perspective on evangelism. God's plan is that His body of believers become a community in which personal witnessing and evangelistic preaching are intensely productive. This study shows participants how to achieve greater unity and fruitfulness, in their lives as well as their churches. Each chapter closes with a "Personal Response" section designed to challenge to action.

Author: Getz, Gene A. **595**
Series:
Title: *Measure of a Man, The*
Publisher: Regal Books, 1974 ISBN: 0-83071-031-0

Num. Sess.	Group Time	Num. Pgs.	Avg. Qst.	Price	Audience	Format	Bible Study
21	45-60	220	Vary	$8.99	New Christian	Book	Topical

Features: Intro to Study
★★★ Personal Application Preparation Time: Low
★★ Relationship Building Ldr. Guide: No Size: 5.25 x 8.0
Subjects: Church Life, Discipleship, Leadership, Men's Issues, Pastoral Epistles, Service, 1 & 2 Timothy/Titus
Comments: This study gives the Apostle Paul's profile for Christian maturity. Through his letters to Timothy and Titus, he spells out in detail the qualifications for men who serve as leaders in the church. Following an introduction are 21 lessons with titles like: "Above Reproach," "Husband of One Wife," "Not Addicted to Wine," "Not Quick-Tempered," and more.

Author: Getz, Gene A. **596**
Series:
Title: *Measure of a Woman, The*
Publisher: Regal Books, 1977 ISBN: 0-83071-386-7

Num. Sess.	Group Time	Num. Pgs.	Avg. Qst.	Price	Audience	Format	Bible Study
14	45-60	140	Vary	$8.99	Beginner	Book	Topical

Features: Intro to Leading a Study, Intro to Study
★★★ Personal Application Preparation Time: Low
★★ Relationship Building Ldr. Guide: No Size: 5.0 x 8.0
Subjects: Family, Women's Issues, Work, 1 & 2 Peter, 1 & 2 Timothy/Titus
Comments: This biblical study of womanhood and femininity offers tested and proven guidelines from 1 Timothy, Titus, and 1 Peter. Among the topics discussed are God's perspective on beauty, what makes a woman worthy of respect, how to feel good about oneself, what makes a wife a good lover, and how career and family mix.

Author: Getz, Gene A. **597**
Series: Biblical Renewal Series
Title: *Praying for One Another*
Publisher: Victor Books, 1982 ISBN: 0-88207-351-6

Num. Sess.	Group Time	Num. Pgs.	Avg. Qst.	Price	Audience	Format	Bible Study
13	60-75	132	N/A	$8.99	New Christian	Book	Topical

Features: Intro to Study, Charts
★★★★ Personal Application Preparation Time: Low
★★★ Relationship Building Ldr. Guide: Yes Size: 5.50 x 8.0
Subjects: Caring, Christian Life, Prayer
Comments: This study focuses on corporate, or "body," prayer, rather than personal, or individual, prayer. Both kinds of prayer are important. Yet in Acts, nearly all references to prayer concern prayer in groups. This study traces the activities and growth of the early Church, demonstrating how "body" praying can be a key to releasing God's power. Topics covered include prayer as a privilege, the meaning of "continuous" prayer, the importance of praise in prayers, and more.

Author: Getz, Gene A. **598**
Series: Biblical Renewal Series
Title: *Serving One Another*
Publisher: Victor Books, 1984 ISBN: 0-88207-612-4

Num. Sess.	Group Time	Num. Pgs.	Avg. Qst.	Price	Audience	Format	Bible Study
13	60-75	153	N/A	$8.99	New Christian	Book	Topical

Features:
★★★★ Personal Application Preparation Time: Low
★★★ Relationship Building Ldr. Guide: Yes Size: 5.50 x 8.0
Subjects: Caring, Church Life, Relationships, Service
Comments: This study explores biblical standards of servanthood, based on selected passages from Paul's letters. Participants will be challenged to complete multiple-choice statements such as: "When I'm asked to take part in some form of Christian ministry I always agree, make excuses, or run for cover"; or "Being a good servant means I will always help, help when I feel like it, do what I'm told, or lose control." No matter what the response, there's always room for improvement.

Author: Gibbs, Eddie **599**
Series: GroupBuilder Resources
Title: *Good News Is for Sharing*
Publisher: Victor Books, 1993 ISBN: 1-56476-200-9

Num. Sess.	Group Time	Num. Pgs.	Avg. Qst.	Price	Audience	Format	Bible Study
8	75-90	139	Vary	$5.99	New Christian	Workbk	Topical

Features: Intro to Study, Objectives, Prayer Helps, Full Scrpt Printed, Ldr's Notes, Drawings
★★★★ Personal Application Preparation Time: None
★★★★ Relationship Building Ldr. Guide: No Size: 6.0 x 9.0
Subjects: Singles' Issues
Comments: This 8-session small group study will provide insights, skill training, and group support to build greater confidence and skill in sharing one's faith. In this study participants will examine 8 aspects of evangelism, including: barriers to evangelism, motivation for evangelism, consequences of keeping silent, sharing your testimony, creating opportunities for sharing one's faith, balancing urgency with patience.

Author: Gibson, Eva & Steve Price **600**
Series: Building Books
Title: *Building Christian Values*
Publisher: Bethany House, 1989 ISBN: 1-55661-024-6

Num. Sess.	Group Time	Num. Pgs.	Avg. Qst.	Price	Audience	Format	Bible Study
34	45-60	68	Vary	$6.99	New Christian	Workbk	Topical

Features: Intro to Study
★★ Personal Application Preparation Time: Low
★★ Relationship Building Ldr. Guide: Yes Size: 8.50 x 11.0
Subjects: Teens: Christian Liv, Teens: Decisions, Teens: Discipleship, Teens: Ethics
Comments: This 34-lesson in-depth study is designed to help young adults develop value systems that harmonize with the holiness of God, and equip them with God's Word to help them make wise decisions. Five major sections track values that can be built by looking at who God is, by participating in the wisdom of Jesus Christ through practical application of God's Word, by seeing how Joseph grew.

Author: Gibson, Eva & Steve Price **601**
Series: Building Books
Title: *Building Christian Confidence*
Publisher: Bethany House, 1987 ISBN: 0-87123-934-5

Num. Sess.	Group Time	Num. Pgs.	Avg. Qst.	Price	Audience	Format	Bible Study
34	45-60	79	Vary	$6.99	New Christian	Workbk	Topical

Features: Intro to Study, Scrpt Memory Helps
★★ Personal Application Preparation Time: Low
★★ Relationship Building Ldr. Guide: Yes Size: 8.50 x 11.0
Subjects: Teens: Discipleship
Comments: This 34-lesson study offers young people a deepened understanding of God and how He has created them. It helps them examine the truth of their own unique position in God's creative design, through consideration of four major issues: "Seeing My Partnership," "Seeing My Person," "Seeing My Potential," and "Seeing My Possibilities."

Author: Gillespie, Mike **602**
Series: Group's Active Bible Curriculum
Title: *Caring for God's Creation*
Publisher: Group Publishing, 1991 ISBN: 1-55945-121-1

Num. Sess.	Group Time	Num. Pgs.	Avg. Qst.	Price	Audience	Format	Bible Study
4	35-60	48	Vary	$9.99	Beginner	Workbk	Topical

Features: Intro to Leading a Study, Intro to Study, Objectives, Study Overview, Ldr's Notes, Handouts, Agenda, Publicity Ideas
★★★★ Personal Application Preparation Time: None
★★★★ Relationship Building Ldr. Guide: No Size: 8.50 x 11.0
Subjects: Teens: Christian Liv, Teens: Junior High, Teens: Values
Comments: In this study, junior highers discover how to be environmentally responsible. Participants learn about environmental concerns—and how Christian faith can help make a difference in solving the earth's "health" problems. Plus, they'll develop an awareness of God's power through creation. It can be adapted for a Bible class or youth meeting. Activity sheets are reproducible.

Author: Gillespie, Mike **603**
Series: Young Teen Feedback
Title: *Character Witnesses—Leader's Book*
Publisher: Victor Books, 1991 ISBN: 0-89693-837-9

Num. Sess.	Group Time	Num. Pgs.	Avg. Qst.	Price	Audience	Format	Bible Study
12	30-45	81	Vary	$13.99	New Christian	Book	Topical

Features: Intro to Study, Handouts
★★★★ Personal Application Preparation Time: None
★★★★ Relationship Building Ldr. Guide: Yes Size: 8.50 x 11.0
Subjects: Teens: Christian Liv, Teens: Discipleship
Comments: This study of 12 Bible characters presents the development of integrity in a way that helps young teens examine their own characters—and develop important traits like honesty, patience, reverence, and love. Each study is based on interviews with youth, including their feedback on personal needs and concerns. The format offers three four-week studies with reproducible student sheets. A student book is available.

Author: Gillespie, Mike **604**
Series:
Title: *Feelings: Frazzled, Frenzied & Frantic*
Publisher: Standard Publishing, 1994 ISBN: 0-87403-766-2

Num. Sess.	Group Time	Num. Pgs.	Avg. Qst.	Price	Audience	Format	Bible Study
12	45-60	96	Vary	$12.99	Beginner	Workbk	Topical

Features: Intro to Leading a Study, Intro to Study, Objectives, Prayer Helps, Handouts
★★★★ Personal Application Preparation Time: None
★★★★ Relationship Building Ldr. Guide: No Size: 8.50 x 11.0
Subjects: Teens: Emotions, Teens: Junior High
Comments: This study focuses on tough, private issues facing teens. Twelve lessons deal with loneliness, fear, differences, dreams, anger, insecurity, frustration, wonder, God's grace, quitting, confusion, and being in love. The book includes reproducible worksheets; teacher activities that make every study exciting for any size group; and debriefing questions for in-depth discussion in each lesson.

Author: Gillespie, Mike **605**
Series:
Title: *Fun Old Testament Bible Studies*
Publisher: Group Publishing, 1989 ISBN: 0-93152-964-6

Num. Sess.	Group Time	Num. Pgs.	Avg. Qst.	Price	Audience	Format	Bible Study
32	30-60	172	N/A	$15.99	New Christian	Book	Book

Features: Intro to Study, Objectives, Prayer Helps, Follow Up, Drawings, Handouts, Maps, Index
★★★★ Personal Application Preparation Time: Low
★★★★ Relationship Building Ldr. Guide: No Size: 8.50 x 11.0
Subjects: Teens: Friends, Teens: Old Testament, Teens: Peer Pressure
Comments: This book provides 32 Old Testament studies on themes important to teenagers, including forgiveness, peer pressure, temptation, friendship, making mistakes, and more. Each session is designed to help teenagers experience Bible drama and then apply what they've learned to their own problems and concerns. The studies include attention-getting openers, activities, reproducible handouts.

Author: Gillespie, Mike **606**
Series: Group's Active Bible Curriculum
Title: *Making Good Decisions*
Publisher: Group Publishing, 1991 ISBN: 1-55945-209-9

Num. Sess.	Group Time	Num. Pgs.	Avg. Qst.	Price	Audience	Format	Bible Study
4	35-60	48	Vary	$9.99	Beginner	Workbk	Topical

Features: Intro to Leading a Study, Intro to Study, Objectives, Study Overview, Ldr's Notes, Drawings, Handouts, Agenda, Publicity Ideas
★★★★ Personal Application Preparation Time: None
★★★★ Relationship Building Ldr. Guide: No Size: 8.50 x 11.0
Subjects: Teens: Christian Liv, Teens: Decisions, Teens: Senior High
Comments: This study helps senior high students make wise, faith-based choices. Its four lessons provide practical skills to help them build confidence in decision making; understand how the Bible helps them exercise good judgment; experience Christian growth as they discover the importance of faith in decision making; and experience hope as they learn how God helps them rebound from past mistakes.

Author: Gillespie, Mike **607**
Series: Group's Active Bible Curriculum
Title: *Movies, Music, TV & Me*
Publisher: Group Publishing, 1991 ISBN: 1-55945-213-7

Num. Sess.	Group Time	Num. Pgs.	Avg. Qst.	Price	Audience	Format	Bible Study
4	35-60	48	Vary	$9.99	Beginner	Workbk	Topical

Features: Intro to Leading a Study, Intro to Study, Objectives, Study Overview, Ldr's Notes, Handouts, Agenda, Publicity Ideas
★★★★ Personal Application Preparation Time: None
★★★★ Relationship Building Ldr. Guide: No Size: 8.50 x 11.0
Subjects: Teens: Christian Liv, Teens: Decisions, Teens: Media, Teens: Music, Teens: Senior High
Comments: This study teaches teenagers to make wise, faith-based choices. Participants learn practical decision-making skills and how to grow beyond bad choices. It helps them build confidence in their decision-making abiblity. It can be adapted for a Bible class or youth meeting. Activity sheets are reproducible. Student books not required.

Author: Gilroy, Mark **608**
Series: Group's Active Bible Curriculum
Title: *Christlike Leadership*
Publisher: Group Publishing, 1992 ISBN: 1-55945-231-5

Num. Sess.	Group Time	Num. Pgs.	Avg. Qst.	Price	Audience	Format	Bible Study
4	35-60	45	Vary	$9.99	Beginner	Workbk	Topical

Features: Intro to Leading a Study, Intro to Study, Objectives, Study Overview, Ldr's Notes, Handouts, Agenda, Publicity Ideas
★★★★ Personal Application Preparation Time: None
★★★★ Relationship Building Ldr. Guide: No Size: 8.50 x 11.0
Subjects: Teens: Christian Liv, Teens: Leadership, Teens: Senior High
Comments: Through this course, teenagers explore leadership, learn to make wise choices about the kind of leaders to follow, see how Christian leadership means serving others, and learn ways to positively influence others. Participants learn they don't need to be popular or charming to be good leaders. It can be adapted for a Bible class or youth meeting. Acitvity sheets are reproducible.

Author: Gilroy, Mark **609**
Series: Group's Active Bible Curriculum
Title: *Exploring Ethical Issues*
Publisher: Group Publishing, 1992 ISBN: 1-55945-225-0

Num. Sess.	Group Time	Num. Pgs.	Avg. Qst.	Price	Audience	Format	Bible Study
4	35-60	48	Vary	$9.99	Beginner	Workbk	Topical

Features: Intro to Leading a Study, Intro to Study, Objectives, Study Overview, Ldr's Notes, Handouts, Agenda, Publicity Ideas
★★★★ Personal Application Preparation Time: None
★★★★ Relationship Building Ldr. Guide: No Size: 8.50 x 11.0
Subjects: Teens: Christian Liv, Teens: Decisions, Teens: Ethics, Teens: Senior High
Comments: In this study teenagers learn how to use God's ideals to make responsible choices. Participants explore the sanctity of human life, develop Scripture-based views on important issues (including abortion and euthanasia), learn to live with others who disagree with them, and discover how to apply biblical principles to their future careers.

Author: Glaphre' **610**
Series: Woman's Workshop Series
Title: *Talking with God: Studies on Prayer*
Publisher: Zondervan, 1985 ISBN: 0-31045-301-1

Num. Sess.	Group Time	Num. Pgs.	Avg. Qst.	Price	Audience	Format	Bible Study
12	90-120	153	Vary	$6.99	New Christian	Workbk	Topical

Features: Intro to Study, Prayer Helps, Scrpt Memory Helps, Worship Helps, Ldr's Notes, Persnl Study Quest
★★★ Personal Application Preparation Time: Low
★★★ Relationship Building Ldr. Guide: No Size: 5.25 x 8.0
Subjects: Prayer, Women's Issues
Comments: This study on prayer helps participants increase the desire and discipline necessary to mature in prayer. However, before beginning this study they should ask, "Do I want to improve my prayer life?" and "Will I pray?" A serious study, it is suited for those who have never prayed, who struggle to pray consistently and fervently, and who already find prayer meaningful but want to improve their prayer life.

Author: Glasser, Arthur F. **611**
Series: Global Issues
Title: *Spiritual Conflict*
Publisher: InterVarsity, 1990 ISBN: 0-83084-901-7

Num. Sess.	Group Time	Num. Pgs.	Avg. Qst.	Price	Audience	Format	Bible Study
6	45-60	48	12	$4.99	Beginner	Workbk	Topical

Features: Intro to Leading a Study, Intro to Study, Bibliography, Prayer Helps, Follow Up
★ Personal Application Preparation Time: Low
★ Relationship Building Ldr. Guide: No Size: 5.50 x 8.25
Subjects: Satan
Comments: This 6-week study helps participants understand spiritual conflict and prepare for battle with principalities and powers. Satan and the battle with supernatural powers are mentioned in all of Paul's epistles. He says these powers have generated a spirit of open revolt against God, and have penetrated all cultures and social structures, blinding people to the Gospel.

Author: Gledhill, Tom **612**
Series: The Bible Speaks Today
Title: *Message of the Song of Songs, The*
Publisher: InterVarsity, 1994 ISBN: 0-83081-235-0

Num. Sess.	Group Time	Num. Pgs.	Avg. Qst.	Price	Audience	Format	Bible Study
6	60-120	250	6	$12.99	New Christian	Book	Book

Features: Intro to Study, Bibliography
★★★ Personal Application Preparation Time: Med
★★ Relationship Building Ldr. Guide: No Size: 5.50 x 8.25
Subjects: Emotions, Love, Old Testament, Song of Solomon
Comments: This commentary for serious Bible students can be studied in 6 or more sessions. In it, Gledhill maintains that the Song of Songs is a literary, poetic exploration of human love that strongly affirms loyalty, beauty, and sexuality. He contends that the songwriter, through metaphor and imagery, spins a tale of human love into the cadence of verse, innocent of readers' quests for historical people behind the text.

Author: Going, Nancy **613**
Series: Group's Active Bible Curriculum
Title: *Boosting Self-Esteem*
Publisher: Group Publishing, 1990 ISBN: 1-55945-100-9

Num. Sess.	Group Time	Num. Pgs.	Avg. Qst.	Price	Audience	Format	Bible Study
4	35-60	44	Vary	$9.99	Beginner	Workbk	Topical

Features: Intro to Leading a Study, Intro to Study, Objectives, Study Overview, Ldr's Notes, Handouts, Agenda, Publicity Ideas
★★★ Personal Application Preparation Time: None
★★★ Relationship Building Ldr. Guide: No Size: 8.50 x 11.0
Subjects: Teens: Junior High, Teens: Psychology, Teens: Relationships, Teens: Self-esteem
Comments: This study helps kids learn to feel good about themselves and develop confidence in their abilities. It includes lessons on evaluation of teen appearances, the difference between pleasing others and caring about others, identification and affirmation of unique abilities, and building self-confidence.

Author: Going, Nancy **614**
Series: Group's Active Bible Curriculum
Title: *Materialism*
Publisher: Group Publishing, 1992 ISBN: 1-55945-130-0

Num. Sess.	Group Time	Num. Pgs.	Avg. Qst.	Price	Audience	Format	Bible Study
4	35-60	47	Vary	$9.99	Beginner	Workbk	Topical

Features: Intro to Leading a Study, Intro to Study, Objectives, Study Overview, Ldr's Notes, Handouts, Agenda, Publicity Ideas
★★★★ Personal Application Preparation Time: None
★★★★ Relationship Building Ldr. Guide: No Size: 8.50 x 11.0
Subjects: Teens: Christian Liv, Teens: Junior High, Teens: Materialism
Comments: This course helps junior highers develop Christlike attitudes toward possessions and success. Participants learn about stewardship and responsibility without getting bored. Plus, they'll learn to celebrate the gifts God has given them. It can be adapted for a Bible class or youth meeting. Activity sheets are reproducible. Student books not required. The instructions are easy to follow.

Author: Gooch, John **615**
Series:
Title: *Is My Nose Growing?: And 29 Other Great Youth Programs*
Publisher: Abingdon Press, 1992 ISBN: 0-68719-707-4

Num. Sess.	Group Time	Num. Pgs.	Avg. Qst.	Price	Audience	Format	Bible Study
	—	104	N/A	$10.95			

Features: Intro to Study, Drawings, Appendix
Personal Application Preparation Time:
Relationship Building Ldr. Guide: Size: 8.50 x 11.0
Subjects: Teens: Resources, Youth Life
Comments: The 30 youth programs in this book are easily implemented, for either youth or adult leaders. Among the 30 programs are: Is My Nose Growing? Do the Good Guys Ever Win? I Don't Like It When You Do That; Showing Your Family You Love Them; Can God Forgive Me? Who Is My Enemy? Is Life Worth Living? Am I manipulated by Advertising? What's the Fuss About Lyrics? It's Not My Fault; My Parents Have Separated; and Praying for Others.

Author: Goodboy, Eadie **616**
Series: Basic Bible Study Series
Title: *God's Daughter: Practical Aspects of a Christian Woman's Life*
Publisher: Aglow, 1980 ISBN: 0-93230-545-8

Num. Sess.	Group Time	Num. Pgs.	Avg. Qst.	Price	Audience	Format	Bible Study
11	60-75	60	Vary	$3.95	New Christian	Workbk	Topical

Features: Intro to Study, Scrpt Memory Helps, Persnl Study Quest
★★★ Personal Application Preparation Time: Low
★★★ Relationship Building Ldr. Guide: No Size: 5.25 x 8.25
Subjects: Charismatic Interest, Relationships, Service, Women's Issues
Comments: This study examines practical aspects of the Christian walk and helps participants attain maturity in their daily lives. Two primary relationships discussed are relationships with God and with one another. Methods of ministry to others that are discussed include: maintaining peace in confusion, laying down lives in submission to one another, using gifts and abilities to serve others, and using the tongue to build up instead of tear down.

Author: Gorman, Julie A. **617**
Series: GroupBuilder Resources
Title: *Community That Is Christian: A Handbook on Small Groups*
Publisher: Victor Books, 1993 ISBN: 0-89693-260-5

Num. Sess.	Group Time	Num. Pgs.	Avg. Qst.	Price	Audience	Format	Bible Study
	—	390	N/A	$12.99			

Features: Bibliography, Appendix
Personal Application Preparation Time:
Relationship Building Ldr. Guide: Size: 6.0 x 9.0
Subjects: Small Group Resource
Comments: This interactive manual for transformation of community living contains a plan, design and instructions for setting up a small group ministry. It discusses self-disclosure that causes a group to bond, the role of leadership in group development, responding to conflict, and other relevant issues. Part 1 frames the big picture of community. Part 2 explains how to sketch desirable goals. Part 3 explores principles for beginning a group; Part 4, special concerns.

Author: Gorman, Julie A. **618**
Series: GroupBuilder Resources
Title: *Let's Get Together*
Publisher: Victor Books, 1991 ISBN: 0-89693-299-0

Num. Sess.	Group Time	Num. Pgs.	Avg. Qst.	Price	Audience	Format	Bible Study
8	75-90	144	Vary	$5.99	New Christian	Workbk	Topical

Features: Intro to Leading a Study, Intro to Study, Worship Helps, Full Scrpt Printed, Ldr's Notes, Drawings
★★★★ Personal Application Preparation Time: Med
★★★★ Relationship Building Ldr. Guide: No Size: 6.0 x 9.0
Subjects: Bible Study, Caring, Commitments, Relationships, Service, Small Group Resource
Comments: In this study participants learn about and experience eight aspects of small group life. Sessions deal with sensitive issues such as choices, commitments, relationships, caring, changes, truth, service, and celebration. Optional activities, hints for leaders, worship ideas, and answers to questions can be found in the leader's guide.

Author: Gorman, Julie A. **619**
Series: GroupBuilder Resources
Title: *No Strangers to God*
Publisher: Victor Books, 1991 ISBN: 0-89693-018-1

Num. Sess.	Group Time	Num. Pgs.	Avg. Qst.	Price	Audience	Format	Bible Study
8	75-90	144	Vary	$5.99	New Christian	Workbk	Topical

Features: Intro to Leading a Study, Objectives, Digging Deeper Quest, Follow Up, Full Scrpt Printed, Ldr's Notes, Cartoons, Persnl Study Quest
★★★★ Personal Application Preparation Time: Low
★★★★ Relationship Building Ldr. Guide: No Size: 6.0 x 9.0
Subjects: Discipleship, God
Comments: This study helps small groups build meaningful relationships with God as together they study how to know Him and become His own. Sessions deal with such topics as spiritual roots, finding God in bad times, fitting in with God's plans, celebrating baptism and the Last Supper, and spiritual growth. Optional activities, hints for leaders, and answers to questions can be found in the leader's guide.

Author: Gorman, Julie A. **620**
Series: GroupBuilder Resources
Title: *Training Manual for Small Group Leaders, A*
Publisher: Victor Books, 1991 ISBN: 0-89693-266-4

Num. Sess.	Group Time	Num. Pgs.	Avg. Qst.	Price	Audience	Format	Bible Study
8	75-90	127	Vary	$7.99	New Christian	Book	Topical

Features: Intro to Leading a Study, Intro to Study, Prayer Helps, Full Scrpt Printed, Ldr's Notes, Drawings
★★★★ Personal Application Preparation Time: Low
★★★★ Relationship Building Ldr. Guide: No Size: 6.0 x 9.0
Subjects: Small Group Resource
Comments: This is an experiential small group training course for new or experienced leaders. It helps develop and enhance skills needed to nurture group members to maturity, including first impressions and safe environments, sharing and building commitments, preparation, using questions effectively, challenging members to grow, listening and ministering through interpersonal relationships.

Author: Gorsuch, Geoff **621**
Series: Promise Keepers
Title: *Brothers! Calling Men Into Vital Relationships*
Publisher: NavPress, 1994 ISBN: 0-89109-858-5

Num. Sess.	Group Time	Num. Pgs.	Avg. Qst.	Price	Audience	Format	Bible Study
8	75-90	109	5	$6.00	New Christian	Book	Topical

Features: Bibliography, Summary, Appendix
★★★★ Personal Application Preparation Time: None
★★ Relationship Building Ldr. Guide: No Size: 5.50 x 8.50
Subjects: Men's Issues, Relationships, Small Group Resource
Comments: Part of the Promise Keepers series, this study can help men develop the kinds of relationships they need to become true brothers in Christ. The lessons use baseball as a visual aid to develop a relational diamond to help men pursue brotherhood with confidence, developing skills to accept one another as acquaintances, to encourage one another as friends, and to exhort one another as brothers. The appendix helps reinforce and apply the purpose of the study.

Author: Granata, Susan and Donna Paulson **622**
Series: Cross Signs
Title: *Why Do We Hope? Living into the Future: Unit 9*
Publisher: Augsburg Fortress Publishers, 1993

Num. Sess.	Group Time	Num. Pgs.	Avg. Qst.	Price	Audience	Format	Bible Study
7	90-105	48	7	$3.75	New Christian	Book	Topical

Features: Intro to Study, Prayer Helps, Worship Helps
★★★ Personal Application Preparation Time: Low
★★ Relationship Building Ldr. Guide: Yes Size: 5.50 x 8.50
Subjects: Hope
Comments: In this study participants see that for Christians, hope is far more than an innate human quality. It springs not from the "human breast," but from faith in God's promise to bring about a good future, which we see most profoundly expressed in Christ's death and resurrection. Christian hope is an act of faith, and sometimes it is truly an act of courage.

Author: Grant, Reg & John Reed **623**
Series: Equipped For Ministry
Title: *Telling Stories To Touch the Heart*
Publisher: Victor Books, 1990 ISBN: 0-89693-820-4

Num. Sess.	Group Time	Num. Pgs.	Avg. Qst.	Price	Audience	Format	Bible Study
	—	131	N/A	$9.99			

Features: Intro to Study, Bibliography, Appendix
Personal Application Preparation Time:
Relationship Building Ldr. Guide: Size: 6.0 x 9.0
Subjects: Small Group Resource
Comments: This book on storytelling encourages those who want to tell stories, but "just can't" because they don't have the right tools. It can strengthen those with storytelling experience by providing a proven method of research, writing, and delivery; and it ignites the imagination of all teachers to be more creative and effective as they relate God's Word to their students. Provides tested story scripts, and can equip Christians to help others see the Lord through the medium of story.

Author: Grayson, Curt & Jan Johnson **624**
Series:
Title: *Healing Hurts That Sabotage the Soul*
Publisher: Victor Books, 1995 ISBN: 1-56476-449-4

Num. Sess.	Group Time	Num. Pgs.	Avg. Qst.	Price	Audience	Format	Bible Study
	—	230	N/A	$9.99		Book	

Features: Persnl Study Quest
Personal Application Preparation Time:
Relationship Building Ldr. Guide: Size: 5.75 x 8.50
Subjects: Christian Living, Relationships, Support
Comments: Emptiness and chaos can provoke a core question: What must a person do to feel loved and valued? To describe processes involved in living an examined Christian life, this book begins with struggles that lead to self-examination, then looks at patterns from the past people set up to protect themselves from hurt. After showing how to break these patterns, the authors explore ways to build safe, authentic relationships, with God and others.

Author: Greenwaldt, Karen A. **625**
Series: Faith Horizons
Title: *Decisions & Dreams*
Publisher: Augsburg Fortress Publishers, 1993

Num. Sess.	Group Time	Num. Pgs.	Avg. Qst.	Price	Audience	Format	Bible Study
6	60-75	40	9	$4.95	Beginner	Workbk	Topical

Features: Intro to Study, Prayer Helps, Worship Helps, Follow Up, Photos
★★ Personal Application Preparation Time: Low
★★ Relationship Building Ldr. Guide: No Size: 5.50 x 8.50
Subjects: Teens: Decisions
Comments: Each book in the Faith Horizons series explores a theme through a topical essay, Bible study, personal reflection and response, and worship. Each offers suggestions for using media (TV, movies, plays, books, newspapers, music recordings, etc.) to enhance interaction. This study explores how God is involved in dreams and decision making.

Author: Greig, Doris W. **626**
Series: Joy of Living
Title: *Courage to Conquer: Studies in Daniel*
Publisher: Regal Books, 1988 ISBN: 0-83071-285-2

Num. Sess.	Group Time	Num. Pgs.	Avg. Qst.	Price	Audience	Format	Bible Study
6	60-90	118	36	$5.99	New Christian	Workbk	Book

Features: Intro to Study, Drawings, Maps
★★★ Personal Application Preparation Time: High
★★ Relationship Building Ldr. Guide: No Size: 6.0 x 9.0
Subjects: Daniel, Ethics, Faith, Major Prophets
Comments: This is a 6-week study of Daniel, who proclaimed everlasting faith in the face of great danger. It reminds participants that God provides strength, insight, and courage to conquer doubts and fears, and helps people uphold Christian values in every area of life. Each lesson features pre-study activities, followed by 6 sets of in-depth questions designed for daily study, and is wrapped up by study notes. Historical background, commentary, maps, and timelines are included.

Author: Greig, Doris W. **627**
Series: Joy of Living
Title: *Walking in God's Way: Studies in Ruth and Esther*
Publisher: Regal Books, 1988 ISBN: 0-83071-284-4

Num. Sess.	Group Time	Num. Pgs.	Avg. Qst.	Price	Audience	Format	Bible Study
7	60-90	131	42	$5.99	New Christian	Workbk	Book

Features: Intro to Study, Drawings, Maps
★★★ Personal Application Preparation Time: High
★★ Relationship Building Ldr. Guide: No Size: 6.0 x 9.0
Subjects: Bible Personalities, Esther, Faith, God, Ruth
Comments: This 7-week study of Ruth and Esther demonstrates to contemporary Christians that listening to God and learning to love is the center of a Christian walk. And, like Ruth, Boaz, Esther, and Mordecai, participants will find that life's difficult times can lead them closer to God. Each lesson begins with pre-study activities, followed by six sets of in-depth questions designed for daily study, and is wrapped up by study notes. Historical background, commentary, maps.

Author: Griffin, Em **628**
Series:
Title: *Getting Together*
Publisher: InterVarsity, 1982 ISBN: 0-87784-390-2

Num. Sess.	Group Time	Num. Pgs.	Avg. Qst.	Price	Audience	Format	Bible Study
11	—	230	N/A	$10.99		Book	No

Features: Intro to Study, Cartoons
Personal Application Preparation Time:
Relationship Building Ldr. Guide: No Size: 5.50 x 8.25
Subjects: Leadership, Small Group Resource
Comments: This book focuses on what makes a good group and discusses 3 types: "task groups," which have a job to do; "relationship groups," which fill a need for community; and "influence groups," which help people change. Topics covered include persuasion, expectations, leadership, and how to lead a good discussion. The "Westwood Food Co-op" is used as an analogy to the development of a small group in the introduction.

Author: Griffith, Stephen & Bill Deckard **629**
Series: Promise Keepers
Title: *What Makes a Man?*
Publisher: NavPress, 1993 ISBN: 0-89109-730-9

Num. Sess.	Group Time	Num. Pgs.	Avg. Qst.	Price	Audience	Format	Bible Study
12	60-75	127	15	$6.00	Beginner	Workbk	Topical

Features: Intro to Leading a Study, Intro to Study, Follow Up, Book Avail
★★★★ Personal Application Preparation Time: Low
★★ Relationship Building Ldr. Guide: No Size: 5.50 x 8.50
Subjects: God's Promises, Men's Issues
Comments: Part of the Promise Keepers series, this study explores key areas of responsibility that men face. The first lesson defines promises, and is followed by promises made to God, to oneself, one's wife, work, family, parents, friends, to worship and fellowship, to neighbors and community, those in need, and one's own future. The study can stimulate lively discussion.

Author: Hadaway, C. Kirk, et al. **630**
Series:
Title: *Home Cell Groups and House Churches*
Publisher: Broadman, 1987 ISBN: 0-80546-944-3

Num. Sess.	Group Time	Num. Pgs.	Avg. Qst.	Price	Audience	Format	Bible Study
10	—	260	N/A	$11.99		Book	No

Features:
Personal Application Preparation Time:
Relationship Building Ldr. Guide: Size: 5.75 x 8.25
Subjects: Small Group Resource
Comments: This book submits that the urban church can be effective. It responds to questions like the following: "How can the urban church effectively take the Gospel to the thousands of people who live near it?" and "Can the urban church hope to reach those who see no relevance in Christianity?" It gives an overview of house groups and addresses issues like the nature and growth of groups, leadership and authority, and the problems and disadvantages of house churches.

Author: Hadsall, Pamela, et al. **631**
Series:
Title: *Faith Matters for Young Adults*
Publisher: Cokesbury, 1992 ISBN: 0-68775-841-6

Num. Sess.	Group Time	Num. Pgs.	Avg. Qst.	Price	Audience	Format	Bible Study
26	30-90	128	Vary	$12.95	Beginner	Book	Topical

Features: Intro to Leading a Study, Intro to Study, Prayer Helps, Handouts
★★★★ Personal Application Preparation Time: Low
★★★ Relationship Building Ldr. Guide: No Size: 10.0 x 7.0
Subjects: Sexual Issues, Singles' Issues, Success, Youth Life
Comments: This study is geared for use with young adults ages 18–30. Each session includes 1 page that can be photocopied and distributed to class members. Topics include: When bad things happen, does God care? What are Christian views of success and possessions? How do different people get different meanings from the same Bible passage? and more.

Author: Hamlin, Dr. Judy **632**
Series: GroupBuilder Resources
Title: *Caring for Your Aging Parents*
Publisher: Victor Books, 1992 ISBN: 0-89693-098-X

Num. Sess.	Group Time	Num. Pgs.	Avg. Qst.	Price	Audience	Format	Bible Study
6	45-60	64	Vary	$4.99	Beginner	Workbk	Topical

Features: Intro to Study, Objectives, Prayer Helps, Full Scrpt Printed, Ldr's Notes, Drawings
★★★★ Personal Application Preparation Time: None
★★★★ Relationship Building Ldr. Guide: No Size: 6.0 x 9.0
Subjects: Aging, Senior Adults, Women's Issues
Comments: This series is written for seekers. Six brief, easy-to-understand lessons cover issues related to being a caregiver. Participants review meeting practical needs such as housing and medical care, finding emotional support for their own needs, identifying their concerns about caregiving and discovering solutions, and more. A helpful witnessing chart is included.

Author: Hamlin, Dr. Judy **633**
Series: GroupBuilder Resources
Title: *Compulsive Consumption*
Publisher: Victor Books, 1993 ISBN: 1-56476-196-7

Num. Sess.	Group Time	Num. Pgs.	Avg. Qst.	Price	Audience	Format	Bible Study
6	45-60	64	Vary	$4.99	Beginner	Workbk	Topical

Features: Intro to Study, Objectives, Prayer Helps, Full Scrpt Printed, Ldr's Notes, Drawings
★★★★ Personal Application Preparation Time: None
★★★★ Relationship Building Ldr. Guide: No Size: 6.0 x 9.0
Subjects: Evangelism, Materialism, Money
Comments: This series is written for seekers. There are 6 brief, easy-to-understand lessons dealing with many aspects of materialism. Participants learn to put possessions in proper perspective, focus on family background and roots, identify and conquer envy and low self-esteem, and let Christ force material things out of the center of their lives. A helpful witnessing chart is included.

Author: Hamlin, Dr. Judy **634**
Series: Leadership Skills For Women
Title: *Group Building Skills*
Publisher: New Hope, 1994 ISBN: 1-56309-083-X

Num. Sess.	Group Time	Num. Pgs.	Avg. Qst.	Price	Audience	Format	Bible Study
8	45-60	56	Vary	$5.95	New Christian	Book	Topical

Features: Intro to Study, Appendix
★★★★ Personal Application Preparation Time: Low
★★ Relationship Building Ldr. Guide: No Size: 5.50 x 8.50
Subjects: Leadership, Missions, Small Group Resource, Women's Issues
Comments: This resource promotes understanding of group dynamics and a sharpening of leadership skills. Lessons explore leadership styles and roles, the importance of a leader's vision, getting to know and understand group members, their personality types and spiritual gifts. Helps identify healthy groups, avoid pitfalls of a group, evaluate a group's progress, details why, when, and how to end a group.

Author: Hamlin, Dr. Judy **635**
Series: GroupBuilder Resources
Title: *Longing For Company*
Publisher: Victor Books, 1993 ISBN: 1-56476-195-9

Num. Sess.	Group Time	Num. Pgs.	Avg. Qst.	Price	Audience	Format	Bible Study
6	45-60	64	Vary	$4.99	Beginner	Workbk	Topical

Features: Intro to Study, Objectives, Prayer Helps, Full Scrpt Printed, Ldr's Notes, Drawings
★★★★ Personal Application Preparation Time: None
★★★★ Relationship Building Ldr. Guide: No Size: 6.0 x 9.0
Subjects: Evangelism, Loneliness, Women's Issues
Comments: This series, written for seekers, deals with subjects in such a way as not to put pressure on but benefit non-Christian participants. Six brief, easy-to-understand sessions identify and deal with loneliness. Participants look at the difference between being lonely and loneliness, learn how loneliness can affect peoples' personalities, how satisfactory relationships can rescue, and how to achieve hope.

Author: Hamlin, Dr. Judy **636**
Series: GroupBuilder Resources
Title: *On The Brink of Divorce*
Publisher: Victor Books, 1992 ISBN: 0-89693-096-3

Num. Sess.	Group Time	Num. Pgs.	Avg. Qst.	Price	Audience	Format	Bible Study
6	45-60	64	Vary	$4.99	Beginner	Workbk	Topical

Features: Intro to Study, Objectives, Prayer Helps, Full Scrpt Printed, Ldr's Notes, Drawings
★★★★ Personal Application Preparation Time: None
★★★★ Relationship Building Ldr. Guide: No Size: 6.0 x 9.0
Subjects: Divorce, Evangelism, Marriage
Comments: This series, written for seekers, deals with subjects in such a way as not to put pressure on but benefit non-Christian participants. Participants look at: removing painful emotional scars, helping children in the middle of struggling marriages, identifying causes for marriage on the brink, reasons to hope for a lasting, fulfilled marriage, and more. A witnessing chart is included.

Author: Hamlin, Dr. Judy 637
Series: GroupBuilder Resources
Title: *Party of One, A*
Publisher: Victor Books, 1992 ISBN: 0-89693-097-1

Num. Sess.	Group Time	Num. Pgs.	Avg. Qst.	Price	Audience	Format	Bible Study
6	45-60	64	Vary	$4.99	Beginner	Workbk	Topical

Features: Intro to Study, Objectives, Prayer Helps, Full Scrpt Printed, Ldr's Notes, Drawings, Charts
★★★★ Personal Application Preparation Time: None
★★★★ Relationship Building Ldr. Guide: No Size: 6.0 x 9.0
Subjects: Singles' Issues, Women's Issues
Comments: This series, written for seekers, deals with subjects in such a way as not to put pressure on but benefit non-Christian participants. Six brief, easy-to-understand lessons cover issues affecting single wholeness. Participants learn how to meet their own needs as they reach out to others, the art of vulnerability, how they can best relate to the opposite sex, living life to the fullest, and more.

Author: Hamlin, Dr. Judy 638
Series: GroupBuilder Resources
Title: *Shedding Light on the New Age*
Publisher: Victor Books, 1993 ISBN: 1-56476-075-8

Num. Sess.	Group Time	Num. Pgs.	Avg. Qst.	Price	Audience	Format	Bible Study
6	45-60	80	Vary	$4.99	Beginner	Workbk	Topical

Features: Intro to Study, Objectives, Prayer Helps, Full Scrpt Printed, Ldr's Notes, Drawings
★★★★ Personal Application Preparation Time: None
★★★★ Relationship Building Ldr. Guide: No Size: 6.0 x 9.0
Subjects: Cults, Evangelism, Spiritual Warfare, Women's Issues
Comments: This series, written for seekers, deals with subjects in ways that don't put pressure on but benefit non-Christian participants. There are 6 brief, easy-to-understand sessions on issues related to the New Age. Participants see astrology as an open door to evil, learn to recognize cults and other New Age snares, evaluate New Age medicine, develop strategies for helping those caught in New Age practices.

Author: Hamlin, Dr. Judy 639
Series:
Title: *Small Group Leaders Training Course, The*
Publisher: NavPress, 1990 ISBN: 0-89109-308-7

Num. Sess.	Group Time	Num. Pgs.	Avg. Qst.	Price	Audience	Format	Bible Study
6	—	210	N/A	$25.00		Book	No

Features: Intro to Study, Drawings, Agenda, Publicity Ideas
Personal Application Preparation Time:
Relationship Building Ldr. Guide: Size: 8.25 x 10.0
Subjects: Evangelism, Leadership, Relationships, Small Group Resource
Comments: Contains all the components for conducting initial leadership training for a small group ministry. Interactive, practical, hands-on experience with fun leadership, communications/questions, witnessing, relationships, promotion, and review are taught and reinforced. A participant manual is available and required. The last chapter covers the development of a leadership handbook specifically for your church.

Author: Hamlin, Dr. Judy 640
Series: GroupBuilder Resources
Title: *Welcome to Your First Small Group*
Publisher: Victor Books, 1993 ISBN: 1-56476-100-2

Num. Sess.	Group Time	Num. Pgs.	Avg. Qst.	Price	Audience	Format	Bible Study
	—	72	N/A	$2.99			

Features: Intro to Study, Charts, Appendix
Personal Application Preparation Time:
Relationship Building Ldr. Guide: Size: 4.25 x 7.0
Subjects: Small Group Resource
Comments: This booklet is designed to reduce the time for new group members to adjust and become comfortable, productive participants. Discover why people participate in small groups; how to get the most out of the experience; practical aspects of group interaction, including fellowship, prayer, study materials, and evaluation; and creating new small groups. It helps prospective unchurched or new church members make informed decisions on participation.

Author: Hamlin, Dr. Judy 641
Series: GroupBuilder Resources
Title: *When You Work Outside The Home*
Publisher: Victor Books, 1993 ISBN: 1-56476-074-X

Num. Sess.	Group Time	Num. Pgs.	Avg. Qst.	Price	Audience	Format	Bible Study
6	45-60	64	Vary	$4.99	Beginner	Workbk	Topical

Features: Intro to Study, Objectives, Prayer Helps, Full Scrpt Printed, Ldr's Notes, Drawings
★★★★ Personal Application Preparation Time: None
★★★★ Relationship Building Ldr. Guide: No Size: 6.0 x 9.0
Subjects: Evangelism, Parenting, Women's Issues
Comments: This series, written for seekers, deals with subjects in such a way as not to put pressure on but benefit non-Christian participants. Six brief sessions cover caring for children while working outside the home. Participants discover what's really important to their children, planning for specific times of the day, how to free oneself from guilt, and ways to share responsibilities with a husband.

Author: Hamlin, Dr. Judy 642
Series: GroupBuilder Resources
Title: *You've Got What It Takes!*
Publisher: Victor Books, 1992 ISBN: 0-89693-095-5

Num. Sess.	Group Time	Num. Pgs.	Avg. Qst.	Price	Audience	Format	Bible Study
6	45-60	64	Vary	$4.99	Beginner	Workbk	Topical

Features: Intro to Study, Objectives, Bibliography, Full Scrpt Printed, Ldr's Notes, Drawings
★★★★ Personal Application Preparation Time: None
★★★★ Relationship Building Ldr. Guide: No Size: 6.0 x 9.0
Subjects: Decision Making, Evangelism, Time, Women's Issues
Comments: This series, written for seekers, deals with subjects in such a way as not to put pressure on but benefit non-Christian participants. Six brief, easy-to-understand lessons help people examine priorities and reorder them if necessary. Participants study making good decisions, putting their lives in balance, getting finances in order, bringing the best to relationships, and more.

Author: Hansen, Cindy S. 643
Series: Group's Active Bible Curriculum
Title: *Knowing God's Will*
Publisher: Group Publishing, 1990 ISBN: 1-55945-205-6

Num. Sess.	Group Time	Num. Pgs.	Avg. Qst.	Price	Audience	Format	Bible Study
4	35-60	43	Vary	$9.99	Beginner	Workbk	Topical

Features: Intro to Leading a Study, Intro to Study, Objectives, Study Overview, Ldr's Notes, Handouts, Agenda, Publicity Ideas
★★★ Personal Application Preparation Time: None
★★★ Relationship Building Ldr. Guide: No Size: 8.50 x 11.0
Subjects: Teens: Christian Liv, Teens: Senior High
Comments: This course challenges teenagers to explore God's direction for their lives. The subject matter covered includes knowing and doing God's will, accepting God's help, and accepting God's forgiveness. It can be adapted for use in a Bible class or youth meeting. Activities and Bible studies are included as separate sheets that can be reproduced. The instructions are easy to follow.

Author: Hanusa, George 644
Series: Small Group Bible Studies
Title: *Faith of the Church, The*
Publisher: Augsburg Fortress Publishers, 1978

Num. Sess.	Group Time	Num. Pgs.	Avg. Qst.	Price	Audience	Format	Bible Study
6	60-75	24	5	$1.35	New Christian	Book	Topical

Features: Intro to Study, Prayer Helps
★★★ Personal Application Preparation Time: None
★★★ Relationship Building Ldr. Guide: No Size: 8.50 x 5.50
Subjects: Church Life, Faith, God, Theology
Comments: This small pamphlet includes 6 sessions on the faith of the Church. The 6 areas covered include God, mankind, salvation, Church, Scripture, and Christian vocation. The study intends to examine the Scriptural dimensions of participants' faith. It is designed to lead them to think through what they believe, as well as to be informed by the Scriptures. The goal is to learn more fully how the faith of the Church applies to their lives.

Author: Hardel, Dick 645
Series: Group's Active Bible Curriculum
Title: *Jesus' Death and Resurrection*
Publisher: Group Publishing, 1991 ISBN: 1-55945-211-0

Num. Sess.	Group Time	Num. Pgs.	Avg. Qst.	Price	Audience	Format	Bible Study
4	35-60	48	Vary	$9.99	New Christian	Workbk	Charctr

Features: Intro to Leading a Study, Intro to Study, Objectives, Study Overview, Ldr's Notes, Drawings, Handouts, Agenda, Publicity Ideas
★★★★ Personal Application Preparation Time: None
★★★★ Relationship Building Ldr. Guide: No Size: 8.50 x 11.0
Subjects: Teens: Jesus Life, Teens: Senior High
Comments: This 4-lesson study helps senior high students understand the relevance of Christ's death and resurrection for their lives. Participants will examine the significance of Jesus' Last Supper with His disciples, learn how He struggled with God's will that He die, gain insights into the strength of His relationship with God the Father, and explore how Jesus' death on the cross provides the way to forgiveness.

Author: Hardel, Dick 646
Series: Group's Active Bible Curriculum
Title: *Who Is Jesus?*
Publisher: Group Publishing, 1991 ISBN: 1-55945-219-6

Num. Sess.	Group Time	Num. Pgs.	Avg. Qst.	Price	Audience	Format	Bible Study
4	35-60	46	Vary	$9.99	Beginner	Workbk	Charctr

Features: Intro to Leading a Study, Intro to Study, Objectives, Study Overview, Ldr's Notes, Handouts, Agenda, Publicity Ideas
★★★★ Personal Application Preparation Time: None
★★★★ Relationship Building Ldr. Guide: No Size: 8.50 x 11.0
Subjects: Teens: Jesus' Life, Teens: Prayer, Teens: Senior High
Comments: Teenagers get to know Jesus as Friend, Teacher, and Savior in this involving 4-week course. Senior high participants learn about the second Person of the Trinity, and explore deeper relationships with Jesus. They'll learn how His death on the cross illustrates the depth of God's love, see Jesus as a friend who desires to walk with them daily, and explore the importance of His humanity and divinity.

Author: Harral, Harriet 647
Series: Leadership Skills For Women
Title: *Communication Skills*
Publisher: New Hope, 1994 ISBN: 1-56309-104-6

Num. Sess.	Group Time	Num. Pgs.	Avg. Qst.	Price	Audience	Format	Bible Study
7	45-60	81	Vary	$5.95	New Christian	Book	Topical

Features: Intro to Study
★★★★ Personal Application Preparation Time: Low
★★ Relationship Building Ldr. Guide: No Size: 5.50 x 8.50
Subjects: Communication, Leadership, Psychology, Women's Issues
Comments: One of 5 books in the Leadership Skills for Women series, this book introduces readers to biblical women who demonstrate some critical communication skill possessed by effective leaders. The book offers evidence that women have been in leadership roles for centuries. Each chapter deals with a particular communication skill needed by a leader. Included in each chapter is a role model, skill explanation, skill assessment, skill practice, and skill evaluation.

Author: Harrison, Dan 648
Series: Global Issues
Title: *Healing for Broken People*
Publisher: InterVarsity, 1990 ISBN: 0-83084-908-4

Num. Sess.	Group Time	Num. Pgs.	Avg. Qst.	Price	Audience	Format	Bible Study
6	45-60	48	13	$4.99	Beginner	Workbk	Topical

Features: Intro to Leading a Study, Intro to Study, Bibliography, Follow Up, Appendix
★★★★ Personal Application Preparation Time: Low
★★★★ Relationship Building Ldr. Guide: No Size: 5.50 x 8.25
Subjects: Addictions, Emotions, Family, Psychology, Relationships, Social Issues, Work
Comments: This 6-week study reveals the fact that most families have problems, sometimes significant ones. It describes the dysfunctional family, as well as negative patterns that affect relationships at work, with friends, and with a spouse. Bitterness, anger, and being overcritical are characteristics ascribed to a codependent person.

Author: Haugen, Doug & Doris **649**
Series: LifeGuide Bible Study
Title: *Jonah, Joel & Amos: Seek the Lord and Live*
Publisher: InterVarsity, 1988 ISBN: 0-83081-032-3

Num. Sess.	Group Time	Num. Pgs.	Avg. Qst.	Price	Audience	Format	Bible Study
13	45-60	64	12	$4.99	New Christian	Workbk	Book

Features: Intro to Leading a Study, Intro to Study, Ldr's Notes
★ Personal Application Preparation Time: Low
★ Relationship Building Ldr. Guide: No Size: 5.50 x 8.25
Subjects: Bible Personalities, God, Minor Prophets, Obedience, Old Testament, Repentance
Comments: In Jonah, Joel, and Amos, God gets people's attention because He desires their fellowship. The study is a constant reminder for twentieth-century believers to turn to God and live according to His teachings. Joel stressed that not only do we turn to God, but we return to Him, seeking God through repentance and obedience. Amos exhorts seeking "good, not evil, that you may live" (Amos 5:14).

Author: Haugk, Kenneth C. **650**
Series:
Title: *Caring for Inactive Members: Leader's Guide*
Publisher: Tebunah Ministries, 1990

Num. Sess.	Group Time	Num. Pgs.	Avg. Qst.8	$29.95 Price	Audience	Format	Bible Study
10	60-75	350	N/A				Topical

Features: Intro to Leading a Study, Prayer Helps, Appendix, Publicity Ideas
Personal Application Preparation Time: Low
Relationship Building Ldr. Guide: Size: 11.50 x 11.50
Subjects: Church Life
Comments: This course has three components: textbook, leader's guide, and participant's manual. The leader's guide has exhaustive helps for the leader. It includes: precourse planning, scheduling, publicity, conducting class sessions, prevention resource suggestions, and course conclusion suggestions. The information is packaged in a three-ring binder and each of the ten modules are divided by tabs.

Author: Haugk, Kenneth C. **651**
Series:
Title: *Caring for Inactive Members: Participant's Manual*
Publisher: Tebunah Ministries, 1990

Num. Sess.	Group Time	Num. Pgs.	Avg. Qst.	Price	Audience	Format	Bible Study
10	60-75	160	Vary	$11.95	New Christian	Workbk	Topical

Features: Prayer Helps, Cartoons
★★★★ Personal Application Preparation Time: Low
★★★★ Relationship Building Ldr. Guide: Yes Size: 10.25 x 11.50
Subjects: Church Life
Comments: This course prepares congregations to relate to inactive members. It shows participants how to minister to inactive members, how to welcome them home, and how to prevent inactivity in the first place. The participant's manual includes outlines of the content for each module, questionnaires and surveys, verbatims, and space for participants to take notes. There are also Focus Notes, which contain sample dialogues, Bible references, and pertinent quotes.

Author: Haugk, Kenneth C. & William J. McKay **652**
Series:
Title: *Christian Caregiving: A Way of Life, Leader's Guide*
Publisher: Augsburg Fortress Publishers, 1994 ISBN: 0-80662-704-2

Num. Sess.	Group Time	Num. Pgs.	Avg. Qst.	Price	Audience	Format	Bible Study
	—	176	N/A	$10.95		Book	

Features: Intro to Study
Personal Application Preparation Time:
Relationship Building Ldr. Guide: Size: 6.0 x 8.50
Subjects: Caring, Christian Life, Leader's Guide, Support
Comments: Leaders of "Christian Caregiving Course" should have copies of this leader's guide. It provides resources for organizing and scheduling the course, publicizing the course in the congregation, recruiting participants for the course, conducting up to 20 exciting sessions, adapting sessions for a retreat, and more. Clearly organized, it provides suggested prayers, carefully planned times for exercises, and gives concise, and complete leader instructions.

Author: Haugk, Kenneth C. **653**
Series:
Title: *Christian Caregiving: A Way of Life*
Publisher: Augsburg Fortress Publishers, 1984 ISBN: 0-80662-123-0

Num. Sess.	Group Time	Num. Pgs.	Avg. Qst.	Price	Audience	Format	Bible Study
20	120-150	157	Vary	$10.95	New Christian	Book	Topical

Features: Prayer Helps, Agenda, Appendix, Publicity Ideas
★★★★ Personal Application Preparation Time: Low
★★★★ Relationship Building Ldr. Guide: Yes Size: 5.25 x 7.75
Subjects: Caring, Christian Life, Support
Comments: This book's purpose is twofold: to describe what makes Christian caregiving distinctive, and to explain how distinctive caregiving can become a way of life for Christians. It is a resource for Christians who wonder what difference their Christianity makes in caring and relating. This practical, "how-to" manual deals with real-life issues in caring and relating, and the leader's guide is thorough and easy to use.

Author: Haugk, Kenneth C. **654**
Series:
Title: *Reopening the Back Door*
Publisher: Tebunah Ministries, 1989 ISBN: 0-96340-930-1

Num. Sess.	Group Time	Num. Pgs.	Avg. Qst.	Price	Audience	Format	Bible Study
	—	190	N/A	$9.95		Book	

Features:
Personal Application Preparation Time:
Relationship Building Ldr. Guide: Size: 5.50 x 8.50
Subjects: Church Life
Comments: The book is part of the course Caring For Inactive Members. This practical book is intended for every member of the congregation. It shows readers how to minister to inactive members, how to welcome them home, and how to prevent inactivity in the first place. This work contains 220 questions drawn from a pool of more than 3,500 original questions asked by both clergy and laity. The questions in the text are those that arose most frequently.

Author: Hawkins, Don **655**
Series:
Title: *Friends In Deed*
Publisher: Moody Press, 1995 ISBN: 0-80242-540-2

Num. Sess.	Group Time	Num. Pgs.	Avg. Qst.	Price	Audience	Format	Bible Study
12	60-90	230	N/A	$9.99	New Christian	Book	Topical

Features: Intro to Study, No Grp Discussion Quest
★★★★ Personal Application Preparation Time: Low
★ Relationship Building Ldr. Guide: No Size: 6.0 x 9.0
Subjects: Friendships, Love, Relationships
Comments: This book reveals that modern society has built roadblocks that keep people from reaching out to one another, such as apathy, fear, materialism, past hurts, prejudice, and selfishness. *Friends in Deed* helps readers reconnect, reach out to others, relate, and care. The author encourages readers to return to agape love, the kind of love Jesus described in the story of the Good Samaritan. A trained leader will be required. Formulate group discussion questions.

Author: Hawkins, Dr. David & Ross A. Tunnell III **656**
Series: The Recovery Bookshelf
Title: *Reclaiming Manhood*
Publisher: Victor Books, 1992 ISBN: 1-56476-027-8

Num. Sess.	Group Time	Num. Pgs.	Avg. Qst.	Price	Audience	Format	Bible Study
12	60-90	166	Vary	$13.99	Beginner	Workbk	Topical

Features: Intro to Leading a Study, Bibliography, Prayer Helps, Drawings, Charts, Glossary,Appendix
★★★★ Personal Application Preparation Time: Med
★★★★ Relationship Building Ldr. Guide: Size: 7.50 x 9.25
Subjects: Ethics, Men's Issues, Parenting, Sexual Issues, Support, Work
Comments: This 12-week study uses the 12-step recovery model to probe crucial issues faced by men, such as marriage, sex and intimacy, work, ethics, fitness, family of origin, money, feelings, faith and spiritual growth, friendship, power and image, and fathering. The Twelve Steps of Alcoholics Anonymous and Scripture are used as bases for the study. Information on a men's Christian 12-step group is helpful.

Author: Haystead, Wesley **657**
Series: Lay Action Ministry
Title: *Touching Tomorrow by Teaching Children*
Publisher: Lay Action Ministry Program, 1989

Num. Sess.	Group Time	Num. Pgs.	Avg. Qst.	Price	Audience	Format	Bible Study
12	60-90	144	Vary	$6.95	New Christian	Workbk	Topical

Features:
★★★ Personal Application Preparation Time: Low
★★★ Relationship Building Ldr. Guide: Yes Size: 5.25 x 8.25
Subjects: Leadership
Comments: This study emphasizes the importance of teaching children; the Bible's relevance to contemporary children; interactive training methods; being prepared to teach; effective use of time; using music in teaching; using a variety of activities, games, and puzzles; discipline of children; and sensitivity to each child. The study is divided into 3 in-depth units covering ministry to children, the teaching session, and teaching methods.

Author: Haystead, Wesley **658**
Series:
Title: *When Life Is a Zoo God Still Loves You: Leader's Guide*
Publisher: Standard Publishing, 1992 ISBN: 0-78470-077-X

Num. Sess.	Group Time	Num. Pgs.	Avg. Qst.	Price	Audience	Format	Bible Study
13	45-60	64	N/A	$5.99	New Christian	Book	Topical

Features: Intro to Study
★★★ Personal Application Preparation Time: Low
★★ Relationship Building Ldr. Guide: Yes Size: 5.25 x 8.50
Subjects: Love
Comments: This book is a collection of Bible stories in which animals are the stars. In each one, participants discover valuable lessons about God's care for His creation, especially the participants themselves. An accompanying leader's guide allows the book to be used in a variety of settings, including small groups, Sunday School, and vacation Bible schools.

Author: Heald, Cynthia **659**
Series:
Title: *Becoming a Woman of Excellence*
Publisher: NavPress, 1986 ISBN: 0-89109-066-5

Num. Sess.	Group Time	Num. Pgs.	Avg. Qst.	Price	Audience	Format	Bible Study
11	60-90	114	10	$6.00	New Christian	Workbk	Topical

Features: Intro to Leading a Study, Scrpt Memory Helps, Charts
★★★ Personal Application Preparation Time: Med
★★ Relationship Building Ldr. Guide: No Size: 5.50 x 8.50
Subjects: Family, Obedience, Singles' Issues, Wisdom, Women's Issues, Work
Comments: This study involves a goal worth pursuing—excellence. Society requires both married and single women to succeed, to achieve excellence in appearance, earning power, and family life. God also urges women to achieve excellence, but what does He ask? Eleven lessons study what excellence means in areas such as surrender, obedience, discipline, discretion, wisdom, purity, and a gentle spirit.

Author: Heald, Cynthia **660**
Series:
Title: *Becoming a Woman of Purpose*
Publisher: NavPress, 1994 ISBN: 0-89109-790-2

Num. Sess.	Group Time	Num. Pgs.	Avg. Qst.	Price	Audience	Format	Bible Study
11	60-90	105	9	$6.00	New Christian	Workbk	Topical

Features: Scrpt Memory Helps
★★★ Personal Application Preparation Time: Med
★★ Relationship Building Ldr. Guide: No Size: 5.50 x 8.50
Subjects: Success, Women's Issues
Comments: This study uses Scripture passages, author's insight, and quotes from Christian thinkers and writers to guide participants to a better understanding of God's intended purposes for Himself and His people. Lessons cover the joy of loving God and others, waiting on Him with hope, trusting Him through suffering, serving Him with reverent fear, and fulfilling His purposes. The study can give particpants new perspectives, and help them meet each day with a sense of hope.

Author: Heald, Cynthia 661
Series:
Title: *Becoming a Woman of Freedom*
Publisher: NavPress, 1992 ISBN: 0-89109-675-2

Num. Sess.	Group Time	Num. Pgs.	Avg. Qst.	Price	Audience	Format	Bible Study
11	60-90	107	8	$6.00	New Christian	Workbk	Topical

Features: Prayer Helps, Scrpt Memory Helps
★★★ Personal Application Preparation Time: Med
★★ Relationship Building Ldr. Guide: No Size: 5.50 x 8.50
Subjects: Christian Life, Self-esteem, Women's Issues
Comments: This study helps participants gain the ability to run life's race freely and unhindered, eliminating the baggage that holds them back and deprives them of freedom in Christ. Lessons help identify past hurt and loss, poor self-image, approval seeking, busyness, doubt and fear, and unhealthy influences. It also offers encouragement to participants through the Word, the thoughts of others who came before, and personal reflection.

Author: Heald, Cynthia 662
Series:
Title: *Intimacy with God*
Publisher: NavPress, 1987 ISBN: 0-89109-140-8

Num. Sess.	Group Time	Num. Pgs.	Avg. Qst.	Price	Audience	Format	Bible Study
12	45-60	93	4	$6.00	Beginner	Workbk	Topical

Features: Intro to Study, Charts
★★★ Personal Application Preparation Time: Low
★★ Relationship Building Ldr. Guide: No Size: 5.50 x 8.50
Subjects: God, Psalms
Comments: This study of the Psalms allows men and women to follow the writers into a deeper experience of God, and to become more honest and vulnerable before Him. The lessons track the psalmists' struggles and triumphs on their way to intimacy with God. Participants can discern fresh, personal observations based on quotes from Christian authors, and spend more time reflecting and less time looking for "right answers."

Author: Heald, Cynthia 663
Series:
Title: *Loving Your Husband*
Publisher: NavPress, 1989 ISBN: 0-89109-544-6

Num. Sess.	Group Time	Num. Pgs.	Avg. Qst.	Price	Audience	Format	Bible Study
12	45-60	112	6	$6.00	New Christian	Workbk	Topical

Features: Intro to Leading a Study
★★★ Personal Application Preparation Time: Low
★★ Relationship Building Ldr. Guide: No Size: 5.50 x 8.50
Subjects: Joy, Marriage, Women's Issues
Comments: This study explores choices in a marriage, such as: How can you be a godly woman outside Eden? What is your role, purpose, and influence as a Christian wife? and How is God's Word relevant to the challenges and temptations of today's society? Key Scriptures help participants apply biblical truths to the joys and struggles of marriage.

Author: Heald, Jack & Cynthia 664
Series:
Title: *Loving Your Wife*
Publisher: NavPress, 1989 ISBN: 0-89109-575-6

Num. Sess.	Group Time	Num. Pgs.	Avg. Qst.	Price	Audience	Format	Bible Study
12	45-60	110	6	$6.00	New Christian	Workbk	Topical

Features: Intro to Leading a Study, Scrpt Memory Helps
★★★ Personal Application Preparation Time: Low
★★ Relationship Building Ldr. Guide: No Size: 5.50 x 8.50
Subjects: Forgiveness, Love, Marriage, Men's Issues, Relationships
Comments: This study explores 12 proven, biblical ways to strengthen and improve marriage, including developing love that's bold, courageous, and true; cultivating a compassionate, self-sacrificial, forgiving spirit toward one's wife; discerning and meeting a wife's needs; overcoming an angry, cynical, or critical spirit; and adopting a leadership style that will build intimacy, confidence, and genuine respect into marriage.

Author: Healey, David 665
Series: LifeGuide Bible Study
Title: *Prayer: An Adventure with God*
Publisher: InterVarsity, 1994 ISBN: 0-83081-053-6

Num. Sess.	Group Time	Num. Pgs.	Avg. Qst.	Price	Audience	Format	Bible Study
12	45-60	78	12	$4.99	New Christian	Workbk	Topical

Features: Intro to Leading a Study, Intro to Study, Prayer Helps, Ldr's Notes
★★ Personal Application Preparation Time: Low
★★ Relationship Building Ldr. Guide: No Size: 5.50 x 8.25
Subjects: Bible Personalities, Prayer
Comments: This study of prayer, focusing on biblical characters like Abraham, Moses, Nehemiah, Daniel, Ezekiel, Paul, David, Hannah, Mary, and Jesus, teaches the "why" of prayer. The principal result is an understanding of the importance of prayer in a relationship with God. Intercession, thanksgiving, repentance, praying for our own needs, and the needs of others are among the different varieties of prayer studied.

Author: Heaner, Linda 666
Series: Group's Active Bible Curriculum
Title: *Making Parents Proud*
Publisher: Group Publishing, 1990 ISBN: 1-55945-107-6

Num. Sess.	Group Time	Num. Pgs.	Avg. Qst.	Price	Audience	Format	Bible Study
4	35-60	46	Vary	$9.99	Beginner	Workbk	Topical

Features: Intro to Leading a Study, Intro to Study, Objectives, Study Overview, Ldr's Notes, Drawings, Handouts, Agenda, Publicity Ideas
★★★★ Personal Application Preparation Time: None
★★★★ Relationship Building Ldr. Guide: No Size: 8.50 x 11.0
Subjects: Teens: Family, Teens: Junior High
Comments: This study encourages junior high youth to develop positive relationships with their parents. Four lessons help them learn to build good communications with parents, develop specific steps to gain parents' trust, explore ways to earn new freedoms, discover creative ways to show love to parents, and examine Jesus' teaching on loving others. Instructions are easy to follow and provide multiple options.

Author: Heidebrecht, Paul & Ted Scheuermann **667**
Series: Fisherman Bible Studyguide
Title: *Men Like Us: Ordinary Men, Extraordinary God*
Publisher: Shaw, 1990 ISBN: 0-87788-544-3

Num. Sess.	Group Time	Num. Pgs.	Avg. Qst.	Price	Audience	Format	Bible Study
13	45-60	94	12	$4.99	Beginner	Workbk	Topical

Features: Intro to Leading a Study, Intro to Study, Prayer Helps, Ldr's Notes
★★★ Personal Application Preparation Time: None
★★★ Relationship Building Ldr. Guide: No Size: 5.0 x 8.25
Subjects: Failure, Grace, Marriage, Men's Issues, Time
Comments: This inductive study deals with issues contemporary men face—materialism, time pressure, godly fathering, keeping marriages strong, and establishing priorities—which were also faced by men in biblical times such as Barnabas, Caleb, Cornelius, Peter, and others. These Bible characters are much like men today. Their failures and weaknesses are not covered up; rather, God's grace transforms them.

Author: Hendricks, Howard G. **668**
Series:
Title: *Heaven Help the Home!*
Publisher: Victor Books, 1973 ISBN: 0-89693-674-0

Num. Sess.	Group Time	Num. Pgs.	Avg. Qst.	Price	Audience	Format	Bible Study
13	45-60	156	N/A	$8.99	Beginner	Book	Topical

Features: Intro to Study
★★★ Personal Application Preparation Time: Low
★★★ Relationship Building Ldr. Guide: Yes Size: 5.50 x 8.0
Subjects: Family, Money, Parenting, Relationships
Comments: This study offers practical advice about family life. It identifies and explores topics from family life conferences, such as the Christian home, convictions, discipline, finances, roles and relationships, attitudes, television, and sexuality. It also provides tools for dealing with these areas inside the home to create effective families. A leader's guide provides reproducible response sheets for participants.

Author: Hendricks, Howard G. **669**
Series:
Title: *Say It with Love*
Publisher: Victor Books, 1972 ISBN: 0-89693-676-7

Num. Sess.	Group Time	Num. Pgs.	Avg. Qst.	Price	Audience	Format	Bible Study
13	60-75	140	N/A	$7.99	New Christian	Book	Topical

Features: Intro to Study
★★★ Personal Application Preparation Time: Low
★★★ Relationship Building Ldr. Guide: Yes Size: 5.50 x 8.0
Subjects: Caring, Evangelism
Comments: This 13-lesson study instructs how to witness in everyday situations and shows how, through communication principles, participants can learn to effectively share the good news of salvation. The study is divided into four parts: "Our Message"; "Sharing the Message"; "Living the Message"; and "A Message to Share (a sample Gospel presentation)." To reach a world uninterested in hearing the Gospel, an emphasis must be placed on communicating through actions.

Author: Hendricks, Jeanne **670**
Series:
Title: *Mother's Legacy, A*
Publisher: NavPress, 1988 ISBN: 0-89109-253-6

Num. Sess.	Group Time	Num. Pgs.	Avg. Qst.	Price	Audience	Format	Bible Study
11	45-60	110	9	$6.00	New Christian	Workbk	Topical

Features: Intro to Study
★★ Personal Application Preparation Time: Low
★★ Relationship Building Ldr. Guide: No Size: 5.50 x 8.50
Subjects: Bible Personalities, Parenting, Women's Issues
Comments: This study of ten Bible mothers focuses on struggles that are real to modern women. Examples bringing godly insights include Mary—faithfully obeying the seemingly impossible; Deborah—a working mom faced with apathy; Samson's mother—praying for her rebellious son; and Eve—living with the results of a wrong choice. Participants will become encouraged in their role of motherhood, and aware of its enormous influence.

Author: Henrichsen, Walter A. **671**
Series:
Title: *Disciples Are Made, Not Born*
Publisher: Victor Books, 1974 ISBN: 0-89693-442-X

Num. Sess.	Group Time	Num. Pgs.	Avg. Qst.	Price	Audience	Format	Bible Study
13	60-90	153	N/A	$8.99	Mature Christian	Book	Topical

Features:
★★★★ Personal Application Preparation Time: Med
★★★ Relationship Building Ldr. Guide: Yes Size: 5.50 x 8.0
Subjects: Discipleship, Evangelism
Comments: This study describes a modern-day disciple and shows participants how to make disciples of others. They review a process that begins with sharing the good news of the Gospel and doesn't end until they've shared so completely that another person becomes fully committed to similar spiritual service. The study is practical and provocative, and is written from effective practical experience. A leader's guide with transparency masters is available.

Author: Hestenes, Roberta **672**
Series:
Title: *Turning Committees Into Communities*
Publisher: NavPress, 1991 ISBN: 0-89109-302-8

Num. Sess.	Group Time	Num. Pgs.	Avg. Qst.	Price	Audience	Format	Bible Study
	—	32	N/A	$4.00			

Features:
Personal Application Preparation Time:
Relationship Building Ldr. Guide: Size: 5.50 x 8.50
Subjects: Church Life, Small Group Resource
Comments: This small group resource was written to help church leaders realize that committees, assuming the relational components of small groups, could have a revolutionary effect on accomplishing the work of the church. People serving on committees without this relational component feel used, burned out, and unappreciated. Using this tool, committees can be redesigned into functioning communities. The result will be more productive meetings and happier workers.

Author: Hestenes, Roberta 673
Series:
Title: *Using the Bible in Groups*
Publisher: The Westminster Press, 1983 ISBN: 0-66424-561-7

Num. Sess.	Group Time	Num. Pgs.	Avg. Qst.	Price	Audience	Format	Bible Study
7	—	118	N/A	$9.99		Book	No

Features: Bibliography, Index
Personal Application Preparation Time:
Relationship Building Ldr. Guide: Size: 6.0 x 9.0
Subjects: Leadership, Small Group Resource
Comments: This is a practical, basic resource for anyone who wants to start a Bible study group. It offers successful, field-tested methods and detailed information about the importance of groups: how to begin, who can lead, how to prepare, and how to build relationships within them. The 20 Bible study methods included can be adapted according to the experience, abilities, and interests of group members. This resource should be available to all potential small group leaders.

Author: Hicks, Cynthia & Robert 674
Series:
Title: *Feminine Journey, The*
Publisher: NavPress, 1994 ISBN: 0-89109-830-5

Num. Sess.	Group Time	Num. Pgs.	Avg. Qst.	Price	Audience	Format	Bible Study
7	60-75	89	Vary	$5.00	Beginner	Book	Topical

Features: Intro to Leading a Study, Prayer Helps, Digging Deeper Quest, Follow Up, Book Avail
★★★★ Personal Application Preparation Time: None
★★★★ Relationship Building Ldr. Guide: No Size: 5.50 x 8.50
Subjects: Relationships, Women's Issues
Comments: Lessons explore 6 Hebrew and Greek terms for "woman" that shed light on the many different characteristics, opportunities, and challenges of each stage of womanhood. No matter what stage of development participants are working through, this guide can help them realize their true identities as individuals designed by their Creator.

Author: Hicks, Robert & Dietrich Gruen 675
Series: Promise Keepers
Title: *Masculine Journey, The*
Publisher: NavPress, 1993 ISBN: 0-89109-734-1

Num. Sess.	Group Time	Num. Pgs.	Avg. Qst.	Price	Audience	Format	Bible Study
8	60-75	95	11	$5.00	Beginner	Workbk	Topical

Features: Digging Deeper Quest, Book Avail
★★★★ Personal Application Preparation Time: None
★★★ Relationship Building Ldr. Guide: No Size: 5.50 x 8.50
Subjects: Men's Issues
Comments: Part of the Promise Keepers series, this study explores biblical roots of masculinity. Drawing from the 6 Hebrew terms for manhood, it presents masculinity as a distinctly powerful asset that can enable men to thrive at and understand every life-stage. Participants can discover their personal levels of masculine development.

Author: Hillis, Don W. 676
Series: Teach Yourself the Bible
Title: *John: The Gospel of Light and Life*
Publisher: Moody Press, 1962 ISBN: 0-80244-375-3

Num. Sess.	Group Time	Num. Pgs.	Avg. Qst.	Price	Audience	Format	Bible Study
12	45-60	64	22	$4.50	New Christian	Workbk	Book

Features: Intro to Leading a Study, Exam
★★ Personal Application Preparation Time: Low
★★ Relationship Building Ldr. Guide: No Size: 5.50 x 8.50
Subjects: God, Grace, Jesus: Life/Teaching, John, Wisdom
Comments: This study of John—part of a 25-book series—concerns Christ as described by John as the "Light" and "Life." Participants will study the glory, righteousness, wisdom, and grace of God. The format includes a series of fill-in-the-blank questions, and checkups to test participants' grasp of Scriptural truths. The series is designed for self-study; however, suggestions for group study, and a four-year plan for using the series, are included.

Author: Hinckley, Karen 677
Series: The Lifechange Series
Title: *Acts*
Publisher: NavPress, 1987 ISBN: 0-89109-112-2

Num. Sess.	Group Time	Num. Pgs.	Avg. Qst.	Price	Audience	Format	Bible Study
20	60-90	220	15	$6.00	New Christian	Workbk	Book

Features: Intro to Leading a Study, Intro to Study, Bibliography, Prayer Helps, Worship Helps, Study Overview, Digging Deeper Quest, Summary, Maps, Cross Ref, Word Study
★★★ Personal Application Preparation Time: Med
★★★ Relationship Building Ldr. Guide: No Size: 5.50 x 8.50
Subjects: Acts, Holy Spirit
Comments: This verse-by-verse study of Acts explores the church, born among Jesus' disciples, which grew into a worldwide force in just a few years. Jesus had left His followers with a mission, and God's Holy Spirit moved through them to fulfill it. Luke's account of how the Gospel challenges participants to know and live out their mission in the world.

Author: Hinckley, Karen 678
Series: The Lifechange Series
Title: *Ephesians*
Publisher: NavPress, 1985 ISBN: 0-89109-054-1

Num. Sess.	Group Time	Num. Pgs.	Avg. Qst.	Price	Audience	Format	Bible Study
14	60-90	127	13	$6.00	New Christian	Workbk	Book

Features: Intro to Leading a Study, Intro to Study, Bibliography, Prayer Helps, Worship Helps, Study Overview, Digging Deeper Quest, Summary, Charts, Maps, Cross Ref, Word Study
★★★ Personal Application Preparation Time: Med
★★★ Relationship Building Ldr. Guide: No Size: 5.50 x 8.50
Subjects: Ephesians, Holiness
Comments: This is a verse-by-verse study of Ephesians, Paul's letter to a young church that needed a fuller knowledge of Christ. It offers participants priceless truths about a believer's new identity in Christ and the special calling included therein. Paul's theme is: know who you are before God through Christ, and live according to that identity.

Author: Hinckley, Karen **679**
Series: The Lifechange Series
Title: *Genesis*
Publisher: NavPress, 1987 ISBN: 0-89109-069-X

Num. Sess.	Group Time	Num. Pgs.	Avg. Qst.	Price	Audience	Format	Bible Study
19	60-90	220	14	$6.00	New Christian	Workbk	Book

Features: Intro to Leading a Study, Intro to Study, Bibliography, Prayer Helps, Worship Helps, Study Overview, Digging Deeper Quest, Summary, Charts, Maps, Cross Ref, Word Study
★★★ Personal Application Preparation Time: Med
★★★ Relationship Building Ldr. Guide: No Size: 5.50 x 8.50
Subjects: Genesis, God
Comments: This verse-by-verse study of Genesis, records God's revelation to humankind from the beginning, through rebellion, then through God's task of mending His relationship with humankind. The events that unfold give form to the entire Bible and offer participants 2 perspectives: 1, a look at God; the other, a look at humanity.

Author: Hinckley, Karen **680**
Series: The Lifechange Series
Title: *Isaiah*
Publisher: NavPress, 1987 ISBN: 0-89109-111-4

Num. Sess.	Group Time	Num. Pgs.	Avg. Qst.	Price	Audience	Format	Bible Study
18	60-90	220	13	$6.00	New Christian	Workbk	Book

Features: Intro to Leading a Study, Intro to Study, Bibliography, Prayer Helps, Worship Helps, Study Overview, Digging Deeper Quest, Follow Up, Charts, Maps, Cross Ref, Word Study
★★★ Personal Application Preparation Time: Med
★★★ Relationship Building Ldr. Guide: No Size: 5.50 x 8.50
Subjects: Christian Living, Isaiah/Jeremiah, Major Prophets, Prophecy
Comments: This is a verse-by-verse study about Isaiah, whose name means "the Lord is salvation," who, for over 40 years, made that his message. Through Isaiah, the Lord judged the proud who sought to save themselves, and comforted the humble. Isaiah's book offers participants a window into God's mind, from 700 years before Christ.

Author: Hinckley, Karen **681**
Series: The Lifechange Series
Title: *James*
Publisher: NavPress, 1988 ISBN: 0-89109-120-3

Num. Sess.	Group Time	Num. Pgs.	Avg. Qst.	Price	Audience	Format	Bible Study
12	60-90	125	15	$6.00	New Christian	Workbk	Book

Features: Intro to Leading a Study, Intro to Study, Bibliography, Prayer Helps, Worship Helps, Study Overview, Digging Deeper Quest, Summary, Cross Ref, Word Study
★★★ Personal Application Preparation Time: Med
★★★ Relationship Building Ldr. Guide: No Size: 5.50 x 8.50
Subjects: Faith, James
Comments: This verse-by-verse study of James offers a challenge to Christians of every age to keep on growing. Participants learn that by faith humankind is reborn into the family of God; but that more than justified infants, He wants mature daughters and sons. The result should be faith that is genuine, proven, and evident to the world.

Author: Hinckley, Karen **682**
Series: The Lifechange Series
Title: *John*
Publisher: NavPress, 1988 ISBN: 0-89109-237-4

Num. Sess.	Group Time	Num. Pgs.	Avg. Qst.	Price	Audience	Format	Bible Study
22	60-90	220	15	$6.00	New Christian	Workbk	Book

Features: Intro to Leading a Study, Intro to Study, Bibliography, Prayer Helps, Worship Helps, Study Overview, Digging Deeper Quest, Summary, Maps, Cross Ref, Word Study
★★★ Personal Application Preparation Time: Med
★★★ Relationship Building Ldr. Guide: No Size: 5.50 x 8.50
Subjects: Jesus: Life/Teaching, John
Comments: This study of John provides a beautiful biography of Christ. During His lifetime, no one truly understood His mission, but using a few carefully chosen incidents, John unfolds the truth. This study uses 22 lessons in a verse-by-verse chronological order to depict John's portrait of the Son of Man. Study aids follow.

Author: Hinckley, Karen **683**
Series: The Lifechange Series
Title: *Joshua*
Publisher: NavPress, 1988 ISBN: 0-89109-121-1

Num. Sess.	Group Time	Num. Pgs.	Avg. Qst.	Price	Audience	Format	Bible Study
16	60-90	173	13	$6.00	New Christian	Workbk	Book

Features: Intro to Leading a Study, Intro to Study, Bibliography, Prayer Helps, Worship Helps, Study Overview, Digging Deeper Quest, Summary, Maps, Cross Ref, Word Study
★★★ Personal Application Preparation Time: Med
★★★ Relationship Building Ldr. Guide: No Size: 5.50 x 8.50
Subjects: God, Joshua
Comments: For centuries God had promised to give the land of Canaan to the family of Abraham. He fulfilled that promise with Joshua as His general. Today as well, the Lord leads His army to take possession of its inheritance. Participants will learn unforgettable lessons about God and what it means to be a citizen of His Kingdom.

Author: Hinckley, Karen **684**
Series: The Lifechange Series
Title: *Philippians*
Publisher: NavPress, 1987 ISBN: 0-89109-072-X

Num. Sess.	Group Time	Num. Pgs.	Avg. Qst.	Price	Audience	Format	Bible Study
11	60-90	113	11	$6.00	New Christian	Workbk	Book

Features: Intro to Leading a Study, Intro to Study, Bibliography, Prayer Helps, Worship Helps, Study Overview, Digging Deeper Quest, Summary, Maps, Cross Ref, Word Study
★★★ Personal Application Preparation Time: Med
★★★ Relationship Building Ldr. Guide: No Size: 5.50 x 8.50
Subjects: Joy, Philippians, Prison Epistles, Suffering, Victorious Living
Comments: In this verse-by-verse study of Philippians, participants will discover Paul's secret joy and experience his triumphant confidence in Christ. In prison for proclaiming Christ, Paul encourages and challenges his "partners in the Gospel." He aims to inspire his ancient readers and modern Christians to persevere in the work of Christ.

Author: Hinckley, Karen 685
Series: The Lifechange Series
Title: *Revelation*
Publisher: NavPress, 1989 ISBN: 0-89109-273-0

Num. Sess.	Group Time	Num. Pgs.	Avg. Qst.	Price	Audience	Format	Bible Study
15	60-90	168	16	$6.00	New Christian	Workbk	Book

Features: Intro to Leading a Study, Intro to Study, Bibliography, Prayer Helps, Worship Helps, Study Overview, Digging Deeper Quest, Summary, Maps, Cross Ref, Word Study
★★★ Personal Application Preparation Time: Med
★★★ Relationship Building Ldr. Guide: No Size: 5.50 x 8.50
Subjects: Faith, Revelation, Satan, Suffering
Comments: This verse-by-verse study of Revelation fortifies believers pressured to deny their faith. God gave the Apostle John a series of visions as a call to stand firm. Revelation unveils events between God and Satan in the end and describes the glory that awaits believers who faithfully endure suffering.

Author: Hinckley, Karen 686
Series: The Lifechange Series
Title: *Romans*
Publisher: NavPress, 1987 ISBN: 0-89109-073-8

Num. Sess.	Group Time	Num. Pgs.	Avg. Qst.	Price	Audience	Format	Bible Study
20	60-90	210	14	$6.00	New Christian	Workbk	Book

Features: Intro to Leading a Study, Intro to Study, Bibliography, Prayer Helps, Worship Helps, Study Overview, Digging Deeper Quest, Summary, Maps, Cross Ref, Word Study
★★★ Personal Application Preparation Time: Med
★★★ Relationship Building Ldr. Guide: No Size: 5.50 x 8.50
Subjects: Grace, Reconciliation, Romans
Comments: This verse-by-verse study on Romans exposes God's path to righteousness and shows how people can be reconciled to God and transformed into the believers He means them to be. Sin, salvation, grace, death, and resurrection are life-changing truths addressed in the study. Participants will gain a firm foundation of Romans.

Author: Hinckley, Karen 687
Series: The Lifechange Series
Title: *Ruth & Esther*
Publisher: NavPress, 1987 ISBN: 0-89109-074-6

Num. Sess.	Group Time	Num. Pgs.	Avg. Qst.	Price	Audience	Format	Bible Study
10	60-90	121	11	$6.00	New Christian	Workbk	Book

Features: Intro to Leading a Study, Intro to Study, Bibliography, Prayer Helps, Worship Helps, Study Overview, Digging Deeper Quest, Summary, Charts, Maps, Cross Ref, Word Study
★★★ Personal Application Preparation Time: Med
★★★ Relationship Building Ldr. Guide: No Size: 5.50 x 8.50
Subjects: Bible Personalities, Esther, God, Obedience, Ruth
Comments: These verse-by-verse studies of Ruth and Esther reveal responses to 2 questions: "Is God really sovereign?" and "Can individual people make a difference in His world?" Ruth and Boaz answer yes and go on to play crucial roles in God's plan. Over 600 years later, Mordecai and his cousin Esther save their nation by also saying yes.

Author: Hinckley, Karen 688
Series: The Lifechange Series
Title: *1 Corinthians*
Publisher: NavPress, 1990 ISBN: 0-89109-559-4

Num. Sess.	Group Time	Num. Pgs.	Avg. Qst.	Price	Audience	Format	Bible Study
17	60-90	168	16	$6.00	New Christian	Workbk	Book

Features: Intro to Leading a Study, Intro to Study, Bibliography, Prayer Helps, Worship Helps, Study Overview, Digging Deeper Quest, Summary, Maps, Cross Ref, Word Study
★★★ Personal Application Preparation Time: Med
★★★ Relationship Building Ldr. Guide: No Size: 5.50 x 8.50
Subjects: Church Life, Sexual Issues, Spiritual Gifts, Worship, 1 Corinthians
Comments: This study of 1 Corinthians is Paul's stern reminder to take our eyes off the external and practice purity, humility, and love. His practical instructions concerning factions, sexuality, spiritual gifts, and worship remain profoundly relevant for contemporary participants.

Author: Hinckley, Karen 689
Series: The Lifechange Series
Title: *1 Peter*
Publisher: NavPress, 1986 ISBN: 0-89109-052-5

Num. Sess.	Group Time	Num. Pgs.	Avg. Qst.	Price	Audience	Format	Bible Study
13	60-90	137	12	$6.00	New Christian	Workbk	Book

Features: Intro to Leading a Study, Intro to Study, Bibliography, Prayer Helps, Worship Helps, Study Overview, Digging Deeper Quest, Summary, Charts, Maps, Cross Ref, Word Study
★★★ Personal Application Preparation Time: Med
★★★ Relationship Building Ldr. Guide: No Size: 5.50 x 8.50
Subjects: Suffering, 1 & 2 Peter
Comments: This verse-by-verse study of 1 Peter reminds modern Christians of their rich identities in Christ. Written for young Christians facing ridicule in a pagan world, it encourages them to focus on their "living hope" and face sufferings with Christlike character. Peter challenges us to meet trials with confidence in "the God of all grace."

Author: Hinckley, Karen 690
Series: The Lifechange Series
Title: *1, 2 & 3 John*
Publisher: NavPress, 1988 ISBN: 0-89109-114-9

Num. Sess.	Group Time	Num. Pgs.	Avg. Qst.	Price	Audience	Format	Bible Study
14	60-90	147	14	$6.00	New Christian	Workbk	Book

Features: Intro to Leading a Study, Intro to Study, Bibliography, Prayer Helps, Worship Helps, Study Overview, Digging Deeper Quest, Summary, Maps, Cross Ref, Word Study
★★★ Personal Application Preparation Time: Med
★★★ Relationship Building Ldr. Guide: No Size: 5.50 x 8.50
Subjects: False Teachers, 1, 2 & 3 John/Jude
Comments: John's letters were circulated among troubled churches to calm members. False teachers were undermining the faith of Christians, and John responded with hard-hitting words about righteousness, love, and truth. His message continues to expose falsehood today and offers Christians confidence in their relationship with God.

Author: Hohensee, Donald Allen Odell **691**
Series:
Title: *Your Spiritual Gifts*
Publisher: Victor Books, 1992 ISBN: 0-89693-069-6

Num. Sess.	Group Time	Num. Pgs.	Avg. Qst.	Price	Audience	Format	Bible Study
12	60-75	167	3	$8.99	New Christian	Book	Topical

Features: Bibliography, Charts
★★★★ Personal Application Preparation Time: Low
★★★ Relationship Building Ldr. Guide: No Size: 5.50 x 8.50
Subjects: Christian Life, Fruit of the Spirit, Psychology, Spiritual Gifts
Comments: While not a Bible study, this booklet offers a comprehensive description of God-given gifts. Used as a part of a small group study, it can help Christians identify their gifts then use them to the fullest. It includes an extensive spiritual gifts questionnaire, detailed descriptions of all 26 gifts found in Scripture, and a 5-step guide to identification. Because the book doesn't provide questions, group leaders will be required to develop a plan for it's use.

Author: Holbert, John **692**
Series:
Title: *Gospel of John, The: Volume 1 & 2*
Publisher: Cokesbury, 1990 ISBN: 0-68776-176-X

Num. Sess.	Group Time	Num. Pgs.	Avg. Qst.	Price	Audience	Format	Bible Study
7	45-60	N/A	Vary	$25.00	New Christian	Video	Book

Features: Intro to Leading a Study, Intro to Study, Ldr's Notes, Video Study Guide
★★★ Personal Application Preparation Time: Low
★★★ Relationship Building Ldr. Guide: Yes Size: 4.75 x 8.0
Subjects: Jesus: Life/Teaching, John
Comments: Even though its sources and origin are yet veiled in mystery, no document has influenced so powerfully the hearts and minds as has the Gospel of John. Nor has any New Testament book received so many diverse interpretations of its meaning. This 2-volume video Bible study of John's Gospel covers some of John's different ideas about how Jesus relates to the world.

Author: Hook, Sue Vander & Rachel Kiepe **693**
Series: Serendipity Support Group
Title: *Infertility: Coping With the Pain of Childlessness*
Publisher: Serendipity House, 1991 ISBN: 1-88341-965-4

Num. Sess.	Group Time	Num. Pgs.	Avg. Qst.	Price	Audience	Format	Bible Study
7	60-90	96	Vary	$5.45	Beginner	Workbk	Topical

Features: Intro to Leading a Study, Objectives, Bibliography, Prayer Helps, Full Scrpt Printed, Ldr's Notes, Drawings, Cartoons, Agenda
★★★★ Personal Application Preparation Time: None
★★★★ Relationship Building Ldr. Guide: No Size: 6.50 x 9.25
Subjects: Grief, Marriage, Medical Issues, Parenting
Comments: This study of infertility explores ways to cope with the pain of childlessness. It considers the following: why being childless can be so difficult; new ways to respond to pressures and comments about childlessness; understanding childlessness as a form of grief and loss; examining medical procedures available to couples; exploring ways to restore intimacy and spontaneity to marriage.

Author: Hoover, James **694**
Series: LifeGuide Bible Study
Title: *Mark: Follow Me*
Publisher: InterVarsity, 1985 ISBN: 0-83081-004-8

Num. Sess.	Group Time	Num. Pgs.	Avg. Qst.	Price	Audience	Format	Bible Study
22	45-75	96	14	$4.99	New Christian	Workbk	Book

Features: Intro to Leading a Study, Intro to Study, Ldr's Notes
★ Personal Application Preparation Time: Low
★ Relationship Building Ldr. Guide: No Size: 5.50 x 8.25
Subjects: Jesus: Life/Teaching, Mark, Service, Suffering
Comments: Mark theologically and pastorally tells the story of Jesus, showing that the Kingdom in its glory comes at the end of a path of suffering and service. Mark portrays Jesus as the Servant-King whom we should follow from suffering to glory (Mark 1:17). This 22-segment study is divided into a 10-part study on "Who Is Jesus?" and a 12-part study on "Why Did Jesus Come?" The last study in each segment serves as a review to tie together major themes.

Author: Horner, Bob & Jan **695**
Series: HomeBuilders Couples
Title: *Resolving Conflict in Your Marriage*
Publisher: Gospel Light Publications, 1991 ISBN: 0-83071-618-1

Num. Sess.	Group Time	Num. Pgs.	Avg. Qst.	Price	Audience	Format	Bible Study
6	60-90	138	Vary	$9.99	Beginner	Workbk	Topical

Features: Intro to Study, Drawings, Appendix
★★★★ Personal Application Preparation Time: Low
★★★★ Relationship Building Ldr. Guide: Yes Size: 5.75 x 8.50
Subjects: Family, Marriage
Comments: This study, which deals with turning conflict into compassion, starts with forgiveness. It's not easy but once people adopt the habit of giving blessings even when hurt, they find the result is a stronger, more exciting marriage. It teaches couples why conflict is inevitable, how to communicate consistently and openly, ways to really hear their mates, how to make confrontation lead to greater love, the secret for replacing conflict with peace.

Author: Horton, T.C. & Charles E. Hurlburt **696**
Series:
Title: *Names of Christ*
Publisher: Moody Press, 1994 ISBN: 0-80246-040-2

Num. Sess.	Group Time	Num. Pgs.	Avg. Qst.	Price	Audience	Format	Bible Study
	—	180	N/A	$3.99	New Christian	Book	Charctr

Features: Intro to Study, Prayer Helps, Index
Personal Application Preparation Time:
Relationship Building Ldr. Guide: Size: 4.25 x 7.0
Subjects: Devotionals, Jesus: Life/Teaching, Small Group Resource
Comments: This book examines the more than 300 names of Christ, each of which reveals an intimate portrait of the Savior. Devotional prayers accompany each name, helping readers meditate on Christ's character and person. "Names of Christ" follows "Names of God" in a series designed to help contemporary Christians better understand the glory, majesty, and power of the triune God. It's a good resource for small group leaders to use to augment other studies.

Author: Hotaling, Scott 697
Series: The TruthSeed Series
Title: *1 Timothy: Leading By Example*
Publisher: Victor Books, 1995 ISBN: 1-56476-328-5

Num. Sess.	Group Time	Num. Pgs.	Avg. Qst.	Price	Audience	Format	Bible Study
10	45-60	80	12	$4.99	Beginner	Workbk	Book

Features: Intro to Leading a Study, Intro to Study, Bibliography, Prayer Helps, Follow Up, Ldr's Notes
★★★ Personal Application Preparation Time: None
★★★ Relationship Building Ldr. Guide: No Size: 6.0 x 9.0
Subjects: 1 & 2 Timothy/Titus
Comments: This new series of inductive Bible studies enables men and women to experience community and develop godliness in either discussion group or personal settings. Questions are designed and field-tested for seekers, new believers, and mature Christians. Enrichment material for further study is provided along with a bibliography. This study of 1 Timothy explores ways to lead by godly example.

Author: Howard, David A. 698
Series: Spiritual Development Work
Title: *Missions Alive: Experiential Games for Youth*
Publisher: Woman's Missionary Union, 1993 ISBN: 1-56309-071-6

Num. Sess.	Group Time	Num. Pgs.	Avg. Qst.	Price	Audience	Format	Bible Study
	—	46	N/A	$5.95		Book	

Features: Intro to Study
Personal Application Preparation Time:
Relationship Building Ldr. Guide: Size: 8.50 x 11.0
Subjects: Teens: Missions, Teens: Resources
Comments: This resource, designed to bring missions alive for youth, offers a new, experiential, encounter-centered approach to missions. Simply by becoming involved in the games and activities suggested, learners will personally encounter missions. It contains experiential games for younger and older teens in missions education or youth group settings. Games emphasize a global viewpoint of missions, an understanding of other cultures, and ministry and witness.

Author: Howard, Walden 699
Series:
Title: *Great Biblical Themes*
Publisher: Faith at Work, 1982

Num. Sess.	Group Time	Num. Pgs.	Avg. Qst.	Price	Audience	Format	Bible Study
12	60-75	38	Vary	$2.50	New Christian	Book	Topical

Features: Intro to Study
★★ Personal Application Preparation Time: Med
★ Relationship Building Ldr. Guide: No Size: 5.50 x 8.50
Subjects: Beliefs, New Testament, Old Testament
Comments: One of a series of 9 booklets, this study deals with great biblical themes. Twelve lessons lead participants through subjects from a "changing/unchanging God" to the Apostle Paul "living through loss." Lesson titles include: "Cocreators with God," "The Kingdom of God," "Dealing with Sin," "Stories of Jesus," "Death and Resurrection," "Life and Death," and more. Each unit deals with its own Scripture and commentary and offers additional suggested reading.

Author: Howard, Walden 700
Series:
Title: *Group Encounters with the Bible*
Publisher: Faith at Work, 1977

Num. Sess.	Group Time	Num. Pgs.	Avg. Qst.	Price	Audience	Format	Bible Study
52	30-45	31	Vary	$2.50	Beginner	Book	Topical

Features: Intro to Study, No Grp Discussion Quest
★★ Personal Application Preparation Time: Low
★★ Relationship Building Ldr. Guide: No Size: 5.50 x 8.50
Subjects: Bible Study, New Testament, Old Testament
Comments: This year-long Old and New Testament study, broken into 52 lessons, is designed to foster personal growth among Christians meeting in small groups. The lessons serve as catalysts for meetings which participants will listen to what God says through the Bible, talk about personal concerns, and pray for group members' growth. Some lessons are entitled: "Where to Find Christ"; "Christian Paradoxes"; "Jesus: God and Man"; "A Model for Prayer"; "The Claims of Christ."

Author: Howard, Walden 701
Series:
Title: *Journeying in the Spirit*
Publisher: Faith at Work, 1982

Num. Sess.	Group Time	Num. Pgs.	Avg. Qst.	Price	Audience	Format	Bible Study
12	60-75	33	Vary	$2.50	New Christian	Book	Topical

Features:
★★ Personal Application Preparation Time: Med
★ Relationship Building Ldr. Guide: No Size: 5.50 x 8.50
Subjects: Holy Spirit, Wisdom
Comments: One of a series of 9 booklets, this study deals with various aspects of the Holy Spirit. Twelve lessons lead participants from Abraham's journey to people's wisdom in old age. Lesson titles include: "The Narrow Way," "Power for the Journey," "Nurturing Spiritual Growth," "Dreams as Guidance," "Growing in Love," "The Call to Leadership," "The Seasons of Life," and more. Each unit deals with its own Scripture and commentary and offers additional suggested reading.

Author: Howard, Walden 702
Series:
Title: *Lessons in the Life of Faith*
Publisher: Faith at Work, 1985

Num. Sess.	Group Time	Num. Pgs.	Avg. Qst.	Price	Audience	Format	Bible Study
52	30-45	37	N/A	$2.50	New Christian	Book	Topical

Features: Intro to Study, No Grp Discussion Quest
★★ Personal Application Preparation Time: Low
★★ Relationship Building Ldr. Guide: No Size: 5.50 x 8.50
Subjects: Faith, New Testament
Comments: This year-long New Testament study, a compilation of 52 lessons, has two unique features. One, it offers 4- and 8-part consecutive studies from particular Bible books, which allows participants to gain a sense of wholeness of each book studied. Two, it offers a comprehensive study of biblical themes, helping participants thoroughly understand the basic tenets of Christian faith and experience. Books covered include Peter, Luke, Colossians, Acts, and Hebrews.

Author: Huddleston, Steven B. **703**
Series: Group's Active Bible Curriculum
Title: *Miracle of Easter, The*
Publisher: Group Publishing, 1993 ISBN: 1-55945-143-2

Num. Sess.	Group Time	Num. Pgs.	Avg. Qst.	Price	Audience	Format	Bible Study
4	35-60	46	Vary	$9.99	Beginner	Workbk	Topical

Features: Intro to Leading a Study, Intro to Study, Objectives, Study Overview, Ldr's Notes, Handouts, Agenda, Publicity Ideas
★★★★ Personal Application Preparation Time: None
★★★★ Relationship Building Ldr. Guide: No Size: 8.50 x 11.0
Subjects: Teens: Jesus' Life, Teens: Junior High
Comments: In this course, junior highers discover that Easter is more than jelly beans and colored eggs, that the true meaning lies in Christ's death and resurrection. Participants learn to comprehend the agony Jesus suffered because of His great love for them, understand that He rose from the dead, and find ways to express the message of Easter all year long. It can be adapted for a Bible class or youth meeting.

Author: Huddleston, Steven B. **704**
Series: Group's Active Bible Curriculum
Title: *What Is God's Purpose for Me?*
Publisher: Group Publishing, 1992 ISBN: 1-55945-132-7

Num. Sess.	Group Time	Num. Pgs.	Avg. Qst.	Price	Audience	Format	Bible Study
4	35-60	41	Vary	$9.99	Beginner	Workbk	Topical

Features: Intro to Leading a Study, Intro to Study, Objectives, Study Overview, Ldr's Notes, Handouts, Agenda, Publicity Ideas
★★★★ Personal Application Preparation Time: None
★★★★ Relationship Building Ldr. Guide: No Size: 8.50 x 11.0
Subjects: Teens: Christian Liv, Teens: Junior High
Comments: This course helps junior highers explore God's will for their lives. Participants learn how God can use their talents and abilities, dicover what makes them valuable and important, and recognize that they can find purpose in life through serving others. It can be adapted for a Bible class or youth meeting. Activity sheets are reproducible. Student books not required.

Author: Huggins, Kevin **705**
Series:
Title: *Parenting Adolescents*
Publisher: NavPress, 1990 ISBN: 9-90073-584-6

Num. Sess.	Group Time	Num. Pgs.	Avg. Qst.	Price	Audience	Format	Bible Study
8	60-120	N/A	Vary	$119.00	Beginner	Video	Topical

Features: Ldr's Notes, Book Incl, Video Study Guide
★★★★ Personal Application Preparation Time: None
★★★★ Relationship Building Ldr. Guide: No Size: 10.0 x 12.75
Subjects: Grace, Parenting, Psychology, Teens: Family
Comments: This 8-week video study features dramatic vignettes, interviews with parents and adolescents, and key insights and principles that provide a launching point into stimulating discussion questions. The series avoids pat answers or formulas and encourages teenagers and their families to adopt biblical principles. It helps participants view teens with grace and love and guide them; it helps them focus their energy and develop their own styles of parenting.

Author: Hulme, Lucy & William **706**
Series: Friendship Bible Study
Title: *Friendship*
Publisher: Augsburg Fortress Publishers, 1987

Num. Sess.	Group Time	Num. Pgs.	Avg. Qst.	Price	Audience	Format	Bible Study
8	60-75	48	10	$3.75	New Christian	Workbk	Topical

Features: Intro to Study, Prayer Helps, Study Overview
★★★★ Personal Application Preparation Time: Low
★★★★ Relationship Building Ldr. Guide: Yes Size: 5.50 x 8.50
Subjects: Family, Friendships
Comments: This 8-lesson study, which invites participants to look at what it means to be a friend, draws upon biblical examples of friendship. Lessons include: "Loyalty in Friendships," "Friends in the Family," "Friendship Between the Sexes," and "Creative Conflict in Friendship." Participants are made aware that love, or friendship, can be the bridge between the secular and the spiritual. The lesson format includes an overview, an opening, a responsive reading.

Author: Humber, Wilson J. **707**
Series:
Title: *Financially Challenged*
Publisher: Moody Press, 1995 ISBN: 0-80242-737-5

Num. Sess.	Group Time	Num. Pgs.	Avg. Qst.	Price	Audience	Format	Bible Study
10	60-90	230	N/A	$8.99	Beginner	Book	Topical

Features: Intro to Study, Bibliography, No Grp Discussion Quest
★★★★ Personal Application Preparation Time: Med
★ Relationship Building Ldr. Guide: No Size: 6.0 x 9.0
Subjects: Money
Comments: This book offers practical steps for steering clear of or emerging from financial disaster. Each chapter presents eye-opening principles that help participants move beyond their financial challenges by learning to adjust habits and attitudes, save money on the 2 largest expenses (housing and transportation), become totally and permanently debt-free in 3 years or less, save money the right way, retire financially secure, and stretch a paycheck 15% or more.

Author: Hummel, Charles & Anne **708**
Series: LifeGuide Bible Study
Title: *Genesis: God's Creative Call*
Publisher: InterVarsity, 1985 ISBN: 0-83081-022-6

Num. Sess.	Group Time	Num. Pgs.	Avg. Qst.	Price	Audience	Format	Bible Study
26	45-75	112	12	$4.99	New Christian	Workbk	Book

Features: Intro to Leading a Study, Intro to Study, Ldr's Notes
★ Personal Application Preparation Time: Low
★ Relationship Building Ldr. Guide: No Size: 5.50 x 8.25
Subjects: Bible Personalities, Genesis, God
Comments: This study guides us through Genesis, focusing on the lives of Abraham, Isaac, Jacob, and Joseph. It's divided into 3 main parts: Genesis 1–11, which includes 7 lessons on the Creation and primeval history; and Genesis 12–36, which includes 12 lessons on Abraham, Isaac, and Jacob and seven lessons on Joseph. The study is designed to stress what is said and not said in the text. Its purpose is to help participants discover the meaning of Genesis.

Author: Hummel, Charles & Anne 709
Series: The Beatitude Series
Title: *Making Peace: Resolving Personal Conflicts*
Publisher: Zondervan, 1993 ISBN: 0-31059-653-X

Num. Sess.	Group Time	Num. Pgs.	Avg. Qst.	Price	Audience	Format	Bible Study
6	45-60	48	14	$4.99	New Christian	Workbk	Topical

Features: Intro to Leading a Study, Intro to Study, Objectives, Prayer Helps, Scrpt Memory Helps, Ldr's Notes
★★★★ Personal Application Preparation Time: Low
★★ Relationship Building Ldr. Guide: No Size: 5.50 x 8.25
Subjects: Sermon on the Mount
Comments: In 6 weeks participants will be challenged to be peacemakers in a world of stained and broken relationships. Lessons cover: the prophet Isaiah's message of judgment and eventual blessings through the Prince of Peace; Jesus' teachings about making peace with enemies and foregoing the use of a sword; principles of peacemaking; and guidelines on mending broken relationships.

Author: Hummel, Charles 710
Series: Christian Basics
Title: *Priorities: Tyranny of The Urgent*
Publisher: InterVarsity, 1994 ISBN: 0-83082-006-X

Num. Sess.	Group Time	Num. Pgs.	Avg. Qst.	Price	Audience	Format	Bible Study
6	30-45	62	7	$4.99	Beginner	Workbk	Topical

Features: Intro to Leading a Study, Intro to Study, Prayer Helps, Follow Up, Full Scrpt Printed, Ldr's Notes
★★★★ Personal Application Preparation Time: None
★★★★ Relationship Building Ldr. Guide: No Size: 5.50 x 8.25
Subjects: Time
Comments: This study is designed to help participants put their lives in order, set new priorities based on the example and instruction of the Lord. The lessons help them identify urgent demands on their time, set priorities under the Lordship of Christ, and experience the power He provides through freedom from "Tyranny of the Urgent."

Author: Hummel, Charles & Anne 711
Series: The Beatitude Series
Title: *Pure Heart, A: The Window to God*
Publisher: Zondervan, 1993 ISBN: 0-31059-643-2

Num. Sess.	Group Time	Num. Pgs.	Avg. Qst.	Price	Audience	Format	Bible Study
6	45-60	48	11	$4.99	New Christian	Workbk	Topical

Features: Intro to Leading a Study, Intro to Study, Objectives, Prayer Helps, Scrpt Memory Helps, Follow Up, Ldr's Notes
★★★★ Personal Application Preparation Time: Low
★★ Relationship Building Ldr. Guide: No Size: 5.50 x 8.25
Subjects: Sermon on the Mount
Comments: In 6 weeks participants will be encouraged to develop moral and spiritual purity so they can see God in a new and fresh way. Lessons look at: Jesus' explanation of what it means to be "pure in heart," David's experience of confession and restoration, instructions for holy living, and preparation to see God both now and in the ultimate vision of the new heaven and earth.

Author: Hummel, Charles & Anne 712
Series: LifeGuide Bible Study
Title: *Spiritual Gifts*
Publisher: InterVarsity, 1989 ISBN: 0-83081-062-5

Num. Sess.	Group Time	Num. Pgs.	Avg. Qst.	Price	Audience	Format	Bible Study
12	45-60	64	12	$4.99	Mature Christian	Workbk	Topical

Features: Intro to Leading a Study, Intro to Study, Ldr's Notes, Appendix
★ Personal Application Preparation Time: Low
★ Relationship Building Ldr. Guide: No Size: 5.50 x 8.25
Subjects: Church Life, New Testament, Spiritual Gifts
Comments: This study explores the nature of spiritual gifts, describes their role in the church, and discusses how to identify one's own gift(s). The authors examine key passages and specific examples of how the gifts were manifested in the early Church. Evangelism, teaching and preaching, healing, prophecy, and tongues are dealt with in specific lessons. Appendices provide a listing of New Testament gifts.

Author: Hummel, Charles & Anne 713
Series: Fisherman Bible Studyguide
Title: *1 Corinthians: Problems & Solutions in a Growing Church*
Publisher: Shaw, 1981 ISBN: 0-87788-137-5

Num. Sess.	Group Time	Num. Pgs.	Avg. Qst.	Price	Audience	Format	Bible Study
16	60-90	94	14	$4.99	Mature Christian	Workbk	Book

Features: Intro to Leading a Study, Intro to Study
★★ Personal Application Preparation Time: Low
★★ Relationship Building Ldr. Guide: No Size: 5.0 x 8.25
Subjects: Accountability, Apologetics, Christian Living, Church Life, Ethics, Obedience, Relationships, Social Issues, 1 Corinthians
Comments: This study of 1 Corinthians discusses Paul's response by letter about disturbing developments in the church at Corinth. Paul spent 18 months discipling the young church; after he left, the church continued to grow, which caused new problems. Concerned about divided loyalties, immorality, and pagan lifestyles, Paul wrote a letter highlighting the principles for balanced church growth.

Author: Hunter, Bob & Carol 714
Series:
Title: *Loving Justice*
Publisher: InterVarsity, 1990 ISBN: 0-83081-066-8

Num. Sess.	Group Time	Num. Pgs.	Avg. Qst.	Price	Audience	Format	Bible Study
12	45-60	59	11	$4.99	Mature Christian	Workbk	Topical

Features: Intro to Leading a Study, Intro to Study, Ldr's Notes
★★ Personal Application Preparation Time: Low
★★ Relationship Building Ldr. Guide: No Size: 5.50 x 8.25
Subjects: Social Issues
Comments: This study concerns the church's social conscience. Scripture includes many themes of liberation and challenges Christians to deal justly with all people. God chose the nation of Israel as His chosen people and illustrated justice through their culture and His instruction. An honest study of the Bible reveals just how far people have strayed. This study is unusual due to topics it addresses, and because of its attempt to interpret subtleties in Scripture.

Author: Hunt, Gladys **715**
Series: The Discipleship Series
Title: *Building Character*
Publisher: Zondervan, 1992 ISBN: 0-31054-711-3

Num. Sess.	Group Time	Num. Pgs.	Avg. Qst.	Price	Audience	Format	Bible Study
6	45-60	48	13	$4.99	New Christian	Workbk	Topical

Features: Intro to Leading a Study, Intro to Study, Objectives, Scrpt Memory Helps, Follow Up, Ldr's Notes
★★★★ Personal Application Preparation Time: Med
★★ Relationship Building Ldr. Guide: No Size: 5.50 x 8.50
Subjects: Discipleship, Faith, Holiness, Integrity, Love
Comments: The lessons focus on those qualities that are at the heart of who Jesus is and what He wants each believer to become. God is no cookie-cutter who stamps out every person the same way. Through the Scriptures and events in one's life, God molds and shapes every Christian into a work of art. Qualities include: Love; Faith; Holiness; Servanthood; Integrity; and Endurance.

Author: Hunt, Gladys **716**
Series: Fisherman Bible Studyguide
Title: *Hebrews: Foundations for Faith*
Publisher: Shaw, 1979 ISBN: 0-87788-338-6

Num. Sess.	Group Time	Num. Pgs.	Avg. Qst.	Price	Audience	Format	Bible Study
13	45-60	80	11	$4.99	Mature Christian	Workbk	Book

Features: Intro to Leading a Study, Intro to Study, Prayer Helps, Summary
★★ Personal Application Preparation Time: Low
★★ Relationship Building Ldr. Guide: No Size: 5.0 x 8.25
Subjects: Faith, Grace, Hebrews, Jesus: Life/Teaching
Comments: This chapter-by-chapter study of Hebrews contrasts Old Testament sacrifices with the abundant, life-changing grace available in Jesus Christ. To profit most, participants need some background in the Gospels, Acts, and the Old Testament. It is a good study for those who want to understand more fully the connection between the Old Testament sacrifices and the death of Jesus Christ.

Author: Hunt, Gladys **717**
Series: Fisherman Bible Studyguide
Title: *Parables of Jesus*
Publisher: Shaw, 1986 ISBN: 0-87788-791-8

Num. Sess.	Group Time	Num. Pgs.	Avg. Qst.	Price	Audience	Format	Bible Study
12	45-60	75	12	$4.99	Beginner	Workbk	Topical

Features: Intro to Leading a Study, Intro to Study, Follow Up
★★ Personal Application Preparation Time: None
★★ Relationship Building Ldr. Guide: No Size: 5.0 x 8.25
Subjects: Jesus: Life/Teaching, Parables
Comments: The parables are the foundation of 12 studies revolving around Jesus, the master teacher and superb storyteller. His speeches weren't dull doctrine or abstract theology, but were lively discourses full of illustrations, metaphors, and stories that caught and held the popular interest. Twelve major parables include familiar things like seed and soil, sheep, coins, and weddings, through which Jesus introduced us to God's Kingdom, its principles, and His people.

Author: Hunt, Gladys **718**
Series: Fisherman Bible Studyguide
Title: *Relationships*
Publisher: Shaw, 1983 ISBN: 0-87788-721-7

Num. Sess.	Group Time	Num. Pgs.	Avg. Qst.	Price	Audience	Format	Bible Study
14	45-60	96	8	$4.99	Beginner	Workbk	Topical

Features: Intro to Leading a Study, Intro to Study, Prayer Helps
★★★ Personal Application Preparation Time: None
★★★ Relationship Building Ldr. Guide: No Size: 5.0 x 8.25
Subjects: Christian Living, God, Relationships
Comments: The primary focus of this study is on human relationships and ways to improve relationships with God by following His example, listening to His truth, and understanding the principles He has established. This study guides the reader to discover biblical foundations for the way people's lives touch, bond, and grow, using examples of Bible relationships—some to emulate and others to avoid.

Author: Hunt, Gladys **719**
Series: Fisherman Bible Studyguide
Title: *Revelation: The Lamb Who Is the Lion*
Publisher: Shaw, 1973 ISBN: 0-87788-486-2

Num. Sess.	Group Time	Num. Pgs.	Avg. Qst.	Price	Audience	Format	Bible Study
13	45-60	80	9	$4.99	Mature Christian	Workbk	Book

Features: Intro to Leading a Study, Intro to Study, Summary, Maps
★★ Personal Application Preparation Time: Low
★★ Relationship Building Ldr. Guide: No Size: 5.0 x 8.25
Subjects: Revelation, Satan
Comments: This advanced inductive study of Revelation, the Bible's final book revealing the age-old conflict between good and evil, shows how believers can be conquerors with the "Victorious Lion." The Revelation demands humility in any attempt at interpretation. Its imagery and symbolism sometimes lead to a contemporary feeling of "this is it." However, after studying Scripture diligently, opinions may be formed, then laid before His sovereignty.

Author: Hunt, Gladys **720**
Series: Fisherman Bible Studyguide
Title: *Sermon on the Mount*
Publisher: Shaw, 1971 ISBN: 0-87788-316-5

Num. Sess.	Group Time	Num. Pgs.	Avg. Qst.	Price	Audience	Format	Bible Study
14	60-90	96	11	$4.99	Mature Christian	Workbk	Book

Features: Intro to Leading a Study, Intro to Study, Prayer Helps, Digging Deeper Quest
★★★ Personal Application Preparation Time: None
★★ Relationship Building Ldr. Guide: No Size: 5.0 x 8.25
Subjects: Christian Living, Matthew, Sermon on the Mount
Comments: This is a verse-by-verse study of Matthew, chapters 5 through 7. Comparison Scriptures from other books of the Bible are used and printed in the text. The study outlines practical principles that enable people to live Christian lives. It differs from other inductive studies in that it features extensive use of material from the apostle's writings to amplify and reinforce Jesus' leading.

Author: Hunt, Gladys 721
Series: LifeGuide Bible Study
Title: *Women of the Old Testament*
Publisher: InterVarsity, 1990 ISBN: 0-83081-064-1

Num. Sess.	Group Time	Num. Pgs.	Avg. Qst.	Price	Audience	Format	Bible Study
12	45-60	63	12	$4.99	Beginner	Workbk	Charctr

Features: Intro to Leading a Study, Intro to Study, Ldr's Notes
★★★★ Personal Application Preparation Time: Low
★★★ Relationship Building Ldr. Guide: No Size: 5.50 x 8.25
Subjects: Bible Personalities, Faith, Obedience, Old Testament, Women's Issues
Comments: This study concerns 12 ordinary women whose choices and actions produced extraordinary results. Through faith and strong character, they rescued their families, led people out of bondage, gave birth to kings, and saved an entire nation. Their lives demonstrate the far-reaching consequences of living every day for God. Among the women studied are Miriam, Rahab, Ruth, Naomi, Hannah, and Esther.

Author: Hunt, Gladys 722
Series:
Title: *You Can Start A Bible Study Group*
Publisher: Shaw, 1971 ISBN: 0-87788-974-0

Num. Sess.	Group Time	Num. Pgs.	Avg. Qst.	Price	Audience	Format	Bible Study
8	—	87	N/A	$4.99		Book	No

Features:
Personal Application Preparation Time:
Relationship Building Ldr. Guide: Size: 5.25 x 8.25
Subjects: Small Group Resource
Comments: For both beginners and experienced leaders, this how-to handbook provides basics as well as fresh ideas for starting home, church, dorm, neighborhood, or office study groups. Questions discussed include: Me, start a Bible study? What is "inductive" Bible study? What should I know about small group dynamics? Exactly how does group Bible study work? What will relationships require of me? What kinds of results will I see? What endures for eternity?

Author: Hunt, Keith 723
Series: The Discipleship Series
Title: *Basic Beliefs*
Publisher: Zondervan, 1992 ISBN: 0-31054-701-6

Num. Sess.	Group Time	Num. Pgs.	Avg. Qst.	Price	Audience	Format	Bible Study
6	45-60	61	13	$4.99	New Christian	Workbk	Topical

Features: Intro to Leading a Study, Intro to Study, Objectives, Scrpt Memory Helps, Follow Up, Ldr's Notes
★★★★ Personal Application Preparation Time: Med
★★ Relationship Building Ldr. Guide: No Size: 5.50 x 8.50
Subjects: Discipleship, Theology
Comments: This is 1 of 8 study guides in the Discipleship series. This guide looks at 6 basic beliefs of Christianity. They provide a practical framework for daily living—how people think, what they value, why they plan, work, and hope. Lesson titles include: "The Greatness of God"; "Revelations"; "Human Nature"; "Jesus Christ"; "The Church"; and "Time and Eternity."

Author: Hurston, Karen 724
Series:
Title: *Growing the World's Largest Church*
Publisher: Chrism (Gospel Pub. House), 1994 ISBN: 0-88243-329-6

Num. Sess.	Group Time	Num. Pgs.	Avg. Qst.	Price	Audience	Format	Bible Study
	—	220	N/A	$8.95			

Features: Intro to Study, Photos, Appendix
Personal Application Preparation Time:
Relationship Building Ldr. Guide: Size: 5.50 x 8.50
Subjects: Church Life, Small Group Resource
Comments: This book tells the story of Seoul, Korea's Yoido Full Gospel Church and its dynamic community of believers, from 5 people meeting in a tent in 1958, to a church with nearly 1 million members. The book highlights the church's emphasis on intense daily prayer, meaningful worship, hope-filled sermons, biblical doctrine, effective lay ministries, evangelism, and outreach to the needy.

Author: Hybels, Bill & Jay Caress 725
Series: SonPower Elective Series
Title: *Caution: Christians Under Construction*
Publisher: Victor Books, 1978 ISBN: 0-88207-759-7

Num. Sess.	Group Time	Num. Pgs.	Avg. Qst.	Price	Audience	Format	Bible Study
12	60-75	143	Vary	$5.99	Beginner	Book	Topical

Features:
★★ Personal Application Preparation Time: None
★★ Relationship Building Ldr. Guide: Yes Size: 4.25 x 7.0
Subjects: Teens: Christian Liv, Teens: Psychology, Teens: Relationships, Teens: Self-image, Teens: Senior High
Comments: This personal, simple, yet challenging study will be helpful in building relationships. It provides a blueprint for growing as a Christian and covers topics such as: exposing misconceptions about Christianity, nailing down your self-image, repairing and maintaining friendships, and building a strong spiritual foundation. A leader's guide with transparency masters is available.

Author: Hybels, Bill 726
Series: Christian Basics
Title: *Character: Who You Are When No One's Looking*
Publisher: InterVarsity, 1994 ISBN: 0-83082-003-5

Num. Sess.	Group Time	Num. Pgs.	Avg. Qst.	Price	Audience	Format	Bible Study
6	30-45	61	7	$4.99	Beginner	Workbk	Topical

Features: Intro to Leading a Study, Intro to Study, Prayer Helps, Follow Up, Full Scrpt Printed, Ldr's Notes
★★★★ Personal Application Preparation Time: None
★★★★ Relationship Building Ldr. Guide: No Size: 5.50 x 8.25
Subjects: Integrity
Comments: Courage, discipline, vision, endurance, compassion, and self-sacrifice are the important qualities discussed in the six studies in this guide. These qualities provide a foundation for character. With this foundation and God's guidance, participants can maintain character even when faced with temptations and troubles. The study also discusses what people are all about when no one's looking.

Author: Hybels, Bill **727**
Series:
Title: *Christians in the Marketplace*
Publisher: Victor Books, 1982 ISBN: 0-88207-314-1

Num. Sess.	Group Time	Num. Pgs.	Avg. Qst.	Price	Audience	Format	Bible Study
13	60-75	144	N/A	$8.99	New Christian	Book	Topical

Features: Cassette Avail
★★★★ Personal Application Preparation Time: Low
★★★ Relationship Building Ldr. Guide: Yes Size: 5.50 x 8.0
Subjects: Evangelism, Faith, Satan, Work
Comments: This study provides practical, biblical guidelines on how to take faith into the secular workplace. Participants are warned about the dangers of being Christian consumers in a materialistic society. When exposed to tactics Satan uses to disarm them, Christians must concentrate on shining Christ's "light" into a darkened world. Many topical questions are answered in this text. A leader's guide with transparency masters is available.

Author: Hybels, Bill **728**
Series:
Title: *Laws of the Heart: 10 Essentials of a Liberated Life*
Publisher: Victor Books, 1985 ISBN: 1-56476-061-8

Num. Sess.	Group Time	Num. Pgs.	Avg. Qst.	Price	Audience	Format	Bible Study
10	60-75	150	11	$9.99	New Christian	Book	Topical

Features: Intro to Leading a Study, Intro to Study, Prayer Helps, Scrpt Memory Helps, Digging Deeper Quest, Follow Up, Ldr's Notes
★★★★ Personal Application Preparation Time: Med
★★★ Relationship Building Ldr. Guide: No Size: 5.50 x 8.50
Subjects: Ten Commandments
Comments: This 10-week study of the Ten Commandments reminds participants that God is not a cosmic killjoy out to keep people from having a good time, but that it really is God's way to add to our relationships with Him, our families, and communities. Leaders notes provide icebreakers, questions, prayer helps, optional activities, and more.

Author: Icenogle, Gareth Weldon **729**
Series:
Title: *Biblical Foundations for Small Group Ministry*
Publisher: InterVarsity, 1994 ISBN: 0-83081-771-9

Num. Sess.	Group Time	Num. Pgs.	Avg. Qst.	Price	Audience	Format	Bible Study
24	—	400	N/A	$12.99			

Features:
Personal Application Preparation Time:
Relationship Building Ldr. Guide: Size: 6.0 x 9.0
Subjects: Small Group Resource
Comments: The author carefully examines Old and New Testament texts and the ministry of the early church in this introduction to the basics of small group ministry. Throughout he offers guidance for applying the principles in study to set up and run biblically based small group ministry programs. A theology of small group ministry, this is written for pastors, parachurch leaders, lay leaders, consultants, teachers, and seminary professors.

Author: Inouye, Arlene R. **730**
Series: GroupBuilder Resources
Title: *Dare To Risk*
Publisher: Victor Books, 1992 ISBN: 1-56476-024-3

Num. Sess.	Group Time	Num. Pgs.	Avg. Qst.	Price	Audience	Format	Bible Study
8	75-90	136	Vary	$5.99	New Christian	Workbk	Topical

Features: Intro to Leading a Study, Intro to Study, Objectives, Digging Deeper Quest, Follow Up, Full Scrpt Printed, Ldr's Notes, Cartoons, Persnl Study Quest
★★★★ Personal Application Preparation Time: Low
★★★★ Relationship Building Ldr. Guide: No Size: 6.0 x 9.0
Subjects: Discipleship, Faith, Victorious Living
Comments: Eight sessions help participants understand the challenges of risk-taking, based on Peter's "out-of-the-boat" experience in Matthew 14:22-33. Questions addressed include: Are you willing to take the risks? What prevents you from taking risks? Are you willing to leave your career to follow Jesus? Are you keeping fellowship with God?

Author: Ishida, Y. Franklin **731**
Series: Youth Talk
Title: *Justice*
Publisher: Augsburg Fortress Publishers, 1994

Num. Sess.	Group Time	Num. Pgs.	Avg. Qst.	Price	Audience	Format	Bible Study
5	45-60	46	Vary	$4.95	Beginner	Book	Topical

Features: Prayer Helps, Worship Helps, Photos
★★★★ Personal Application Preparation Time: Low
★★★★ Relationship Building Ldr. Guide: Yes Size: 8.0 x 11.0
Subjects: Teens: Senior High, Teens: Values
Comments: An alternative to the "textbook approach," these studies are energetic, contemporary, and modeled after popular teen magazines. Advice columns, fiction, poetry, and other features are mostly written by youth. Bringing justice to the world means listening to and feeling for all people. This course helps students recognize stereotypes that cause indifference, misunderstanding, and discrimination.

Author: Jackman, David **732**
Series: The Bible Speaks Today
Title: *Message of John's Letters, The*
Publisher: InterVarsity, 1988 ISBN: 0-83081-226-1

Num. Sess.	Group Time	Num. Pgs.	Avg. Qst.	Price	Audience	Format	Bible Study
11	60-120	210	6	$12.99	New Christian	Book	Book

Features: Intro to Study, Bibliography
★★★ Personal Application Preparation Time: Med
★★ Relationship Building Ldr. Guide: No Size: 5.50 x 8.25
Subjects: John, New Testament
Comments: This series of Old and New Testament expositions are characterized by three goals: to expound the biblical text with accuracy, relate it to contemporary life, and be readable. In this contemporary retelling of John's message, David Jackman describes John's first letter as an upwardly spiraling staircase that circles and broadens out around the twin themes of truth and love, mind and heart, Word and Spirit. It is a message both timeless and timely for the church today.

Author: Jacks, Bob & Betty 733
Series:
Title: *Your Home, A Lighthouse*
Publisher: NavPress, 1986 ISBN: 0-89109-127-0

Num. Sess.	Group Time	Num. Pgs.	Avg. Qst.	Price	Audience	Format	Bible Study
13	—	156	N/A	$8.00		Book	No

Features: Bibliography, Appendix
Personal Application Preparation Time:
Relationship Building Ldr. Guide: Size: 5.25 x 8.0
Subjects: Evangelism, Small Group Resource
Comments: This book describes the simple concept of using the warmth of a home as a relaxed setting in which people can consider God, His Word, and the implications for their lives. Subject matter includes how to start a group, who to invite, what to study, how to ask and answer good questions, and when to encourage a decision for Christ. The appendix section includes many "helps," such as how to explain the Gospel.

Author: Jacks, Bob & Betty 734
Series:
Title: *Your Home, A Lighthouse Video*
Publisher: NavPress, 1990 ISBN: 8-90073-028-2

Num. Sess.	Group Time	Num. Pgs.	Avg. Qst.	Price	Audience	Format	Bible Study
3	60-90	N/A	8	$79.00	New Christian	Video	Topical

Features: Book Incl
★★★★ Personal Application Preparation Time: None
★★★ Relationship Building Ldr. Guide: No Size: 10.50 x 12.50
Subjects: Evangelism, Small Group Resource
Comments: This 3-part video offers insights, principles, and suggestions to equip and motivate participants to use their homes to reach others for Christ. The 40" tapes combine lecture with situational vignettes. The guide helps participants apply principles illustrated in the video. Each session opens with a warm-up question, followed by a question on which to focus while viewing the video. Group discussion questions follow a review of the video's points.

Author: Jackson, Dave and Neta 735
Series: Family Growth Electives
Title: *Growing Together With Your Teens: Studies for Parents of Teens*
Publisher: David C. Cook Publishing Co., 1993 ISBN: 0-78145-023-3

Num. Sess.	Group Time	Num. Pgs.	Avg. Qst.	Price	Audience	Format	Bible Study
13	45-60	128	Vary	$19.95	Beginner	Workbk	Topical

Features: Intro to Study, Bibliography, Prayer Helps, Drawings, Handouts, Persnl Study Quest
★★★ Personal Application Preparation Time: Low
★★★ Relationship Building Ldr. Guide: Yes Size: 8.50 x 11.0
Subjects: Family, Parenting, Relationships, Teens: Self-esteem
Comments: This study helps modern parents explore the key issues of adolescence. They learn how to enhance their teens' self-esteem while teaching responsibility and independence. They also learn to cope with their own mid-life concerns while working with their teens. Appropriate for married or single parents, beginners, new or mature Christians.

Author: Jackson, Dave and Neta 736
Series: Family Growth Electives
Title: *Starting Out Together: Studies for New Couples*
Publisher: David C. Cook Publishing Co., 1993 ISBN: 0-78145-021-7

Num. Sess.	Group Time	Num. Pgs.	Avg. Qst.	Price	Audience	Format	Bible Study
13	45-60	128	Vary	$19.95	New Christian	Workbk	Topical

Features: Intro to Study, Objectives, Bibliography, Prayer Helps, Drawings, Handouts, Persnl Study Quest
★★★★ Personal Application Preparation Time: Low
★★★★ Relationship Building Ldr. Guide: Yes Size: 8.50 x 11.0
Subjects: Decision Making, Marriage, Money, Relationships, Self-esteem, Sexual Issues, Time
Comments: This study helps newly married couples establish Christ-centered homes, handle unmet expectations and conflict, understand biblical roles, develop time and financial management skills, communicate in love and truth, and learn how to make decisions as a couple. Every session includes reproducible handouts.

Author: Jackson, Neta 737
Series: Building Books
Title: *Building Christian Relationships*
Publisher: Bethany House, 1984 ISBN: 0-87123-407-6

Num. Sess.	Group Time	Num. Pgs.	Avg. Qst.	Price	Audience	Format	Bible Study
34	45-60	63	Vary	$6.99	New Christian	Workbk	Topical

Features: Intro to Leading a Study
★★ Personal Application Preparation Time: Low
★★ Relationship Building Ldr. Guide: Yes Size: 8.50 x 11.0
Subjects: Teens: Christian Liv, Teens: Family, Teens: Relationships
Comments: This 34-lesson study for young people deals with getting along with others, with God, with oneself, with family, and with friends. It is divided into four sections: (1) attitudes that build barriers, such as pride, fear, gossip, materialism; (2) strengthening the foundation on which to build good friendships; (3) the building blocks of Christian relationships; and (4) application to specific relationships, such as parent and peers.

Author: Jacobson, Donald O. 738
Series: Small Group Bible Studies
Title: *People Who Care*
Publisher: Augsburg Fortress Publishers, 1980

Num. Sess.	Group Time	Num. Pgs.	Avg. Qst.	Price	Audience	Format	Bible Study
5	60-75	16	9	$1.30	New Christian	Book	Topical

Features: Intro to Study, Prayer Helps
Personal Application Preparation Time: None
Relationship Building Ldr. Guide: No Size: 8.50 x 5.50
Subjects: Caring, Emotions, Joy, Relationships
Comments: This small pamphlet includes five sessions on human relationships. It examines the human emotions of joy, fear, grief, anger, and guilt. It differs from traditional Bible studies because it begins with human needs and looks to the Bible for affirmation rather than taking the more common approach of starting with a biblical passage. Each session begins with someone reading aloud a true account about people experiencing intense human emotions.

Author: James, Edgar C. 739
Series: Teach Yourself the Bible
Title: *Epistles of Peter, The*
Publisher: Moody Press, 1964 ISBN: 0-80242-355-8

Num. Sess.	Group Time	Num. Pgs.	Avg. Qst.	Price	Audience	Format	Bible Study
8	60-75	48	28	$4.50	New Christian	Workbk	Book

Features: Intro to Leading a Study, Intro to Study, Exam
★★ Personal Application Preparation Time: Low
★★ Relationship Building Ldr. Guide: No Size: 5.50 x 8.50
Subjects: False Teachers, 1 & 2 Peter
Comments: This study of 1 and 2 Peter—part of a 25-book series—provides practical advice for the "last days." Peter responds to churches and believers under persecution and assault from false teachers with words of comfort and counsel. The format includes a series of fill-in-the-blank questions, and checkups to test participants' grasp of Scriptural truths. The series, although designed for self-study, also includes suggestions for group study.

Author: James, Edgar C. 740
Series: Teach Yourself the Bible
Title: *2 Corinthians: Keys to Triumphant Living*
Publisher: Moody Press, 1964 ISBN: 0-80247-680-5

Num. Sess.	Group Time	Num. Pgs.	Avg. Qst.	Price	Audience	Format	Bible Study
12	60-75	64	29	$4.50	New Christian	Workbk	Book

Features: Intro to Leading a Study, Intro to Study, Exam
★★ Personal Application Preparation Time: Low
★★ Relationship Building Ldr. Guide: No Size: 5.50 x 8.50
Subjects: Church Life, Hope, Integrity, Leadership, Repentance, Service, Suffering, Victorious Living, 2 Corinthians
Comments: In this study, Paul's confidence in God is shown through topics such as: confidence through difficulty, testimony, ministry, conduct, repentance, and death. The format includes a series of fill-in-the-blank questions; and checkups test participants' grasp of Scriptural truths. This 25-book series is designed for self-study; however, suggestions for group study are included.

Author: Jayaprakash, Eva & Joshi 741
Series: Global Issues
Title: *Fundamentalistic Religion*
Publisher: InterVarsity, 1990 ISBN: 0-83084-910-6

Num. Sess.	Group Time	Num. Pgs.	Avg. Qst.	Price	Audience	Format	Bible Study
6	45-60	48	11	$4.99	New Christian	Workbk	Topical

Features: Intro to Leading a Study, Intro to Study, Prayer Helps, Digging Deeper Quest
★★ Personal Application Preparation Time: Low
★ Relationship Building Ldr. Guide: No Size: 5.50 x 8.25
Subjects: Cults
Comments: This six-session study explores characteristics of fundamentalistic religions, including the Shi'ite, Marxist, Hindu, and Christian fundamentalistic movements. The lessons lead participants to consider what the real "fundamentals" of faith should be and how they can be implemented. Participants use Scripture to distinguish the difference between commitment and fanaticism.

Author: Jeffress, Robert 742
Series:
Title: *Choose Your Attitudes, Change Your Life*
Publisher: Victor Books, 1992 ISBN: 0-89693-123-4

Num. Sess.	Group Time	Num. Pgs.	Avg. Qst.	Price	Audience	Format	Bible Study
12	60-90	190	12	$8.99	New Christian	Book	Topical

Features: Prayer Helps, Ldr's Notes
★★★★ Personal Application Preparation Time: Med
★★★★ Relationship Building Ldr. Guide: No Size: 5.50 x 8.50
Subjects: Christian Life, Psychology
Comments: Identifying attitude as the key to changes people desire in their lives, this book shows readers biblical bases and practical suggestions for choices, including purpose over aimlessness, perseverance over defeat, faith over anxiety, repentance over guilt, relaxation over stress, contentment over comparison, and forgiveness over bitterness. It also compares productivity with laziness, humility with pride, companionship with loneliness, and intimacy with God with isolation.

Author: Jensen, Irving L. 743
Series: Bible Self-study Guides
Title: *Acts*
Publisher: Moody Press, 1969 ISBN: 0-80244-452-0

Num. Sess.	Group Time	Num. Pgs.	Avg. Qst.	Price	Audience	Format	Bible Study
21	60-75	104	Vary	$4.99	Mature Christian	Workbk	Book

Features: Intro to Leading a Study, Intro to Study, Bibliography, Study Overview, Digging Deeper Quest, Follow Up, Summary, Charts, Maps, Topical Index, Word Study
★★★★ Personal Application Preparation Time: Med
★★ Relationship Building Ldr. Guide: No Size: 5.50 x 8.50
Subjects: Acts, Church Life, Holy Spirit
Comments: This academic study of Acts—part of a 39-book series—concerns Luke's account of the Holy Spirit working through the apostles. The 28 chapters of Acts fall into 3 main divisions: the church established, the church scattered, and the church extended. Ideal for individual, small group, or class use.

Author: Jensen, Irving L. 744
Series: Bible Self-study Guides
Title: *Colossians and Philemon*
Publisher: Moody Press, 1973 ISBN: 0-80244-469-5

Num. Sess.	Group Time	Num. Pgs.	Avg. Qst.	Price	Audience	Format	Bible Study
8	60-75	64	Vary	$4.99	Mature Christian	Workbk	Book

Features: Intro to Leading a Study, Intro to Study, Bibliography, Digging Deeper Quest, Follow Up, Summary, Charts, Maps, Word Study
★★★★ Personal Application Preparation Time: Med
★★ Relationship Building Ldr. Guide: No Size: 5.50 x 8.50
Subjects: Colossians/Philemon, False Teachers, Forgiveness, Prison Epistles
Comments: This academic study of Colossians and Philemon—part of a 39-book series—covers 2 of Paul's Prison Epistles. Colossians was written to Colossae concerning heresy in the church. The letter to Philemon, is a masterpiece of graceful, tactful, pleading for a forgiving spirit between slave and master.

Author: Jensen, Irving L. 745
Series: Bible Self-study Guides
Title: *Ecclesiastes and the Song of Solomon*
Publisher: Moody Press, 1974 ISBN: 0-80244-472-5

Num. Sess.	Group Time	Num. Pgs.	Avg. Qst.	Price	Audience	Format	Bible Study
12	60-75	96	Vary	$4.99	Mature Christian	Workbk	Book

Features: Intro to Leading a Study, Intro to Study, Bibliography, Digging Deeper Quest, Follow Up, Summary, Charts, Maps, Word Study
★★★★ Personal Application Preparation Time: Med
★★ Relationship Building Ldr. Guide: No Size: 5.50 x 8.50
Subjects: Ecclesiastes, Song of Solomon
Comments: Ecclesiastes and Song of Solomon deal with life and love. Ecclesiastes evaluates life and outlines worthwhile living (the way to God); Song of Solomon is the classic book on love (the way of God). This 39-book series of Bible self-studies is ideal for individual, small group, or class use. Outlines, diagrams, and explanations keep participants challenged.

Author: Jensen, Irving L. 746
Series: Bible Self-study Guides
Title: *Ephesians*
Publisher: Moody Press, 1973 ISBN: 0-80244-454-7

Num. Sess.	Group Time	Num. Pgs.	Avg. Qst.	Price	Audience	Format	Bible Study
10	60-75	96	Vary	$4.99	Mature Christian	Workbk	Book

Features: Intro to Leading a Study, Intro to Study, Bibliography, Digging Deeper Quest, Follow Up, Summary, Charts, Maps, Word Study
★★★★ Personal Application Preparation Time: Med
★★ Relationship Building Ldr. Guide: No Size: 5.50 x 8.50
Subjects: Discipleship, Ephesians
Comments: This academic study of Ephesians—part of a 39-book series—covers Paul's letter to the church at Ephesus in great detail. Ten lessons move participants from the letter's background and setting to Paul's encouraging final words on Christians' armor. This series of Bible self-studies is ideal for individual, small group, or class use. Outlines, diagrams, and explanations keep participants challenged.

Author: Jensen, Irving L. 747
Series: Bible Self-study Guides
Title: *Epistles of John & Jude*
Publisher: Moody Press, 1971 ISBN: 0-80244-461-X

Num. Sess.	Group Time	Num. Pgs.	Avg. Qst.	Price	Audience	Format	Bible Study
13	60-75	112	Vary	$4.99	Mature Christian	Workbk	Book

Features: Intro to Leading a Study, Intro to Study, Bibliography, Digging Deeper Quest, Follow Up, Summary, Charts, Maps, Word Study
★★★★ Personal Application Preparation Time: Med
★★ Relationship Building Ldr. Guide: No Size: 5.50 x 8.50
Subjects: Church Life, Satan, 1, 2 & 3 John/Jude
Comments: In this academic study of 1, 2, and 3 John and Jude—part of a 39-book series—John and Jude address Christians who fell prey to the same deceptive devices of Satan common today. The studies deal with real problems in local churches, sound solutions, and the surety of tragic judgment. Participants will be challenged to persevere.

Author: Jensen, Irving L. 748
Series: Bible Self-study Guides
Title: *Exodus*
Publisher: Moody Press, 1967 ISBN: 0-80244-457-1

Num. Sess.	Group Time	Num. Pgs.	Avg. Qst.	Price	Audience	Format	Bible Study
12	60-75	112	Vary	$4.99	Mature Christian	Workbk	Book

Features: Intro to Leading a Study, Intro to Study, Bibliography, Digging Deeper Quest, Follow Up, Summary, Charts, Maps, Word Study
★★★★ Personal Application Preparation Time: Med
★★ Relationship Building Ldr. Guide: No Size: 5.50 x 8.50
Subjects: Bible Personalities, Exodus, God, Leadership
Comments: This academic study of Exodus—part of a 39-book series—covers Moses' account of a nation's problem and closes with its redemption by God. This redemption unfolds in the following way: God appoints a leader for Israel (Moses); He makes Israel's enemy impotent through plagues; He delivers Israel from Egypt and confirms the covenant relationship.

Author: Jensen, Irving L. 749
Series: Bible Self-study Guides
Title: *Ezekiel/Daniel*
Publisher: Moody Press, 1968 ISBN: 0-80244-458-X

Num. Sess.	Group Time	Num. Pgs.	Avg. Qst.	Price	Audience	Format	Bible Study
12	60-75	96	Vary	$4.99	Mature Christian	Workbk	Book

Features: Intro to Leading a Study, Intro to Study, Bibliography, Digging Deeper Quest, Follow Up, Summary, Charts, Maps, Word Study
★★★★ Personal Application Preparation Time: Med
★★ Relationship Building Ldr. Guide: No Size: 5.50 x 8.50
Subjects: Daniel, Eschatology, Ezekiel, Major Prophets
Comments: The books of Ezekiel and Daniel, the accounts of 2 prophets living in exile, give attention to end-time events of world history scheduled on God's timetable. This 39-book series of Bible self-studies is ideal for individual, small group, or class use. Outlines, diagrams, and explanations keep participants challenged.

Author: Jensen, Irving L. 750
Series: Bible Self-study Guides
Title: *Ezra, Nehemiah and Esther*
Publisher: Moody Press, 1970 ISBN: 0-80244-478-4

Num. Sess.	Group Time	Num. Pgs.	Avg. Qst.	Price	Audience	Format	Bible Study
14	60-75	96	Vary	$4.99	Mature Christian	Workbk	Book

Features: Intro to Leading a Study, Intro to Study, Bibliography, Digging Deeper Quest, Follow Up, Summary, Charts, Maps, Word Study
★★★★ Personal Application Preparation Time: Med
★★ Relationship Building Ldr. Guide: No Size: 5.50 x 8.50
Subjects: Esther, Ezra/Nehemiah, Faith
Comments: The books of Ezra, Nehemiah, and Esther deal with the last events recorded in the Old Testament. Ezra shows how the Lord fulfilled His promises and restored Israel to their own land; Nehemiah shows the restoration of the failing faith of the Jews; and Esther shows how the Jews were saved from extermination. This series of academic Bible self-studies is ideal for individual, small group, or class use.

Author: Jensen, Irving L. 751
Series: Bible Self-study Guides
Title: *Galatians*
Publisher: Moody Press, 1973 ISBN: 0-80244-468-7

Num. Sess.	Group Time	Num. Pgs.	Avg. Qst.	Price	Audience	Format	Bible Study
10	60-75	96	Vary	$4.99	Mature Christian	Workbk	Book

Features: Intro to Leading a Study, Intro to Study, Bibliography, Digging Deeper Quest, Follow Up, Summary, Charts, Maps, Appendix, Word Study
★★★★ Personal Application Preparation Time: Med
★★ Relationship Building Ldr. Guide: No Size: 5.50 x 8.50
Subjects: Galatians, Holy Spirit
Comments: This academic study of Galatians—part of a 39-book series—covers Paul's first inspired letter, written to combat heresy and to confirm Gospel truth. More than a doctrinal study, it will encourage and inspire participants to move forward spiritually in the power and direction of the Holy Spirit, enjoying the freedom of new life in Christ.

Author: Jensen, Irving L. 752
Series: Bible Self-study Guides
Title: *Genesis*
Publisher: Moody Press, 1967 ISBN: 0-80244-450-4

Num. Sess.	Group Time	Num. Pgs.	Avg. Qst.	Price	Audience	Format	Bible Study
12	60-75	96	Vary	$4.99	Mature Christian	Workbk	Book

Features: Intro to Leading a Study, Intro to Study, Bibliography, Digging Deeper Quest, Follow Up, Summary, Charts, Maps, Word Study
★★★★ Personal Application Preparation Time: Med
★★ Relationship Building Ldr. Guide: No Size: 5.50 x 8.50
Subjects: Bible Personalities, Genesis, God
Comments: This academic study of Genesis—part of a 39-book series—covers Moses' account of "the beginnings." It moves from Creation to the Fall, the Flood, Abraham's life, Isaac's life, and Jacob's life, and concludes with Joseph's life. This series of Bible self-studies is ideal for individual, small group, or class use. Outlines, diagrams, and explanations keep participants challenged.

Author: Jensen, Irving L. 753
Series: Bible Self-study Guides
Title: *Haggai, Zechariah, Malachi*
Publisher: Moody Press, 1976 ISBN: 0-80244-487-3

Num. Sess.	Group Time	Num. Pgs.	Avg. Qst.	Price	Audience	Format	Bible Study
11	60-75	96	Vary	$4.99	Mature Christian	Workbk	Book

Features: Intro to Leading a Study, Intro to Study, Bibliography, Digging Deeper Quest, Follow Up, Summary, Charts, Maps
★★★★ Personal Application Preparation Time: Med
★★ Relationship Building Ldr. Guide: No Size: 5.50 x 8.50
Subjects: Bible Personalities, Christian Living, Minor Prophets, Prophecy, Reconciliation
Comments: This academic study of Haggai, Zechariah, and Malachi covers the last of the Old Testament prophets. Haggai's major theme is, "put first things first in your life" to renew a relationship with the Lord. Haggai and Zechariah exhort the Jews to finish rebuilding the Temple. Malachi offers timeless commands about everyday living.

Author: Jensen, Irving L. 754
Series: Bible Self-study Guides
Title: *Hebrews*
Publisher: Moody Press, 1970 ISBN: 0-80244-460-1

Num. Sess.	Group Time	Num. Pgs.	Avg. Qst.	Price	Audience	Format	Bible Study
13	60-75	104	Vary	$4.99	Mature Christian	Workbk	Book

Features: Intro to Leading a Study, Intro to Study, Bibliography, Digging Deeper Quest, Follow Up, Summary, Charts, Maps, Word Study
★★★★ Personal Application Preparation Time: Med
★★ Relationship Building Ldr. Guide: No Size: 5.50 x 8.50
Subjects: Faith, Hebrews
Comments: This academic study of Hebrews—part of a 39-book series—covers the threat of apostasy. Thirteen lessons move participants from a background of Hebrews to confidence of faith, examples of faith, endurance of faith, and workings of faith. This series of Bible self-studies is ideal for individual, small group, or class use. Outlines, diagrams, and explanations keep participants challenged.

Author: Jensen, Irving L. 755
Series: Bible Self-study Guides
Title: *Isaiah/Jeremiah*
Publisher: Moody Press, 1968 ISBN: 0-80244-464-4

Num. Sess.	Group Time	Num. Pgs.	Avg. Qst.	Price	Audience	Format	Bible Study
12	60-75	112	Vary	$4.99	Mature Christian	Workbk	Book

Features: Intro to Leading a Study, Intro to Study, Bibliography, Digging Deeper Quest, Follow Up, Summary, Charts, Maps, Word Study
★★★★ Personal Application Preparation Time: Med
★★ Relationship Building Ldr. Guide: No Size: 5.50 x 8.50
Subjects: Isaiah/Jeremiah, Major Prophets, Prophecy
Comments: This 12-lesson academic study of Isaiah and Jeremiah—part of a 39-book series—begins with a thorough overview of prophets in general. It then proceeds to Isaiah, whose message was twofold: a warning of judgment for sin, and comfort of salvation for righteousness. It concludes with Jeremiah, whose message is also twofold: "to destroy" (destruction) and "to build" (construction).

Author: Jensen, Irving L. 756
Series: Bible Self-study Guides
Title: *James*
Publisher: Moody Press, 1971 ISBN: 0-80244-455-5

Num. Sess.	Group Time	Num. Pgs.	Avg. Qst.	Price	Audience	Format	Bible Study
10	60-75	112	Vary	$4.99	Mature Christian	Workbk	Book

Features: Intro to Leading a Study, Intro to Study, Bibliography, Digging Deeper Quest, Follow Up, Summary, Charts, Maps, Word Study
★★★★ Personal Application Preparation Time: Med
★★ Relationship Building Ldr. Guide: No Size: 5.50 x 8.50
Subjects: Christian Living, Faith, James, Prayer, Wisdom
Comments: This academic study covers James' letter to Christians who have been reconciled to God through Christ. It specifically instructs them in how to walk with God in this present life. Subjects include: patience, prayer, love, liberty, equality, humility, peace, steadfastness, self-control, and wisdom. Outlines, diagrams, and explanations keep participants challenged.

Author: Jensen, Irving L. 757
Series: Bible Self-study Guides
Title: *Job*
Publisher: Moody Press, 1975 ISBN: 0-80244-479-2

Num. Sess.	Group Time	Num. Pgs.	Avg. Qst.	Price	Audience	Format	Bible Study
13	60-75	104	Vary	$4.99	Mature Christian	Workbk	Book

Features: Intro to Leading a Study, Intro to Study, Bibliography, Digging Deeper Quest, Follow Up, Summary, Charts, Maps, Word Study
★★★★ Personal Application Preparation Time: Med
★★ Relationship Building Ldr. Guide: No Size: 5.50 x 8.50
Subjects: Faith, God, Job, Satan
Comments: Part of a 39-book series, this academic study covers the person of Job and his physical and spiritual experience, in which his faith was supremely tested. Its purposes are to reveal who God is, to show the kind of trust He wants for His children, and to reveal His favor toward His children, and His absolute control over Satan.

Author: Jensen, Irving L. 758
Series: Bible Self-study Guides
Title: *John*
Publisher: Moody Press, 1970 ISBN: 0-80244-451-2

Num. Sess.	Group Time	Num. Pgs.	Avg. Qst.	Price	Audience	Format	Bible Study
19	60-75	112	Vary	$4.99	Mature Christian	Workbk	Book

Features: Intro to Leading a Study, Intro to Study, Bibliography, Digging Deeper Quest, Follow Up, Summary, Charts, Maps, Word Study
★★★★ Personal Application Preparation Time: Med
★★ Relationship Building Ldr. Guide: No Size: 5.50 x 8.50
Subjects: Evangelism, Jesus: Life/Teaching, John
Comments: This academic study of John—part of a 39-book series—covers John's writings on the evangelistic founding of the church. It was primarily written to win unbelievers to a saving faith. This series of Bible self-studies is ideal for individual, small group, or class use. Outlines, diagrams, and explanations keep participants challenged.

Author: Jensen, Irving L. 759
Series: Bible Self-study Guides
Title: *Joshua*
Publisher: Moody Press, 1968 ISBN: 0-80244-470-9

Num. Sess.	Group Time	Num. Pgs.	Avg. Qst.	Price	Audience	Format	Bible Study
11	60-75	80	Vary	$4.99	Mature Christian	Workbk	Book

Features: Intro to Leading a Study, Intro to Study, Bibliography, Digging Deeper Quest, Follow Up, Summary, Charts, Maps, Word Study
★★★★ Personal Application Preparation Time: Med
★★ Relationship Building Ldr. Guide: No Size: 5.50 x 8.50
Subjects: Joshua
Comments: This academic study of Joshua—part of a 39-book series—is the account of the conquest of Canaan. It is a history of the military campaign, and is divided into five study segments: introduction, preparation, conquest, inheritances, and consecration. This study is full of encouragement for the spiritual soldier. This series of Bible self-studies is ideal for individual, small group, or class use.

Author: Jensen, Irving L. 760
Series: Bible Self-study Guides
Title: *Judges and Ruth*
Publisher: Moody Press, 1968 ISBN: 0-80244-484-9

Num. Sess.	Group Time	Num. Pgs.	Avg. Qst.	Price	Audience	Format	Bible Study
11	60-75	96	Vary	$4.99	Mature Christian	Workbk	Book

Features: Intro to Leading a Study, Intro to Study, Bibliography, Digging Deeper Quest, Follow Up, Summary, Charts, Maps, Word Study
★★★★ Personal Application Preparation Time: Med
★★ Relationship Building Ldr. Guide: No Size: 5.50 x 8.50
Subjects: Bible Personalities, Failure, Judges, Ruth, Women's Issues
Comments: Judges covers a period of failure, and Ruth completes the biblical history of the period of Judges. In Judges, participants learn the woes of walking outside fellowship with Christ and how fellowship can be restored. Ruth, the only book of the Bible devoted to the domestic history of a woman, presents the genealogy through which comes the Savior-King.

Author: Jensen, Irving L. 761
Series: Bible Self-study Guides
Title: *Leviticus*
Publisher: Moody Press, 1967 ISBN: 0-80244-482-2

Num. Sess.	Group Time	Num. Pgs.	Avg. Qst.	Price	Audience	Format	Bible Study
10	60-75	80	Vary	$4.99	Mature Christian	Workbk	Book

Features: Intro to Leading a Study, Intro to Study, Bibliography, Digging Deeper Quest, Follow Up, Summary, Charts, Maps, Word Study
★★★★ Personal Application Preparation Time: Med
★★ Relationship Building Ldr. Guide: No Size: 5.50 x 8.50
Subjects: Leviticus, Worship
Comments: Leviticus, Moses' third installment to the Pentateuch, records God's instructions to Israel on how they might have access to Him in worship, and walk with Him in fellowship. This academic study, part of a 39-book series of Bible self-studies, is ideal for individual, small group, or class use. Outlines, diagrams, and explanations keep participants challenged.

Author: Jensen, Irving L. 762
Series: Bible Self-study Guides
Title: *Life of Christ*
Publisher: Moody Press, 1969 ISBN: 0-80244-462-8

Num. Sess.	Group Time	Num. Pgs.	Avg. Qst.	Price	Audience	Format	Bible Study
15	60-75	112	Vary	$4.99	Mature Christian	Workbk	Book

Features: Intro to Leading a Study, Intro to Study, Bibliography, Digging Deeper Quest, Follow Up, Summary, Charts, Maps, Word Study
★★★★ Personal Application Preparation Time: Med
★★ Relationship Building Ldr. Guide: No Size: 5.50 x 8.50
Subjects: Gospels, Jesus: Life/Teaching
Comments: This academic study of Christ's life covers the 33 years of His earthly biography. It begins before Bethlehem and ends with His resurrection. A comparative analysis of all 4 Gospels is presented. This 39-book series of Bible self-studies is ideal for individual, small group, or class use. Outlines, diagrams, and explanations keep participants challenged.

Author: Jensen, Irving L. 763
Series: Bible Self-study Guides
Title: *Luke*
Publisher: Moody Press, 1970 ISBN: 0-80244-466-0

Num. Sess.	Group Time	Num. Pgs.	Avg. Qst.	Price	Audience	Format	Bible Study
13	60-75	104	Vary	$4.99	Mature Christian	Workbk	Book

Features: Intro to Leading a Study, Intro to Study, Bibliography, Digging Deeper Quest, Follow Up, Summary, Charts, Maps, Word Study
★★★★ Personal Application Preparation Time: Med
★★ Relationship Building Ldr. Guide: No Size: 5.50 x 8.50
Subjects: Jesus: Life/Teaching, Luke
Comments: This academic study—part of a 39-book series—covers Luke's account of the full truth of Jesus' ministry. Jesus is revealed as the "Son of Man," and the book's prominent theme is "grace." A key verse is 19:10: "For the Son of man is come to seek and to save that which was lost." The key phrase, "Son of Man," is found 25 times in the Gospel.

Author: Jensen, Irving L. 764
Series: Bible Self-study Guides
Title: *Mark*
Publisher: Moody Press, 1972 ISBN: 0-80244-465-2

Num. Sess.	Group Time	Num. Pgs.	Avg. Qst.	Price	Audience	Format	Bible Study
14	60-75	112	Vary	$4.99	Mature Christian	Workbk	Book

Features: Intro to Leading a Study, Intro to Study, Bibliography, Digging Deeper Quest, Follow Up, Summary, Charts, Maps, Word Study
★★★★ Personal Application Preparation Time: Med
★★ Relationship Building Ldr. Guide: No Size: 5.50 x 8.50
Subjects: Jesus: Life/Teaching, Mark
Comments: This academic study—part of a 39-book series—covers Mark's account of the Gospel, which was directed to a Roman mind more impressed by action and power than discourse and dialogue. Mark therefore stressed "the actions, not so much the words of Jesus," to reach such an audience. Outlines, diagrams, and explanations keep participants challenged.

Author: Jensen, Irving L. 765
Series: Bible Self-study Guides
Title: *Matthew*
Publisher: Moody Press, 1974 ISBN: 0-80244-459-8

Num. Sess.	Group Time	Num. Pgs.	Avg. Qst.	Price	Audience	Format	Bible Study
15	60-75	112	Vary	$4.99	Mature Christian	Workbk	Book

Features: Intro to Leading a Study, Intro to Study, Bibliography, Digging Deeper Quest, Follow Up, Summary, Charts, Maps, Appendix, Word Study
★★★★ Personal Application Preparation Time: Med
★★ Relationship Building Ldr. Guide: No Size: 5.50 x 8.50
Subjects: Jesus: Life/Teaching, Matthew
Comments: This academic study of Matthew discusses the historical connecting link between the Old and New Testaments. The Gospel narrative begins with the story of Jesus' birth and concludes with His Great Commission. This 39-book series of Bible self-studies is ideal for individual, small group, or class use.

Author: Jensen, Irving L. 766
Series: Bible Self-study Guides
Title: *Minor Prophets of Israel*
Publisher: Moody Press, 1975 ISBN: 0-80244-480-6

Num. Sess.	Group Time	Num. Pgs.	Avg. Qst.	Price	Audience	Format	Bible Study
13	60-75	112	Vary	$4.99	Mature Christian	Workbk	Book

Features: Intro to Leading a Study, Intro to Study, Bibliography, Digging Deeper Quest, Follow Up, Summary, Charts, Maps, Word Study
★★★★ Personal Application Preparation Time: Med
★★ Relationship Building Ldr. Guide: No Size: 5.50 x 8.50
Subjects: Minor Prophets, Prophecy
Comments: This academic study of Israel's minor prophets Jonah, Amos, and Hosea—part of a 39-book series—covers prophecy delivered in response to urgent situations when God called upon them to deliver the "Thus saith the Lord" messages. The 3 prophets have been compared this way: Jonah, prophet of a broken ministry; Amos, prophet of the broken law; and Hosea, prophet of a broken heart.

Author: Jensen, Irving L. 767
Series: Bible Self-study Guides
Title: *Minor Prophets of Judah*
Publisher: Moody Press, 1975 ISBN: 0-80244-486-5

Num. Sess.	Group Time	Num. Pgs.	Avg. Qst.	Price	Audience	Format	Bible Study
13	60-75	104	Vary	$4.99	Mature Christian	Workbk	Book

Features: Intro to Leading a Study, Intro to Study, Bibliography, Digging Deeper Quest, Follow Up, Summary, Charts, Maps, Word Study
★★★★ Personal Application Preparation Time: Med
★★ Relationship Building Ldr. Guide: No Size: 5.50 x 8.50
Subjects: Ethics, Minor Prophets, Prophecy
Comments: Part of a 39-book series, this academic study of Judah's minor prophets—Obadiah, Joel, Micah, Nahum, Zephaniah, and Habakkuk—reveals that each spoke to people's definite needs, as disclosed by God through revelation. The subjects—materialism, rising crime, adultery, general disregard for God, and more—are timeless and speak to contemporary Christians as well.

Author: Jensen, Irving L. 768
Series: Bible Self-study Guides
Title: *Numbers and Deuteronomy*
Publisher: Moody Press, 1967 ISBN: 0-80244-483-0

Num. Sess.	Group Time	Num. Pgs.	Avg. Qst.	Price	Audience	Format	Bible Study
14	60-75	112	Vary	$4.99	Mature Christian	Workbk	Book

Features: Intro to Leading a Study, Intro to Study, Bibliography, Digging Deeper Quest, Follow Up, Summary, Charts, Maps
★★★★ Personal Application Preparation Time: Med
★★ Relationship Building Ldr. Guide: No Size: 5.50 x 8.50
Subjects: Christian Living, God, Numbers/Deuteronomy
Comments: This academic study of Numbers and Deuteronomy covers Moses' account of truths about God, about God's people, and about the blessed everyday living God wants His children to enjoy. Prominent teachings of Numbers include probation and pilgrimage; and Deuteronomy features instruction and prospects. Outlines, diagrams, and explanations keep participants challenged.

Author: Jensen, Irving L. 769
Series: Bible Self-study Guides
Title: *Philippians*
Publisher: Moody Press, 1973 ISBN: 0-80244-474-1

Num. Sess.	Group Time	Num. Pgs.	Avg. Qst.	Price	Audience	Format	Bible Study
8	60-75	64	Vary	$4.99	Mature Christian	Workbk	Book

Features: Intro to Leading a Study, Intro to Study, Bibliography, Digging Deeper Quest, Follow Up, Summary, Charts, Maps, Word Study
★★★★ Personal Application Preparation Time: Med
★★ Relationship Building Ldr. Guide: No Size: 5.50 x 8.50
Subjects: Joy, Philippians, Prison Epistles, Suffering
Comments: This academic study—part of a 39-book series—covers Paul's letter to the saints at Philippi. Paul's purpose in writing was more practical than doctrinal; therefore a detailed outline is not apparent in the letter's structure. Paul does teach about the doctrines of the person and work of Christ, however, in this, the last of the Prison Epistles.

Author: Jensen, Irving L. 770
Series: Bible Self-study Guides
Title: *Proverbs*
Publisher: Moody Press, 1976 ISBN: 0-80244-471-7

Num. Sess.	Group Time	Num. Pgs.	Avg. Qst.	Price	Audience	Format	Bible Study
13	60-75	88	Vary	$4.99	Mature Christian	Workbk	Book

Features: Intro to Leading a Study, Intro to Study, Bibliography, Digging Deeper Quest, Follow Up, Summary, Charts, Maps, Appendix, Word Study
★★★★ Personal Application Preparation Time: Med
★★ Relationship Building Ldr. Guide: No Size: 5.50 x 8.50
Subjects: Christian Living, Ethics, Proverbs, Wisdom
Comments: The book of Proverbs reveals God's detailed instructions and exhortations to His people concerning their thought-and-deed life. Proverbs mainly addresses personal ethics, including believers' walks with God on this earth. The Proverbs are profitable for all people, saved and unsaved.

Author: Jensen, Irving L. 771
Series: Bible Self-study Guides
Title: *Psalms*
Publisher: Moody Press, 1968 ISBN: 0-80244-463-6

Num. Sess.	Group Time	Num. Pgs.	Avg. Qst.	Price	Audience	Format	Bible Study
11	60-75	128	Vary	$4.99	Mature Christian	Workbk	Book

Features: Intro to Leading a Study, Intro to Study, Bibliography, Digging Deeper Quest, Follow Up, Summary, Charts, Maps, Word Study
★★★★ Personal Application Preparation Time: Med
★★ Relationship Building Ldr. Guide: No Size: 5.50 x 8.50
Subjects: Psalms
Comments: This psalm-by-psalm review is divided into 11 lessons. Psalms, 73 of which are ascribed to David, is a practical book that provides two benefits: it furnishes models of devotion, and it teaches truth in terms of human experience. This series of 39 Bible self-studies is ideal for individual, small group, or class use. Outlines, diagrams, and explanations keep participants challenged.

Author: Jensen, Irving L. 772
Series: Bible Self-study Guides
Title: *Revelation*
Publisher: Moody Press, 1971 ISBN: 0-80244-456-3

Num. Sess.	Group Time	Num. Pgs.	Avg. Qst.	Price	Audience	Format	Bible Study
14	60-75	142	Vary	$4.99	Mature Christian	Workbk	Book

Features: Intro to Leading a Study, Intro to Study, Bibliography, Digging Deeper Quest, Follow Up, Summary, Charts, Maps, Word Study
★★★★ Personal Application Preparation Time: Med
★★ Relationship Building Ldr. Guide: No Size: 5.50 x 8.50
Subjects: Revelation, Stress
Comments: Revelation is a record of John's dramatic God-inspired visions. Addressed to believers during a time of troubles and darkness, Revelation also encourages contemporary Christians to persevere under the stress of persecution. The hope is for justice which ultimately triumphs at the enthronement of Christ. Outlines, diagrams, and explanations keep participants challenged.

Author: Jensen, Irving L. 773
Series: Bible Self-study Guides
Title: *Romans*
Publisher: Moody Press, 1969 ISBN: 0-80244-453-9

Num. Sess.	Group Time	Num. Pgs.	Avg. Qst.	Price	Audience	Format	Bible Study
14	60-75	112	Vary	$4.99	Mature Christian	Workbk	Book

Features: Intro to Leading a Study, Intro to Study, Bibliography, Digging Deeper Quest, Follow Up, Summary, Charts, Maps, Word Study
★★★★ Personal Application Preparation Time: Med
★★ Relationship Building Ldr. Guide: No Size: 5.50 x 8.50
Subjects: Grace, Romans
Comments: In Romans, Paul writes to tell Roman Christians of his plan to visit them, and to enlist their support for his proposed trip to Spain. The underlying purpose of this academic study is to give a comprehensive interpretation of the Gospel. This 39-book series of Bible self-studies is ideal for individual, small group, or class use. Outlines, diagrams, and explanations keep participants challenged.

Author: Jensen, Irving L. 774
Series: Bible Self-study Guides
Title: *1 Corinthians*
Publisher: Moody Press, 1972 ISBN: 0-80244-467-9

Num. Sess.	Group Time	Num. Pgs.	Avg. Qst.	Price	Audience	Format	Bible Study
14	60-75	112	Vary	$4.99	Mature Christian	Workbk	Book

Features: Intro to Leading a Study, Intro to Study, Bibliography, Digging Deeper Quest, Follow Up, Summary, Charts, Maps, Word Study
★★★★ Personal Application Preparation Time: Med
★★ Relationship Building Ldr. Guide: No Size: 5.50 x 8.50
Subjects: Christian Living, 1 Corinthians
Comments: Part of a 39-book series, this academic study covers Paul's first letter to a Corinthian church plagued with problems. Two main benefits of studying 1 Corinthians are seeing God's diagnosis of modern Christians' spiritual maladies, and learning His prescriptions for cure. This series of Bible self-studies is ideal for individual, small group, or class use.

Author: Jensen, Irving L. 775
Series: Bible Self-study Guides
Title: *1 Kings with Chronicles*
Publisher: Moody Press, 1968 ISBN: 0-80244-477-6

Num. Sess.	Group Time	Num. Pgs.	Avg. Qst.	Price	Audience	Format	Bible Study
10	60-75	112	Vary	$4.99	Mature Christian	Workbk	Book

Features: Intro to Leading a Study, Intro to Study, Bibliography, Digging Deeper Quest, Follow Up, Summary, Charts, Maps, Word Study
★★★★ Personal Application Preparation Time: Med
★★ Relationship Building Ldr. Guide: No Size: 5.50 x 8.50
Subjects: Kings/Chronicles
Comments: This academic study of 1 Kings and Chronicles—part of a 39-book series—traces the course of Israel's history from the division of the nation after the death of King Solomon. The study is organized around 1 Kings, and since parts of Chronicles cover the same time period, parallel accounts will be followed. This series of Bible self-studies is ideal for individual, small group, or class use.

Author: Jensen, Irving L. 776
Series: Bible Self-study Guides
Title: *1 & 2 Peter*
Publisher: Moody Press, 1971 ISBN: 0-80244-475-X

Num. Sess.	Group Time	Num. Pgs.	Avg. Qst.	Price	Audience	Format	Bible Study
12	60-75	96	Vary	$4.99	Mature Christian	Workbk	Book

Features: Intro to Leading a Study, Intro to Study, Bibliography, Digging Deeper Quest, Follow Up, Summary, Charts, Maps, Word Study
★★★★ Personal Application Preparation Time: Med
★★ Relationship Building Ldr. Guide: No Size: 5.50 x 8.50
Subjects: Faith, False Teachers, Suffering, 1 & 2 Peter
Comments: This academic study of 1 and 2 Peter—part of a 39-book series—covers Peter's letter to exiles, mostly Jewish believers persecuted by dispersion for their Christian faith. The themes of 1 and 2 Peter are hope in the midst of severe trial. While it also addresses external opposition to Christians, it addresses dangers originating inside—namely, apostasy and false teaching.

Author: Jensen, Irving L. 777
Series: Bible Self-study Guides
Title: *1 & 2 Samuel*
Publisher: Moody Press, 1968 ISBN: 0-80244-476-8

Num. Sess.	Group Time	Num. Pgs.	Avg. Qst.	Price	Audience	Format	Bible Study
16	60-75	112	Vary	$4.99	Mature Christian	Workbk	Book

Features: Intro to Leading a Study, Intro to Study, Bibliography, Digging Deeper Quest, Follow Up, Summary, Charts, Maps, Word Study
★★★★ Personal Application Preparation Time: Med
★★ Relationship Building Ldr. Guide: No Size: 5.50 x 8.50
Subjects: Bible Personalities, 1 & 2 Samuel
Comments: The 2 books of Samuel record the history of the kingdom era of Israel, including the kingdom of David, a foreteller of Christ's Kingdom. The 16 lessons of this academic study move participants from the background and survey of 1 Samuel to 2 Samuel and a review of David's reign, sin, and troubles. The study concludes with restoration from the hand of God.

Author: Jensen, Irving L. 778
Series: Bible Self-study Guides
Title: *1 & 2 Thessalonians*
Publisher: Moody Press, 1974 ISBN: 0-80244-488-1

Num. Sess.	Group Time	Num. Pgs.	Avg. Qst.	Price	Audience	Format	Bible Study
12	60-75	96	Vary	$4.99	Mature Christian	Workbk	Book

Features: Intro to Leading a Study, Intro to Study, Bibliography, Digging Deeper Quest, Follow Up, Summary, Charts, Maps, Appendix, Word Study
★★★★ Personal Application Preparation Time: Med
★★ Relationship Building Ldr. Guide: No Size: 5.50 x 8.50
Subjects: Faith, Theology, 1 & 2 Thessalonians
Comments: This academic study covers Paul's 2 letters to the Thessalonians. The first letter commends Christians for their faith, exposes sin, exhorts young converts, and responds to false charges against Paul. The second letter goes one step further, instructing, exhorting, commending, and addressing doctrinal and practical correction.

Author: Jensen, Irving L. 779
Series: Bible Self-study Guides
Title: *1 & 2 Timothy and Titus*
Publisher: Moody Press, 1973 ISBN: 0-80244-481-4

Num. Sess.	Group Time	Num. Pgs.	Avg. Qst.	Price	Audience	Format	Bible Study
16	60-75	96	Vary	$4.99	Mature Christian	Workbk	Book

Features: Intro to Leading a Study, Intro to Study, Bibliography, Digging Deeper Quest, Follow Up, Summary, Charts, Maps, Appendix, Word Study
★★★★ Personal Application Preparation Time: Med
★★ Relationship Building Ldr. Guide: No Size: 5.50 x 8.50
Subjects: Pastoral Epistles, 1 & 2 Timothy/Titus
Comments: This academic study begins with 1 Timothy, moves to Titus, and closes with 2 Timothy, Paul's last recorded words of urgency, triumph, and tender care. This 39-book series of Bible self-studies is ideal for individual, small group, or class use. Outlines, diagrams, and explanations keep participants challenged.

Author: Jensen, Irving L. 780
Series: Bible Self-study Guides
Title: *2 Corinthians*
Publisher: Moody Press, 1972 ISBN: 0-80244-473-3

Num. Sess.	Group Time	Num. Pgs.	Avg. Qst.	Price	Audience	Format	Bible Study
13	60-75	112	Vary	$4.99	Mature Christian	Workbk	Book

Features: Intro to Leading a Study, Intro to Study, Bibliography, Digging Deeper Quest, Follow Up, Summary, Charts, Maps, Word Study
★★★★ Personal Application Preparation Time: Med
★★ Relationship Building Ldr. Guide: No Size: 5.50 x 8.50
Subjects: Church Life, Hope, Integrity, Leadership, Repentance, Service, Suffering, 2 Corinthians
Comments: This academic study of 2 Corinthians—part of a 39-book series—covers Paul's letter to Corinthians who encountered obstacles in proclaiming the Gospel. Emphasizing solutions to problems, Paul discusses his dilemma of convincing Corinthian brethren that he was a true apostle of Christ, preaching the true Gospel of God.

Author: Jensen, Irving L. **781**
Series: Bible Self-study Guides
Title: *2 Kings with Chronicles*
Publisher: Moody Press, 1968 ISBN: 0-80244-485-7

Num. Sess.	Group Time	Num. Pgs.	Avg. Qst.	Price	Audience	Format	Bible Study
11	60-75	112	Vary	$4.99	Mature Christian	Workbk	Book

Features: Intro to Leading a Study, Intro to Study, Bibliography, Digging Deeper Quest, Follow Up, Summary, Charts, Maps, Word Study
★★★★ Personal Application Preparation Time: Med
★★ Relationship Building Ldr. Guide: No Size: 5.50 x 8.50
Subjects: Kings/Chronicles, Victorious Living
Comments: This academic study of 2 Kings and 1 and 2 Chronicles helps participants sort out items of lesser importance in order to concentrate on the important. At the conclusion of the study—part of a 39-book series—participants see that only Christ, the King of Kings, can provide permanent peace. This series of Bible self-studies is ideal for individual, small group, or class use.

Author: Jeremiah, David **782**
Series: The Turning Point Series
Title: *Turning Toward Joy*
Publisher: Victor Books, 1992 ISBN: 1-56476-009-X

Num. Sess.	Group Time	Num. Pgs.	Avg. Qst.	Price	Audience	Format	Bible Study
12	60-90	240	7	$8.99	New Christian	Book	Book

Features: Intro to Study, Prayer Helps, Follow Up, Ldr's Notes, Persnl Study Quest
★★★★ Personal Application Preparation Time: Low
★★★★ Relationship Building Ldr. Guide: No Size: 5.50 x 8.50
Subjects: Joy, Philippians
Comments: This study of Phillippians concerns the Apostle Paul's most personal letter, sent to the Christians of Philippi—believers who lived in the shadow of the Roman tyrant Nero. Paul was in a Roman prison, facing an uncertain future, when he wrote it. As people came together in a worshiping community, in the midst of their difficulties, they could experience the joy Jesus promised those who follow Him.

Author: Jeremiah, David **783**
Series: The Turning Point Series
Title: *Turning Toward Integrity*
Publisher: Victor Books, 1993 ISBN: 1-56476-070-7

Num. Sess.	Group Time	Num. Pgs.	Avg. Qst.	Price	Audience	Format	Bible Study
12	60-75	240	11	$9.99	New Christian	Book	Topical

Features: Intro to Leading a Study, Intro to Study, Prayer Helps, Scrpt Memory Helps, Follow Up, Ldr's Notes
★★★★ Personal Application Preparation Time: Low
★★★ Relationship Building Ldr. Guide: No Size: 5.50 x 8.50
Subjects: Integrity, James, New Testament
Comments: This study is about the integrity of faith, the kind of faith that perseveres in persecution, resists temptation, responds obediently to God's Word, overcomes prejudice, produces good works, controls the tongue, follows God's wisdom, considers God in all its plans, depends on God rather than wealth, waits patiently for the return of the Lord, and makes prayer, not personal effort, its spiritual resource.

Author: Jessen, Nancy and Dan **784**
Series: Serendipity Support Group
Title: *Learning Disabilities: Parenting the Misunderstood*
Publisher: Serendipity House, 1991 ISBN: 1-88341-962-X

Num. Sess.	Group Time	Num. Pgs.	Avg. Qst.	Price	Audience	Format	Bible Study
7	60-90	112	12	$5.45	Beginner	Workbk	Topical

Features: Intro to Leading a Study, Objectives, Bibliography, Prayer Helps, Full Scrpt Printed, Ldr's Notes, Cartoons, Agenda
★★★★ Personal Application Preparation Time: None
★★★★ Relationship Building Ldr. Guide: No Size: 6.50 x 9.0
Subjects: Parenting, Support
Comments: This study is for parents of children with learning disabilities, interested relatives, and friends or teachers of LD children. It examines possible causes, difficulties and stresses in families, problems at school with "the system," education, relationships, communication, and LD teens. The format includes icebreakers, Bible study and prayer. Timelines are provided. It can be adapted for a 7 or 14 week study.

Author: Johnson, David W. & Frank P. **785**
Series:
Title: *Joining Together: Group Theory and Group Skills*
Publisher: Prentice-Hall, 1994 ISBN: 0-20515-846-3

Num. Sess.	Group Time	Num. Pgs.	Avg. Qst.	Price	Audience	Format	Bible Study
13	—	490	N/A	$46.00		Book	No

Features: Bibliography, Summary, Drawings, Cartoons, Photos, Charts, Index, Appendix
Personal Application Preparation Time:
Relationship Building Ldr. Guide: Size: 7.0 x 9.25
Subjects: Small Group Resource
Comments: This book on skills-oriented group dynamics integrates research, theory, skill-building exercises, and applications into specific group situations. It provides the theory and experience needed to develop high skill levels of group interaction, by offering an interdisciplinary perspective, appealing pedagogical aids, diagnostic materials to evaluate knowledge and skills, and much more.

Author: Johnson, Greg & Susie Shellenberger **786**
Series:
Title: *Keeping Your Cool While Sharing Your Faith*
Publisher: Tyndale House, 1993 ISBN: 0-84237-036-6

Num. Sess.	Group Time	Num. Pgs.	Avg. Qst.	Price	Audience	Format	Bible Study
43	30-60	220	3	$7.99	New Christian	Workbk	Topical

Features: Cartoons
★★★ Personal Application Preparation Time: None
★★ Relationship Building Ldr. Guide: No Size: 6.0 x 9.0
Subjects: Teens: Christian Liv, Teens: Evangelism, Teens: Friends
Comments: This book both inspires and instructs young people on how to lead Christian lives and share their faith with others. The chapters are short and easy to read. It discusses different reasons to share faith, and talks about things that get in the way of witnessing. Finally, it talks about how to share faith, and includes practical suggestions. It could be used as resource material for a small group but is too long for a stand alone Bible study.

Author: Johnson, Jan 787
Series:
Title: *Creative Groups Guide: A Call to Prayer*
Publisher: Standard Publishing, 1995 ISBN: 0-78470-309-4

Num. Sess.	Group Time	Num. Pgs.	Avg. Qst.	Price	Audience	Format	Bible Study
7	60-75	96	14	$12.99	New Christian	Workbk	Topical

Features: Intro to Leading a Study, Intro to Study, Prayer Helps, Scrpt Memory Helps, Worship Helps, Follow Up, Summary, Ldr's Notes, Handouts, Transpcy Masters, Agenda, Publicity Ideas, Book Avail
★★★★ Personal Application Preparation Time: None
★★★★ Relationship Building Ldr. Guide: No Size: 8.50 x 11.0
Subjects: Prayer
Comments: This 7-week course shows participants why and how to pray, and what to pray for. Based on a book, *A Call to Prayer: A Season of Harvest,* it addresses power in prayer, hindrances to prayer, and intercessory prayer. Contains easy-to-use lesson plans for Sunday School classes, discussion questions, and reproducible resources.

Author: Johnson, Jan 788
Series: The TruthSeed Series
Title: *Habakkuk: Staying Sane in a Crazy World*
Publisher: Victor Books, 1995 ISBN: 1-56476-257-2

Num. Sess.	Group Time	Num. Pgs.	Avg. Qst.	Price	Audience	Format	Bible Study
8	45-60	64	12	$4.99	Beginner	Workbk	Book

Features: Intro to Leading a Study, Intro to Study, Bibliography, Follow Up, Ldr's Notes, Persnl Study Quest
★★★ Personal Application Preparation Time: None
★★★ Relationship Building Ldr. Guide: No Size: 6.0 x 9.0
Subjects: Bible Personalities, Minor Prophets
Comments: This new series of inductive Bible studies enables men and women to experience community and develop godliness in either discussion group or personal settings. Questions are designed and field-tested for seekers, new believers, and mature Christians. Includes enrichment material for further study. Uses God's responses to Habakkuk to help us maintain sanity in modern chaotic times.

Author: Johnson, Jan, and David Mains 789
Series: Christian Lifestyle Series
Title: *Jump-Starting Your Devotional Life*
Publisher: David C. Cook Publishing Co., 1991 ISBN: 1-55513-376-2

Num. Sess.	Group Time	Num. Pgs.	Avg. Qst.	Price	Audience	Format	Bible Study
7	45-60	92	Vary	$14.95	New Christian	Workbk	Topical

Features: Intro to Study, Prayer Helps, Drawings, Handouts, Persnl Study Quest
★★★ Personal Application Preparation Time: None
★★★ Relationship Building Ldr. Guide: Yes Size: 8.50 x 11.0
Subjects: Devotionals, Prayer, Worship
Comments: This study combines biblical teaching, small group interaction, and practical application. It helps adults of all ages, especially Boomers and younger, talk honestly about their devotional frustrations/misconceptions, and discover the joy of getting closer to God. It's appropriate for singles or marrieds, new or mature Christians.

Author: Johnson, Jan & Warren W. Wiersbe 790
Series: Christian Lifestyle Series
Title: *Preparing for Battle In the War That's Won*
Publisher: David C. Cook Publishing Co., 1993 ISBN: 0-78145-025-X

Num. Sess.	Group Time	Num. Pgs.	Avg. Qst.	Price	Audience	Format	Bible Study
7	45-60	96	Vary	$14.95	New Christian	Workbk	Topical

Features: Intro to Study, Bibliography, Prayer Helps, Study Overview, Drawings, Handouts, Persnl Study Quest
★★★★ Personal Application Preparation Time: None
★★★★ Relationship Building Ldr. Guide: Yes Size: 8.50 x 11.0
Subjects: Satan, Spiritual Warfare, Victorious Living
Comments: This study helps adults of all ages, especially Boomers and younger, own up to their questions and misperceptions about spiritual warfare. They will discover biblical truths that will equip them for living in ways that honor God and defeat Satan. Specifically they will understand the reality of spiritual warfare, examine Satan's personality and strategies, explore the role of angels, handle temptation.

Author: Johnson, Jan 791
Series: A Bible Study for Women
Title: *When It Hurts to Grow*
Publisher: Victor Books, 1991 ISBN: 0-89693-197-8

Num. Sess.	Group Time	Num. Pgs.	Avg. Qst.	Price	Audience	Format	Bible Study
8	60-75	96	15	$5.99	New Christian	Workbk	Book

Features: Intro to Study, Prayer Helps, Ldr's Notes
★★★★ Personal Application Preparation Time: Med
★★★ Relationship Building Ldr. Guide: No Size: 6.0 x 9.0
Subjects: Faith, Hebrews, Suffering, Women's Issues
Comments: This in-depth 8-week study of Hebrews 12:1-17 deals with "discipline of the Lord." It shows that God's discipline includes both specific acts He initiates and the typical daily hardships through which believers grow. Like a parent, God teaches, loves, and disciplines so that a person's relationship with Him will grow deeper. Participants are encouraged as they learn to endure suffering and conquer trials with God's help.

Author: Johnson, Lin 792
Series: Fisherman Bible Studyguide
Title: *Encouraging Others: Biblical Models for Caring*
Publisher: Shaw, 1991 ISBN: 0-87788-221-5

Num. Sess.	Group Time	Num. Pgs.	Avg. Qst.	Price	Audience	Format	Bible Study
12	45-60	72	12	$4.99	New Christian	Workbk	Topical

Features: Intro to Leading a Study, Intro to Study, Prayer Helps, Follow Up
★★★ Personal Application Preparation Time: None
★★★ Relationship Building Ldr. Guide: No Size: 5.0 x 8.25
Subjects: Bible Personalities, Caring, Christian Living, Faith
Comments: These studies provide models from Scripture for encouraging people and building them up in their faith. It shows the needs God's people have for advice and encouragement, as they live their faith in this world; it helps them persevere in their goals to become more like Christ. Participants will learn to become and practice being "spiritual cheerleaders" to other believers.

Author: Johnson, Lin 793
Series: A Bible Study for Women
Title: *Growing Season, The*
Publisher: Victor Books, 1987 ISBN: 0-89693-009-2

Num. Sess.	Group Time	Num. Pgs.	Avg. Qst.	Price	Audience	Format	Bible Study
9	60-90	95	15	$5.99	New Christian	Workbk	Topical

Features: Intro to Leading a Study, Intro to Study, Objectives, Scrpt Memory Helps, Summary, Ldr's Notes, Charts
★★★ Personal Application Preparation Time: Med
★★ Relationship Building Ldr. Guide: No Size: 6.0 x 9.0
Subjects: Christian Living, Fruit of the Spirit, Women's Issues
Comments: This study explores nine "fruits of the Spirit." Love, joy, peace, patience, kindness, goodness, faithfulness, gentleness, and self-control are qualities of character that believers must seek. Such character is grown through cooperation of the Holy Spirit, who prepares, plants, prunes, and produces His fruit in believers. God expects Christians to work at developing fruit.

Author: Johnson, Lin 794
Series: The Knowing God Series
Title: *Our Good Provider: Delighting in God's Gifts*
Publisher: Zondervan, 1994 ISBN: 0-31048-321-2

Num. Sess.	Group Time	Num. Pgs.	Avg. Qst.	Price	Audience	Format	Bible Study
6	45-60	64	12	$4.99	Beginner	Workbk	Topical

Features: Intro to Leading a Study, Intro to Study, Objectives, Prayer Helps, Scrpt Memory Helps, Follow Up, Ldr's Notes
★★★★ Personal Application Preparation Time: Low
★★★ Relationship Building Ldr. Guide: No Size: 5.50 x 8.50
Subjects: God, Victorious Living
Comments: One of eight in a series, this guide focuses on God's amazing goodness, and helps participants realize that every good and perfect gift comes from Him. It explores how to keep from worrying about finances, job security, health, and the future, and how to trust God to provide for all of one's needs. The study is good for people who don't reflect on God and His provisions.

Author: Johnson, Lin 795
Series: Tapestry Collection
Title: *Prayer Patterns*
Publisher: Victor Books, 1993 ISBN: 1-56476-193-2

Num. Sess.	Group Time	Num. Pgs.	Avg. Qst.	Price	Audience	Format	Bible Study
10	60-90	96	16	$6.99	New Christian	Workbk	Topical

Features: Intro to Study, Objectives, Prayer Helps
★★★★ Personal Application Preparation Time: Low
★★★ Relationship Building Ldr. Guide: No Size: 6.0 x 9.0
Subjects: Prayer
Comments: This study focuses on prayers in the Bible, and what participants can learn from their structure and content in relating to modern situations. Each lesson includes a series of questions to help participants interact with the text of a biblical prayer, a narrative that illustrates how this biblical prayer relates to today's needs, a week's worth of prayer suggestions related to that prayer, and small group helps.

Author: Johnson, Victoria & Mike Murphy 796
Series: Family Growth Electives
Title: *Parenting Streetwise Kids: Studies for Parents of Kids at Risk*
Publisher: David C. Cook Publishing Co., 1995 ISBN: 0-78145-137-X

Num. Sess.	Group Time	Num. Pgs.	Avg. Qst.	Price	Audience	Format	Bible Study
13	45-60	144	Vary	$19.95	Beginner	Workbk	Topical

Features: Intro to Study, Objectives, Bibliography, Prayer Helps, Drawings, Handouts, Persnl Study Quest
★★★★ Personal Application Preparation Time: Low
★★★★ Relationship Building Ldr. Guide: Yes Size: 8.50 x 11.0
Subjects: Family, Parenting, Relationships, Self-esteem, Social Issues, Teens: Peer Pressure
Comments: This study combines sound biblical teaching, small group interaction, and practical application. Written by and for African-American parents (plus inner-city and other parents) who understand their kids' world, combat the influences of the media, recognize at-risk behavior and signs of gang violence, and hold their kids accountable.

Author: Joiner, Barbara, et al. 797
Series:
Title: *With A Servant Heart*
Publisher: Woman's Missionary Union, 1992 ISBN: 1-56309-048-1

Num. Sess.	Group Time	Num. Pgs.	Avg. Qst.	Price	Audience	Format	Bible Study
	—	86	Vary	$3.95		Book	

Features: Intro to Study, Ldr's Notes
Personal Application Preparation Time:
Relationship Building Ldr. Guide: No Size: 5.50 x 8.50
Subjects: Leadership, Missions, Women's Issues
Comments: Drawing on the leadership experiences and varying styles of 6 authors, this book takes a look at servant leadership, the kind of leadership symbolized more by a towel and basin than a throne and scepter. It focuses on how women can and should lead as Christians called by God. It challenges each woman to use her leadership skills in her own spheres of influence and to follow the model taught by Jesus. It was written to assist Woman's Missionary Union leaders.

Author: Jones, Kenneth E. 798
Series:
Title: *Divorce & Remarriage: In The Bible*
Publisher: Warner Press, 1989 ISBN: 0-87162-503-2

Num. Sess.	Group Time	Num. Pgs.	Avg. Qst.	Price	Audience	Format	Bible Study
13	60-75	112	6	$3.95	New Christian	Book	Topical

Features: Intro to Study, Bibliography
★★★ Personal Application Preparation Time: Low
★★★ Relationship Building Ldr. Guide: Yes Size: 4.25 x 7.0
Subjects: Divorce, Marriage
Comments: This study maps out a path that leads participants to a clear understanding of God's full intent for family living. Everything is supported by Scripture. Areas covered include the following: modern problems with marriage, marriage in the Bible, divorce in the Old Testament, divorce in the Gospels, divorced and remarried pastors, and more. A leader's guide includes Bible passages, teaching goals, an introduction, questions for discussion, and a plan for each session.

Author: Jones, Timothy & Jill Zook-Jones **799**
Series: Fisherman Bible Studyguide
Title: *Prayer: Discovering What Scripture Says*
Publisher: Shaw, 1993 ISBN: 0-87788-709-8

Num. Sess.	Group Time	Num. Pgs.	Avg. Qst.	Price	Audience	Format	Bible Study
12	45-60	75	12	$4.99	Beginner	Workbk	Topical

Features: Intro to Leading a Study, Intro to Study, Prayer Helps, Ldr's Notes
★★★★ Personal Application Preparation Time: Low
★★ Relationship Building Ldr. Guide: No Size: 5.25 x 8.25
Subjects: Prayer
Comments: This realistic 12-week prayer study, filled with guidance for praying, addresses the longing expressed by Jesus' disciples, "Lord, teach us to pray." Topics include: "Praying Like Jesus"; "How Shall We Come?" "Great is the Lord!" "A Cry for Forgiveness"; "Don't Be Afraid to Ask"; "Prayers for the Kingdom"; "A Listening Heart"; "Two Are Better Than One"; "When the Door Won't Open."

Author: Joy, Donald **800**
Series: Personal Growth Bookshelf
Title: *Men Under Construction*
Publisher: Victor Books, 1989 ISBN: 1-56476-053-7

Num. Sess.	Group Time	Num. Pgs.	Avg. Qst.	Price	Audience	Format	Bible Study
9	60-75	190	3	$8.99	Beginner	Book	Topical

Features: Intro to Study, Bibliography, Persnl Study Quest, Index
★★★★ Personal Application Preparation Time: Low
★★★★ Relationship Building Ldr. Guide: No Size: 5.50 x 8.50
Subjects: Men's Issues, Support
Comments: This expanded paperback version of "unfinished business" examines men's unique needs and concerns. It includes an agenda for use in men's support groups. Peeling away cultural and un-Christian trappings that accompany the secular movement, the author cuts to the core of men's true needs and concerns. Among the subjects covered are father-son, mother-son, and husband-wife relationships, celebrating our male/female distinctives, our need to compete.

Author: Juel, Donald **801**
Series: Search Weekly Bible
Title: *Unit 5/Matthew 1–16*
Publisher: Augsburg Fortress Publishers, 1984

Num. Sess.	Group Time	Num. Pgs.	Avg. Qst.	Price	Audience	Format	Bible Study
8	90-105	64	Vary	$5.50	New Christian	Book	Book

Features: Intro to Study, Objectives, Prayer Helps, Worship Helps, Follow Up, Summary
★★ Personal Application Preparation Time: Med
★★ Relationship Building Ldr. Guide: Yes Size: 8.50 x 11.0
Subjects: Matthew
Comments: This review of Matthew is 1 of 20 units of a 5-year study titled "Search." The series is divided into 5 themes: Beginnings, Journey, Struggles, Experiences, and Hopes. This study of Matthew covers: "The Birth of a King"; "A Time of Testing"; "The Paths of Righteousness—Part 1 (Matthew 5)"; Part 2 (Matthew 6–7); "The Deliverer"; "Heralding the News"; "The Provider"; and "A Confession of Faith."

Author: Juel, Donald **802**
Series: Search Weekly Bible
Title: *Unit 6/Matthew 17–28*
Publisher: Augsburg Fortress Publishers, 1984

Num. Sess.	Group Time	Num. Pgs.	Avg. Qst.	Price	Audience	Format	Bible Study
8	90-105	64	Vary	$5.50	New Christian	Book	Book

Features: Intro to Study, Objectives, Prayer Helps, Worship Helps, Follow Up, Summary
★★ Personal Application Preparation Time: Med
★★ Relationship Building Ldr. Guide: Yes Size: 8.50 x 11.0
Subjects: Matthew
Comments: This review of Matthew is 1 of 20 units of a 5-year study titled "Search." The series is divided into 5 themes: Beginnings, Journey, Struggles, Experiences, and Hopes. This study of Matthew covers 8 session. This second half of Matthew's Gospel changes tones as the story moves toward Jerusalem and the cross. They become darker and more somber. The story is played out in the shadow of the cross.

Author: Kaplan, David B. **803**
Series: Small Group Bible Studies
Title: *Psalm 23*
Publisher: Augsburg Fortress Publishers, 1986

Num. Sess.	Group Time	Num. Pgs.	Avg. Qst.	Price	Audience	Format	Bible Study
4	60-75	16	12	$1.15	New Christian	Book	Topical

Features: Intro to Study, Prayer Helps, Full Scrpt Printed
★★★★ Personal Application Preparation Time: None
★★★★ Relationship Building Ldr. Guide: No Size: 8.50 x 5.50
Subjects: God, Psalms, Worship
Comments: This short, 4-session study analyzes the phrases in Psalm 23. The session titles include "The Lord Is My Shepherd," "In Green Pastures," "Through the Dark Valley," and "All the Days of My Life." God's preserving, providing, and protecting activities are brought to light, and participants are encouraged to share throughout the study about how God has provided in their lives. The study also discusses the use of Psalm 23 in corporate worship.

Author: Kaplan, David B. **804**
Series: Search Weekly Bible
Title: *Unit 7/Exodus 1–18*
Publisher: Augsburg Fortress Publishers, 1984

Num. Sess.	Group Time	Num. Pgs.	Avg. Qst.	Price	Audience	Format	Bible Study
8	90-105	64	Vary	$5.50	New Christian	Book	Book

Features: Intro to Study, Objectives, Prayer Helps, Worship Helps, Follow Up, Summary
★★ Personal Application Preparation Time: Med
★★ Relationship Building Ldr. Guide: Yes Size: 8.50 x 11.0
Subjects: Exodus
Comments: The series is divided into 5 themes: Beginnings, Journey, Struggles, Experiences, and Hopes. The study of Exodus covers 8 sessions looking at the Exodus deliverance. Participants will understand the plight of an enslaved and oppressed people. They will see how God revealed Himself to a reluctant Moses and commissioned him for the task of leader. Then explore the plagues, Passover, the deliverance.

Author: Kaplan, David B. **805**
Series: Search Weekly Bible
Title: *Unit 8/Exodus 19–40, Leviticus, Numbers*
Publisher: Augsburg Fortress Publishers, 1985

Num. Sess.	Group Time	Num. Pgs.	Avg. Qst.	Price	Audience	Format	Bible Study
8	90-105	64	Vary	$5.50	New Christian	Book	Book

Features: Intro to Study, Objectives, Prayer Helps, Worship Helps, Follow Up, Summary

★★ Personal Application Preparation Time: Med

★★ Relationship Building Ldr. Guide: Yes Size: 8.50 x 11.0

Subjects: Exodus, Leviticus, Numbers/Deuteronomy

Comments: This review of Exodus, Leviticus, and Numbers is 1 of 20 units of a 5-year study titled "Search." The series is divided into 5 themes: Beginnings, Journey, Struggles, Experiences, and Hopes. This study is set within the framework of Israel's wilderness journey. Through the journey, participants get a glimpse of their own journeys as God's people. Individual lessons help them make the connection.

Author: Karssen, Gien **806**
Series:
Title: *Her Name Is Woman—Book 2*
Publisher: NavPress, 1977 ISBN: 0-89109-424-5

Num. Sess.	Group Time	Num. Pgs.	Avg. Qst.	Price	Audience	Format	Bible Study
24	60-75	240	6	$9.00	New Christian	Book	Charctr

Features: Intro to Leading a Study, Intro to Study, Full Scrpt Printed, Cross Ref

★★★ Personal Application Preparation Time: Med

★★ Relationship Building Ldr. Guide: No Size: 5.25 x 8.0

Subjects: Bible Personalities, Failure, Success, Women's Issues

Comments: This continuing study offers participants 25 more Bible women to explore. Deborah, Delilah, Ruth, Bathsheba, Jezebel, Mary Magdalene, and others become alive and relevant to contemporary women. Participants will discover why some women succeed while others fail. For group study, a notebook is needed for responses and prayer requests.

Author: Karssen, Gien **807**
Series:
Title: *Her Name Is Woman—Book 1*
Publisher: NavPress, 1975 ISBN: 0-89109-420-2

Num. Sess.	Group Time	Num. Pgs.	Avg. Qst.	Price	Audience	Format	Bible Study
24	60-75	200	6	$9.00	New Christian	Book	Charctr

Features: Intro to Leading a Study, Intro to Study, Full Scrpt Printed, Cross Ref

★★★ Personal Application Preparation Time: Med

★★ Relationship Building Ldr. Guide: No Size: 5.25 x 8.0

Subjects: Bible Personalities, Singles' Issues, Women's Issues

Comments: This study of 24 Old and New Testament women illustrates the importance of a woman's spiritual side. Some of the women studied include Lydia (businesswoman), Priscilla (spiritual leader), Sarah (honored wife and mother), and Anna (aging widow). Married or single, happy or brokenhearted, secure or shaken, participants will identify with one of these women.

Author: Keefauver, Larry **808**
Series: Group's Apply-It-To-Life
Title: *Faith In The Workplace*
Publisher: Group Publishing, 1993 ISBN: 1-55945-299-4

Num. Sess.	Group Time	Num. Pgs.	Avg. Qst.	Price	Audience	Format	Bible Study
4	35-60	48	Vary	$9.99	Beginner	Workbk	Topical

Features: Intro to Leading a Study, Intro to Study, Objectives, Prayer Helps, Digging Deeper Quest, Ldr's Notes, Handouts, Agenda, Publicity Ideas

★★★★ Personal Application Preparation Time: Low

★★★★ Relationship Building Ldr. Guide: No Size: 8.50 x 11.0

Subjects: Communication, Ethics, Work

Comments: This 4-week study helps adults learn: how to respond to people they don't like at work; where to turn when a supervisor asks them to lie; how to succeed at work without compromising personal beliefs; the importance of forgiveness in the workplace; and ways to apply Christian principles to ethical dilemmas.

Author: Keefauver, Larry **809**
Series: Group's Active Bible Curriculum
Title: *Who Is the Holy Spirit?*
Publisher: Group Publishing, 1992 ISBN: 1-55945-217-X

Num. Sess.	Group Time	Num. Pgs.	Avg. Qst.	Price	Audience	Format	Bible Study
4	35-60	48	Vary	$9.99	Beginner	Workbk	Charctr

Features: Intro to Leading a Study, Intro to Study, Objectives, Study Overview, Ldr's Notes, Handouts, Agenda, Publicity Ideas

★★★★ Personal Application Preparation Time: None

★★★★ Relationship Building Ldr. Guide: No Size: 8.50 x 11.0

Subjects: Teens: Holy Spirit, Teens: Senior High

Comments: This course helps teenagers understand and know the Holy Spirit. Through these lessons, senior high participants develop personal relationships with the third Person of the Trinity. They'll discover who the Holy Spirit is, examine His gifts, learn how to be empowered and taught by the personal presence of God, and explore ways to receive guidance from the Holy Spirit.

Author: Keffer, Lois **810**
Series: Group's Active Bible Curriculum
Title: *Getting Along With Your Family*
Publisher: Group Publishing, 1992 ISBN: 1-55945-233-1

Num. Sess.	Group Time	Num. Pgs.	Avg. Qst.	Price	Audience	Format	Bible Study
4	35-60	48	Vary	$9.99	Beginner	Workbk	Topical

Features: Intro to Leading a Study, Intro to Study, Objectives, Study Overview, Ldr's Notes, Handouts, Agenda, Publicity Ideas

★★★★ Personal Application Preparation Time: None

★★★★ Relationship Building Ldr. Guide: No Size: 8.50 x 11.0

Subjects: Teens: Christian Liv, Teens: Family, Teens: Relationships, Teens: Senior High

Comments: This course helps senior highers explore family relationships and the importance of their roles in the family structure. Participants learn to accept responsibility for helping create healthy family environments, understand typical family roles and explore God's standards for family relationships, resolve conflict in positive.

Author: Keller, Carolyn M. and Vern Jahnke **811**
Series: Cross Signs
Title: *How Does the Spirit Lead? Portraits of Faith: Unit 5*
Publisher: Augsburg Fortress Publishers, 1992

Num. Sess.	Group Time	Num. Pgs.	Avg. Qst.	Price	Audience	Format	Bible Study
7	90-105	48	6	$3.75	New Christian	Book	Topical

Features: Intro to Study, Prayer Helps, Worship Helps, Photos, Maps
★★★ Personal Application Preparation Time: Low
★★ Relationship Building Ldr. Guide: Yes Size: 5.50 x 8.50
Subjects: Holy Spirit
Comments: In this study, participants investigate key texts from Acts and the Epistles to gain insight into activities of the Holy Spirit. Specifically it explores the fulfillment of God's words spoken by the prophet Joel at Pentecost, how the Spirit encounters and works through resistance, how the Spirit carries out God's urgent task of saving people, how the Spirit calls people to do specific tasks, how the Spirit makes people free.

Author: Kelly, Paul **812**
Series: Group's Active Bible Curriculum
Title: *Deciphering Jesus' Parables*
Publisher: Group Publishing, 1993 ISBN: 1-55945-237-4

Num. Sess.	Group Time	Num. Pgs.	Avg. Qst.	Price	Audience	Format	Bible Study
4	35-60	45	Vary	$9.99	Beginner	Workbk	Topical

Features: Intro to Leading a Study, Intro to Study, Objectives, Study Overview, Ldr's Notes, Handouts, Agenda, Publicity Ideas
★★★★ Personal Application Preparation Time: None
★★★★ Relationship Building Ldr. Guide: No Size: 8.50 x 11.0
Subjects: Teens: Bible Study, Teens: Christian Liv, Teens: Jesus Life, Teens: New Testament, Teens: Senior High
Comments: Teenagers learn to apply Jesus' parables to everyday life, using stories rather than statements of faith to make points. Senior highers understand God's love for them, recognize the importance of using their talents faithfully, understand the value of their places in the kingdom of God, and see the joy of eternity with God.

Author: Kelly, Paul **813**
Series: Group's Active Bible Curriculum
Title: *Forgiveness*
Publisher: Group Publishing, 1992 ISBN: 1-55945-223-4

Num. Sess.	Group Time	Num. Pgs.	Avg. Qst.	Price	Audience	Format	Bible Study
4	35-60	48	Vary	$9.99	Beginner	Workbk	Topical

Features: Intro to Leading a Study, Intro to Study, Objectives, Study Overview, Ldr's Notes, Handouts, Agenda, Publicity Ideas
★★★★ Personal Application Preparation Time: None
★★★★ Relationship Building Ldr. Guide: No Size: 8.50 x 11.0
Subjects: Teens: Christian Liv, Teens: Relationships, Teens: Senior High
Comments: This 4-week course teaches senior highers to give and receive forgiveness. Participants learn to accept and understand their own mistakes and the mistakes of others, explore ways to ask for forgiveness from God and others, examine ways to mend broken relationships, and experience God's loving forgiveness.

Author: Kelly, Paul **814**
Series: Group's Active Bible Curriculum
Title: *1 & 2 Corinthians: Christian Discipleship*
Publisher: Group Publishing, 1992 ISBN: 1-55945-230-7

Num. Sess.	Group Time	Num. Pgs.	Avg. Qst.	Price	Audience	Format	Bible Study
4	35-60	42	Vary	$9.99	Beginner	Workbk	Book

Features: Intro to Leading a Study, Intro to Study, Objectives, Study Overview, Ldr's Notes, Handouts, Agenda, Publicity Ideas
★★★★ Personal Application Preparation Time: None
★★★★ Relationship Building Ldr. Guide: No Size: 8.50 x 11.0
Subjects: Teens: Christian Liv, Teens: Discipleship, Teens: Senior High
Comments: Through this action-packed course, teenagers determine specific ways to live out the ministry of Christ and set goals for Christian living. This course will challenge teenagers to follow Jesus in a fantastic life-journey of unity, love, and ministry. It can be adapted for a Bible class or youth meeting. Activity sheets are reproducible. Student books not required, and instructions are easy to follow.

Author: Kendrick, Michael **815**
Series:
Title: *Supper Club*
Publisher: Baker Book House, 1994 ISBN: 0-80105-263-7

Num. Sess.	Group Time	Num. Pgs.	Avg. Qst.	Price	Audience	Format	Bible Study
	—	119	N/A	$7.99			

Features: Intro to Study
Personal Application Preparation Time:
Relationship Building Ldr. Guide: Size: 6.0 x 9.0
Subjects: Church Life, Small Group Resource
Comments: This resource provides creative ideas using supper clubs for small-group fellowship. Supper clubs are imaginative theme evenings that provide ideas for food and fellowship to draw newcomers into the church and deepen small group relationships. Everything you need to host a memorable evening: suggestions for music, thrifty decorations, mood-setting special effects, rousing mixers and games, stimulating small group questions, and menus complete with recipes.

Author: Kent, Carol **816**
Series:
Title: *Secret Longings of the Heart*
Publisher: NavPress, 1991 ISBN: 0-89109-614-0

Num. Sess.	Group Time	Num. Pgs.	Avg. Qst.	Price	Audience	Format	Bible Study
6	60-75	96	18	$6.00	Beginner	Workbk	Topical

Features: Intro to Leading a Study, Intro to Study, Prayer Helps, Scrpt Memory Helps, Follow Up, Full Scrpt Printed, Cassette Avail, Book Avail
★★★★ Personal Application Preparation Time: None
★★★★ Relationship Building Ldr. Guide: No Size: 5.50 x 8.50
Subjects: Emotions, Women's Issues
Comments: This study, with candid questions and revealing insights, is an ideal discussion guide for women of all ages. Self-contained, it can be used with or without its book counterpart. It explores longings for fulfillment and victory in five areas: significance, security, intimacy, success, and spirituality. Participants compare their own expectations, disappointments, longings, emotions, decisions, drives, and actions.

Author: Kerr, John S. 817
Series: Friendship Bible Study
Title: *Discipleship*
Publisher: Augsburg Fortress Publishers, 1988

Num. Sess.	Group Time	Num. Pgs.	Avg. Qst.	Price	Audience	Format	Bible Study
8	60-75	48	18	$3.75	New Christian	Workbk	Topical

Features: Intro to Study, Prayer Helps, Study Overview
★★★★ Personal Application Preparation Time: Low
★★★★ Relationship Building Ldr. Guide: Yes Size: 5.50 x 8.50
Subjects: Discipleship, Faith
Comments: This 8-lesson study is a biblical guide for contemporary disciples who seek to follow Christ and live out their commitment of faith. It asks, in various ways, one basic question: "What does that mean for me?" The lesson format includes an overview, an opening, a responsive reading, Bible background, questions for reflection, a key verse, a prayer response, and an "our faith" response.

Author: Keyes, Sharrel 818
Series: Fisherman Bible Studyguide
Title: *Luke: Following Jesus*
Publisher: Shaw, 1983 ISBN: 0-87788-511-7

Num. Sess.	Group Time	Num. Pgs.	Avg. Qst.	Price	Audience	Format	Bible Study
20	45-60	94	12	$4.99	New Christian	Workbk	Book

Features: Intro to Leading a Study, Intro to Study, Prayer Helps, Persnl Study Quest, Maps
★★★ Personal Application Preparation Time: Low
★★ Relationship Building Ldr. Guide: No Size: 5.0 x 8.25
Subjects: Caring, Faith, Jesus: Life/Teaching, Luke, Obedience
Comments: This study follows Luke's account of Jesus caring and healing people, righting injustice and teaching people spiritual and moral truth. Jesus teaches faithfulness to Him; putting aside personal priorities; learning to love people who are unkind; freeing oneself from hypocrisy, greed, and ambition. The study is a topical approach to Luke.

Author: Kiepe, Rachel 819
Series: Serendipity Support Group
Title: *Parents of Preschoolers: From Car Seats to Kindergarten*
Publisher: Serendipity House, 1992 ISBN: 1-88341-973-5

Num. Sess.	Group Time	Num. Pgs.	Avg. Qst.	Price	Audience	Format	Bible Study
7	60-90	80	12	$5.45	Beginner	Workbk	Topical

Features: Intro to Leading a Study, Objectives, Bibliography, Prayer Helps, Full Scrpt Printed, Ldr's Notes, Cartoons, Agenda
★★★★ Personal Application Preparation Time: None
★★★★ Relationship Building Ldr. Guide: No Size: 6.50 x 9.0
Subjects: Marriage, Parenting, Support, Work
Comments: This study is for anyone who has young children, or is about to have children. Subjects dealt with include stress and conflict, money problems, being consistent, building independence and self-control, setting priorities, stress in marriage, keeping a sense of humor, being flexible, dealing with guilt, and building security and love in the home. The format includes icebreakers, Bible study, and prayer.

Author: Kimbrough, Marjorie 820
Series:
Title: *Matthew: Volume 1 & 2*
Publisher: Cokesbury, 1990 ISBN: 0-68776-182-4

Num. Sess.	Group Time	Num. Pgs.	Avg. Qst.	Price	Audience	Format	Bible Study
8	45-60	N/A	Vary	$25.00	New Christian	Video	Book

Features: Intro to Leading a Study, Intro to Study, Ldr's Notes, Video Study Guide
★★★ Personal Application Preparation Time: Low
★★★ Relationship Building Ldr. Guide: Yes Size: 4.75 x 8.0
Subjects: Jesus: Life/Teaching, Matthew
Comments: This 2-volume video lecture series discusses Matthew, which scholars believe was the favorite and most used Gospel by the early Church, and perhaps the first recorded Gospel. It concerns not only Christ's story, but why, to whom, and by whom it was written. In each volume, 4 lessons give participants a verse-by-verse exposition. A comprehensive leader's guide is included.

Author: Kimmel, Tim 821
Series:
Title: *Surviving Life in the Fast Lane*
Publisher: NavPress, 1990 ISBN: 0-89109-293-5

Num. Sess.	Group Time	Num. Pgs.	Avg. Qst.	Price	Audience	Format	Bible Study
9	45-60	96	9	$6.00	New Christian	Book	Topical

Features: Intro to Study, Prayer Helps, Scrpt Memory Helps, Pre-discussion Quest, Follow Up, Full Scrpt Printed, Ldr's Notes
★★★★ Personal Application Preparation Time: None
★★★★ Relationship Building Ldr. Guide: No Size: 5.50 x 8.50
Subjects: Christian Living, Family, Forgiveness, Friendships, Relationships, Stress, Suffering, Work
Comments: This study helps participants explore and apply six keys to genuine rest for the family in life, marriage, friendships, work, and in their relationship with God. Include forgiveness, living within the boundaries of God's Word, having an eternal perspective, resting in the midst of suffering, learning contentment, and managing our resources.

Author: Kinley, Jeff 822
Series: Main Thing Series
Title: *Never the Same*
Publisher: David C. Cook Publishing Co., 1994ISBN: 0-78145-110-8

Num. Sess.	Group Time	Num. Pgs.	Avg. Qst.	Price	Audience	Format	Bible Study
15	60-90	144	15	$9.95	Mature Christian	Workbk	Topical

Features: Intro to Study, Prayer Helps, Worship Helps, Study Overview, Pre-discussion Quest, Full Scrpt Printed, Cartoons, Persnl Study Quest
★★★★ Personal Application Preparation Time: Med
★★★★ Relationship Building Ldr. Guide: Yes Size: 7.25 x 9.25
Subjects: Teens: God, Teens: Holy Spirit
Comments: This 15-week study helps participant know God in a deeper way. They'll find answers to questions like: What's God really like? How can I get closer to Him? What are the Father, Son, and Holy Spirit really like? How can God be three entities, yet one? How do I defend what I believe? What's my spiritual gift? and How can I get more of God in my life? The studies begin with an activity or story.

Author: Kinley, Jeff 823
Series: Main Thing Series
Title: *No Turning Back*
Publisher: David C. Cook Publishing Co., 1994 ISBN: 0-78145-112-4

Num. Sess.	Group Time	Num. Pgs.	Avg. Qst.	Price	Audience	Format	Bible Study
15	60-90	144	15	$9.95	Mature Christian	Workbk	Topical

Features: Intro to Study, Prayer Helps, Worship Helps, Study Overview, Pre-discussion Quest, Full Scrpt Printed, Ldr's Notes, Cartoons, Persnl Study Quest
★★★★ Personal Application Preparation Time: Med
★★★★ Relationship Building Ldr. Guide: Yes Size: 7.25 x 9.25
Subjects: Teens: Discipleship, Teens: Evangelism, Teens: Prayer, Teens: Senior High
Comments: This study challenges youth to push their walk with God to the limit, seek His best, and be nothing but their best for Him. It includes 15 studies to be used over 3 weeks. A "Pray About It" page serves as a prayer journal.

Author: Klug, Ron 824
Series: Fisherman Bible Studyguide
Title: *Job: Trusting Through Trials*
Publisher: Shaw, 1982 ISBN: 0-87788-430-7

Num. Sess.	Group Time	Num. Pgs.	Avg. Qst.	Price	Audience	Format	Bible Study
13	45-60	96	9	$4.99	Mature Christian	Workbk	Book

Features: Intro to Leading a Study, Intro to Study, Prayer Helps, Follow Up
★★ Personal Application Preparation Time: None
★★ Relationship Building Ldr. Guide: No Size: 5.0 x 8.25
Subjects: Faith, Job, Suffering
Comments: In this study, participants will identify with Job as he wrestles with deep personal questions on illness, loss, disappointment, suffering, and death. Job maintains faith in the God of strength and love who cares for him in the midst of suffering. Some of the questions posed by the study include: Why, God? Why has this happened to me? Why do good people suffer? Why doesn't God do something about pain?

Author: Klug, Ron 825
Series: Fisherman Bible Studyguide
Title: *Philippians: God's Guide to Joy*
Publisher: Shaw, 1979 ISBN: 0-87788-680-6

Num. Sess.	Group Time	Num. Pgs.	Avg. Qst.	Price	Audience	Format	Bible Study
8	45-60	64	13	$4.99	Beginner	Workbk	Book

Features: Intro to Leading a Study, Intro to Study, Prayer Helps
★★ Personal Application Preparation Time: Low
★★ Relationship Building Ldr. Guide: No Size: 5.0 x 8.25
Subjects: Joy, Philippians, Prison Epistles, Suffering
Comments: This study presents the meaning of joy from Paul, who faced head-on all the troubles of the world—supernatural evil as well as human misunderstanding, sickness, abandonment, persecution, imprisonment, doubt, and despair—and still could say, "Rejoice in the Lord always!" The apostle's letter to the church at Philippi is filled with joy, gladness, and rejoicing. At the end of each study is a section titled "Focus on Joy."

Author: Klug, Ron 826
Series: Fisherman Bible Studyguide
Title: *Psalms: A Guide to Prayer & Praise*
Publisher: Shaw, 1979 ISBN: 0-87788-699-7

Num. Sess.	Group Time	Num. Pgs.	Avg. Qst.	Price	Audience	Format	Bible Study
12	45-60	80	12	$4.99	Beginner	Workbk	Book

Features: Intro to Study, Prayer Helps, Worship Helps, Digging Deeper Quest, Follow Up
★★ Personal Application Preparation Time: None
★★ Relationship Building Ldr. Guide: No Size: 5.0 x 8.25
Subjects: God, Psalms
Comments: This study of 16 representative psalms and their literary types leads participants on an exploration of the most beloved book of the Bible. It offers insights into who God is and how to experience deepening growth in a relationship with Him.

Author: Koester, Craig and Nancy 827
Series: Search Weekly Bible
Title: *Unit 15/John 1–8*
Publisher: Augsburg Fortress Publishers, 1986

Num. Sess.	Group Time	Num. Pgs.	Avg. Qst.	Price	Audience	Format	Bible Study
8	90-105	64	Vary	$5.50	New Christian	Book	Book

Features: Intro to Study, Objectives, Prayer Helps, Worship Helps, Follow Up, Summary
★★ Personal Application Preparation Time: Med
★★ Relationship Building Ldr. Guide: Yes Size: 8.50 x 11.0
Subjects: John
Comments: This review of John 1–8 is 1 of 20 units of a 5-year study titled "Search." The outline of unit 15: "The Word"; "Come and See"; "The Sign"; "To Be Born Anew"; "Living Water"; "From Death to Life"; "The Bread of Life"; "The Light of the World." Each of the episodes explored in this unit reveals something about Christ and something about His hearers.

Author: Koester, Craig and Nancy 828
Series: Search Weekly Bible
Title: *Unit 16/John 9–21*
Publisher: Augsburg Fortress Publishers, 1986

Num. Sess.	Group Time	Num. Pgs.	Avg. Qst.	Price	Audience	Format	Bible Study
8	90-105	64	Vary	$5.50	New Christian	Book	Book

Features: Intro to Study, Objectives, Prayer Helps, Worship Helps, Follow Up, Summary
★★ Personal Application Preparation Time: Med
★★ Relationship Building Ldr. Guide: Yes Size: 8.50 x 11.0
Subjects: Holy Spirit, John
Comments: This review of John 9–20 is 1 of 20 units of a 5-year study titled "Search." Unit 16 will build on Unit 15 and particularly develop discipleship, the Holy Spirit, and the mission of the church. Sessions include: "Now I See"; "The Resurrection and the Life"; "A Grain of Wheat"; "Discipleship"; "Abiding Presence"; "The World on Trial"; "It Is Completed"; and "Seeing and Believing."

Author: Koester, Nancy **829**
Series: Small Group Bible Studies
Title: *By Grace Through Faith*
Publisher: Augsburg Fortress Publishers, 1982

Num. Sess.	Group Time	Num. Pgs.	Avg. Qst.	Price	Audience	Format	Bible Study
6	60-75	24	14	$1.35	New Christian	Book	Book

Features: Intro to Study, Prayer Helps
★★★ Personal Application Preparation Time: None
★★★ Relationship Building Ldr. Guide: No Size: 8.50 x 5.50
Subjects: Christian Living, Church Life, Ephesians, Faith, Grace
Comments: This small pamphlet includes 6 sessions on Ephesians. The themes of Ephesians are varied, from lofty heights of praise to practical instruction for living. Major concerns include unity among believers, the purpose of the Church, and the proper Christian path; however, the heartbeat of the letter is found in Ephesians 2:8-9: "grace through faith." Ephesians divides into 2 parts: chapters 1–3 describe God's plan; chapters 4–6 instruct Christians in daily living.

Author: Koester, Nancy **830**
Series: Friendship Bible Study
Title: *1, 2, 3 John*
Publisher: Augsburg Fortress Publishers, 1986

Num. Sess.	Group Time	Num. Pgs.	Avg. Qst.	Price	Audience	Format	Bible Study
8	60-75	48	10	$3.75	New Christian	Workbk	Book

Features: Intro to Study, Prayer Helps, Study Overview
★★★★ Personal Application Preparation Time: Low
★★★★ Relationship Building Ldr. Guide: Yes Size: 5.50 x 8.50
Subjects: Faith, Love, Marriage, 1, 2 & 3 John/Jude
Comments: This 8-lesson study emphasizes Christian love and considers how that love can be realized in daily life. Questions explored in this study include: "What is the Christian message?" "What does it mean to be a child of God?" and "How can we put our faith into practice?" The lesson format includes an overview, an opening, a responsive reading, Bible background, questions for reflection, a key verse, a prayer response, and an "our faith" response.

Author: Kohlhafer, Mina **831**
Series:
Title: *Rees Howells Workbook*
Publisher: Christian Literature Crusade, 1989 ISBN: 0-87508-299-8

Num. Sess.	Group Time	Num. Pgs.	Avg. Qst.	Price	Audience	Format	Bible Study
16	105-120	105	Vary	$3.95	Mature Christian	Workbk	Topical

Features: Intro to Study, Ldr's Notes
★★ Personal Application Preparation Time: Med
★★ Relationship Building Ldr. Guide: No Size: 5.50 x 8.50
Subjects: Faith, Prayer
Comments: This study guide, based on the biography of Rees Howells, shows participants how to deal with total surrender, learn to love the unlovely, and find the key to prevailing prayer. They see Howells become the channel of a mighty revival in Africa, teach the principles of divine healing, and progress in faith until world events seemed affected by his prayers.

Author: Korth, Russ, et al. **832**
Series: God in You
Title: *Alive! God in Intimate Relationship with You*
Publisher: NavPress, 1986 ISBN: 0-89109-093-2

Num. Sess.	Group Time	Num. Pgs.	Avg. Qst.	Price	Audience	Format	Bible Study
12	45-60	65	6	$5.00	Beginner	Workbk	Topical

Features: Intro to Study, Cartoons, Charts
★★★ Personal Application Preparation Time: Low
★★ Relationship Building Ldr. Guide: Yes Size: 7.0 x 9.0
Subjects: Christian Living, Discipleship, Evangelism, God, Prayer, Relationships
Comments: This study shows participants the benefits of a deepening relationship with God. Old and New Testament passages provide the basis for lessons on giving new life, lighting the way, residing in God, providing fullness, granting access, giving guidance, being a companion, assuring triumph, reviving by His Word, and responding to prayers. Participants will learn how to keep relationships fresh and meaningful.

Author: Korth, Russ, et al. **833**
Series: God in You
Title: *Changed! Reflecting Your Love for God*
Publisher: NavPress, 1986 ISBN: 0-89109-096-7

Num. Sess.	Group Time	Num. Pgs.	Avg. Qst.	Price	Audience	Format	Bible Study
12	45-60	65	6	$5.00	Beginner	Workbk	Topical

Features: Intro to Study, Cartoons, Charts
★★★ Personal Application Preparation Time: Low
★★ Relationship Building Ldr. Guide: Yes Size: 7.0 x 9.0
Subjects: Christian Living, Discipleship, Evangelism, Family, God
Comments: This study concerns changes in people which allow them to reflect their love for God. Changes God makes on the inside, which are revealed on the outside, don't come automatically. Many are slow in coming. Lessons cover renewing; loving; being humble, generous, submissive, and uncompromising; purity; sensitivity; being a good family member; and being worshipful. Each lesson contains a cartoon, summary statement, hymn verse, Scripture reference, or quote.

Author: Korth, Russ, et al. **834**
Series: God in You
Title: *Fulfilled! Enjoying God's Purpose for You*
Publisher: NavPress, 1986 ISBN: 0-89109-097-5

Num. Sess.	Group Time	Num. Pgs.	Avg. Qst.	Price	Audience	Format	Bible Study
12	45-60	65	5	$5.00	Beginner	Workbk	Topical

Features: Intro to Study, Cartoons, Charts, Maps
★★★ Personal Application Preparation Time: Low
★★ Relationship Building Ldr. Guide: Yes Size: 7.0 x 9.0
Subjects: Christian Living, Discipleship, Evangelism, Faith, God, Service, Work
Comments: This study is designed to help Christians lead a more fulfilled life. In this study, the Scriptures lead participants to God's purpose for their lives, and fulfillment. Lesson titles include: "Offering Yourself," "Working Together," "Helping Others Grow," "Balancing Your Faith," "Caring Enough to Act," and "Praying as a Body." Lessons begin with a cartoon.

Author: Korth, Russ, et al. **835**
Series: God in You
Title: *Jesus! God in You Made Possible*
Publisher: NavPress, 1986 ISBN: 0-89109-092-4

Num. Sess.	Group Time	Num. Pgs.	Avg. Qst.	Price	Audience	Format	Bible Study
12	45-60	71	7	$5.00	Beginner	Workbk	Charctr

Features: Intro to Study, Cartoons, Charts
★★★ Personal Application Preparation Time: Low
★★ Relationship Building Ldr. Guide: Yes Size: 7.0 x 9.0
Subjects: Discipleship, Evangelism, God, Gospels
Comments: This study examines Jesus through eyewitness accounts of His life. Each lesson deals with one specific portion of Scripture, from Matthew, Mark, Luke, John, or Acts. Participants will see Jesus called Immanuel, the Word, Savior, Friend of Sinners, Master, Christ, Servant, Bread of Life, Great High Priest, Man of Sorrows, Lord God Omnipotent, and King of Kings. Each lesson begins with a cartoon and concludes with a summary statement, hymn verse, Scripture reference.

Author: Korth, Russ, et al. **836**
Series: God in You
Title: *Powerful! God Enabling You*
Publisher: NavPress, 1986 ISBN: 0-89109-095-9

Num. Sess.	Group Time	Num. Pgs.	Avg. Qst.	Price	Audience	Format	Bible Study
12	45-60	63	7	$5.00	Beginner	Workbk	Topical

Features: Intro to Study, Objectives, Summary, Cartoons, Charts
★★★ Personal Application Preparation Time: Low
★★ Relationship Building Ldr. Guide: Yes Size: 7.0 x 9.0
Subjects: Christian Living, Discipleship, Evangelism, Faith, God, Prayer, Suffering
Comments: This study explores 12 Scriptural passages in short lessons and introduces participants to God's power and His armor: the Scriptures, prayer, and faith. Through His Holy Spirit, and through cooperation with others, participants can find strength to testify and persevere. This study proves that God's power can enable one to overcome adversity and accomplish great things.

Author: Korth, Russ, et al. **837**
Series: God in You
Title: *Rich! God Meeting Your Deepest Needs*
Publisher: NavPress, 1986 ISBN: 0-89109-094-0

Num. Sess.	Group Time	Num. Pgs.	Avg. Qst.	Price	Audience	Format	Bible Study
12	45-60	63	7	$5.00	Beginner	Workbk	Topical

Features: Intro to Study, Cartoons, Charts
★★★ Personal Application Preparation Time: Low
★★ Relationship Building Ldr. Guide: Yes Size: 7.0 x 9.0
Subjects: Christian Living, Discipleship, Evangelism, God, Grace, Hope, Wisdom
Comments: This study shows how God touches people's lives by meeting their deepest needs, including love, grace, peace, acceptance, clear conscience, wisdom, comfort, freedom, provision, family, courage, and hope. Each lesson begins with a cartoon and concludes with a summary statement, hymn verse, additional Scripture reference, or a quote from a famous theologian.

Author: Korth, Russ, et. al. **838**
Series: God in You
Title: *Leader's Guide: God In You Series*
Publisher: NavPress, 1986 ISBN: 0-89109-098-3

Num. Sess.	Group Time	Num. Pgs.	Avg. Qst.	Price	Audience	Format	Bible Study
7	—	151	N/A	$7.00			

Features: Intro to Study
Personal Application Preparation Time:
Relationship Building Ldr. Guide: Size: 5.50 x 8.50
Subjects: Leader's Guide
Comments: This leader's guide, supporting every lesson of every study in the series, includes brief background information related to each Scripture passage, additional group discussion questions, and suggestions for the leader that will make the small group experience most helpful to the members. A teaching objective and summary are also given.

Author: Kuhatschek, Jack **839**
Series: LifeGuide Bible Study
Title: *David: A Heart for God*
Publisher: InterVarsity, 1990 ISBN: 0-83081-063-3

Num. Sess.	Group Time	Num. Pgs.	Avg. Qst.	Price	Audience	Format	Bible Study
12	45-60	62	11	$4.99	Beginner	Workbk	Charctr

Features: Intro to Leading a Study, Intro to Study, Ldr's Notes
★★★ Personal Application Preparation Time: Low
★★★ Relationship Building Ldr. Guide: No Size: 5.50 x 8.25
Subjects: Bible Personalities, God, 1 & 2 Samuel
Comments: This 12-week study of David's life helps participants discover what it means to have a passionate heart for God. It observes David from childhood to the end of his life, selecting key events which reveal his multifaceted character. Contemporary role models are desperately needed—not comic-book superheroes impossible to imitate, but flesh-and-blood people. David is such a role model.

Author: Kuhatschek, Jack **840**
Series: LifeGuide Bible Study
Title: *Galatians: Why God Accepts Us*
Publisher: InterVarsity, 1990 ISBN: 0-83081-011-0

Num. Sess.	Group Time	Num. Pgs.	Avg. Qst.	Price	Audience	Format	Bible Study
12	45-60	64	11	$4.99	Beginner	Workbk	Topical

Features: Intro to Leading a Study, Intro to Study, Ldr's Notes
★★★ Personal Application Preparation Time: Low
★★★ Relationship Building Ldr. Guide: No Size: 5.50 x 8.25
Subjects: Christian Living, Galatians, God, Repentance
Comments: This study is a testimony to the futility of people trying to earn God's acceptance when they are already accepted in Christ. Since the world often accepts only the attractive, smart, wealthy, or powerful, many people think they must work harder, live better, pray longer, and witness more to impress God. Paul's message frees Christians from living with guilt, offers fresh assurance of God's love, and provides renewed power to serve Him.

Author: Kuhatschek, Jack **841**
Series: The Knowing God Series
Title: *Our Glorius Lord: Beholding God's Majesty*
Publisher: Zondervan, 1994 ISBN: 0-31048-361-1

Num. Sess.	Group Time	Num. Pgs.	Avg. Qst.	Price	Audience	Format	Bible Study
6	45-60	64	11	$4.99	Beginner	Workbk	Topical

Features: Intro to Leading a Study, Intro to Study, Objectives, Prayer Helps, Scrpt Memory Helps, Follow Up, Ldr's Notes
★★★★ Personal Application Preparation Time: Low
★★★ Relationship Building Ldr. Guide: No Size: 5.50 x 8.50
Subjects: God
Comments: One of eight in a series, this guide explores the majesty and glory of God. It reveals how participants can be personally transformed from one degree of glory to another. Lessons include: "God's Glory in Creation"; "A Vision of God's Glory"; "Revealing God's Glory"; "Declaring God's Glory"; "The Glory of God's Son"; and "Transformed By Glory."

Author: Kuhatschek, Jack **842**
Series: The Knowing God Series
Title: *Our Loving Father: Feeling God's Embrace*
Publisher: Zondervan, 1994 ISBN: 0-31048-291-7

Num. Sess.	Group Time	Num. Pgs.	Avg. Qst.	Price	Audience	Format	Bible Study
6	45-60	64	13	$4.99	New Christian	Workbk	Topical

Features: Intro to Leading a Study, Intro to Study, Objectives, Prayer Helps, Scrpt Memory Helps, Follow Up, Ldr's Notes, Charts
★★★★ Personal Application Preparation Time: Low
★★★ Relationship Building Ldr. Guide: No Size: 5.50 x 8.50
Subjects: Faith, God
Comments: One of 8 in a series, this guide explores the depth of God's love for His children. For many Christians, God's love seems more like a cold "concept" than a warm reality. The Bible presents an astounding portrait of the heavenly Father. The lessons in this guide reveal a God who will always love, who will never leave, who takes care of, comforts, disciplines, and wants His people to be like Him.

Author: Kuhatschek, Jack **843**
Series: Fruit of the Spirit
Title: *Peace: Overcoming Anxiety and Conflict*
Publisher: Zondervan, 1991 ISBN: 0-31053-741-X

Num. Sess.	Group Time	Num. Pgs.	Avg. Qst.	Price	Audience	Format	Bible Study
6	45-60	48	12	$4.99	New Christian	Workbk	Topical

Features: Intro to Study, Ldr's Notes
★★★ Personal Application Preparation Time: None
★★ Relationship Building Ldr. Guide: No Size: 5.50 x 8.50
Subjects: Christian Living, Emotions, Fruit of the Spirit, God, Relationships, Stress
Comments: This 6-week study, using selected Psalms and New Testament passages, explores God's prescription for peace. It helps participants discover how to cope with anxiety, feel safe in God's care, and live at peace with others. It helps answer these questions: How can one experience the "peace which transcends all understanding"? and, How can we guard our hearts and minds from the stress of everyday life?

Author: Kuhatschek, Jack **844**
Series: LifeGuide Bible Study
Title: *Romans: Becoming New in Christ*
Publisher: InterVarsity, 1986 ISBN: 0-83081-008-0

Num. Sess.	Group Time	Num. Pgs.	Avg. Qst.	Price	Audience	Format	Bible Study
21	45-60	94	10	$4.99	New Christian	Workbk	Book

Features: Intro to Leading a Study, Intro to Study, Ldr's Notes
★ Personal Application Preparation Time: Low
★ Relationship Building Ldr. Guide: No Size: 5.50 x 8.25
Subjects: Jesus: Life/Teaching, Romans
Comments: Romans is the clearest and fullest explanation of the Gospel in the Bible. Today, many preach a Gospel which lacks clarity and substance. People make decisions to "follow Christ" without clear understanding of the meaning of His death and resurrection. Paul, in his letter to the Romans, expresses what he would have liked to have said in person. This guide is divided into 2 parts, one containing 12 studies and the other with 9.

Author: Kuhatschek, Jack **845**
Series: Fruit of the Spirit
Title: *Self-Control: Mastering Our Passions*
Publisher: Zondervan, 1991 ISBN: 0-31053-731-2

Num. Sess.	Group Time	Num. Pgs.	Avg. Qst.	Price	Audience	Format	Bible Study
6	45-60	48	12	$4.99	New Christian	Workbk	Topical

Features: Intro to Study, Ldr's Notes
★★★ Personal Application Preparation Time: None
★★ Relationship Building Ldr. Guide: No Size: 5.50 x 8.50
Subjects: Accountability, Christian Living, Fruit of the Spirit, Money
Comments: This 6-week study, using passages from Proverbs and the New Testament, helps participants master self-control over their passions. It explores five crucial areas of control: the tongue, the body, desires, appetites, and finances. The final study considers what it means to clothe oneself with Jesus Christ.

Author: Kuhatschek, Jack **846**
Series: LifeGuide Bible Study
Title: *Self-Esteem: Seeing Ourselves As God Sees Us*
Publisher: InterVarsity, 1990 ISBN: 0-83081-065-X

Num. Sess.	Group Time	Num. Pgs.	Avg. Qst.	Price	Audience	Format	Bible Study
9	45-60	62	11	$4.99	New Christian	Workbk	Topical

Features: Intro to Leading a Study, Intro to Study, Prayer Helps, Ldr's Notes
★★★ Personal Application Preparation Time: Low
★★ Relationship Building Ldr. Guide: No Size: 5.50 x 8.25
Subjects: God, Psychology, Self-esteem
Comments: This 9-week study on self-esteem helps participants gain a biblically balanced vision of who they are in Christ. The first 5 studies provide a foundation for healthy self-esteem. The next 4 reveal the multifaceted and sometimes contradictory nature of Christians: old yet new, weak yet strong, poor yet rich, dying yet alive. Not a resource for those seeking recovery from badly wounded self-esteem.

Author: Kuhatschek, Jack **847**
Series: The Beatitude Series
Title: *Spiritual Poverty: The Path to True Riches*
Publisher: Zondervan, 1993 ISBN: 0-31059-603-3

Num. Sess.	Group Time	Num. Pgs.	Avg. Qst.	Price	Audience	Format	Bible Study
6	45-60	48	11	$4.99	New Christian	Workbk	Topical

Features: Intro to Leading a Study, Intro to Study, Objectives, Prayer Helps, Follow Up, Ldr's Notes
★★★★ Personal Application Preparation Time: Low
★★ Relationship Building Ldr. Guide: No Size: 5.50 x 8.25
Subjects: Sermon on the Mount
Comments: This is 1 of 8 guides in the Beatitude series. The 6 passages in this study help participants develop a humble dependence on God. They strip away pride and shatter a false sense of security. The purpose is not to wound but heal. Lesson titles include: "Who Are the Poor?"; "Admitting Our Need"; "Seeing Our Blindness"; "Seeking God's Mercy"; "Treasures in Heaven"; and more.

Author: Kuhatschek, Jack **848**
Series: LifeGuide Bible Study
Title: *Suffering: Receiving God's Comfort*
Publisher: InterVarsity, 1992 ISBN: 0-83081-067-6

Num. Sess.	Group Time	Num. Pgs.	Avg. Qst.	Price	Audience	Format	Bible Study
10	45-60	64	12	$4.99	New Christian	Workbk	Topical

Features: Intro to Leading a Study, Intro to Study, Prayer Helps, Ldr's Notes
★★ Personal Application Preparation Time: Low
★★ Relationship Building Ldr. Guide: No Size: 5.50 x 8.25
Subjects: Suffering
Comments: This study of suffering helps participants discover how to meet God in their struggles, and receive His strength and grace. Participants learn not to analyze suffering and its varied effects, but to focus on people who suffer and why they respond well or poorly. Lessons cover such Bible personalities as Job, Paul, David, and the Lord Himself.

Author: Kuniholm, Whitney **849**
Series: Fisherman Bible Studyguide
Title: *Galatians, Titus & Philemon*
Publisher: Shaw, 1989 ISBN: 0-87788-307-6

Num. Sess.	Group Time	Num. Pgs.	Avg. Qst.	Price	Audience	Format	Bible Study
13	45-60	63	10	$4.99	New Christian	Workbk	Book

Features: Intro to Leading a Study, Intro to Study, Ldr's Notes, Maps
★★★★ Personal Application Preparation Time: Low
★★ Relationship Building Ldr. Guide: No Size: 5.25 x 8.25
Subjects: Colossians/Philemon, Galatians, 1 & 2 Timothy/Titus
Comments: This study covers three letters that Paul wrote so believers could rejoice in the true freedom Christ gives. Paul wrote Galatians to defend the Gospel—the Good News that we are saved by faith alone. Titus enforces this truth—we have been saved not because of good deeds, but to do good deeds. And Philemon continues the freedom theme with the account of a slave whose story is a parable of our redemption.

Author: Kuniholm, Whitney **850**
Series: Fisherman Bible Studyguide
Title: *John: The Living Word*
Publisher: Shaw, 1992 ISBN: 0-87788-429-3

Num. Sess.	Group Time	Num. Pgs.	Avg. Qst.	Price	Audience	Format	Bible Study
23	45-60	94	12	$4.99	Beginner	Workbk	Book

Features: Intro to Leading a Study, Intro to Study, Ldr's Notes
★★★★ Personal Application Preparation Time: None
★★ Relationship Building Ldr. Guide: No Size: 5.25 x 8.25
Subjects: Jesus: Life/Teaching, John
Comments: This 23 week study is a concise, simplified study of Jesus' life and teachings as chronicled in the Gospel of John. It helps participants come face-to-face with the Son of God—who He is and what it means to follow Him. If used with beginners, the study probably should be divided into 6-lesson sections, using each 7th week as a break. With new Christians it could be covered in a year.

Author: LaHaye, Tim **851**
Series:
Title: *Spirit Controlled Temperament*
Publisher: Tyndale House, 1992 ISBN: 0-84236-220-7

Num. Sess.	Group Time	Num. Pgs.	Avg. Qst.	Price	Audience	Format	Bible Study
14	60-75	250	8	$8.99	Beginner	Book	Topical

Features: Intro to Study, Bibliography, Drawings
★★★★ Personal Application Preparation Time: None
★ Relationship Building Ldr. Guide: No Size: 5.25 x 8.25
Subjects: Christian Living, Leadership, Relationships
Comments: This book, a 14-week study of basic temperaments and how God can use them, has been revised with new chapters and questions for group study. Everyone is born with a temperament that includes strengths as well as weaknesses that can impede spiritual growth. This study helps participants determine their predominant temperament—Sanguine, Choleric, Melancholy, or Phlegmatic. Available in Spanish.

Author: Lake, Vicki **852**
Series: A Bible Study for Women
Title: *Firming Up Your Flabby Faith*
Publisher: Victor Books, 1990 ISBN: 0-89693-783-6

Num. Sess.	Group Time	Num. Pgs.	Avg. Qst.	Price	Audience	Format	Bible Study
8	60-75	95	10	$5.99	New Christian	Workbk	Topical

Features: Intro to Study, Prayer Helps, Scrpt Memory Helps, Follow Up, Ldr's Notes
★★★★ Personal Application Preparation Time: Med
★★★★ Relationship Building Ldr. Guide: No Size: 6.0 x 9.0
Subjects: Faith, James, Women's Issues
Comments: This study on firming up faith helps participants recognize that their spiritual fitness needs shaping up. By applying the practical principles of James, they can restore spiritual health by the daily discipline of reading, applying, and memorizing God's Word. Each lesson contains a series of inductive questions, a narrative section, and a journaling section.

Author: Lake, Vicki **853**
Series: Tapestry Collection
Title: *Restored in the Ruins*
Publisher: Victor Books, 1992 ISBN: 0-89693-877-8

Num. Sess.	Group Time	Num. Pgs.	Avg. Qst.	Price	Audience	Format	Bible Study
8	75-90	95	9	$5.99	New Christian	Workbk	Book

Features: Intro to Leading a Study, Intro to Study, Objectives, Prayer Helps, Scrpt Memory Helps, Follow Up, Ldr's Notes, Persnl Study Quest
★★★★ Personal Application Preparation Time: Med
★★★ Relationship Building Ldr. Guide: No Size: 6.0 x 9.0
Subjects: Ezra/Nehemiah, Women's Issues
Comments: This 8-week study helps participants who panic and feel powerless in the face of obstacles, who have disorganized lives, or who've forgotten how to praise God. Nehemiah takes on an impossible task, mobilizes and organizes helpers, then praises God. Participants learn how following Nehemiah's example can generate power, purpose, and praise in their lives. The study includes journaling exercises.

Author: Lambert, David **854**
Series: The Beatitude Series
Title: *Joy In Suffering: Receiving Your Reward*
Publisher: Zondervan, 1993 ISBN: 0-31059-673-4

Num. Sess.	Group Time	Num. Pgs.	Avg. Qst.	Price	Audience	Format	Bible Study
6	45-60	63	13	$4.99	New Christian	Workbk	Topical

Features: Intro to Leading a Study, Intro to Study, Objectives, Scrpt Memory Helps, Follow Up, Ldr's Notes
★★★★ Personal Application Preparation Time: Low
★★ Relationship Building Ldr. Guide: No Size: 5.50 x 8.25
Subjects: Sermon on the Mount, Suffering
Comments: This is 1 of 8 guides in the Beatitude series. Everyone suffers in one way or another. But not everyone responds to suffering in the same way. Some people become bitter and cynical. They think life is against them and God has abandoned them. Others have a more positive response. They feel closer to God and actually feel joy—not because of their sufferings but in spite of them.

Author: Lambert, David **855**
Series: The Beatitude Series
Title: *Showing Mercy: Getting What You Give*
Publisher: Zondervan, 1993 ISBN: 0-31059-663-7

Num. Sess.	Group Time	Num. Pgs.	Avg. Qst.	Price	Audience	Format	Bible Study
6	45-60	62	12	$4.99	New Christian	Workbk	Topical

Features: Intro to Leading a Study, Intro to Study, Objectives, Scrpt Memory Helps, Follow Up, Ldr's Notes
★★★★ Personal Application Preparation Time: Low
★★ Relationship Building Ldr. Guide: No Size: 5.50 x 8.25
Subjects: Caring, Mercy, Sermon on the Mount
Comments: This study highlights why those who want to receive mercy—from God and others—must be willing to give it. For the Christian, mercy is not an option. God does not demand that we follow pharisaical rules and laws, but rather desires mercy, justice, and humble fellowship with Him. Lesson titles include: "God's Great Mercy to Us"; "Being Merciful to Others"; "Models of Mercy."

Author: Larsen, Dale & Sandy **856**
Series: Shaw Contemporary Issues
Title: *Managing Money*
Publisher: Shaw, 1993 ISBN: 0-87788-520-6

Num. Sess.	Group Time	Num. Pgs.	Avg. Qst.	Price	Audience	Format	Bible Study
8	30-45	48	8	$4.99	New Christian	Workbk	Topical

Features: Intro to Leading a Study, Intro to Study, Objectives, Bibliography, Follow Up, Ldr's Notes
★★★★ Personal Application Preparation Time: Low
★★★ Relationship Building Ldr. Guide: No Size: 5.25 x 8.25
Subjects: Accountability, Materialism, Money
Comments: Eight brief lessons help participants consider how to view money in a way that is both practical and Christ-centered. Lessons focus on participants' personal lives: "I want it, but do I need it?" "How much should I give?" "When am I too attached to my paycheck?" "Giving: With Grace or a Grimace?" "Is It Saving or Is It Hoarding?" The author suggests journaling and provides guidelines.

Author: Larsen, Dale & Sandy **857**
Series: Teamwork Discipleship
Title: *Maturing in Christ*
Publisher: InterVarsity, 1993 ISBN: 0-83081-127-3

Num. Sess.	Group Time	Num. Pgs.	Avg. Qst.	Price	Audience	Format	Bible Study
6	30-60	92	5	$4.99	Beginner	Workbk	Topical

Features: Intro to Leading a Study, Prayer Helps
★★★★ Personal Application Preparation Time: Med
★★★★ Relationship Building Ldr. Guide: No Size: 5.50 x 8.25
Subjects: Christian Life, Discipleship, God's Promises
Comments: Teamwork guides are designed to help mature Christians mentor people exploring the Christian faith. Each of 6 studies is divided into 5 sections for weekday Bible reading and study. Mentor and new Christians meet to discuss highlights of the week's studies. This study looks closely at what it means in practical terms to live in Christ and have Christ living in you. It also deals with questions about forgiveness, suffering, sexuality, and obedience.

Author: Larsen, Dale & Sandy **858**
Series: Fisherman Bible Studyguide
Title: *Moneywise: Biblical Spending, Saving, Sharing*
Publisher: Shaw, 1992 ISBN: 0-87788-550-8

Num. Sess.	Group Time	Num. Pgs.	Avg. Qst.	Price	Audience	Format	Bible Study
12	45-60	61	11	$4.99	Beginner	Workbk	Topical

Features: Intro to Leading a Study, Intro to Study, Bibliography, Ldr's Notes
★★★★ Personal Application Preparation Time: None
★★ Relationship Building Ldr. Guide: No Size: 5.25 x 8.25
Subjects: Christian Living, Materialism, Money
Comments: This 12-week study examines key biblical texts concerning money, stewardship, and use of resurces. Lessons include: "What Good Is Money?" "God or Money (Do We Have to Choose?)" "The Love of Money"; "When Money Lies"; "Rich and Poor"; "Spending"; "The Costly Cost of Credit"; "Saving for a Rainy Day . . . or Even Dry One"; "Giving: With Grace or a Grimace?" "The Tithe: Still in Effect?"

Author: Larsen, Dale & Sandy **859**
Series: Fisherman Bible Studyguide
Title: *One Body, One Spirit*
Publisher: Shaw, 1988 ISBN: 0-87788-619-9

Num. Sess.	Group Time	Num. Pgs.	Avg. Qst.	Price	Audience	Format	Bible Study
12	45-60	80	10	$4.99	New Christian	Workbk	Topical

Features: Intro to Leading a Study, Intro to Study, Prayer Helps, Follow Up, Ldr's Notes
★★ Personal Application Preparation Time: None
★★ Relationship Building Ldr. Guide: No Size: 5.0 x 8.25
Subjects: Christian Living, Church Life, Holy Spirit
Comments: These studies explore how Christians can discern the difference between Christian unity and simple conformity to practices within the church. Concepts regarding "unity among Christians" include: merging into one superchurch, celebrating communion exactly the same way, saying identical prayers, singing the same kind of music, meeting in the same building, and more.

Author: Larsen, Dale & Sandy **860**
Series: Teamwork Discipleship
Title: *Starting With Christ*
Publisher: InterVarsity, 1993 ISBN: 0-83081-126-5

Num. Sess.	Group Time	Num. Pgs.	Avg. Qst.	Price	Audience	Format	Bible Study
6	30-60	104	5	$4.99	Beginner	Workbk	Topical

Features: Intro to Leading a Study, Prayer Helps
★★★★ Personal Application Preparation Time: Med
★★★★ Relationship Building Ldr. Guide: No Size: 5.50 x 8.25
Subjects: Apologetics, Discipleship, Singles' Issues
Comments: Teamwork guides are designed to help mature Christians mentor people exploring the Christian faith. Each of 6 studies is divided into 5 sections for weekday Bible reading and study. Mentors and new Christian meet to discuss highlights of the week's studies. This guide is for participants who want to learn more about Christian faith. It explores topics like "Who is Jesus Christ?" "Why the Cross?" "Who's a Christian?" and "What Makes Faith Confident?"

Author: Larsen, Dale & Sandy **861**
Series: Shaw Contemporary Issues
Title: *Tending Creation*
Publisher: Shaw, 1991 ISBN: 0-87788-806-X

Num. Sess.	Group Time	Num. Pgs.	Avg. Qst.	Price	Audience	Format	Bible Study
8	30-45	48	5	$4.99	Beginner	Workbk	Topical

Features: Intro to Leading a Study, Intro to Study, Bibliography, Follow Up, Ldr's Notes
★★★★ Personal Application Preparation Time: Low
★★★ Relationship Building Ldr. Guide: No Size: 5.25 x 8.25
Subjects: Social Issues
Comments: Eight short lessons help participants become more aware of their responsibilities for tending the earth. Questions include: What is our responsibility toward God's world? What does it mean to have dominion over the earth? and How can we enjoy creation without exploiting it? As a result of this study, participants will question years of silence, pollution, and waste.

Author: Larson, Ellen E. & David V. Esterline **862**
Series: Tapestry Collection
Title: *More Than a Story*
Publisher: Victor Books, 1991 ISBN: 0-89693-813-1

Num. Sess.	Group Time	Num. Pgs.	Avg. Qst.	Price	Audience	Format	Bible Study
9	60-90	96	Vary	$5.99	New Christian	Workbk	Topical

Features: Intro to Leading a Study, Intro to Study, Prayer Helps, Digging Deeper Quest, Follow Up, Ldr's Notes, Persnl Study Quest
★★★★ Personal Application Preparation Time: Low
★★★ Relationship Building Ldr. Guide: No Size: 6.0 x 9.0
Subjects: Parables, Prayer, Women's Issues
Comments: This inductive Bible study for women examines 8 parables of Jesus. Each lesson includes a narrative, application questions, and exercises in prayer. These parables challenge women at every stage of life, and every level of Christian maturity.

Author: Larson, Knute **863**
Series: Equipped For Ministry
Title: *Growing Adults on Sunday Morning*
Publisher: Victor Books, 1991 ISBN: 0-89693-822-0

Num. Sess.	Group Time	Num. Pgs.	Avg. Qst.	Price	Audience	Format	Bible Study
9	—	119	N/A	$9.99		Book	Topical

Features: Bibliography, No Grp Discussion Quest, Appendix
Personal Application Preparation Time:
Relationship Building Ldr. Guide: Size: 6.0 x 9.0
Subjects: Church Life, Small Group Resource
Comments: This book emphasizes the need for believers to meet together regularly, to care for each other and study God's Word. The author shows how this can be done by establishing Adult Bible Fellowships (ABFs). A step beyond traditional adult Sunday School classes, these groups provide organized fellowship, defined caring, accountability in ministry, teaching time, and outreach opportunities. ABFs are congregations within a congregation. A variety of groups are described.

Author: Larson, Ruth H. **864**
Series:
Title: *Beginning to Study the Bible: Student*
Publisher: Cokesbury, 1993 ISBN: 0-68778-210-4

Num. Sess.	Group Time	Num. Pgs.	Avg. Qst.	Price	Audience	Format	Bible Study
8	60-90	32	Vary	$3.95	Beginner	Workbk	Topical

Features:
★★★★ Personal Application Preparation Time: None
★★★★ Relationship Building Ldr. Guide: Yes Size: 8.25 x 11.0
Subjects: Bible Study
Comments: This study helps adults with low reading skills who are just beginning to learn English grow spiritually while improving their English reading skills. Written on a third grade reading level, it can also be used with intergenerational groups. Adults can learn to find references in the Bible and to identify major parts of the Bible. They can grow spiritually as they begin to read and study the Bible for themselves.

Author: Larson, Ruth H. **865**
Series:
Title: *Beginning to Study the Bible: Teacher*
Publisher: Cokesbury, 1993 ISBN: 0-68778-211-2

Num. Sess.	Group Time	Num. Pgs.	Avg. Qst.	Price	Audience	Format	Bible Study
8	60-90	48	Vary	$6.95	Beginner	Workbk	Topical

Features: Intro to Study, Bibliography
Personal Application Preparation Time:
Relationship Building Ldr. Guide: Size: 8.25 x 11.0
Subjects: Bible Study
Comments: This study helps adults with low reading skills and adults who are just beginning to learn English grow spiritually while improving their English reading skills. Written on a third grade reading level, it can also be used with intergenerational groups. This teacher book includes an introductory section, the text of the student book with answers for the exercises, and brief guidance for teaching each lesson.

Author: Lawrence, Rick **866**
Series: Group's Active Bible Curriculum
Title: *Evil and the Occult*
Publisher: Group Publishing, 1990 ISBN: 1-55945-102-5

Num. Sess.	Group Time	Num. Pgs.	Avg. Qst.	Price	Audience	Format	Bible Study
4	35-60	46	Vary	$9.99	Beginner	Workbk	Topical

Features: Intro to Leading a Study, Intro to Study, Objectives, Study Overview, Ldr's Notes, Handouts, Agenda, Publicity Ideas
★★★ Personal Application Preparation Time: None
★★★ Relationship Building Ldr. Guide: No Size: 8.50 x 11.0
Subjects: Teens: Junior High, Teens: Occult
Comments: In this study, teenagers will learn to protect themselves against the trap of satanism, and discover how to draw strength from God to overcome fears of evil and the unknown. Four lessons outline the attraction of the occult and warning signs of occult involvement, and recognize the differences between Christianity and the occult. It can be adapted for a Bible class or youth meeting.

Author: Lawson, LeRoy **867**
Series:
Title: *Come to the Party! Celebrate Jesus*
Publisher: Standard Publishing, 1994 ISBN: 0-78470-144-X

Num. Sess.	Group Time	Num. Pgs.	Avg. Qst.	Price	Audience	Format	Bible Study
13	30-60	190	9	$5.99	New Christian	Book	Topical

Features: Intro to Study
★★★ Personal Application Preparation Time: None
★★★ Relationship Building Ldr. Guide: Yes Size: 5.25 x 8.50
Subjects: Worship
Comments: In this study the author defines "celebrating" using modern terms and interpretations. Biblical events discussed include Luke's birth in the city of Mesa, Jesus at the wedding, the feeding of five thousand people, and more. Chapter 10 deals with "The Big Event" (the story of end times) as told in Luke and Revelation.

Author: Lawson, LeRoy **868**
Series:
Title: *Strength Not My Own*
Publisher: Standard Publishing, 1992 ISBN: 0-87403-746-8

Num. Sess.	Group Time	Num. Pgs.	Avg. Qst.	Price	Audience	Format	Bible Study
13	60-75	160	N/A	$5.99	New Christian	Book	Topical

Features: Intro to Study
★★ Personal Application Preparation Time: Low
★★ Relationship Building Ldr. Guide: Yes Size: 5.25 x 8.50
Subjects: Christian Life
Comments: This book reflects the author's own physical struggles, and shows how personally true and fulfilling are Paul's words to the Corinthians, "with a strength not my own" (2 Cor. 12). It traces a scared, asthmatic youth through one revelation after another, using memorized Scripture to hold each point, until he embodies the truth that if we hand over our handicaps and weaknesses, God will transform them into strengths and assets. A leader's guide is available.

Author: Lebar, Lois E. & James E. Plueddemann **869**
Series: GroupBuilder Resources
Title: *Education That Is Christian*
Publisher: Victor Books, 1995 ISBN: 1-56476-412-5

Num. Sess.	Group Time	Num. Pgs.	Avg. Qst.	Price	Audience	Format	Bible Study
	—	320	N/A	$12.99		Book	

Features:
Personal Application Preparation Time:
Relationship Building Ldr. Guide: Size: 6.0 x 9.0
Subjects: Church Life, Family, Small Group Resource
Comments: Anyone interested in revitalizing the teaching of the Bible will benefit from this book, which provides a strategic vision for education that will produce Christlike people. Each chapter is updated with implications for families, churches, and schools by Plueddemann, former chairman of educational ministries at Wheaton (IL) College.

Author: Lee, Harris W. **870**
Series: Small Group Bible Studies
Title: *That You May Have Life*
Publisher: Augsburg Fortress Publishers, 1976

Num. Sess.	Group Time	Num. Pgs.	Avg. Qst.	Price	Audience	Format	Bible Study
8	60-75	32	Vary	$1.45	New Christian	Book	Topical

Features: Intro to Study, Prayer Helps
★★★ Personal Application Preparation Time: None
★★★ Relationship Building Ldr. Guide: No Size: 8.50 x 5.50
Subjects: Jesus: Life/Teaching, John
Comments: This small pamphlet contains eight lessons taken from the Book of John. Among the unique features of this Gospel are Jesus' "I am" sayings: "I am the door . . . the way, the truth, and the life . . . the light of the world . . . the vine . . . the bread of life . . . the good shepherd . . . the resurrection and the life." Participants are reminded, as they pursue these sayings' meanings for today, of the promise of "life" which runs through John's entire book.

Author: Lee-Thorp, Karen **871**
Series: Thinking Through Disciple
Title: *Exploring the Essentials*
Publisher: NavPress, 1993 ISBN: 0-89109-736-8

Num. Sess.	Group Time	Num. Pgs.	Avg. Qst.	Price	Audience	Format	Bible Study
8	60-75	77	12	$5.00	New Christian	Workbk	Topical

Features: Prayer Helps, Scrpt Memory Helps, Follow Up, Ldr's Notes
★★★★ Personal Application Preparation Time: None
★★★ Relationship Building Ldr. Guide: No Size: 5.50 x 8.50
Subjects: Jesus: Life/Teaching
Comments: This study, 1 of 4 in a series, provides a look at what it means to follow Christ in modern culture. The lessons explore what the Gospel is and its personal implications. Participants look at what the Bible says about who we are, what God is like, who Jesus is, the reasons for the cross, what it means to be part of God's kingdom now, and what we set our hopes on. Christ's impact on daily situations is discussed.

Author: Lee-Thorp, Karen **872**
Series: Thinking Through Disciple
Title: *Who's in Control*
Publisher: NavPress, 1993 ISBN: 0-89109-739-2

Num. Sess.	Group Time	Num. Pgs.	Avg. Qst.	Price	Audience	Format	Bible Study
8	60-75	73	10	$5.00	New Christian	Workbk	Topical

Features: Prayer Helps, Scrpt Memory Helps, Follow Up, Ldr's Notes
★★★★ Personal Application Preparation Time: None
★★★ Relationship Building Ldr. Guide: No Size: 5.50 x 8.50
Subjects: Relationships
Comments: This study, 1 of 4 in a series, provides a look at what it means to follow Christ in modern culture. Eight lessons examine some of the reasons behind the battle for control that everyone faces. Participants explore what it means to let Christ take charge of their past, struggles with sin, the pain life throws, money, and nature and the environment. Leader's notes are in the margin of this study.

Author: Le Peau, Andrew T. & Phyllis J. **873**
Series: LifeGuide Bible Study
Title: *Ephesians: Wholeness for a Broken World*
Publisher: InterVarsity, 1985 ISBN: 0-83081-012-9

Num. Sess.	Group Time	Num. Pgs.	Avg. Qst.	Price	Audience	Format	Bible Study
13	45-60	64	13	$4.99	Beginner	Workbk	Book

Features: Intro to Leading a Study, Intro to Study, Ldr's Notes
★ Personal Application Preparation Time: Low
★ Relationship Building Ldr. Guide: No Size: 5.50 x 8.25
Subjects: Ephesians, Friendships, Marriage, Prison Epistles, Relationships, Wholeness
Comments: Broken marriages, shattered friendships, racial divisions, rifts between nations—we live in a fractured world. How can the pieces be put back together? In Ephesians Paul lifts the veil of the future to show God's new creation; His plan to right everyone and everything in Christ. This study helps people handle the present by putting their problems and lives in the context of eternity.

Author: Le Peau, Andrew T. & Phyllis J. **874**
Series: LifeGuide Bible Study
Title: *James: Faith That Works*
Publisher: InterVarsity, 1987 ISBN: 0-83081-018-8

Num. Sess.	Group Time	Num. Pgs.	Avg. Qst.	Price	Audience	Format	Bible Study
11	45-60	62	12	$4.99	New Christian	Workbk	Book

Features: Intro to Leading a Study, Intro to Study, Ldr's Notes
★ Personal Application Preparation Time: Low
★ Relationship Building Ldr. Guide: No Size: 5.50 x 8.25
Subjects: Christian Living, Faith, James, Money, Time
Comments: James is a practical study built around life's imperfections. How does one handle trouble when it hits? In terminology easy to understand, James treats subjects like "words"—how to talk to others; "money"—how to handle it; and "time"—the use of it. The opening study, an overview, helps put the next nine studies in perspective, while the final chapter adds cohesion. James calls for living a consistent Christian life and developing a practical faith.

Author: Le Peau, Andrew T. & Phyllis J. **875**
Series:
Title: *One Plus One Equals One*
Publisher: InterVarsity, 1981 ISBN: 0-87784-803-3

Num. Sess.	Group Time	Num. Pgs.	Avg. Qst.	Price	Audience	Format	Bible Study
16	60-75	130	11	$6.99	Beginner	Workbk	Topical

Features: Intro to Study, Ldr's Notes, Appendix
★★★ Personal Application Preparation Time: Med
★★★ Relationship Building Ldr. Guide: No Size: 5.50 x 8.25
Subjects: Divorce, Family, Love, Marriage, Sexual Issues
Comments: This 16-week study helps couples or small groups of couples work to improve their marriages. Topics covered include expectations, self-image, sex, family life, submission, communication, forgiveness, divorce, children, possessions, and priorities. An appendix offers practical suggestions for planning in marriage. The final part focuses on love, which binds an entire marriage together. Leader's notes include objectives and questions for each lesson.

Author: Le Peau, Phyllis J. **876**
Series: LifeGuide Bible Study
Title: *Acts*
Publisher: InterVarsity, 1992 ISBN: 0-83081-007-2

Num. Sess.	Group Time	Num. Pgs.	Avg. Qst.	Price	Audience	Format	Bible Study
24	45-60	112	12	$4.99	New Christian	Workbk	Book

Features: Intro to Leading a Study, Intro to Study, Ldr's Notes
★★ Personal Application Preparation Time: Low
★★ Relationship Building Ldr. Guide: No Size: 5.50 x 8.25
Subjects: Acts
Comments: Still pertinent today, Acts confirms that the power which transformed the disciples' lives is the same power that can transform modern lives. That power is God Himself, coming through the Holy Spirit. The benefits of studying Acts are that it serves as a mirror for today's church, emphasizes evangelism as the primary task of the church, calls believers to a vital experience with the Holy Spirit, and forges a new sense of Christian identity.

Author: Le Peau, Phyllis J. 877
Series: Caring People Bible Study
Title: *Caring for Emotional Needs*
Publisher: InterVarsity, 1991 ISBN: 0-83081-195-8

Num. Sess.	Group Time	Num. Pgs.	Avg. Qst.	Price	Audience	Format	Bible Study
9	45-60	64	12	$4.99	New Christian	Workbk	Topical

Features: Intro to Leading a Study, Intro to Study, Ldr's Notes
★★★ Personal Application Preparation Time: Low
★★★ Relationship Building Ldr. Guide: No Size: 5.50 x 8.50
Subjects: Caring, Emotions, Loneliness, Support
Comments: This inductive 9-week study helps participants understand there's nothing unspiritual about recognizing their own emotional needs, such as fear, loneliness, and depression. They will find that increased openness will attract people to them and to Christ through them. A series of questions leads participants to discover what the Bible says about this issue. Participants are challenged to make a commitment at the end of the study.

Author: Le Peau, Phyllis J. 878
Series: Caring People Bible Study
Title: *Caring for People in Grief*
Publisher: InterVarsity, 1991 ISBN: 0-83081-193-1

Num. Sess.	Group Time	Num. Pgs.	Avg. Qst.	Price	Audience	Format	Bible Study
9	45-60	64	12	$4.99	New Christian	Workbk	Topical

Features: Intro to Leading a Study, Intro to Study, Ldr's Notes
★★★ Personal Application Preparation Time: Low
★★★ Relationship Building Ldr. Guide: No Size: 5.50 x 8.50
Subjects: Caring, Emotions, Grace, Grief, Hope, Support
Comments: This 9-week study helps participants understand the conflicting thoughts and emotions that consume the grieving. It considers fear, peace, grace, hope, comfort, and more. Participants learn to find genuine comfort for their own pain and to offer that comfort to others. This inductive study's format is a series of questions which lead participants to discover what the Bible says. Participants are challenged to make a commitment at the end of the study.

Author: Le Peau, Phyllis J. 879
Series: Caring People Bible Study
Title: *Caring for People in Conflict*
Publisher: InterVarsity, 1991 ISBN: 0-83081-192-3

Num. Sess.	Group Time	Num. Pgs.	Avg. Qst.	Price	Audience	Format	Bible Study
9	45-60	64	12	$4.99	New Christian	Workbk	Topical

Features: Intro to Leading a Study, Intro to Study, Ldr's Notes
★★★ Personal Application Preparation Time: Low
★★★ Relationship Building Ldr. Guide: No Size: 5.50 x 8.50
Subjects: Caring, Marriage, Parenting, Reconciliation, Relationships, Support
Comments: This 9-week study examines conflict in divided churches, broken friendships, angry children, and damaged marriages. It helps participants approach conflict in a godly way by showing how God can bring healing and reconciliation to their lives and to the lives of their loved ones. In this inductive study a series of questions leads participants to discover what the Bible says.

Author: Le Peau, Phyllis J. 880
Series: Caring People Bible Study
Title: *Caring for Physical Needs*
Publisher: InterVarsity, 1991 ISBN: 0-83081-196-6

Num. Sess.	Group Time	Num. Pgs.	Avg. Qst.	Price	Audience	Format	Bible Study
8	45-60	64	12	$4.99	New Christian	Workbk	Topical

Features: Intro to Leading a Study, Intro to Study, Ldr's Notes
★★★ Personal Application Preparation Time: Low
★★★ Relationship Building Ldr. Guide: No Size: 5.50 x 8.50
Subjects: Caring, Medical Issues, Support
Comments: This inductive 8-week study helps participants learn to be effective caregivers to the poor and the sick. God cares about our physical needs—food, clothing, shelter, and medical treatment. As participants attend to the physical needs of others, they show God's care and learn how He cares for them. A series of questions leads participants to discover what the Bible says about this issue. Participants are challenged to make a commitment at the end of the study.

Author: Le Peau, Phyllis J. 881
Series: Caring People Bible Study
Title: *Caring for Spiritual Needs*
Publisher: InterVarsity, 1991 ISBN: 0-83081-194-X

Num. Sess.	Group Time	Num. Pgs.	Avg. Qst.	Price	Audience	Format	Bible Study
9	45-60	64	12	$4.99	New Christian	Workbk	Topical

Features: Intro to Leading a Study, Intro to Study, Ldr's Notes
★★★ Personal Application Preparation Time: Low
★★★ Relationship Building Ldr. Guide: No Size: 5.50 x 8.50
Subjects: Caring, Support
Comments: This 9-week study helps participants discover how God meets their spiritual needs and how He helps them minister to others' spiritual needs. Purpose, assurance, belonging, and love are some of the spiritual needs addressed which are common to every person. This inductive study's format is a series of questions which lead participants to discover what the Bible says. Participants are challenged to make a commitment at the end of the study.

Author: Le Peau, Phyllis J. 882
Series: Caring People Bible Study
Title: *Character of Caring People, The*
Publisher: InterVarsity, 1991 ISBN: 0-83081-197-4

Num. Sess.	Group Time	Num. Pgs.	Avg. Qst.	Price	Audience	Format	Bible Study
8	45-60	64	12	$4.99	New Christian	Workbk	Topical

Features: Intro to Leading a Study, Intro to Study, Ldr's Notes
★★★ Personal Application Preparation Time: Low
★★★ Relationship Building Ldr. Guide: No Size: 5.50 x 8.50
Subjects: Caring, Service, Support
Comments: This 8-week study helps participants identify character traits of caring people and develop them in their own lives. It covers hospitality, generosity, encouragment, and more. This inductive study's format is a series of questions which lead participants to discover what the Bible says. Participants are challenged to make a commitment at the end of the study.

Author: Le Peau, Phyllis J. **883**
Series: Fruit of the Spirit
Title: *Gentleness: The Strength of Being Tender*
Publisher: Zondervan, 1991 ISBN: 0-31053-691-X

Num. Sess.	Group Time	Num. Pgs.	Avg. Qst.	Price	Audience	Format	Bible Study
6	45-60	48	12	$4.99	New Christian	Workbk	Topical

Features: Intro to Study, Ldr's Notes
★★★ Personal Application Preparation Time: None
★★ Relationship Building Ldr. Guide: No Size: 5.50 x 8.50
Subjects: Caring, Christian Living, Fruit of the Spirit
Comments: This 6-week study, using passages from Proverbs and the New Testament, helps participants discover the strength of being tender. It dispels the myth that gentle people are weak. They would rather persuade than force, are self-giving rather than self-assertive, and prefer a kind word more than a cutting remark; these qualities reveal quiet power. A strong person may not be gentle, but a gentle person must be strong.

Author: Le Peau, Phyllis J. & Bonnie J. Miller **884**
Series: Caring People Bible Study
Title: *Handbook for Caring People*
Publisher: InterVarsity, 1991 ISBN: 0-83081-198-2

Num. Sess.	Group Time	Num. Pgs.	Avg. Qst.	Price	Audience	Format	Bible Study
10	45-60	64	12	$4.99	New Christian	Book	Topical

Features: Intro to Leading a Study, Intro to Study, Bibliography, Ldr's Notes
Personal Application Preparation Time:
Relationship Building Ldr. Guide: No Size: 5.50 x 8.50
Subjects: Caring, Grief, Loneliness, Medical Issues, Relationships, Small Group Resource, Support, Work
Comments: This 10-chapter book covers principles of care and communication that help participants minister to friends and neighbors. It takes away fears by providing simple, time-tested principles for dealing with people's pain. It addresses what one should say to a friend who just lost a job or to someone who is terminally ill.

Author: Le Peau, Phyllis J. **885**
Series: Fruit of the Spirit
Title: *Joy: How to Rejoice in Any Situation*
Publisher: Zondervan, 1991 ISBN: 0-31053-711-8

Num. Sess.	Group Time	Num. Pgs.	Avg. Qst.	Price	Audience	Format	Bible Study
6	45-60	48	12	$4.99	New Christian	Workbk	Topical

Features: Intro to Study, Ldr's Notes
★★★ Personal Application Preparation Time: None
★★ Relationship Building Ldr. Guide: No Size: 5.50 x 8.50
Subjects: Christian Living, Fruit of the Spirit, Joy
Comments: This 6-week study helps participants discover how to rejoice in any situation. Lessons use Psalms and New Testament passages and deal with joy in trials and in weakness, God's Word, the Gospel, and God's discipline. Although hospital rooms, work around the house, and announcements of bad news are seldom "fun," they can be occasions of joy.

Author: Le Peau, Phyllis J. **886**
Series: Fruit of the Spirit
Title: *Kindness: Reaching Out to Others*
Publisher: Zondervan, 1991 ISBN: 0-31053-701-0

Num. Sess.	Group Time	Num. Pgs.	Avg. Qst.	Price	Audience	Format	Bible Study
6	45-60	48	12	$4.99	New Christian	Workbk	Topical

Features: Intro to Study, Ldr's Notes
★★★ Personal Application Preparation Time: None
★★ Relationship Building Ldr. Guide: No Size: 5.50 x 8.50
Subjects: Bible Personalities, Caring, Christian Living, Fruit of the Spirit, Relationships
Comments: This 6-week study on kindness helps participants appreciate God's kindness to them so that they will be motivated to show kindness to others. The lessons illustrate kindness through the lives of Boaz and Ruth, and David and Mephibosheth. A lesson on reaching out to the poor and needy makes participants aware of the many modern opportunities to reach out in kindness to others.

Author: Le Peau, Phyllis J. **887**
Series: Caring People Bible Study
Title: *Resources for Caring People*
Publisher: InterVarsity, 1991 ISBN: 0-83081-191-5

Num. Sess.	Group Time	Num. Pgs.	Avg. Qst.	Price	Audience	Format	Bible Study
8	45-60	64	12	$4.99	New Christian	Workbk	Topical

Features: Intro to Leading a Study, Intro to Study, Ldr's Notes
★★★ Personal Application Preparation Time: Low
★★★ Relationship Building Ldr. Guide: No Size: 5.50 x 8.50
Subjects: Caring, Emotions, Support
Comments: This inductive 8-week study guide uncovers God's many resources for ministering to people. Participants learn that healing comes when God works through them, and not from their own wisdom or strength. God works through them even though they don't have all the answers. A series of questions leads participants to discover what the Bible says. Participants are challenged to make a commitment at the end of the study.

Author: Lewis, Robert **888**
Series: HomeBuilders Couples
Title: *Building Teamwork in Your Marriage*
Publisher: Gospel Light Publications, 1989 ISBN: 0-83071-614-9

Num. Sess.	Group Time	Num. Pgs.	Avg. Qst.	Price	Audience	Format	Bible Study
7	60-90	140	Vary	$9.99	Beginner	Workbk	Topical

Features: Intro to Study, Summary, Drawings, Appendix
★★★★ Personal Application Preparation Time: Low
★★★★ Relationship Building Ldr. Guide: Yes Size: 5.75 x 8.50
Subjects: Family, Marriage, Women's Issues
Comments: This study helps married participants understand their different but complementary roles, by discerning and meeting a mate's unique needs. Couples learn how men and women are truly different, what a wife needs most in her life, what a husband needs in order to feel like a man, how to fulfill responsibilities and bring increased love, how to resolve differences using God's supernatural help, and how to be a godly role model for children.

Author: Limburg, James 889
Series: Friendship Bible Study
Title: *Jonah and Ruth*
Publisher: Augsburg Fortress Publishers, 1989

Num. Sess.	Group Time	Num. Pgs.	Avg. Qst.	Price	Audience	Format	Bible Study
8	60-75	48	13	$3.75	New Christian	Workbk	Book

Features: Intro to Study, Prayer Helps, Study Overview
★★★★ Personal Application Preparation Time: Low
★★★★ Relationship Building Ldr. Guide: Yes Size: 5.50 x 8.50
Subjects: Bible Personalities, God, Jonah, Ruth
Comments: This 8-lesson study prompts adults to study 2 of the best-known stories from the Bible. The stories of Ruth and of Jonah are different in many ways, but they share a common theme: God's love is for all people, even those outside the chosen people of God. Specific suggestions in the introduction show how to approach the study. Includes an overview, an opening, a responsive reading, Bible background, questions for reflection, a key verse, prayer response.

Author: Limburg, James 890
Series: Search Weekly Bible
Title: *Unit 3/Genesis 1–17*
Publisher: Augsburg Fortress Publishers, 1983

Num. Sess.	Group Time	Num. Pgs.	Avg. Qst.	Price	Audience	Format	Bible Study
8	90-105	64	Vary	$5.50	New Christian	Book	Book

Features: Intro to Study, Objectives, Prayer Helps, Worship Helps, Follow Up, Summary
★★ Personal Application Preparation Time: Med
★★ Relationship Building Ldr. Guide: Yes Size: 8.50 x 11.0
Subjects: Genesis
Comments: This review of Genesis is 1 of 20 units of a 5-year study titled "Search." This study of Genesis covers 8 weeks and 8 sessions: "Beginnings"; "Creation and the Care of the Earth"; "The Earthlings"; "The Breakdown of the Family"; "Amazing Grace"; "Our Gathering and Our Scattering"; "Blessed to Be a Blessing"; and "In God We Trust."

Author: Limburg, James 891
Series: Search Weekly Bible
Title: *Unit 4/Genesis 18–50*
Publisher: Augsburg Fortress Publishers, 1983

Num. Sess.	Group Time	Num. Pgs.	Avg. Qst.	Price	Audience	Format	Bible Study
8	90-105	64	Vary	$5.50	New Christian	Book	Book

Features: Intro to Study, Objectives, Prayer Helps, Worship Helps, Follow Up, Summary
★★ Personal Application Preparation Time: Med
★★ Relationship Building Ldr. Guide: Yes Size: 8.50 x 11.0
Subjects: Genesis
Comments: This review of Genesis is 1 of 20 units of a 5-year study titled "Search. This study of Genesis covers 8 sessions: "Birth Announcements"; "When God Tests Us"; "Matchmaker, Matchmaker"; "The Struggle for Success Part 1—Winning Isn't Everything"; "Part 2—Welcome Home!" "God Is Working His Purpose Out: Part 1—Shalom Shattered," Part 2—"Success," and Part 3—"Shalom Restored."

Author: Little, Paul E. 892
Series:
Title: *How to Give Away Your Faith*
Publisher: InterVarsity, 1988 ISBN: 0-83081-217-2

Num. Sess.	Group Time	Num. Pgs.	Avg. Qst.	Price	Audience	Format	Bible Study
10	60-75	190	10	$9.99	New Christian	Book	Topical

Features: Intro to Study, Ldr's Notes, Drawings, Cassette Avail
★★★★ Personal Application Preparation Time: Med
★★★★ Relationship Building Ldr. Guide: No Size: 5.50 x 8.25
Subjects: Apologetics, Evangelism, Small Group Resource
Comments: The down-to-earth approach of this 10-week study helps participants show how friendly and natural evangelism can really be. The study has been updated and expanded, making it more practical and contemporary. Chapters are followed by probing questions and suggestions for a group leader. Two chapters—"Hurdling Social Barriers," and "Christ Is Relevant Today"—deal with many questions Christians face when witnessing today.

Author: Little, Paul E. 893
Series:
Title: *Know What You Believe*
Publisher: Victor Books, 1970 ISBN: 0-89693-045-9

Num. Sess.	Group Time	Num. Pgs.	Avg. Qst.	Price	Audience	Format	Bible Study
13	60-75	139	N/A	$8.99	New Christian	Book	Topical

Features: Intro to Study
★★★★ Personal Application Preparation Time: Low
★★★★ Relationship Building Ldr. Guide: Yes Size: 5.50 x 8.0
Subjects: Angels, Church Life, Faith, God, Holy Spirit, Jesus: Life/Teaching, Satan, Theology
Comments: This 13-week study helps participants understand the basic truths of Christian faith. The lessons describe God, Jesus Christ, Christ's death and resurrection, man and sin, the Holy Spirit, the Church, God's Word, angels, Satan, demons, salvation, and coming events. The leader's guide offers many helps and reproducible transparency masters.

Author: Little, Paul E. 894
Series:
Title: *Know Why You Believe*
Publisher: Victor Books, 1967 ISBN: 0-89693-080-7

Num. Sess.	Group Time	Num. Pgs.	Avg. Qst.	• Price	Audience	Format	Bible Study
13	60-75	144	N/A	$8.99	New Christian	Book	Topical

Features: Intro to Study
★★★★ Personal Application Preparation Time: Low
★★★★ Relationship Building Ldr. Guide: Yes Size: 5.50 x 8.0
Subjects: Faith, God, Miracles, Psychology, Theology
Comments: This 13-week study helps participants examine the claims of Christian faith. It responds to such questions as: "How do I know there's a God?" "Are miracles really possible?" "Why is there pain and evil?" "Did Christ really rise from the dead?" "Do science and Scripture conflict?" and "How can I know the truth, since some claim that Christian experience is psychological?" The leader's guide offers many helps and reproducible transparency masters.

Author: Littleton, Mark R. **895**
Series:
Title: *Battle Ready*
Publisher: Victor Books, 1992 ISBN: 0-89693-577-9

Num. Sess.	Group Time	Num. Pgs.	Avg. Qst.	Price	Audience	Format	Bible Study
18	60-90	180	N/A	$8.99	New Christian	Book	Topical

Features: Intro to Study, No Grp Discussion Quest
★★★★ Personal Application Preparation Time: Med
★ Relationship Building Ldr. Guide: No Size: 5.0 x 8.50
Subjects: Spiritual Warfare
Comments: This book encourages readers to move in the right direction to maturity, to the point of resisting temptation more and sinning less. It helps them gain daily victories through hard, rational, Spirit-guided choices. It can be used in 5 sessions for small group gatherings. Since no leader's guide is available leaders will have to prepare review questions.

Author: Lloyd, Debbie **896**
Series: Leadership Skills For Women
Title: *Time Management*
Publisher: New Hope, 1994 ISBN: 1-56309-102-X

Num. Sess.	Group Time	Num. Pgs.	Avg. Qst.	Price	Audience	Format	Bible Study
8	45-60	72	Vary	$5.95	New Christian	Book	Topical

Features: Intro to Study
★★★★ Personal Application Preparation Time: Low
★★ Relationship Building Ldr. Guide: No Size: 5.50 x 8.50
Subjects: Christian Living, Time, Women's Issues
Comments: One of 5 books in the Leadership Skills for Women series, this book's lessons cover prioritizing, dealing with interruptions, saying "no," and making deliberate choices about the use of time. It also includes practical helps and suggestions for finding time to be more involved in missions. Lesson titles include: "A Time for Everything?" "First Things First"; "Planning in the Quiet Time"; "Seize Control of Your Time"; "Walk Wisely"; "Battling Overcommitment."

Author: Louthan, Andrea Sterk & Howard **897**
Series: Christian Character
Title: *Staying Faithful*
Publisher: InterVarsity, 1992 ISBN: 0-83081-146-X

Num. Sess.	Group Time	Num. Pgs.	Avg. Qst.	Price	Audience	Format	Bible Study
6	30-90	64	23	$4.99	New Christian	Workbk	Topical

Features: Intro to Leading a Study, Intro to Study, Bibliography, Ldr's Notes
★★★★ Personal Application Preparation Time: None
★★★ Relationship Building Ldr. Guide: No Size: 5.50 x 8.25
Subjects: Discipleship
Comments: This study offers 7 options for either individual or group study, ranging from 6–12 weeks and 30″–90″ depending on the number of questions covered. The first lesson introduces the theme of Christian identity, examines ways in which people are pressured to compromise their convictions, and what it means to stand firm, aspects of living as disciples of Christ.

Author: Lum, Ada **898**
Series: LifeGuide Bible Study
Title: *Luke: New Hope, New Joy*
Publisher: InterVarsity, 1992 ISBN: 0-83081-005-6

Num. Sess.	Group Time	Num. Pgs.	Avg. Qst.	Price	Audience	Format	Bible Study
26	45-60	111	10	$4.99	New Christian	Workbk	Book

Features: Intro to Leading a Study, Intro to Study, Ldr's Notes
★★ Personal Application Preparation Time: Low
★ Relationship Building Ldr. Guide: No Size: 5.50 x 8.25
Subjects: Luke
Comments: The 26 studies of Luke are divided into 2 parts. The first part shows how Jesus progressively revealed His full identity. The second shows how He prepared His disciples to continue His divine mission to the rest of the world. Luke's portrait of Jesus is strong, warm, compassionate, and cosmopolitan.

Author: Lutz, Charles P. and John Kerr **899**
Series: Cross Signs
Title: *Who Is My Neighbor? Living as God's People: Unit 6*
Publisher: Augsburg Fortress Publishers, 1993

Num. Sess.	Group Time	Num. Pgs.	Avg. Qst.	Price	Audience	Format	Bible Study
7	90-105	48	7	$3.75	New Christian	Book	Topical

Features: Intro to Study, Prayer Helps, Worship Helps
★★★ Personal Application Preparation Time: Low
★★ Relationship Building Ldr. Guide: Yes Size: 5.50 x 8.50
Subjects: Christian Living, Faith
Comments: Cross Signs, a Bible study series for adult small groups, features 9 units of study that focus on key faith questions. This study looks at how Christians should live with others in response to Christ's love and care. It focuses on chief biblical themes that deal with daily behavior of God's people in the world. Christians should live under the sign of the cross, the sign of love and life.

Author: Lutzer, Erwin W. **900**
Series: Life-in-Perspective
Title: *Chiseled By The Master's Hand*
Publisher: Victor Books, 1993 ISBN: 1-56476-059-6

Num. Sess.	Group Time	Num. Pgs.	Avg. Qst.	Price	Audience	Format	Bible Study
12	60-75	153	N/A	$7.99	New Christian	Book	Charctr

Features: Intro to Study
★★★ Personal Application Preparation Time: Med
★★ Relationship Building Ldr. Guide: Yes Size: 5.50 x 8.0
Subjects: Bible Personalities
Comments: Through this contemporary portrait of Peter, participants can relive the experiences Christ used to mold the raw fisherman into a giant for God. They can learn how Christ motivated Christians to change their character, how He intentionally puts them into tight places to develop their faith, how to learn important lessons from past mistakes and sins, and that Christ's sovereignty extends to every detail of a believer's life.

Author: Lutzer, Erwin W. **901**
Series:
Title: *Christ Among Other Gods*
Publisher: Moody Press, 1994 ISBN: 0-80241-648-9

Num. Sess.	Group Time	Num. Pgs.	Avg. Qst.	Price	Audience	Format	Bible Study
12	60-75	210	N/A	$12.99	New Christian	Book	Topical

Features: Intro to Study
★★ Personal Application Preparation Time: Low
★ Relationship Building Ldr. Guide: No Size: 6.0 x 9.0
Subjects: God, Jesus: Life/Teaching
Comments: This book explains why Christ shatters the idea that various religions are spokes of a wheel that unite at the hub of inner experience. He shows why combining Christ with other religions is to profoundly misunderstand Him. Readers can understand Christ better, defend Him with more confidence, and worship Him with more single-mindedness. A trained leader will need to plan agendas and formulate group study questions.

Author: Lutzer, Erwin W. **902**
Series: Lutzer Study Series
Title: *Getting Closer To God*
Publisher: Victor Books, 1994 ISBN: 1-56476-119-3

Num. Sess.	Group Time	Num. Pgs.	Avg. Qst.	Price	Audience	Format	Bible Study
13	75-90	210	10	$8.99	New Christian	Book	Topical

Features: Intro to Leading a Study, Prayer Helps, Scrpt Memory Helps, Digging Deeper Quest,Follow Up, Ldr's Notes
★★★★ Personal Application Preparation Time: Low
★★★ Relationship Building Ldr. Guide: No Size: 5.50 x 8.0
Subjects: Bible Personalities, Discipleship
Comments: In this study the author explains that becoming better acquainted with God should be a Christian's single motivating passion. It can also motivate readers to know God even though they may be in their own deserts, help them expose excuses they use to retreat from close walks with God, help them identify idols so they can uproot them from their hearts, and offer hope to those discouraged by past failures.

Author: Lutzer, Erwin W. **903**
Series: Life-in-Perspective
Title: *Growing Through Conflict*
Publisher: Victor Books, 1992 ISBN: 0-89693-063-7

Num. Sess.	Group Time	Num. Pgs.	Avg. Qst.	Price	Audience	Format	Bible Study
12	60-75	156	N/A	$7.99	Mature Christian	Book	Charctr

Features: Intro to Study
★★★★ Personal Application Preparation Time: Med
★★ Relationship Building Ldr. Guide: Yes Size: 5.50 x 8.0
Subjects: Bible Personalities, Christian Living, Conflict, Devotionals, Failure, 1 & 2 Samuel
Comments: This 12-week study, which follows the life of David, is designed to help participants benefit from his mistakes and failures, and to learn how to manage conflict. Participants will learn that, like David, they can grow spiritually through conflict, realizing it is a normal part of life. Teaches that spiritual growth usually doesn't happen when things are going smoothly; that doing God's will is not always peaceful.

Author: Lutzer, Erwin W. **904**
Series:
Title: *How to Say No to a Stubborn Habit*
Publisher: Victor Books, 1979 ISBN: 0-88207-787-2

Num. Sess.	Group Time	Num. Pgs.	Avg. Qst.	Price	Audience	Format	Bible Study
13	60-75	143	5	$8.99	New Christian	Book	Topical

Features: Intro to Study
★★★★ Personal Application Preparation Time: Low
★★★★ Relationship Building Ldr. Guide: Yes Size: 5.50 x 8.0
Subjects: Addictions, Christian Living, Satan, Self-help
Comments: This 13-week study helps participants fight stubborn, trouble-causing habits. It offers the good news that people can say no to sin and yes to God. Issues discussed include why temptation is so powerful and attractive; why God doesn't always curtail Satan's power; what to do when a temptation turns into a sin; and why God doesn't dull your passions. A leader's guide includes reproducible transparency masters.

Author: Lutzer, Erwin W. **905**
Series: Life-in-Perspective
Title: *Keep Your Dream Alive*
Publisher: Victor Books, 1991 ISBN: 0-89693-811-5

Num. Sess.	Group Time	Num. Pgs.	Avg. Qst.	Price	Audience	Format	Bible Study
12	60-75	141	N/A	$7.99	New Christian	Book	Charctr

Features:
★★★ Personal Application Preparation Time: Med
★★ Relationship Building Ldr. Guide: Yes Size: 5.50 x 8.0
Subjects: Bible Personalities, Christian Life, Genesis, Old Testament
Comments: This study is about dreams, shattered or fulfilled, past or present. It is also about Joseph, a man who kept his dream alive through 20 years on an emotional roller coaster, from prison to palace, slave to savior of his people. Participants discover that everyone has unfulfilled dreams, that God provides dreams for all, that we must let God expose all to their dreams, and that nothing can thwart dreams God has created.

Author: Lutzer, Erwin W. **906**
Series: Critical Issues Series
Title: *Living with Your Passions*
Publisher: Victor Books, 1983 ISBN: 0-88207-294-3

Num. Sess.	Group Time	Num. Pgs.	Avg. Qst.	Price	Audience	Format	Bible Study
13	60-75	151	5	$8.99	New Christian	Book	Topical

Features:
★★★ Personal Application Preparation Time: Med
★★ Relationship Building Ldr. Guide: Yes Size: 5.50 x 8.0
Subjects: Counseling, Psychology, Sexual Issues, Support
Comments: This book provides a strong rationale for sexual purity. Questions answered include: "What happens when passion gets out of control?" "How do we reconcile sexual sin?" and "Are there legitimate expressions of passion?" Adultery, lust, homosexuality, and masturbation are dealt with specifically. Some areas should not be discussed in a group setting. Leaders must be sensitive to participants who have experienced, or been victims of, sexual sin.

Author: Lutzer, Erwin W. **907**
Series:
Title: *Managing Your Emotions*
Publisher: Victor Books, 1983 ISBN: 0-88207-386-9

Num. Sess.	Group Time	Num. Pgs.	Avg. Qst.	Price	Audience	Format	Bible Study
13	60-75	152	6	$8.99	New Christian	Book	Topical

Features:
★★★ Personal Application Preparation Time: Med
★★ Relationship Building Ldr. Guide: Yes Size: 5.50 x 8.0
Subjects: Emotions, Psychology, Wholeness
Comments: This study shows participants how to regain emotional control by finding God's answer for emotional needs. They will learn how to defeat depression, survive sorrow, control anger, conquer fear, and enjoy life to its fullest. They will also learn why only God can completely heal emotional wounds and put people back on the road to emotional wholeness. Each chapter concludes with several application questions. A leader's guide with transparency masters is available.

Author: Lutzer, Erwin W. **908**
Series:
Title: *Matters of Life and Death*
Publisher: Moody Press, 1994 ISBN: 0-80245-292-2

Num. Sess.	Group Time	Num. Pgs.	Avg. Qst.	Price	Audience	Format	Bible Study
10	60-90	290	N/A	$8.99	New Christian	Book	Topical

Features: Prayer Helps, No Grp Discussion Quest
★★★★ Personal Application Preparation Time: Med
★★ Relationship Building Ldr. Guide: No Size: 5.50 x 8.50
Subjects: Heaven/Hell, Homosexuality, Social Issues, Work
Comments: All Christians have fundamental questions. This book about 10 such questions helps prepare Christians to respond to non-Christians, advise friends, and gain confidence in their own knowledge and understanding of important biblical and social issues. Subjects include heaven, hell, unanswered prayer, death and dying, God's discipline of the believer, Satan's plan for people's lives, marital conflict, sexual pasts, homosexuality, and roles in the workplace.

Author: Lutzer, Erwin W. **909**
Series: Life-in-Perspective
Title: *Overcoming the Grasshopper Complex*
Publisher: Victor Books, 1991 ISBN: 0-89693-826-3

Num. Sess.	Group Time	Num. Pgs.	Avg. Qst.	Price	Audience	Format	Bible Study
14	60-75	155	N/A	$7.99	New Christian	Book	Topical

Features: Intro to Study
★★★ Personal Application Preparation Time: Med
★★ Relationship Building Ldr. Guide: Yes Size: 5.50 x 8.0
Subjects: Bible Personalities, Devotionals, Joshua
Comments: This book helps readers grasp principles for applying God's promises. It teaches through the life of Joshua, who focused on God, not circumstances, and was not paralyzed by fear of his enemies. Through this study, participants can identify pitfalls of spiritual growth, capture territory from Satan, and use it for the glory of God. They can take giant steps toward spiritual maturity, discover that God is all-powerful and worthy of trust, and conquer fear of failure and defeat.

Author: MacArthur, Jr., John **910**
Series: MacArthur Study Series
Title: *Alone With God*
Publisher: Victor Books, 1995 ISBN: 1-56476-488-5

Num. Sess.	Group Time	Num. Pgs.	Avg. Qst.	Price	Audience	Format	Bible Study
9	60-75	190	11	$8.99	New Christian	Book	Topical

Features: Intro to Leading a Study, Intro to Study, Follow Up, Persnl Study Quest, Index
★★★★ Personal Application Preparation Time: Low
★★★ Relationship Building Ldr. Guide: No Size: 5.50 x 8.50
Subjects: Prayer
Comments: This study helps participants discover power and passion that can be found in truly biblical prayer. The author first explores patterns and attitudes of prayer given to Christians in Scripture, then provides practical, biblical means of activating them.

Author: MacArthur, Jr., John **911**
Series: MacArthur Study Series
Title: *Anxiety Attacked*
Publisher: Victor Books, 1993 ISBN: 1-56476-128-2

Num. Sess.	Group Time	Num. Pgs.	Avg. Qst.	Price	Audience	Format	Bible Study
9	60-75	190	12	$8.99	New Christian	Book	Topical

Features: Intro to Leading a Study, Intro to Study, Prayer Helps, Follow Up, Summary, Persnl Study Quest, Index, Appendix
★★★★ Personal Application Preparation Time: Med
★★★★ Relationship Building Ldr. Guide: No Size: 5.50 x 8.50
Subjects: Emotions
Comments: In 9 chapters readers discover how God cares for them: how to avoid anxiety through prayer; how to cast cares on God; how to live a life of faith and trust; recognize that others are looking out for them; how to deal with problem people; how to have peace in every circumstance; how to do all things without complaining; and learning to be content.

Author: MacArthur, Jr., John **912**
Series: John MacArthur's
Title: *Believer's Armor, The*
Publisher: Moody Press, 1981 ISBN: 0-80245-092-X

Num. Sess.	Group Time	Num. Pgs.	Avg. Qst.	Price	Audience	Format	Bible Study
12	60-75	230	19	$7.99	Mature Christian	Book	Topical

Features: Intro to Study, Scrpt Index, Study Overview, Cassette Avail
★★ Personal Application Preparation Time: Med
★ Relationship Building Ldr. Guide: No Size: 5.50 x 8.50
Subjects: Ephesians, Satan
Comments: This study describes every piece of the believer's armor. Participants will explore the Apostle Paul's teaching that Christians who live as believers will be severly tempted. Paul concludes Ephesians with an impressive list of armor to protect believers in the battle against Satan. Each lesson has an introduction, the lesson, questions about the lesson, and two statements that reflect on the lesson's principles. Optional companion tape messages are available.

Author: MacArthur, Jr., John **913**
Series: MacArthur Study Series
Title: *Different By Design*
Publisher: Victor Books, 1994 ISBN: 1-56476-247-5

Num. Sess.	Group Time	Num. Pgs.	Avg. Qst.	Price	Audience	Format	Bible Study
9	60-75	210	11	$8.99	New Christian	Book	Topical

Features: Intro to Leading a Study, Intro to Study, Follow Up, Persnl Study Quest, Index
★★★★ Personal Application Preparation Time: Low
★★★ Relationship Building Ldr. Guide: No Size: 5.50 x 8.50
Subjects: Social Issues
Comments: This book offers hope for bridging gaps and finding fulfillment and success in family and church amid the secular definition of sex-roles. In his thorough, no-nonsense style, MacArthur sets aside prevailing cultural standards and helps participants understand and apply biblical principles for men's and women's roles. Readers can discover the beauty and benefits of God's unique roles for them.

Author: MacArthur, Jr., John **914**
Series: MacArthur Study Series
Title: *First Love: The Joy and Simplicity of Life in Christ*
Publisher: Victor Books, 1995 ISBN: 1-56476-344-7

Num. Sess.	Group Time	Num. Pgs.	Avg. Qst.	Price	Audience	Format	Bible Study
10	60-75	190	9	$8.99	New Christian	Book	Topical

Features: Intro to Leading a Study, Intro to Study, Prayer Helps, Follow Up, Persnl Study Quest, Index
★★★★ Personal Application Preparation Time: Low
★★★ Relationship Building Ldr. Guide: No Size: 5.50 x 8.50
Subjects: Christian Life, Faith, Worship
Comments: Revelation 2:1-7 crystallizes the danger of becoming so busy in activity for Christ that one forgets the necessity of maintaining a rich, loving relationship with Him. It can help Christians restore the fire and conviction of their first love for Christ by helping them develop a clearer understanding of His character, His glory, and His love for them.

Author: MacArthur, Jr., John **915**
Series: John MacArthur's
Title: *Fulfilled Family, The*
Publisher: Moody Press, 1981 ISBN: 0-80245-318-X

Num. Sess.	Group Time	Num. Pgs.	Avg. Qst.	Price	Audience	Format	Bible Study
8	60-75	146	19	$6.99	Mature Christian	Book	Topical

Features: Intro to Study, Scrpt Index, Study Overview, Cassette Avail
★★ Personal Application Preparation Time: Med
★ Relationship Building Ldr. Guide: No Size: 5.50 x 8.50
Subjects: Ephesians, Family, Marriage, Relationships
Comments: This verse-by-verse study of Ephesians 5:21–6:4 clearly presents the divine pattern of authority, submission, and godly love that should guide family relationships. Participants will learn how to understand and apply that pattern to achieve more meaningful, rewarding, and fulfilling family life. Preceding each lesson is an introduction, and succeeding each are questions and summarizing statements. Optional companion tape messages are available.

Author: MacArthur, Jr., John **916**
Series: MacArthur Study Series
Title: *God: Coming Face to Face with His Majesty*
Publisher: Victor Books, 1993 ISBN: 1-56476-071-5

Num. Sess.	Group Time	Num. Pgs.	Avg. Qst.	Price	Audience	Format	Bible Study
12	60-75	190	8	$8.99	New Christian	Book	Charctr

Features: Intro to Leading a Study, Intro to Study, Prayer Helps, Follow Up, Persnl Study Quest, Index
★★★★ Personal Application Preparation Time: Low
★★★ Relationship Building Ldr. Guide: No Size: 5.50 x 8.50
Subjects: God
Comments: This book chisels away centuries of cultural residue from people's understanding of Who God is. Readers can witness the glory and majesty of divine attributes through the eyes of prophets, kings, mighty men of faith, and God's own Son, Jesus Christ. Packed with Scripture references and day-to-day applications, this book enhances readers' worship, and compels them to praise.

Author: MacArthur, Jr., John **917**
Series: John MacArthur's
Title: *God's High Calling for Women*
Publisher: Moody Press, 1987 ISBN: 0-80245-308-2

Num. Sess.	Group Time	Num. Pgs.	Avg. Qst.	Price	Audience	Format	Bible Study
4	45-60	57	13	$5.99	Mature Christian	Book	Topical

Features: Intro to Study, Scrpt Index, Study Overview, Topical Index, Cassette Avail
★★ Personal Application Preparation Time: Med
★ Relationship Building Ldr. Guide: No Size: 5.50 x 8.50
Subjects: Theology, Women's Issues, 1 & 2 Timothy/Titus
Comments: This verse-by-verse study of 1 Timothy 2:9-15 covers major concerns for women in the church as outlined by the Apostle Paul: attitude, appearance, testimony, roles, design, and contribution. Each lesson opens with an introduction, followed by the lesson itself, questions focusing on the facts, and 2 statements that reflect on the lesson's principles. Optional companion tape messages are available.

Author: MacArthur, Jr., John **918**
Series: John MacArthur's
Title: *Heaven*
Publisher: Moody Press, 1988 ISBN: 0-80245-383-X

Num. Sess.	Group Time	Num. Pgs.	Avg. Qst.	Price	Audience	Format	Bible Study
8	45-60	128	16	$6.99	New Christian	Book	Topical

Features: Intro to Study, Scrpt Index, Study Overview, Summary, Topical Index
★★★ Personal Application Preparation Time: Med
★ Relationship Building Ldr. Guide: No Size: 5.50 x 8.50
Subjects: Heaven/Hell
Comments: This study of selected Scriptures presents a comprehensive viewpoint of Heaven. It shows what Heaven is; where it is; what it is like; what people will be like there; how they'll relate with one another; what God will be like; and what saints will do. Each lesson has an introduction, questions focusing on the lesson, and two statements that reflect on the lesson's principles.

Author: MacArthur, Jr., John 919
Series: MacArthur Study Series
Title: *How to Meet the Enemy: Arming Yourself for Spiritual Warfare*
Publisher: Victor Books, 1992 ISBN: 1-56476-016-2

Num. Sess.	Group Time	Num. Pgs.	Avg. Qst.	Price	Audience	Format	Bible Study
12	60-75	220	10	$8.99	New Christian	Book	Topical

Features: Intro to Leading a Study, Intro to Study, Prayer Helps, Follow Up, Persnl Study Quest, Index
★★★★ Personal Application Preparation Time: Low
★★★ Relationship Building Ldr. Guide: No Size: 5.50 x 8.50
Subjects: Materialism, Satan, Spiritual Warfare
Comments: This study takes a detailed look at each piece of spiritual armor, which the author points out is primarily defensive, not offensive in nature. This biblically based study responds to Christians who believe Satan and his army of demons should be ignored and others who say Christians should learn how to fight them and seek to engage them in battle.

Author: MacArthur, Jr., John 920
Series: John MacArthur's
Title: *How to Study The Bible*
Publisher: Moody Press, 1982 ISBN: 0-80245-105-5

Num. Sess.	Group Time	Num. Pgs.	Avg. Qst.	Price	Audience	Format	Bible Study
4	60-75	82	27	$5.99	New Christian	Book	Topical

Features: Intro to Leading a Study, Scrpt Index, Study Overview, Cassette Avail
★★ Personal Application Preparation Time: Med
★ Relationship Building Ldr. Guide: No Size: 5.50 x 8.50
Subjects: Bible Study, Small Group Resource
Comments: This study examines not only how to study the Bible, but why Bible study is so important in every believer's life. Participants will learn that the Bible offers the Word of life, as well as hope in death. Each lesson consists of an introduction, the lesson, questions focusing on the facts, and two statements that reflect on the lesson's principles. Optional companion tape messages are available.

Author: MacArthur, Jr., John 921
Series: MacArthur Study Series
Title: *Power of Suffering, The*
Publisher: Victor Books, 1995 ISBN: 1-56476-429-X

Num. Sess.	Group Time	Num. Pgs.	Avg. Qst.	Price	Audience	Format	Bible Study
10	60-75	190	Vary	$8.99	New Christian	Book	Topical

Features: Intro to Leading a Study, Intro to Study, Praver Helps, Follow Up, Persnl Study Quest, Index
★★★★ Personal Application Preparation Time: Low
★★★ Relationship Building Ldr. Guide: No Size: 5.75 x 8.50
Subjects: Faith, Suffering
Comments: Modern Christians often have difficulty accepting persecution and suffering that often seem inevitable parts of life. The author discusses reasons that trials and persecutions occur, providing examples from Scripture. He recommends ways that believers should face suffering, and shows how to learn valuable lessons from God as a result.

Author: MacArthur, Jr., John 922
Series: MacArthur Study Series
Title: *Saved Without A Doubt: How to Be Sure of Your Salvation*
Publisher: Victor Books, 1992 ISBN: 1-56476-017-0

Num. Sess.	Group Time	Num. Pgs.	Avg. Qst.	Price	Audience	Format	Bible Study
9	60-90	190	8	$8.99	New Christian	Book	Topical

Features: Intro to Study, Prayer Helps, Follow Up, Ldr's Notes, Persnl Study Quest, Index
★★★★ Personal Application Preparation Time: Low
★★★★ Relationship Building Ldr. Guide: No Size: 5.50 x 8.50
Subjects: Evangelism, Theology
Comments: This study answers such questions as "Do you ever struggle with doubt that you are sure you will go to heaven?" and "Is there any way to overcome that doubt?" Shows how Bible truths apply to Christians, by presenting 11 biblical tests that help them determine once and for all whether they have experienced salvation. The author concludes by describing victory in the Spirit.

Author: Mack, Michael C. & Mark A. Taylor 923
Series:
Title: *Creative Groups Guide: Hearing God*
Publisher: Standard Publishing, 1994 ISBN: 0-78470-286-1

Num. Sess.	Group Time	Num. Pgs.	Avg. Qst.	Price	Audience	Format	Bible Study
6	30-60	96	Vary	$12.99	New Christian	Workbk	Topical

Features: Intro to Leading a Study, Objectives, Scrpt Memory Helps, Worship Helps, Full Scrpt Printed, Handouts, Transpcy Masters, Agenda, Book Avail
★★★★ Personal Application Preparation Time: None
★★★★ Relationship Building Ldr. Guide: No Size: 8.50 x 11.0
Subjects: Bible Study
Comments: This resource is for leaders of small groups or Sunday school classes. It provides complete lesson plans, a full small group study guide with thought-provoking discussion questions, reproducible worksheets, and overhead transparency masters. This course can show participants how to read God's Word and truly understand it.

Author: Mack, Michael C. & Mark A. Taylor 924
Series:
Title: *Creative Groups Guide: Claiming Your Place*
Publisher: Standard Publishing, 1994 ISBN: 0-78470-285-3

Num. Sess.	Group Time	Num. Pgs.	Avg. Qst.	Price	Audience	Format	Bible Study
7	30-60	96	Vary	$12.99	New Christian	Workbk	Topical

Features: Intro to Leading a Study, Objectives, Scrpt Memory Helps, Worship Helps, Full Scrpt Printed, Handouts, Transpcy Masters, Agenda, Book Avail
★★★★ Personal Application Preparation Time: None
★★★★ Relationship Building Ldr. Guide: No Size: 8.50 x 11.0
Subjects: Church Life
Comments: It provides complete lesson plans, a full small group study guide complete with thought-provoking discussion questions, reproducible worksheets, and overhead transparency masters. This course can show participants how God wants to use them in their local congregations, keeping them from feeling lost in their churches.

Author: Madsen, Keith **925**
Series: Serendipity Support Group
Title: *Divorce Recovery: Life After Divorce*
Publisher: Serendipity House, 1991 ISBN: 1-88341-961-1

Num. Sess.	Group Time	Num. Pgs.	Avg. Qst.	Price	Audience	Format	Bible Study
7	60-90	96	12	$5.45	Beginner	Workbk	Topical

Features: Intro to Leading a Study, Objectives, Bibliography, Prayer Helps, Full Scrpt Printed, Ldr's Notes, Cartoons, Agenda
★★★★ Personal Application Preparation Time: None
★★★★ Relationship Building Ldr. Guide: No Size: 6.50 x 9.0
Subjects: Divorce, Grief, Self-esteem, Support
Comments: This study concerns common issues for those going through divorce. Lessons deal with the mourning/grieving process, conflict and anger in divorce, children in divorce, forgiveness, building self-image, and building support systems. The format includes ice-breakers, Bible study, and prayer. Timelines are provided. It can be adapted for a 7- or 14-week study.

Author: Madsen, Keith **926**
Series: Serendipity Support Group
Title: *Stress Management: Finding the Balance*
Publisher: Serendipity House, 1992 ISBN: 1-88341-964-6

Num. Sess.	Group Time	Num. Pgs.	Avg. Qst.	Price	Audience	Format	Bible Study
7	60-90	94	12	$5.45	Beginner	Workbk	Topical

Features: Intro to Leading a Study, Objectives, Bibliography, Prayer Helps, Full Scrpt Printed, Ldr's Notes, Cartoons, Agenda
★★★★ Personal Application Preparation Time: None
★★★★ Relationship Building Ldr. Guide: No Size: 6.50 x 9.0
Subjects: Stress, Support
Comments: This study allows participants to learn about stress, set a new activity pace, see how stress affects physical ailments, be focused, content in their circumstances, develop healthy relationships, and look to God for help in managing stress. The format includes icebreakers, Bible study, and prayer. Timelines are provided. It can be adapted for a 7- or 14-week study.

Author: Madsen, Keith and Jan Johnson **927**
Series: Serendipity Support Group
Title: *Waist Watchers: Trimming Down to Size*
Publisher: Serendipity House, 1994 ISBN: 1-88341-975-1

Num. Sess.	Group Time	Num. Pgs.	Avg. Qst.	Price	Audience	Format	Bible Study
14	60-90	85	12	$5.45	Beginner	Workbk	Topical

Features: Intro to Leading a Study, Objectives, Bibliography, Prayer Helps, Full Scrpt Printed, Ldr's Notes, Cartoons, Agenda
★★★★ Personal Application Preparation Time: None
★★★★ Relationship Building Ldr. Guide: No Size: 6.50 x 9.0
Subjects: Addictions, Self-help, Support, Victorious Living
Comments: This study is for people who want to control their eating behavior. It deals with guilt that can contribute to eating disorders, healthy and unhealthy eating, compulsive overeating, anorexia, bulimia, self-discipline, and forgiveness. It helps participants realize that eating can be a response to unfulfilled emotional needs, and that they have to make basic life changes, before diet changes will work.

Author: Maeder, Gary **928**
Series:
Title: *God's Will for Your Life*
Publisher: Tyndale House, 1991 ISBN: 0-84231-097-5

Num. Sess.	Group Time	Num. Pgs.	Avg. Qst.	Price	Audience	Format	Bible Study
16	60-75	300	Vary	$8.99	New Christian	Book	Topical

Features: Intro to Study, Follow Up, Drawings
★★★ Personal Application Preparation Time: Med
★★★ Relationship Building Ldr. Guide: No Size: 6.0 x 9.0
Subjects: Christian Life
Comments: This book for highly motivated New Christians provides Bible teaching about 16 aspects of God's will for people today. Each chapter includes many Scripture references to answer such questions as: "Discovering God's will for you. Is it really possible?" "Studying the Bible. How can I make it interesting?" "Spending time in prayer. Does God really answer?" Finding and using your spiritual gifts. What gift have I been given? Sharing your faith. How can I do it more naturally?

Author: Mains, David **929**
Series: The Recovery Bookshelf
Title: *Healing the Dysfunctional Church Family*
Publisher: Victor Books, 1992 ISBN: 0-89693-050-5

Num. Sess.	Group Time	Num. Pgs.	Avg. Qst.	Price	Audience	Format	Bible Study
8	60-75	156	6	$10.99	New Christian	Book	Topical

Features: Intro to Study, Prayer Helps, Ldr's Notes
★★★ Personal Application Preparation Time: Low
★★ Relationship Building Ldr. Guide: No Size: 5.50 x 8.50
Subjects: Church Life
Comments: This book explores the humanness of the Church. It explores 8 common dysfunctions. Chapters include: "Love That Has to Be Earned"; "Blaming and Shaming"; "Unhealthy Comparisons and Competition"; "Compulsive/Addictive Behavior"; "Perfectionism"; "Frozen Feelings"; and "The Inability to Celebrate." The author urges Christians to reaffirm the church as a place where people can feel loved, helped, forgiven, and receive hope.

Author: Malotky, Catherine **930**
Series: Youth Talk
Title: *Violence*
Publisher: Augsburg Fortress Publishers, 1993

Num. Sess.	Group Time	Num. Pgs.	Avg. Qst.	Price	Audience	Format	Bible Study
5	45-60	46	Vary	$4.95	Beginner	Book	Topical

Features: Prayer Helps, Worship Helps, Photos
★★★★ Personal Application Preparation Time: Low
★★★★ Relationship Building Ldr. Guide: Yes Size: 8.0 x 11.0
Subjects: Teens: Senior High
Comments: An alternative to the "textbook approach," these studies are energetic, contemporary, and modeled after popular teen magazines. Advice columns, fiction, poetry, and other features are mostly written by youth. By the time young people have reached high school, they have experienced some kind of violence. This course increases students' awareness of violence in their lives and in the world around them, and helps them establish non-violent strategies for living.

Author: Marcum, Walt **931**
Series: Group's Active Bible Curriculum
Title: *Sex: A Christian Perspective*
Publisher: Group Publishing, 1990 ISBN: 1-55945-206-4

Num. Sess.	Group Time	Num. Pgs.	Avg. Qst.	Price	Audience	Format	Bible Study
4	35-60	46	Vary	$9.99	New Christian	Workbk	Topical

Features: Intro to Leading a Study, Intro to Study, Objectives, Study Overview, Ldr's Notes, Drawings, Handouts, Agenda, Publicity Ideas
★★★★ Personal Application Preparation Time: None
★★★★ Relationship Building Ldr. Guide: No Size: 8.50 x 11.0
Subjects: Teens: Senior High, Teens: Sexuality
Comments: This study provides biblical guidance for senior high students living in a sexually confused world. Its 4 lessons discuss the Bible's view of premarital sex, sexuality as a gift from God, creative ways to resist sexual pressure, and how to avoid the negative consequences of sex outside marriage. Instructions are easy to follow and provide multiple options for teachers. No student books are required.

Author: Marian, Jim **932**
Series: SonPower Youth Sources
Title: *Growing Up Christian*
Publisher: Victor Books, 1992 ISBN: 0-89693-802-6

Num. Sess.	Group Time	Num. Pgs.	Avg. Qst.	Price	Audience	Format	Bible Study
10	—	156	5	$7.99	New Christian	Book	Topical

Features: Intro to Study, Drawings, Persnl Study Quest
★★★★ Personal Application Preparation Time: None
★★ Relationship Building Ldr. Guide: No Size: 6.0 x 9.0
Subjects: Teens: Resources
Comments: This book explores special characteristics of "church kids," and the struggles they face, and provides hope, encouragement, and practical advice for meeting their special needs. It is divided into three parts: "Youth who have grown up in the church"; "Struggles that emerge"; and "Strategies for ministry." Specific lessons address: "Born belivers"; "the Christian home"; "Measuring up to Christian standards"; "Conversion and converting"; "Playing with Sin."

Author: Marler, Malcolm **933**
Series:
Title: *Ideas for Homebound Ministries*
Publisher: New Hope, 1993 ISBN: 1-56309-072-4

Num. Sess.	Group Time	Num. Pgs.	Avg. Qst.	Price	Audience	Format	Bible Study
	—	41	N/A	$4.95		Book	

Features:
Personal Application Preparation Time:
Relationship Building Ldr. Guide: Size: 8.50 x 11.0
Subjects: Missions, Small Group Resource, Support
Comments: The lives of homebound people can be extremely limited and lonely. They often can't go to grocery stores for food, to the movies or church, or to visit friends. They may depend on others for even the most basic necessities of life. This resource book contains a host of ideas to help groups and individuals minister to the homebound, as well as to people who care for them. It's a good resource for small group mission projects.

Author: Martin, George & Paul Thigpen **934**
Series: Catholic Bible Study Guide
Title: *Praying the Scriptures: A Guide to Talking with God*
Publisher: Servant Publications, 1990 ISBN: 0-89283-647-4

Num. Sess.	Group Time	Num. Pgs.	Avg. Qst.	Price	Audience	Format	Bible Study
9	60-75	84	10	$5.99	Beginner	Workbk	Topical

Features: Intro to Leading a Study, Intro to Study, Prayer Helps, Scrpt Memory Helps, Summary, Charts
★★★★ Personal Application Preparation Time: Low
★★★ Relationship Building Ldr. Guide: No Size: 5.25 x 8.0
Subjects: God, Prayer
Comments: The focus of this 9-lesson study on passages of Scripture used as the basis for different types of prayer. Its subject matter varies from prayers of thanksgiving to stories of Jesus' life to theological statements of mystery. It's divided into three topical areas: "praying prayers of scripture"; "Scriptural conversation starters"; and "praying beyond the words."

Author: Martin, Sara Hines **935**
Series:
Title: *Meeting Needs Through Support Groups*
Publisher: New Hope, 1992 ISBN: 1-56309-053-8

Num. Sess.	Group Time	Num. Pgs.	Avg. Qst.	Price	Audience	Format	Bible Study
	—	96	N/A	$5.95		Book	

Features: Intro to Study, Bibliography
Personal Application Preparation Time:
Relationship Building Ldr. Guide: Size: 5.50 x 8.50
Subjects: Small Group Resource, Support
Comments: This book describes true accounts of people involved in a variety of support groups. It shows Christians who are willing to listen and learn, how to lead these groups, which include adult children of alchoholics, divorced people, single parents, chemically dependent people, bereaved persons, and others. Also included are guidelines for learning how to sponsor support groups and meet the needs of members.

Author: Matthias-Long, Karen **936**
Series: Youth Talk
Title: *Health*
Publisher: Augsburg Fortress Publishers, 1994

Num. Sess.	Group Time	Num. Pgs.	Avg. Qst.	Price	Audience	Format	Bible Study
5	45-60	46	N/A	$4.95	Beginner	Book	Topical

Features: Prayer Helps, Worship Helps, Photos
★★★★ Personal Application Preparation Time: Low
★★★★ Relationship Building Ldr. Guide: Yes Size: 8.0 x 11.0
Subjects: Teens: Emotions, Teens: Senior High, Teens: Youth Life
Comments: These studies are energetic, contemporary, and modeled after popular teen magazines. Advice columns, fiction, poetry, and other features are mostly written by youth. Good health is the combination of physical, emotional, and spiritual well-being. This course helps students set personal goals related to establishing and maintaining good health. Students study and compare lifestyles as they are shaped by contemporary culture, family traditions, and Jesus.

Author: Mauney, Jim 937
Series: Small Group Bible Studies
Title: *First Peter*
Publisher: Augsburg Fortress Publishers, 1988

Num. Sess.	Group Time	Num. Pgs.	Avg. Qst.	Price	Audience	Format	Bible Study
4	60-75	22	22	$1.15	New Christian	Book	Book

Features: Intro to Study, Prayer Helps
★★★ Personal Application Preparation Time: None
★★★ Relationship Building Ldr. Guide: No Size: 8.50 x 5.50
Subjects: Baptism, Relationships, Suffering, 1 & 2 Peter
Comments: This short, 4-session study on 1 Peter helps participants discover the baptismal imagery and understand the rite of baptism and its meaning for their lives. Secondly, it deals with references to suffering. Thirdly, it wrestles with 1 Peter's constant theme of being "sojourners." Finally, it speaks to relationships, then leads participants to redefine and recovenant their own relationships.

Author: Mayhue, Richard 938
Series:
Title: *Unmasking Satan*
Publisher: Victor Books, 1988 ISBN: 0-89693-603-1

Num. Sess.	Group Time	Num. Pgs.	Avg. Qst.	Price	Audience	Format	Bible Study
13	60-75	166	N/A	$8.99	New Christian	Book	Charctr

Features: Intro to Study, Bibliography
★★★★ Personal Application Preparation Time: Low
★★★ Relationship Building Ldr. Guide: Yes Size: 5.50 x 8.0
Subjects: Cults, Satan
Comments: This 13-week study unmasks the Adversary and exposes the tricks of the temptation trade. For each devilish tactic, biblical countertactics are given to combat schemes of sensationalism, ecumenicism, rationalism, situationalism, individualism, isolationism, pessimism, negativism, defeatism, cultism, egoism, and antagonism. This study can properly arm participants to triumph over Satan. A leader's guide includes reproducible transparency masters.

Author: McAllister, Dawson & Jim Lamb 939
Series:
Title: *Discussion Manual for Student Relationships—Volume 2*
Publisher: Shepherd Ministries, 1976 ISBN: 0-86606-402-8

Num. Sess.	Group Time	Num. Pgs.	Avg. Qst.	Price	Audience	Format	Bible Study
26	45-60	210	Vary	$8.95	New Christian	Workbk	Topical

Features: Intro to Study, Drawings, Cartoons
★★★★ Personal Application Preparation Time: None
★★★ Relationship Building Ldr. Guide: Yes Size: 8.50 x 11.0
Subjects: Teens: Discipleship, Teens: Friends, Teens: Peer Pressure, Teens: Psychology, Teens: Relationships, Teens: Sexuality
Comments: This study, second in a series of 3 youth-oriented discussion manuals, is appealing and relevant to the needs of youth. Topics covered include glorifying God, discipleship, love, what's not love, dating, peer pressure, making friends, and honesty. The format is discussion-oriented, contemporary, and uses cartoon characters. It can be used one-on-one or with a large or small group.

Author: McAllister, Dawson & Dan Webster 940
Series:
Title: *Discussion Manual for Student Relationships—Volume 1*
Publisher: Shepherd Ministries, 1975 ISBN: 0-86606-400-1

Num. Sess.	Group Time	Num. Pgs.	Avg. Qst.	Price	Audience	Format	Bible Study
26	45-60	174	Vary	$8.95	New Christian	Workbk	Topical

Features: Intro to Study, Drawings, Cartoons
★★★★ Personal Application Preparation Time: None
★★ Relationship Building Ldr. Guide: Yes Size: 8.50 x 11.0
Subjects: Teens: Christian Liv, Teens: Discipleship, Teens: Peer Pressure, Teens: Psychology, Teens: Relationships, Teens: Self-image, Teens: Sexuality
Comments: This study, first in a series of 3 youth-oriented discussion manuals, is appealing and relevant to the needs of youth. Topics include the Bible, God's will, self-image, loneliness, parents, sex, dating, love, clearing the mind, and temptation. The format promotes discussion, is contemporary, and uses cartoon characters.

Author: McAllister, Dawson & Jim Lamb 941
Series:
Title: *Discussion Manual for Student Relationships—Volume 3*
Publisher: Shepherd Ministries, 1978 ISBN: 0-86606-404-4

Num. Sess.	Group Time	Num. Pgs.	Avg. Qst.	Price	Audience	Format	Bible Study
26	45-60	240	Vary	$8.95	New Christian	Workbk	Topical

Features: Intro to Study, Drawings, Cartoons
★★★★ Personal Application Preparation Time: None
★★ Relationship Building Ldr. Guide: Yes Size: 8.50 x 11.0
Subjects: Teens: Christian Liv, Teens:Drugs/Drinking, Teens: Family, Teens: Friends, Teens: Music, Teens: Peer Pressure, Teens: Psychology, Teens: Relationships, Teens: Self-image
Comments: This study, third in a series of 3 youth-oriented discussion manuals, is appealing and relevant to the needs of youth. Topics include dealing with cliques, breaking up, drugs and alcohol, bad habits, healthy habits, broken homes, guilt, rock music, using time, and death. The format is discussion-oriented.

Author: McAllister, Dawson 942
Series:
Title: *Discussion Manual for Student Discipleship—Volume 2*
Publisher: Shepherd Ministries, 1978 ISBN: 0-86606-407-9

Num. Sess.	Group Time	Num. Pgs.	Avg. Qst.	Price	Audience	Format	Bible Study
8	45-60	162	Vary	$8.95	New Christian	Workbk	Topical

Features: Intro to Study, Cartoons, Index
★★★★ Personal Application Preparation Time: None
★★ Relationship Building Ldr. Guide: No Size: 8.50 x 11.0
Subjects: Teens: Discipleship, Teens: Youth Life
Comments: This study, second in a 2-volume series for new Christians, is formatted in easy-to-use, discussion-oriened, fill-in-the-blank style. Material is presented in a concise, interesting manner and includes cartoon characters. Topics covered include the importance of obedience, learning to obey God, worship, the Christian and the lordship of Christ, the Christian life and endurance, and more. This study of basic biblical principles is designed for new Christians.

Author: McAllister, Dawson & Dan Webster **943**
Series:
Title: *Discussion Manual for Student Discipleship—Volume 1*
Publisher: Shepherd Ministries, 1975 ISBN: 0-86606-406-0

Num. Sess.	Group Time	Num. Pgs.	Avg. Qst.	Price	Audience	Format	Bible Study
10	45-60	200	Vary	$8.95	New Christian	Workbk	Topical

Features: Intro to Study, Drawings, Cartoons
★★★★ Personal Application Preparation Time: None
★★ Relationship Building Ldr. Guide: No Size: 8.50 x 11.0
Subjects: Teens: Discipleship, Teens: Prayer, Teens: Relationships, Teens: Youth Life
Comments: This study, first in a two-volume series for new Christians, is formatted in easy-to-use, discussion-oriented, fill-in-the-blank style. Material is presented in a concise, interesting manner and includes cartoon characters. Chapter titles include: "Your New Life," "God's Love and Forgiveness," "Your Trials," "Your Quiet Time," "The Word," "Your Prayer," and more. Designed for use in small groups of new Christians.

Author: McAllister, Dawson **944**
Series:
Title: *How to Get Along with Your Parents*
Publisher: Word, 1983 ISBN: 0-84998-249-9

Num. Sess.	Group Time	Num. Pgs.	Avg. Qst.	Price	Audience	Format	Bible Study
4	45-60	33	20	$1.99	Beginner	Workbk	Topical

Features: Worship Helps, Full Scrpt Printed, Cartoons
★★★ Personal Application Preparation Time: None
★★★ Relationship Building Ldr. Guide: No Size: 8.50 x 11.0
Subjects: Teens: Family
Comments: This discussion manual is a tool designed to be used with a 4-part videocassette series, which was created by American Student Ministries in conjunction with Western Bible College. The 4-part study includes: "Seeing God Through Your Parents' Eyes," "Being a Peacemaker in Your Home," "Learning How to Obey Your Parents," and "Seeing Life from Your Parents' Points of View." The 4-part video costs $159.95; the student workbooks (set of 5), $9.75 each.

Author: McAllister, Dawson **945**
Series:
Title: *Preparing Your Teenager for Sexuality*
Publisher: Shepherd Ministries, 1988 ISBN: 0-92341-700-1

Num. Sess.	Group Time	Num. Pgs.	Avg. Qst.	Price	Audience	Format	Bible Study
6	45-60	61	Vary	$8.95	Beginner	Workbk	Topical

Features: Intro to Study, Prayer Helps, Full Scrpt Printed, Drawings
★★★ Personal Application Preparation Time: None
★★★ Relationship Building Ldr. Guide: No Size: 8.50 x 11.0
Subjects: Parenting, Teens: Ethics, Teens: Peer Pressure, Teens: Relationships, Teens: Sexuality
Comments: This study is a resource to help parents communicate an often neglected topic, sexual morality. Unit 1, directed toward the parent, discusses the need for preparing children for adulthood, the common barriers, and biblical principles to help break down those barriers. Unit 2, directed toward youth, points out God's positive viewpoint on sex. A companion 6-part video is available for $189.95.

Author: McAllister, Dawson & Robert S. McGee **946**
Series:
Title: *Search for Significance: Youth Edition*
Publisher: Shepherd Ministries, 1990 ISBN: 0-92341-712-5

Num. Sess.	Group Time	Num. Pgs.	Avg. Qst.	Price	Audience	Format	Bible Study
7	60-90	147	Vary	$8.95	Beginner	Workbk	Topical

Features: Intro to Study, Full Scrpt Printed, Drawings
★★★ Personal Application Preparation Time: None
★★ Relationship Building Ldr. Guide: No Size: 8.50 x 11.0
Subjects: Teens: Emotions, Teens: Psychology, Teens: Relationships, Teens: Self-esteem
Comments: This 7-lesson study on low self-esteem concerns one of the most critical problems students face today. How people perceive themselves affects their abilities and relationships. The study goes beyond theory and offers practical work projects to bring about positive results. Four specific areas covered include: the performance, approval, blame game, and shame trap.

Author: McAllister, Dawson **947**
Series:
Title: *Walk with Christ Through the Resurrection, A*
Publisher: Shepherd Ministries, 1981 ISBN: 0-92341-714-1

Num. Sess.	Group Time	Num. Pgs.	Avg. Qst.	Price	Audience	Format	Bible Study
9	60-75	220	Vary	$8.95	Beginner	Workbk	Charctr

Features: Bibliography, Full Scrpt Printed, Drawings
★★★ Personal Application Preparation Time: None
★★ Relationship Building Ldr. Guide: No Size: 8.50 x 11.0
Subjects: Teens: Christian Liv, Teens: Jesus Life, Teens: Theology
Comments: This 9-part study describes the profound story of God's victory over death, as Jesus Christ arose from the darkness of a tomb to the glory of Heaven. It traces Christ's walk, from the intense agony of the Cross, through the exciting moments of the Resurrection, to the glorious event of the Ascension.

Author: McAllister, Dawson **948**
Series:
Title: *Walk with Christ to the Cross, A*
Publisher: Shepherd Ministries, 1980 ISBN: 0-92341-709-5

Num. Sess.	Group Time	Num. Pgs.	Avg. Qst.	Price	Audience	Format	Bible Study
12	60-75	270	Vary	$8.95	Beginner	Workbk	Charctr

Features: Bibliography, Full Scrpt Printed, Drawings
★★★ Personal Application Preparation Time: None
★★ Relationship Building Ldr. Guide: Yes Size: 8.50 x 11.0
Subjects: Teens: Jesus' Life, Teens: Theology
Comments: This 12-lesson study takes a close look at the last 13 hours of Christ's life and the suffering and humiliation He endured. It does so in order to help participants understand why Jesus should be put at the center of people's lives. A 6-part video is available for $189.95. Transparency masters are also available for $24.95.

Author: McAllister, Dawson & Rich Miller 949
Series:
Title: *Who Are You, God? and What Are You Like?*
Publisher: Shepherd Ministries, 1988 ISBN: 0-92341-711-7

Num. Sess.	Group Time	Num. Pgs.	Avg. Qst.	Price	Audience	Format	Bible Study
11	45-60	112	Vary	$8.95	Beginner	Workbk	Topical

Features: Intro to Study, Full Scrpt Printed, Drawings
★★★ Personal Application Preparation Time: None
★★ Relationship Building Ldr. Guide: Yes Size: 8.50 x 11.0
Subjects: Teens: Christian Liv, Teens: Peer Pressure, Teens: Theology
Comments: This study provides biblical answers that stand the test, practical answers that probe the heart, and realistic answers that satisfy youth's search for the identify of God. Titles include "False ideas people have about God"; "Your God must be strong, know everything, be big, be in control, be holy, be loving, be merciful and gracious, and be trustworthy"; and "Your God must be a person." The closing lesson calls for youth to make up their minds about God's place in their lives.

Author: McAllister, Dawson 950
Series:
Title: *Who Are You Jesus?*
Publisher: Shepherd Ministries, 1986 ISBN: 0-92341-705-2

Num. Sess.	Group Time	Num. Pgs.	Avg. Qst.	Price	Audience	Format	Bible Study
10	45-60	141	Vary	$8.95	Beginner	Workbk	Charctr

Features: Intro to Study, Full Scrpt Printed, Drawings
★★★ Personal Application Preparation Time: None
★★ Relationship Building Ldr. Guide: Yes Size: 8.50 x 11.0
Subjects: Teens: Family, Teens: Friends, Teens: Jesus Life, Teens: Relationships, Teens: Theology, Teens: Youth Life
Comments: This study introduces Jesus Christ as the answer to one of America's top problems—teenage suicides. It challenges searching students to consider Christ as the provider of purpose, hope, and satisfaction. The format consists of simple, basic, and hard-hitting discussions for which American students are looking.

Author: McAllister, Dawson 951
Series:
Title: *You, God, and Your Sexuality*
Publisher: Shepherd Ministries, 1988 ISBN: 0-92341-701-X

Num. Sess.	Group Time	Num. Pgs.	Avg. Qst.	Price	Audience	Format	Bible Study
4	45-60	61	Vary	$8.95	Beginner	Workbk	Topical

Features: Intro to Study, Prayer Helps, Full Scrpt Printed, Drawings
★★★ Personal Application Preparation Time: None
★★★ Relationship Building Ldr. Guide: No Size: 8.50 x 11.0
Subjects: Teens: Ethics, Teens: Peer Pressure, Teens: Relationships, Teens: Sexuality
Comments: This study, which helps students understand an often neglected topic—sexual morality—demonstrates God's positive viewpoint on sex. It also helps participants understand the counterfeit being portrayed as love, and offers practical steps to a life of real love. At the conclusion, participants will understand how God protects their dignity, shields them from lust, and guards their future marriage.

Author: McBride, Neil F. 952
Series:
Title: *How to Build a Small Group Ministry*
Publisher: NavPress, 1995 ISBN: 0-89109-769-4

Num. Sess.	Group Time	Num. Pgs.	Avg. Qst.	Price	Audience	Format	Bible Study
	—	200	N/A	$20.00			

Features:
Personal Application Preparation Time:
Relationship Building Ldr. Guide: Size: 7.0 x 10.25
Subjects: Small Group Resource
Comments: This book walks readers through the critical steps in planning and coordinating a successful small group program in a local church. This hands-on handbook includes three essential features: 12 logical steps for organizing and administrating a small groups ministry, a case study of a church in the process of implementing this plan, and worksheets for developing a plan for a local church. Readers are encouraged to personalize the information.

Author: McBride, Neil F. 953
Series:
Title: *How to Lead Small Groups*
Publisher: NavPress, 1990 ISBN: 0-89109-303-6

Num. Sess.	Group Time	Num. Pgs.	Avg. Qst.	Price	Audience	Format	Bible Study
7	—	141	N/A	$6.00		Book	No

Features: Intro to Study
Personal Application Preparation Time:
Relationship Building Ldr. Guide: Size: 5.25 x 8.0
Subjects: Small Group Resource
Comments: This book studies leadership skills for all types of small groups—Bible study, fellowship, task, and support groups. It includes practical exercises to help readers group the critical aspects of small group leadership and dynamics, including: defining your group's purpose; covenanting; understanding group stages; evaluating your group; handling conflict; asking good discussion questions; and stimulating healthy fellowship, sharing, and prayer.

Author: McCall, Emmanuel 954
Series: The Contact Series
Title: *Son, The! His Redemptive Sacrifice*
Publisher: New Hope, 1991 ISBN: 1-56309-043-0

Num. Sess.	Group Time	Num. Pgs.	Avg. Qst.	Price	Audience	Format	Bible Study
12	60-75	220	Vary	$21.95	New Christian	Book	Charctr

Features: Intro to Study, Objectives, Prayer Helps, Scrpt Memory Helps, Cassette Avail
★★★ Personal Application Preparation Time: High
★★★ Relationship Building Ldr. Guide: Yes Size: 10.25 x 11.75
Subjects: Jesus: Life/Teaching, Old Testament
Comments: Contact is a 12-week experience in Bible study, prayer, and personal reflection. Each week, participants spend 5 days in personal learning, using a learner's notebook that contains 60 daily sessions. This study is a simple but profound look at the world through the eyes of Jesus, the Redeemer. Evaluates people's redemptive roles as related to sacrifice, in the design of the Father's plan.

Author: McCann, Michael D. 955
Series:
Title: *Creative Groups Guide: Find Us Faithful*
Publisher: Standard Publishing, 1995 ISBN: 0-78470-308-6

Num. Sess.	Group Time	Num. Pgs.	Avg. Qst.	Price	Audience	Format	Bible Study
13	75-105	160	16	$14.99	New Christian	Workbk	Topical

Features: Intro to Leading a Study, Intro to Study, Scrpt Memory Helps, Worship Helps, Follow Up, Summary, Ldr's Notes, Handouts, Transpcy Masters, Agenda, Publicity Ideas, Book Avail
★★★★ Personal Application Preparation Time: None
★★★★ Relationship Building Ldr. Guide: No Size: 8.50 x 11.0
Subjects: Faith
Comments: This 13-week course helps participants pass their faith to their children and others in their spheres of influence. Based on a book by the same title. For each session leaders have complete lesson plans with a small group study guide with questions, reproducible worksheets, and transparency masters.

Author: McCartney, Dan & Charles Clayton 956
Series:
Title: *Let The Reader Understand*
Publisher: Victor Books, 1994 ISBN: 1-56476-266-1

Num. Sess.	Group Time	Num. Pgs.	Avg. Qst.	Price	Audience	Format	Bible Study
	—	360	N/A	$15.99		Book	

Features: Intro to Study, Bibliography, Index, Appendix
Personal Application Preparation Time:
Relationship Building Ldr. Guide: Size: 6.0 x 9.0
Subjects: Small Group Resource
Comments: This book serves as an introduction for students and laypeople to philosophical and technical matters involved in Bible interpretation. It tries to provide a basis for confidence in understanding Scripture. The material is organized into several parts: "presuppositions," the things we assume when we begin trying to understand a text; the theory of interpretation; the practice of interpretation the application of interpretation, and how to use the Bible.

Author: McCullough, Steven 957
Series: Group's Active Bible Curriculum
Title: *Becoming Responsible*
Publisher: Group Publishing, 1991 ISBN: 1-55945-109-2

Num. Sess.	Group Time	Num. Pgs.	Avg. Qst.	Price	Audience	Format	Bible Study
4	35-60	48	Vary	$9.99	New Christian	Workbk	Topical

Features: Intro to Leading a Study, Intro to Study, Objectives, Study Overview, Ldr's Notes, Drawings, Handouts, Agenda, Publicity Ideas
★★★★ Personal Application Preparation Time: None
★★★★ Relationship Building Ldr. Guide: No Size: 8.50 x 11.0
Subjects: Teens: Junior High, Teens: Relationships
Comments: This study helps junior high students discover the importance of being responsible. Examines the following topics: how being responsible can build trust in relationships; how it can result in positive ways of gaining independence; learn biblical reasons why youth should submit to proper authority; and how they can grow in faith as they learn the importance of honesty in relationships.

Author: McDowell, Dr. Clyde B. 958
Series: Lay Action Ministry
Title: *Equipping for Leadership*
Publisher: Lay Action Ministry Program, 1992

Num. Sess.	Group Time	Num. Pgs.	Avg. Qst.	Price	Audience	Format	Bible Study
12	60-75	112	Vary	$6.95	New Christian	Workbk	Topical

Features: Bibliography
★★★ Personal Application Preparation Time: Low
★★★ Relationship Building Ldr. Guide: Yes Size: 5.50 x 8.50
Subjects: Leadership
Comments: This Lamp lay publication is a practical training course designed to encourage, equip, and train Christian men and women for increased effectiveness in leadership. Areas addressed include: characteristics, strategies, biblical models, biblical principles, spiritual gifts, major tasks of leadership. Also included are motivating others, learning from conflict, treating group illness, organizing the church's vision, implementing the church's vision, and creating a climate for growth.

Author: McDowell, Dr. Clyde B. 959
Series: Lay Action Ministry
Title: *How to Discover Your Spiritual Gifts*
Publisher: Lay Action Ministry Program, 1988 ISBN: 1-55513-016-X

Num. Sess.	Group Time	Num. Pgs.	Avg. Qst.	Price	Audience	Format	Bible Study
12	60-90	112	Vary	$6.95	New Christian	Workbk	Topical

Features: Objectives, Prayer Helps, Ldr's Notes
★★★ Personal Application Preparation Time: Low
★★ Relationship Building Ldr. Guide: Yes Size: 5.25 x 8.25
Subjects: Church Life, Service, Spiritual Gifts
Comments: This practical study helps Christians identify who they are in the body of Christ—and how their spiritual gifts contribute to the ongoing life of the Church. Participants learn how the speaking, serving, and sign gifts differ from their natural talents, and identify the gifts God blesses in their life. They learn which areas of service and ministry match their spiritual gifts. Homework is required.

Author: McDowell, Josh 960
Series:
Title: *Don't Check Your Brains At the Door*
Publisher: Word, 1992 ISBN: 0-84991-155-9

Num. Sess.	Group Time	Num. Pgs.	Avg. Qst.	Price	Audience	Format	Bible Study
4	60-90	N/A	Vary	$79.99	New Christian	Video	Topical

Features: Intro to Leading a Study, Objectives, Prayer Helps, Handouts, Agenda, Book Incl
★★★★ Personal Application Preparation Time: None
★★★★ Relationship Building Ldr. Guide: Yes Size: 10.25 x 12.50
Subjects: Teens: Apologetics, Teens: Junior High, Teens: Senior High
Comments: This 4-session video course helps youth understand and apply the evidences for their faith. Sessions include: "Know Why You Believe"; "Defending the Faith"; "The Uniqueness of the Bible"; and "The Reliability of Scripture." The video uses dramatic vignettes, and intersperses music throughout McDowell's presentation. The drama is set in a situation comedy format.

Author: McDowell, Josh 961
Series: Video Curriculum Resource
Title: *Evidence for Faith*
Publisher: Word, 1984 ISBN: 8-01910-079-2

Num. Sess.	Group Time	Num. Pgs.	Avg. Qst.	Price	Audience	Format	Bible Study
13	60-75	N/A	Vary	$99.99	New Christian	Video	Topical

Features: Prayer Helps, Study Overview, Appendix, Video Study Guide
★★★★ Personal Application Preparation Time: Low
★★ Relationship Building Ldr. Guide: Yes Size: 11.0 x 12.0
Subjects: Apologetics, Christian Life, Faith, God
Comments: This 13-session video study addresses uncertainty over the reliability of Scripture. Archaeological discoveries, physical and historical findings, and easy-to-understand proofs are quoted to reinforce faith. Participants learn that the Bible is reliable, that God is trustworthy and will meet their basic needs for love, acceptance, and security. The kit includes 2 audio cassettes, a book, *Unlocking the Secrets of Being Loved, Accepted and Secure,* and a leader's study guide.

Author: McDowell, Josh 962
Series: Video Curriculum Resource
Title: *How to Help Your Child Say "No" to Sexual Pressure*
Publisher: Word, 1987 ISBN: 8-01890-079-5

Num. Sess.	Group Time	Num. Pgs.	Avg. Qst.	Price	Audience	Format	Bible Study
8	50-60	N/A	Vary	$129.99	Beginner	Video	Topical

Features: Intro to Leading a Study, Prayer Helps, Study Overview, Publicity Ideas, Book Incl, Video Study Guide
★★★★ Personal Application Preparation Time: Low
★★★ Relationship Building Ldr. Guide: Yes Size: 11.0 x 12.0
Subjects: Parenting, Sexual Issues
Comments: This 8-session video study for parents of preteens and teens is designed to help them provide their children with a Christian understanding of sexuality. This video curriculum kit contains 8 video segments on 2 video cassettes, a leader's guide, a paperback book by the same title, a third video containing a 22″ promotional program, and an audio cassette of popular Christian music.

Author: McDowell, Josh 963
Series: Video Curriculum Resource
Title: *Let's Talk About Love & Sex*
Publisher: Word, 1988 ISBN: 8-01506-079-6

Num. Sess.	Group Time	Num. Pgs.	Avg. Qst.	Price	Audience	Format	Bible Study
3	45-60	N/A	Vary	$39.95	Beginner	Video	Topical

Features: Book Incl
★★★★ Personal Application Preparation Time: None
★★★★ Relationship Building Ldr. Guide: Yes Size: 7.50 x 10.50
Subjects: Parenting, Teens: Junior High, Teens: Psychology, Teens: Self-image, Teens: Senior High, Teens: Sexuality
Comments: This fast-paced 35″ video study is designed to be used as a conversation tool by parents, teens, and preteens. It covers three important issues regarding sexuality: forming a healthy self-image, adopting biblical values, and establishing rules and standards; and is a modern approach to presenting traditional values. A companion book, *Love, Dad,* will be read by teens.

Author: McDowell, Josh 964
Series:
Title: *More Than a Carpenter*
Publisher: Tyndale House, 1977 ISBN: 0-84234-552-3

Num. Sess.	Group Time	Num. Pgs.	Avg. Qst.	Price	Audience	Format	Bible Study
11	30-60	128	N/A	$3.99	Beginner	Book	Topical

Features: No Grp Discussion Quest, Cassette Avail
★★★★ Personal Application Preparation Time: Low
★ Relationship Building Ldr. Guide: No Size: 4.0 x 7.0
Subjects: Jesus: Life/Teaching
Comments: This best seller is a hard-hitting book for those skeptical about Jesus' deity, resurrection, and claim on people's lives. Written by a former skeptic of Christianity, it poses and answers questions such as: "What Makes Jesus So Different?" "Lord, Liar, or Lunatic?" "What Good Is a Dead Messiah?" and "Will the Real Messiah Please Stand Up?" It is also available in Spanish.

Author: McDowell, Josh 965
Series:
Title: *No! The Positive Answer*
Publisher: Word, 1993 ISBN: 0-84998-074-7

Num. Sess.	Group Time	Num. Pgs.	Avg. Qst.	Price	Audience	Format	Bible Study
4	60-75	N/A	N/A	$59.99	Beginner	Video	Topical

Features: Intro to Leading a Study, Objectives, Bibliography, Prayer Helps, Handouts, Book Incl
★★★★ Personal Application Preparation Time: None
★★★★ Relationship Building Ldr. Guide: Yes Size: 10.25 x 12.50
Subjects: Teens: Ethics, Teens: Junior High, Teens: Senior High, Teens: Sexuality
Comments: In this video, McDowell helps equip youth with biblically based and emotionally sound reasons to say "no" to sexual pressure. Included are all-new teaching sessions, contemporary vignettes, interviews with young people, music videos. Kit includes: an 82″ video cassette (4 sessions), leader's guide, and book.

Author: McDowell, Josh 966
Series:
Title: *See You At The Party!*
Publisher: Word, 1992 ISBN: 0-84998-055-0

Num. Sess.	Group Time	Num. Pgs.	Avg. Qst.	Price	Audience	Format	Bible Study
5	60-75	N/A	Vary	$89.99	New Christian	Video	Topical

Features: Objectives, Handouts, Agenda, Publicity Ideas, Book Incl
★★★★ Personal Application Preparation Time: Low
★★★★ Relationship Building Ldr. Guide: Yes Size: 10.75 x 12.75
Subjects: Teens: Evangelism, Teens: Junior High, Teens: Senior High
Comments: This interactive video helps youth leaders motivate and equip their entire group to conduct evangelistic parties in a non-threatening atmosphere of fun, food, and fellowship. Powerful dramatic vignettes, music videos, video teaching, and creative activities help students adopt effective outreach strategies. Booklets, devotionals, and a New Testament are provided.

Author: McDowell, Josh **967**
Series:
Title: *Teenage Q & A Video Series, The*
Publisher: Word, 1990 ISBN: 0-84991-157-5

Num. Sess.	Group Time	Num. Pgs.	Avg. Qst.	Price	Audience	Format	Bible Study
4	45-75	N/A	11	$79.99	Beginner	Video	Topical

Features: Intro to Leading a Study, Bibliography, Handouts, Publicity Ideas, Book Incl
★★★★ Personal Application Preparation Time: None
★★★★ Relationship Building Ldr. Guide: Yes Size: 10.25 x 12.50
Subjects: Teens: Friends, Teens: Junior High, Teens: Relationships, Teens: Senior High
Comments: This 4-session video (23″ each) is about forming biblically based boy-girl relationships, emotionally, physically, and spiritually. The program is designed not simply to answer young people's practical questions, but also to ground them in biblical concepts of real love. The kit includes a companion book and reproducible handouts.

Author: McDowell, Josh and Dann Spader **968**
Series:
Title: *Won By One*
Publisher: Word, 1993 ISBN: 0-84998-078-X

Num. Sess.	Group Time	Num. Pgs.	Avg. Qst.	Price	Audience	Format	Bible Study
4	60-75	N/A	Vary	$49.99	New Christian	Video	Topical

Features: Intro to Leading a Study, Objectives, Bibliography, Prayer Helps, Scrpt Memory Helps, Handouts, Agenda, Cassette Avail
★★★★ Personal Application Preparation Time: Low
★★★★ Relationship Building Ldr. Guide: Yes Size: 7.50 x 11.0
Subjects: Teens: Evangelism, Teens: Junior High, Teens: Senior High
Comments: This interactive training video helps youth leaders equip junior and senior high students to personally share their faith. The 26″ evangelistic video features testimonies directly from students, and dramatic vignettes in a fast-paced format of student-to-student interaction. The series will empower students to discover the real purpose of outreach and understand the true message of the Gospel.

Author: McKay, William J., et al. **969**
Series:
Title: *Caring Evangelism: Leader's Guide*
Publisher: Stephen Ministries, 1992

Num. Sess.	Group Time	Num. Pgs.	Avg. Qst.	Price	Audience	Format	Bible Study
16	60-75	250	N/A	$34.95	New Christian	Book	Topical

Features: Intro to Leading a Study, Intro to Study, Objectives, Prayer Helps, Study Overview, Book Avail
★★★★ Personal Application Preparation Time: Low
★★★★ Relationship Building Ldr. Guide: Size: 11.0 x 12.0
Subjects: Evangelism
Comments: This guide includes concise instructions for teaching, time frames for each lecture or activity, detailed instructions for leading exercises, prayers to begin and end class sessions, and numerous hints for conducting the class sessions most effectively. The format includes: central Bible passages, goals and objectives, how to teach each module, and opening and closing prayers.

Author: McKay, William J. **970**
Series:
Title: *Me, An Evangelist? Every Christian's Guide to Caring Evangelism*
Publisher: Stephen Ministries, 1992 ISBN: 0-96338-310-8

Num. Sess.	Group Time	Num. Pgs.	Avg. Qst.	Price	Audience	Format	Bible Study
	—	240	N/A	$11.95	New Christian	Book	

Features:
Personal Application Preparation Time:
Relationship Building Ldr. Guide: Size: 5.50 x 8.50
Subjects: Evangelism
Comments: This book, the required text for the "Me, an Evangelist?" is for people who never dreamed they could be evangelists. Its goal is to help equip Christians to effectively and compassionately live and share their love of Jesus for others. The story revolves around a Christian couple who never thought they could be evangelists, but learn that they can. It unfolds in the couple's relationship with Andy and Sarah and their neighbor, Margaret.

Author: McNulty, Edward N. **971**
Series: Group's Active Bible Curriculum
Title: *Hazardous to Your Health*
Publisher: Group Publishing, 1990 ISBN: 1-55945-200-5

Num. Sess.	Group Time	Num. Pgs.	Avg. Qst.	Price	Audience	Format	Bible Study
4	35-60	46	Vary	$9.99	Beginner	Workbk	Topical

Features: Intro to Leading a Study, Intro to Study, Objectives, Study Overview, Ldr's Notes, Handouts, Agenda, Publicity Ideas
★★★★ Personal Application Preparation Time: None
★★★★ Relationship Building Ldr. Guide: No Size: 8.50 x 11.0
Subjects: Teens: Decisions, Teens: Discipleship, Teens: Senior High
Comments: This study helps young people learn, from a Christian perspective, to avoid destructive lifestyles. The four lessons, which explore the AIDS crisis, the dangers of steroids, eating disorders, and the importance of a healthy physical and spiritual life, can be used in a Bible class or youth meeting. Activities and Bible studies are included as separate reproducible sheets. No student books are required.

Author: McQuay, Dr. Earl P. **972**
Series: Lay Action Ministry
Title: *Panorama of the Bible, A*
Publisher: Lay Action Ministry Program, 1988 ISBN: 0-89191-511-7

Num. Sess.	Group Time	Num. Pgs.	Avg. Qst.	Price	Audience	Format	Bible Study
12	60-90	128	Vary	$6.95	New Christian	Workbk	Topical

Features: Prayer Helps, Ldr's Notes, Maps
★★★ Personal Application Preparation Time: Low
★★★ Relationship Building Ldr. Guide: Yes Size: 5.25 x 8.25
Subjects: Bible Study, Church Life
Comments: This study helps participants trace God's dealings with humankind through the ages, from Genesis to Revelation. Participants will be encouraged to follow God's call to Christian living and service as they study His work in the lives of faithful men and women before them. A visual memory system helps participants understand and remember 12 important segments of Bible history. Includes a test on the material and symbols covered over the 12 weeks.

Author: Meek, James A. 973
Series: Discover Life
Title: *Did Jesus Say That? Leader's Guide*
Publisher: Church Development Resources, 1993

Num. Sess.	Group Time	Num. Pgs.	Avg. Qst.	Price	Audience	Format	Bible Study
7	45-60	30	5	$4.40	Beginner	Book	Topical

Features: Intro to Leading a Study, Intro to Study, Follow Up, Summary, Full Scrpt Printed
★★★★ Personal Application Preparation Time: None
★★ Relationship Building Ldr. Guide: Yes Size: 8.50 x 11.0
Subjects: Jesus: Life/Teaching
Comments: Jesus, the Teacher from heaven, often said some astonishing things. His words stung the pride of His religious enemies; they soothed the pains of His closest friends. He was a master teacher and His message is as relevant today as it was 2,000 years ago. This study can help participants learn how to live today and how to prepare for tomorrow. The participant book costs $2.70.

Author: Meek, James A. 974
Series: Discover Life
Title: *Ecclesiastes: Finding Meaning In Life: Leader's Guide*
Publisher: Church Development Resources, 1992

Num. Sess.	Group Time	Num. Pgs.	Avg. Qst.	Price	Audience	Format	Bible Study
7	45-60	30	5	$4.40	Beginner	Book	Topical

Features: Intro to Leading a Study, Intro to Study, Follow Up, Summary, Full Scrpt Printed
★★★★ Personal Application Preparation Time: None
★★ Relationship Building Ldr. Guide: Yes Size: 8.50 x 11.0
Subjects: Ecclesiastes, Hope, Suffering, Time, Work
Comments: This 7-lesson study points the way to Jesus Christ Who alone provides true meaning in life. Participants will find this study relevant as they explore the lessons: "Life Is Disappointing"; "Work and Play"; "Time and Change"; "Wealth"; "Justice"; "Suffering and Death"; "Beyond Disappointment to Hope." It closes with the author of Ecclesiastes having complete trust in God. Participant book is $2.70.

Author: Meek, James A. 975
Series: Discover Life
Title: *Evil Seeds, Deadly Fruit: Leader's Guide*
Publisher: Church Development Resources, 1994

Num. Sess.	Group Time	Num. Pgs.	Avg. Qst.	Price	Audience	Format	Bible Study
7	45-60	N/A	6	$17.95	Beginner	Book	Topical

Features: Intro to Leading a Study, Intro to Study, Follow Up, Full Scrpt Printed
★★★★ Personal Application Preparation Time: None
★★ Relationship Building Ldr. Guide: Yes Size: 8.50 x 11.0
Subjects: Christian Living
Comments: The "seven deadly sins" have held men and women captive since the beginning of time. Participants will learn how to break free from the power of pride, envy, anger, sloth, greed, gluttony, and lust. This study book contains within it 2 leader guides and 8 discovery guides (participant sheets). Homework is not required. Lessons are distributed prior to each study.

Author: Meek, James A. 976
Series: Discover Life
Title: *Growing Together: Leader's Guide*
Publisher: Church Development Resources, 1990

Num. Sess.	Group Time	Num. Pgs.	Avg. Qst.	Price	Audience	Format	Bible Study
7	45-60	30	7	$4.40	Beginner	Book	Topical

Features: Intro to Leading a Study, Follow Up, Summary, Full Scrpt Printed
★★★★ Personal Application Preparation Time: None
★★ Relationship Building Ldr. Guide: Yes Size: 8.50 x 11.0
Subjects: Church Life, Leadership, Missions, Worship
Comments: This study allows participants to explore growing together as one body in the church. Lessons cover: "The Church"; "Worship"; "Fellowship"; "Giving"; "Serving"; "Leadership"; and "Missions." Bible passages are printed, eliminating embarrassment over trying to find a passage, or bringing a Bible to a public place. Brief follow-up articles are included. The participant book costs $2.70.

Author: Meek, James A. 977
Series: Discover Life
Title: *New Kind of Life, A: Leader's Guide*
Publisher: Church Development Resources, 1990

Num. Sess.	Group Time	Num. Pgs.	Avg. Qst.	Price	Audience	Format	Bible Study
9	45-60	38	6	$5.60	Beginner	Book	Topical

Features: Intro to Leading a Study, Follow Up, Summary, Full Scrpt Printed
★★★★ Personal Application Preparation Time: None
★★ Relationship Building Ldr. Guide: Yes Size: 8.50 x 11.0
Subjects: Christian Living, New Testament, Suffering
Comments: This 9-lesson study taken from Peter's letters covers topics ranging from holy living to unjust suffering. Lessons include: "An Eternal Inheritance"; "A Christian Lifestyle"; "Submission to Authority"; "Suffering For Doing Right"; "Rejoicing While Suffering"; "Qualities of Greatness"; "Everything We Need"; "Protected by the Truth"; and "The Return of Christ." The participant book costs $3.40.

Author: Meek, James A. 978
Series: Discover Life
Title: *Spiritual Fitness: Exercise for the Soul: Leader's Guide*
Publisher: Church Development Resources, 1991

Num. Sess.	Group Time	Num. Pgs.	Avg. Qst.	Price	Audience	Format	Bible Study
6	45-60	26	6	$3.75	Beginner	Book	Topical

Features: Intro to Leading a Study, Follow Up, Summary, Full Scrpt Printed
★★★★ Personal Application Preparation Time: None
★★ Relationship Building Ldr. Guide: Yes Size: 8.50 x 11.0
Subjects: 1, 2 & 3 John/Jude
Comments: This 6-lesson study from 1 John is full of insights from God's Word about shaping up spiritually. Lessons cover how one can be spiritually alive, identifing if a person has spiritual cancer, how to live life, how to have stamina and insight, how to love others, and how to be confident in Christ. The participant book costs $2.30 and pages are perforated for easy distribution prior to each small group meeting.

Author: Meek, James A. **979**
Series: Discover Life
Title: *Steps to Success: Leader's Guide*
Publisher: Church Development Resources, 1990

Num. Sess.	Group Time	Num. Pgs.	Avg. Qst.	Price	Audience	Format	Bible Study
7	45-60	30	6	$4.40	Beginner	Book	Topical

Features: Intro to Leading a Study, Intro to Study, Follow Up, Summary, Full Scrpt Printed
★★★★ Personal Application Preparation Time: None
★★ Relationship Building Ldr. Guide: Yes Size: 8.50 x 11.0
Subjects: Faith, Love, Success
Comments: In 2 Peter 1:5-7, we are told to make every effort to add the increasing presence of faith, goodness, knowledge, self-control, perseverance, godliness, and love. This study examines each of these qualities as participants meet men who "made every effort" to build these qualities into their own lives and see how God honored their commitment. The participant book costs $2.70.

Author: Mees, Jr., Walter H. **980**
Series: Group's Active Bible Curriculum
Title: *Counterfeit Religions*
Publisher: Group Publishing, 1990 ISBN: 1-55945-207-2

Num. Sess.	Group Time	Num. Pgs.	Avg. Qst.	Price	Audience	Format	Bible Study
4	35-60	48	Vary	$9.99	Beginner	Workbk	Topical

Features: Intro to Leading a Study, Intro to Study, Objectives, Study Overview, Ldr's Notes, Handouts, Agenda, Publicity Ideas
★★★★ Personal Application Preparation Time: None
★★★★ Relationship Building Ldr. Guide: No Size: 8.50 x 11.0
Subjects: Teens: Christian Liv, Teens: Cults, Teens: Occult, Teens: Senior High
Comments: In this course, senior highers learn how to identify non-Christian beliefs and avoid the traps of cults, the New Age, and the occult. Participants learn the tactics cults use to recruit members and how to avoid them, and explore ways to build faith that will stand up to counterfeit religions.

Author: Mees, Jr., Walter H. **981**
Series: Group's Active Bible Curriculum
Title: *Who Is God?*
Publisher: Group Publishing, 1991 ISBN: 1-55945-218-8

Num. Sess.	Group Time	Num. Pgs.	Avg. Qst.	Price	Audience	Format	Bible Study
4	35-60	43	Vary	$9.99	Beginner	Workbk	Charctr

Features: Intro to Leading a Study, Intro to Study, Objectives, Study Overview, Ldr's Notes, Handouts, Agenda, Publicity Ideas
★★★★ Personal Application Preparation Time: None
★★★★ Relationship Building Ldr. Guide: No Size: 8.50 x 11.0
Subjects: Teens: Discipleship, Teens: God, Teens: Senior High
Comments: In this course, teenagers get to know God as Creator, Merciful Judge, Father, and Conqueror. Senior high participants learn about the first Person of the Trinity, and explore deeper relationships with God. They'll explore how God balances mercy and justice, discover how to have a close relationship with God, and learn to trust that He is in control of the world.

Author: Menconi, Peter **982**
Series: Serendipity Support Group
Title: *Mid Life: The Crisis That Brings Renewal*
Publisher: Serendipity House, 1990 ISBN: 1-88341-968-9

Num. Sess.	Group Time	Num. Pgs.	Avg. Qst.	Price	Audience	Format	Bible Study
14	60-90	80	12	$5.45	Beginner	Workbk	Topical

Features: Intro to Leading a Study, Objectives, Bibliography, Prayer Helps, Full Scrpt Printed, Ldr's Notes, Cartoons, Agenda
★★★★ Personal Application Preparation Time: None
★★★★ Relationship Building Ldr. Guide: No Size: 6.50 x 9.0
Subjects: Men's Issues, Renewal, Social Issues, Women's Issues
Comments: This study is written for anyone approaching, in, or just through midlife. The book of Ecclesiastes is the source of insights into the nature and dynamics of midlife. Everyone has to face midlife questions of mortality, crazy decisions, dumb moves, and crises of all sorts. This study leads participants through reevaluation, rediscovery, reaffirmation, and redirection.

Author: Meyer, Lester **983**
Series: Search Weekly Bible
Title: *Unit 18/Isaiah*
Publisher: Augsburg Fortress Publishers, 1987

Num. Sess.	Group Time	Num. Pgs.	Avg. Qst.	Price	Audience	Format	Bible Study
8	90-105	64	Vary	$5.50	New Christian	Book	Book

Features: Intro to Study, Objectives, Prayer Helps, Worship Helps, Follow Up, Summary
★★ Personal Application Preparation Time: Med
★★ Relationship Building Ldr. Guide: Yes Size: 8.50 x 11.0
Subjects: Isaiah/Jeremiah
Comments: This review of Isaiah is 1 of 20 units of a 5-year study titled "Search." There are 3 main divisions of the Book of Isaiah. Chapters 1–39 contains the messages delivered to God's people in Jerusalem and Judah during a time of great uncertainty and insecurity. Chapters 40–55 are addressed to those who have experienced defeat and destruction. In Chapters 56–66, God speaks to those in Jerusalem.

Author: Miles, Mary Dell **984**
Series: LifeSearch
Title: *Stress*
Publisher: Abingdon Press, 1994 ISBN: 0-68777-876-X

Num. Sess.	Group Time	Num. Pgs.	Avg. Qst.	Price	Audience	Format	Bible Study
6	60-90	62	Vary	$4.95	Beginner	Workbk	Topical

Features: Intro to Leading a Study, Intro to Study, Prayer Helps, Worship Helps, Ldr's Notes
★★★★ Personal Application Preparation Time: None
★★★★ Relationship Building Ldr. Guide: No Size: 7.0 x 10.0
Subjects: Stress
Comments: This 6-session study helps participants look at sources of stress in their lives, at ways they currently deal with stress, and at finding help and developing skills for reducing stress. Participants are encouraged to view topics, not only from personal concern, but also from a communal/congregational concern. The book contains leader aids and marginal notes.

Author: Miles, M. Scott **985**
Series: GroupBuilder Resources
Title: *Confronting a World Gone Wrong*
Publisher: Victor Books, 1992 ISBN: 1-56476-023-5

Num. Sess.	Group Time	Num. Pgs.	Avg. Qst.	Price	Audience	Format	Bible Study
8	75-90	143	Vary	$5.99	New Christian	Workbk	Charctr

Features: Intro to Leading a Study, Intro to Study, Objectives, Full Scrpt Printed, Ldr's Notes, Drawings, Persnl Study Quest, Charts
★★★★ Personal Application Preparation Time: Med
★★★★ Relationship Building Ldr. Guide: No Size: 6.0 x 9.0
Subjects: Bible Personalities, Christian Living, Kings/Chronicles
Comments: This eight-week study looks at Elijah's life, on his being God's person for God's purposes. Eight aspects of Elijah's life are discussed, including learning to live convictions, living freely in God's power, trusting Him in specific situations, dealing with divided spiritual loyalties, and developing a prayer life. Also covered are seeking God's care when depressed, and leaving a legacy that impacts the world.

Author: Miles, M. Scott **986**
Series: GroupBuilder Resources
Title: *Someone In My Corner*
Publisher: Victor Books, 1995 ISBN: 1-56476-409-5

Num. Sess.	Group Time	Num. Pgs.	Avg. Qst.	Price	Audience	Format	Bible Study
8	75-90	144	Vary	$5.99	New Christian	Workbk	Topical

Features: Intro to Leading a Study, Intro to Study, Objectives, Full Scrpt Printed, Ldr's Notes, Drawings, Persnl Study Quest, Charts
★★★★ Personal Application Preparation Time: Med
★★★★ Relationship Building Ldr. Guide: No Size: 6.0 x 9.0
Subjects: Self-esteem, Support
Comments: This 8-week study takes a look at how God touches the lives of people who need someone to believe in them. Topics discussed include turning dreams into reality, taking risks, abandonment, and failure. Participants will discover how God can use them to empower others.

Author: Miles, M. Scott **987**
Series: GroupBuilder Resources
Title: *When The Walls are Closing In*
Publisher: Victor Books, 1993 ISBN: 1-56476-104-5

Num. Sess.	Group Time	Num. Pgs.	Avg. Qst.	Price	Audience	Format	Bible Study
8	75-90	144	Vary	$5.99	New Christian	Workbk	Book

Features: Intro to Leading a Study, Intro to Study, Objectives, Digging Deeper Quest, Follow Up, Full Scrpt Printed, Ldr's Notes, Cartoons, Persnl Study Quest
★★★★ Personal Application Preparation Time: Low
★★★★ Relationship Building Ldr. Guide: No Size: 6.0 x 9.0
Subjects: 1 & 2 Peter
Comments: In this study participants examine 8 aspects of courage and hope from the Book of 1 Peter. It includes positive responses during troubled times, a reflection of God's holiness during difficult circumstances, character qualities for painful trials, principles of submission and responses to abusive authority.

Author: Millard, Kent **988**
Series: LifeSearch
Title: *Spiritual Gifts*
Publisher: Abingdon Press, 1994 ISBN: 0-68777-866-2

Num. Sess.	Group Time	Num. Pgs.	Avg. Qst.	Price	Audience	Format	Bible Study
6	60-90	62	Vary	$4.95	New Christian	Workbk	Topical

Features: Intro to Leading a Study, Intro to Study, Prayer Helps, Worship Helps, Ldr's Notes
★★★★ Personal Application Preparation Time: None
★★★★ Relationship Building Ldr. Guide: No Size: 7.0 x 10.0
Subjects: Spiritual Gifts
Comments: This 6-week study helps adults concretely identify and cultivate their spiritual gifts, both individually and corporately, as members of their small groups. Participants are encouraged to view topics, not only from personal concern, but also from a communal/congregational concern. The book contains leader aids and marginal notes. A section called Quick Lead.

Author: Miller, Katherine S. **989**
Series: Youth Talk
Title: *Heroes & Role Models*
Publisher: Augsburg Fortress Publishers, 1994

Num. Sess.	Group Time	Num. Pgs.	Avg. Qst.	Price	Audience	Format	Bible Study
5	45-60	46	N/A	$4.95	Beginner	Book	Topical

Features: Prayer Helps, Worship Helps, Photos
★★★★ Personal Application Preparation Time: Low
★★★★ Relationship Building Ldr. Guide: Yes Size: 8.0 x 11.0
Subjects: Teens: Self-image, Teens: Senior High
Comments: These studies are energetic, contemporary, and modeled after popular teen magazines. Advice columns, fiction, poetry, and other features are mostly written by youth. Oftentimes heroes are confused with idols. In this course, students identify people they admire and discover heroic qualities that they themselves may have and are called to share as followers of Jesus Christ. Topics: Heroes and Role Models To Watch.

Author: Miller, Kathy Collard **990**
Series: Daughters of the King
Title: *Character of the King*
Publisher: David C. Cook Publishing Co., 1994 ISBN: 0-89636-310-4

Num. Sess.	Group Time	Num. Pgs.	Avg. Qst.	Price	Audience	Format	Bible Study
11	60-75	94	12	$5.49	New Christian	Workbk	Charctr

Features: Charts
★★★★ Personal Application Preparation Time: Low
★★ Relationship Building Ldr. Guide: No Size: 6.0 x 9.0
Subjects: God, Women's Issues
Comments: This study is about the character of the King, Who can be trusted, Who is timeless, infinite, and eternal. The study speaks of His character in "I Am" statements including I am "love," "eternal," "patient," "just," "faithful," "immutable," "sovereign," "omnipotent," "omnipresent," "omniscient," and "merciful." Participants can learn together why they can trust the King.

Author: Miller, Kathy Collard **991**
Series: Daughters of the King
Title: *Choices of the Heart*
Publisher: David C. Cook Publishing Co., 1993 ISBN: 0-89636-295-7

Num. Sess.	Group Time	Num. Pgs.	Avg. Qst.	Price	Audience	Format	Bible Study
10	60-75	92	20	$5.49	New Christian	Workbk	Topical

Features:
★★★★ Personal Application Preparation Time: Low
★★ Relationship Building Ldr. Guide: No Size: 6.0 x 9.0
Subjects: Bible Personalities, Women's Issues
Comments: This study reviews choices women face, including jealousy, obedience, power, prayer, forgiveness, and temptation. Biblical women include "Rebekah and Rahab," "Job's Wife and the Woman of Shunem," "Jezebel and Deborah," "Naomi and the Syrophoenician Woman," "Gomer and the Forgiven Woman," "Sarah and Lydia," "Sapphira and The Samaritan Woman," "Bathsheba and Hannah," "Miriam and Leah," and "Martha and Mary.

Author: Miller, Kathy Collard **992**
Series: Daughters of the King
Title: *Contentment*
Publisher: David C. Cook Publishing Co., 1993 ISBN: 0-89636-294-9

Num. Sess.	Group Time	Num. Pgs.	Avg. Qst.	Price	Audience	Format	Bible Study
9	60-75	64	10	$5.49	New Christian	Workbk	Topical

Features:
★★★★ Personal Application Preparation Time: Low
★★ Relationship Building Ldr. Guide: No Size: 6.0 x 9.0
Subjects: Women's Issues
Comments: This study reflects how elusive contentment can seem and how it really looks in the light of life's stress. There are enemies and fruits of contentment. In between is the Father's plan that enables Christians to be content with who they are, right now, in the midst of trials, relationships, physical problems, financial plenty or lack, even while growing older. Participants glean principles and encouragement in all areas.

Author: Miller, Kathy Collard **993**
Series: Daughters of the King
Title: *My Father in Me*
Publisher: David C. Cook Publishing Co., 1994 ISBN: 0-89636-309-0

Num. Sess.	Group Time	Num. Pgs.	Avg. Qst.	Price	Audience	Format	Bible Study
11	60-75	88	10	$5.49	New Christian	Workbk	Topical

Features: Charts
★★★★ Personal Application Preparation Time: Low
★★ Relationship Building Ldr. Guide: No Size: 6.0 x 9.0
Subjects: Women's Issues
Comments: This study helps participants assess godly characteristics others may see in them, including strength, love, goodness, generosity, faith, perseverance, courage, wisdom, self-control, kindness, and peace. Charts throughout the study help participants apply the lessons.

Author: Miller, Keith **994**
Series:
Title: *Hunger for Healing, A*
Publisher: NavPress, 1991 ISBN: 8-90073-182-3

Num. Sess.	Group Time	Num. Pgs.	Avg. Qst.	Price	Audience	Format	Bible Study
12	75-90	N/A	5	$129.00	Beginner	Video	Topical

Features: Intro to Study, Follow Up, Book Incl, Video Study Guide
★★★★ Personal Application Preparation Time: Low
★★★★ Relationship Building Ldr. Guide: Yes Size: 10.25 x 12.25
Subjects: Addictions, Counseling, Emotions, Relationships, Support
Comments: In this 12-week video series designed for small groups (25″ segments on 3 cassettes), Keith brings the Twelve Step model into focus for the church. Relating each of the steps to biblical principles, he demonstrates how they serve as spiritual disciplines. Each session offers lessons in recovery and self-assessment—a way out of a world marked for compulsion, fear, and broken relationships and into a new world of serenity, service, and healthy interaction with God and others.

Author: Milne, Bruce **995**
Series: The Bible Speaks Today
Title: *Message of John, The*
Publisher: InterVarsity, 1993 ISBN: 0-83081-233-4

Num. Sess.	Group Time	Num. Pgs.	Avg. Qst.	Price	Audience	Format	Bible Study
9	60-120	350	Vary	$14.99	New Christian	Book	Book

Features: Intro to Study, Bibliography
★★★ Personal Application Preparation Time: Med
★★ Relationship Building Ldr. Guide: No Size: 5.50 x 8.25
Subjects: John, New Testament
Comments: This series of Old and New Testament expositions is characterized by three goals: to expound the biblical text with accuracy, relate it to contemporary life, and be readable. This study of John is written for lay people who seek a deeper appreciation of the Gospel's text and want to apply it. The study guide lists possible discussion questions and requires leader preparation prior to study sessions.

Author: Mitcham, Jane T. **996**
Series: Faith Horizons
Title: *Intimacy & Identity*
Publisher: Augsburg Fortress Publishers, 1993

Num. Sess.	Group Time	Num. Pgs.	Avg. Qst.	Price	Audience	Format	Bible Study
6	60-75	40	9	$4.95	Beginner	Workbk	Topical

Features: Intro to Study, Prayer Helps, Worship Helps, Follow Up, Photos
★★ Personal Application Preparation Time: Low
★★ Relationship Building Ldr. Guide: No Size: 5.50 x 8.50
Subjects: Teens: Relationships
Comments: Each book in the Faith Horizons series explores a theme through a topical essay, Bible study, personal reflection and response, and worship. This study explores central questions: Who are we as individuals? How can we become more comfortable with ourselves, with God, with others? What is intimacy? How does our ability to be intimate affect relationships in our lives?

Author: Mitcham, Jr., L. William **997**
Series: Youth Talk
Title: *Sexuality*
Publisher: Augsburg Fortress Publishers, 1994

Num. Sess.	Group Time	Num. Pgs.	Avg. Qst.	Price	Audience	Format	Bible Study
5	45-60	46	N/A	$4.95	Beginner	Book	Topical

Features: Prayer Helps, Worship Helps, Photos
★★★★ Personal Application Preparation Time: Low
★★★★ Relationship Building Ldr. Guide: Yes Size: 8.0 x 11.0
Subjects: Teens: Junior High, Teens: Sexuality
Comments: An alternative to the "textbook approach," these studies are energetic, contemporary, and modeled after popular teen magazines. Advice columns, fiction, poetry, and other features are mostly written by youth. Decisions regarding sexual behavior can have a long-term impact on the lives of youth. This course acknowledges God's gift of sexuality, and helps youth value that gift. Topics: Created equal but different, Sexuality and dating, date rape, and more.

Author: Moberg, Frederick J. **998**
Series: Small Group Bible Studies
Title: *Parables*
Publisher: Augsburg Fortress Publishers, 1978

Num. Sess.	Group Time	Num. Pgs.	Avg. Qst.	Price	Audience	Format	Bible Study
6	60-75	24	20	$1.35	New Christian	Book	Topical

Features: Intro to Study, Prayer Helps
★★★ Personal Application Preparation Time: None
★★★ Relationship Building Ldr. Guide: No Size: 8.50 x 5.50
Subjects: Parables
Comments: This short, 6-session study looks at the parables of Jesus in three ways. It determines the real-life situation Jesus addressed in a particular parable; what question He answered, to which audience He spoke, and their need. It determines the parable's central idea and how it is related to the audience and the situation. Finally, it examines the parables in light of modern problems or needs.

Author: Money, Royce **999**
Series:
Title: *Building Stronger Families*
Publisher: Victor Books, 1984 ISBN: 0-88207-244-7

Num. Sess.	Group Time	Num. Pgs.	Avg. Qst.	Price	Audience	Format	Bible Study
13	60-90	165	N/A	$7.99	Beginner	Book	Topical

Features:
★★★★ Personal Application Preparation Time: Med
★★★★ Relationship Building Ldr. Guide: Yes Size: 5.50 x 8.0
Subjects: Church Life, Family, Parenting, Relationships
Comments: This book helps families develop good communication patterns, spend time togther, express appreciation, affirm spiritual values, and deal positively with crises. The same principles that strengthen family relationships also strengthen the church family. The second part of the book shows how a church can develop a family ministry, so that church and family can work together. A thorough leader's guide with transparency masters is available.

Author: Monge, David and Kathy Haugeisen **1000**
Series: Cross Signs
Title: *Who Are We? Being Children of God: Unit 2*
Publisher: Augsburg Fortress Publishers, 1992

Num. Sess.	Group Time	Num. Pgs.	Avg. Qst.	Price	Audience	Format	Bible Study
7	90-105	48	7	$3.75	New Christian	Book	Topical

Features: Intro to Study, Prayer Helps, Worship Helps
★★★ Personal Application Preparation Time: Low
★★ Relationship Building Ldr. Guide: Yes Size: 5.50 x 8.50
Subjects: Christian Living, Faith
Comments: Cross Signs, a Bible study series for adult small groups, includes 9 units of study that focus on key faith questions. In 7 sessions, participants consider what it means to be human in the closing years of the twentieth century. People's identities, theologically understood, are tied up with things like baptism, being created in the image of God, justification by faith, new creation, reconciliation, gifts, and hope.

Author: Moore, James "Trip" **1001**
Series: IBC Discussion Guide
Title: *Self-Image*
Publisher: NavPress, 1992 ISBN: 0-89109-684-1

Num. Sess.	Group Time	Num. Pgs.	Avg. Qst.	Price	Audience	Format	Bible Study
5	60-90	64	9	$5.00	Beginner	Workbk	Topical

Features: Intro to Leading a Study, Intro to Study, Prayer Helps, Follow Up, Ldr's Notes
★★★★ Personal Application Preparation Time: None
★★★★ Relationship Building Ldr. Guide: No Size: 5.25 x 8.25
Subjects: Counseling, Self-esteem, Support
Comments: "Self-Image" is one of 6 studies that identify how life struggles affect the way participants relate to themselves, others, and God. Five lessons look at what self-image is really all about, including: stories from one's past that emotionally fuel self-image, the benefits of clinging to a poor self-image, the unhealthy control that it can exert over one's daily life, and how to pursue change.

Author: Moore, James W. **1002**
Series: Bible Study for Christian
Title: *1 Corinthians—Volumes 1-3*
Publisher: Cokesbury, 1989 ISBN: 0-68776-138-7

Num. Sess.	Group Time	Num. Pgs.	Avg. Qst.	Price	Audience	Format	Bible Study
9	45-60	N/A	Vary	$40.00	New Christian	Video	Book

Features: Intro to Leading a Study, Intro to Study, Ldr's Notes, Video Study Guide
★★★ Personal Application Preparation Time: Low
★★★ Relationship Building Ldr. Guide: Yes Size: 4.75 x 8.0
Subjects: Christian Living, 1 Corinthians
Comments: This 3-volume video lecture study covers Paul's first letter to the Corinthian Christians, rugged individualists eager to be free of the apostle's traditional standards of personal conduct. He knew that if the church were to mature, the individualists would have to share one Lord, and one common life. It's valid, relevant subject matter for contemporary Christians. A leader's guide contains helpful insights.

Author: Moravec, Marilyn **1003**
Series: Growing Together Studies
Title: *Balancing Your Priorities*
Publisher: David C. Cook Publishing Co., 1989 ISBN: 1-55513-189-1

Num. Sess.	Group Time	Num. Pgs.	Avg. Qst.	Price	Audience	Format	Bible Study
6	50-60	64	10	$5.95	Beginner	Workbk	Topical

Features: Intro to Leading a Study, Intro to Study, Bibliography, Prayer Helps, Drawings
★★★ Personal Application Preparation Time: None
★★★★ Relationship Building Ldr. Guide: No Size: 5.25 x 8.25
Subjects: Caring, Christian Living, Wisdom
Comments: This study, part of a 4-book series, shows participants how to balance priorities by: deciding what's really important; listening to God in a noisy world; understanding personal needs without being self-centered; and taking time to express love to others. Warm, genuine fellowship will result. Complete with easy-to-follow instructions for leaders and group members, the study can last from 6 to 12 weeks.

Author: Moravec, Marilyn **1004**
Series: Growing Together Studies
Title: *Getting Along with People You Love*
Publisher: David C. Cook Publishing Co., 1989 ISBN: 1-55513-195-6

Num. Sess.	Group Time	Num. Pgs.	Avg. Qst.	Price	Audience	Format	Bible Study
6	50-60	64	8	$5.95	Beginner	Workbk	Topical

Features: Intro to Leading a Study, Intro to Study, Bibliography, Prayer Helps, Drawings
★★★ Personal Application Preparation Time: None
★★★★ Relationship Building Ldr. Guide: No Size: 5.25 x 8.25
Subjects: Christian Living, Commitments, Relationships
Comments: This study, part of a 4-book series, shows participants how to get along with loved ones by: easing tension in relationships; understanding what loved ones really mean; accepting and comforting loved ones; and letting commitment to Christ change relationships with loved ones. Complete with easy-to-follow instructions for leaders and group members, the study can last from 6 to 12 weeks.

Author: Moravec, Marilyn **1005**
Series: Growing Together Studies
Title: *Getting Your Act Together*
Publisher: David C. Cook Publishing Co., 1989 ISBN: 1-55513-194-8

Num. Sess.	Group Time	Num. Pgs.	Avg. Qst.	Price	Audience	Format	Bible Study
6	50-60	66	12	$5.95	Beginner	Workbk	Topical

Features: Intro to Leading a Study, Intro to Study, Bibliography, Prayer Helps, Drawings
★★★ Personal Application Preparation Time: None
★★★★ Relationship Building Ldr. Guide: No Size: 5.25 x 8.25
Subjects: Christian Living, Emotions, Stress, Success
Comments: This study, part of a 4-book series, shows participants how to get their acts together by: achieving goals through self-management; overcoming disabling fears; counting the cost of achievement; and caring for the "inner world" of biblical self-management. Complete with easy-to-follow instructions for leaders and group members, the study can last from 6 to 12 weeks.

Author: Moravec, Marilyn **1006**
Series: Growing Together Studies
Title: *Living in Harmony*
Publisher: David C. Cook Publishing Co., 1989 ISBN: 1-55513-190-5

Num. Sess.	Group Time	Num. Pgs.	Avg. Qst.	Price	Audience	Format	Bible Study
6	50-60	61	8	$5.95	Beginner	Workbk	Topical

Features: Intro to Leading a Study, Intro to Study, Bibliography, Prayer Helps, Drawings
★★★ Personal Application Preparation Time: None
★★★★ Relationship Building Ldr. Guide: No Size: 5.25 x 8.25
Subjects: Christian Living, Emotions, Relationships, Stress
Comments: This study, part of a 4-book series, shows participants how to live in harmony by: identifying their style for handling conflicts; taming their anger; stating needs clearly and competing fairly; and turning conflict into spiritual growth instead of revenge. Complete with easy-to-follow instructions for leaders and group members, the study can last from 6 to 12 weeks.

Author: Mork, Carol J. **1007**
Series: Friendship Bible Study
Title: *Sermon on the Mount*
Publisher: Augsburg Fortress Publishers, 1987

Num. Sess.	Group Time	Num. Pgs.	Avg. Qst.	Price	Audience	Format	Bible Study
8	60-75	48	13	$3.75	New Christian	Workbk	Topical

Features: Intro to Study, Prayer Helps, Study Overview
★★★★ Personal Application Preparation Time: Low
★★★★ Relationship Building Ldr. Guide: Yes Size: 5.50 x 8.0
Subjects: Matthew, Sermon on the Mount
Comments: This 8-lesson study challenges contemporary participants to explore what Jesus' Sermon on the Mount means for them as Christians in North America. The first lesson consists of the first 10 verses of Jesus' sermon called the Beatitudes. The lesson format includes an overview, an opening, a responsive reading, Bible background, questions for reflection, a key verse, a prayer response, and an "our faith" response.

Author: Mouser, William **1008**
Series: LifeGuide Bible Study
Title: *Proverbs*
Publisher: InterVarsity, 1990 ISBN: 0-83081-026-9

Num. Sess.	Group Time	Num. Pgs.	Avg. Qst.	Price	Audience	Format	Bible Study
13	45-60	95	11	$4.99	Beginner	Workbk	Topical

Features: Intro to Leading a Study, Intro to Study, Ldr's Notes
★★★ Personal Application Preparation Time: Low
★★★ Relationship Building Ldr. Guide: No Size: 5.50 x 8.25
Subjects: Family, Friendships, Proverbs, Relationships, Wisdom, Work
Comments: This thirteen-week study introduces participants to selected proverbs from Solomon's collection, grouped together under 13 different themes. They teach how to be successful and prosperous in work, in dealings with family and friends, and in a relationship with God. Direction and guidance from Proverbs is practical, concrete, reasonable, and fruitful; it will teach participants to live more wisely.

Author: Mowchan, Carolyn M. **1009**
Series: Friendship Bible Study
Title: *Prayer*
Publisher: Augsburg Fortress Publishers, 1989

Num. Sess.	Group Time	Num. Pgs.	Avg. Qst.	Price	Audience	Format	Bible Study
8	60-75	48	14	$3.75	New Christian	Workbk	Topical

Features: Intro to Study, Prayer Helps, Study Overview
★★★★ Personal Application Preparation Time: Low
★★★★ Relationship Building Ldr. Guide: Yes Size: 5.50 x 8.50
Subjects: Faith, Prayer
Comments: This eight-lesson study helps participants explore issues of prayer and spirituality. It encourages the practice of individual and corporate prayer which deepen faith and enrich spiritual life. The lesson format includes an overview, an opening, a responsive reading, Bible background, questions for reflection, a key verse, a prayer response, and an "our faith" response.

Author: Mullins, Terence Y. **1010**
Series: Friendship Bible Study
Title: *Isaiah*
Publisher: Augsburg Fortress Publishers, 1988

Num. Sess.	Group Time	Num. Pgs.	Avg. Qst.	Price	Audience	Format	Bible Study
8	60-75	48	10	$3.75	New Christian	Workbk	Book

Features: Intro to Study, Prayer Helps, Study Overview
★★★★ Personal Application Preparation Time: Low
★★★★ Relationship Building Ldr. Guide: Yes Size: 5.50 x 8.50
Subjects: Isaiah/Jeremiah, Major Prophets, Prophecy
Comments: This 8-lesson study examines the Old Testament prophecy of Isaiah. Three sections are viewed. The first (chapters 1–39) is about the acts and words of the prophet; the second (chapters 40–55) speaks of "comfort, comfort My people, says your God" (40:1); and the third (chapters 56–66) emphasizes righteousness. The lesson format includes an overview, an opening, a responsive reading, Bible background, questions for reflection, a key verse, a prayer response.

Author: Munger, Robert Boyd **1011**
Series: Christian Basics
Title: *Commitment: My Heart—Christ's Home*
Publisher: InterVarsity, 1994 ISBN: 0-83082-005-1

Num. Sess.	Group Time	Num. Pgs.	Avg. Qst.	Price	Audience	Format	Bible Study
6	30-45	61	7	$4.99	Beginner	Workbk	Topical

Features: Intro to Leading a Study, Intro to Study, Full Scrpt Printed, Ldr's Notes
★★★★ Personal Application Preparation Time: None
★★★★ Relationship Building Ldr. Guide: No Size: 5.50 x 8.25
Subjects: Christian Life, Commitments
Comments: This study leads participants on a "walk through 6 of the heart's rooms," helping them see aspects of their Christian life as Jesus sees them. The lessons move participants from room to room discovering God's desires for them. Lessons cover the parts of these rooms which need to be changed or cleaned out in order to be places in which Christ can be at home.

Author: Murphy, Mike & Victoria Johnson **1012**
Series: Family Growth Electives
Title: *Raising Kids in a Violent Culture: Studies for Today's Parents*
Publisher: David C. Cook Publishing Co., 1995 ISBN: 0-78145-139-6

Num. Sess.	Group Time	Num. Pgs.	Avg. Qst.	Price	Audience	Format	Bible Study
13	45-60	144	Vary	$19.95	Beginner	Workbk	Topical

Features: Intro to Study, Objectives, Bibliography, Prayer Helps, Drawings, Handouts, Persnl Study Quest
★★★★ Personal Application Preparation Time: Low
★★★★ Relationship Building Ldr. Guide: Yes Size: 8.50 x 11.0
Subjects: Family, Parenting, Relationships, Social Issues
Comments: This 13-week self-contained leader's guide helps modern parents who are concerned about the impact of America's violent culture on their children. It helps parents assess and compare culture today and yesterday, handle the influence of the media, understand and recognize signs of at-risk behavior, develop effective parenting skills, and equip children to resist violence.

Author: Myers, Bill **1013**
Series: SonPower Elective Series
Title: *Hot Topics, Tough Questions*
Publisher: Victor Books, 1987 ISBN: 0-89693-517-5

Num. Sess.	Group Time	Num. Pgs.	Avg. Qst.	Price	Audience	Format	Bible Study
13	60-75	159	Vary	$5.99	Beginner	Book	Topical

Features: Drawings
★★★★ Personal Application Preparation Time: None
★★★★ Relationship Building Ldr. Guide: Yes Size: 4.25 x 7.0
Subjects: Teens: Christian Liv, Teens: Emotions, Teens: Senior High
Comments: This book responds to a series of tough questions asked by teenagers, such as: How do I find God's will? Sex—why not? How do I handle anger, fear, depression? Answers are found in the Bible. A leader's guide with transparency masters is available. Rip-out sheets for students are also available.

Author: Myers, Martha L. **1014**
Series: Search Weekly Bible
Title: *Unit 12/Galatians*
Publisher: Augsburg Fortress Publishers, 1985

Num. Sess.	Group Time	Num. Pgs.	Avg. Qst.	Price	Audience	Format	Bible Study
8	90-105	64	Vary	$5.50	New Christian	Book	Book

Features: Intro to Study, Objectives, Prayer Helps, Worship Helps, Follow Up, Summary
★★ Personal Application Preparation Time: Med
★★ Relationship Building Ldr. Guide: Yes Size: 8.50 x 11.0
Subjects: Galatians
Comments: This review of Galatians is 1 of 20 units of a 5-year study titled "Search. Paul's letter centers mainly on 2 issues: What is the Gospel? What difference does the Gospel make in the way that Christians live with other people? The three-part outline includes: "Paul and His Gospels"; "The Law Never Was the Gospel"; and "Living in the Freedom of the Spirit."

Author: Nagy, Martin, et al. **1015**
Series:
Title: *130 Ways To Involve Parents in Youth Ministry*
Publisher: Group Publishing, 1994 ISBN: 1-55945-250-1

Num. Sess.	Group Time	Num. Pgs.	Avg. Qst.	Price	Audience	Format	Bible Study
	—	127	N/A	$13.99			

Features: Intro to Study, Handouts
Personal Application Preparation Time:
Relationship Building Ldr. Guide: Size: 6.0 x 9.0
Subjects: Teens: Resources
Comments: This book provides over 100 innovative ideas to help parents play vital roles in youth ministries. This book includes: ideas for making parents partners in ministry; tips for coordinating successful parent meetings and support groups; activities that give parents and kids opportunities to grow together, have fun together, communicate, and serve together; creative ways to encourage and inform parents; strategies for handling conflict with parents; and reproducible forms.

Author: Nappa, Amy **1016**
Series: Group's Active Bible Curriculum
Title: *Dealing With Disappointment*
Publisher: Group Publishing, 1992 ISBN: 1-55945-139-4

Num. Sess.	Group Time	Num. Pgs.	Avg. Qst.	Price	Audience	Format	Bible Study
4	35-60	47	Vary	$9.99	Beginner	Workbk	Topical

Features: Intro to Leading a Study, Intro to Study, Objectives, Study Overview, Ldr's Notes, Handouts, Agenda, Publicity Ideas
★★★★ Personal Application Preparation Time: None
★★★★ Relationship Building Ldr. Guide: No Size: 8.50 x 11.0
Subjects: Teens: Christian Liv, Teens: Family, Teens: Junior High, Teens: Relationships
Comments: In this course, teenagers explore examples from the Bible of people with problems and learn from these Bible characters' struggles and mistakes. Participants explore how to deal with disappointments in relationships, find healthy ways to deal with family problems, learn to overcome obstacles at school.

Author: Nappa, Amy **1017**
Series: Group's Active Bible Curriculum
Title: *Exodus: Following God*
Publisher: Group Publishing, 1992 ISBN: 1-55945-226-9

Num. Sess.	Group Time	Num. Pgs.	Avg. Qst.	Price	Audience	Format	Bible Study
4	35-60	48	Vary	$9.99	Beginner	Workbk	Book

Features: Intro to Leading a Study, Intro to Study, Objectives, Study Overview, Ldr's Notes, Handouts, Agenda, Publicity Ideas
★★★★ Personal Application Preparation Time: None
★★★★ Relationship Building Ldr. Guide: No Size: 8.50 x 11.0
Subjects: Teens: Christian Liv, Teens: Senior High
Comments: Four participatory sessions show teenagers the plans God has for their lives, and how to trust God even when things seem impossible. They'll learn that some risks are worth taking when God provides protection, recognize the value of trusting Him, explore God's laws and apply them to choices they make today, and see how He provides for them each day.

Author: Nappa, Amy **1018**
Series: Group's Active Bible Curriculum
Title: *Love or Infatuation?*
Publisher: Group Publishing, 1992 ISBN: 1-55945-128-9

Num. Sess.	Group Time	Num. Pgs.	Avg. Qst.	Price	Audience	Format	Bible Study
4	35-60	46	Vary	$9.99	Beginner	Workbk	Topical

Features: Intro to Leading a Study, Intro to Study, Objectives, Study Overview, Handouts, Agenda, Publicity Ideas
★★★★ Personal Application Preparation Time: None
★★★★ Relationship Building Ldr. Guide: No Size: 8.50 x 11.0
Subjects: Teens: Christian Liv, Teens: Friends, Teens: Junior High, Teens: Sexuality
Comments: This course helps teenagers learn to sort out feelings while exploring myths and realities about love, infatuation, and friends of the opposite sex. It teaches the difference between having a crush and being in love and helps teens discover what the Bible says about sex's proper place in relationships.

Author: Nappa, Mike **1019**
Series: Group's Active Bible Curriculum
Title: *Accepting Others: Beyond Barriers & Stereotypes*
Publisher: Group Publishing, 1992 ISBN: 1-55945-126-2

Num. Sess.	Group Time	Num. Pgs.	Avg. Qst.	Price	Audience	Format	Bible Study
4	35-60	43	Vary	$9.99	Beginner	Workbk	Topical

Features: Intro to Leading a Study, Intro to Study, Objectives, Study Overview, Ldr's Notes, Handouts, Agenda, Publicity Ideas
★★★★ Personal Application Preparation Time: None
★★★★ Relationship Building Ldr. Guide: No Size: 8.50 x 11.0
Subjects: Teens: Christian Liv, Teens: Junior High, Teens: Relationships, Teens: Values
Comments: Junior highers learn to accept and relate to people of different races, cultures, beliefs, and social status. Participants learn to accept and love others while experiencing and exploring the consequences of racism and prejudice, discovering ways to reach out to people of different cultures, and developing a sense of unity.

Author: Nappa, Mike **1020**
Series: Group's Active Bible Curriculum
Title: *Reaching Out to a Hurting World*
Publisher: Group Publishing, 1992 ISBN: 1-55945-140-8

Num. Sess.	Group Time	Num. Pgs.	Avg. Qst.	Price	Audience	Format	Bible Study
4	35-60	46	Vary	$9.99	Beginner	Workbk	Topical

Features: Intro to Leading a Study, Intro to Study, Objectives, Study Overview, Ldr's Notes, Handouts, Agenda, Publicity Ideas
★★★★ Personal Application Preparation Time: None
★★★★ Relationship Building Ldr. Guide: No Size: 8.50 x 11.0
Subjects: Teens: Christian Liv, Teens: Junior High, Teens: Missions
Comments: Through this course, junior highers reach out to people in need to make a positive impact on the world around them. Participants discover the reality of poverty and are challenged to help the poor, grow in compassion for suffering people, join in meeting the world's need to know Jesus, and stand firm in the face of oppression. It can be adapted for a Bible class or youth meeting. Activity sheets are reproducible.

Author: Nappa, Mike and Paul Neale Lessard **1021**
Series:
Title: *Super Plays For Worship and Special Occasions*
Publisher: Group Publishing, 1994 ISBN: 1-55945-254-4

Num. Sess.	Group Time	Num. Pgs.	Avg. Qst.	Price	Audience	Format	Bible Study
	20-30	144	N/A	$15.99		Book	

Features: Intro to Study, Drawings, Handouts
Personal Application Preparation Time:
Relationship Building Ldr. Guide: Size: 7.0 x 10.0
Subjects: Small Group Resource, Teens: Resources
Comments: This collection of 12 one-act plays concerns worship or special themes such as faith, the church, and new life in Christ. Other plays for special occasions include: Easter, Lent, Mothers day, Fathers day, Thanksgiving, and Christmas. Each play comes with guidelines for simple staging, props, and costumes. It also provides photocopiable scripts, guidelines for planning auditions and rehearsals, plans to guide actors on stage, and ideas for light and sound resources.

Author: Nappa, Mike, et al. **1022**
Series:
Title: *Youth Worker's Encyclopedia of Bible Teaching Ideas, The: Old Testament*
Publisher: Group Publishing, 1994 ISBN: 1-55945-184-X

Num. Sess.	Group Time	Num. Pgs.	Avg. Qst.	Price	Audience	Format	Bible Study
	—	420	N/A	$19.99		Book	

Features: Intro to Study, Summary, Handouts, Index
Personal Application Preparation Time:
Relationship Building Ldr. Guide: Size: 6.0 x 9.0
Subjects: Teens: Old Testament, Teens: Resources
Comments: This resource for youth includes over 365 presentations on Old Testament Scripture. Three indexes make it easy to use: Scripture, themes, and teaching ideas index. The Old Testament theme index is helpful in selecting topical presentations such as "Advice" and "A friend loves at all times." Includes: adventures, affirmations, creative prayers, creative readings, devotions, group projects, skits, and more.

Author: Nappa, Mike, et al. **1023**
Series:
Title: *Youth Worker's Encyclopedia of Bible Teaching Ideas, The: New Testament*
Publisher: Group Publishing, 1994 ISBN: 1-55945-183-1

Num. Sess.	Group Time	Num. Pgs.	Avg. Qst.	Price	Audience	Format	Bible Study
	—	420	N/A	$19.99		Book	

Features: Intro to Study, Summary, Handouts, Index
Personal Application Preparation Time:
Relationship Building Ldr. Guide: Size: 6.0 x 9.0
Subjects: Teens: New Testament, Teens: Resources
Comments: This resource for youth includes over 365 presentations on New Testament Scripture. Three indexes make it easy to use: Scripture, themes, and teaching ideas index. The New Testament theme index is helpful in selecting topical presentations such as "being beautiful inside" and "bragging." Includes: adventures, affirmations, creative prayers, creative readings, devotions, learning games, projects.

Author: Neff, Miriam **1024**
Series:
Title: *Women and Their Emotions*
Publisher: Moody Press, 1995 ISBN: 0-80249-531-1

Num. Sess.	Group Time	Num. Pgs.	Avg. Qst.	Price	Audience	Format	Bible Study
14	60-90	175	5	$8.99	Beginner	Book	Topical

Features: Intro to Study, Charts
★★★★ Personal Application Preparation Time: Med
★★ Relationship Building Ldr. Guide: No Size: 5.50 x 8.50
Subjects: Emotions, Women's Issues
Comments: This book helps readers focus on emotional wounds, hard-to-break habits, and pitfalls, and learn how to overcome them. Covering anger, bitterness, fear, contentment, loneliness, love, anxiety, discouragement, depression, and grief, the author shows how emotions can be transformed to become helpful and useful. Exercises help women who are ready to restructure their emotions. Experienced leaders are required, as questions are more for personal reflection.

Author: Nelson, Jonathan **1025**
Series: Lay Action Ministry
Title: *Panorama of Christian History, A*
Publisher: Lay Action Ministry Program, 1993

Num. Sess.	Group Time	Num. Pgs.	Avg. Qst.	Price	Audience	Format	Bible Study
12	60-75	152	Vary	$6.95	New Christian	Workbk	Topical

Features:
★★★ Personal Application Preparation Time: Low
★★★ Relationship Building Ldr. Guide: Yes Size: 5.50 x 8.50
Subjects: Church Life
Comments: This Lamp lay training publication offers a "big picture" view of the church from the 1st through the 20th century. Lessons include: "The Young Church"; "Catholic Christianity and the Age of Councils"; "Constantine and Augustine"; "The Church of the Barbarians"; "The Church at the Height of Its Power"; "Theologians and Reformers in the Middle Ages"; "The Renaissance and German Reformation"; and more.

Author: Nelson, Randy A. and Virginia Knueppel **1026**
Series: Cross Signs
Title: *How Do I Decide? Making Faithful Choices: Unit 7*
Publisher: Augsburg Fortress Publishers, 1993

Num. Sess.	Group Time	Num. Pgs.	Avg. Qst.	Price	Audience	Format	Bible Study
7	90-105	48	5	$3.75	New Christian	Book	Topical

Features: Intro to Study, Prayer Helps, Worship Helps
★★★ Personal Application Preparation Time: Low
★★ Relationship Building Ldr. Guide: Yes Size: 5.50 x 8.50
Subjects: Decision Making
Comments: Cross Signs, a Bible study series for adult small groups, features nine units of study which focus on key faith questions. This study invites participants to join with other Christians in discovering what it means to be faithful to God in daily choices that confront everyone.

Author: Nelson, Richard D. **1027**
Series: Search Weekly Bible
Title: *Unit 17/Amos & Hosea*
Publisher: Augsburg Fortress Publishers, 1987

Num. Sess.	Group Time	Num. Pgs.	Avg. Qst.	Price	Audience	Format	Bible Study
8	90-105	64	Vary	$5.50	New Christian	Book	Book

Features: Intro to Study, Objectives, Prayer Helps, Worship Helps, Follow Up, Summary
★★ Personal Application Preparation Time: Med
★★ Relationship Building Ldr. Guide: Yes Size: 8.50 x 11.0
Subjects: Minor Prophets
Comments: This review of Amos and Hosea is one of twenty units of a 5-year study titled "Search." Amos and Hosea were two prophets, or preachers of God's Word, in the Old Testament kingdom of Israel. They worked between about 760 and 720 B.C., Amos first, and then Hosea. The word they brought was a word of judgment on a people who richly deserved it, but they also spoke of a hope for a new future from God.

Author: Nelson, Wayne S. **1028**
Series: The Lifechange Series
Title: *Exodus*
Publisher: NavPress, 1989 ISBN: 0-89109-283-8

Num. Sess.	Group Time	Num. Pgs.	Avg. Qst.	Price	Audience	Format	Bible Study
18	60-90	166	17	$6.00	New Christian	Workbk	Book

Features: Intro to Leading a Study, Intro to Study, Bibliography, Prayer Helps, Worship Helps, Study Overview, Digging Deeper Quest, Summary, Maps, Cross Ref, Word Study
★★★ Personal Application Preparation Time: Med
★★★ Relationship Building Ldr. Guide: No Size: 5.50 x 8.50
Subjects: Exodus, God, Worship
Comments: This verse-by-verse study of Exodus examines God's methods for dealing with rebellion, His shaping of Moses into a leader, governing principles for just treatment of others, and guidelines for pure and wholehearted worship. It covers the story of humanity's redemption, showing how God brought Israel out of slavery.

Author: Nelson, Wayne S. **1029**
Series: The Lifechange Series
Title: *1 Samuel*
Publisher: NavPress, 1989 ISBN: 0-89109-277-3

Num. Sess.	Group Time	Num. Pgs.	Avg. Qst.	Price	Audience	Format	Bible Study
16	60-90	168	17	$6.00	New Christian	Workbk	Book

Features: Intro to Leading a Study, Intro to Study, Bibliography, Prayer Helps, Worship Helps, Study Overview, Digging Deeper Quest, Summary, Maps, Cross Ref, Word Study
★★★ Personal Application Preparation Time: Med
★★★ Relationship Building Ldr. Guide: No Size: 5.50 x 8.50
Subjects: Bible Personalities, Commitments, Leadership, 1 & 2 Samuel
Comments: This study looks at 3 men chosen by God to guide Israel's military attacks on moral corruption. The 3 are Samuel, a prophet who directs Israel's transition from judgeship to monarchy; Saul, Israel's first king; and David, a man after God's own heart.

Author: Nielson, Kathleen B. **1030**
Series: Challenge Bible Study
Title: *Resting Secure*
Publisher: Baker Book House, 1993 ISBN: 0-80106-789-8

Num. Sess.	Group Time	Num. Pgs.	Avg. Qst.	Price	Audience	Format	Bible Study
7	60-75	106	Vary	$4.99	New Christian	Workbk	Topical

Features: Intro to Leading a Study, Intro to Study
★★★ Personal Application Preparation Time: Med
★★★ Relationship Building Ldr. Guide: No Size: 5.50 x 8.50
Subjects: Bible Personalities, Proverbs, Psalms
Comments: This 7-lesson study deals with Old Testament poetry. The goal of the study is to help participants know God better through the imaginative experience of Old Testament poems. Included are: "Psalm 16: Resting Secure"; "Psalm 36: Two Ways of Seeing"; "Psalm 48: In the City of Our God"; "Poetry from the Book of Proverbs: Lips and Tongues and Words"; "A Poem of Isaiah: Come to the Water"; and "A Poem of Habakkuk: I will Wait Patiently."

Author: Nielson, Kathleen B. **1031**
Series: Challenge Bible Study
Title: *This God We Worship*
Publisher: Baker Book House, 1993 ISBN: 0-80106-787-1

Num. Sess.	Group Time	Num. Pgs.	Avg. Qst.	Price	Audience	Format	Bible Study
6	60-75	92	Vary	$4.99	New Christian	Workbk	Charctr

Features: Intro to Leading a Study, Intro to Study
★★★ Personal Application Preparation Time: Med
★★★ Relationship Building Ldr. Guide: No Size: 5.50 x 8.50
Subjects: Bible Personalities
Comments: This 7-lesson study deals with Old Testament poetry. The goal of the study is to help participants know God better through the imaginative experience of Old Testament poems. Included are: "A Poem of Moses: God's Strong Hand"; "A Poem of Hannah: No One Besides You"; "Psalm 19: God is Speaking"; "Psalm 32: Blessed Forgiveness"; "Psalm 33: Look at This God We Worship"; and "A Poem of Hosea: Loving Father God."

Author: Niguette, Alan & Beth **1032**
Series: Building Books
Title: *Building Your Christian Defense System*
Publisher: Bethany House, 1988 ISBN: 1-55661-015-7

Num. Sess.	Group Time	Num. Pgs.	Avg. Qst.	Price	Audience	Format	Bible Study
34	45-60	54	Vary	$6.99	New Christian	Workbk	Topical

Features: Intro to Study
★★ Personal Application Preparation Time: Low
★★ Relationship Building Ldr. Guide: Yes Size: 8.50 x 11.0
Subjects: Teens: Cults
Comments: This 34-lesson study is designed to train young people to think biblically and uncover the subtle tactics of cults. It helps equip participants to discern truth from falsehood by treating 6 major topics: deception of the cults, warning signs of deception, 4 common threads of deception, how counterfeit things look real, the attractive but deadly nature of cults, and how to overcome error with truth.

Author: Nilsen, Mary Y. **1033**
Series: Friendship Bible Study
Title: *Proverbs*
Publisher: Augsburg Fortress Publishers, 1987

Num. Sess.	Group Time	Num. Pgs.	Avg. Qst.	Price	Audience	Format	Bible Study
8	60-75	48	10	$3.75	New Christian	Workbk	Book

Features: Intro to Study, Prayer Helps, Study Overview
★★★★ Personal Application Preparation Time: Low
★★★★ Relationship Building Ldr. Guide: Yes Size: 5.50 x 8.50
Subjects: Proverbs, Wisdom
Comments: This 8-lesson study enhances Christian growth and friendship. A study of Proverbs helps participants "recognize wisdom . . . and live intelligently." It can make them "clever" and "resourceful," and even add knowledge to those already wise or educated. The lesson format includes an overview, an opening, a responsive reading, Bible background, questions for reflection, a key verse, a prayer response, and an "our faith" response.

Author: Nyquist, James F. & Jack Kuhatschek **1034**
Series: LifeGuide Bible Study
Title: *Leading Bible Discussion*
Publisher: InterVarsity, 1985 ISBN: 0-83081-000-5

Num. Sess.	Group Time	Num. Pgs.	Avg. Qst.	Price	Audience	Format	Bible Study
9	—	64	N/A	$4.99	New Christian	Book	No

Features: Intro to Study, Appendix
Personal Application Preparation Time:
Relationship Building Ldr. Guide: Size: 5.50 x 8.25
Subjects: Leadership, Small Group Resource
Comments: The suggestions in this book can enable potential leaders to effectively and enjoyably fulfill their leadership roles. Subjects covered include how to: start a group, decide what to study, prepare to lead, study the Bible, use a study guide, write your own questions, lead a discussion, and evaluate a study. An appendix reviews a model study on humility.

Author: Nystrom, Carolyn **1035**
Series: Christian Character
Title: *Finding Contentment*
Publisher: InterVarsity, 1992 ISBN: 0-83081-145-1

Num. Sess.	Group Time	Num. Pgs.	Avg. Qst.	Price	Audience	Format	Bible Study
6	30-90	64	23	$4.99	New Christian	Workbk	Topical

Features: Intro to Leading a Study, Intro to Study, Ldr's Notes
★★★★ Personal Application Preparation Time: None
★★★ Relationship Building Ldr. Guide: No Size: 5.50 x 8.25
Subjects: Christian Life, Hope
Comments: This study offers 7 options for either individual or group study, ranging from 6–12 weeks and 30″–90″ depending on the number of questions covered. The lessons help participants define contentment that is found in the Christian life, including intangibles such as trust, love, joy, peace, comfort and hope. These intangibles introduce participants to the keys to complete fulfillment in Christ.

Author: Nystrom, Carolyn **1036**
Series: The TruthSeed Series
Title: *Jonah & Ruth: A Friend for the Journey*
Publisher: Victor Books, 1995 ISBN: 1-56476-363-3

Num. Sess.	Group Time	Num. Pgs.	Avg. Qst.	Price	Audience	Format	Bible Study
8	45-60	96	12	$4.99	Beginner	Workbk	Book

Features: Intro to Leading a Study, Intro to Study, Bibliography, Prayer Helps, Worship Helps, Follow Up, Ldr's Notes
★★★ Personal Application Preparation Time: None
★★★ Relationship Building Ldr. Guide: No Size: 6.0 x 9.0
Subjects: Bible Personalities, Ruth
Comments: This new series of inductive Bible studies enables men and women to experience community and develop godliness in either discussion group or personal settings. Questions are designed and field-tested for seekers, new believers, and mature Christians. In this study participants travel alongside Jonah and Ruth to learn from their individual experiences that God is their Friend for the journey.

Author: Nystrom, Carolyn **1037**
Series: The Discipleship Series
Title: *Knowing Scripture*
Publisher: Zondervan, 1992 ISBN: 0-31054-721-0

Num. Sess.	Group Time	Num. Pgs.	Avg. Qst.	Price	Audience	Format	Bible Study
6	45-60	63	14	$4.99	New Christian	Workbk	Topical

Features: Intro to Leading a Study, Intro to Study, Objectives, Scrpt Memory Helps, Follow Up, Ldr's Notes
★★★★ Personal Application Preparation Time: Med
★★ Relationship Building Ldr. Guide: No Size: 5.50 x 8.50
Subjects: Bible Study, Discipleship, Prayer
Comments: This study is for Christians who find the Bible difficult to understand. This guide not only stresses the importance of Scripture but also teaches how to study the Bible on one's own. Lesson titles include: "Why Study Scripture?"; "Getting an Overview"; "Looking for Details"; "Discovering Meaning"; "Learning to Apply"; and "Praying the Scriptures."

Author: Nystrom, Carolyn **1038**
Series: Christian Character
Title: *Living in the World*
Publisher: InterVarsity, 1992 ISBN: 0-83081-143-5

Num. Sess.	Group Time	Num. Pgs.	Avg. Qst.	Price	Audience	Format	Bible Study
6	30-90	64	24	$4.99	New Christian	Workbk	Topical

Features: Intro to Leading a Study, Intro to Study, Bibliography, Ldr's Notes
★★★★ Personal Application Preparation Time: None
★★★ Relationship Building Ldr. Guide: No Size: 5.50 x 8.25
Subjects: Christian Life
Comments: This study helps participants discover their roles in God's world, from valuing the sanctity of life, to sharing their faith, to helping society's outcasts, to protecting the environment. These conscience-raising lessons include: "Valuing Life"; "Meeting Physical Needs"; "Relieving the Oppressed"; "Practicing Hospitality"; and more.

Author: Nystrom, Carolyn **1039**
Series: Christian Character
Title: *Loving God*
Publisher: InterVarsity, 1992 ISBN: 0-83081-141-9

Num. Sess.	Group Time	Num. Pgs.	Avg. Qst.	Price	Audience	Format	Bible Study
6	30-90	64	21	$4.99	New Christian	Workbk	Topical

Features: Intro to Leading a Study, Intro to Study, Bibliography, Ldr's Notes
★★★★ Personal Application Preparation Time: None
★★★ Relationship Building Ldr. Guide: No Size: 5.50 x 8.25
Subjects: God, Love
Comments: In this study, the first 3 sessions discuss examples of how God's character of love is displayed: gracious, stubborn, and victorious. The last 3 lessons treat Christians response of love to Him: a love with heart and soul, a love with mind, and a love with strength.

Author: Nystrom, Carolyn **1040**
Series: Christian Character
Title: *Loving One Another*
Publisher: InterVarsity, 1992 ISBN: 0-83081-142-7

Num. Sess.	Group Time	Num. Pgs.	Avg. Qst.	Price	Audience	Format	Bible Study
6	30-90	64	24	$4.99	New Christian	Workbk	Topical

Features: Intro to Leading a Study, Intro to Study, Bibliography, Ldr's Notes
★★★★ Personal Application Preparation Time: None
★★★ Relationship Building Ldr. Guide: No Size: 5.50 x 8.25
Subjects: Christian Living, Love, Relationships
Comments: This study offers 7 options for either individual or group study, ranging from 6–12 weeks and 30″–90″ depending on the number of questions covered. Lessons instruct on worshiping together, encouraging one another, caring for the weak, holding one another accountable, and how to be "one" in Christ.

Author: Nystrom, Carolyn **1041**
Series: Christian Character
Title: *Loving the World*
Publisher: InterVarsity, 1992 ISBN: 0-83081-144-3

Num. Sess.	Group Time	Num. Pgs.	Avg. Qst.	Price	Audience	Format	Bible Study
6	30-90	64	25	$4.99	New Christian	Workbk	Topical

Features: Intro to Leading a Study, Intro to Study, Bibliography, Ldr's Notes
★★★★ Personal Application Preparation Time: None
★★★ Relationship Building Ldr. Guide: No Size: 5.50 x 8.25
Subjects: Materialism, Work
Comments: This study offers 7 options for either individual or group study, ranging form 6–12 weeks and 30″–90″. Lessons deal with being Christians in a secular world, facing tensions between the world's values and God's values. Subjects include: "How do we glorify God in secular work?" "How should we spend our money?" and "What is our responsibility as citizens?

Author: Nystrom, Carolyn **1042**
Series: LifeGuide Bible Study
Title: *Old Testament Kings*
Publisher: InterVarsity, 1993 ISBN: 0-83081-070-6

Num. Sess.	Group Time	Num. Pgs.	Avg. Qst.	Price	Audience	Format	Bible Study
12	45-60	64	13	$4.99	New Christian	Workbk	Charctr

Features: Intro to Leading a Study, Intro to Study, Ldr's Notes, Maps
★★ Personal Application Preparation Time: Low
★★ Relationship Building Ldr. Guide: No Size: 5.50 x 8.25
Subjects: Bible Personalities
Comments: This study looks at the Hebrew kings, including Solomon, Jeroboam, Rehoboam, Asa, Ahab, Jehoshaphat, Ahaz, Hoshea, Hezekiah, Manasseh, Josiah, and Zedekiah, the last Hebrew king. The forty-two kings ruled for four centuries. Some ruled only days, others for a lifetime. Some were evil, some good. In the study, participants will see that none of the kings were perfect and neither are they, but that God is sovereign, over kings and over modern mankind as well.

Author: Nystrom, Carolyn **1043**
Series: LifeGuide Bible Study
Title: *Peter & Jude*
Publisher: InterVarsity, 1992 ISBN: 0-83081-019-6

Num. Sess.	Group Time	Num. Pgs.	Avg. Qst.	Price	Audience	Format	Bible Study
12	45-60	64	12	$4.99	New Christian	Workbk	Book

Features: Intro to Leading a Study, Intro to Study, Ldr's Notes
★★ Personal Application Preparation Time: Low
★★ Relationship Building Ldr. Guide: No Size: 5.50 x 8.25
Subjects: 1 & 2 Peter, 1, 2 & 3 John/Jude
Comments: This study of Peter and Jude discusses the difficulty of growing into maturity. But it also shows participants how God provides direction and comfort when things are bad and what it takes to be mature in Christ. These letters do not promote an escape from suffering, but instead tell people to expect it. They tell Christians to balance holy living with correct doctrine, nurture spiritual growth, work within exisiting authority structures, and take care of one another.

Author: Nystrom, Carolyn **1044**
Series: Christian Character
Title: *Pursuing Holiness*
Publisher: InterVarsity, 1992 ISBN: 0-83081-147-8

Num. Sess.	Group Time	Num. Pgs.	Avg. Qst.	Price	Audience	Format	Bible Study
6	30-90	64	25	$4.99	New Christian	Workbk	Topical

Features: Intro to Leading a Study, Intro to Study, Bibliography, Ldr's Notes
★★★★ Personal Application Preparation Time: None
★★★ Relationship Building Ldr. Guide: No Size: 5.50 x 8.25
Subjects: Holiness, Integrity
Comments: This study offers 7 options for either individual or group study, ranging from 6–12 weeks and 30″–90″. Lessons help participants pursue the traits of holiness: honesty, self-control, sexual purity, integrity, and facing temptation. This study attempts to capture some of the joy, awe, worship, love, and submission that grow from what the Bible says about holiness.

Author: Nystrom, Carolyn **1045**
Series: The Discipleship Series
Title: *Sharing Your Faith*
Publisher: Zondervan, 1992 ISBN: 0-31054-741-5

Num. Sess.	Group Time	Num. Pgs.	Avg. Qst.	Price	Audience	Format	Bible Study
6	45-60	64	13	$4.99	New Christian	Workbk	Topical

Features: Intro to Leading a Study, Intro to Study, Objectives, Scrpt Memory Helps, Follow Up, Ldr's Notes
★★★★ Personal Application Preparation Time: Med
★★ Relationship Building Ldr. Guide: No Size: 5.50 x 8.50
Subjects: Singles' Issues
Comments: This is one of 8 study guides in the Discipleship series. It is a study for people who realize the Good News is too good to keep to themselves. It helps participants face their fears about sharing their faith. It considers Christ's command about evangelism, analyzes a nutshell version of the Gospel message, walks with Peter and John to jail—and out again—with new courage to share the Gospel.

Author: O'Donnell, Peter, et al. **1046**
Series: Life Application
Title: *Philippians & Colossians*
Publisher: Tyndale House, 1989 ISBN: 0-84232-733-9

Num. Sess.	Group Time	Num. Pgs.	Avg. Qst.	Price	Audience	Format	Bible Study
13	60-90	82	12	$4.99	New Christian	Workbk	Book

Features: Intro to Leading a Study, Intro to Study, Study Overview, Digging Deeper Quest, Full Scrpt Printed, Drawings, Charts, Maps, Cross Ref
★★★ Personal Application Preparation Time: Med
★★★ Relationship Building Ldr. Guide: No Size: 6.50 x 9.0
Subjects: Church Life, Colossians/Philemon, False Teachers, Forgiveness, Joy, Philippians, Prison Epistles, Service, Suffering
Comments: Although Paul wrote from prison, joy is the dominant theme of Philippians; lessons cover joy in suffering, serving, believing, and giving. Colossians was written to combat errors in the church and to show that believers have everything they need in Christ.

Author: O'Donnell, Peter, et al. **1047**
Series: Life Application
Title: *Romans*
Publisher: Tyndale House, 1989 ISBN: 0-84232-718-5

Num. Sess.	Group Time	Num. Pgs.	Avg. Qst.	Price	Audience	Format	Bible Study
13	60-90	88	13	$4.99	New Christian	Workbk	Book

Features: Intro to Leading a Study, Intro to Study, Study Overview, Digging Deeper Quest, Full Scrpt Printed, Drawings, Charts, Maps, Cross Ref
★★★ Personal Application Preparation Time: Med
★★★ Relationship Building Ldr. Guide: No Size: 6.50 x 9.0
Subjects: Commitments, Faith, Relationships, Romans
Comments: In this study, which contains the complete text of Romans, Paul clearly sets forth the foundations of Christian faith. He also provides clear, practical guidelines for believers in Rome. The study allows participants to reexamine their commitments to Christ and reconfirm their relationships with other believers.

Author: Offner, Hazel **1048**
Series: LifeGuide Bible Study
Title: *Fruit of the Spirit*
Publisher: InterVarsity, 1987 ISBN: 0-83081-058-7

Num. Sess.	Group Time	Num. Pgs.	Avg. Qst.	Price	Audience	Format	Bible Study
9	45-60	57	10	$4.99	New Christian	Workbk	Topical

Features: Intro to Leading a Study, Intro to Study, Ldr's Notes
★ Personal Application Preparation Time: Low
★ Relationship Building Ldr. Guide: No Size: 5.50 x 8.25
Subjects: Christian Living, Discipleship, Fruit of the Spirit
Comments: This study draws on Old and New Testament verses to define, describe, and challenge believers to a Christlike maturity, and help them display the fruits of the Spirit, including love, joy, peace, patience, kindness, goodness, faithfulness, gentleness, and self-control. Strong emphasis is given to God's meaning of the "fruits of the Spirit" and the way each fruit can be worked out in our own lives. Optional passages are included for further study.

Author: Ogilvie, Lloyd John **1049**
Series:
Title: *Autobiography of God: God Revealed in the Parables of Jesus*
Publisher: Regal Books, 1979 ISBN: 0-83070-791-3

Num. Sess.	Group Time	Num. Pgs.	Avg. Qst.	Price	Audience	Format	Bible Study
29	45-60	320	Vary	$9.99	New Christian	Book	Charctr

Features: Intro to Study
★★★★ Personal Application Preparation Time: Low
★★ Relationship Building Ldr. Guide: Yes Size: 5.50 x 8.0
Subjects: God, Parables
Comments: This contemporary commentary on 29 parables offers a fresh look at God's nature. The author exposes the main point of each parable and what it says about God. He describes actions for those reached by the parables, the contexts that motivated them, and how Christians can live out the parables as citizens of God's kingdom. In a world confused about God and beguiled by distorted images of His nature, participants learn much from this resource.

Author: Olshine, David **1050**
Series:
Title: *Staying On Top: How to Know God in an Upside-Down World*
Publisher: Standard Publishing, 1994 ISBN: 0-78470-100-8

Num. Sess.	Group Time	Num. Pgs.	Avg. Qst.	Price	Audience	Format	Bible Study
12	45-60	80	Vary	$12.99	Beginner	Workbk	Topical

Features: Intro to Leading a Study, Intro to Study, Objectives, Digging Deeper Quest, Summary, Drawings
★★★★ Personal Application Preparation Time: None
★★ Relationship Building Ldr. Guide: No Size: 8.50 x 11.0
Subjects: Philippians, Teens: Christian Liv, Teens: Junior High, Teens: Senior High
Comments: This study utilizes the Book of Philippians to address everyday problems of young people. It draws young people into God's Word, engages them in discovering truth, and pushes them to lifestyle changes. Teens can gain insight and wisdom into living for Christ in radical ways.

Author: Olson, Edmund E. **1051**
Series: Small Group Bible Studies
Title: *Open the Door*
Publisher: Augsburg Fortress Publishers, 1975

Num. Sess.	Group Time	Num. Pgs.	Avg. Qst.	Price	Audience	Format	Bible Study
4	60-75	16	13	$1.15	New Christian	Book	Topical

Features: Intro to Study, Prayer Helps
★★★ Personal Application Preparation Time: None
★★★ Relationship Building Ldr. Guide: No Size: 8.50 x 5.50
Subjects: Prayer
Comments: This short, 4-session study on prayer begins with a personal evaluation of participants' prayer ideas and experiences. Session 2 examines the Lord's Prayer in different versions, Matthew 6:9-13 and Luke 11:1-4. Session 3 reviews Jesus in prayer, using John 17—sometimes called the "High Priestly Prayer." Jesus prays not just for Himself, but also for His own disciples and for the Church. The final lesson deals with the development of personal prayer life.

Author: Olson, Stanley N. & Peter A. Sethre **1052**
Series: Youth Talk
Title: *Family Life*
Publisher: Augsburg Fortress Publishers, 1994

Num. Sess.	Group Time	Num. Pgs.	Avg. Qst.	Price	Audience	Format	Bible Study
5	45-60	46	N/A	$4.95	Beginner	Book	Topical

Features: Prayer Helps, Worship Helps, Photos
★★★★ Personal Application Preparation Time: Low
★★★★ Relationship Building Ldr. Guide: Yes Size: 8.0 x 11.0
Subjects: Teens: Family, Teens: Senior High
Comments: An alternative to the "textbook approach," these studies are energetic, contemporary, and modeled after popular teen magazines. Advice columns, fiction, poetry, and other features are mostly written by youth. Successful family life demands a willingness to listen and the ability to communicate. This course gives students the opportunity to examine the dynamics of their own families. It challenges students to ask the Holy Spirit to guide their attitudes and actions.

Author: Olson, Stanley N. **1053**
Series: Friendship Bible Study
Title: *Romans*
Publisher: Augsburg Fortress Publishers, 1986

Num. Sess.	Group Time	Num. Pgs.	Avg. Qst.	Price	Audience	Format	Bible Study
8	60-75	48	10	$3.75	New Christian	Workbk	Book

Features: Intro to Study, Prayer Helps, Study Overview
★★★★ Personal Application Preparation Time: Low
★★★★ Relationship Building Ldr. Guide: Yes Size: 5.50 x 8.50
Subjects: Christian Living, God, Grace, Relationships, Romans
Comments: This 8-week study of Romans stresses justification by faith, not law, and emphasizes the interplay between Christian freedom and concern for others. The lesson format includes an overview, an opening, a responsive reading, Bible background, questions for reflection, a key verse, a prayer response, and an "our faith" response. Lesson titles include: "At Peace and Free," "Unbelief and the Promise of God," "Confident in the Gospel," and "God Creates Trust."

Author: Olson, Stanley N. **1054**
Series: Search Weekly Bible
Title: *Unit 11/1 Corinthians*
Publisher: Augsburg Fortress Publishers, 1985

Num. Sess.	Group Time	Num. Pgs.	Avg. Qst.	Price	Audience	Format	Bible Study
8	90-105	64	Vary	$5.50	New Christian	Book	Book

Features: Intro to Study, Objectives, Prayer Helps, Worship Helps, Follow Up, Summary
★★ Personal Application Preparation Time: Med
★★ Relationship Building Ldr. Guide: Yes Size: 8.50 x 11.0
Subjects: Faith, 1 Corinthians
Comments: Paul begins 1 Corinthians by concentrating on the certainties of the faith he shares with the Corinthians. This unit considers the foundation of the Christian faith and the faithfulness of God. Sessions include: "Laying the Foundations"; "Authority: From God Alone"; "Some Things Don't Fit"; "Single or Married: Serve God!"; "Love: For the Good of the Other"; "In Love: One Spirit, Many Gifts"; and more.

Author: Ortlund, Anne **1055**
Series: Proven Word
Title: *Disciplines of the Beautiful Woman*
Publisher: Word, 1977 ISBN: 0-84992-983-0

Num. Sess.	Group Time	Num. Pgs.	Avg. Qst.	Price	Audience	Format	Bible Study
14	45-60	144	6	$10.99	Beginner	Book	Topical

Features: Intro to Leading a Study, Intro to Study, Ldr's Notes
★★★ Personal Application Preparation Time: Low
★★ Relationship Building Ldr. Guide: No Size: 5.50 x 8.0
Subjects: Prayer, Time, Women's Issues
Comments: This study is for every woman who wants to be truly beautiful, from the inside out. It offers practical, specific suggestions: hints for managing schedules, maintaining wardrobes, organizing personal notebooks. Sections on prayer, meditation, and discipline combine practical "hows" with thoughtful and considered "whys." Young and old, homemakers and career women, all can profit from this sound advice on living beautifully.

Author: Osterhaus, Dr. James **1056**
Series: Men of Integrity Series
Title: *Bonds of Iron*
Publisher: Moody Press, 1994 ISBN: 0-80247-129-3

Num. Sess.	Group Time	Num. Pgs.	Avg. Qst.	Price	Audience	Format	Bible Study
14	45-60	220	N/A	$16.99	Beginner	Book	Topical

Features: Intro to Study
★★★★ Personal Application Preparation Time: Low
★★ Relationship Building Ldr. Guide: No Size: 6.25 x 9.25
Subjects: Friendships, Men's Issues
Comments: Modern Christian men are waking up to an amazing fact that God created them for friendships with other men, and that without them they miss the abundant life God promises. Osterhaus puts what he's seen into a potentially life-changing look at men who learned to overcome barriers and formed lasting friendships. This book shows how to make deeper friendships. A trained leader will be required, to formulate group discussion questions.

Author: Owens, Virginia Stem & Karen Lee-Thorp 1057
Series:
Title: *Daughters of Eve: Study Guide*
Publisher: NavPress, 1995 ISBN: 0-89109-825-9

Num. Sess.	Group Time	Num. Pgs.	Avg. Qst.	Price	Audience	Format	Bible Study
10	75-90	96	9	$5.00	New Christian	Workbk	Charctr

Features: Intro to Leading a Study, Prayer Helps
★★★★ Personal Application Preparation Time: None
★★★★ Relationship Building Ldr. Guide: No Size: 5.50 x 8.50
Subjects: Bible Personalities
Comments: This companion study guide takes an in-depth look at the stories of ten biblical women: Mary, the mother of Jesus; Michal; woman with the issue of blood; Martha; Rizpah; Mary of Bethany; Rebekah; Jezebel; Sapphira; and the necromancer of Endor. Designed to be used with or without the book, each session contains an excerpt. Each session includes the following: "Scripture Passages"; "One Woman's Story"; "Your Thoughts"; and "A Response of Prayer."

Author: Packer, J.I. 1058
Series:
Title: *Knowing God*
Publisher: InterVarsity, 1993 ISBN: 0-83081-649-6

Num. Sess.	Group Time	Num. Pgs.	Avg. Qst.	Price	Audience	Format	Bible Study
22	30-60	32	11	$4.99	Beginner	Book	Charctr

Features: Objectives, Digging Deeper Quest, Book Avail
★★★★ Personal Application Preparation Time: Low
★★★★ Relationship Building Ldr. Guide: No Size: 5.50 x 8.25
Subjects: God, Theology
Comments: This study guide outlines 2 11-week series of discussions on J. I. Packer's text. Christians can use the entire book or various chapters, according to their purposes, interest, and time limitations. Participants will learn both who God is and how a human being can relate to Him. Three sections describe the hows and whys of knowing God, His attributes, and the benefits of being a child of God.

Author: Packer, J. I. 1059
Series: LifeGuide Bible Study
Title: *Meeting God*
Publisher: InterVarsity, 1986 ISBN: 0-83081-057-9

Num. Sess.	Group Time	Num. Pgs.	Avg. Qst.	Price	Audience	Format	Bible Study
12	45-60	64	11	$4.99	New Christian	Workbk	Topical

Features: Intro to Leading a Study, Intro to Study, Ldr's Notes
★ Personal Application Preparation Time: Low
★ Relationship Building Ldr. Guide: No Size: 5.50 x 8.25
Subjects: God, Holiness, Marriage, Theology
Comments: Twelve key Bible passages are explored which enlarge humanity's vision of God. The studies help refocus attention on God whenever the Bible is read, not on the principles of daily personal godliness. Exodus offers a fresh vision of God's glory and goodness. In John the Father is known through the Son. The remaining lessons challenge humanity's tiny thoughts of God's greatness, love, holiness, delivering power, comfort, control, mercy, and triumph.

Author: Parker, Margaret 1060
Series: GroupBuilder Resources
Title: *How to Hear The Living Word*
Publisher: Victor Books, 1994 ISBN: 1-56476-270-X

Num. Sess.	Group Time	Num. Pgs.	Avg. Qst.	Price	Audience	Format	Bible Study
12	60-75	152	7	$5.99	Mature Christian	Workbk	Topical

Features: Intro to Leading a Study, Intro to Study, Digging Deeper Quest, Ldr's Notes
★★★ Personal Application Preparation Time: Low
★★★ Relationship Building Ldr. Guide: No Size: 6.0 x 9.0
Subjects: Bible Study
Comments: Participants explore Scripture with creative abilities, "seeing" pictures painted by parable or hyperbole, "hearing" the tone of God's voice in the printed page, "feeling" the rhythms of poetry pulsing with grief or love or praise. In 12 sessions, they examine literary elements, such as imagery, conflict, tone, contrast, analogy, repetition, omission, and more.

Author: Parolini, Stephen 1061
Series: Group's Active Bible Curriculum
Title: *Peace & War*
Publisher: Group Publishing, 1991 ISBN: 1-55945-123-8

Num. Sess.	Group Time	Num. Pgs.	Avg. Qst.	Price	Audience	Format	Bible Study
4	35-60	48	Vary	$9.99	Beginner	Workbk	Topical

Features: Intro to Leading a Study, Intro to Study, Objectives, Study Overview, Ldr's Notes, Handouts, Agenda, Publicity Ideas
★★★★ Personal Application Preparation Time: None
★★★★ Relationship Building Ldr. Guide: No Size: 8.50 x 11.0
Subjects: Teens: Emotions, Teens: Junior High
Comments: Through this course, junior highers discover God's faithfulness in times of peace and war and see how the Bible provides answers to questions of peace and war. Plus, participants explore their own fears about war and how to overcome them. It can be adapted for a Bible class or youth meeting. Activity sheets are reproducible. Student books not required, and instructions are easy to follow.

Author: Parolini, Stephen 1062
Series: Group's Active Bible Curriculum
Title: *Sermon on the Mount*
Publisher: Group Publishing, 1992 ISBN: 1-55945-129-7

Num. Sess.	Group Time	Num. Pgs.	Avg. Qst.	Price	Audience	Format	Bible Study
4	35-60	48	Vary	$9.99	Beginner	Workbk	Topical

Features: Intro to Leading a Study, Intro to Study, Objectives, Study Overview, Ldr's Notes, Handouts, Agenda, Publicity Ideas
★★★★ Personal Application Preparation Time: None
★★★★ Relationship Building Ldr. Guide: No Size: 8.50 x 11.0
Subjects: Teens: Bible Study, Teens: Junior High, Teens: New Testament
Comments: This course helps junior highers understand the core of Jesus' teaching on the law, money, prayer, lifestyles, and judging others. Participants explore the Beatitudes, examine how Jesus brought new light to the Old Testament laws, learn how to pray, and discover how to live as Christians. Activity sheets are reproducible.

Author: Parolini, Stephen **1063**
Series: Group's Active Bible Curriculum
Title: *Today's Music: Good or Bad?*
Publisher: Group Publishing, 1990 ISBN: 1-55945-101-7

Num. Sess.	Group Time	Num. Pgs.	Avg. Qst.	Price	Audience	Format	Bible Study
4	35-60	45	Vary	$9.99	Beginner	Workbk	Topical

Features: Intro to Leading a Study, Intro to Study, Objectives, Study Overview, Ldr's Notes, Handouts, Agenda, Publicity Ideas
★★★ Personal Application Preparation Time: None
★★★ Relationship Building Ldr. Guide: No Size: 8.50 x 11.0
Subjects: Teens: Junior High, Teens: Music
Comments: This study helps teenagers understand and evaluate contemporary music, and learn how their music can help them build a stronger relationship with God. It takes a look at the messages and controversy in music, alternative types of music, accepting opposing music tastes, and how to talk with parents and become selective listeners.

Author: Patterson, Ben **1064**
Series:
Title: *Serving God: The Grand Essentials of Work & Worship*
Publisher: InterVarsity, 1994 ISBN: 0-83081-399-3

Num. Sess.	Group Time	Num. Pgs.	Avg. Qst.	Price	Audience	Format	Bible Study
10	30-60	178	5	$9.99	New Christian	Book	Topical

Features:
★★★★ Personal Application Preparation Time: Low
★★ Relationship Building Ldr. Guide: No Size: 5.50 x 8.25
Subjects: Christian Life, Work, Worship
Comments: The author shows how work and worship are interrelated and treats them both theologically and psychologically. He points out that in worship people find community with God, while in work people live out His purposes for them. He also writes that beyond work and worship there is a universal longing for something better in the future. This book offers ways to find hope both for now and the hereafter, even in seemingly hopeless situations.

Author: Patterson, Ben **1065**
Series: Christian Basics
Title: *Work: Serving God by What We Do*
Publisher: InterVarsity, 1994 ISBN: 0-83082-007-8

Num. Sess.	Group Time	Num. Pgs.	Avg. Qst.	Price	Audience	Format	Bible Study
6	30-45	64	6	$4.99	Beginner	Workbk	Topical

Features: Intro to Leading a Study, Intro to Study, Prayer Helps, Follow Up, Full Scrpt Printed, Ldr's Notes
★★★★ Personal Application Preparation Time: None
★★★★ Relationship Building Ldr. Guide: No Size: 5.50 x 8.25
Subjects: Work
Comments: These 6 studies deal with how an "honest day's work" fits into God's plan for people. They show participants that work, even when mundane, is ordained by God; and show how to make work become more meaningful and satisfying. The 6 segments, through inductive study, help participants discover what Scripture says about jobs, "our daily bread," work levels and reasons for work.

Author: Patterson, Ben **1066**
Series: Christian Basics
Title: *Worship: Serving God With Our Praise*
Publisher: InterVarsity, 1994 ISBN: 0-83082-008-6

Num. Sess.	Group Time	Num. Pgs.	Avg. Qst.	Price	Audience	Format	Bible Study
6	30-45	63	8	$4.99	New Christian	Workbk	Topical

Features: Intro to Leading a Study, Intro to Study, Prayer Helps, Follow Up, Full Scrpt Printed, Ldr's Notes
★★★★ Personal Application Preparation Time: None
★★★★ Relationship Building Ldr. Guide: No Size: 5.50 x 8.25
Subjects: Worship
Comments: People's deepest needs can be filled only through coming to the Creator in worship. True worship can transform lives and these studies help participants understand and experience the glory of praising God. It has been written that duty makes people do things well, but love makes them do them beautifully. Worship can turn duty into love and good works into things of beauty.

Author: Peace, Richard **1067**
Series: Serendipity Support Group
Title: *Addictive Lifestyles: Breaking Free*
Publisher: Serendipity House, 1991 ISBN: 1-88341-971-9

Num. Sess.	Group Time	Num. Pgs.	Avg. Qst.	Price	Audience	Format	Bible Study
7	60-90	112	12	$5.45	Beginner	Workbk	Topical

Features: Intro to Leading a Study, Objectives, Bibliography, Prayer Helps, Full Scrpt Printed, Ldr's Notes, Cartoons, Agenda
★★★★ Personal Application Preparation Time: None
★★★★ Relationship Building Ldr. Guide: No Size: 6.50 x 9.0
Subjects: Addictions, Self-help, Support, Victorious Living
Comments: This study helps participants learn about addictive behavior. It covers a widespread number of substances, activities, emotions and objects to which one can become addicted. It describes addictive behavior, the difference between habits and addictions, denial, obsession and lack of control, and God's grace in healing and recovery. The format includes icebreakers, Bible study, and prayer.

Author: Peace, Richard **1068**
Series: Serendipity Support Group
Title: *Co-Dependency: Breaking Free from Entangled Relationships*
Publisher: Serendipity House, 1991 ISBN: 1-88341-972-7

Num. Sess.	Group Time	Num. Pgs.	Avg. Qst.	Price	Audience	Format	Bible Study
7	60-90	112	12	$5.45	Beginner	Workbk	Topical

Features: Intro to Leading a Study, Objectives, Bibliography, Prayer Helps, Full Scrpt Printed, Ldr's Notes, Cartoons, Agenda
★★★★ Personal Application Preparation Time: None
★★★★ Relationship Building Ldr. Guide: No Size: 6.50 x 9.0
Subjects: Addictions, Emotions, Relationships, Self-help, Support, Victorious Living
Comments: This study is for anyone interested in learning about co-dependency. Lessons include: "What is Co-dependency?"; "Letting Others Use Us"; "Letting Others Define Who We Are"; "Letting My Feelings Go Numb"; "Getting in Touch with My History"; "Getting in Touch with the Present"; and "Getting in Touch with God.

Author: Peace, Richard, et al. 1069
Series: Christian Lifestyle Series
Title: *Facing Your Fears about Sharing Your Faith*
Publisher: David C. Cook Publishing Co., 1991 ISBN: 1-55513-382-7

Num. Sess.	Group Time	Num. Pgs.	Avg. Qst.	Price	Audience	Format	Bible Study
7	45-60	92	Vary	$14.95	New Christian	Workbk	Topical

Features: Intro to Study, Prayer Helps, Drawings, Handouts, Persnl Study Quest
★★★ Personal Application Preparation Time: None
★★★ Relationship Building Ldr. Guide: Yes Size: 8.50 x 11.0
Subjects: Discipleship, Evangelism
Comments: This study combines biblical teaching, small group interaction, and practical application. It helps adults of all ages, especially Boomers and younger, face their fears of witnessing, understand the needs and attitudes of non-Christians, and learn how to relax and be themselves when telling others what they really feel and believe about Jesus.

Author: Peace, Richard 1070
Series: Learning To Love
Title: *Learning to Love God*
Publisher: NavPress, 1994 ISBN: 0-89109-841-0

Num. Sess.	Group Time	Num. Pgs.	Avg. Qst.	Price	Audience	Format	Bible Study
7	60-90	88	Vary	$6.00	New Christian	Book	Topical

Features: Intro to Leading a Study, Intro to Study, Bibliography, Prayer Helps, Digging Deeper Quest, Full Scrpt Printed, Ldr's Notes, Persnl Study Quest
★★★★ Personal Application Preparation Time: None
★★★★ Relationship Building Ldr. Guide: No Size: 6.0 x 9.0
Subjects: God, Jesus: Life/Teaching, Love
Comments: Points out that having a relationship with God is different than having a relationship with any other person. God is alive and personal, but He is also Spirit. Lessons examine: "Encountering God"; "Knowing God"; "Being Sure We Know God"; "Learning About God"; "Conversing with God"; "Worshiping God"; and "Following God."

Author: Peace, Richard 1071
Series: Learning To Love
Title: *Learning to Love Ourselves*
Publisher: NavPress, 1994 ISBN: 0-89109-842-9

Num. Sess.	Group Time	Num. Pgs.	Avg. Qst.	Price	Audience	Format	Bible Study
7	60-90	89	Vary	$6.00	New Christian	Book	Topical

Features: Intro to Leading a Study, Intro to Study, Bibliography, Prayer Helps, Digging Deeper Quest, Full Scrpt Printed, Ldr's Notes, Persnl Study Quest
★★★★ Personal Application Preparation Time: None
★★★★ Relationship Building Ldr. Guide: No Size: 6.0 x 9.0
Subjects: Love, Self-esteem
Comments: Points out that failing to love ourselves adequately can be self-destructive. Without proper self-esteem, people fail to use their God-given gifts and have difficulty loving others. Topics covered include: "Loving Ourselves"; "Valuing Ourselves"; "Understanding Ourselves"; "Behaving Ourselves."

Author: Peace, Richard 1072
Series: Learning To Love
Title: *Learning to Love Others*
Publisher: NavPress, 1994 ISBN: 0-89109-840-2

Num. Sess.	Group Time	Num. Pgs.	Avg. Qst.	Price	Audience	Format	Bible Study
7	60-90	88	Vary	$6.00	New Christian	Book	Topical

Features: Intro to Leading a Study, Intro to Study, Bibliography, Prayer Helps, Digging Deeper Quest, Full Scrpt Printed, Ldr's Notes, Persnl Study Quest
★★★★ Personal Application Preparation Time: None
★★★★ Relationship Building Ldr. Guide: No Size: 6.0 x 9.0
Subjects: Love, Relationships
Comments: This study helps participants learn to love others the way Jesus desires, while understanding that difficult people are not always lovable and loving them can interfere with our own self-interests. Lessons cover: "Loving Others"; "Loving Our Families"; "Fellowship with Others"; "Getting Along with Others"; "Opposition from Others."

Author: Peace, Richard & Lyman Coleman 1073
Series: Mastering the Basics
Title: *1 John*
Publisher: Serendipity House, 1988 ISBN: 1-88341-935-2

Num. Sess.	Group Time	Num. Pgs.	Avg. Qst.	Price	Audience	Format	Bible Study
7	60-75	64	Vary	$4.95	Beginner	Workbk	Book

Features: Intro to Leading a Study, Intro to Study, Digging Deeper Quest, Summary, Full Scrpt Printed, Photos, Maps, Agenda
★★★ Personal Application Preparation Time: Low
★★★ Relationship Building Ldr. Guide: Yes Size: 9.50 x 8.0
Subjects: 1, 2 & 3 John/Jude
Comments: The book of 1 John is John's record of his final thoughts on the nature of faith. It's written so that those leaning toward strange doctrine can, once and for all, get it straight. It records the essentials of Christianity as seen by the last of the 12 disciples. This verse-by-verse, 7- or 13-week study is part of Mastering the Basics, a comprehensive, integrated program for personal or small group study.

Author: Peace, Richard 1074
Series: Serendipity Support Group
Title: *12 Steps: The Path to Wholeness*
Publisher: Serendipity House, 1990 ISBN: 1-88341-955-7

Num. Sess.	Group Time	Num. Pgs.	Avg. Qst.	Price	Audience	Format	Bible Study
7	60-90	96	Vary	$5.45	Beginner	Workbk	Topical

Features: Intro to Leading a Study, Objectives, Bibliography, Full Scrpt Printed, Cartoons,Agenda
★★★★ Personal Application Preparation Time: None
★★★★ Relationship Building Ldr. Guide: No Size: 6.50 x 9.25
Subjects: Addictions, God, Repentance, Support, Wholeness
Comments: This study offers a path to wholeness using the 12 step program. The first lesson defines the 12 step approach. Others include: "Naming the Addiction," "Naming the Higher Power," "Coming to God," "Being Open," "Being Repentant," and "Living Addiction-free." The format includes icebreakers, Bible study, and prayer. Timelines are provided for each lesson.

Author: Peel, William Carr **1075**
Series: Promise Keepers
Title: *What God Does When Men Pray*
Publisher: NavPress, 1993 ISBN: 0-89109-729-5

Num. Sess.	Group Time	Num. Pgs.	Avg. Qst.	Price	Audience	Format	Bible Study
8	30-60	95	16	$5.00	Beginner	Workbk	Topical

Features: Ldr's Notes, Appendix
★★★★ Personal Application Preparation Time: Med
★★★★ Relationship Building Ldr. Guide: No Size: 5.50 x 8.50
Subjects: Men's Issues, Prayer
Comments: Part of the Promise Keepers series, this study provides encouragement, inspiration, and practical tips on how a group of men can get together and affect their world through prayer. Lessons cover: God's open invitation for us to talk to Him, how to break through personal barriers toward prayer, the adventure of praying together with other men, the 30-day prayer experiment, praying over your personal worries, and the joy of watching God at work.

Author: Peskett, Howard **1076**
Series: LifeGuide Bible Study
Title: *Isaiah: Trusting God in Troubled Times*
Publisher: InterVarsity, 1991 ISBN: 0-83081-029-3

Num. Sess.	Group Time	Num. Pgs.	Avg. Qst.	Price	Audience	Format	Bible Study
24	45-60	109	11	$4.99	New Christian	Workbk	Book

Features: Intro to Leading a Study, Intro to Study, Ldr's Notes, Charts
★★ Personal Application Preparation Time: Low
★★ Relationship Building Ldr. Guide: No Size: 5.50 x 8.25
Subjects: Isaiah/Jeremiah
Comments: This study of Isaiah addresses how the prophet raises a cry for revival in the midst of a rotting society and how to find comfort in troubled times. Lessons include a study of: hard-hitting criticisms of empty religion; some of the most famous Messianic prophecies; dramatic narratives of times of national crisis; the famous story of Isaiah's call and mysterious commission, and meditations on what it means for us to be trustful, faithful servants of God.

Author: Petersen, J. Allan **1077**
Series:
Title: *Before You Marry*
Publisher: Tyndale House, 1974 ISBN: 0-84231-221-8

Num. Sess.	Group Time	Num. Pgs.	Avg. Qst.	Price	Audience	Format	Bible Study
13	75-90	210	Vary	$4.99	Beginner	Workbk	Topical

Features: Intro to Leading a Study, Follow Up, Summary
★★★★ Personal Application Preparation Time: Low
★★★★ Relationship Building Ldr. Guide: No Size: 4.25 x 7.0
Subjects: Love, Marriage
Comments: For 20 years, this study guide has provided Christian counsel on the decision-making process of courtship and marriage. Each lesson demonstrates a specific principle with examples, application questions, and Bible truth about love, engagements, and wedding vows. Numerous self-evaluations help prepare couples for one of life's most important decisions. A suggestion for recommended reading follows each chapter. Also available in Spanish.

Author: Petersen, Randy & Stuart Briscoe **1078**
Series: Christian Lifestyle Series
Title: *Attacking Your Me-Attitudes*
Publisher: David C. Cook Publishing Co., 1991 ISBN: 1-55513-377-0

Num. Sess.	Group Time	Num. Pgs.	Avg. Qst.	Price	Audience	Format	Bible Study
7	45-60	102	Vary	$14.95	New Christian	Workbk	Topical

Features: Intro to Study, Prayer Helps, Drawings, Handouts, Persnl Study Quest
★★★ Personal Application Preparation Time: None
★★★ Relationship Building Ldr. Guide: Yes Size: 8.50 x 11.0
Subjects: Discipleship, Materialism
Comments: This study combines biblical teaching, small group interaction, and practical application. It helps adults of all ages, especially Boomers and younger, root out tendencies toward materialism, instant gratification, and escapism, in exchange for Christlike attitudes that bring real fulfillment in today's world. It's appropriate for singles or marrieds, new or mature Christians.

Author: Petersen, Randy & Calvin Miller **1079**
Series: Christian Lifestyle Series
Title: *Being Totally True When You're In The Pew*
Publisher: David C. Cook Publishing Co., 1992 ISBN: 0-78140-003-1

Num. Sess.	Group Time	Num. Pgs.	Avg. Qst.	Price	Audience	Format	Bible Study
7	45-60	91	Vary	$14.95	New Christian	Workbk	Topical

Features: Intro to Study, Prayer Helps, Drawings, Handouts, Persnl Study Quest
★★★ Personal Application Preparation Time: None
★★★ Relationship Building Ldr. Guide: Yes Size: 8.50 x 11.0
Subjects: Church Life, Worship
Comments: This study combines biblical teaching, small group interaction, and practical application. It helps adults of all ages, especially Boomers and younger, be honest with God about how they feel in His "house," want to go to church each week, discover real meaning in church music, and learn how to worship "in Spirit and in truth." It's appropriate for singles or marrieds, new or mature Christians.

Author: Petersen, Randy & Don Cousins **1080**
Series: Christian Lifestyle Series
Title: *Giving the Body a Lift by Using Your Spiritual Gift*
Publisher: David C. Cook Publishing Co., 1993 ISBN: 0-78145-026-8

Num. Sess.	Group Time	Num. Pgs.	Avg. Qst.	Price	Audience	Format	Bible Study
7	45-60	96	Vary	$14.95	New Christian	Workbk	Topical

Features: Intro to Study, Bibliography, Prayer Helps, Study Overview, Drawings, Handouts, Persnl Study Quest
★★★★ Personal Application Preparation Time: None
★★★★ Relationship Building Ldr. Guide: Yes Size: 8.50 x 11.0
Subjects: Spiritual Gifts
Comments: This study helps adults of all ages, especially Boomers and younger, answer questions like: What are spiritual gifts? How do I know what my spiritual gift is? Why does God give spiritual gifts? What is the difference between gifts and talents? How do I use my gifts in ministry? and How do gifts fit in the ministry of the church? Reproducible resource sheets for students are included.

Author: Petersen, Randy & John Trent **1081**
Series: Christian Lifestyle Series
Title: *Growing in Faith When Challenged by Change*
Publisher: David C. Cook Publishing Co., 1995 ISBN: 0-78145-128-0

Num. Sess.	Group Time	Num. Pgs.	Avg. Qst.	Price	Audience	Format	Bible Study
7	45-60	96	Vary	$14.95	New Christian	Workbk	Topical

Features: Intro to Study, Bibliography, Prayer Helps, Study Overview, Drawings, Handouts, Persnl Study Quest
★★★★ Personal Application Preparation Time: None
★★★★ Relationship Building Ldr. Guide: Yes Size: 8.50 x 11.0
Subjects: Stress
Comments: This study helps adults of all ages, especially Boomers and younger, face change with confidence in an unchanging God. It helps participants understand why they react to change as they do, overcome fear and indecision when facing good changes, avoid anger and bitterness when facing bad changes, feel less stressful about negative changes in society, and be equipped as God's agents of change.

Author: Petersen, Randy & Ray C. Stedman **1082**
Series: Christian Lifestyle Series
Title: *Staying on Fire in a Wet-Blanket World*
Publisher: David C. Cook Publishing Co., 1992 ISBN: 0-78140-004-X

Num. Sess.	Group Time	Num. Pgs.	Avg. Qst.	Price	Audience	Format	Bible Study
7	45-60	96	Vary	$14.95	New Christian	Workbk	Topical

Features: Intro to Study, Prayer Helps, Drawings, Handouts, Persnl Study Quest
★★★ Personal Application Preparation Time: None
★★★ Relationship Building Ldr. Guide: Yes Size: 8.50 x 11.0
Subjects: Apocalyptic, Christian Living, Discipleship, False Teachers, Integrity, Morals
Comments: This study combines biblical teaching, small group interaction, and practical application. It helps adults of all ages, especially Boomers and younger, keep their love for Christ alive, deal with distractions such as persecution and false teaching, and focus on Christ's return.

Author: Peterson, Eugene H. **1083**
Series: LifeGuide Bible Study
Title: *Psalms: Prayers of the Heart*
Publisher: InterVarsity, 1987 ISBN: 0-83081-034-X

Num. Sess.	Group Time	Num. Pgs.	Avg. Qst.	Price	Audience	Format	Bible Study
12	45-60	64	11	$4.99	New Christian	Workbk	Book

Features: Intro to Leading a Study, Intro to Study, Ldr's Notes
★ Personal Application Preparation Time: Low
★ Relationship Building Ldr. Guide: No Size: 5.50 x 8.25
Subjects: Emotions, Prayer, Psalms
Comments: This is a book of poetry and prayer: the poetry exposes and sharpens what it means to be a human being before God; prayer is the language used to relate to and communicate with God. The Psalms do not teach about God but train response to Him. Areas dealt with include inattention, intimidation, trouble, creation, sin, salvation, fear, hate, tears, doubt, death, and praise. This introspective study allows growth in personal prayer life and dependence on God.

Author: Peterson, Judy **1084**
Series:
Title: *Something of Your Own*
Publisher: Victor Books, 1991 ISBN: 0-89693-898-0

Num. Sess.	Group Time	Num. Pgs.	Avg. Qst.	Price	Audience	Format	Bible Study
7	75-90	160	N/A	$7.99	Beginner	Workbk	Topical

Features:
★★★ Personal Application Preparation Time: Med
★ Relationship Building Ldr. Guide: No Size: 5.50 x 8.50
Subjects: Psychology, Women's Issues, Work
Comments: This book helps women who struggle with what to do with their lives and resources. It shows readers how to move from personal vision to development of a life/work plan. Women working together in a small group can enhance the study's benefits. With a seasoned leader a group can discover their personal path, engage their hearts with vision, dream to find a direction, design a creative venture, write a start-up plan, make their dreams reality and fill in a life/work chart.

Author: Peterson, Lorraine **1085**
Series:
Title: *If God Loves Me, Why Can't I Get My Locker Open?*
Publisher: Bethany House, 1980 ISBN: 0-87123-251-0

Num. Sess.	Group Time	Num. Pgs.	Avg. Qst.	Price	Audience	Format	Bible Study
13	45-60	153	N/A	$7.99	New Christian	Book	Topical

Features: Intro to Leading a Study, Prayer Helps, Scrpt Memory Helps, Drawings
★★★ Personal Application Preparation Time: Med
★★ Relationship Building Ldr. Guide: Yes Size: 5.50 x 8.50
Subjects: Teens: Devotionals, Teens: Junior High, Teens: Psychology, Teens: Self-image, Teens: Senior High
Comments: This teen devotional has been adapted for group study through use of a companion teacher's guide. Twenty-five lessons incorporate 91 devotionals from the book. Examples include: "Do I Have to Forgive My Sister For Ruining My Good Jeans?" and "How Can I Get Rid of Self-Consciousness?"

Author: Petro, Sandy **1086**
Series:
Title: *Discover Your Gift of Fragrance*
Publisher: Victor Books, 1991 ISBN: 0-89693-693-7

Num. Sess.	Group Time	Num. Pgs.	Avg. Qst.	Price	Audience	Format	Bible Study
10	60-90	163	N/A	$7.99	New Christian	Book	Topical

Features: Intro to Study, Prayer Helps, Scrpt Memory Helps, Persnl Study Quest, Charts
★★★★ Personal Application Preparation Time: Med
★3 Relationship Building Ldr. Guide: No Size: 5.50 x 8.50
Subjects: Spiritual Gifts, Women's Issues
Comments: By showing readers how to savor the aromas of truth found in God's Word, the author guides participants through a life-changing process which will enable them to accept and love unconditionally, be free from guilt and negativity, identify and begin fulfilling God's purpose, discover and develop spiritual gifts, develop personal worship, and respond with faith, not fear.

Author: Petro, Sandy **1087**
Series: A Bible Study for Women
Title: *Spice Up Your Life With Joy*
Publisher: Victor Books, 1990 ISBN: 0-89693-817-4

Num. Sess.	Group Time	Num. Pgs.	Avg. Qst.	Price	Audience	Format	Bible Study
8	60-75	92	12	$5.99	New Christian	Workbk	Book

Features: Intro to Leading a Study, Intro to Study, Objectives, Bibliography, Prayer Helps,Study Overview, Follow Up, Ldr's Notes
★★★★ Personal Application Preparation Time: Med
★★★ Relationship Building Ldr. Guide: No Size: 6.0 x 9.0
Subjects: Joy, Philippians, Women's Issues
Comments: In these 8 studies from the Book of Philippians, participants can uncover Paul's recipe for increasing joy in Christ. They don't have to feel trapped in flat, tasteless existences. Paul gives readers a recipe for life that never fails, regardless of daily circumstances. Lessons cover joyful prayer, praise, purpose, and pursuit; partnership in joy; pattern for joy; peace and joy; and power and joy.

Author: Petro, Sandy **1088**
Series: A Bible Study for Women
Title: *Word Pictures Painted By Paul*
Publisher: Victor Books, 1993 ISBN: 1-56476-034-0

Num. Sess.	Group Time	Num. Pgs.	Avg. Qst.	Price	Audience	Format	Bible Study
8	60-90	113	13	$6.99	New Christian	Workbk	Book

Features: Intro to Study, Objectives, Prayer Helps
★★★ Personal Application Preparation Time: Med
★★★ Relationship Building Ldr. Guide: No Size: 6.0 x 9.0
Subjects: 2 Corinthians
Comments: This is an inductive study of 8 metaphors or "word pictures" from 2 Corinthians. Paul paints clay pots hiding infinite treasures, leading readers to recognize themselves as mundane creatures housing the holy Christ. Paul paints a thorn rammed into delicate flesh, and readers wince from their own inescapable jabs of pain. Paul paints the human body as a flimsy tent, and readers groan with longing for new bodies—fit for heaven.

Author: Phillips, John L. **1089**
Series: Teach Yourself the Bible
Title: *How to Live Forever*
Publisher: Moody Press, 1964 ISBN: 0-80243-700-1

Num. Sess.	Group Time	Num. Pgs.	Avg. Qst.	Price	Audience	Format	Bible Study
8	45-60	48	18	$4.50	Beginner	Workbk	Topical

Features: Intro to Leading a Study, Exam
★★ Personal Application Preparation Time: Low
★★ Relationship Building Ldr. Guide: No Size: 5.50 x 8.50
Subjects: Evangelism, Theology
Comments: This study on how to live forever—part of a 25-book series—is a step-by-step study of God's nature. Participants will learn that eternal life is a gift from God, and learn why to accept that gift. The format includes a series of fill-in-the-blank questions, and check-ups to test participants' grasp of Scriptural truths. The series is designed for self-study; however, suggestions for group study, and a 4-year plan for using the series, are included.

Author: Picardi, Patricia **1090**
Series: The TruthSeed Series
Title: *Ephesians: Living Toward Eternity*
Publisher: Victor Books, 1995 ISBN: 1-56476-327-7

Num. Sess.	Group Time	Num. Pgs.	Avg. Qst.	Price	Audience	Format	Bible Study
12	45-60	96	12	$4.99	Beginner	Workbk	Book

Features: Intro to Leading a Study, Intro to Study, Bibliography, Prayer Helps, Worship Helps, Follow Up, Ldr's Notes, Persnl Study Quest
★★★ Personal Application Preparation Time: None
★★★ Relationship Building Ldr. Guide: No Size: 6.0 x 9.0
Subjects: Ephesians, New Testament
Comments: These inductive Bible studies enable men and women to experience community and develop godliness in either discussion group or personal settings. Questions are designed and field-tested for seekers, new believers, and mature Christians. Examines questions such as "How do I fit into God's great cosmic plan?" and "How can I experience Christian unity with people who are under my authority?"

Author: Pilgrim, Walter E. **1091**
Series: Search Weekly Bible
Title: *Unit 20/Revelation*
Publisher: Augsburg Fortress Publishers, 1988

Num. Sess.	Group Time	Num. Pgs.	Avg. Qst.	Price	Audience	Format	Bible Study
8	90-105	64	Vary	$5.50	New Christian	Book	Book

Features: Intro to Study, Objectives, Prayer Helps, Worship Helps, Follow Up, Summary
★★ Personal Application Preparation Time: Med
★★ Relationship Building Ldr. Guide: Yes Size: 8.50 x 11.0
Subjects: Hope, Revelation
Comments: This is the last of four units on the theme of "Hopes." Revelation is a book of hope for the people of God. It was first written during a period of crisis, when suffering and persecution were threatening the Christian communities in the cities of Asia Minor. Ever since, the message of Revelation has brought powerful words of encouragement and hope in God during difficult times.

Author: Pippert, Rebecca & Ruth Siemens **1092**
Series: LifeGuide Bible Study
Title: *Evangelism: A Way of Life*
Publisher: InterVarsity, 1985 ISBN: 0-83081-050-1

Num. Sess.	Group Time	Num. Pgs.	Avg. Qst.	Price	Audience	Format	Bible Study
12	45-60	75	11	$4.99	Mature Christian	Workbk	Topical

Features: Intro to Leading a Study, Intro to Study, Ldr's Notes
★ Personal Application Preparation Time: Low
★ Relationship Building Ldr. Guide: No Size: 5.50 x 8.25
Subjects: Commitments, Evangelism
Comments: This is a practical guide for communicating the Gospel. Evangelism can be intimidating for Christians as well as non-Christians, but with proper understanding it can be an exciting way of life. Topics covered include the "why" of sharing, reluctant evangelists, seeking the lost, getting people interested, creative communication, friendship evangelism, talking with strangers, cross-cultural evangelism, presenting the cost of commitment, facing opposition, and balanced expectations.

Author: Pippert, Rebecca **1093**
Series:
Title: *Hope Has Its Reasons*
Publisher: NavPress, 1991 ISBN: 9-90073-804-7

Num. Sess.	Group Time	Num. Pgs.	Avg. Qst.	Price	Audience	Format	Bible Study
6	60-90	32	10	$79.00	New Christian	Video	No

Features: Intro to Leading a Study, Intro to Study, Objectives, Prayer Helps, Pre-discussion Quest, Follow Up, Full Scrpt Printed, Ldr's Notes, Glossary, Video Study Guide
★★★★ Personal Application Preparation Time: None
★★★★ Relationship Building Ldr. Guide: No Size: 8.50 x 11.0
Subjects: Christian Living, Emotions, Hope, Relationships
Comments: Does being a Christian make a practical difference to our lives? In 6 30″ talks, Pippert shows how the Cross and the Resurrection are vitally relevant to modern life and how to live in light of them. We are forgiven people, and resurrection power to overcome our bondages is available to us.

Author: Plueddemann, Carol **1094**
Series: Fisherman Bible Studyguide
Title: *Great Passages of the Bible*
Publisher: Shaw, 1987 ISBN: 0-87788-332-7

Num. Sess.	Group Time	Num. Pgs.	Avg. Qst.	Price	Audience	Format	Bible Study
14	45-60	94	12	$4.99	Beginner	Workbk	Topical

Features: Intro to Leading a Study, Intro to Study, Prayer Helps
★★ Personal Application Preparation Time: None
★★ Relationship Building Ldr. Guide: No Size: 5.0 x 8.25
Subjects: Jesus: Life/Teaching, New Testament, Old Testament, Ten Commandments
Comments: This study, which presents an overview of main themes of the Bible, focuses on 14 individual, chronological passages from the Old and New Testaments. They include the Ten Commandments, Psalm 23, and the birth, death, and resurrection of Christ. God's plan for all people and each person's part in that design is made clearer by this study.

Author: Plueddemann, Carol, et. al. **1095**
Series: Fisherman Bible Studyguide
Title: *Great People of the Bible*
Publisher: Shaw, 1988 ISBN: 0-87788-333-5

Num. Sess.	Group Time	Num. Pgs.	Avg. Qst.	Price	Audience	Format	Bible Study
15	45-60	78	11	$4.99	Beginner	Workbk	Charctr

Features: Intro to Leading a Study, Intro to Study, Prayer Helps, Follow Up
★★ Personal Application Preparation Time: None
★★ Relationship Building Ldr. Guide: No Size: 5.0 x 8.25
Subjects: Bible Personalities, Failure, God, Hope, Loneliness, Relationships
Comments: These 15 character studies look into the lives of well-known Bible characters, including Adam and Eve, Moses, Ruth, Mary, Peter, and Barnabas. The great heroes of the past struggled with difficult family relationships, failure, illness, poverty, death, war, temptation, and loneliness—the same challenges we face today.

Author: Plueddemann, Carol **1096**
Series: Fisherman Bible Studyguide
Title: *Great Prayers of the Bible*
Publisher: Shaw, 1991 ISBN: 0-87788-334-3

Num. Sess.	Group Time	Num. Pgs.	Avg. Qst.	Price	Audience	Format	Bible Study
12	45-60	80	12	$4.99	New Christian	Workbk	Topical

Features: Intro to Leading a Study, Intro to Study, Prayer Helps, Follow Up
★★★ Personal Application Preparation Time: None
★★★ Relationship Building Ldr. Guide: No Size: 5.0 x 8.25
Subjects: Bible Personalities, Prayer
Comments: These lessons help participants understand the discipline of prayer and God's character, through the lives of His praying people throughout history. Participants see how people like David, Daniel, and Mary talked to God and what can be learned from their examples. Through the prayers of Hannah, Job, and Paul, they will discover much about God's character.

Author: Plueddemann, Carol and Jim **1097**
Series: The TruthSeed Series
Title: *James: Growing in Maturity*
Publisher: Victor Books, 1995 ISBN: 1-56476-366-8

Num. Sess.	Group Time	Num. Pgs.	Avg. Qst.	Price	Audience	Format	Bible Study
6	45-60	64	12	$4.99	Beginner	Workbk	Book

Features: Intro to Leading a Study, Intro to Study, Bibliography, Prayer Helps, Follow Up, Ldr's Notes, Persnl Study Quest
★★★ Personal Application Preparation Time: None
★★★ Relationship Building Ldr. Guide: No Size: 6.0 x 9.0
Subjects: Faith, James, Wisdom
Comments: This new series of inductive Bible studies enables men and women to experience community and develop godliness in either discussion group or personal settings. Questions are designed and field-tested for seekers, new believers, and mature Christians. This study explores how to endure trials, discern real wisdom, control tongues, and put faith to work.

Author: Plueddemann, Jim & Carol **1098**
Series: The Beatitude Series
Title: *Meekness: Claiming Your Inheritance*
Publisher: Zondervan, 1993 ISBN: 0-31059-623-8

Num. Sess.	Group Time	Num. Pgs.	Avg. Qst.	Price	Audience	Format	Bible Study
6	45-60	48	12	$4.99	New Christian	Workbk	Topical

Features: Intro to Leading a Study, Intro to Study, Objectives, Follow Up, Ldr's Notes, Charts
★★★★ Personal Application Preparation Time: Low
★★ Relationship Building Ldr. Guide: No Size: 5.50 x 8.25
Subjects: Sermon on the Mount
Comments: This study guide explains the biblical definition of meekness. Meekness requires unusual strength. Jesus described Himself as meek and demands meekness in each of His followers. Participants discover why meekness results in eternal rewards. Lesson titles include: "The Dangers of Pride"; "The Meekness of Christ"; "Meekness in Action"; "Meekness is Not Weakness"; and more.

Author: Plueddemann, Jim & Carol **1099**
Series:
Title: *Pilgrims in Progress*
Publisher: Shaw, 1990 ISBN: 0-87788-647-4

Num. Sess.	Group Time	Num. Pgs.	Avg. Qst.	Price	Audience	Format	Bible Study
12	—	165	N/A	$8.99		Book	No

Features: Intro to Study, Bibliography, Index, Appendix
Personal Application Preparation Time:
Relationship Building Ldr. Guide: Size: 5.25 x 8.25
Subjects: Leadership, Small Group Resource
Comments: This book concerns why small groups work and how they can be most effective. It provides a historical perspective; speaks to the purpose, nature, and aim, of small groups; and discusses the methods by which Christians (pilgrims) form them. "Pilgrim" leaders are discussed in a narrow context, as only authoritarian and laissez-faire styles are addressed. Remaining chapters include "Benefits and Pitfalls," "Profiles of Pilgrim Groups," and "Strengthening Pilgrim Groups."

Author: Plueddemann, Jim & Carol **1100**
Series: The Beatitude Series
Title: *Spiritual Hunger: Filling Your Deepest Longings*
Publisher: Zondervan, 1993 ISBN: 0-31059-633-5

Num. Sess.	Group Time	Num. Pgs.	Avg. Qst.	Price	Audience	Format	Bible Study
6	45-60	47	13	$4.99	New Christian	Workbk	Topical

Features: Intro to Leading a Study, Intro to Study, Objectives, Follow Up, Ldr's Notes
★★★★ Personal Application Preparation Time: Low
★★ Relationship Building Ldr. Guide: No Size: 5.50 x 8.25
Subjects: Sermon on the Mount
Comments: This is 1 of 8 guides in the Beatitude series. In 6 weeks participants can develop a healthy spiritual appetite and fill their deepest longings in Christ. Lesson titles include: "A Thirst for God"; "Longing for Home"; "Satisfying Your Hunger"; "Quenching Your Thirst"; "Food for the Soul"; and "Filled to Overflowing." A "Between Studies" assignment is provided in each lesson.

Author: Plueddemann, Jim **1101**
Series: Fisherman Bible Studyguide
Title: *Strengthened to Serve: 2 Corinthians*
Publisher: Shaw, 1991 ISBN: 0-87788-783-7

Num. Sess.	Group Time	Num. Pgs.	Avg. Qst.	Price	Audience	Format	Bible Study
12	45-60	80	12	$4.99	New Christian	Workbk	Book

Features: Intro to Leading a Study, Intro to Study, Prayer Helps, Follow Up
★★★ Personal Application Preparation Time: None
★★ Relationship Building Ldr. Guide: No Size: 5.0 x 8.25
Subjects: Service, Success, 2 Corinthians
Comments: These lessons discuss service, a great theme of Paul's second letter to the Corinthian Christians. They help participants sort out society's concepts of success and develop biblical views of successful ministry and service to a needy world.

Author: Porter, Jane **1102**
Series: Shaw Contemporary Issues
Title: *Parenting Alone*
Publisher: Shaw, 1992 ISBN: 0-87788-639-3

Num. Sess.	Group Time	Num. Pgs.	Avg. Qst.	Price	Audience	Format	Bible Study
8	30-45	48	8	$4.99	Beginner	Workbk	Topical

Features: Intro to Leading a Study, Intro to Study, Objectives, Bibliography, Follow Up, Ldr's Notes
★★★★ Personal Application Preparation Time: Low
★★★ Relationship Building Ldr. Guide: No Size: 5.25 x 8.25
Subjects: Loneliness, Parenting, Singles' Issues
Comments: Eight brief lessons help participants find secure foundations and godly perspectives for single parenting. These lessons deal with the tough challenges of single parenting, by pointing to God, the perfect Father and source of boundless love and security. Topics addressed include: loneliness, needing help, worring, opportunities, forgiveness, overcoming bad choices, being the victim, and hope.

Author: Potter, Eric, et al. **1103**
Series: Christian Lifestyle Series
Title: *Walking With God When You Have Feet of Clay*
Publisher: David C. Cook Publishing Co., 1991 ISBN: 1-55513-381-9

Num. Sess.	Group Time	Num. Pgs.	Avg. Qst.	Price	Audience	Format	Bible Study
7	45-60	96	Vary	$14.95	New Christian	Workbk	Topical

Features: Intro to Study, Prayer Helps, Drawings, Handouts, Persnl Study Quest
★★★ Personal Application Preparation Time: None
★★★ Relationship Building Ldr. Guide: Yes Size: 8.50 x 11.0
Subjects: Bible Personalities, Failure
Comments: This study combines sound biblical teaching, small group interaction, and practical application. By studying the lives of Peter, Abraham, Sarah, Rebekah, David, Solomon, and Elijah, it helps adults of all ages, especially Boomers and younger, discover that God can use them in spite of personal failures and weaknesses. It's appropriate for singles or marrieds, new or mature Christians.

Author: Potter, Juanita Wright, et al. **1104**
Series: Moving Toward Maturity
Title: *Moving Toward Maturity: Leader's Guide*
Publisher: Victor Books, 1991 ISBN: 0-89693-298-2

Num. Sess.	Group Time	Num. Pgs.	Avg. Qst.	Price	Audience	Format	Bible Study
	—	260	N/A	$9.99		Book	

Features: Intro to Study, Study Overview
Personal Application Preparation Time:
Relationship Building Ldr. Guide: Size: 5.50 x 8.50
Subjects: Leader's Guide
Comments: This leader's guide provides a complete study plan for each chapter of the series, as well as reproducible "Time Alone With God" sheets for participants to use in personal devotions. For each session there is an "Overview" outlining key concepts and goals, "Before the Meeting" instructions for leaders, a "Building the Group" getting acquainted exercise, a thought-provoking "Focusing on Life" section, and sections on "Exploring" and "Applying God's Word."

Author: Powell, Dr. Terry D. **1105**
Series: Lay Action Ministry
Title: *Learning to Serve: Jesus As Role Model*
Publisher: Lay Action Ministry Program, 1989 ISBN: 0-89191-489-7

Num. Sess.	Group Time	Num. Pgs.	Avg. Qst.	Price	Audience	Format	Bible Study
12	60-90	112	Vary	$6.95	New Christian	Workbk	Topical

Features: Prayer Helps, Ldr's Notes
★★★ Personal Application Preparation Time: Low
★★★ Relationship Building Ldr. Guide: Yes Size: 5.25 x 8.25
Subjects: Accountability, Church Life, Jesus: Life/Teaching, Service
Comments: This study helps participants understand and follow the example of Jesus, the greatest servant. They discover how servanthood begins in the heart; how a true servant prays, loves, trusts, and faces temptation; and how to be accountable to others, who can help them grow. The leader's guide includes perspectives and objectives for each lesson, suggestions for accountability, a focusing activity, and a discovering and responding to the Word section. Homework is required.

Author: Powell, Dr. Terry D. **1106**
Series: Lay Action Ministry
Title: *Welcome to the Church*
Publisher: Lay Action Ministry Program, 1987 ISBN: 0-89191-514-1

Num. Sess.	Group Time	Num. Pgs.	Avg. Qst.	Price	Audience	Format	Bible Study
12	60-90	96	Vary	$6.95	New Christian	Workbk	Topical

Features: Prayer Helps, Scrpt Memory Helps
★★★ Personal Application Preparation Time: Low
★★★ Relationship Building Ldr. Guide: Yes Size: 5.25 x 8.25
Subjects: Church Life, Prayer, Service
Comments: This practical study helps participants respond to several questions: How do I tell others about salvation? How can I know God better? How do I tap the power of prayer? How do I "fit in" at my church? Participants learn how to search Scripture for guidance. A Christian service inventory is included. Homework is required. An accompanying book, *Daily Time With God,* focuses on scheduled Bible reading, Bible memory, prayer, and notetaking from sermons.

Author: Powell, Dr. Terry D. **1107**
Series: Lay Action Ministry
Title: *Welcome to Your Ministry*
Publisher: Lay Action Ministry Program, 1987 ISBN: 0-89191-515-X

Num. Sess.	Group Time	Num. Pgs.	Avg. Qst.	Price	Audience	Format	Bible Study
12	60-90	96	Vary	$6.95	New Christian	Workbk	Topical

Features:
★★★ Personal Application Preparation Time: Low
★★★ Relationship Building Ldr. Guide: Yes Size: 5.25 x 8.25
Subjects: Church Life, Service, Spiritual Gifts
Comments: This practical study helps participants identify and develop their spiritual gifts. They learn that God has called them—not just pastors and church leaders—to minister on His behalf and leave distinctive marks for Christ wherever they go. The study provides biblical foundations for lay ministry; students will be excited by the opportunities and rewards of serving Christ. The ministries of encouragement, intercession, and evangelism are among subjects covered.

Author: Powell, Terry D. **1108**
Series:
Title: *Balanced Living On a Tightrope*
Publisher: Victor Books, 1990 ISBN: 0-89693-145-5

Num. Sess.	Group Time	Num. Pgs.	Avg. Qst.	Price	Audience	Format	Bible Study
12	60-75	151	N/A	$7.99	New Christian	Book	Book

Features: No Grp Discussion Quest
★★★★ Personal Application Preparation Time: Low
★ Relationship Building Ldr. Guide: Yes Size: 5.50 x 8.0
Subjects: Christian Life, Money, Proverbs
Comments: This book helps challenge participants to deepen their walks with the Lord. Drawing insights from the Book of Proverbs, the author addresses such questions as: How does a Christian respond when criticized? When pressed to make decisions about job changes or parenting issues, what guidelines can help? What's the best way to use and invest money? In what specific ways does the tongue get people in trouble? What are some tips for getting along with problem people?

Author: Pratt, Lonni Collins **1109**
Series: Family Growth Electives
Title: *Making Two Halves a Whole*
Publisher: David C. Cook Publishing Co., 1995 ISBN: 0-78145-138-8

Num. Sess.	Group Time	Num. Pgs.	Avg. Qst.	Price	Audience	Format	Bible Study
13	45-60	136	Vary	$19.95	Beginner	Workbk	Topical

Features: Intro to Study, Objectives, Bibliography, Prayer Helps, Drawings, Handouts, Persnl Study Quest
★★★★ Personal Application Preparation Time: Low
★★★★ Relationship Building Ldr. Guide: Yes Size: 8.50 x 11.0
Subjects: Conflict, Divorce, Family, Parenting, Relationships, Time
Comments: This 13-week self-contained leader's guide helps remarried couples with children deal with the past, develop realistic expectations, place priority on their marriage relationship, understand and handle conflict, build trust and new family traditions, and grow together spiritually. Every session includes reproducible handouts for group members and step-by-step plans for the leader.

Author: Preston, Don and Rhoda **1110**
Series:
Title: *Before They Ask: Talking About Sex From a Christian Perspective*
Publisher: Graded Press, 1989 ISBN: 0-68775-344-9

Num. Sess.	Group Time	Num. Pgs.	Avg. Qst.	Price	Audience	Format	Bible Study
5	45-60	112	6	$3.10	Beginner	Book	Topical

Features: Bibliography, Prayer Helps, Ldr's Notes, Drawings, Glossary
★★★ Personal Application Preparation Time: None
★★ Relationship Building Ldr. Guide: No Size: 5.25 x 8.50
Subjects: Sexual Issues, Teens: Sexuality
Comments: This book serves as a guide for parents of children from birth through age 12. Chapter titles include: "Hopes and Expectations"; "Knowing, Deciding, and Being in Control"; "Understanding Our Children's Sexuality"; "The Question Box"; "The Real World"; and "Suggested Activities for Group Study."

Author: Prior, David **1111**
Series: The Bible Speaks Today
Title: *Message of 1 Corinthians, The*
Publisher: InterVarsity, 1985 ISBN: 0-87784-297-3

Num. Sess.	Group Time	Num. Pgs.	Avg. Qst.	Price	Audience	Format	Bible Study
16	60-120	310	Vary	$12.99	New Christian	Book	Book

Features: Intro to Study
★★★ Personal Application Preparation Time: Med
★★ Relationship Building Ldr. Guide: No Size: 5.50 x 8.25
Subjects: New Testament, 1 Corinthians
Comments: This series of Old and New Testament expositions is characterized by three goals: to expound the biblical text with accuracy, relate it to contemporary life, and be readable. This exposition of 1 Corinthians plainly shows modern relevance of Paul's letter. The prophet, upon hearing of the difficulties in the Corinthian church, wrote an intense and pointed letter concerning snobbishness, factionalism, insensitivity to other believers, doctrinal looseness, and more.

Author: Quanbeck, Philip A. **1112**
Series: Search Weekly Bible
Title: *Unit 19/1 Peter & 1 John*
Publisher: Augsburg Fortress Publishers, 1987

Num. Sess.	Group Time	Num. Pgs.	Avg. Qst.	Price	Audience	Format	Bible Study
8	90-105	64	Vary	$5.50	New Christian	Book	Book

Features: Intro to Study, Objectives, Prayer Helps, Worship Helps, Follow Up, Summary
★★ Personal Application Preparation Time: Med
★★ Relationship Building Ldr. Guide: Yes Size: 8.50 x 11.0
Subjects: 1 & 2 Peter, 1, 2 & 3 John/Jude
Comments: This review of 1 Peter and 1 John is 1 of 20 units of a 5-year study titled "Search. To remain faithful is the reoccuring theme. The outline includes four sessions for 1 Peter: "The Basis for Hope"; "Called to Be Obedient"; "Living in Relationship"; "Suffering and Hope"; and four sessions for 1 John: "God Has Come in the Flesh"; "Fellowship: Boast or Gift"; "Love: In Deed and Truth."

Author: Raguse, Dan **1113**
Series: Group's Active Bible Curriculum
Title: *Prayer*
Publisher: Group Publishing, 1990 ISBN: 1-55945-104-1

Num. Sess.	Group Time	Num. Pgs.	Avg. Qst.	Price	Audience	Format	Bible Study
4	35-60	45	Vary	$9.99	Beginner	Workbk	Topical

Features: Intro to Leading a Study, Intro to Study, Objectives, Study Overview, Ldr's Notes, Handouts, Agenda, Publicity Ideas
★★★ Personal Application Preparation Time: None
★★★ Relationship Building Ldr. Guide: No Size: 8.50 x 11.0
Subjects: Teens: Junior High, Teens: Prayer
Comments: Christian teenagers will learn how to unleash the power of prayer and develop active prayer lives. This study explores topics like "Why Pray?" "How to Pray," "God's Answer to Prayer," and "Developing a Prayer Attitude." This course can be adapted for use in a Bible class or youth meeting. Activities and Bible studies are included as separate sheets that can be reproduced. The instructions are easy to follow.

Author: Rainey, Dennis **1114**
Series: HomeBuilders Couples
Title: *Building Your Marriage*
Publisher: Gospel Light Publications, 1989 ISBN: 0-83071-612-2

Num. Sess.	Group Time	Num. Pgs.	Avg. Qst.	Price	Audience	Format	Bible Study
7	60-90	164	Vary	$9.99	Beginner	Workbk	Topical

Features: Intro to Study, Bibliography, Appendix, Cassette Avail
★★★★ Personal Application Preparation Time: Low
★★★★ Relationship Building Ldr. Guide: Yes Size: 5.75 x 8.50
Subjects: Family, Marriage, Women's Issues
Comments: This study recognizes that married people can still feel lonely or isolated. Participants will understand that their feelings of isolation can be overcome as they become one. Lessons address rekindling romance, growing together spiritually, the uniqueness of one's mate, and that intimacy and transparency result from commitment. It provides biblical guidelines for husbands and wives, describes the Holy Spirit's role, and more.

Author: Rainey, Dennis & Barbara **1115**
Series: HomeBuilders Couples
Title: *Building Your Mate's Self-Esteem*
Publisher: Gospel Light Publications, 1989 ISBN: 0-83071-616-5

Num. Sess.	Group Time	Num. Pgs.	Avg. Qst.	Price	Audience	Format	Bible Study
8	60-90	200	Vary	$9.99	Beginner	Workbk	Topical

Features: Intro to Study, Prayer Helps, Appendix
★★★★ Personal Application Preparation Time: Low
★★★ Relationship Building Ldr. Guide: Yes Size: 5.75 x 8.50
Subjects: Family, Marriage, Self-esteem
Comments: This study helps participants focus on practical ways to strengthen marriage by building up and encouraging one another. Couples learn how to accept a mate unconditionally, how to put aside past hurts and negative feelings, what encouraging words to use with a mate, and ways to help a mate separate self-worth from performance. It teaches how to defeat stress and keep life manageable, and how to meet a mate's specific needs.

Author: Rainey, Dennis & Robert Lewis **1116**
Series: HomeBuilders Couples
Title: *Managing Pressure in Your Marriage*
Publisher: Gospel Light Publications, 1993 ISBN: 0-83071-630-0

Num. Sess.	Group Time	Num. Pgs.	Avg. Qst.	Price	Audience	Format	Bible Study
6	60-90	148	Vary	$9.99	Beginner	Workbk	Topical

Features: Intro to Study, Appendix
★★★★ Personal Application Preparation Time: Low
★★★★ Relationship Building Ldr. Guide: Yes Size: 5.75 x 8.50
Subjects: Family, Marriage
Comments: This study shows couples how to make better choices, plan for the future, and find new solutions as they mature. It teaches how wise decision making is essential to resolving pressure, why poor financial decisions stress marriages, and how to relieve weariness even when free time is limited. It shows how to face pressures that come with each marriage "season," how to understand a mate's needs and sexual frustrations, and how living biblically strengthens marriage.

Author: Rainey, Shannon B. **1117**
Series: IBC Discussion Guide
Title: *Anger*
Publisher: NavPress, 1992 ISBN: 0-89109-687-6

Num. Sess.	Group Time	Num. Pgs.	Avg. Qst.	Price	Audience	Format	Bible Study
6	60-90	67	7	$5.00	Beginner	Workbk	Topical

Features: Intro to Leading a Study, Intro to Study, Prayer Helps, Follow Up, Ldr's Notes, Charts
★★★★ Personal Application Preparation Time: None
★★★★ Relationship Building Ldr. Guide: No Size: 5.25 x 8.25
Subjects: Anger, Counseling, Emotions, Support
Comments: "Anger" is one of 6 studies that identify how life struggles affect the way participants relate to themselves, others, and God. Six lessons review: the symptoms and styles of anger, where anger comes from, what motives of the heart are served when you get angry, and how to get rid of distorted ways of dealing with anger. A "During the Week" section helps participants apply the lesson.

Author: Reames, Cheryl **1118**
Series: LifeSearch
Title: *Parenting*
Publisher: Abingdon Press, 1994 ISBN: 0-68777-868-9

Num. Sess.	Group Time	Num. Pgs.	Avg. Qst.	Price	Audience	Format	Bible Study
6	60-90	62	Vary	$4.95	Beginner	Workbk	Topical

Features: Intro to Leading a Study, Intro to Study, Prayer Helps, Worship Helps, Ldr's Notes
★★★★ Personal Application Preparation Time: None
★★★★ Relationship Building Ldr. Guide: No Size: 7.0 x 10.0
Subjects: Parenting
Comments: This 6-week study focuses on helping parents of children and youth find support in sharing problems with ideas for parenting their children, as well as developing principles and skills for parenting. Participants are encouraged to view topics, not only from personal concern, but also from a communal/congregational concern. The book contains leader aids and marginal notes.

Author: Reapsome, James & Martha **1119**
Series: Fisherman Bible Studyguide
Title: *Discipleship: The Growing Christian's Lifestyle*
Publisher: Shaw, 1984 ISBN: 0-87788-175-8

Num. Sess.	Group Time	Num. Pgs.	Avg. Qst.	Price	Audience	Format	Bible Study
12	45-60	80	14	$4.99	New Christian	Workbk	Topical

Features: Intro to Leading a Study, Intro to Study, Prayer Helps
★★ Personal Application Preparation Time: None
★★ Relationship Building Ldr. Guide: No Size: 5.0 x 8.25
Subjects: Bible Personalities, Discipleship
Comments: This study explores Jesus' requirements of those who want to be His disciples. Selected passages address the life of discipleship under the lordship of Jesus Christ. Ten studies discuss principles of discipleship, while two studies show how New Testament personalities demonstrate the characteristics of discipleship. In total, the study explores ways to become a true follower of Jesus, by identifying with His character, attitudes, and priorities, and by drawing on His resources.

Author: Reapsome, James & Martha **1120**
Series: The Discipleship Series
Title: *Effective Prayer*
Publisher: Zondervan, 1992 ISBN: 0-31054-731-8

Num. Sess.	Group Time	Num. Pgs.	Avg. Qst.	Price	Audience	Format	Bible Study
6	45-60	48	13	$4.99	New Christian	Workbk	Topical

Features: Intro to Leading a Study, Intro to Study, Objectives, Scrpt Memory Helps, Follow Up, Ldr's Notes
★★★★ Personal Application Preparation Time: Med
★★ Relationship Building Ldr. Guide: No Size: 5.50 x 8.50
Subjects: Discipleship, Prayer
Comments: This is 1 of 8 study guides in the Discipleship series. This study is practical and down to earth. It will help participants discover the essence of prayer from the Lord's Prayer, why worship is a vital part of prayer, how confession can help one be humble and honest with the Lord, how to pray for one's own needs (petition) and for the needs of others (intercession).

Author: Reapsome, James **1121**
Series: LifeGuide Bible Study
Title: *Exodus: Learning to Trust God*
Publisher: InterVarsity, 1989 ISBN: 0-83081-023-4

Num. Sess.	Group Time	Num. Pgs.	Avg. Qst.	Price	Audience	Format	Bible Study
24	45-75	110	14	$4.99	New Christian	Workbk	Book

Features: Intro to Leading a Study, Intro to Study, Ldr's Notes
★ Personal Application Preparation Time: Low
★ Relationship Building Ldr. Guide: No Size: 5.50 x 8.25
Subjects: Exodus, God
Comments: This study shows how Israel's struggle to trust God mirrors that of modern man. It's divided into 2 parts: the first 12 lessons concern liberating God's people (Exodus 1-19); the second 12 lessons teach God's people (Exodus 20-40). The study covers 100 years of Hebrew history and is organized around major events, their significance for Israel and the insights and practical values relevant today. It is a good study for those with only a basic knowledge of Hebrew history.

Author: Reapsome, James **1122**
Series: Fisherman Bible Studyguide
Title: *Growing Through Life's Challenges*
Publisher: Shaw, 1995 ISBN: 0-87788-381-5

Num. Sess.	Group Time	Num. Pgs.	Avg. Qst.	Price	Audience	Format	Bible Study
12	50-60	96	12	$4.99	Beginner	Workbk	Topical

Features: Intro to Leading a Study, Intro to Study, Prayer Helps, Ldr's Notes
★★★ Personal Application Preparation Time: None
★★ Relationship Building Ldr. Guide: No Size: 5.0 x 8.25
Subjects: Failure, Faith, Grief
Comments: This studyguide explores 11 challenges including rejection, grief, sin and guilt, failure, and disappointments, common to people in the Bible and today. In each study participants can witness an individual's faith struggle, and watch how fears and frustrations are brought before God. Faith can grow as they see how God's character and presence are sufficient to meet the needs of His children.

Author: Reapsome, James & Martha 1123
Series: LifeGuide Bible Study
Title: *Marriage: God's Design for Intimacy*
Publisher: InterVarsity, 1986 ISBN: 0-83081-056-0

Num. Sess.	Group Time	Num. Pgs.	Avg. Qst.	Price	Audience	Format	Bible Study
12	45-60	63	11	$4.99	New Christian	Workbk	Topical

Features: Intro to Leading a Study, Intro to Study, Ldr's Notes
★★★ Personal Application Preparation Time: Med
★★ Relationship Building Ldr. Guide: No Size: 5.50 x 8.25
Subjects: God, Marriage, Money, Relationships
Comments: This study begins with the view of God's purpose and plan for marriage, as well as the source of broken relationship between husband and wife as shown in Genesis. In Galatians, God's design is restored. In Ephesians, the role of the man and woman is explored. The remaining lessons deal with God's design for communication, conflict, and handling money. The final study explores God's demand for faithfulness and love in marriage.

Author: Reapsome, James and Martha 1124
Series: The TruthSeed Series
Title: *Money: How Much Is Enough?*
Publisher: Victor Books, 1995 ISBN: 1-56476-309-9

Num. Sess.	Group Time	Num. Pgs.	Avg. Qst.	Price	Audience	Format	Bible Study
11	45-60	96	12	$4.99	Beginner	Workbk	Book

Features: Intro to Leading a Study, Intro to Study, Bibliography, Prayer Helps, Digging Deeper Quest, Follow Up, Ldr's Notes, Persnl Study Quest
★★★ Personal Application Preparation Time: None
★★★ Relationship Building Ldr. Guide: No Size: 6.0 x 9.0
Subjects: Money
Comments: This new series of inductive Bible studies enables men and women to experience community and develop godliness in either discussion group or personal settings. Questions are designed and field-tested for seekers, new believers, and mature Christians. Examines contemporary pressures and biblical texts that deal with money.

Author: Reapsome, James 1125
Series: Fisherman Bible Studyguide
Title: *Romans: The Christian Story*
Publisher: Shaw, 1989 ISBN: 0-87788-734-9

Num. Sess.	Group Time	Num. Pgs.	Avg. Qst.	Price	Audience	Format	Bible Study
16	45-60	92	10	$4.99	Beginner	Workbk	Book

Features: Intro to Leading a Study, Intro to Study, Ldr's Notes
★★ Personal Application Preparation Time: Low
★★ Relationship Building Ldr. Guide: No Size: 5.0 x 8.25
Subjects: Romans
Comments: This study inseparably binds theology and practice. After Paul drills theology into the minds and hearts of his readers, he calls them to transformed living. The study includes justification, reconciliation, righteousness, sin, and redemption. Other topics covered are how to be holy in daily conduct, how to live under government, and how to get along with fellow believers in church and unbelieving neighbors across the street.

Author: Reapsome, James & Martha 1126
Series: Fisherman Bible Studyguide
Title: *Senior Saints: Growing Older in God's Family*
Publisher: Shaw, 1993 ISBN: 0-87788-746-2

Num. Sess.	Group Time	Num. Pgs.	Avg. Qst.	Price	Audience	Format	Bible Study
12	45-60	77	14	$4.99	Beginner	Workbk	Topical

Features: Intro to Leading a Study, Intro to Study, Prayer Helps, Ldr's Notes
★★★★ Personal Application Preparation Time: None
★★★ Relationship Building Ldr. Guide: No Size: 5.25 x 8.25
Subjects: Aging, Senior Adults
Comments: This 12-week study explores how to develop a godly perspective toward aging. Two important focuses of this study are biblical promises to claim and examples to follow. Included are: "Continuing Significance"; "Telling the Next Generation"; "Trusting God in Changing Circumstances"; "Finding New Opportunities"; and more. Encourages Christians to still bear fruit in old age.

Author: Reapsome, James & Martha 1127
Series: The Discipleship Series
Title: *Spiritual Warfare*
Publisher: Zondervan, 1992 ISBN: 0-31054-771-7

Num. Sess.	Group Time	Num. Pgs.	Avg. Qst.	Price	Audience	Format	Bible Study
6	45-60	48	14	$4.99	New Christian	Workbk	Topical

Features: Intro to Leading a Study, Intro to Study, Objectives, Prayer Helps, Scrpt Memory Helps, Follow Up, Ldr's Notes
★★★★ Personal Application Preparation Time: Med
★★ Relationship Building Ldr. Guide: No Size: 5.50 x 8.50
Subjects: Discipleship, Spiritual Warfare
Comments: Becoming a Christian is like joining the armed services. After one declares his allegiance to Jesus Christ and willingness to serve Him, he begins a lifetime of spiritual training and combat. This study guide presents the superb "tactics and weaponry" God has made available. Participants learn how to know the enemy, choose weapons, confront doubts, face temptations, overcome struggles against sin.

Author: Reapsome, Martha 1128
Series: LifeGuide Bible Study
Title: *Colossians & Philemon*
Publisher: InterVarsity, 1989 ISBN: 0-83081-014-5

Num. Sess.	Group Time	Num. Pgs.	Avg. Qst.	Price	Audience	Format	Bible Study
10	45-60	63	12	$4.99	New Christian	Workbk	Book

Features: Intro to Leading a Study, Intro to Study, Ldr's Notes
★ Personal Application Preparation Time: Low
★ Relationship Building Ldr. Guide: No Size: 5.50 x 8.25
Subjects: Church Life, Colossians/Philemon, False Teachers, Forgiveness, Hope, Prison Epistles, Relationships, Service, Suffering
Comments: The 20th century teaches "more" is better—more wisdom, maturity, power, faith, and material goods. Paul responded to Colossian Christians with similar longings by pointing to the fullness in Christ—which they had—and away from false teachers. The study of Colossians defines the scope, reality, and implications of fullness of life in Christ. Philemon offers principles for mending relationships.

Author: Reeder, W. Donald **1129**
Series: Teach Yourself the Bible
Title: *Letters of John and Jude, The*
Publisher: Moody Press, 1965 ISBN: 0-80244-674-4

Num. Sess.	Group Time	Num. Pgs.	Avg. Qst.	Price	Audience	Format	Bible Study
8	60-75	64	37	$4.50	New Christian	Workbk	Book

Features: Intro to Leading a Study, Exam
★★ Personal Application Preparation Time: Low
★★ Relationship Building Ldr. Guide: No Size: 5.50 x 8.50
Subjects: Church Life, False Teachers, 1, 2 & 3 John/Jude
Comments: This study is part of a 25-book series and concerns four letters addressed to members of the early Church. Their problems, similar to those faced by contemporary Christians, include struggling with false teachers, heresy, and intrachurch personalities. The format includes a series of fill-in-the-blank questions, and checkups to test participants' grasp of Scriptural truths. The series is designed for self-study; however, suggestions for group study are included.

Author: Reinicke, Melinda **1130**
Series:
Title: *Parables for Personal Growth*
Publisher: Recovery Publications, 1993 ISBN: 0-94140-522-2

Num. Sess.	Group Time	Num. Pgs.	Avg. Qst.	Price	Audience	Format	Bible Study
20	60-75	180	Vary	$12.95	Beginner	Workbk	Topical

Features: Intro to Study, Bibliography, Drawings, Appendix
★★★★ Personal Application Preparation Time: Low
★ Relationship Building Ldr. Guide: No Size: 7.0 x 9.25
Subjects: Forgiveness, Grief, Parables, Self-help, Support
Comments: This book includes 19 original parables to engage participants' heads and hearts. It combines writing, drawing, imagination, and other exercises with inventive tools for opening and understanding closed-off feelings and using insights for personal growth. The parables address self-defeating behavior, depression, self-concept, loss of childhood, recovery from childhood abuse, dysfunctional family interactions, fears, anxiety, and much more.

Author: Resta, M.D., Bartholomew **1131**
Series: LifeSearch
Title: *Health and Wholeness*
Publisher: Abingdon Press, 1994 ISBN: 0-68777-869-7

Num. Sess.	Group Time	Num. Pgs.	Avg. Qst.	Price	Audience	Format	Bible Study
6	60-90	62	Vary	$4.95	Beginner	Workbk	Topical

Features: Intro to Leading a Study, Intro to Study, Prayer Helps, Worship Helps, Ldr's Notes
★★★★ Personal Application Preparation Time: None
★★★★ Relationship Building Ldr. Guide: No Size: 7.0 x 10.0
Subjects: Wholeness
Comments: This 6-week study explores health and wholeness in ways that affect the whole person, including physical, spiritual, emotional, mental, and moral dimensions. It also provides concrete suggestions for enhancing personal and communal health and wholeness. The book contains leader aids and marginal notes. A section on how to lead with minimal preparation time, is also included.

Author: Reuss, Edith A. **1132**
Series: Small Group Bible Studies
Title: *Mary*
Publisher: Augsburg Fortress Publishers, 1978

Num. Sess.	Group Time	Num. Pgs.	Avg. Qst.	Price	Audience	Format	Bible Study
4	60-75	16	18	$1.15	New Christian	Book	Charctr

Features: Intro to Study, Prayer Helps
★★★ Personal Application Preparation Time: None
★★ Relationship Building Ldr. Guide: No Size: 8.50 x 5.50
Subjects: Bible Personalities, Faith, Jesus: Life/Teaching, Prophecy
Comments: This small pamphlet includes four sessions on Mary, the Lord's mother. The study portrays the unfolding drama of Jesus' birth and life from her point of view. It gives a clearer picture of Mary as a real person. Sessions include: "Mary, an Example of Faith"; "Mary, Fulfiller of Prophecy"; "Mary, the Mother of the Christ"; and "Mary, Follower of the Christ." Starred questions are especially recommended for group discussion.

Author: Reynolds, Randy **1133**
Series: Serendipity Support Group
Title: *Compassion Fatigue: Worn Out from Caring*
Publisher: Serendipity House, 1990 ISBN: 1-88341-966-2

Num. Sess.	Group Time	Num. Pgs.	Avg. Qst.	Price	Audience	Format	Bible Study
7	60-90	80	Vary	$5.45	Beginner	Workbk	Topical

Features: Intro to Leading a Study, Objectives, Bibliography, Prayer Helps, Full Scrpt Printed, Cartoons, Agenda
★★★★ Personal Application Preparation Time: None
★★★★ Relationship Building Ldr. Guide: No Size: 6.50 x 9.25
Subjects: Caring, Stress, Support
Comments: This study is for caregivers who face the danger of burnout from giving of themselves. Issues covered include: the gift of caring, the causes of burnout, dependency, self-protection, recovery, and how to handle the feeling of being indispensable. The format includes icebreakers, Bible study, and prayer. Timelines are provided for each lesson.

Author: Rhodes, Ron **1134**
Series: The Lifechange Series
Title: *Hebrews*
Publisher: NavPress, 1989 ISBN: 0-89109-272-2

Num. Sess.	Group Time	Num. Pgs.	Avg. Qst.	Price	Audience	Format	Bible Study
19	60-90	190	18	$6.00	New Christian	Workbk	Book

Features: Intro to Leading a Study, Intro to Study, Bibliography, Prayer Helps, Worship Helps, Study Overview, Digging Deeper Quest, Summary, Cross Ref, Word Study
★★★ Personal Application Preparation Time: Med
★★★ Relationship Building Ldr. Guide: No Size: 5.50 x 8.50
Subjects: Faith, Hebrews, Obedience
Comments: This study of Hebrews challenges participants to live wholeheartedly for Christ in every situation. They see Jewish Christians faced with hostility and loss of jobs and tempted to revert to Jewish customs. Then they see a trusted mentor remind them that Christ is far superior to anything Judaism offers.

Author: Rhodes, Ron **1135**
Series: The Lifechange Series
Title: *Proverbs*
Publisher: NavPress, 1990 ISBN: 0-89109-348-6

Num. Sess.	Group Time	Num. Pgs.	Avg. Qst.	Price	Audience	Format	Bible Study
15	60-90	149	15	$6.00	New Christian	Workbk	Book

Features: Intro to Leading a Study, Intro to Study, Bibliography, Prayer Helps, Worship Helps, Study Overview, Digging Deeper Quest, Summary, Charts, Cross Ref, Word Study
★★★ Personal Application Preparation Time: Med
★★★ Relationship Building Ldr. Guide: No Size: 5.50 x 8.50
Subjects: Christian Living, Proverbs, Wisdom
Comments: This verse-by-verse study of Proverbs offers helpful advice on nearly every aspect—both good and bad—of personal conduct imaginable, including goodness, folly, sin, wealth and poverty, the tongue, pride and humility, justice, vengeance, strife, gluttony, love, lust, laziness, friendship, the family, life, and death.

Author: Rhodes, Ron **1136**
Series: Fisherman Bible Studyguide
Title: *When Servants Suffer: Finding Purpose in Pain*
Publisher: Shaw, 1989 ISBN: 0-87788-929-5

Num. Sess.	Group Time	Num. Pgs.	Avg. Qst.	Price	Audience	Format	Bible Study
13	45-60	79	12	$4.99	New Christian	Workbk	Topical

Features: Intro to Leading a Study, Intro to Study, Objectives, Bibliography, Ldr's Notes
★★★★ Personal Application Preparation Time: Low
★★ Relationship Building Ldr. Guide: No Size: 5.25 x 8.25
Subjects: Suffering
Comments: This 13-week study deals with issues like feeling as though God is ignoring your pain, wondering if your faith is deficient because no miracle has come, and secret doubts that God is truly all-powerful and all-loving. The study searches the Scriptures for comfort and encouragement regarding the purposes of suffering and reaffirms the wisdom and love of God.

Author: Richards, Lawrence O. **1137**
Series: GroupBuilder Resources
Title: *Small Group Member's Commentary*
Publisher: Victor Books, 1992 ISBN: 0-89693-055-6

Num. Sess.	Group Time	Num. Pgs.	Avg. Qst.	Price	Audience	Format	Bible Study
	—	650	N/A	$17.99		Book	

Features: Prayer Helps, Maps, Index
Personal Application Preparation Time:
Relationship Building Ldr. Guide: Size: 6.0 x 9.25
Subjects: Small Group Resource
Comments: This commentary divides Bible text into nearly 100 different units or "chapters," study-sized portions of Scripture that cover the entire New Testament and 10 Psalms. Each unit concludes with a group resource guide that provides step-by-step instructions for conducting small group meetings. It features activities that encourage sharing, fellowship-building, exploration and application of Scriptures, ministry, and worship.

Author: Richards, Lawrence O. **1138**
Series:
Title: *Victor Bible Background Commentary, The: New Testament*
Publisher: Victor Books, 1994 ISBN: 0-89693-507-8

Num. Sess.	Group Time	Num. Pgs.	Avg. Qst.	Price	Audience	Format	Bible Study
	—	640	N/A	$27.99			

Features: Intro to Study
Personal Application Preparation Time:
Relationship Building Ldr. Guide: Size: 6.50 x 9.50
Subjects: New Testament, Small Group Resource
Comments: This commentary is intended to provide enriching information for communicators of God's Word. Seventy-seven teachable units cover the whole of the New Testament. It draws on a variety of sources to provide background which illuminates the text and guides its modern application. Because the book's goal is to serve lay Bible teachers and preachers, special attention is paid to those passages which are most teachable and preachable.

Author: Rickerson, Wayne **1139**
Series:
Title: *This Is the Thanks I Get? A Guide to Raising Teenagers*
Publisher: Standard Publishing, 1988 ISBN: 0-87403-406-X

Num. Sess.	Group Time	Num. Pgs.	Avg. Qst.	Price	Audience	Format	Bible Study
13	60-120	142	10	$5.99	Beginner	Book	Topical

Features: Intro to Leading a Study, Intro to Study, Drawings
★★★ Personal Application Preparation Time: Low
★★ Relationship Building Ldr. Guide: Yes Size: 5.25 x 8.50
Subjects: Parenting, Relationships, Support
Comments: This study, part of a 2-book series on rearing children, is designed to prepare parents, through Bible-inspired instruction and by encouraging the development of parenting support groups, for the task of parenting teenagers. Three sections take participants from laying a firm foundation for understanding and preparation, to developing a structure and skills for dealing with teens, to building a positive relationship involving give-and-take and communication.

Author: Rickerson, Wayne **1140**
Series:
Title: *What Should I Do Now? A Guide to Raising Children*
Publisher: Standard Publishing, 1988 ISBN: 0-87403-405-1

Num. Sess.	Group Time	Num. Pgs.	Avg. Qst.	Price	Audience	Format	Bible Study
13	60-120	176	10	$5.99	Beginner	Book	Topical

Features: Intro to Study, Drawings
★★★ Personal Application Preparation Time: Low
★★ Relationship Building Ldr. Guide: Yes Size: 5.25 x 8.50
Subjects: Ethics, Family, Parenting, Relationships, Support
Comments: This study, part of a two-book series on rearing children, is designed to prepare parents for parenting, through Bible-inspired instruction and by encouraging the development of parenting support groups. Three sections take participants through the following topics: family foundations, Christian values, and family togetherness; the basics of parenting, dealing with authority; and what to do when the kids fight. Discussion questions follow each section.

Author: Ridenour, Fritz **1141**
Series: LifeTouch
Title: *How to Be a Christian and Still Enjoy Life*
Publisher: Regal Books, 1988 ISBN: 0-83071-218-6

Num. Sess.	Group Time	Num. Pgs.	Avg. Qst.	Price	Audience	Format	Bible Study
13	60-75	190	Vary	$8.99	New Christian	Book	Topical

Features: Prayer Helps, Drawings
★★★★ Personal Application Preparation Time: Med
★★★★ Relationship Building Ldr. Guide: Yes Size: 5.50 x 8.50
Subjects: Christian Life, Integrity, Joy, Philippians, Prison Epistles, Success, Victorious Living
Comments: This study examines what Paul's letter to the Philippians says about integrity, perseverance, and true success. Philippians shows participants why life can be joyous. The format combines Bible commentary with life-related questions to challenge participants to incorporate their spiritual discoveries into daily living. The separate leader's guide offers an 8- to 13-week study format.

Author: Ridenour, Fritz **1142**
Series: The Light Force
Title: *How to Be a Christian Without Being Religious: Youth Edition*
Publisher: Regal Books, 1967 ISBN: 0-83071-026-4

Num. Sess.	Group Time	Num. Pgs.	Avg. Qst.	Price	Audience	Format	Bible Study
14	45-60	166	3	$6.99	New Christian	Book	Topical

Features: Intro to Study, Scrpt Memory Helps, Drawings
★★★ Personal Application Preparation Time: Low
★★★ Relationship Building Ldr. Guide: Yes Size: 5.25 x 8.0
Subjects: Teens: Discipleship, Teens: New Testament, Teens: Youth Life
Comments: Paul, in Romans, writes that while most people try to reach God through their own efforts (like keeping their noses clean), Christianity is just the opposite. In Christianity, God reaches out to people so together they can enjoy rich and meaningful relationships. Cartoons and a humorous approach provide a guide that helps youth understand Paul's message about God's purpose for their lives.

Author: Ridley, Ruthann **1143**
Series: Tapestry Collection
Title: *Every Marriage is Different*
Publisher: Victor Books, 1993 ISBN: 1-56476-051-0

Num. Sess.	Group Time	Num. Pgs.	Avg. Qst.	Price	Audience	Format	Bible Study
8	120-150	104	13	$5.99	New Christian	Workbk	Topical

Features: Intro to Leading a Study, Intro to Study, Objectives, Prayer Helps, Follow Up, Ldr's Notes, Persnl Study Quest
★★★★ Personal Application Preparation Time: Low
★★★★ Relationship Building Ldr. Guide: No Size: 6.0 x 9.0
Subjects: Marriage
Comments: This 8-week study is designed to help participants discover the personalities of their marriages and what will work for them. Points of marital tension discussed include unity and diversity, growth and stagnation, action and passivity, communication and silence, love and indifference, and submission and leadership. Husband and wife discussions are encouraged.

Author: Robbins, Duffy **1144**
Series: SonPower Youth Sources
Title: *Youth Ministry That Works*
Publisher: Victor Books, 1991 ISBN: 0-89693-918-9

Num. Sess.	Group Time	Num. Pgs.	Avg. Qst.	Price	Audience	Format	Bible Study
	—	121	N/A	$7.99		Book	

Features: Intro to Study, Bibliography, Charts
Personal Application Preparation Time:
Relationship Building Ldr. Guide: Size: 6.0 x 9.0
Subjects: Teens: Discipleship, Teens: Resources
Comments: This book for youth ministers who struggle with effectiveness in their ministry offers professional advice on balancing priorities between personal life and ministry. The author reaches beyond the statistical goal of increasing attendance at youth meetings, stressing Christ's compelling mandate to make disciples. Robbins recognizes that kids are at different stages of development, analyzes their levels of receptivity to the Gospel claims, and proposes ways to meet them.

Author: Robinson, Haddon **1145**
Series:
Title: *Decision Making By The Book*
Publisher: Victor Books, 1991 ISBN: 0-89693-913-8

Num. Sess.	Group Time	Num. Pgs.	Avg. Qst.	Price	Audience	Format	Bible Study
12	60-75	166	N/A	$13.99	New Christian	Book	Topical

Features: Intro to Study, No Grp Discussion Quest
★★★★ Personal Application Preparation Time: Low
★ Relationship Building Ldr. Guide: No Size: 6.0 x 9.0
Subjects: Decision Making
Comments: This book exposes how some Christians seek godly wisdom in misguided ways, then explains how they can handle God's Word with confidence as they strive to make choices that please Him and strengthen them and their families. Specifically discussed are: making sense of the circumstances, seeking godly counsel, understanding the place of divine revelation today, how our freedom to decide fits alongside God's sovereign will, and how our personality can help us.

Author: Roen, Scott D. **1146**
Series: Lay Action Ministry
Title: *Outreach As a Life-Style*
Publisher: Lay Action Ministry Program, 1989 ISBN: 0-89191-484-6

Num. Sess.	Group Time	Num. Pgs.	Avg. Qst.	Price	Audience	Format	Bible Study
12	60-90	142	Vary	$6.95	New Christian	Workbk	Topical

Features: Intro to Study, Prayer Helps, Scrpt Memory Helps, Ldr's Notes
★★★ Personal Application Preparation Time: Low
★★★ Relationship Building Ldr. Guide: Yes Size: 5.25 x 8.25
Subjects: Accountability, Evangelism
Comments: This study shows Christians how to take the terror out of sharing their faith. Participants discover how to listen to nonbelievers, sense their needs, and gauge their levels of interest. They also learn how to clarify their own personal testimony, explain the Gospel, and handle objections. The leaders's guide includes perspectives and objectives for each lesson, suggestion for accountability, a focusing activity.

Author: Root, Jerry & Claudia **1147**
Series: Shaw Contemporary Issues
Title: *Friendship Evangelism*
Publisher: Shaw, 1990 ISBN: 0-87788-273-8

Num. Sess.	Group Time	Num. Pgs.	Avg. Qst.	Price	Audience	Format	Bible Study
8	30-45	48	5	$4.99	Beginner	Workbk	Topical

Features: Intro to Leading a Study, Intro to Study, Bibliography, Follow Up, Ldr's Notes
★★★★ Personal Application Preparation Time: Low
★★★ Relationship Building Ldr. Guide: No Size: 5.25 x 8.25
Subjects: Christian Life, Evangelism
Comments: A practical short study on friendship evangelism, this guide will prepare participants for reaching out to coworkers or neighbors with the good news of Jesus. Helpful sections include: a list of suggestions for starting conversations about Christ, components of an effective testimony, suggestions for using a church for evangelism, and the 3 essential elements of a Christian life.

Author: Roper, Harlin J. **1148**
Series: Through the Bible
Title: *And You Shall Be Witnesses: Acts—Youth*
Publisher: Roper Press, 1978 ISBN: 0-86606-370-6

Num. Sess.	Group Time	Num. Pgs.	Avg. Qst.	Price	Audience	Format	Bible Study
26	30-45	64	10	$4.50	New Christian	Workbk	Book

Features: Intro to Leading a Study, Intro to Study, Scrpt Memory Helps, Maps
★★★ Personal Application Preparation Time: Low
★★ Relationship Building Ldr. Guide: Yes Size: 5.50 x 8.0
Subjects: Teens: Evangelism, Teens: New Testament
Comments: This chapter-by-chapter study encourages youth to develop inductive Bible study skills by answering questions, thus learning to interpret the Word and discover its message. This study covers Acts, the great bridge between fulfillment of Old Testament prophecy about Christ and the commission following His death and resurrection. Crossword puzzles enhance the study.

Author: Roper, Harlin J. **1149**
Series: Through the Bible
Title: *And You Shall Be Witnesses*
Publisher: Roper Press, 1978 ISBN: 0-86606-358-7

Num. Sess.	Group Time	Num. Pgs.	Avg. Qst.	Price	Audience	Format	Bible Study
26	45-60	52	20	$4.50	New Christian	Workbk	Book

Features: Intro to Study, Scrpt Memory Helps, Maps
★★★ Personal Application Preparation Time: Med
★ Relationship Building Ldr. Guide: Yes Size: 5.50 x 8.25
Subjects: Acts, Church Life, Evangelism
Comments: In this chapter-by-chapter study of Acts, participants will develop inductive Bible study skills by answering questions, thus learning to interpret the Word and discover its message. This study, the 10th of a 13-unit series, covers Acts, which serves as a bridge between the fulfillment of Old Testament prophecy about Christ and His commission following death and resurrection. An in-depth leader's guide is available.

Author: Roper, Harlin J. **1150**
Series: Through the Bible
Title: *Consider Jesus: Hebrews—Revelation*
Publisher: Roper Press, 1988 ISBN: 0-86606-361-7

Num. Sess.	Group Time	Num. Pgs.	Avg. Qst.	Price	Audience	Format	Bible Study
26	45-60	52	20	$4.50	New Christian	Workbk	Book

Features: Intro to Study, Scrpt Memory Helps, Maps
★★★ Personal Application Preparation Time: Med
★ Relationship Building Ldr. Guide: Yes Size: 5.50 x 8.25
Subjects: Faith, Hebrews, James, Jesus: Life/Teaching, Revelation, 1 & 2 Peter, 1, 2 & 3 John/Jude
Comments: This chapter-by-chapter study encourages participants to develop inductive Bible study skills by answering questions, thus learning to interpret the Word and discover its message. The last in a 13-unit series, this study covers the last 9 books of the New Testament—Hebrews, James, 1 and 2 Peter, 1, 2, and 3 John, Jude, and Revelation. An in-depth leader's guide is available.

Author: Roper, Harlin J. **1151**
Series: Through the Bible
Title: *Consider Jesus: Hebrews—Revelation—Youth*
Publisher: Roper Press, 1988 ISBN: 0-86606-373-0

Num. Sess.	Group Time	Num. Pgs.	Avg. Qst.	Price	Audience	Format	Bible Study
26	30-45	64	10	$4.50	New Christian	Workbk	Book

Features: Intro to Leading a Study, Intro to Study, Scrpt Memory Helps, Maps
★★★ Personal Application Preparation Time: Low
★★ Relationship Building Ldr. Guide: Yes Size: 5.50 x 8.0
Subjects: Teens: Jesus Life, Teens: New Testament
Comments: This chapter-by-chapter study encourages participants to develop inductive Bible study skills by responding to true/false, fill-in-the-blank, and application questions, thus learning to interpret the Word and discover its message. This study covers the last 9 books of the New Testament—Hebrews, James, 1 and 2 Peter, 1, 2, and 3 John, Jude, and Revelation.

Author: Roper, Harlin J. **1152**
Series: Through the Bible
Title: *Declaring His Deity: John—Youth*
Publisher: Roper Press, 1978 ISBN: 0-86606-062-6

Num. Sess.	Group Time	Num. Pgs.	Avg. Qst.	Price	Audience	Format	Bible Study
26	30-45	40	10	$4.50	New Christian	Workbk	Book

Features: Intro to Leading a Study, Intro to Study, Scrpt Memory Helps, Maps
★★★ Personal Application Preparation Time: Low
★★ Relationship Building Ldr. Guide: Yes Size: 5.50 x 8.0
Subjects: Teens: Jesus Life, Teens: New Testament
Comments: This chapter-by-chapter study of John encourages youth to develop inductive Bible study skills. They will respond to true/false, fill-in-the-blank, and application questions to learn to interpret the Word and discover its message. John deals with Jesus' humanity, using His human name 247 times. Crossword puzzles enhance the study.

Author: Roper, Harlin J. **1153**
Series: Through the Bible
Title: *Declaring His Deity: John*
Publisher: Roper Press, 1978 ISBN: 0-86606-357-9

Num. Sess.	Group Time	Num. Pgs.	Avg. Qst.	Price	Audience	Format	Bible Study
26	45-60	52	20	$4.50	New Christian	Workbk	Book

Features: Intro to Study, Scrpt Memory Helps, Maps
★★★ Personal Application Preparation Time: Med
★ Relationship Building Ldr. Guide: Yes Size: 5.50 x 8.25
Subjects: Jesus: Life/Teaching, John
Comments: This chapter-by-chapter study of John encourages participants to develop inductive Bible study skills by answering questions, thus learning to interpret the Word and discover its message. The 9th of a 13-unit series, this study covers the Gospel of John, a book different from Matthew, Mark, and Luke, being theological and interpretive rather than historical and factual. John deals with Jesus' humanity, using His human name 247 times.

Author: Roper, Harlin J. **1154**
Series: Through the Bible
Title: *Disruption and Dispersion: 1 Kings 9—Job—Youth*
Publisher: Roper Press, 1978 ISBN: 0-86606-054-5

Num. Sess.	Group Time	Num. Pgs.	Avg. Qst.	Price	Audience	Format	Bible Study
26	30-45	40	10	$4.50	New Christian	Workbk	Book

Features: Intro to Leading a Study, Intro to Study, Scrpt Memory Helps, Maps
★★★ Personal Application Preparation Time: Low
★★ Relationship Building Ldr. Guide: Yes Size: 5.50 x 8.0
Subjects: Teens: Bible/Pers., Teens: Old Testament
Comments: This chapter-by-chapter study encourages youth to develop inductive Bible study skills by responding to true/false, fill-in-the-blank and application questions. This will teach them to interpret the Word and discover its message. This study covers 1 and 2 Kings, showing that, despite warnings, sin brings ruin without remedy; and Job.

Author: Roper, Harlin J. **1155**
Series: Through the Bible
Title: *God Leads His People: Exodus 19—Deuteronomy—Youth*
Publisher: Roper Press, 1978 ISBN: 0-86606-363-3

Num. Sess.	Group Time	Num. Pgs.	Avg. Qst.	Price	Audience	Format	Bible Study
26	30-45	64	10	$4.50	New Christian	Workbk	Book

Features: Intro to Leading a Study, Intro to Study, Scrpt Memory Helps, Maps
★★★ Personal Application Preparation Time: Low
★★ Relationship Building Ldr. Guide: Yes Size: 5.50 x 8.0
Subjects: Teens: Bible/Pers., Teens: Old Testament
Comments: This chapter-by-chapter study of Exodus 19 through Deuteronomy encourages youth to develop inductive Bible study skills by responding to true/false, fill-in-the-blank, and application questions. Thus they will learn to interpret the Word and discover its message. This study shows the Israelites preparing for the Promised Land and receiving the Law from Moses. Crossword puzzles enhance the study.

Author: Roper, Harlin J. **1156**
Series: Through the Bible
Title: *God Leads His People: Exodus 19—Deuteronomy*
Publisher: Roper Press, 1978 ISBN: 0-86606-351-X

Num. Sess.	Group Time	Num. Pgs.	Avg. Qst.	Price	Audience	Format	Bible Study
26	45-60	52	20	$4.50	New Christian	Workbk	Book

Features: Intro to Study, Scrpt Memory Helps, Maps
★★★ Personal Application Preparation Time: Med
★ Relationship Building Ldr. Guide: Yes Size: 5.50 x 8.25
Subjects: Bible Personalities, Exodus, God, Leviticus, Numbers/Deuteronomy
Comments: This chapter-by-chapter study, the 2nd of a 13-unit series, covers the last half of Exodus and all of Leviticus, Numbers, Deuteronomy, the Israelites preparation for the Promised Land, and the Law from Moses. Participants are encouraged to develop inductive Bible study skills by answering questions, thus learning to interpret the Word and discover its message.

Author: Roper, Harlin J. **1157**
Series: Through the Bible
Title: *God's Salvation and Grace: Romans—Galatians—Youth*
Publisher: Roper Press, 1978 ISBN: 0-86606-371-4

Num. Sess.	Group Time	Num. Pgs.	Avg. Qst.	Price	Audience	Format	Bible Study
26	30-45	64	10	$4.50	New Christian	Workbk	Book

Features: Intro to Leading a Study, Intro to Study, Scrpt Memory Helps, Maps
★★★ Personal Application Preparation Time: Low
★★ Relationship Building Ldr. Guide: Yes Size: 5.50 x 8.0
Subjects: Teens: Evangelism, Teens: Jesus Life, Teens: New Testament
Comments: This chapter-by-chapter study encourages youth to develop inductive Bible study skills by answering questions, thus learning to interpret the Word and discover its message. This study covers Romans, 1 and 2 Corinthians, and Galatians. It deals with the apostle Paul's letters to Christians in those cities, supports the Gospel, and lifts up Christ as the only true example. Crossword puzzles enhance the study.

Author: Roper, Harlin J. **1158**
Series: Through the Bible
Title: *God's Salvation and Grace: Romans—Galatians*
Publisher: Roper Press, 1978 ISBN: 0-86606-359-5

Num. Sess.	Group Time	Num. Pgs.	Avg. Qst.	Price	Audience	Format	Bible Study
26	45-60	52	20	$4.50	New Christian	Workbk	Book

Features: Intro to Study, Scrpt Memory Helps, Maps
★★★ Personal Application Preparation Time: Med
★ Relationship Building Ldr. Guide: Yes Size: 5.50 x 8.25
Subjects: Galatians, Grace, Repentance, Romans, Service, Suffering, 1 Corinthians, 2 Corinthians
Comments: This chapter-by-chapter study of Romans through Galatians encourages participants to develop inductive Bible study skills by answering questions, thus learning to interpret the Word and discover its message. This study, the 11th of a 13-unit series, deals with 4 of the apostle Paul's letters that support the Gospel and lifting up Christ as the only true example.

Author: Roper, Harlin J. **1159**
Series: Through the Bible
Title: *Golden Years of the Kingdom, The: Joshua—1 Kings 8—Youth*
Publisher: Roper Press, 1978 ISBN: 0-86606-053-7

Num. Sess.	Group Time	Num. Pgs.	Avg. Qst.	Price	Audience	Format	Bible Study
26	30-45	40	10	$4.50	New Christian	Workbk	Book

Features: Intro to Leading a Study, Intro to Study, Scrpt Memory Helps, Maps
★★★ Personal Application Preparation Time: Low
★★ Relationship Building Ldr. Guide: Yes Size: 5.50 x 8.0
Subjects: Teens: Bible/Pers., Teens: Old Testament
Comments: This chapter-by-chapter study of Joshua through 1 Kings 8 encourages youth to develop inductive Bible study skills by responding to true/false, fill-in-the-blank, and application questions. Joshua begins this study with the Israelites gaining the Promised land moving then to the people of Israel demanding a new king; the rule of David, God's king; the record of David's last days; and the glory of Solomon's reign.

Author: Roper, Harlin J. **1160**
Series: Through the Bible
Title: *In the Beginning God: Genesis—Exodus 18*
Publisher: Roper Press, 1978 ISBN: 0-86606-350-1

Num. Sess.	Group Time	Num. Pgs.	Avg. Qst.	Price	Audience	Format	Bible Study
26	45-60	52	20	$4.50	New Christian	Workbk	Book

Features: Intro to Study, Objectives, Scrpt Memory Helps, Maps
★★★ Personal Application Preparation Time: Med
★ Relationship Building Ldr. Guide: Yes Size: 5.50 x 8.25
Subjects: Exodus, Genesis, God
Comments: This chapter-by-chapter study of Genesis 1 through Exodus 18 encourages participants to develop inductive Bible study skills. By answering questions, participants will learn to interpret the Word and discover its message. This study, the 1st of 13 units in the series, deals with the Creation, the Flood, the tower of Babel, Abraham and the Jewish nation, Joseph, and the Exodus. An in-depth leader's guide is available.

Author: Roper, Harlin J. **1161**
Series: Through the Bible
Title: *In the Beginning God: Genesis—Exodus 18—Youth*
Publisher: Roper Press, 1988 ISBN: 0-86606-362-5

Num. Sess.	Group Time	Num. Pgs.	Avg. Qst.	Price	Audience	Format	Bible Study
26	30-45	64	10	$4.50	New Christian	Workbk	Book

Features: Intro to Leading a Study, Intro to Study, Scrpt Memory Helps, Maps
★★★ Personal Application Preparation Time: Low
★★ Relationship Building Ldr. Guide: Yes Size: 5.50 x 8.0
Subjects: Teens: Bible/Pers., Teens: Old Testament
Comments: This chapter-by-chapter study encourages youth to develop inductive Bible study skills. They will respond to true/false, fill-in-the-blank, and application questions and learn to interpret the Word and discover its message. This study deals with Genesis—the Creation, the Flood, the tower of Babel, Abraham and the Jewish nation, Joseph—and Exodus—the deliverance from Egypt.

Author: Roper, Harlin J. **1162**
Series: Through the Bible
Title: *Jesus Christ the Son of God: Matthew thru Luke—Youth*
Publisher: Roper Press, 1978 ISBN: 0-86606-060-X

Num. Sess.	Group Time	Num. Pgs.	Avg. Qst.	Price	Audience	Format	Bible Study
26	30-45	40	10	$4.50	New Christian	Workbk	Book

Features: Intro to Leading a Study, Intro to Study, Scrpt Memory Helps, Maps
★★★ Personal Application Preparation Time: Low
★★ Relationship Building Ldr. Guide: Yes Size: 5.50 x 8.0
Subjects: Teens: Jesus Life, Teens: New Testament
Comments: This chapter-by-chapter study of Matthew, Mark, and Luke encourages youth to interpret the Word and discover its message by responding to true/false, fill-in-the-blank, and application questions. It covers Luke chronologically, leading up to and including the final days of Christ's earthly ministry—the trial, Crucifixion, and Resurrection, interweaving Matthew and Mark when appropriate.

Author: Roper, Harlin J. **1163**
Series: Through the Bible
Title: *Jesus Christ the Son of God: Matthew thru Luke*
Publisher: Roper Press, 1978 ISBN: 0-86606-012-X

Num. Sess.	Group Time	Num. Pgs.	Avg. Qst.	Price	Audience	Format	Bible Study
26	45-60	48	20	$4.50	New Christian	Workbk	Book

Features: Intro to Study, Scrpt Memory Helps, Maps
★★★ Personal Application Preparation Time: Med
★ Relationship Building Ldr. Guide: Yes Size: 5.50 x 8.25
Subjects: Jesus: Life/Teaching, Luke, Mark, Matthew
Comments: This chapter-by-chapter study of Matthew through Luke encourages participants to develop inductive Bible study skills by answering questions, thus learning to interpret the Word and discover its message. This study covers Luke chronologically, interweaving Matthew and Mark when appropriate. It also includes the final days of Christ's earthly ministry—the trial, crucifixion, and resurrection. An in-depth leader's guide is available.

Author: Roper, Harlin J. **1164**
Series: Through the Bible
Title: *Land and the Kingdom, The: Joshua—1 Kings 8*
Publisher: Roper Press, 1978 ISBN: 0-86606-352-8

Num. Sess.	Group Time	Num. Pgs.	Avg. Qst.	Price	Audience	Format	Bible Study
26	45-60	52	20	$4.50	New Christian	Workbk	Book

Features: Intro to Study, Scrpt Memory Helps, Maps
★★★ Personal Application Preparation Time: Med
★ Relationship Building Ldr. Guide: Yes Size: 5.50 x 8.25
Subjects: Bible Personalities, Joshua, Judges, Kings/Chronicles, Ruth, 1 & 2 Samuel
Comments: This chapter-by-chapter study of Joshua through 1 Kings 8 encourages participants to develop inductive Bible study skills. Students will learn to interpret the Word and discover its message. This study, 3rd of a 13-unit series, covers the Israelites gaining the Promised Land and the great lessons in Judges, Ruth, 1 and 2 Samuel, and the first half of Kings, from David to Solomon.

Author: Roper, Harlin J. **1165**
Series: Through the Bible
Title: *Letters to Believers: Ephesians—Titus*
Publisher: Roper Press, 1978 ISBN: 0-86606-360-9

Num. Sess.	Group Time	Num. Pgs.	Avg. Qst.	Price	Audience	Format	Bible Study
26	45-60	52	20	$4.50	New Christian	Workbk	Book

Features: Intro to Study, Scrpt Memory Helps, Maps
★★★ Personal Application Preparation Time: Med
★ Relationship Building Ldr. Guide: Yes Size: 5.50 x 8.25
Subjects: Church Life, Colossians/Philemon, Ephesians, Leadership, Pastoral Epistles, Philippians, Prison Epistles, 1 & 2 Thessalonians, 1 & 2 Timothy/Titus
Comments: This chapter-by-chapter study encourages participants to develop inductive Bible study skills. This study, the 12th in a 13-unit series, covers Ephesians, Philippians, Colossians, Philemon, 1 and 2 Thessalonians, 1 and 2 Timothy, and Titus. It deals with the apostle Paul's letters to churches and to his fellow Christian leaders.

Author: Roper, Harlin J. **1166**
Series: Through the Bible
Title: *Letters to Believers: Ephesians—Titus—Youth*
Publisher: Roper Press, 1978 ISBN: 0-86606-372-2

Num. Sess.	Group Time	Num. Pgs.	Avg. Qst.	Price	Audience	Format	Bible Study
26	30-45	64	10	$4.50	New Christian	Workbk	Book

Features: Intro to Leading a Study, Intro to Study, Scrpt Memory Helps, Maps
★★★ Personal Application Preparation Time: Low
★★ Relationship Building Ldr. Guide: Yes Size: 5.50 x 8.0
Subjects: Teens: Christian Liv, Teens: New Testament
Comments: This chapter-by-chapter study encourages youth to develop inductive Bible study skills by answering questions, thus learning to interpret the Word and discover its message. This study covers Ephesians, Philippians, Colossians, Philemon, 1 and 2 Thessalonians, 1 and 2 Timothy, and Titus. It deals with the apostle Paul's letters to churches and to his fellow Christian leaders.

Author: Roper, Harlin J. **1167**
Series: Through the Bible
Title: *Let the Wicked Be Warned: Lamentations—Malachi—Youth*
Publisher: Roper Press, 1978 ISBN: 0-86606-059-6

Num. Sess.	Group Time	Num. Pgs.	Avg. Qst.	Price	Audience	Format	Bible Study
26	30-45	40	10	$4.50	New Christian	Workbk	Book

Features: Intro to Leading a Study, Intro to Study, Scrpt Memory Helps, Maps
★★★ Personal Application Preparation Time: Low
★★ Relationship Building Ldr. Guide: Yes Size: 5.50 x 8.0
Subjects: Teens: Bible/Pers., Teens: Old Testament
Comments: In this chapter-by-chapter study, youth are encouraged to develop inductive Bible study skills by responding to true/false, fill-in-the-blank, and application questions. Thus they learn to interpret the Word and discover its message. This study covers the writings of the major prophets Ezekiel and Daniel, and minor prophets from Hosea to Malachi. Crossword puzzles enhance the study.

Author: Roper, Harlin J. **1168**
Series: Through the Bible
Title: *Predictions of Judgment and Glory: Psalm—Jeremiah—Youth*
Publisher: Roper Press, 1978 ISBN: 0-86606-057-X

Num. Sess.	Group Time	Num. Pgs.	Avg. Qst.	Price	Audience	Format	Bible Study
26	30-45	40	10	$4.50	New Christian	Workbk	Book

Features: Intro to Leading a Study, Intro to Study, Scrpt Memory Helps, Maps
★★★ Personal Application Preparation Time: Low
★★ Relationship Building Ldr. Guide: Yes Size: 5.50 x 8.0
Subjects: Teens: Bible/Pers., Teens: Old Testament
Comments: This chapter-by-chapter study of Isaiah and Jeremiah encourages youth to develop inductive Bible study skills by responding to true/false, fill-in-the-blank, and application questions. This study covers Psalms, Proverbs, Ecclesiastes, Song of Solomon, Lamentations—a group of books generally called "the poetry"—and major prophets Isaiah and Jeremiah. Crossword puzzles enhance the study.

Author: Roper, Harlin J. **1169**
Series: Through the Bible
Title: *Prophecy Out of Captivity: Lamentations—Malachi—Youth*
Publisher: Roper Press, 1978 ISBN: 0-86606-058-8

Num. Sess.	Group Time	Num. Pgs.	Avg. Qst.	Price	Audience	Format	Bible Study
26	30-45	40	10	$4.50	New Christian	Workbk	Book

Features: Intro to Leading a Study, Intro to Study, Scrpt Memory Helps, Maps
★★★ Personal Application Preparation Time: Low
★★ Relationship Building Ldr. Guide: Yes Size: 5.50 x 8.0
Subjects: Teens: Bible/Pers., Teens: Old Testament
Comments: This chapter-by-chapter study encourages youth to develop inductive Bible study skills. They will respond to true/false, fill-in-the-blank, and application questions and thus learn to interpret the Word and discover its message. This study covers Lamentations, Ezekiel, Daniel, and Hosea, completing study of the Major Prophets and the Minor Prophets from Hosea to Malachi.

Author: Roper, Harlin J. **1170**
Series: Through the Bible
Title: *Return and Restoration: 1 Kings 9—Job—Youth*
Publisher: Roper Press, 1978 ISBN: 0-86606-055-3

Num. Sess.	Group Time	Num. Pgs.	Avg. Qst.	Price	Audience	Format	Bible Study
26	30-45	40	10	$4.50	New Christian	Workbk	Book

Features: Intro to Leading a Study, Intro to Study, Scrpt Memory Helps,
Maps
★★★ Personal Application Preparation Time: Low
★★ Relationship Building Ldr. Guide: Yes Size: 5.50 x 8.0
Subjects: Teens: Bible/Pers., Teens: Old Testament
Comments: This chapter-by-chapter study of 1 Kings 9 through Job encourages youth to interpret the Word and discover its message by responding to true/false, fill-in-the-blank, and application questions. This study covers Ezra, Nehemiah, Esther, and Job, dealing with great historical records in the Old Testament.

Author: Roper, Harlin J. 1171
Series: Through the Bible
Title: *Songs, Sayings and Searches: Psalms—Jeremiah—Youth*
Publisher: Roper Press, 1978 ISBN: 0-86606-056-1

Num. Sess.	Group Time	Num. Pgs.	Avg. Qst.	Price	Audience	Format	Bible Study
26	30-45	40	10	$4.50	New Christian	Workbk	Book

Features: Intro to Leading a Study, Intro to Study, Scrpt Memory Helps, Maps
★★★ Personal Application Preparation Time: Low
★★ Relationship Building Ldr. Guide: Yes Size: 5.50 x 8.0
Subjects: Teens: Old Testament
Comments: In this chapter-by-chapter study, youth are encouraged to develop inductive Bible study skills by responding to true/false, fill-in-the-blank, and application questions, thus learning to interpret the Word and discover its message. This study covers the Psalms, Proverbs, Ecclesiastes, Song of Solomon, Lamentations—a group of books generally called "the poetry"—and major prophets Isaiah and Jeremiah.

Author: Roper, Harlin J. 1172
Series: Through the Bible
Title: *Wisdom and Prophecy: Psalms—Jeremiah*
Publisher: Roper Press, 1978 ISBN: 0-86606-354-4

Num. Sess.	Group Time	Num. Pgs.	Avg. Qst.	Price	Audience	Format	Bible Study
26	45-60	52	20	$4.50	New Christian	Workbk	Book

Features: Intro to Study, Scrpt Memory Helps, Maps
★★★ Personal Application Preparation Time: Med
★ Relationship Building Ldr. Guide: Yes Size: 5.50 x 8.25
Subjects: Ecclesiastes, Isaiah/Jeremiah, Major Prophets, Prophecy, Proverbs, Psalms, Song of Solomon, Wisdom
Comments: This chapter-by-chapter study of Psalms through Jeremiah encourages participants to develop inductive Bible study skills by answering questions. This study, 5th of a 13-unit series, covers Psalms, Proverbs, Ecclesiastes, Song of Solomon, Lamentations—a group of books generally called "the poetry"—and major prophets Isaiah and Jeremiah. An in-depth leader's guide is available.

Author: Rosenberger, Margaret 1173
Series:
Title: *Issues in Focus*
Publisher: Regal Books, 1989 ISBN: 0-83071-332-8

Num. Sess.	Group Time	Num. Pgs.	Avg. Qst.	Price	Audience	Format	Bible Study
15	60-90	230	Vary	$6.99	Beginner	Book	Topical

Features: Bibliography, No Grp Discussion Quest, Appendix
★★★ Personal Application Preparation Time: Low
★★★ Relationship Building Ldr. Guide: Yes Size: 5.0 x 8.0
Subjects: Divorce, Ethics, Medical Issues, Occult, Sexual Issues, Women's Issues
Comments: This study forces participants to take an informed stand on 15 controversial contemporary topics. The topics, themselves clouded with emotion and controversy, include AIDS, drug abuse, sexual sin, the New Age movement, aging, divorce, and women in the church. The leader's material includes a study overview, insights and guide sheets, session plans, and reproducible in-session handouts.

Author: Ross, Linda and Sandy Kline 1174
Series: Serendipity Support Group
Title: *Support and Recovery Training Manual*
Publisher: Serendipity House, 1992 ISBN: 1-88341-974-3

Num. Sess.	Group Time	Num. Pgs.	Avg. Qst.	Price	Audience	Format	Bible Study
6	60-90	64	Vary	$5.00	Mature Christian	Workbk	Topical

Features: Intro to Leading a Study, Intro to Study, Objectives, Drawings
Personal Application Preparation Time:
Relationship Building Ldr. Guide: Size: 6.50 x 9.0
Subjects: Small Group Resource, Support
Comments: This manual is recommended for all leaders, prospective leaders, supervisors and trainers, to make them more effective in ministry. It helps define a support group targeted at people who function well in most areas of life but need support when facing specific challenges; and a recovery group, aimed at people who are hurting and powerless in a particular area.

Author: Ross, Ron 1175
Series:
Title: *When I Grow Up . . . I Want to Be an Adult*
Publisher: Recovery Publications, 1990 ISBN: 0-94140-515-X

Num. Sess.	Group Time	Num. Pgs.	Avg. Qst.	Price	Audience	Format	Bible Study
10	120-150	200	Vary	$12.95	New Christian	Workbk	Topical

Features: Intro to Leading a Study, Intro to Study, Bibliography, Prayer Helps, Ldr's Notes, Agenda, Appendix, Publicity Ideas
★★★★ Personal Application Preparation Time: Med
★★★★ Relationship Building Ldr. Guide: No Size: 7.0 x 9.25
Subjects: Counseling, Support
Comments: This empowering workbook introduces the value of the 12-step recovery process to Christians raised in dysfunctional families. It offers a means of support to those struggling with the pain of their upbringing and guides them toward bringing their healing home. Helps provided for starting a recovery group.

Author: Rowlands, Gerald & JoAnne Sekowsky 1176
Series: Basic Bible Study Series
Title: *Coming Alive in the Spirit: The Spirit-Led Life*
Publisher: Aglow, 1985 ISBN: 0-93075-690-8

Num. Sess.	Group Time	Num. Pgs.	Avg. Qst.	Price	Audience	Format	Bible Study
8	75-90	63	20	$3.95	New Christian	Workbk	Topical

Features: Intro to Study, Prayer Helps, Scrpt Memory Helps, Persnl Study Quest
★★★ Personal Application Preparation Time: Med
★★★ Relationship Building Ldr. Guide: No Size: 5.25 x 8.25
Subjects: Charismatic Interest, Fruit of the Spirit, Holy Spirit
Comments: This 8-week study reveals how the Holy Spirit renews believers. It teaches about the new life in Christ, the renewed mind, one's spiritual senses, and the fruit of the Spirit. Lessons include: "Possessing the Mind of Christ"; "Walking in the Spirit"; "Marching to Victory"; and more. It is not a theoretical study; rather, it is practical and calls for personal application.

Author: Rowlands, Gerald & JoAnne Sekowsky **1177**
Series: Basic Bible Study Series
Title: *Holy Spirit and His Gifts, The: A Study of the Spiritual Gifts*
Publisher: Aglow, 1984 ISBN: 0-93075-683-5

Num. Sess.	Group Time	Num. Pgs.	Avg. Qst.	Price	Audience	Format	Bible Study
10	75-90	64	20	$3.95	New Christian	Workbk	Topical

Features: Intro to Study, Prayer Helps, Scrpt Memory Helps, Persnl Study Quest
★★★ Personal Application Preparation Time: Med
★★★ Relationship Building Ldr. Guide: No Size: 5.25 x 8.25
Subjects: Charismatic Interest, Holy Spirit, Spiritual Gifts
Comments: This 10-week study leads participants to an understanding of the Holy Spirit, His work in the present age, and the spiritual gifts He makes available to every believer. Lessons include: "Who Is the Holy Spirit?"; "The Fullness of the Spirit Predicted"; "The Initial Evidence of the Holy Spirit"; "The Holy Spirit and the Believer"; "Why Speak in Tongues?"; "The Gifts of the Spirit"; "The Gift of Prophecy."

Author: Rudie, Carol Veldman **1178**
Series: Discover Your Bible
Title: *Discover: Genesis—Creation to Abraham*
Publisher: Church Development Resources, 1987

Num. Sess.	Group Time	Num. Pgs.	Avg. Qst.	Price	Audience	Format	Bible Study
11	60-75	38	8	$2.10	Beginner	Workbk	Book

Features: Intro to Study, Summary, Glossary
★★★ Personal Application Preparation Time: None
★★ Relationship Building Ldr. Guide: Yes Size: 5.50 x 8.50
Subjects: Genesis, God
Comments: This inductive study of Genesis chapters 1–12 explores the creation of the world, the animal kingdom, and the first humans. It records humanity's fall into sin and God's first promise of a Savior. It tells of the spread of civilization and the birth of the Jewish nation, and leads participants up to Abraham, the "father of all believers." A comprehensive study guide is available.

Author: Rudie, Carol Veldman **1179**
Series: Discover Your Bible
Title: *Discover: Genesis—Abraham and Sarah*
Publisher: Church Development Resources, 1989

Num. Sess.	Group Time	Num. Pgs.	Avg. Qst.	Price	Audience	Format	Bible Study
13	60-75	38	8	$2.45	Beginner	Workbk	Book

Features: Intro to Study, Glossary
★★★ Personal Application Preparation Time: None
★★ Relationship Building Ldr. Guide: Yes Size: 5.50 x 8.50
Subjects: Bible Personalities, Faith, Genesis, God
Comments: This inductive study of Genesis 1–25 introduces participants to Abraham, "father" of the Jewish nation and of all who believe in God. Participants will study his weaknesses as well as his faith. They will learn about Abraham's God, who is loving and just and faithful, who understands weakness, and who calls people to faith in Him. A comprehensive leader's guide is available.

Author: Rudie, Carol Veldman **1180**
Series: Discover Your Bible
Title: *Discover: God in the Psalms*
Publisher: Church Development Resources, 1988

Num. Sess.	Group Time	Num. Pgs.	Avg. Qst.	Price	Audience	Format	Bible Study
7	60-75	23	9	$1.50	Beginner	Workbk	Book

Features: Intro to Study, Summary, Glossary
★★★ Personal Application Preparation Time: None
★★ Relationship Building Ldr. Guide: Yes Size: 5.50 x 8.50
Subjects: God, Holiness, Marriage, Psalms
Comments: This inductive study of Psalms explores the depths of the relationship between God and humankind. It focuses on psalms that teach the character of God, His holiness, power, majesty, and love. An underlying theme is God's continual pursuit of the human heart and His kindness to those who find Him. Uses word pictures to compare God to things like thunderstorms, fathers with small children, kings, rocks, or refuge.

Author: Rudie, Carol Veldman **1181**
Series: Discover Your Bible
Title: *Discovering God In The Psalms*
Publisher: Church Development Resources, 1988

Num. Sess.	Group Time	Num. Pgs.	Avg. Qst.	Price	Audience	Format	Bible Study
14	60-70	48	9	$1.50	Beginner	Workbk	Book

Features: Intro to Study
★★★ Personal Application Preparation Time: None
★★ Relationship Building Ldr. Guide: Yes Size: 5.50 x 8.50
Subjects: Psalms
Comments: The Book of Psalms is a collection of songs that explore depths of relationships between God and humankind. This study focuses on psalms that teach us about God—His holiness, power, majesty, and love. Woven through is the theme of God's continual pursuit of the human heart and His kindness to those who find Him. Participants can meet a God who brings healing to a world broken by sin, a holy and righteous God who has deep compassion for His world.

Author: Rundstrom, G. B. **1182**
Series: Small Group Bible Studies
Title: *Lord's Prayer, The*
Publisher: Augsburg Fortress Publishers, 1984

Num. Sess.	Group Time	Num. Pgs.	Avg. Qst.	Price	Audience	Format	Bible Study
6	60-75	24	12	$1.35	New Christian	Book	Topical

Features: Intro to Study, Prayer Helps
★★★ Personal Application Preparation Time: None
★★★ Relationship Building Ldr. Guide: No Size: 8.50 x 5.50
Subjects: God, Prayer
Comments: This short, 6-session study on the Lord's Prayer will enlarge participants' conception of the 7 petitions that make up the prayer. Various passages of Scripture are related to the different petitions. The Lord's Prayer is found in two forms in the Bible, but Matthew 6:9-13 is used for this study. The primary focus is on what it says to individuals, and the response to God as they pray the prayer.

Author: Russell, Bob **1183**
Series:
Title: *When Life Is a Zoo God Still Loves You*
Publisher: Standard Publishing, 1992 ISBN: 0-78470-078-8

Num. Sess.	Group Time	Num. Pgs.	Avg. Qst.	Price	Audience	Format	Bible Study
13	45-60	158	N/A	$4.49	New Christian	Book	Topical

Features: Objectives, No Grp Discussion Quest
★★★ Personal Application Preparation Time: Low
★★ Relationship Building Ldr. Guide: Yes Size: 5.50 x 8.50
Subjects: Love
Comments: This book is a refreshing change of pace from heavily theological and exegetical studies. While thoroughly biblical, it is topical in nature. It looks at familiar events in biblical history from the interesting perspective of animals involved. With the available leader's guide, some Sunday school classes might use it for a quarter of study. Vacation Bible School may use 5 or 10 of the lessons for youth or adult courses. Midweek study groups can also enjoy the study.

Author: Ryan, Dale & Juanita **1184**
Series: Life Recovery Guides
Title: *Recovery from Family Dysfunctions*
Publisher: InterVarsity, 1990 ISBN: 0-83081-151-6

Num. Sess.	Group Time	Num. Pgs.	Avg. Qst.	Price	Audience	Format	Bible Study
6	45-60	64	8	$4.99	Beginner	Workbk	Topical

Features: Intro to Leading a Study, Intro to Study, Prayer Helps, Full Scrpt Printed, Ldr's Notes
★★★★ Personal Application Preparation Time: Low
★★ Relationship Building Ldr. Guide: No Size: 5.50 x 8.25
Subjects: Counseling, Family, Relationships, Support
Comments: Dysfunctional relationship patterns learned early in life can affect all future relationships. People can become guarded and defensive, talk little about what really matters, and become reluctant to trust others...and God. This study shows participants how to break these patterns and learn the vital skills of building relationships. Offers healing from the pain of the past, and acceptance into God's family.

Author: Ryan, Dale & Juanita **1185**
Series: Life Recovery Guides
Title: *Recovery from Bitterness*
Publisher: InterVarsity, 1990 ISBN: 0-83081-154-0

Num. Sess.	Group Time	Num. Pgs.	Avg. Qst.	Price	Audience	Format	Bible Study
6	45-60	63	9	$4.99	Beginner	Workbk	Topical

Features: Intro to Leading a Study, Intro to Study, Prayer Helps, Full Scrpt Printed, Ldr's Notes
★★★ Personal Application Preparation Time: Low
★★ Relationship Building Ldr. Guide: No Size: 5.50 x 8.25
Subjects: Counseling, Emotions, Forgiveness, Support
Comments: This study is pertinent for those who have tried to forgive and become frustrated because they were unable to do so. Sometimes forgiveness is blocked, stuck, restrained, and entangled, and hearts turn to bitterness and revenge. The inability to forgive can result in a feeling of spiritual failure. This guide helps provide the strength to change bitterness into forgiveness.

Author: Ryan, Dale & Juanita **1186**
Series: Life Recovery Guides
Title: *Recovery from Loss*
Publisher: InterVarsity, 1990 ISBN: 0-83081-157-5

Num. Sess.	Group Time	Num. Pgs.	Avg. Qst.	Price	Audience	Format	Bible Study
6	45-60	63	8	$4.99	Beginner	Workbk	Topical

Features: Intro to Leading a Study, Intro to Study, Prayer Helps, Full Scrpt Printed, Ldr's Notes
★★★★ Personal Application Preparation Time: Low
★★ Relationship Building Ldr. Guide: No Size: 5.50 x 8.25
Subjects: Counseling, Emotions, Grief, Support
Comments: Disappointment, unmet expectations, physical or emotional illness, and death are all examples of losses. Working through grief does not help people forget what has been lost, but it does help people grow in understanding, compassion, and courage in the midst of loss. This study encourages participants to lean on God for comfort, strength, and purpose.

Author: Ryan, Dale & Juanita **1187**
Series: Life Recovery Guides
Title: *Recovery from Shame*
Publisher: InterVarsity, 1990 ISBN: 0-83081-153-2

Num. Sess.	Group Time	Num. Pgs.	Avg. Qst.	Price	Audience	Format	Bible Study
6	45-60	64	9	$4.99	Beginner	Workbk	Topical

Features: Intro to Leading a Study, Intro to Study, Prayer Helps, Full Scrpt Printed, Ldr's Notes
★★★★ Personal Application Preparation Time: Low
★★ Relationship Building Ldr. Guide: No Size: 5.50 x 8.25
Subjects: Counseling, Emotions, Self-esteem, Support
Comments: This study has been written for people who have experienced shame and need to realize God's unconditional love. Whatever its source—public humiliation, personal rejection—shame affects self-image, producing feelings of being unlovable or unworthy. Because shame wounds deeply, recovery requires deep healing—the kind only God can provide.

Author: Ryan, Dale & Juanita **1188**
Series: Life Recovery Guides
Title: *Recovery from Codependency*
Publisher: InterVarsity, 1990 ISBN: 0-83081-156-7

Num. Sess.	Group Time	Num. Pgs.	Avg. Qst.	Price	Audience	Format	Bible Study
6	45-60	64	8	$4.99	Beginner	Workbk	Topical

Features: Intro to Leading a Study, Intro to Study, Prayer Helps, Full Scrpt Printed, Ldr's Notes
★★★★ Personal Application Preparation Time: Low
★★ Relationship Building Ldr. Guide: No Size: 5.50 x 8.25
Subjects: Addictions, Counseling, Psychology, Support
Comments: Fear, anger, and helplessness concerning an addicted loved one can lead a person to attempt to control that loved one. Both the addicted person's and codependent's behavior can become a destructive spiral of denial and blame. This study shows how to relinquish overresponsibility and entrust those one loves to God. An enclosed response card may be returned for networking purposes.

Author: Ryan, Dale & Juanita **1189**
Series: Life Recovery Guides
Title: *Recovery from Abuse*
Publisher: InterVarsity, 1990 ISBN: 0-83081-158-3

Num. Sess.	Group Time	Num. Pgs.	Avg. Qst.	Price	Audience	Format	Bible Study
6	45-60	63	9	$4.99	Beginner	Workbk	Topical

Features: Intro to Leading a Study, Intro to Study, Prayer Helps, Full Scrpt Printed, Ldr's Notes
★★★★ Personal Application Preparation Time: Low
★★ Relationship Building Ldr. Guide: No Size: 5.50 x 8.25
Subjects: Counseling, Emotions, Self-esteem, Sexual Issues, Support
Comments: This study presents a series of practical, positive steps from abuse to health and happiness. Questions addressed include: Does the nightmare of abuse ever end? Is it possible to be called terrible names thoughout childhood and later develop a healthy self-esteem? Is it possible to be physically beaten by a loved one and later develop a capacity for intimacy?

Author: Ryan, Dale & Juanita **1190**
Series: Life Recovery Guides
Title: *Recovery from Addictions*
Publisher: InterVarsity, 1990 ISBN: 0-83081-155-9

Num. Sess.	Group Time	Num. Pgs.	Avg. Qst.	Price	Audience	Format	Bible Study
6	45-60	63	8	$4.99	Beginner	Workbk	Topical

Features: Intro to Leading a Study, Intro to Study, Prayer Helps, Full Scrpt Printed, Ldr's Notes
★★★★ Personal Application Preparation Time: Low
★★ Relationship Building Ldr. Guide: No Size: 5.50 x 8.25
Subjects: Addictions, Counseling, Money, Psychology, Sexual Issues, Support
Comments: Addiction to chemicals, food, sex, work, spending, gambling, religious practices, etc. can enslave and lead to spiritual, emotional, or physical death. This guide is structured like the Alcoholics Anonymous 12 Step program; it explores biblical principles which are rich sources of help and healing for those struggling with addiction.

Author: Ryan, Dale & Juanita **1191**
Series: Life Recovery Guides
Title: *Recovery from Distorted Images of God*
Publisher: InterVarsity, 1990 ISBN: 0-83081-152-4

Num. Sess.	Group Time	Num. Pgs.	Avg. Qst.	Price	Audience	Format	Bible Study
6	45-60	63	8	$4.99	Beginner	Workbk	Topical

Features: Intro to Leading a Study, Intro to Study, Prayer Helps, Full Scrpt Printed, Ldr's Notes
★★★★ Personal Application Preparation Time: Low
★★ Relationship Building Ldr. Guide: No Size: 5.50 x 8.25
Subjects: Counseling, Family, God, Psychology, Support
Comments: This study helps participants identify distorted images of God, meditate on true Scriptural images of God, and exchange the distortions for biblically accurate portraits. The distortions interfere with the ability to talk honestly with God, express feelings to Him, and trust Him. Distorted images of God are often rooted in family and cultural backgrounds; this study can lead to recovery.

Author: Ryan, Juanita **1192**
Series: LifeGuide Bible Study
Title: *Psalms II: Heart Cries to God*
Publisher: InterVarsity, 1995 ISBN: 0-83081-038-2

Num. Sess.	Group Time	Num. Pgs.	Avg. Qst.	Price	Audience	Format	Bible Study
12	45-60	64	12	$4.99	New Christian	Workbk	Book

Features: Intro to Leading a Study, Intro to Study, Ldr's Notes
★★★ Personal Application Preparation Time: Low
★★★ Relationship Building Ldr. Guide: No Size: 5.50 x 8.25
Subjects: Psalms
Comments: The Psalms do not attempt to be "nice," "polite," or even "theologically correct." Instead, they give Christians permission to talk to God without holding back, and be exactly where and who they are with God. Joy, anger, distress, hope, and trust are feelings expressed in the Psalms. By studying and praying through 12 that deal with emotions, participants can learn to be honest with God and allow Him to meet their needs.

Author: Ryan, Juanita & Dale **1193**
Series: Life Recovery Guides
Title: *Recovery: A Lifelong Journey*
Publisher: InterVarsity, 1993 ISBN: 0-83081-166-4

Num. Sess.	Group Time	Num. Pgs.	Avg. Qst.	Price	Audience	Format	Bible Study
6	30-45	60	11	$4.99	Beginner	Workbk	Topical

Features: Intro to Leading a Study, Intro to Study, Prayer Helps, Full Scrpt Printed, Ldr's Notes
★★★★ Personal Application Preparation Time: None
★★★★ Relationship Building Ldr. Guide: No Size: 5.50 x 8.25
Subjects: Counseling, Support
Comments: Recovery requires a commitment to keep growing and changing through prayer and discipline. In this guide you'll see how the last 3 steps of the 12 Steps provide a model for a lifelong journey of recovery. By following the disciplines of self-awareness, confession, seeking God, and asking for guidance, participants can find continued healing and growth.

Author: Ryan, Juanita & Dale **1194**
Series: Life Recovery Guides
Title: *Recovery from Spiritual Abuse*
Publisher: InterVarsity, 1992 ISBN: 0-83081-159-1

Num. Sess.	Group Time	Num. Pgs.	Avg. Qst.	Price	Audience	Format	Bible Study
6	30-45	64	11	$4.99	Beginner	Workbk	Topical

Features: Intro to Leading a Study, Intro to Study, Prayer Helps, Full Scrpt Printed, Ldr's Notes
★★★★ Personal Application Preparation Time: None
★★★★ Relationship Building Ldr. Guide: No Size: 5.50 x 8.25
Subjects: Counseling, Support
Comments: Because of negative teachings from parents, pastors, or others, many Christians feel they must earn their way with God. They can come to experience the Christian life as a burden, a source of deep shame. Through these 6 lessons, participants can discover a healing of spiritual abuse and find freedom and grace in Christ. Includes an introduction and more.

Author: Ryan, Juanita & Dale **1195**
Series: Life Recovery Guides
Title: *Recovery from Distorted Images of Self*
Publisher: InterVarsity, 1993 ISBN: 0-83081-162-1

Num. Sess.	Group Time	Num. Pgs.	Avg. Qst.	Price	Audience	Format	Bible Study
6	30-45	58	11	$4.99	Beginner	Workbk	Topical

Features: Intro to Leading a Study, Intro to Study, Prayer Helps, Full Scrpt Printed, Ldr's Notes
★★★★ Personal Application Preparation Time: None
★★★★ Relationship Building Ldr. Guide: No Size: 5.50 x 8.25
Subjects: Counseling, Self-esteem, Support
Comments: God created man to be loved, valued, and capable. But often people don't feel these positive emotions. Rather, they mentally replay negative feedback: "You're not good enough . . . strong enough . . . attractive enough." These lessons show participants how to escape negatives and regain a positive self-image as people of immense worth.

Author: Ryan, Juanita & Dale **1196**
Series: Life Recovery Guides
Title: *Recovery from Depression*
Publisher: InterVarsity, 1993 ISBN: 0-83081-161-3

Num. Sess.	Group Time	Num. Pgs.	Avg. Qst.	Price	Audience	Format	Bible Study
6	30-45	60	11	$4.99	Beginner	Workbk	Topical

Features: Intro to Leading a Study, Intro to Study, Prayer Helps, Full Scrpt Printed, Ldr's Notes
★★★★ Personal Application Preparation Time: None
★★★★ Relationship Building Ldr. Guide: No Size: 5.50 x 8.25
Subjects: Counseling, Hope, Support
Comments: Hopelessness can affect anyone. It can arise due to difficult events such as broken relationships, death of a loved one, unemployment, or other crises. Sometimes victims are unable to work through their feelings alone, getting stuck in a cycle of sadness and suffering. They need to be pointed toward the Source of hope. These lessons can help show the way.

Author: Ryan, Juanita & Dale **1197**
Series: Life Recovery Guides
Title: *Recovery from Guilt*
Publisher: InterVarsity, 1993 ISBN: 0-83081-163-X

Num. Sess.	Group Time	Num. Pgs.	Avg. Qst.	Price	Audience	Format	Bible Study
6	30-45	62	15	$4.99	Beginner	Workbk	Topical

Features: Intro to Leading a Study, Intro to Study, Prayer Helps, Full Scrpt Printed, Ldr's Notes
★★★★ Personal Application Preparation Time: None
★★★★ Relationship Building Ldr. Guide: No Size: 5.50 x 8.25
Subjects: Counseling, Emotions, Support
Comments: Guilt is a distress signal that warns of something gone wrong. If not heeded it can continue in destructive patterns. These 6 lessons help participants work through the pain of what they may have done to themselves or others. Using steps 4–9 of the 12 Steps in conjunction with Scripture, these studies offer hope and assistance in getting beyond guilt to forgiveness.

Author: Ryan, Juanita & Dale **1198**
Series: Life Recovery Guides
Title: *Recovery from Workaholism*
Publisher: InterVarsity, 1993 ISBN: 0-83081-164-8

Num. Sess.	Group Time	Num. Pgs.	Avg. Qst.	Price	Audience	Format	Bible Study
6	30-45	60	12	$4.99	Beginner	Workbk	Topical

Features: Intro to Leading a Study, Intro to Study, Prayer Helps, Full Scrpt Printed, Ldr's Notes
★★★★ Personal Application Preparation Time: None
★★★★ Relationship Building Ldr. Guide: No Size: 5.50 x 8.25
Subjects: Counseling, Support, Work
Comments: Hard work results in promotions, raises, and the respect of colleagues. More important, it fills the need we have to be needed. But overwork also eats away at marriage and family relationships, while making friendships outside the office nearly non-existent. It can create health problems as well as spiritual struggles. Helps participants break free of workaholism and accept the rest that God offers.

Author: Ryan, Juanita & Dale **1199**
Series: Life Recovery Guides
Title: *Recovery from Broken Relationships*
Publisher: InterVarsity, 1993 ISBN: 0-83081-165-6

Num. Sess.	Group Time	Num. Pgs.	Avg. Qst.	Price	Audience	Format	Bible Study
6	30-45	62	11	$4.99	Beginner	Workbk	Topical

Features: Intro to Leading a Study, Intro to Study, Prayer Helps, Full Scrpt Printed, Ldr's Notes
★★★★ Personal Application Preparation Time: None
★★★★ Relationship Building Ldr. Guide: No Size: 5.50 x 8.25
Subjects: Counseling, Relationships, Support
Comments: This guide is designed to explore biblical insights into recovering from the deep wound of a broken relationship, whether that relationship was with a friend, spouse, family member, or business associate. Victims learn to fear closeness because they don't want to experience another separation from someone close. Lessons help participants discover how to risk love again.

Author: Ryan, Juanita & Dale **1200**
Series: Life Recovery Guides
Title: *Recovery from Fear*
Publisher: InterVarsity, 1992 ISBN: 0-83081-160-5

Num. Sess.	Group Time	Num. Pgs.	Avg. Qst.	Price	Audience	Format	Bible Study
6	30-45	64	12	$4.99	Beginner	Workbk	Topical

Features: Intro to Leading a Study, Intro to Study, Prayer Helps, Full Scrpt Printed, Ldr's Notes
★★★★ Personal Application Preparation Time: None
★★★★ Relationship Building Ldr. Guide: No Size: 5.50 x 8.25
Subjects: Counseling, Emotions, Failure, Loneliness, Support
Comments: The world today is violent. Fear is a natural response to many of life's experiences. Sometimes it offers a healthy layer of protection; other times it limits and stifles opportunities. Fear results from certain basic issues: intimacy, risk, failure, loneliness, inadequacy, and danger. But God offers support, empowerment, and courage for facing fear in all areas of life.

Author: Rydberg, Denny 1201
Series:
Title: *Creative Bible Studies for Young Adults*
Publisher: Group Publishing, 1990 ISBN: 0-93152-999-9

Num. Sess.	Group Time	Num. Pgs.	Avg. Qst.	Price	Audience	Format	Bible Study
20	45-60	154	Vary	$12.99	New Christian	Book	Topical

Features: Intro to Leading a Study, Intro to Study, Prayer Helps, Study Overview, Drawings,Handouts, Charts
★★★★ Personal Application Preparation Time: Low
★★★★ Relationship Building Ldr. Guide: No Size: 6.0 x 9.0
Subjects: Christian Living, Emotions, Faith, Sexual Issues, Singles' Issues, Stress, Success, Youth Life
Comments: This study provides 20 faith-building Bible studies for people 18 to 35 years old. Divided into 5 4-week studies, topics include: "Handling Stress"; "Sex: God's Good Idea"; "Christians and Success"; "Discipleship and God's Will"; and "Growing in Faith." Each study is designed to address young adults' daily needs.

Author: Ryrie, Charles C. 1202
Series:
Title: *Balancing the Christian Life*
Publisher: Moody Press, 1994 ISBN: 0-80240-887-7

Num. Sess.	Group Time	Num. Pgs.	Avg. Qst.	Price	Audience	Format	Bible Study
18	60-90	250	4	$8.99	New Christian	Book	Topical

Features: Index
★★★ Personal Application Preparation Time: Low
★★ Relationship Building Ldr. Guide: No Size: 6.0 x 9.0
Subjects: Christian Life
Comments: In this study Ryrie reminds readers that "the Bible must be the guide and test for all their experiences in the spiritual life . . . and if any experience fails to pass that test, it must be discarded." He warns that unbalanced application of doctrines related to spirituality can result in an unbalanced Christian life. Issues examined include old and new lives, sanctification, using one's gifts, routine faithfulness, wiles of the devil, temptation, and confession and forgiveness.

Author: Ryrie, Charles C. 1203
Series:
Title: *So Great Salvation: What It Means to Believe in Jesus Christ*
Publisher: Victor Books, 1989 ISBN: 0-89693-127-7

Num. Sess.	Group Time	Num. Pgs.	Avg. Qst.	Price	Audience	Format	Bible Study
13	60-90	166	N/A	$9.99	New Christian	Book	Topical

Features: Scrpt Index
★★★ Personal Application Preparation Time: Med
★★★ Relationship Building Ldr. Guide: Yes Size: 5.50 x 8.0
Subjects: Evangelism, Jesus: Life/Teaching, Theology
Comments: This study clarifies the meaning and evidences of salvation. It is clear, concise, and authoritative, when the tendency today is to water down the Gospel or add nonscriptural requirements to it. It addresses specific questions, including: "What exactly is the Gospel?" "What is spiritual fruit?" "Can a born-again Christian be carnal and, if so, for how long?" and "What is eternal security?" Participants will find clear implications for their spiritual lives.

Author: Salerno, Tony, et. al. 1204
Series:
Title: *Life in Christ: A Manual for Disciples*
Publisher: Bethany House, 1983 ISBN: 0-87123-887-X

Num. Sess.	Group Time	Num. Pgs.	Avg. Qst.	Price	Audience	Format	Bible Study
10	60-90	290	Vary	$13.99	New Christian	Workbk	Topical

Features: Intro to Study, Bibliography, Prayer Helps, Scrpt Memory Helps, Photos
★★ Personal Application Preparation Time: High
★★ Relationship Building Ldr. Guide: No Size: 8.50 x 11.0
Subjects: Baptism, Discipleship, Faith, God, Prayer, Repentance
Comments: This in-depth study helps new Christians understand their faith, read the Word of God, and fellowship with other believers. Topics include repentance, faith, restitution, baptism, the Church, prayer, the Word of God, love of God, witnessing, and spiritual power. References to the teachings of well-known Christians, past and present, help illuminate the material. Illustrations are elaborate.

Author: Salsgiver, Tom 1205
Series:
Title: *Complete Youth Group Checkup, The: And Other Great Retreats*
Publisher: Abingdon Press, 1992 ISBN: 0-68736-171-0

Num. Sess.	Group Time	Num. Pgs.	Avg. Qst.	Price	Audience	Format	Bible Study
	—	108	N/A	$10.95			

Features: Intro to Study, Drawings
Personal Application Preparation Time:
Relationship Building Ldr. Guide: Size: 8.50 x 11.0
Subjects: Teens: Resources, Youth Life
Comments: This book is a collection of 15 effective retreats which have been "youth tested," refined, practical and easy to follow. Includes adaptable schedules and planning guides for effective retreats, helps for older and younger youth, worship that's integrated with the topic, and creative and meaningful activities. Some of the retreats are planned to help youth learn about the way a group functions. Others challenge youth to learn about life issues.

Author: Samms, Dr. Robert L. 1206
Series: Lay Action Ministry
Title: *How to Study the Bible—Part 2*
Publisher: Lay Action Ministry Program, 1987 ISBN: 0-89191-517-6

Num. Sess.	Group Time	Num. Pgs.	Avg. Qst.	Price	Audience	Format	Bible Study
12	60-90	112	Vary	$6.95	New Christian	Workbk	Topical

Features: Full Scrpt Printed, Ldr's Notes
★★★ Personal Application Preparation Time: Low
★★★ Relationship Building Ldr. Guide: Yes Size: 5.25 x 8.25
Subjects: Bible Study, Ephesians, Small Group Resource
Comments: This study, the 2nd of a 2-part series on Bible study, will improve participants' abilities to study Scripture inductively, and lead their own Bible studies. This continuation of an in-depth look at Ephesians covers the following: looking for the big ideas; observing the text; asking the text questions; studying the context; using cross-references, concordances, Bible atlases, Bible dictionaries, and commentaries; and more. Homework is required.

Author: Samms, Dr. Robert L. **1207**
Series: Lay Action Ministry
Title: *How to Study the Bible—Part 1*
Publisher: Lay Action Ministry Program, 1987 ISBN: 0-89191-516-8

Num. Sess.	Group Time	Num. Pgs.	Avg. Qst.	Price	Audience	Format	Bible Study
12	60-90	90	Vary	$6.95	New Christian	Workbk	Topical

Features: Prayer Helps, Full Scrpt Printed
★★★ Personal Application Preparation Time: Low
★★★ Relationship Building Ldr. Guide: Yes Size: 5.25 x 8.25
Subjects: Bible Study, Ephesians, Small Group Resource
Comments: This study, the 1st of a 2-part series on Bible study, introduces inductive study techniques and helps participants practice them in examing Ephesians. This book includes the following: study tools; guidelines for understanding, applying, and teaching Bible portions; ideas for developing a personal study plan; and an in-depth study of Ephesians 1. Homework is required. One leader's guide covers both parts 1 and 2.

Author: Samms, Dr. Robert L. **1208**
Series: Lay Action Ministry
Title: *Truth That Transforms: A Study in Christian Doctrine*
Publisher: Lay Action Ministry Program, 1990 ISBN: 0-89191-486-2

Num. Sess.	Group Time	Num. Pgs.	Avg. Qst.	Price	Audience	Format	Bible Study
12	60-90	142	Vary	$6.95	New Christian	Workbk	Topical

Features: Intro to Study, Ldr's Notes
★★★ Personal Application Preparation Time: Low
★★★ Relationship Building Ldr. Guide: Yes Size: 5.25 x 8.25
Subjects: Beliefs, Faith, God, Theology, Worship
Comments: This study examines God: who He is, what He has done, and what He wants everyone to know through His Word. Participants will benefit from an explanation of the story upon which Christianity and its doctrines are founded: the story of Jesus Christ. Doctrine provides Christians common ground concerning faith, belief, and worship, and a study of doctrines provide a basis for the way they live. Homework is required.

Author: Samms, Dr. Robert L. & Maryann E. **1209**
Series: Lay Action Ministry
Title: *Your Ministry at Home*
Publisher: Lay Action Ministry Program, 1988 ISBN: 0-89191-487-0

Num. Sess.	Group Time	Num. Pgs.	Avg. Qst.	Price	Audience	Format	Bible Study
12	60-90	112	Vary	$6.95	New Christian	Workbk	Topical

Features: Prayer Helps, Scrpt Memory Helps, Ldr's Notes
★★★ Personal Application Preparation Time: Low
★★★ Relationship Building Ldr. Guide: Yes Size: 5.25 x 8.25
Subjects: Devotionals, Family, Money, Time
Comments: This study, designed for younger couples, provides many practical "how-to's" for establishing a Christian home. Included are instructions on developing family quiet times; improving communication at home; and managing time, money, and nutrition. Participants are asked to start, maintain, and be accountable for daily quiet times; begin a spiritual journal; memorize a key verse each week; and keep a prayer list.

Author: Sanders, J. Oswald **1210**
Series: Commitment To Spiritual
Title: *Spiritual Leadership*
Publisher: Moody Press, 1994 ISBN: 0-80246-799-7

Num. Sess.	Group Time	Num. Pgs.	Avg. Qst.	Price	Audience	Format	Bible Study
6	60-75	190	10	$10.99	New Christian	Book	Topical

Features: Index
★★★★ Personal Application Preparation Time: Low
★★★★ Relationship Building Ldr. Guide: No Size: 6.0 x 9.0
Subjects: Discipleship, Leadership
Comments: This book, which teaches the principles of leadership, presents and illustrates them through biographies of eminent men of God, men such as Moses, Nehemiah, Paul, David Livingstone, and Charles Spurgeon. The book encourages readers to place their talents and powers at God's disposal so they can become leaders used for His glory.

Author: Scanlon, Michael, T.O.R. **1211**
Series: Catholic Bible Study Guide
Title: *Repentance: A Guide to Receiving God's Forgiveness*
Publisher: Servant Publications, 1989 ISBN: 0-89283-398-X

Num. Sess.	Group Time	Num. Pgs.	Avg. Qst.	Price	Audience	Format	Bible Study
9	60-75	85	10	$5.99	Beginner	Workbk	Topical

Features: Intro to Leading a Study, Intro to Study, Scrpt Memory Helps, Summary, Charts
★★★★ Personal Application Preparation Time: Low
★★★ Relationship Building Ldr. Guide: No Size: 5.25 x 8.0
Subjects: Christian Life, Forgiveness, Repentance
Comments: This 9-lesson study shows participants how to turn away from sin and receive God's abundant mercy. It provides a biblical basis for the sacrament of reconciliation, including a practical tip on how to prepare for confession. The lessons are divided into three parts: "Responding to the Call to Repent"; "Common Pitfalls That Hinder Us from Repenting"; and "A Life of Ongoing Conversion."

Author: Scazzero, Peter **1212**
Series: Fruit of the Spirit
Title: *Love: Building Healthy Relationships*
Publisher: Zondervan, 1991 ISBN: 0-31053-721-5

Num. Sess.	Group Time	Num. Pgs.	Avg. Qst.	Price	Audience	Format	Bible Study
6	45-60	48	12	$4.99	New Christian	Workbk	Topical

Features: Intro to Study, Ldr's Notes
★★★ Personal Application Preparation Time: None
★★ Relationship Building Ldr. Guide: No Size: 5.50 x 8.50
Subjects: Christian Living, Forgiveness, Fruit of the Spirit, Love, Marriage, Relationships
Comments: This 6-week study explores the "most excellent way" into the hearts of those we care about. It considers how to develop a love that affirms, that forgives, and that lasts. Using New Testament passages, lessons look at loving Jesus, God's family, our neighbors, and more.

Author: Scazzero, Peter 1213
Series: The Discipleship Series
Title: *New Life in Christ*
Publisher: Zondervan, 1992 ISBN: 0-31054-761-X

Num. Sess.	Group Time	Num. Pgs.	Avg. Qst.	Price	Audience	Format	Bible Study
6	45-60	63	13	$4.99	New Christian	Workbk	Topical

Features: Intro to Leading a Study, Intro to Study, Objectives, Prayer Helps, Scrpt Memory Helps, Follow Up, Ldr's Notes, Charts
★★★★ Personal Application Preparation Time: Med
★★ Relationship Building Ldr. Guide: No Size: 5.50 x 8.50
Subjects: Christian Life, Discipleship, Jesus: Life/Teaching
Comments: This is 1 of 8 study guides in the Discipleship series. This study guide helps participants grasp the hope, the riches, and the great power God has given each of us through His Son. Lesson titles include: "Welcome to the Family"; "Getting to Know Jesus"; "Finding Strength in God's Family"; "Being Filled with the Spirit"; "Resisting the Enemy"; and "Following Jesus."

Author: Scazzero, Peter 1214
Series: LifeGuide Bible Study
Title: *Old Testament Characters*
Publisher: InterVarsity, 1988 ISBN: 0-83081-059-5

Num. Sess.	Group Time	Num. Pgs.	Avg. Qst.	Price	Audience	Format	Bible Study
12	45-60	63	12	$4.99	Beginner	Workbk	Topical

Features: Intro to Leading a Study, Intro to Study, Ldr's Notes, Charts, Maps
★★ Personal Application Preparation Time: Low
★ Relationship Building Ldr. Guide: No Size: 5.50 x 8.25
Subjects: Bible Personalities, Marriage, Old Testament, Prayer
Comments: A study of real men and women of the Old Testament who, with both weaknesses and strengths, provide excellent role models. Biblical characters—including Jonah, Hannah, Samuel, Abraham, Caleb and Joshua, Elijah, Achan, King Saul, Daniel, Esther, David, and Moses—exemplify different themes relevant to following Jesus today, including prayer, temptation, lordship, and unconditional love.

Author: Schaap, Mary Nelle 1215
Series: Challenge Bible Study
Title: *David's Lord: Seeing God in the Life of David the King*
Publisher: Baker Book House, 1993 ISBN: 0-80108-348-6

Num. Sess.	Group Time	Num. Pgs.	Avg. Qst.	Price	Audience	Format	Bible Study
7	60-75	134	Vary	$4.99	New Christian	Workbk	Charctr

Features: Intro to Leading a Study
★★★ Personal Application Preparation Time: Med
★★★ Relationship Building Ldr. Guide: No Size: 5.50 x 8.50
Subjects: Bible Personalities, God, 1 & 2 Samuel
Comments: This 7-lesson study is designed to help you delve into the life of David as he learned to know God and rely on what he knew of God. Israel's shepherd king knew success and failure, but throughout he knew God's reassuring, convicting, forgiving, and completing power through fellowship. The study plan includes questions prior to each lesson, Scripture passages, commentary, and direction for using the questions.

Author: Schaap, Mary Nelle 1216
Series: Challenge Bible Study
Title: *David's Lord: Seeing God in the Life of Young David*
Publisher: Baker Book House, 1993 ISBN: 0-80108-347-8

Num. Sess.	Group Time	Num. Pgs.	Avg. Qst.	Price	Audience	Format	Bible Study
7	60-75	112	Vary	$4.99	New Christian	Workbk	Charctr

Features: Intro to Leading a Study
★★★ Personal Application Preparation Time: Med
★★★ Relationship Building Ldr. Guide: No Size: 5.50 x 8.50
Subjects: Bible Personalities, God, 1 & 2 Samuel
Comments: This 7-lesson study of David focuses on his life as a young man, as he learned to know God and rely on that knowledge. The study poses this question: What does it mean to be chosen and directed, softened and corrected? The life of the future king of Israel offers sound principles for spiritual growth. The study plan includes questions prior to each lesson, Scripture passages, commentary, and direction for using the questions.

Author: Schaap, Mary Nelle 1217
Series: Challenge Bible Study
Title: *Portraits of Jesus: From Luke and John*
Publisher: Baker Book House, 1992 ISBN: 0-80108-345-1

Num. Sess.	Group Time	Num. Pgs.	Avg. Qst.	Price	Audience	Format	Bible Study
7	60-75	110	Vary	$4.99	New Christian	Workbk	Charctr

Features: Intro to Leading a Study
★★★ Personal Application Preparation Time: Med
★★★ Relationship Building Ldr. Guide: No Size: 5.50 x 8.50
Subjects: Jesus: Life/Teaching, John, Luke
Comments: This 7-lesson study explores Jesus' humanity and majesty as described from the vantage points of Luke and John. Luke focuses on Jesus' profound compassion and concern for individuals, emphasizing Jesus' warm human personality and how He identified with people. John takes a distinctly different tack than the other Gospels. His main focus is that he saw Jesus as the glorious Son of God.

Author: Schaap, Mary Nelle 1218
Series: Challenge Bible Study
Title: *Portraits of Jesus: From Matthew and Mark*
Publisher: Baker Book House, 1992 ISBN: 0-80108-333-8

Num. Sess.	Group Time	Num. Pgs.	Avg. Qst.	Price	Audience	Format	Bible Study
7	60-75	112	Vary	$4.99	New Christian	Workbk	Charctr

Features: Intro to Leading a Study
★★★ Personal Application Preparation Time: Med
★★★ Relationship Building Ldr. Guide: No Size: 5.50 x 8.50
Subjects: Jesus: Life/Teaching, Mark, Matthew
Comments: This 7-lesson study explores Jesus' humanity and majesty as seen from 2 vantage points: those of Matthew and Mark. Mark portrays Jesus as an energetic and forceful leader, as embodied by His whirlwind Galilean ministry. Mark also describes Jesus as God's obedient servant. Matthew leads an exploration of Jesus' role as the Master Teacher, through the complete record of the teachings of Jesus.

Author: Schaap, Ward B. **1219**
Series: Challenge Bible Study
Title: *Character of the King: Studies in the Parables*
Publisher: Baker Book House, 1994 ISBN: 0-80108-369-9

Num. Sess.	Group Time	Num. Pgs.	Avg. Qst.	Price	Audience	Format	Bible Study
7	60-75	119	Vary	$4.99	New Christian	Workbk	Topical

Features: Intro to Leading a Study
★★★ Personal Application Preparation Time: Med
★★★ Relationship Building Ldr. Guide: No Size: 5.50 x 8.50
Subjects: Parables
Comments: This 7-lesson study examines the traits of Jesus as He describes in 7 parables. Parables covered include: the friend at midnight, the prodigal son, the rich man and Lazarus, the persistent widow, the workers in the vineyard, the royal wedding banquet, and the parable of the talents. The study plan includes questions prior to each lesson, Scripture passage, commentary, and directions for using the questions.

Author: Schaap, Ward B. **1220**
Series: Challenge Bible Study
Title: *Character of the Kingdom: Studies in the Parables*
Publisher: Baker Book House, 1994 ISBN: 0-80108-370-2

Num. Sess.	Group Time	Num. Pgs.	Avg. Qst.	Price	Audience	Format	Bible Study
7	60-75	123	Vary	$4.99	New Christian	Workbk	Topical

Features: Intro to Leading a Study
★★★ Personal Application Preparation Time: Med
★★★ Relationship Building Ldr. Guide: No Size: 5.50 x 8.50
Subjects: Parables
Comments: This 7-lesson study examines aspects of the kingdom of heaven as Jesus described it in 12 parables. Parables covered include: "Jesus, the Master Teacher"; "The Parables of the Patch and the Wineskins"; "The Parable of the Sower"; "Six Parables of the Kingdom"; "The Parable of the Two Debtors"; and more. The goal of the studies is to help participants understand Jesus' parables in their original time and setting-to.

Author: Schaeffer, Dr. Francis A. **1221**
Series:
Title: *How Should We Then Live?*
Publisher: Gospel Films, 1977 ISBN: 1-55568-109-3

Num. Sess.	Group Time	Num. Pgs.	Avg. Qst.	Price	Audience	Format	Bible Study
12	60-75	N/A	3	$99.95	Beginner	Video	Topical

Features: Follow Up, Video Study Guide, Book Avail
★★★★ Personal Application Preparation Time: None
★★ Relationship Building Ldr. Guide: No Size: 14.0 x 9.0
Subjects: Church Life, Suffering
Comments: In 10 30″ episodes, Dr. Schaeffer analyzes the historical period from the Roman age to the modern era (period scenes add to the video impact) and shows how man's only hope for escaping the consequences of authoritarian society and arbitrary absolutes is a return to biblical truth revealed in Christ. Two additional segments present in-depth interviews with Francis and Edith Schaeffer.

Author: Schaeffer, Dr. Francis A. & Dr. C. Everett Koop **1222**
Series:
Title: *Whatever Happened to the Human Race?*
Publisher: Gospel Films, 1980

Num. Sess.	Group Time	Num. Pgs.	Avg. Qst.	Price	Audience	Format	Bible Study
6	90-120	62	Vary	$99.95	Beginner	Video	Topical

Features: Intro to Study, Digging Deeper Quest, Photos, Video Study Guide
★★★★ Personal Application Preparation Time: None
★★★★ Relationship Building Ldr. Guide: No Size: 7.0 x 10.0
Subjects: Abortion, Medical Issues, Social Issues
Comments: This dramatic 6-part comprehensive video study has a twofold purpose: to inform the public, whether Christian or not, of the actual facts of abortion on demand, infanticide, and euthanasia; and to encourage decisive, sacrificial action within the generous boundaries provided by the U.S. Constitution. The study guide clarifies the facts and arguments presented.

Author: Schaeffer, Frank **1223**
Series:
Title: *Religious Apartheid*
Publisher: Gospel Films, 1994

Num. Sess.	Group Time	Num. Pgs.	Avg. Qst.	Price	Audience	Format	Bible Study
4	60-90	N/A	5	$49.95	Beginner	Video	Topical

Features: Intro to Study, Book Incl, Video Study Guide
★★★★ Personal Application Preparation Time: None
★★ Relationship Building Ldr. Guide: Yes Size: 12.0 x 9.75
Subjects: Beliefs, Divorce, Ethics, Family, Morals
Comments: This 30″ video featuring John W. Whitehead chronicles many examples of religious discrimination: a child reprimanded for praying over her public school cafeteria meal, a Florida pastor forbidden to place a cross in his own front yard, a university ban of religious symbols as "offensive." These examples point out the need for a thoughtful and direct response to such discrimination. Designed to inform belivers and non-belivers, and to encourage decisive action.

Author: Schaller, Lyle E. **1224**
Series:
Title: *Getting Things Done*
Publisher: Abingdon Press, 1986 ISBN: 0-68714-142-7

Num. Sess.	Group Time	Num. Pgs.	Avg. Qst.	Price	Audience	Format	Bible Study
8	—	270	N/A	$13.95		Book	No

Features: Drawings, Cartoons
Personal Application Preparation Time:
Relationship Building Ldr. Guide: Size: 5.25 x 8.50
Subjects: Leadership, Small Group Resource
Comments: This book proposes that "anyone" can learn to be a leader, and discusses various aspects about leadership: leadership can be learned; leaders know how to organize, accept responsibility, enlist allies, and institute change when necessary; authoritarian and laissez-faire leadership styles are obsolete; leaders share certain qualities; and it's never too late to learn to become a leader. Cartoons and a fictional character are used to illustrate assumptions about effective leadership.

Author: Schiller, Barbara 1225
Series: Singles Ministry Resources
Title: *Just Me & the Kids: Building Healthy Single-Parent Families*
Publisher: David C. Cook Publishing Co., 1994 ISBN: 6-12508-391-8

Num. Sess.	Group Time	Num. Pgs.	Avg. Qst.	Price	Audience	Format	Bible Study
12	60-75	N/A	N/A	$299.00	Beginner	Video	Topical

Features: Intro to Study, Bibliography, Handouts, Publicity Ideas, Book Incl
★★★★ Personal Application Preparation Time: Low
★★★★ Relationship Building Ldr. Guide: Yes Size: 8.50 x 11.0
Subjects: Divorce, Emotions, Family, Grief, Parenting, Relationships, Singles' Issues, Wholeness
Comments: This 12-week program, for divorced single parents and pre-school through grade 6 children, is ideal for community outreach. The kit includes materials for each session, including videos, training materials, promotional brochures, posters, director's handbook, children's group leader's guide, single-parent study book, leader's guide.

Author: Schmidt, Doug 1226
Series: Good Word Series
Title: *Gospel On the Go*
Publisher: David C. Cook Publishing Co., 1994 ISBN: 0-78145-129-9

Num. Sess.	Group Time	Num. Pgs.	Avg. Qst.	Price	Audience	Format	Bible Study
15	60-90	144	15	$9.95	Beginner	Workbk	Charctr

Features: Intro to Study, Prayer Helps, Worship Helps, Study Overview, Pre-discussion Quest, Full Scrpt Printed, Cartoons, Persnl Study Quest
★★★★ Personal Application Preparation Time: Med
★★★★ Relationship Building Ldr. Guide: Yes Size: 7.25 x 9.25
Subjects: Teens: New Testament
Comments: This study challenges youth to push their walk with God to the limit, to seek His best, and be nothing but their best for Him. They will come to know more about Jesus as they walk with Mark. Fifteen studies, over three weeks, begin with an activity or story and include some Scripture, but participants are encouraged to use Bibles. Space is provided for written responses to each question.

Author: Schoberg, Gerry & R. Paul Stevens 1227
Series: Shaw Contemporary Issues
Title: *Servant Leadership*
Publisher: Shaw, 1990 ISBN: 0-87788-755-1

Num. Sess.	Group Time	Num. Pgs.	Avg. Qst.	Price	Audience	Format	Bible Study
8	30-45	48	5	$4.99	Beginner	Workbk	Topical

Features: Intro to Leading a Study, Intro to Study, Bibliography, Follow Up, Ldr's Notes
★★★★ Personal Application Preparation Time: Low
★★★ Relationship Building Ldr. Guide: No Size: 5.25 x 8.25
Subjects: Christian Living, Church Life, Family, Leadership, Work
Comments: Eight short studies on mixing leader and servant qualities help participants focus on Christian response to everyday challenges of both. Qualities considered include what it means to be a servant in the marketplace, how to value oneself without becoming proud, and how to balance the competing agendas of work, family, church, and friends.

Author: Schooley, Shirley 1228
Series: Leadership Skills For Women
Title: *Conflict Management*
Publisher: New Hope, 1994 ISBN: 1-56309-103-8

Num. Sess.	Group Time	Num. Pgs.	Avg. Qst.	Price	Audience	Format	Bible Study
6	45-60	54	Vary	$5.95	New Christian	Book	Topical

Features: Intro to Study
★★★★ Personal Application Preparation Time: Low
★★ Relationship Building Ldr. Guide: No Size: 5.50 x 8.50
Subjects: Conflict, Leadership, Psychology, Women's Issues
Comments: One of five books in the Leadership Skills for Women Series, this book shows readers how to understand the impact conflict has on their lives. It shows how conflict can be used creatively and constructively, making their lives and more effective and successful. It defines conflict, identifies sources and types of conflict, exposes ways people deal with conflict, discusses leadership and conflict, and finally, clarifies the role of conflict in a small group.

Author: Schrag, Dr Lyle, et. al. 1229
Series: Life Application
Title: *Revelation*
Publisher: Tyndale House, 1989 ISBN: 0-84232-719-3

Num. Sess.	Group Time	Num. Pgs.	Avg. Qst.	Price	Audience	Format	Bible Study
13	60-90	96	12	$4.99	New Christian	Workbk	Book

Features: Intro to Leading a Study, Intro to Study, Study Overview, Digging Deeper Quest, Full Scrpt Printed, Drawings, Charts, Maps, Cross Ref
★★★ Personal Application Preparation Time: Med
★★★ Relationship Building Ldr. Guide: No Size: 6.50 x 9.0
Subjects: Church Life, Hope, Revelation
Comments: This study contains the complete text of Revelation. Participants will marvel with John at the panorama of God's revealed plan, listen as Christ warns the churches, and root out any sin that blocks their relationships with Him. They are urged to have hope, knowing that God is in control.

Author: Schramm, Mary 1230
Series: Small Group Bible Studies
Title: *Peacemaking*
Publisher: Augsburg Fortress Publishers, 1986

Num. Sess.	Group Time	Num. Pgs.	Avg. Qst.	Price	Audience	Format	Bible Study
8	60-75	32	11	$1.45	New Christian	Book	Topical

Features: Intro to Study, Prayer Helps
★★★ Personal Application Preparation Time: None
★★★ Relationship Building Ldr. Guide: No Size: 8.50 x 5.50
Subjects: Relationships, Wholeness
Comments: This small pamphlet includes 8 sessions on peacemaking, using Scripture as a guide. Peacemaking begins with and is an integral part of the vision of shalom—God's plan for the world. This Hebrew word is a way to say hello and goodby. It means prosperity and health, security and well-being, but its best definition is "wholeness" or "completeness." God is interested in an inner peace. These sessions reflect peacemaking as a call upon Christians' lives.

Author: Schreur, Jack & Jerry **1231**
Series:
Title: *Family Fears*
Publisher: Gospel Films, 1994 ISBN: 1-55568-152-2

Num. Sess.	Group Time	Num. Pgs.	Avg. Qst.	Price	Audience	Format	Bible Study
6	45-75	N/A	Vary	$79.95	Beginner	Video	Topical

Features: Intro to Leading a Study, Book Incl, Video Study Guide
★★★★ Personal Application Preparation Time: Med
★★★★ Relationship Building Ldr. Guide: Yes Size: 12.0 x 9.50
Subjects: Family
Comments: This package contains the "Family Fears" book from Victor Books, a 5-part video (20″ each part) and complete leader's guide for a 5 or 10-session curriculum. It helps participants confront 4 common family fears: What if our children make life-dominating mistakes? What if our children don't "turn out right?" Are we failing as a family? and What if our children decide not to live out our values and faith?

Author: Schreur, Jerry, Judy, & Jack **1232**
Series:
Title: *Creative Grandparenting*
Publisher: Gospel Films, 1994

Num. Sess.	Group Time	Num. Pgs.	Avg. Qst.	Price	Audience	Format	Bible Study
4	30-60	N/A	Vary	$39.95	Beginner	Video	Topical

Features: Intro to Study, Prayer Helps, Book Incl, Video Study Guide
★★★★ Personal Application Preparation Time: Low
★★★★ Relationship Building Ldr. Guide: No Size: 6.0 x 9.0
Subjects: Aging, Parenting, Senior Adults, Teens: Family
Comments: This study includes a 4 part video, book, and a study guide. The 4 15″ video segments answer questions such as: What do children need from grandparents? How much responsibility can I assume without overstepping bounds? How can I relate to teenage grandchildren? A fun series with a serious purpose, it's based on solid principles of child development and anchored in the truth of the Bible. The speakers are Jerry, Judy, and Jack Schreur.

Author: Schreur, Tamera Veenstra **1233**
Series: Discover Your Bible
Title: *Discover: Ephesians*
Publisher: Church Development Resources, 1984

Num. Sess.	Group Time	Num. Pgs.	Avg. Qst.	Price	Audience	Format	Bible Study
12	60-75	43	5	$2.30	Beginner	Workbk	Book

Features: Intro to Study, Summary, Glossary
★★★ Personal Application Preparation Time: None
★★ Relationship Building Ldr. Guide: Yes Size: 5.50 x 8.50
Subjects: Ephesians, Marriage, Parenting, Relationships
Comments: This inductive study of Ephesians deals with the transformation from the "old self" to the "new." Paul offers contemporary participants practical, candid guidance on parenting, marriage, and other relationships. Ephesian Christians had previously lived to gratify their own selfish desires and thoughts. Their lifestyles had opposed God's will, but now they were alive in Christ. Participants will find the letter encouraging and relevant.

Author: Schreur, Tamera Veenstra **1234**
Series: Discover Your Bible
Title: *Discover: Galatians*
Publisher: Church Development Resources, 1986

Num. Sess.	Group Time	Num. Pgs.	Avg. Qst.	Price	Audience	Format	Bible Study
8	60-75	46	6	$1.60	Beginner	Workbk	Book

Features: Intro to Study, Summary, Glossary
★★★ Personal Application Preparation Time: None
★★ Relationship Building Ldr. Guide: Yes Size: 5.50 x 8.50
Subjects: Church Life, Faith, Galatians
Comments: This inductive study of Galatians discusses the issues and customs that concerned the early Church. It uncovers universal Christian principles that have become foundations of the Church's life, and shows their modern application. Paul's letter helps answer basic questions about Christian faith, such as: "How is one saved—by believing or by achieving?" "Does Jesus save us or do we save ourselves?" A comprehensive leader's guide is available.

Author: Schreur, Tamera Veenstra **1235**
Series: Discover Your Bible
Title: *Discover Luke: Jesus' Parables and Miracles*
Publisher: Church Development Resources, 1983

Num. Sess.	Group Time	Num. Pgs.	Avg. Qst.	Price	Audience	Format	Bible Study
9	60-75	35	6	$1.75	Beginner	Workbk	Book

Features: Intro to Study, Summary, Glossary
★★★ Personal Application Preparation Time: None
★★ Relationship Building Ldr. Guide: Yes Size: 5.50 x 8.50
Subjects: Jesus: Life/Teaching, Luke, Miracles, Parables
Comments: This study on Jesus' parables and miracles is 2nd in a 3-part series on Luke. An inductive study, it helps participants discover Bible truth themselves, in this case, verse by verse through Luke 13–19. Each of 9 lessons consists of a series of questions which, when answered, give participants a clear, personal understanding of the Scripture. Application of the message in their lives and sharing with others are encouraged.

Author: Schreur, Tamera Veenstra **1236**
Series: Discover Your Bible
Title: *Discover Luke: Jesus' Last Days*
Publisher: Church Development Resources, 1983

Num. Sess.	Group Time	Num. Pgs.	Avg. Qst.	Price	Audience	Format	Bible Study
9	60-75	36	6	$1.75	Beginner	Workbk	Book

Features: Intro to Study, Summary
★★★ Personal Application Preparation Time: None
★★ Relationship Building Ldr. Guide: Yes Size: 5.50 x 8.50
Subjects: Jesus: Life/Teaching, Luke
Comments: This study on Jesus' last days is last in a 3-part series on Luke. An inductive study, it helps participants discover Bible truth themselves, in this case, verse by verse through Luke 19–24. Each of 7 lessons consists of a series of questions which, when answered, give participants a clear, personal understanding of the Scripture. Application of the message in their lives and sharing with others are encouraged.

Author: Schreur, Tamera Veenstra **1237**
Series: Discover Your Bible
Title: *Discover Luke: Jesus' Early Life*
Publisher: Church Development Resources, 1989

Num. Sess.	Group Time	Num. Pgs.	Avg. Qst.	Price	Audience	Format	Bible Study
7	60-75	40	6	$1.50	Beginner	Workbk	Book

Features: Glossary
★★★ Personal Application Preparation Time: None
★★ Relationship Building Ldr. Guide: Yes Size: 5.50 x 8.50
Subjects: Luke
Comments: Luke, the story of Jesus' life, has been called the "most beautiful book ever written." Luke's purpose is to convince readers that Jesus is both Lord and Christ. "Discover Luke" is part of a basic Bible study series, and there are 3 study booklets in the series: "Jesus' Early Life," "Jesus' Parables and Miracles," and "Jesus' Last Days." Taken together, they provide an overview of Christ's life and ministry.

Author: Schreur, Tamera Veenstra **1238**
Series: Discover Your Bible
Title: *Discover: The Sermon on the Mount*
Publisher: Church Development Resources, 1985

Num. Sess.	Group Time	Num. Pgs.	Avg. Qst.	Price	Audience	Format	Bible Study
8	60-75	31	6	$1.60	Beginner	Workbk	Book

Features: Intro to Study, Summary, Glossary
★★★ Personal Application Preparation Time: None
★★ Relationship Building Ldr. Guide: Yes Size: 5.50 x 8.50
Subjects: Christian Living, Sermon on the Mount, Ten Commandments
Comments: This inductive study of the Sermon on the Mount deals with murder, adultery, peacemaking, ambition, and righteousness. Putting the Ten Commandments into perspective, Jesus shows His listeners what God intended the Law to be. He presents it as a guide to a believer's new life that comes from a changed heart, not from following a set of rules. It is a practical study.

Author: Schultze, Dr. Quentin J. **1239**
Series:
Title: *Winning Your Kids Back From the Media*
Publisher: Gospel Films, 1994 ISBN: 1-55568-153-0

Num. Sess.	Group Time	Num. Pgs.	Avg. Qst.	Price	Audience	Format	Bible Study
5	45-60	N/A	5	$49.95	Beginner	Video	Topical

Features: Intro to Study, Book Incl
★★★★ Personal Application Preparation Time: Low
★★★ Relationship Building Ldr. Guide: Yes Size: 11.25 x 9.0
Subjects: Parenting, Teens: Communication, Teens: Family, Teens: Music
Comments: This package contains a 5 (20″) session video, book, and leader's guide. Dr. Schultze reaches out to teens through adults with humorous anecdotes, straight-forward teaching and warm encouragement. This video helps participants tone down the media racket and tune into each other and God, find more family time, find the best media for young children, and answer why MTV appeals to teens.

Author: Schultz, Thom & Joanni **1240**
Series: Group's Active Bible Curriculum
Title: *Is Marriage in Your Future?*
Publisher: Group Publishing, 1990 ISBN: 1-55945-203-X

Num. Sess.	Group Time	Num. Pgs.	Avg. Qst.	Price	Audience	Format	Bible Study
4	35-60	46	Vary	$9.99	Beginner	Workbk	Topical

Features: Intro to Leading a Study, Intro to Study, Objectives, Study Overview, Ldr's Notes, Handouts, Agenda, Publicity Ideas
★★★ Personal Application Preparation Time: None
★★★ Relationship Building Ldr. Guide: No Size: 8.50 x 11.0
Subjects: Teens: Family, Teens: Relationships, Teens: Senior High
Comments: This study offers senior high students the secrets of a great marriage, how to have a continuing successful marriage and family life. It defines marriage, discusses how friendship builds a foundation for marriage, deals with God's idea of love, and outlines what makes a marriage work. It can be adapted for use in a Bible class or youth meeting.

Author: Schultz, Thom & Joanni **1241**
Series:
Title: *Why Nobody Learns Much of Anything at Church*
Publisher: Group Publishing, 1993 ISBN: 1-55945-907-7

Num. Sess.	Group Time	Num. Pgs.	Avg. Qst.	Price	Audience	Format	Bible Study
	—	240	N/A	$12.99			

Features: Intro to Study
Personal Application Preparation Time:
Relationship Building Ldr. Guide: Size: 6.0 x 9.0
Subjects: Small Group Resource
Comments: This evaluation of learning in the church includes practical solutions for improving how a church educates. Teachers of all ages will see evidence why people aren't learning in church; discover why Sunday School attendance is plummeting; why people don't learn from sermons; understand how some teaching styles may be crippling; and explore how curriculum materials may not be achieving the proper goal.

Author: Schultz, Yvonne **1242**
Series: The Lifechange Series
Title: *Colossians & Philemon*
Publisher: NavPress, 1988 ISBN: 0-89109-119-X

Num. Sess.	Group Time	Num. Pgs.	Avg. Qst.	Price	Audience	Format	Bible Study
11	60-90	139	15	$6.00	New Christian	Workbk	Book

Features: Intro to Leading a Study, Intro to Study, Bibliography, Prayer Helps, Worship Helps, Study Overview, Digging Deeper Quest, Summary, Maps, Word Study
★★★ Personal Application Preparation Time: Med
★★★ Relationship Building Ldr. Guide: No Size: 5.50 x 8.50
Subjects: Church Life, Colossians/Philemon, False Teachers, Forgiveness, Prison Epistles
Comments: Visitors to Paul in prison recount news of false teachers belittling Christ, laying down rules, and boasting of secret knowledge beyond the Gospel. Paul's words exalt Christ, refocus the Colossians' attention, and affirm a Christian lifestyle.

Author: Sciacca, Fran & Jill **1243**
Series: Lifelines
Title: *Are Families Forever? Strengthening Family Ties*
Publisher: Zondervan, 1992 ISBN: 0-31048-071-X

Num. Sess.	Group Time	Num. Pgs.	Avg. Qst.	Price	Audience	Format	Bible Study
6	45-60	48	Vary	$3.99	Beginner	Workbk	Topical

Features: Intro to Study, Scrpt Memory Helps, Persnl Study Quest
★★★★ Personal Application Preparation Time: Low
★★★★ Relationship Building Ldr. Guide: No Size: 5.25 x 8.25
Subjects: Teens: Family, Teens: Relationships
Comments: This contemporary study for young adults concerns family. Lessons include: "May I Speak to the Manager, Please?"—(God chooses parents); "I Can't Wait Until I Graduate!"—(obeying one's parents); "Technical Difficulties . . . Please Stand By"—("how" to talk to my parents); "Did You Hear Me?"—(listening); "After the Bomb Drops"—(children of divorce) and "Who Does He Think He Is Anyway?"—(Stepparents). Each lesson begins with a true story.

Author: Sciacca, Fran & Jill **1244**
Series: Lifelines
Title: *Burger, Fries and a Friend to Go: Making Friends*
Publisher: Zondervan, 1992 ISBN: 0-31048-041-8

Num. Sess.	Group Time	Num. Pgs.	Avg. Qst.	Price	Audience	Format	Bible Study
6	45-60	45	Vary	$3.99	Beginner	Workbk	Topical

Features: Intro to Study, Scrpt Memory Helps, Persnl Study Quest
★★★★ Personal Application Preparation Time: Low
★★★★ Relationship Building Ldr. Guide: No Size: 5.25 x 8.25
Subjects: Teens: Christian Liv, Teens: Friends
Comments: This study concerns young adults building friendships. Lessons deal with selecting friends, identifying genuine friends, ingredients in true friendships, non-Christian friends, conflict among friends, and the ultimate friend—Jesus. Each lesson begins with a true story from the life of a teenager. An inductive study approach is used and group discussion questions are provided.

Author: Sciacca, Fran & Jill **1245**
Series: Lifelines
Title: *Cliques & Clones: Facing Peer Pressure*
Publisher: Zondervan, 1992 ISBN: 0-31048-031-0

Num. Sess.	Group Time	Num. Pgs.	Avg. Qst.	Price	Audience	Format	Bible Study
6	45-60	54	Vary	$3.99	Beginner	Workbk	Topical

Features: Intro to Study, Scrpt Memory Helps, Persnl Study Quest
★★★★ Personal Application Preparation Time: Low
★★★★ Relationship Building Ldr. Guide: No Size: 5.25 x 8.25
Subjects: Teens: Decisions, Teens: Peer Pressure
Comments: This study deals with peer pressure on young adults. Lessons include: "Who's Pushing Me?"; "When the Party's Over"; "It's Your Choice"; "Why Won't God Help Me?"; "Surprise!"; and "Standing Alone." Each lesson begins with a true story from the life of a teenager. An inductive study approach is used and group discussion questions are provided.

Author: Sciacca, Fran & Jill **1246**
Series: Lifelines
Title: *Does Anyone Else Feel This Way?*
Publisher: Zondervan, 1992 ISBN: 0-31048-021-3

Num. Sess.	Group Time	Num. Pgs.	Avg. Qst.	Price	Audience	Format	Bible Study
6	45-60	59	Vary	$3.99	Beginner	Workbk	Topical

Features: Intro to Leading a Study, Intro to Study, Scrpt Memory Helps, Persnl Study Quest
★★★★ Personal Application Preparation Time: Low
★★★★ Relationship Building Ldr. Guide: No Size: 5.25 x 8.25
Subjects: Teens: Emotions, Teens: Psychology
Comments: This contemporary study for young adults concerns loneliness, depression, and thoughts of suicide. Lessons address honesty about loneliness, causes of loneliness and depression, understanding one's inner and outer focus, talking about thoughts of suicide, and why suicide is no solution. A chart titled "What to Say to a Suicidal Friend" outlines what to say and why, as well as what to do and why.

Author: Sciacca, Fran & Jill **1247**
Series: Lifelines
Title: *Good News for a Bad News World: Understanding the Gospel*
Publisher: Zondervan, 1992 ISBN: 0-31048-061-2

Num. Sess.	Group Time	Num. Pgs.	Avg. Qst.	Price	Audience	Format	Bible Study
6	45-60	70	Vary	$3.99	Beginner	Workbk	Topical

Features: Intro to Study, Scrpt Memory Helps, Full Scrpt Printed, Drawings, Persnl Study Quest
★★★★ Personal Application Preparation Time: Low
★★★★ Relationship Building Ldr. Guide: No Size: 5.25 x 8.25
Subjects: Teens: Discipleship, Teens: Evangelism
Comments: This contemporary study for young adults is subtitled "Understanding the Gospel." Lessons include: "Who Am I? And Why Am I Here?"; "I Feel Guilty"; "Enough Is Never Enough"; "The Painless Paddling"; "Take It or Leave It"; "Paid in Full." A brief tract and some drawings in the back of the study review the steps to salvation. Each lesson begins with a true story from the life of a teenager.

Author: Sciacca, Fran & Jill **1248**
Series: Lifelines
Title: *Is This the Real Thing? What Love Is and Isn't*
Publisher: Zondervan, 1992 ISBN: 0-31048-081-7

Num. Sess.	Group Time	Num. Pgs.	Avg. Qst.	Price	Audience	Format	Bible Study
6	45-60	59	Vary	$3.99	Beginner	Workbk	Topical

Features: Intro to Study, Scrpt Memory Helps, Drawings, Persnl Study Quest
★★★★ Personal Application Preparation Time: Low
★★★★ Relationship Building Ldr. Guide: No Size: 5.25 x 8.25
Subjects: Teens: Emotions, Teens: Friends
Comments: This contemporary study for young adults concerns what love is and what it isn't. Lessons include: "Give and Take"; "Love Is Not a Feeling!"; "Plugging In and Turning On"; "Philadelphia Friends"; "Is This the Real Thing?"; "Eros Defiled!" Each lesson begins with a true story from the life of a teenager. An inductive study approach is used and group discussion questions are provided.

Author: Sciacca, Fran & Jill **1249**
Series: Lifelines
Title: *So What's Wrong with a Big Nose? Building Self-Esteem*
Publisher: Zondervan, 1992 ISBN: 0-31048-051-5

Num. Sess.	Group Time	Num. Pgs.	Avg. Qst.	Price	Audience	Format	Bible Study
6	45-60	56	Vary	$3.99	Beginner	Workbk	Topical

Features: Intro to Study, Scrpt Memory Helps, Persnl Study Quest
★★★★ Personal Application Preparation Time: Low
★★★★ Relationship Building Ldr. Guide: No Size: 5.25 x 8.25
Subjects: Teens: Psychology, Teens: Self-esteem
Comments: This contemporary study on self-esteem is for young adults. Lessons deal with subjects like the need for self-worth, where self-worth comes from, God's love, God's perfect plan, preoccupation with self, and self-sacrifice. Each lesson begins with a true story from the life of a teenager. An inductive study approach is used and group discussion questions are provided.

Author: Sciacca, Fran **1250**
Series:
Title: *To Run and Not Grow Tired*
Publisher: NavPress, 1991 ISBN: 0-89109-393-1

Num. Sess.	Group Time	Num. Pgs.	Avg. Qst.	Price	Audience	Format	Bible Study
12	75-90	91	11	$5.00	New Christian	Workbk	Charctr

Features: Intro to Study, Scrpt Memory Helps
★★★★ Personal Application Preparation Time: None
★★★ Relationship Building Ldr. Guide: No Size: 5.50 x 8.50
Subjects: Bible Personalities, Emotions, Faith
Comments: Through 12 Bible characters, this study helps participants understand how God cares about every problem, and how He guides people into balanced, timely solutions. Characters examined include: Hannah, Peter, Sarah, Cain, Jezebel, Paul, Martha, King Saul, the Ten Spies, Joseph, Jesus, and the Holy Spirit. This study will help those who have inner wounds-and not sure how to heal them.

Author: Sciacca, Fran **1251**
Series:
Title: *To Walk and Not Grow Weary*
Publisher: NavPress, 1985 ISBN: 0-89109-034-7

Num. Sess.	Group Time	Num. Pgs.	Avg. Qst.	Price	Audience	Format	Bible Study
12	45-60	81	10	$5.00	New Christian	Workbk	Topical

Features: Intro to Study, Bibliography, Scrpt Memory Helps, Digging Deeper Quest
★★★ Personal Application Preparation Time: Low
★★ Relationship Building Ldr. Guide: No Size: 5.50 x 8.50
Subjects: Bible Personalities, Emotions, Loneliness, Psychology, Success
Comments: This study presents cameos of 12 godly people under pressure. Each contrasts human problems with God's solutions, under chapter titles such as: "Job—When the Lights Go Out"; "David—Dealing with Guilt"; "Jesus—How to Handle Rejection"; and "Barnabas—Encouraging Others.

Author: Sciacca, Fran & Jill **1252**
Series: Lifelines
Title: *What Really Matters? Setting Priorites*
Publisher: Zondervan, 1992 ISBN: 0-31048-091-4

Num. Sess.	Group Time	Num. Pgs.	Avg. Qst.	Price	Audience	Format	Bible Study
6	45-60	50	Vary	$3.99	Beginner	Workbk	Topical

Features: Intro to Study, Scrpt Memory Helps, Persnl Study Quest
★★★★ Personal Application Preparation Time: Low
★★★★ Relationship Building Ldr. Guide: No Size: 5.25 x 8.25
Subjects: Teens: Christian Liv, Teens: Values
Comments: This contemporary study for young adults concerns setting priorities. Lessons include: "Some Treasures Don't Stay Buried"; "Who Sets Your Price Tags?"; "Mirror, Mirror, On My Wall . . ."; "What Does God Value?"; "Who's Number One on Your List?"; "Standing Alone." Each lesson begins with a true story from the life of a teenager. Several checklists and rating scales help direct the study. An inductive study approach is used and group discussion questions are provided.

Author: Seamands, David A. **1253**
Series: The Recovery Bookshelf
Title: *Freedom from the Performance Trap*
Publisher: Victor Books, 1988 ISBN: 0-89693-986-3

Num. Sess.	Group Time	Num. Pgs.	Avg. Qst.	Price	Audience	Format	Bible Study
12	—	200	N/A	$9.99		Book	Topical

Features:
Personal Application Preparation Time:
Relationship Building Ldr. Guide: Size: 5.50 x 8.50
Subjects: Grace
Comments: This book is for Christians who have exchanged the joy and security of God's unconditional grace for the guilt and anxiety of what David Seamands calls "dys-grace." Dys-grace is a type of twisted message people receive from family members, an achievement-oriented society, and even some churches—proclaiming that they will be accepted and loved, and feel worthwhile only when they have delivered a perfect performance.

Author: Seamands, David A. and Beth Funk **1254**
Series: The Recovery Bookshelf
Title: *Healing for Damaged Emotions Workbook*
Publisher: Victor Books, 1992 ISBN: 1-56476-025-1

Num. Sess.	Group Time	Num. Pgs.	Avg. Qst.	Price	Audience	Format	Bible Study
13	90-120	240	4	$15.99	Beginner	Workbk	Topical

Features: Intro to Leading a Study, Intro to Study, Prayer Helps, Persnl Study Quest, Appendix
★★★★ Personal Application Preparation Time: None
★★★★ Relationship Building Ldr. Guide: No Size: 7.50 x 9.50
Subjects: Addictions, Emotions, Support
Comments: This workbook provides tools for examining the rings of life, and finding healing for painful scars that cripple emotions. In it, participants can find the entire text of the book by the same title, Scripture meditation and memorization, prayer exercises, journaling exercises, a small group guide, and recovery resources.

Author: Seamands, David A. **1255**
Series: The Recovery Bookshelf
Title: *Healing for Damaged Emotions*
Publisher: Victor Books, 1981 ISBN: 0-89693-938-3

Num. Sess.	Group Time	Num. Pgs.	Avg. Qst.	Price	Audience	Format	Bible Study
12	60-90	144	N/A	$9.99	New Christian	Book	Topical

Features:
★★★★ Personal Application Preparation Time: Med
★★★ Relationship Building Ldr. Guide: Yes Size: 5.50 x 8.0
Subjects: Emotions, Psychology, Self-esteem, Support
Comments: Whether through fallen temperament, willful disobedience, or as victims of others' hurtful actions, many Christians struggle with crippling emotions—among them perfectionism, depression, and low self-worth. Pain is present even though the incidents and relationships that caused it may be long past. This study helps Christians deal honestly and successfully with their inner hurts and become agents of healing for fellow strugglers.

Author: Seamands, David A. **1256**
Series:
Title: *If Only*
Publisher: Victor Books, 1995 ISBN: 1-56476-173-8

Num. Sess.	Group Time	Num. Pgs.	Avg. Qst.	Price	Audience	Format	Bible Study
	60-90	156	N/A	$8.99	New Christian	Book	Topical

Features: No Grp Discussion Quest
★★★★ Personal Application Preparation Time: Med
★★★ Relationship Building Ldr. Guide: Yes Size: 5.75 x 8.50
Subjects: Emotions, Failure, Faith
Comments: This book combats an increasing trend toward evasion of responsibility in dealing with life's regrets and disappointments. Observing many instances in society in which people blame everything from their own dysfunctional family lives to calculated murder on past problems, the author explores what the Bible has to say about the "If only . . ." way of thinking. The Bible's response is Jesus' response to Martha and Mary in John 11.

Author: Seamands, David A. **1257**
Series:
Title: *Putting Away Childish Things*
Publisher: Victor Books, 1982 ISBN: 0-88207-308-7

Num. Sess.	Group Time	Num. Pgs.	Avg. Qst.	Price	Audience	Format	Bible Study
13	60-90	144	N/A	$8.99	New Christian	Book	Topical

Features:
★★★★ Personal Application Preparation Time: Med
★★★ Relationship Building Ldr. Guide: Yes Size: 5.50 x 8.0
Subjects: Christian Living, Discipleship, Grace, Marriage, Psychology
Comments: This study helps participants progress toward the maturity God desires for all believers. These lessons identify outdated childish patterns and suggest ways of breaking their grip, so there can be growth in Christ. Lessons include: "The Hidden Child in Us All," "The Healing of the Memories," "Childish Ideas of Love and Marriage," "Childish Ideas of God and His Will," and "Reprogramming Grace." A leader's guide with transparency masters is available.

Author: Seemuth, David P. **1258**
Series: GroupBuilder Resources
Title: *Defeating Those Dragons*
Publisher: Victor Books, 1991 ISBN: 0-89693-924-3

Num. Sess.	Group Time	Num. Pgs.	Avg. Qst.	Price	Audience	Format	Bible Study
8	75-90	144	Vary	$5.99	New Christian	Workbk	Topical

Features: Intro to Leading a Study, Objectives, Pre-discussion Quest, Digging Deeper Quest,Full Scrpt Printed, Ldr's Notes, Cartoons, Persnl Study Quest
★★★ Personal Application Preparation Time: Low
★★★ Relationship Building Ldr. Guide: No Size: 6.0 x 9.0
Subjects: Emotions, Failure
Comments: This study helps small groups gain insight and support as they study how to put to death (or at least mortally wound) hindrances to their spiritual growth. Sessions deal with such dragons as anxiety, doubt, temptation, discouragement, hopelessness, fear, bitterness, and failure. Includes optional activities and hints for leaders.

Author: Seemuth, David P. **1259**
Series: GroupBuilder Resources
Title: *Don't Look Back*
Publisher: Victor Books, 1992 ISBN: 1-56476-032-4

Num. Sess.	Group Time	Num. Pgs.	Avg. Qst.	Price	Audience	Format	Bible Study
8	75-90	144	Vary	$5.99	New Christian	Workbk	Topical

Features: Intro to Leading a Study, Intro to Study, Objectives, Full Scrpt Printed, Ldr's Notes, Drawings, Persnl Study Quest
★★★★ Personal Application Preparation Time: Med
★★★★ Relationship Building Ldr. Guide: No Size: 6.0 x 9.0
Subjects: Faith, Relationships, Service
Comments: This study examines 8 aspects of developing a bold testimony for Christ, including putting priorities in line with Christ's will, learning to focus on Him and understand His discipline, tune daily life with God's desires, make positive changes in relationships, and value one another. It studies developing humility, adopting Christ's attitude toward possessions, and resting in God's strength.

Author: Seemuth, David P. **1260**
Series: GroupBuilder Resources
Title: *How Dynamic is Your Small Group?*
Publisher: Victor Books, 1991 ISBN: 0-89693-880-8

Num. Sess.	Group Time	Num. Pgs.	Avg. Qst.	Price	Audience	Format	Bible Study
11	—	156	6	$7.99		Book	

Features: Charts
Personal Application Preparation Time:
Relationship Building Ldr. Guide: Size: 6.0 x 9.0
Subjects: Commitments, Small Group Resource
Comments: This book allows leaders to evaluate their small groups according to 7 criteria, including communication, acceptance, commitment, standards, purpose, recognition of people and their backgrounds, and cohesion. Forms provided include a sample covenant and guidelines for developing neighborhood groups. Questions at the close of each chapter aid in review and reflection on the text. Sections may be used effectively in ongoing small-group leadership training.

Author: Seemuth, David P. **1261**
Series: GroupBuilder Resources
Title: *One Plus One*
Publisher: Victor Books, 1995 ISBN: 1-56476-415-X

Num. Sess.	Group Time	Num. Pgs.	Avg. Qst.	Price	Audience	Format	Bible Study
8	75-90	144	N/A	$5.99	New Christian	Workbk	Topical

Features: Intro to Leading a Study, Intro to Study, Objectives, Full Scrpt Printed, Ldr's Notes, Drawings, Persnl Study Quest
★★★★ Personal Application Preparation Time: Med
★★★★ Relationship Building Ldr. Guide: No Size: 6.0 x 9.0
Subjects: Commitments, Marriage
Comments: Many couples say their marital vows, convinced that nothing could ever threaten their marriage. They vow "for better or for worse" but know they will have the best. They say "for richer or for poorer" but see only upward mobility as a possibility, until reality hits, sometime as soon as the honeymoon. Eight sessions for small groups help couples move toward greater love, transparency, commitment.

Author: Senter, III, Mark **1262**
Series: SonPower Youth Sources
Title: *Coming Revolution in Youth Ministry, The*
Publisher: Victor Books, 1992 ISBN: 0-89693-917-0

Num. Sess.	Group Time	Num. Pgs.	Avg. Qst.	Price	Audience	Format	Bible Study
	—	220	N/A	$12.99		Book	

Features: Intro to Study, Bibliography, Index
Personal Application Preparation Time:
Relationship Building Ldr. Guide: Size: 6.0 x 9.0
Subjects: Teens: Resources
Comments: This book offers a prophetic vision for future efforts required to reach young people. The author describes the forces which shaped youth ministry in the past; societal and global influences of the present; megatrends of the emerging revolution; models for future ministry; and probing questions for youth workers, local churches, parachurch agencies, and Christian colleges and media who want to be prepared to face the coming revolution.

Author: Senter, III, Mark **1263**
Series: Equipped For Ministry
Title: *Recruiting Volunteers In The Church*
Publisher: Victor Books, 1990 ISBN: 0-89693-799-2

Num. Sess.	Group Time	Num. Pgs.	Avg. Qst.	Price	Audience	Format	Bible Study
	—	167	N/A	$9.99			

Features:
Personal Application Preparation Time:
Relationship Building Ldr. Guide: Size: 6.0 x 9.0
Subjects: Church Life, Leadership, Small Group Resource
Comments: This book offers step-by-step procedures and abundant resource materials to help leaders recruit. It includes information for nurturing, and keeping (or dismissing if necessary) a strong staff of volunteers. It is intended to counter the lack of volunteers in many modern churches, which have nearly died under the impact of cultural fragmentation, the exaltation of individualism, and heavy economic pressures on the average American family.

Author: Serratt, Mary Lou **1264**
Series: Spiritual Development Work
Title: *Light Journey: Adventures In Personal Witnessing*
Publisher: Woman's Missionary Union, 1993 ISBN: 1-56309-063-5

Num. Sess.	Group Time	Num. Pgs.	Avg. Qst.	Price	Audience	Format	Bible Study
5	—	32	Vary	$4.95	New Christian	Workbk	Topical

Features: Ldr's Notes
Personal Application Preparation Time:
Relationship Building Ldr. Guide: No Size: 8.50 x 11.0
Subjects: Teens: Discipleship, Teens: Evangelism
Comments: This workbook helps youths prepare to actively share their faith and develop skills in lifestyle evangelism. The "SDW" series is 3 workbooks containing Bible study material that will strengthen youths' prayer life, stretch their involvement in peer ministry, and exercise their personal witnessing skills. Included in this book are ideas, suggestions, and reproducible learning activities for group and individual study.

Author: Sethre, Peter A. **1265**
Series: Friendship Bible Study
Title: *James*
Publisher: Augsburg Fortress Publishers, 1987

Num. Sess.	Group Time	Num. Pgs.	Avg. Qst.	Price	Audience	Format	Bible Study
8	60-75	48	13	$3.75	New Christian	Workbk	Book

Features: Intro to Study, Prayer Helps, Study Overview
★★★★ Personal Application Preparation Time: Low
★★★★ Relationship Building Ldr. Guide: Yes Size: 5.0 x 8.50
Subjects: Faith, James, Joy, Relationships, Suffering
Comments: This 8-lesson study stresses to those who profess faith in Christ that they are called to let that faith govern their actions and relationships. Participants learn what it means to count various trials and circumstances as "all joy" (James 1:2), and receive practical guidelines for their walk in Christian faith. The lesson format includes an overview, an opening, a responsive reading, Bible background, questions for reflection, a key verse, prayer response, and more.

Author: Seversen, Beth Donigan **1266**
Series: Tapestry Collection
Title: *Mirror Image*
Publisher: Victor Books, 1992 ISBN: 1-56476-018-9

Num. Sess.	Group Time	Num. Pgs.	Avg. Qst.	Price	Audience	Format	Bible Study
8	75-90	95	14	$5.99	New Christian	Workbk	Book

Features: Intro to Leading a Study, Intro to Study, Objectives, Prayer Helps, Scrpt Memory Helps, Digging Deeper Quest, Follow Up, Ldr's Notes, Persnl Study Quest, Charts
★★★★ Personal Application Preparation Time: Med
★★★ Relationship Building Ldr. Guide: No Size: 6.0 x 9.0
Subjects: Colossians/Philemon, Women's Issues
Comments: In this 8-week study of Colossians, women examine a recurring theme of the outworking of Christ's life as He resides in them. Participants learn how to survive as Christians in the battle against heresy, persecution, materialism, and deteriorating relationships.

Author: Shaw, Luci **1267**
Series: Fisherman Bible Studyguide
Title: *Colossians: Focus on Christ*
Publisher: Shaw, 1982 ISBN: 0-87788-132-4

Num. Sess.	Group Time	Num. Pgs.	Avg. Qst.	Price	Audience	Format	Bible Study
8	45-60	75	12	$4.99	Mature Christian	Workbk	Book

Features: Intro to Leading a Study, Intro to Study, Prayer Helps
★★ Personal Application Preparation Time: Low
★★ Relationship Building Ldr. Guide: No Size: 5.0 x 8.25
Subjects: Church Life, Colossians/Philemon, False Teachers, Forgiveness, Hope, Occult, Prison Epistles, Service
Comments: In this verse-by-verse study of Colossians, Paul provides a defense-warning, teaching, and encouraging growth and maturity in Christ. Also dealt with are the same heresies of the young Asian church—threat of legalism and Gnosticism—that are still active today. Eager to investigate other power sources, the Colossians allowed false emphases to erode their view of Jesus Christ.

Author: Sheely, Steve, et al. **1268**
Series: Small Group Resources
Title: *Director's Workbook for Small Groups*
Publisher: Serendipity House, 1994 ISBN: 1-88341-981-6

Num. Sess.	Group Time	Num. Pgs.	Avg. Qst.	Price	Audience	Format	Bible Study
	—	157	N/A	$10.00		Workbk	

Features: Intro to Leading a Study
★★★★ Personal Application Preparation Time:
★★★★ Relationship Building Ldr. Guide: Size: 8.50 x 11.0
Subjects: Small Group Resource
Comments: This manual provides practical surveys, assessment questionnaires, orientation, and kick off material for launching small groups in a church. The contents include: "Clarifying Your Strategy"; "Forming Your Vision"; "Creating Your Small Group Dream"; "Developing Your Small Group Format"; "Building Your Small Group Team"; "Establishing Special Leadership Skills"; "Designing Your Small Group Lifecycle"; "Reinforcing the Ministry"; "Sharing Your Small Group Dream."

Author: Sheely, Steve, et al. **1269**
Series: Small Group Resources
Title: *Ice-Breakers and Heart-Warmers*
Publisher: Serendipity House, 1994 ISBN: 1-88341-979-4

Num. Sess.	Group Time	Num. Pgs.	Avg. Qst.	Price	Audience	Format	Bible Study
	—	127	N/A	$7.95	Beginner		

Features: Intro to Study, Drawings
Personal Application Preparation Time:
Relationship Building Ldr. Guide: Size: 6.50 x 9.0
Subjects: Small Group Resource
Comments: This book, a collection of "ice-breakers" and "heart-warmers" especially written for Christian small groups, includes some Serendipity classics, but many which are brand new. Begun with "ice-breakers" and ended with effective closing activities (heart-warmers), small groups can be well on the way to becoming trusting, loving communities. Ice-breakers encourage everyone to communicate in lively, non-threatening ways.

Author: Sheely, Steve, et al. **1270**
Series: Small Group Resources
Title: *Leader's Handbook for Small Groups*
Publisher: Serendipity House, 1994 ISBN: 1-88341-980-8

Num. Sess.	Group Time	Num. Pgs.	Avg. Qst.	Price	Audience	Format	Bible Study
6	30-60	64	12	$5.00	Mature Christian	Workbk	Topical

Features: Intro to Leading a Study, Intro to Study, Prayer Helps
★★★★ Personal Application Preparation Time: Low
★★★★ Relationship Building Ldr. Guide: No Size: 8.50 x 11.0
Subjects: Small Group Resource
Comments: Six sessions offer training for potential leaders. Lessons deal with different aspects of beginning, maintaining, and closing a group. Session 1 answers the "why" and "what." Session 2 covers leaders' responsibilities and covenanting. Session 3 covers communication, choosing study material, and selecting mission projects. Session 4 identifing healthy groups, dealing with problems, and having fun. Session 5 developing community, and Session 6 starting/ending groups.

Author: Shelley, Marshall **1271**
Series: The Knowing God Series
Title: *Our Merciful Judge: Trusting God's Fairness*
Publisher: Zondervan, 1994 ISBN: 0-31048-351-4

Num. Sess.	Group Time	Num. Pgs.	Avg. Qst.	Price	Audience	Format	Bible Study
6	45-60	64	12	$4.99	Beginner	Workbk	Topical

Features: Intro to Leading a Study, Intro to Study, Objectives, Scrpt Memory Helps, Follow Up, Ldr's Notes
★★★★ Personal Application Preparation Time: Low
★★★ Relationship Building Ldr. Guide: No Size: 5.50 x 8.50
Subjects: Faith, God, Suffering
Comments: One of 8 in the series, this guide explores why the Judge of the universe can be counted on to treat people fairly. Experiences such as the loss of a loved one, a personal injury, or a layoff from work can cause people to question God's goodness and fairness. Why does He allow such things to happen? Can He be trusted in the future? The study reveals why the Lord is worthy of our trust.

Author: Shelley, Marshall **1272**
Series: The Knowing God Series
Title: *Our Powerful Helper: Relying on God's Strength*
Publisher: Zondervan, 1994 ISBN: 0-31048-341-7

Num. Sess.	Group Time	Num. Pgs.	Avg. Qst.	Price	Audience	Format	Bible Study
6	45-60	48	12	$4.99	Beginner	Workbk	Topical

Features: Intro to Leading a Study, Intro to Study, Objectives, Scrpt Memory Helps, Follow Up, Ldr's Notes
★★★★ Personal Application Preparation Time: Low
★★★ Relationship Building Ldr. Guide: No Size: 5.50 x 8.50
Subjects: God, Grief, Hope
Comments: One of 8 in a series, these 6 studies focus on sections of the Bible that offer fresh glimpses into how God works. When faced with challenges that seem beyond human abilities, how does one receive God's help? When strength is needed to make it through the day, how can one experience God's power? This guide encourages participants to rely on God's strength daily.

Author: Shelton, Chuck 1273
Series: Global Issues
Title: *Voiceless People*
Publisher: InterVarsity, 1990 ISBN: 0-83084-912-2

Num. Sess.	Group Time	Num. Pgs.	Avg. Qst.	Price	Audience	Format	Bible Study
6	45-60	48	10	$4.99	Beginner	Workbk	Topical

Features: Intro to Leading a Study, Intro to Study, Bibliography, Prayer Helps, Follow Up
★★ Personal Application Preparation Time: Low
★★ Relationship Building Ldr. Guide: No Size: 5.50 x 8.25
Subjects: Medical Issues, Social Issues
Comments: This 6-week study describes the homeless, minorities, the illiterate, terminally ill, and those who live under oppressive governments, among others. It poses questions such as: "How have they become so helpless?" "What can we do to improve life for these people?" and "What does God want us to do?" Participants are challenged to help the world's voiceless people.

Author: Sherman, Doug & William Hendricks 1274
Series:
Title: *Your Work Matters to God*
Publisher: NavPress, 1988 ISBN: 0-89109-226-9

Num. Sess.	Group Time	Num. Pgs.	Avg. Qst.	Price	Audience	Format	Bible Study
16	60-75	112	Vary	$6.00	New Christian	Workbk	Topical

Features: Intro to Leading a Study, Intro to Study, Follow Up, Book Avail
★★★★ Personal Application Preparation Time: Low
★★ Relationship Building Ldr. Guide: No Size: 5.50 x 8.50
Subjects: Work
Comments: This study guide, based on a book by the same title, helps assure participants that work matters to God. They can discover practical ideas and strategies for living out their faith on the job, find moral courage to maintain ethical integrity at work, sort through daily work issues, opportunities, and frustrations in a relaxed environment, and build relationships with others with similar concerns.

Author: Shields, Ann 1275
Series: Catholic Bible Study Guide
Title: *Intercession: A Guide to Effective Prayer*
Publisher: Servant Publications, 1988 ISBN: 0-89283-397-1

Num. Sess.	Group Time	Num. Pgs.	Avg. Qst.	Price	Audience	Format	Bible Study
9	60-75	76	10	$5.99	Beginner	Workbk	Topical

Features: Intro to Study, Scrpt Memory Helps, Charts
★★★ Personal Application Preparation Time: Low
★ Relationship Building Ldr. Guide: No Size: 5.0 x 8.0
Subjects: Prayer
Comments: This 9-lesson study on intercessory prayer is designed to prepare students for more effective prayer. It offers practical, Scripture-based teaching that will enable the student to pray for family, friends, relatives, neighbors, and his or her church. Structurally, it is divided into three topical areas and features Scripture texts, commentary on the Scripture, questions and exercises, and tips for practical application.

Author: Shores, Steve 1276
Series: IBC Discussion Guide
Title: *Stress*
Publisher: NavPress, 1992 ISBN: 0-89109-686-8

Num. Sess.	Group Time	Num. Pgs.	Avg. Qst.	Price	Audience	Format	Bible Study
5	60-90	64	7	$5.00	Beginner	Workbk	Topical

Features: Intro to Leading a Study, Intro to Study, Prayer Helps, Follow Up, Ldr's Notes
★★★★ Personal Application Preparation Time: None
★★★★ Relationship Building Ldr. Guide: No Size: 5.25 x 8.25
Subjects: Counseling, Stress, Support
Comments: "Stress" is 1 of 6 studies that identify how life struggles affect the way participants relate to themselves, others, and God. Five lessons explore the common sources of stress, the weariness that accompanies stress, which kinds of stress leads to burnout and which don't, how to avoid stress you bring on yourself, and how faith can help you transform your exhaustion from stress into endurance.

Author: Sibley, Larry 1277
Series: Fisherman Bible Studyguide
Title: *Matthew: People of the Kingdom*
Publisher: Shaw, 1988 ISBN: 0-87788-537-0

Num. Sess.	Group Time	Num. Pgs.	Avg. Qst.	Price	Audience	Format	Bible Study
14	45-60	96	10	$4.99	Beginner	Workbk	Book

Features: Intro to Leading a Study, Intro to Study, Prayer Helps, Ldr's Notes, Charts, Maps
★★ Personal Application Preparation Time: None
★★ Relationship Building Ldr. Guide: No Size: 5.0 x 8.25
Subjects: Jesus: Life/Teaching, Matthew, Obedience
Comments: This chapter-by-chapter study of Matthew will help participants discover how to submit to Jesus Christ, the Father, and the Holy Spirit. It defines what it means to be a citizen of the Kingdom of God; it defines submission to human authority, a point of tension or confusion for many; it defines what human life and community look like when they come under the gracious rule of God.

Author: Sibley, Larry 1278
Series: Shaw Contemporary Issues
Title: *Spiritual Disciplines*
Publisher: Shaw, 1992 ISBN: 0-87788-776-4

Num. Sess.	Group Time	Num. Pgs.	Avg. Qst.	Price	Audience	Format	Bible Study
8	30-45	48	8	$4.99	Beginner	Workbk	Topical

Features: Intro to Leading a Study, Intro to Study, Objectives, Bibliography, Prayer Helps,Follow Up, Ldr's Notes
★★★★ Personal Application Preparation Time: Low
★★★ Relationship Building Ldr. Guide: No Size: 5.25 x 8.25
Subjects: Fasting, Prayer, Worship
Comments: Eight brief lessons explore the disciplines of a joyful life in Christ. Those disciplines include: "Time for God"; "Meditation: Soaking up God's Words"; "Prayer: Bringing Our Lives into God's Presence"; "Fasting: The Hunger that Satisfies"; "The Healing Sollitude"; "Receiving Spiritual Direction"; "Sabbath Time and Worship: Going to Jerusalem." The author suggests journaling.

Author: Sibley, Larry **1279**
Series: Fisherman Bible Studyguide
Title: *Worship: Discovering What Scripture Says*
Publisher: Shaw, 1993 ISBN: 0-87788-911-2

Num. Sess.	Group Time	Num. Pgs.	Avg. Qst.	Price	Audience	Format	Bible Study
13	45-60	78	12	$4.99	New Christian	Workbk	Topical

Features: Intro to Leading a Study, Intro to Study, Ldr's Notes
★★★★ Personal Application Preparation Time: None
★★ Relationship Building Ldr. Guide: No Size: 5.25 x 8.25
Subjects: Worship
Comments: To help participants understand what Scripture teaches about worshiping "in spirit and truth" and how to enter God's presence, this study uses stories of godly people to show what God desires from His people. Readers join Abraham as he prays under a lonely tree; hear God's Word from Moses; rejoice in procession with David; cry out in pain and praise with the psalmist; welcome children as they come to Jesus; bless God in prayer with Paul.

Author: Simundson, Daniel J. **1280**
Series: Friendship Bible Study
Title: *Esther*
Publisher: Augsburg Fortress Publishers, 1987

Num. Sess.	Group Time	Num. Pgs.	Avg. Qst.	Price	Audience	Format	Bible Study
8	60-75	48	8	$3.75	New Christian	Workbk	Book

Features: Intro to Study, Prayer Helps, Study Overview
★★★★ Personal Application Preparation Time: Low
★★★★ Relationship Building Ldr. Guide: Yes Size: 5.50 x 8.50
Subjects: Bible Personalities, Esther, God's Promises, Women's Issues
Comments: This 8-lesson study of Esther raises questions about how Christians and Jews relate to one another, how governments are often hostile to religious people, how (directly or indirectly) God works in the world to keep promises, and how God chooses women as well as men for important tasks. The lesson format includes an overview, an opening, a responsive reading, Bible background, questions for reflection, a key verse, a prayer response, and an "our faith" response.

Author: Simundson, Daniel J. **1281**
Series: Search Weekly Bible
Title: *Unit 14/Job*
Publisher: Augsburg Fortress Publishers, 1986

Num. Sess.	Group Time	Num. Pgs.	Avg. Qst.	Price	Audience	Format	Bible Study
8	90-105	64	Vary	$5.50	New Christian	Book	Book

Features: Intro to Study, Objectives, Prayer Helps, Worship Helps, Follow Up, Summary
★★ Personal Application Preparation Time: Med
★★ Relationship Building Ldr. Guide: Yes Size: 8.50 x 11.0
Subjects: Job, Suffering
Comments: Key passages of Job are examined in-depth. Goals for this unit include: to learn the story of Job, his counselors, and his God; to increase awareness of how a sufferer thinks and feels; to become better ministers to one another in times of suffering. Sessions include: "God and Satan Make a Deal"; "The Impatience of Job"; "Eliphaz Gives Job Some Answers"; "The Ingratitude of Job"; "What Is Job's Hope?"

Author: Singleton, James **1282**
Series: Serendipity Support Group
Title: *Single Again: Life After Divorce*
Publisher: Serendipity House, 1991 ISBN: 1-88341-970-0

Num. Sess.	Group Time	Num. Pgs.	Avg. Qst.	Price	Audience	Format	Bible Study
7	60-90	96	12	$5.45	Beginner	Workbk	Topical

Features: Intro to Leading a Study, Objectives, Bibliography, Prayer Helps, Full Scrpt Printed, Ldr's Notes, Cartoons, Agenda
★★★★ Personal Application Preparation Time: None
★★★★ Relationship Building Ldr. Guide: No Size: 6.50 x 9.0
Subjects: Anger, Divorce, Forgiveness, Loneliness, Singles' Issues
Comments: This study is for any divorced person who is ready and willing to embrace a new life of singleness. It deals with failure of marriage, blame, handling anger, power of forgiveness, releasing the past, loneliness and self-pity, refocusing, trust and new friendships. The format includes icebreakers, Bible study, and prayer. Timelines are provided. It can be adapted for a 7- or 14-week study.

Author: Sittser, Jerry **1283**
Series:
Title: *Adventure, The: Putting Energy into Your Walk With God*
Publisher: InterVarsity, 1985 ISBN: 0-87784-335-X

Num. Sess.	Group Time	Num. Pgs.	Avg. Qst.	Price	Audience	Format	Bible Study
19	30-60	240	5	$10.99	New Christian	Book	Topical

Features:
★★★ Personal Application Preparation Time: Low
★★ Relationship Building Ldr. Guide: No Size: 5.50 x 8.25
Subjects: Christian Living
Comments: This book uses group questions and the author's personal stories to springboard into lessons on how discipleship should transform every part of life. It is divided into 6 parts titled: "Making Sense out of Discipleship"; "Beginning With God"; "God's Goal for Our Growth"; "Knowing the Enemy"; and "Saint-Making." Groups can cover more than one chapter at a time.

Author: Sloan, John D. **1284**
Series: The Knowing God Series
Title: *Our Faithful Friend: Building Intimacy with God*
Publisher: Zondervan, 1994 ISBN: 0-31048-301-8

Num. Sess.	Group Time	Num. Pgs.	Avg. Qst.	Price	Audience	Format	Bible Study
6	45-60	64	12	$4.99	Beginner	Workbk	Topical

Features: Intro to Leading a Study, Intro to Study, Objectives, Prayer Helps, Scrpt Memory Helps, Follow Up, Ldr's Notes
★★★★ Personal Application Preparation Time: Low
★★★ Relationship Building Ldr. Guide: No Size: 5.50 x 8.50
Subjects: God
Comments: One of 8 in a series, this guide can help participants build a stronger and deeper friendship with God. It looks at the examples of those who knew God intimately—Abraham, Sarah, David, Joshua, Jeremiah, Paul, and the Lord Jesus Himself. Also studied are God's promises to those seeking His friendship: in Genesis, Joshua, the Psalms, Lamentations, 1 Corinthians, and the Gospel of John.

Author: Smalley, Gary & John Trent, Ph.D. **1285**
Series:
Title: *Blessing, The: A Study Guide for Small Groups*
Publisher: NavPress, 1988 ISBN: 0-89109-275-7

Num. Sess.	Group Time	Num. Pgs.	Avg. Qst.	Price	Audience	Format	Bible Study
12	60-90	102	Vary	$6.00	Beginner	Workbk	Topical

Features: Intro to Study, Digging Deeper Quest
★★★ Personal Application Preparation Time: Med
★★★ Relationship Building Ldr. Guide: No Size: 5.50 x 8.50
Subjects: Emotions, Relationships
Comments: This study's message, that everyone has a God-given need to feel blessed, helps participants find emotional healing and experience restored relationships with God, family, and friends. A companion book is optional; however, key principles from the companion book are presented. The format includes excerpts from the book, paraphrased stories, self-tests, and application-oriented exercises. Designed for group study, it is also suited for personal study.

Author: Smalley, Gary & John Trent **1286**
Series: LifeTopics
Title: *Home Remedies*
Publisher: David C. Cook Publishing Co., 1992 ISBN: 0-78149-137-1

Num. Sess.	Group Time	Num. Pgs.	Avg. Qst.	Price	Audience	Format	Bible Study
13	45-60	136	Vary	$19.95	Beginner	Workbk	Topical

Features: Intro to Leading a Study, Intro to Study, Objectives, Prayer Helps, Drawings, Handouts, Persnl Study Quest, Publicity Ideas
★★★ Personal Application Preparation Time: None
★★★ Relationship Building Ldr. Guide: Yes Size: 8.50 x 11.0
Subjects: Family, Relationships
Comments: This self-contained leader's guide combines learning activities for small group interaction and practical application, with excerpts and biblical teaching from the Smalley and Trent's "Home Remedies." It helps adults of all ages establish and build loving relationships within their families, and is appropriate for singles or marrieds, and beginners through mature Christians. Student books are not required.

Author: Smalley, Gary **1287**
Series: Video Curriculum Resource
Title: *Love Is A Decision*
Publisher: Word, 1991 ISBN: 0-84998-004-6

Num. Sess.	Group Time	Num. Pgs.	Avg. Qst.	Price	Audience	Format	Bible Study
6	60-90	N/A	7	$129.99	Beginner	Video	Topical

Features: Book Incl, Video Study Guide
★★★★ Personal Application Preparation Time: None
★★★ Relationship Building Ldr. Guide: No Size: 10.0 x 12.50
Subjects: Love, Marriage, Relationships, Singles' Issues, Young Marrieds
Comments: This 6-part Bible-centered video series outlines a clear action plan that points the way to vital, healthy, growing relationships for engaged couples, newlyweds, and veteran marrieds. The 35″–50″ sessions include: "The Incredible Worth of a Woman," "How to Energize Your Mate in 60 Seconds," "The Tremendous Value of a Man," and more. The brief study guide is reproducible.

Author: Smith, Harold Ivan **1288**
Series:
Title: *One Is a Whole Number*
Publisher: Gospel Films, 1990 ISBN: 1-55568-112-3

Num. Sess.	Group Time	Num. Pgs.	Avg. Qst.	Price	Audience	Format	Bible Study
4	75-90	19	13	$59.95	Beginner	Video	Topical

Features: Bibliography, Follow Up, Photos, Video Study Guide
★★★ Personal Application Preparation Time: None
★★ Relationship Building Ldr. Guide: No Size: 8.50 x 11.0
Subjects: Commitments, Divorce, Marriage, Sexual Issues, Singles' Issues
Comments: This 4-part video series presents Christ as the prime example of the single adult lifestyle. There are 4 40″ episodes that present biblical truths about singleness, marriage, divorce, and sexuality through lecture and drama. The study guide includes a key quote, Scripture, and question; something to talk about, and think about; and an activity for each video segment.

Author: Smith, Joseph E. **1289**
Series:
Title: *How to Win in Spiritual Warfare—Volume 1*
Publisher: Maranatha Publications, 1984 ISBN: 0-91892-301-8

Num. Sess.	Group Time	Num. Pgs.	Avg. Qst.	Price	Audience	Format	Bible Study
13	60-90	98	Vary	$7.95	Beginner	Workbk	Topical

Features: Intro to Study
★★★ Personal Application Preparation Time: Med
★★ Relationship Building Ldr. Guide: No Size: 8.50 x 11.0
Subjects: Emotions, Grief, Joy, Love, Marriage, Relationships, Satan
Comments: This is the first volume in a 3-part study on winning in spiritual warfare. It points out that Satan often succeeds because Christians don't know their authority and how to use it. This study examines principles and concepts for developing and using that authority. Topics include how the war began and ended, love, envy, fear, covetousness, joy, depression, grief, worry, and more. Each of the 13 lessons ends with a series of fill-in-the-blank questions.

Author: Smith, Joseph E. **1290**
Series:
Title: *How to Win in Spiritual Warfare—Volume 2*
Publisher: Maranatha Publications, 1988 ISBN: 0-91892-302-6

Num. Sess.	Group Time	Num. Pgs.	Avg. Qst.	Price	Audience	Format	Bible Study
13	60-90	172	Vary	$8.95	Beginner	Workbk	Topical

Features: Intro to Study
★★★ Personal Application Preparation Time: Med
★★ Relationship Building Ldr. Guide: No Size: 8.50 x 11.0
Subjects: Emotions, Relationships, Satan
Comments: This is the second volume in a 3-part study on winning in spiritual warfare. It points out that Satan often succeeds because Christians don't know their authority and how to use it. This study examines principles and concepts for developing and using that authority. Topics include the invisible war, long-suffering, anger, resentment, impatience, gentleness, judgment, goodness, rejection, and more. Each of the 13 lessons ends with fill-in-the-blank questions.

Author: Smith, Joyce Marie **1291**
Series: New Life Bible Studies
Title: *Learning to Talk with God*
Publisher: Tyndale House, 1976 ISBN: 0-84232-140-3

Num. Sess.	Group Time	Num. Pgs.	Avg. Qst.	Price	Audience	Format	Bible Study
12	45-60	62	10	$3.95	New Christian	Workbk	Topical

Features: Intro to Leading a Study, Intro to Study, Bibliography, Prayer Helps
★★★ Personal Application Preparation Time: Low
★★ Relationship Building Ldr. Guide: No Size: 5.0 x 7.50
Subjects: Prayer, Women's Issues
Comments: This 12-lesson study on prayer is especially designed for Christian women. It is recommended for groups of 10 to 12. The structure of each lesson includes Scripture reading, definitions, discussion questions, and group interaction. Study subject matter includes the importance of prayer, the elements of prayer, praise in prayer, hindrances to prayer, Old and New Testament prayer examples.

Author: Smith, Joyce Marie **1292**
Series: New Life Bible Studies
Title: *Understanding Your Emotions*
Publisher: Tyndale House, 1977 ISBN: 0-84237-770-0

Num. Sess.	Group Time	Num. Pgs.	Avg. Qst.	Price	Audience	Format	Bible Study
12	45-60	60	10	$3.99	New Christian	Workbk	Topical

Features: Intro to Leading a Study, Intro to Study, Bibliography, Prayer Helps
★★★ Personal Application Preparation Time: Low
★★ Relationship Building Ldr. Guide: No Size: 5.0 x 7.50
Subjects: Emotions, Women's Issues
Comments: This study, a comprehensive guide to freedom from the negative side effects of emotions, is a liberating look at how God deals with His people when their hearts are right before Him. It explores emotions such as worry, anxiety, fear, anger, guilt, jealousy, pride, criticism, and gossip. Also included are prayers to help people commit one emotion each week to God.

Author: Smith, Joyce Marie **1293**
Series: New Life Bible Studies
Title: *Woman's Priorities, A*
Publisher: Tyndale House, 1976 ISBN: 0-84238-380-8

Num. Sess.	Group Time	Num. Pgs.	Avg. Qst.	Price	Audience	Format	Bible Study
12	45-60	63	10	$3.99	Beginner	Workbk	Charctr

Features: Intro to Leading a Study, Intro to Study, Bibliography, Summary
★★ Personal Application Preparation Time: Low
★★ Relationship Building Ldr. Guide: No Size: 5.0 x 7.50
Subjects: Bible Personalities, Failure, Success, Women's Issues
Comments: This study uses the lives of 11 women in the Bible—Rahab, Ruth, Sarah, Hannah, Priscilla, and others—to lead to a description of the "ideal woman" of Proverbs 31. The study portrays the Bible examples honestly, without glossing over their weaknesses or exaggerating their virtues.

Author: Smith, Tim **1294**
Series: SonPower Youth Sources
Title: *Eight Habits of an Effective Youth Worker*
Publisher: Victor Books, 1995 ISBN: 1-56476-406-0

Num. Sess.	Group Time	Num. Pgs.	Avg. Qst.	Price	Audience	Format	Bible Study
	—	190	N/A	$8.99		Book	

Features:
Personal Application Preparation Time:
Relationship Building Ldr. Guide: Size: 6.0 x 9.0
Subjects: Teens: Resources
Comments: This book introduces an entirely new paradigm for youth ministry. The author evaluates the best material in the fields of leadership and human performance against the authority of Scripture, then develops concepts which are distinctive and biblical.

Author: Smith, Tim **1295**
Series:
Title: *"Hi, I'm Bob and I'm the Parent of a Teenager."*
Publisher: Gospel Light Publications, 1991 ISBN: 0-83071-465-0

Num. Sess.	Group Time	Num. Pgs.	Avg. Qst.	Price	Audience	Format	Bible Study
7	60-75	128	Vary	$14.99	Beginner	Workbk	Topical

Features: Intro to Leading a Study, Bibliography, Drawings
★★★★ Personal Application Preparation Time: None
★★★★ Relationship Building Ldr. Guide: No Size: 8.50 x 11.0
Subjects: Parenting, Support, Teens: Family
Comments: This 7-session course focuses on biblical principles of parenting, and explains 7 building blocks to becoming effective parents. It's designed to help youth ministers launch peer-led parent support groups. Parents will learn how to: understand changes of both parents and teens, build a teen's self-esteem, avoid unnecessary conflicts, help teens become independent and responsible, stop trying to control teens and start to influence them instead, and more.

Author: Snowden, Mark, et al. **1296**
Series:
Title: *Meeting The World: Ministering Cross-Culturally*
Publisher: New Hope, 1992 ISBN: 1-56309-020-1

Num. Sess.	Group Time	Num. Pgs.	Avg. Qst.	Price	Audience	Format	Bible Study
	—	71	N/A	$3.95			

Features:
Personal Application Preparation Time:
Relationship Building Ldr. Guide: No Size: 5.50 x 8.50
Subjects: Cults, New Age, Singles' Issues, Small Group Resource
Comments: This book offers advice on how to understand people of other cultures and religions, and how to form relationships with them that exemplify Jesus' saving love. Chapters deal with meeting the Hispanic world, Chinese world, Hindu world, Muslims, people involved in the New Age movement, the Mormons, Jehovah's witnesses, and members of the Way International. It helps participants understand diverse cultures, needs, and viewpoints.

Author: Snyder, Linda **1297**
Series: Group's Active Bible Curriculum
Title: *School Struggles*
Publisher: Group Publishing, 1990 ISBN: 1-55945-201-3

Num. Sess.	Group Time	Num. Pgs.	Avg. Qst.	Price	Audience	Format	Bible Study
4	35-60	46	Vary	$9.99	Beginner	Workbk	Topical

Features: Intro to Leading a Study, Intro to Study, Objectives, Study Overview, Ldr's Notes, Handouts, Agenda, Publicity Ideas
★★★ Personal Application Preparation Time: None
★★★ Relationship Building Ldr. Guide: No Size: 8.50 x 11.0
Subjects: Teens: Decisions, Teens: Senior High, Teens: Youth Life
Comments: This study will help teenagers discover practical tips on studying more effectively, improving grades, resisting cheating, and balancing their active schedules. It also helps teenagers set school and extracurricular priorities and attainable goals. The course can be adapted for use in a Bible class or youth meeting. Activities and Bible studies are included as separate sheets that can be reproduced.

Author: Sorenson, Stephen and Amanda **1298**
Series:
Title: *Living Smart, Spending Less Workbook*
Publisher: Moody Press, 1994 ISBN: 0-80244-931-X

Num. Sess.	Group Time	Num. Pgs.	Avg. Qst.	Price	Audience	Format	Bible Study
14	90-120	190	Vary	$12.99	Beginner	Workbk	Topical

Features: No Grp Discussion Quest, Charts
★★★★ Personal Application Preparation Time: Med
★★★ Relationship Building Ldr. Guide: No Size: 7.50 x 10.0
Subjects: Family, Materialism, Money, Self-help, Support
Comments: This workbook helps participants discover how to take steps toward financial improvement, spend and save wisely. It covers areas in which people make daily financial decisions, and provides money-saving tips on life's big decisions. Subjects include shopping smart, buying homes, reducing home energy costs, buying and caring for clothing, saving money on food, caring for cars, saving on car insurance, and reducing the expense of flying.

Author: Sproul, R.C. **1299**
Series:
Title: *Ultimate Issues: Right Answers to Wrong Thinking*
Publisher: Gospel Films, 1990

Num. Sess.	Group Time	Num. Pgs.	Avg. Qst.	Price	Audience	Format	Bible Study
4	60-75	N/A	10	$19.95	Beginner	Video	Topical

Features: Intro to Study, Objectives, Video Study Guide
★★★★ Personal Application Preparation Time: None
★★★★ Relationship Building Ldr. Guide: No Size: 4.25 x 7.50
Subjects: Teens: Bible Study, Teens: Evangelism, Teens: Theology
Comments: In this 4-part video series (30″ messages), Dr. Sproul answers the deepest challenges confronting young people today. Interspersed with teen interviews from across the country, Sproul shows that there are only 2 worldviews, that God exists and we disregard His Word, and that Christ is the only way to God. Young people who want to stand for God are faced with opposition and false thinking. They need ammunition, and this series can help.

Author: Stanley, Charles F. **1300**
Series:
Title: *Handle with Prayer*
Publisher: Victor Books, 1982 ISBN: 0-88207-309-5

Num. Sess.	Group Time	Num. Pgs.	Avg. Qst.	Price	Audience	Format	Bible Study
13	60-75	120	N/A	$8.99	New Christian	Book	Topical

Features:
★★★★ Personal Application Preparation Time: Low
★★★★ Relationship Building Ldr. Guide: Yes Size: 5.50 x 8.0
Subjects: Prayer, Time
Comments: In this 13-week study, participants will realize that prayer and waiting go hand in hand. Lesson titles include "Praying with Authority"; "Answered Prayer"; "How to Pray in the Will of God"; "A Time to Wait, a Time to Act"; "Praying for Others"; "The Warfare of Prayer"; and more. A leader's guide includes many helps and reproducible transparency masters.

Author: Stark, Tom & Joan **1301**
Series: Fisherman Bible Studyguide
Title: *Guidance & God's Will*
Publisher: Shaw, 1978 ISBN: 0-87788-324-6

Num. Sess.	Group Time	Num. Pgs.	Avg. Qst.	Price	Audience	Format	Bible Study
11	45-60	78	9	$4.99	Beginner	Workbk	Topical

Features: Intro to Leading a Study, Intro to Study, Follow Up, Full Scrpt Printed
★★ Personal Application Preparation Time: None
★ Relationship Building Ldr. Guide: No Size: 5.0 x 8.25
Subjects: Christian Living, God, Holy Spirit
Comments: Searching the life of Paul, this study exposes principles which apply to daily life. The first three segments deal with God's will; 4–5, the Holy Spirit's guidance; studies 6–10, God's guidance and personal preference, good sense, circumstances, counsel, and sovereignty; 11–12 trusting God for guidance.

Author: St. Clair, Barry **1302**
Series:
Title: *Building Leaders For Strategic Youth Ministry*
Publisher: Victor Books, 1991 ISBN: 0-89693-288-5

Num. Sess.	Group Time	Num. Pgs.	Avg. Qst.	Price	Audience	Format	Bible Study
36	45-60	144	5		New Christian	Workbk	Topical

Features: Intro to Study, Scrpt Memory Helps, Drawings, Charts, Appendix
★★★★ Personal Application Preparation Time: Low
★★★★ Relationship Building Ldr. Guide: No Size: 8.50 x 11.0
Subjects: Teens: Resources
Comments: This book is for training adults willing to work with youth. The workbook provides 3 12-session units for individual or small group study, instructions for group leaders and a list of additional or optional resources. The study addresses a leader's personal relationship with Jesus Christ, vision for life and ministry, and knowledge and skills for working with youth.

Author: St. Clair, Barry & Bill Jones 1303
Series: SonPower Youth Sources
Title: *Dating: Going Out in Style*
Publisher: Victor Books, 1993 ISBN: 1-56476-189-4

Num. Sess.	Group Time	Num. Pgs.	Avg. Qst.	Price	Audience	Format	Bible Study
12	45-75	154	Vary	$5.99	New Christian	Workbk	Topical

Features: Intro to Study, Objectives, Scrpt Memory Helps
★★★★ Personal Application Preparation Time: Med
★★★ Relationship Building Ldr. Guide: Yes Size: 6.0 x 9.0
Subjects: Teens: Sexuality
Comments: This study offers biblical, practical, humorous advice on dating and not dating, with creative ideas and alternatives for date activities. It addresses the following questions: How do I decide who to go out with? What should I do if I'm not dating? When should I go out with just one person? How can I make sure I date a winner? Should I date non-Christians? How can I break up with someone without anyone getting hurt? and Just how many creative ideas are there for dates?

Author: St. Clair, Barry 1304
Series: Moving Toward Maturity
Title: *Following Jesus—Book 1*
Publisher: Victor Books, 1983 ISBN: 0-88207-301-X

Num. Sess.	Group Time	Num. Pgs.	Avg. Qst.	Price	Audience	Format	Bible Study
10	60-90	132	Vary	$5.99	Beginner	Workbk	Topical

Features: Objectives, Scrpt Memory Helps, Drawings, Cartoons
★★★ Personal Application Preparation Time: Low
★★★ Relationship Building Ldr. Guide: Yes Size: 5.25 x 8.0
Subjects: Teens: Bible Study, Teens: Discipleship, Teens: Junior High, Teens: New Testament
Comments: This study introduces participants to the basics of discipleship: becoming children of God; developing relationships with Christ; discovering God's purposes, love, and will; learning Bible study and prayer; and putting God first. It contains ten Bible studies, ten memory verse cards, and a "Bible Response Sheet" for use in a daily study of 1 John. A leader's guide gives an overview.

Author: St. Clair, Barry 1305
Series: Moving Toward Maturity
Title: *Giving Away Your Faith--Book 4*
Publisher: Victor Books, 1991 ISBN: 0-89693-297-4

Num. Sess.	Group Time	Num. Pgs.	Avg. Qst.	Price	Audience	Format	Bible Study
10	75-90	166	Vary	$5.99	Mature Christian	Workbk	Topical

Features: Intro to Study, Scrpt Memory Helps, Drawings, Persnl Study Quest
★★★★ Personal Application Preparation Time: Med
★★★★ Relationship Building Ldr. Guide: Yes Size: 5.50 x 8.50
Subjects: Teens: Christian Liv, Teens: Discipleship, Teens: Evangelism, Teens: Friends
Comments: This 10-lesson study helps students as they begin sharing their testimony with non-Christians. It helps them overcome fears and know exactly what to say as they express their faith to their friends. Lessons prepare youth to: build relationships with non-Christians, start conversations about Jesus Christ, lead others to Christ.

Author: St. Clair, Barry 1306
Series: Moving Toward Maturity
Title: *Influencing Your World—Book 5*
Publisher: Victor Books, 1991 ISBN: 0-89693-294-X

Num. Sess.	Group Time	Num. Pgs.	Avg. Qst.	Price	Audience	Format	Bible Study
10	60-90	168	Vary	$5.99	New Christian	Workbk	Topical

Features: Prayer Helps, Scrpt Memory Helps, Follow Up, Drawings
★★★★ Personal Application Preparation Time: Med
★★★★ Relationship Building Ldr. Guide: Yes Size: 5.50 x 8.50
Subjects: Teens: Friends, Teens: Relationships, Teens:Spiritual Gift
Comments: Through this 10 week study youth can learn how to respond as God calls them to help others, build loving relationships, identify and use spiritual gifts, serve unselfishly, minister to the overlooked and neglected, and multiply their lives by helping others grow in Christ. This is the final book in the Moving Toward Maturity series. For best results begin with Book 1 and work consecutively through all 5 books. This book can be used in group, individual, or buddy studies.

Author: St. Clair, Barry 1307
Series: SonPower Youth Sources
Title: *Love: Making it Last*
Publisher: Victor Books, 1993 ISBN: 1-56476-188-6

Num. Sess.	Group Time	Num. Pgs.	Avg. Qst.	Price	Audience	Format	Bible Study
12	45-75	147	Vary	$5.99	New Christian	Workbk	Topical

Features: Intro to Study, Objectives, Scrpt Memory Helps
★★★★ Personal Application Preparation Time: Med
★★★ Relationship Building Ldr. Guide: Yes Size: 6.0 x 9.0
Subjects: Teens: Sexuality
Comments: This book offers practical discussion about the pursuit of love and a lasting relationship. It answers such questions as: What does falling in love really mean? What should I do if someone breaks up with me? What qualities does true love have? How do I build a relationship with someone of the opposite sex? What should I do if we get into a fight? and How do I know if I've found the "right one"? The leader's guide outlines a five lesson plan.

Author: St. Clair, Barry 1308
Series: Moving Toward Maturity
Title: *Making Jesus Lord—Book 3*
Publisher: Victor Books, 1991 ISBN: 0-89693-293-1

Num. Sess.	Group Time	Num. Pgs.	Avg. Qst.	Price	Audience	Format	Bible Study
10	60-90	144	Vary	$5.99	New Christian	Workbk	Topical

Features: Prayer Helps, Scrpt Memory Helps, Follow Up, Drawings
★★★★ Personal Application Preparation Time: Med
★★★★ Relationship Building Ldr. Guide: Yes Size: 5.50 x 8.50
Subjects: Teens: Discipleship, Teens: Youth Life
Comments: This 10-week study helps youth develop clearer understanding of the awesomeness of God the Father, Jesus, and the Holy Spirit, and examines Jesus' credentials to see why He wants to call the shots in their day-to-day lives (grades, sports, possesions, friends, dating, and habits). It helps them learn how Jesus' power can become their power. This is the third book in the series, and for best results they should be studied in numerical order.

Author: St. Clair, Barry & Keith Naylor **1309**
Series: SonPower Youth Sources
Title: *Penetrating The Campus: Reaching Kids Where They Are*
Publisher: Victor Books, 1993 ISBN: 1-56476-085-5

Num. Sess.	Group Time	Num. Pgs.	Avg. Qst.	Price	Audience	Format	Bible Study
12	45-60	220	4	$8.99	New Christian	Workbk	Topical

Features: Appendix
★★★★ Personal Application Preparation Time: Low
★★ Relationship Building Ldr. Guide: No Size: 6.0 x 9.0
Subjects: Teens: Evangelism, Teens: Resources, Teens: Senior High
Comments: This book gives in-depth, practical advice for communicating God's love to high school students. The detailed strategy presented helps youth leaders bridge the gap between their ministry and the public school campus, probably the most important mission field in America today. Youth leaders can study this book in several ways: alone, with other youth workers in a small group, or with youth workers in their church. Questions are provided for group discussion.

Author: St. Clair, Barry & Bill Jones **1310**
Series: SonPower Youth Sources
Title: *Sex: Desiring the Best*
Publisher: Victor Books, 1993 ISBN: 1-56476-190-8

Num. Sess.	Group Time	Num. Pgs.	Avg. Qst.	Price	Audience	Format	Bible Study
12	45-75	179	5	$5.99	New Christian	Workbk	Topical

Features: Intro to Study, Objectives
★★★★ Personal Application Preparation Time: Med
★★★ Relationship Building Ldr. Guide: Yes Size: 6.0 x 9.0
Subjects: Teens: Sexuality
Comments: This study provides straight answers to young people's most common question about sex, and explains why God designed sex to be confined to marriage. It responds to the following questions: How far is too far? How do I keep from being pressured into sex? Why is it so difficult to figure out the opposite sex? Is lust abnormal? How do I straighten out the past? We're pregnant—What do we do? and How do I get my sexual desires under control?

Author: St. Clair, Barry **1311**
Series: Moving Toward Maturity
Title: *Spending Time Alone with God—Book 2*
Publisher: Victor Books, 1984 ISBN: 0-88207-302-8

Num. Sess.	Group Time	Num. Pgs.	Avg. Qst.	Price	Audience	Format	Bible Study
10	60-90	144	Vary	$5.99	New Christian	Workbk	Topical

Features: Intro to Study, Prayer Helps, Scrpt Memory Helps, Drawings, Cartoons, Appendix
★★★ Personal Application Preparation Time: Low
★★★ Relationship Building Ldr. Guide: Yes Size: 5.25 x 8.0
Subjects: Teens: Bible Study, Teens: Junior High, Teens: Prayer
Comments: This study helps participants discover the value of time alone with God, what it can do in their lives, and how to achieve it. It is a workable plan for developing personal Bible study, and covers communicating with God through praise, thanksgiving, confession, petition, and intercession. It also covers Scripture memory. A leader's guide is available, as well as notebook inserts.

Author: St. Clair, Barry and Carol **1312**
Series: SonPower Youth Sources
Title: *Talking With Your Kids About Love, Sex, and Dating*
Publisher: Victor Books, 1993 ISBN: 1-56476-230-0

Num. Sess.	Group Time	Num. Pgs.	Avg. Qst.	Price	Audience	Format	Bible Study
12	45-75	180	N/A	$7.99	New Christian	Workbk	Topical

Features: Intro to Study, Objectives
★★★★ Personal Application Preparation Time: Med
★★★ Relationship Building Ldr. Guide: Yes Size: 6.0 x 9.0
Subjects: Parenting, Teens: Communication, Teens: Sexuality
Comments: This book moves parents beyond the often-dreaded "talk" with their children to a series of conversations designed to build positive biblical values. Parents discover how to: provide straight answers for young questioners, discuss body changes, deal with dating decisions, create in children a desire to wait until marriage, help develop convictions in a world of sexual pressure, and discuss serious relationships.

Author: Stepp, Rex **1313**
Series: Group's Active Bible Curriculum
Title: *Angels, Demons, Miracles & Prayer*
Publisher: Group Publishing, 1993 ISBN: 1-55945-235-8

Num. Sess.	Group Time	Num. Pgs.	Avg. Qst.	Price	Audience	Format	Bible Study
4	35-60	45	Vary	$9.99	Beginner	Workbk	Topical

Features: Intro to Leading a Study, Intro to Study, Objectives, Study Overview, Ldr's Notes, Handouts, Agenda, Publicity Ideas
★★★★ Personal Application Preparation Time: None
★★★★ Relationship Building Ldr. Guide: No Size: 8.50 x 11.0
Subjects: Teens: Heaven/Hell, Teens: Prayer, Teens: Senior High
Comments: Modern teenagers have many questions about the supernatural. In this 4-week course, participants explore the role that angels play, understand demons and how to protect themselves from demonic influences, recognize modern miracles, and understand prayer by exploring ways to express themselves to God. Senior highers will find biblical answers to questions about angels and demons.

Author: Sterk, Andrea & Peter Scazzero **1314**
Series: LifeGuide Bible Study
Title: *Christian Character*
Publisher: InterVarsity, 1985 ISBN: 0-83081-054-4

Num. Sess.	Group Time	Num. Pgs.	Avg. Qst.	Price	Audience	Format	Bible Study
12	45-60	64	12	$4.99	New Christian	Workbk	Topical

Features: Intro to Leading a Study, Intro to Study, Ldr's Notes
★ Personal Application Preparation Time: Low
★ Relationship Building Ldr. Guide: No Size: 5.50 x 8.25
Subjects: Christian Living, Discipleship, Holiness, Holy Spirit, Jesus: Life/Teaching, Obedience, Service
Comments: This study of Christian character focuses on certain qualities which lead one to become the person God wants him to be. Such character comes as the Spirit of God transforms through the Word of God. Discusses justification, establishes the lordship of Jesus Christ, issues a challenge to consider and understand temptation, holiness, compassion, servanthood, self-image, perseverance.

Author: Sterk, Andrea & Peter Scazzero **1315**
Series: LifeGuide Bible Study
Title: *Christian Disciplines*
Publisher: InterVarsity, 1985 ISBN: 0-83081-055-2

Num. Sess.	Group Time	Num. Pgs.	Avg. Qst.	Price	Audience	Format	Bible Study
12	45-60	64	13	$4.99	New Christian	Workbk	Topical

Features: Intro to Leading a Study, Intro to Study, Ldr's Notes
★ Personal Application Preparation Time: Low
★ Relationship Building Ldr. Guide: No Size: 5.50 x 8.25
Subjects: Accountability, Bible Study, Discipleship, Missions, Prayer, Social Issues, Stewardship, Time, Worship
Comments: This is a discussion of the discipline required to achieve spiritual depth. Strengthening character and deepening one's relationship with Christ in the areas of prayer, Bible study, quiet time, evangelism, social justice, the church, missions, managing time and gifts, guidance, worship, giving, and discipling all help build depth, strength, wisdom, and maturity.

Author: Stevens, Paul **1316**
Series: LifeGuide Bible Study
Title: *End Times: Practical Heavenly Mindedness*
Publisher: InterVarsity, 1994 ISBN: 0-83081-072-2

Num. Sess.	Group Time	Num. Pgs.	Avg. Qst.	Price	Audience	Format	Bible Study
13	45-60	80	11	$4.99	New Christian	Workbk	Topical

Features: Intro to Leading a Study, Intro to Study, Ldr's Notes
★★ Personal Application Preparation Time: Low
★★ Relationship Building Ldr. Guide: No Size: 5.50 x 8.25
Subjects: Apocalyptic
Comments: This study provides an overview of biblical teaching on the end times, thus helping participants prepare to face the future. It deals with fundamental questions, such as: What will happen when I die? Will the world end with a fizzle or a bang? Will things get worse or better? Does my work in this world have any lasting significance? Why be good if the world will be blown up anyway? What will heaven be like? Who will go there?

Author: Stevens, Paul **1317**
Series: LifeGuide Bible Study
Title: *Revelation: The Triumph of God*
Publisher: InterVarsity, 1987 ISBN: 0-83081-021-8

Num. Sess.	Group Time	Num. Pgs.	Avg. Qst.	Price	Audience	Format	Bible Study
12	45-60	64	12	$4.99	New Christian	Workbk	Book

Features: Intro to Leading a Study, Intro to Study, Ldr's Notes
★ Personal Application Preparation Time: Low
★ Relationship Building Ldr. Guide: No Size: 5.50 x 8.25
Subjects: Church Life, God, Hope, Revelation
Comments: This study of Revelation is divided into 3 parts. Part 1 includes 5 studies on Christ and the 7 churches (Rev. 1–5). In Part 2, 4 studies focus on key themes (Rev. 6–18); while Part 3 contains 3 studies on the concluding visions (Rev. 19–22). Jesus gave John the vision he recorded in the Book of Revelation, to offer hope. Revelation, which deals with future shock, fear of persecution, and collaboration with a sick society, is relevant today.

Author: Stevens, Paul & Gerry Schoberg **1318**
Series: Fisherman Bible Studyguide
Title: *Satisfying Work: Christian Living from Nine to Five*
Publisher: Shaw, 1989 ISBN: 0-87788-752-7

Num. Sess.	Group Time	Num. Pgs.	Avg. Qst.	Price	Audience	Format	Bible Study
13	45-60	92	10	$4.99	Beginner	Workbk	Topical

Features: Intro to Leading a Study, Intro to Study, Prayer Helps, Ldr's Notes
★★★ Personal Application Preparation Time: None
★★ Relationship Building Ldr. Guide: No Size: 5.0 x 8.25
Subjects: Christian Living, Ethics, Success, Women's Issues, Work
Comments: This study from Genesis to Revelation will help answer the question, What is a Christian view of work? It explores issues such as ethics, success and prosperity, creative rest, the value of homemaking, and meaningful ministry. Discovering God's design for modern-day work in the Scriptures is not simple because a new set of satisfactions exists today. Today jobs must be appropriate to a person's talents.

Author: Stevens, Paul & Dan Williams **1319**
Series: LifeGuide Bible Study
Title: *1 Corinthians: The Challenges of Life Together*
Publisher: InterVarsity, 1988 ISBN: 0-83081-009-9

Num. Sess.	Group Time	Num. Pgs.	Avg. Qst.	Price	Audience	Format	Bible Study
13	45-60	80	12	$4.99	New Christian	Workbk	Book

Features: Intro to Leading a Study, Intro to Study, Ldr's Notes
★ Personal Application Preparation Time: Low
★ Relationship Building Ldr. Guide: No Size: 5.50 x 8.25
Subjects: Marriage, Relationships, Singles' Issues, Spiritual Gifts, 1 Corinthians
Comments: Paul's advice to the Corinthians is practical for people today who seek fellowship with others in and out of a church setting. Paul deals with issues such as cliques and power struggles, people who think they are spiritually or intellectually superior, immorality, exercising one's rights, marriage, singleness, and spiritual gifts. Paul specifically addresses matters which distressed the church at Corinth.

Author: Stevens, Paul **1320**
Series: LifeGuide Bible Study
Title: *2 Corinthians: Finding Strength in Weakness*
Publisher: InterVarsity, 1990 ISBN: 0-83081-010-2

Num. Sess.	Group Time	Num. Pgs.	Avg. Qst.	Price	Audience	Format	Bible Study
12	45-60	75	10	$4.99	New Christian	Workbk	Topical

Features: Intro to Leading a Study, Intro to Study, Ldr's Notes
★★★ Personal Application Preparation Time: Low
★★★ Relationship Building Ldr. Guide: No Size: 5.50 x 8.25
Subjects: God's Promises, Grace, Hope, Leadership, Relationships, Repentance, Service, Suffering, 2 Corinthians
Comments: This study on finding strength in weakness concerns real relationships, not perfect ones. The apostle Paul delighted in his weaknesses, welcomed hardships and difficulties, and thanked God for obstacles that provided opportunities for experiencing His power. In 2 Corinthians, Paul turns many contemporary values upside down and teaches that in all circumstances.

Author: Stevens, R. Paul & Gerry Schoberg **1321**
Series: Shaw Contemporary Issues
Title: *Fulfilling Work*
Publisher: Shaw, 1991 ISBN: 0-87788-271-1

Num. Sess.	Group Time	Num. Pgs.	Avg. Qst.	Price	Audience	Format	Bible Study
8	30-45	48	5	$4.99	Beginner	Workbk	Topical

Features: Intro to Leading a Study, Intro to Study, Bibliography, Follow Up, Ldr's Notes
★★★★ Personal Application Preparation Time: Low
★★★ Relationship Building Ldr. Guide: No Size: 5.25 x 8.25
Subjects: Ethics, Success, Work
Comments: Eight short lessons help participants answer questions that focus on issues like workplace ethics, creative rest, the value of homemaking, and meaningful ministry. Questions include: What is a Christian's view of work? What is success and prosperity? What makes work fulfilling?

Author: Stevens, R. Paul & Gail **1322**
Series: Fisherman Bible Studyguide
Title: *Marriage: Learning from Couples in Scripture*
Publisher: Shaw, 1991 ISBN: 0-87788-533-8

Num. Sess.	Group Time	Num. Pgs.	Avg. Qst.	Price	Audience	Format	Bible Study
12	45-60	92	12	$4.99	New Christian	Workbk	Topical

Features: Intro to Leading a Study, Intro to Study, Prayer Helps, Follow Up
Personal Application Preparation Time: None
Relationship Building Ldr. Guide: No Size: 5.0 x 8.25
Subjects: Bible Personalities, Marriage
Comments: These lessons explore stories of couples in the Bible, people whose life experiences are amazingly similar to those contemporary couples face. It shows examples of both good and bad relationships. Participants will gain deeper understanding of the marriage covenant, and strengthen the spiritual dimension of their lives together.

Author: Stewart, Ruth Goring **1323**
Series: Global Issues
Title: *Environmental Stewardship*
Publisher: InterVarsity, 1990 ISBN: 0-83084-903-3

Num. Sess.	Group Time	Num. Pgs.	Avg. Qst.	Price	Audience	Format	Bible Study
6	45-60	48	12	$4.99	Beginner	Workbk	Topical

Features: Intro to Leading a Study, Intro to Study, Bibliography
★ Personal Application Preparation Time: Low
★ Relationship Building Ldr. Guide: No Size: 5.50 x 8.25
Subjects: Social Issues
Comments: This 6-week study helps participants examine crucial issues involved in caring for the environment. It helps them become responsible leaders in restoring God's creation to wholeness. Subjects discussed include oil spills, dangerous pesticides, unsanitary sewage dumps, toxic landfills, and nuclear waste. Two important questions explored are ""What attitudes and values have led to the poisoning of our planet?" and "What does this have to do with Christianity?"

Author: Stirrat, Kevin **1324**
Series: Good Word Series
Title: *First Family Tree*
Publisher: David C. Cook Publishing Co., 1994 ISBN: 0-78145-131-0

Num. Sess.	Group Time	Num. Pgs.	Avg. Qst.	Price	Audience	Format	Bible Study
15	60-90	144	15	$9.95	New Christian	Workbk	Book

Features: Intro to Study, Prayer Helps, Worship Helps, Study Overview, Pre-discussion Quest, Full Scrpt Printed, Ldr's Notes, Cartoons, Persnl Study Quest
★★★★ Personal Application Preparation Time: Med
★★★★ Relationship Building Ldr. Guide: Yes Size: 7.25 x 9.25
Subjects: Teens: Discipleship, Teens: Old Testament, Teens: Senior High
Comments: This study includes 15 studies to be used over a 3-week period. As youths study Genesis they will develop important skills for studying the Bible, focusing on observation, interpretation, and application. The study approach is an "overview."

Author: Stokes, Penelope J. **1325**
Series: Fisherman Bible Studyguide
Title: *Ruth & Daniel: God's People in an Alien Society*
Publisher: Shaw, 1986 ISBN: 0-87788-735-7

Num. Sess.	Group Time	Num. Pgs.	Avg. Qst.	Price	Audience	Format	Bible Study
8	45-60	60	10	$4.99	New Christian	Workbk	Charctr

Features: Intro to Leading a Study, Intro to Study, Prayer Helps, Follow Up
★★★ Personal Application Preparation Time: Low
★★ Relationship Building Ldr. Guide: No Size: 5.0 x 8.25
Subjects: Bible Personalities, Daniel, Faith, God, Integrity, Major Prophets, Obedience, Ruth
Comments: This is a character study of Ruth and Daniel. Part 1 portrays Ruth as a woman of faithfulness, humility, obedience, and fruitfulness. Part 2 shows Daniel to be a man of integrity, prayer, witness, submission, trust, and reputation. Part 3 shows participants how to follow the examples, learning from Ruth and Daniel.

Author: Stolpe, Norman D. **1326**
Series: Group's Active Bible Curriculum
Title: *Genesis: The Beginnings*
Publisher: Group Publishing, 1991 ISBN: 1-55945-111-4

Num. Sess.	Group Time	Num. Pgs.	Avg. Qst.	Price	Audience	Format	Bible Study
4	35-60	47	Vary	$9.99	Beginner	Workbk	Book

Features: Intro to Leading a Study, Intro to Study, Objectives, Study Overview, Ldr's Notes, Drawings, Handouts, Agenda, Publicity Ideas
★★★★ Personal Application Preparation Time: None
★★★★ Relationship Building Ldr. Guide: No Size: 8.50 x 11.0
Subjects: Teens: Christian Liv, Teens: Junior High, Teens: Old Testament, Teens: Self-esteem
Comments: This 4-lesson study helps junior high youth learn powerful lessons from familiar stories in Genesis. Students will build self-esteem, as they uncover what it means to be created in God's image, grow in faith as they discover how to overcome temptation, discover what it means to give their best to God, and learn hope.

Author: Stott, John **1327**
Series: Christian Basics
Title: *Christ: Basic Christianity*
Publisher: InterVarsity, 1994 ISBN: 0-83082-002-7

Num. Sess.	Group Time	Num. Pgs.	Avg. Qst.	Price	Audience	Format	Bible Study
6	30-45	59	7	$4.99	Beginner	Workbk	Topical

Features: Intro to Leading a Study, Intro to Study, Prayer Helps, Follow Up, Full Scrpt Printed, Ldr's Notes
★★★★ Personal Application Preparation Time: None
★★★★ Relationship Building Ldr. Guide: No Size: 5.50 x 8.25
Subjects: Jesus: Life/Teaching, Singles' Issues
Comments: This study is for seekers or Christians meeting Christ anew or in a fresh and deeper way. It explains that direct statements of God's initiative summarize the message of Scripture: He has created, spoken, and acted. These lessons deal with the second and third actions of God, because basic Christianity begins with the historical figure of Jesus Christ.

Author: Stott, John **1328**
Series: Christian Basics
Title: *Scripture: God's Word for Contemporary Christians*
Publisher: InterVarsity, 1994 ISBN: 0-83082-001-9

Num. Sess.	Group Time	Num. Pgs.	Avg. Qst.	Price	Audience	Format	Bible Study
6	30-45	61	7	$4.99	New Christian	Workbk	Topical

Features: Intro to Leading a Study, Intro to Study, Prayer Helps, Follow Up, Full Scrpt Printed, Ldr's Notes
★★★★ Personal Application Preparation Time: None
★★★★ Relationship Building Ldr. Guide: No Size: 5.50 x 8.25
Subjects: Bible Study
Comments: These 6 studies position the Bible as mankind's anchor to God in the face of constant temptation and widespread corruption. It explores the role of Scripture in Christian's lives and how it can make a daily difference. Specifically it looks at: "Power of God's Word"; "Standing in the Word"; "Continuing in the Word"; "Submitting to the Word"; "Sharing the Word"; and "Understanding the Word."

Author: Stott, John **1329**
Series: LifeGuide Bible Study
Title: *Sermon on the Mount*
Publisher: InterVarsity, 1987 ISBN: 0-83081-036-6

Num. Sess.	Group Time	Num. Pgs.	Avg. Qst.	Price	Audience	Format	Bible Study
13	45-60	80	12	$4.99	New Christian	Workbk	Topical

Features: Intro to Leading a Study, Intro to Study, Ldr's Notes
★ Personal Application Preparation Time: Low
★ Relationship Building Ldr. Guide: No Size: 5.50 x 8.25
Subjects: Ethics, Jesus: Life/Teaching, Matthew, Money, Relationships, Sermon on the Mount
Comments: Matthew's Gospel recounts Jesus' greatest sermon, preached near the beginning of His public ministry. In this study, a contrast is drawn between the standards of Christians and non-Christians. Christian values, ethical standards, religious devotion, attitudes about money, ambition, lifestyles, and relationships are all discussed. It calls for students to be challenged by this great sermon.

Author: Stott, John R. W. **1330**
Series: The Bible Speaks Today
Title: *Message of Acts, The*
Publisher: InterVarsity, 1994 ISBN: 0-83081-236-9

Num. Sess.	Group Time	Num. Pgs.	Avg. Qst.	Price	Audience	Format	Bible Study
19	60-120	430	20	$14.99	New Christian	Book	Book

Features: Intro to Study, Bibliography
★★★ Personal Application Preparation Time: Med
★★ Relationship Building Ldr. Guide: No Size: 5.50 x 8.25
Subjects: Acts, New Testament
Comments: This series of Old and New Testament expositions are characterized by 3 goals: to expound the biblical text with accuracy, relate it to contemporary life, and be readable. This study of the early church has much to say about issues that concern modern day Christians such as: What can Acts tell us about tongues and other extraordinary manifestations of the Spirit? How should churches structure themselves—with elders, deacons, pastors, or all 3?

Author: Stott, John R. W. **1331**
Series: The Bible Speaks Today
Title: *Message of 1 & 2 Thessalonians, The*
Publisher: InterVarsity, 1994 ISBN: 0-83081-237-7

Num. Sess.	Group Time	Num. Pgs.	Avg. Qst.	Price	Audience	Format	Bible Study
8	60-120	220	13	$12.99	New Christian	Book	Book

Features: Intro to Study, Bibliography
★★★ Personal Application Preparation Time: Med
★★ Relationship Building Ldr. Guide: No Size: 5.50 x 8.25
Subjects: New Testament, 1 & 2 Thessalonians
Comments: This series of Old and New Testament expositions are characterized by 3 goals: to expound the biblical text with accuracy, relate it to contemporary life, and be readable. Newly planted, the Thessalonian church grew in strength as it spread the Gospel in the surrounding area. But some theological and moral problems also grew. To build up these believers Paul addressed many issues which concern Christians today—how the church spreads the Gospel, and more.

Author: Stout, Diane **1332**
Series: Tapestry Collection
Title: *De-Stressing Your Life*
Publisher: Victor Books, 1995 ISBN: 1-56476-325-0

Num. Sess.	Group Time	Num. Pgs.	Avg. Qst.	Price	Audience	Format	Bible Study
8	45-60	96	14	$5.99	New Christian	Workbk	Topical

Features: Intro to Leading a Study, Intro to Study, Prayer Helps, Digging Deeper Quest, Follow Up, Persnl Study Quest
★★★ Personal Application Preparation Time: Med
★★★ Relationship Building Ldr. Guide: No Size: 6.0 x 9.0
Subjects: Stress
Comments: This study helps women learn to corral stress inherent in modern fast-paced lifestyles, and bring it under God's control. It shows participants how to do things that have always been difficult, such as set priorities, release perfectionism, say "no," develop good habits, and invite and claim peace and calm that come from God alone.

Author: Stowell, Joseph M. **1333**
Series:
Title: *Perilous Pursuits*
Publisher: Moody Press, 1994 ISBN: 0-80247-842-5

Num. Sess.	Group Time	Num. Pgs.	Avg. Qst.	Price	Audience	Format	Bible Study
4	90-120	200	6	$16.99	New Christian	Book	Topical

Features:
★★★★ Personal Application Preparation Time: Med
★★ Relationship Building Ldr. Guide: No Size: 6.25 x 9.50
Subjects: Social Issues, Suffering, Victorious Living
Comments: This book calls Christians to trade the powers of pleasure, pride, and passion for productive energies that separate them from those who compete in a "me-first" world. The author helps readers refocus on true significance in the person and work of Christ. Thirteen chapters are divided into regret, reunion, refocus, and response. Dedicated participants could cover the book in 4 sessions, using questions provided at the end of each of the 4 parts.

Author: Stowell, Joseph M. **1334**
Series:
Title: *Tongue in Check*
Publisher: Victor Books, 1994 ISBN: 1-56476-308-0

Num. Sess.	Group Time	Num. Pgs.	Avg. Qst.	Price	Audience	Format	Bible Study
12	75-90	163	11	$8.99	New Christian	Book	Topical

Features: Prayer Helps, Scrpt Memory Helps, Digging Deeper Quest, Follow Up, Ldr's Notes
★★★★ Personal Application Preparation Time: Med
★★★ Relationship Building Ldr. Guide: No Size: 5.50 x 8.50
Subjects: Communication
Comments: The purpose of this 12-week study is to help participants develop Spirit-controlled tongues that will serve God, speech patterns that will heal, help, warm, and encourage others. Not learning to hold a tongue in check can lead to lies, deceit, gossip, slander, boasts, murmurs, and many more. Leaders notes provide icebreakers, questions, prayer helps, optional activities, and assignments.

Author: Strom, Kay Marshall **1335**
Series: Woman's Workshop Series
Title: *Perfect in His Eyes: Studies on Self-esteem*
Publisher: Zondervan, 1988 ISBN: 0-31033-691-0

Num. Sess.	Group Time	Num. Pgs.	Avg. Qst.	Price	Audience	Format	Bible Study
13	60-90	112	Vary	$5.99	Beginner	Workbk	Topical

Features: Intro to Leading a Study, Intro to Study, Ldr's Notes, Drawings, Charts
★★★ Personal Application Preparation Time: None
★★ Relationship Building Ldr. Guide: No Size: 5.25 x 8.0
Subjects: Christian Living, Self-esteem, Women's Issues
Comments: This study shows that the solution to low self-esteem is understanding how precious each person is to God, who creates and molds him or her into His own likeness. It defines self-esteem, identifies true values, promotes learning about oneself and shedding guilt, and outlines steps for attaining healthy self-esteem.

Author: Suggs, Rob **1336**
Series: LifeGuide Bible Study
Title: *Christian Community*
Publisher: InterVarsity, 1994 ISBN: 0-83081-071-4

Num. Sess.	Group Time	Num. Pgs.	Avg. Qst.	Price	Audience	Format	Bible Study
12	45-60	61	8	$4.99	New Christian	Workbk	Topical

Features: Intro to Leading a Study, Intro to Study, Ldr's Notes
★★ Personal Application Preparation Time: Low
★★ Relationship Building Ldr. Guide: No Size: 5.50 x 8.25
Subjects: Church Life
Comments: This 12-week study explores what it means to partake in the unique fellowship of the body of Christ. Through His body, the church, participants can identify their gifts and experience worship, healing, and power. People's yearning for a sense of community is stymied by busyness, lack of friends, and demands on time. The Bible promotes a community in which people can experience unconditional love, coupled with uncompromising accountability.

Author: Sunde, David **1337**
Series: HomeBuilders Couples
Title: *Growing Together In Christ*
Publisher: Gospel Light Publications, 1991 ISBN: 0-83071-628-9

Num. Sess.	Group Time	Num. Pgs.	Avg. Qst.	Price	Audience	Format	Bible Study
6	60-90	132	Vary	$9.99	Beginner	Workbk	Topical

Features: Intro to Study, Appendix
★★★★ Personal Application Preparation Time: Low
★★★★ Relationship Building Ldr. Guide: Yes Size: 5.75 x 8.50
Subjects: Family, Marriage
Comments: This study guides couples, helping them experience the joy of exciting daily relationships with God. Its messages are that Jesus provides the foundation for marriage, and that prayer can make them one with God. It suggests ways to read the Bible together, shows how to draw upon the power of the Holy Spirit, how to serve Christ and one another, and how God can use people to influence others for Christ. Homework assignments enhance application of the study.

Author: Swaby-Ellis, E. Dawn **1338**
Series: Global Issues
Title: *Sanctity of Life*
Publisher: InterVarsity, 1990 ISBN: 0-83084-911-4

Num. Sess.	Group Time	Num. Pgs.	Avg. Qst.	Price	Audience	Format	Bible Study
6	45-60	48	11	$4.99	Beginner	Workbk	Topical

Features: Intro to Leading a Study, Intro to Study, Bibliography, Follow Up
★★ Personal Application Preparation Time: Low
★★ Relationship Building Ldr. Guide: No Size: 5.50 x 8.25
Subjects: Abortion, Ethics, Social Issues
Comments: This 6-week study exposes participants to tough questions on abortion, war, and capital punishment. Questions explored include: "Does being created in God's image suggest anything to us about capital punishment for murderers?" "What if the person in question is a serial killer?" "What about a drug kingpin?" and "What biblical principles would Christians base their decision on?"

Author: Swanson, Richard W. and Janet Grant **1339**
Series: Cross Signs
Title: *Who Is Jesus? Gospel Portraits: Unit 4*
Publisher: Augsburg Fortress Publishers, 1992

Num. Sess.	Group Time	Num. Pgs.	Avg. Qst.	Price	Audience	Format	Bible Study
7	90-105	48	5	$3.75	New Christian	Book	Charctr

Features: Intro to Study, Prayer Helps, Worship Helps
★★★ Personal Application Preparation Time: Low
★★ Relationship Building Ldr. Guide: Yes Size: 5.50 x 8.50
Subjects: Jesus: Life/Teaching
Comments: Cross Signs, a Bible study series for adult small groups, features nine units of study that focus on key faith questions. This study, explores the identity of Jesus using text taken primarily from Mark's Gospel.

Author: Swanson, Richard W. **1340**
Series: Youth Talk
Title: *Work & Play*
Publisher: Augsburg Fortress Publishers, 1994

Num. Sess.	Group Time	Num. Pgs.	Avg. Qst.	Price	Audience	Format	Bible Study
5	45-60	46	N/A	$4.95	Beginner	Book	Topical

Features: Prayer Helps, Worship Helps, Photos
★★★★ Personal Application Preparation Time: Low
★★★★ Relationship Building Ldr. Guide: Yes Size: 8.0 x 11.0
Subjects: Teens: Senior High, Teens: Youth Life
Comments: An alternative to the "textbook approach," these studies are energetic, contemporary, and modeled after popular teen magazines. Advice columns, fiction, poetry, and other features are mostly written by youth. This course helps students identify the demands on their time. Recognizing the value of work and the importance of play, students will find a balance between the two that will nourish them both spiritually and physically.

Author: Swanson, Sandi **1341**
Series: Woman's Workshop Series
Title: *Fruit of the Spirit, The: Studies on Galatians 5:22-23*
Publisher: Zondervan, 1989 ISBN: 0-31052-241-2

Num. Sess.	Group Time	Num. Pgs.	Avg. Qst.	Price	Audience	Format	Bible Study
12	60-90	156	Vary	$6.99	New Christian	Workbk	Book

Features: Intro to Leading a Study, Intro to Study, Scrpt Memory Helps, Study Overview, Ldr's Notes, Charts, Word Study
★★★ Personal Application Preparation Time: Med
★★★ Relationship Building Ldr. Guide: No Size: 5.25 x 8.0
Subjects: Faith, Fruit of the Spirit, Galatians, Women's Issues
Comments: This is a study on the fruit of the Spirit: love, joy, goodness, kindness, patience, faithfulness, gentleness, peace, and self-control. In his letter to the Galatians, Paul paints a picture of faithful Christians' potential under the New Covenant; and the study reveals how such pictures are to be interpreted. A comparison is made between works of the flesh and the fruit of the Spirit.

Author: Swanson, Steve **1342**
Series: Faith Horizons
Title: *Values & Vocation*
Publisher: Augsburg Fortress Publishers, 1993

Num. Sess.	Group Time	Num. Pgs.	Avg. Qst.	Price	Audience	Format	Bible Study
6	60-75	40	9	$4.95	Beginner	Workbk	Topical

Features: Intro to Study, Prayer Helps, Worship Helps, Follow Up
★★ Personal Application Preparation Time: Low
★★ Relationship Building Ldr. Guide: No Size: 5.50 x 8.50
Subjects: Teens: Decisions, Teens: Values
Comments: Each book in the Faith Horizons series explores a theme through a topical essay, Bible study, personal reflection and response, and worship. Each offers suggestions for using media (TV, movies, plays, books, newpapers, music recordings, etc.) to enhance interaction. This study explores how values can affect decisions regarding vocations, and responds to a central question: How can we live out our values in the workplace and in all our relationships?

Author: Swindoll, Charles R. **1343**
Series: Insight for Living
Title: *Abraham: The Friend of God*
Publisher: Word, 1986 ISBN: 0-84998-329-0

Num. Sess.	Group Time	Num. Pgs.	Avg. Qst.	Price	Audience	Format	Bible Study
25	45-60	174	2	$4.99	Mature Christian	Workbk	Charctr

Features: Intro to Study, Bibliography, Digging Deeper Quest, Charts, Cassette Avail
★★ Personal Application Preparation Time: Med
★★ Relationship Building Ldr. Guide: No Size: 5.50 x 8.50
Subjects: Bible Personalities, Faith, God
Comments: This study motivates participants to replace theoretical talk about God with practical, daily walks with God. The story of Abraham, "father of a multitude," is a story of faith in action. Even though he lived in ancient times, he modeled an enviable walk with his Lord. Far from perfect, he still demonstrated faith and sincerity seldom found today. A 2-page chart depicts Abraham's life.

Author: Swindoll, Charles R. **1344**
Series: Insight for Living
Title: *Behold Christ the Lamb of God: A Study of John 15–21*
Publisher: Word, 1975 ISBN: 0-84998-297-9

Num. Sess.	Group Time	Num. Pgs.	Avg. Qst.	Price	Audience	Format	Bible Study
16	45-60	130	2	$4.99	New Christian	Workbk	Book

Features: Intro to Study, Bibliography, Charts, Cassette Avail
★★ Personal Application Preparation Time: Med
★★ Relationship Building Ldr. Guide: No Size: 5.50 x 8.50
Subjects: Jesus: Life/Teaching, John
Comments: This study of John's Gospel chapters 15–21, covers the Lamb—Jesus Christ—on display. After an intimate last supper with His disciples, He faces the horrors of illegal trials, scourging, crucifixion, and death. The Lamb is slain—but He is later raised! Participants' attention is focused on the Christ who bore humankind's sin. A chart depicting 6 trials of Jesus lists the pertinent Scripture, the officiating authority, accusation, legality, type, and result.

Author: Swindoll, Charles R. **1345**
Series: Insight for Living
Title: *Birth of an Existing Vision, The: A Study of Acts 1:1–9:43*
Publisher: Word, 1992 ISBN: 0-84998-439-4

Num. Sess.	Group Time	Num. Pgs.	Avg. Qst.	Price	Audience	Format	Bible Study
20	45-60	173	Vary	$4.99	New Christian	Workbk	Book

Features: Intro to Study, Bibliography, Drawings, Charts, Maps, Cassette Avail
★★★ Personal Application Preparation Time: Med
★★ Relationship Building Ldr. Guide: No Size: 5.50 x 8.50
Subjects: Acts
Comments: This, the 1st of 2 volumes covering the Book of Acts, begins with a survey of Acts and goes through Chapter 9, from the leadership of Peter to the conversion of Saul of Tarsus. The scenes are both disturbing and exciting, as participants witness everything from the Spirit's arrival at Pentecost to the persecution of the apostles; from the horrible stoning of Stephen to the remarkable change in Saul en route.

Author: Swindoll, Charles R. **1346**
Series: Insight for Living
Title: *Calm Answers for a Confused Church*
Publisher: Word, 1973 ISBN: 0-84998-400-9

Num. Sess.	Group Time	Num. Pgs.	Avg. Qst.	Price	Audience	Format	Bible Study
16	45-60	114	2	$4.99	Mature Christian	Workbk	Book

Features: Intro to Study, Bibliography, Charts, Cassette Avail
★★ Personal Application Preparation Time: Med
★★ Relationship Building Ldr. Guide: No Size: 5.50 x 8.50
Subjects: Church Life, Hope, Love, Marriage, 1 Corinthians
Comments: This study is Paul's response to Corinthian Christians who were confused over spiritual issues. Their disagreements led to cliques and splinter groups, each going in a different direction and listening to a different leader. Interwoven through this final segment in a 3-part study of 1 Corinthians are the themes of unity, assurance, hope, and love.

Author: Swindoll, Charles R. **1347**
Series: Insight for Living
Title: *Christ At The Crossroads*
Publisher: Word, 1991 ISBN: 0-84998-427-0

Num. Sess.	Group Time	Num. Pgs.	Avg. Qst.	Price	Audience	Format	Bible Study
18	45-60	162	Vary	$4.99	New Christian	Workbk	Topical

Features: Intro to Study, Bibliography, Cassette Avail
★★★★ Personal Application Preparation Time: Med
★★ Relationship Building Ldr. Guide: No Size: 5.50 x 8.50
Subjects: Decision Making, Hope, Jesus: Life/Teaching, Suffering
Comments: This study is about Christ's presence in Christian lives, at times when they are hard-pressed, squeezed into corners, and unsure about the next step. While examining crossroads in Jesus' own life and ministry, participants can be equipped with wisdom and strength necessary to make life changing decisions. Crossroads examined include temptation, misunderstanding, anxiety, shame, ambition, death, doubt, divorce, remarriage, pain, prejudice, hypocrisy, and integrity.

Author: Swindoll, Charles R. **1348**
Series: Insight for Living
Title: *Conquering Through Conflict: A Study of 2 Peter*
Publisher: Word, 1990 ISBN: 0-84998-422-X

Num. Sess.	Group Time	Num. Pgs.	Avg. Qst.	Price	Audience	Format	Bible Study
10	45-60	93	Vary	$4.99	New Christian	Workbk	Book

Features: Intro to Study, Bibliography, Charts, Cassette Avail
★★★ Personal Application Preparation Time: Med
★★ Relationship Building Ldr. Guide: No Size: 5.50 x 8.50
Subjects: False Teachers, Morals, 1 & 2 Peter
Comments: In this study of 2 Peter participants are reminded of intense warnings found in the New Testament, about moral corruption, doctrinal compromise, and false prophecy. It can protect Christians from being hoodwinked by false teachers and corrupt leaders who infiltrate the local church. Alongside the warnings, faith-building encouragement is included in this study. It concludes that, despite conflicts within the church, Christians can emerge triumphant in the end.

Author: Swindoll, Charles R. **1349**
Series: Insight for Living
Title: *Contagious Christianity: A Study of First Thessalonians*
Publisher: Word, 1993 ISBN: 0-84998-481-5

Num. Sess.	Group Time	Num. Pgs.	Avg. Qst.	Price	Audience	Format	Bible Study
12	45-60	109	Vary	$4.99	New Christian	Workbk	Book

Features: Intro to Study, Bibliography, Cassette Avail
★★ Personal Application Preparation Time: Med
★★ Relationship Building Ldr. Guide: No Size: 5.50 x 8.50
Subjects: Christian Living, Church Life, Joy, Work, 1 & 2 Thessalonians
Comments: This study is drawn from Paul's first letter to the Thessalonians, which has a remarkably 20th-century ring to it. The first of Paul's letters, Thessalonians establishes his style of ministry, provides insights into the rapture of the church, offers needed balance regarding the Lord's imminent return, and emphasizes vocational diligence. Paul discusses a pastor's heart and burden. A chart breaks down 1 Thessalonians chapter by chapter.

Author: Swindoll, Charles R. **1350**
Series: Insight for Living
Title: *Daniel: God's Pattern For The Future*
Publisher: Word, 1986 ISBN: 0-84998-219-7

Num. Sess.	Group Time	Num. Pgs.	Avg. Qst.	Price	Audience	Format	Bible Study
18	45-60	123	2	$4.99	Mature Christian	Book	Charctr

Features: Intro to Study, Bibliography, Digging Deeper Quest, Charts, Cassette Avail
★★ Personal Application Preparation Time: Med
★★ Relationship Building Ldr. Guide: No Size: 5.50 x 8.50
Subjects: Bible Personalities, Daniel, Integrity, Major Prophets, Prophecy
Comments: This study allows participants to gain a deeper understanding of Daniel, a true biblical model of integrity. It takes the reader from the pit of peer pressure to the pinnacle of prophecy, as Daniel endures the rigors of "boot camp" in Babylon and emerges as premier counselor to the king.

Author: Swindoll, Charles R. **1351**
Series: Insight for Living
Title: *David: A Man After God's Own Heart*
Publisher: Word, 1988 ISBN: 0-84998-328-2

Num. Sess.	Group Time	Num. Pgs.	Avg. Qst.	Price	Audience	Format	Bible Study
24	45-60	167	2	$4.99	New Christian	Workbk	Charctr

Features: Intro to Study, Bibliography, Charts, Cassette Avail
★★ Personal Application Preparation Time: Med
★★ Relationship Building Ldr. Guide: No Size: 5.50 x 8.50
Subjects: Bible Personalities, Leadership, 1 & 2 Samuel
Comments: This study helps participants apply biblical facts about David in concrete, personal ways. It helps build the realization that devotion—not perfection—is the secret of living a life that pleases God. Perhaps the most popular Old Testament character, David is a study in contrasts: an unknown shepherd lad who became the king; a rugged warrior who wrote tender psalms; a strong leader who was weak at home; a man of God with a rebellious son.

Author: Swindoll, Charles R. **1352**
Series: Insight for Living
Title: *Esther: A Woman for Such a Time as This*
Publisher: Word, 1990 ISBN: 0-84998-416-5

Num. Sess.	Group Time	Num. Pgs.	Avg. Qst.	Price	Audience	Format	Bible Study
12	45-60	111	Vary	$4.99	New Christian	Workbk	Charctr

Features: Intro to Study, Cassette Avail
★★ Personal Application Preparation Time: Med
★★ Relationship Building Ldr. Guide: No Size: 5.50 x 8.50
Subjects: Bible Personalities, Esther
Comments: This 12-week study is a verse-by-verse exposition of Esther. It opens with a survey of the book and includes a chart describing God's providence among His people during hard times and happy times. The key thought in Esther is God at work behind the scenes. The uniqueness is that the name of God is never once mentioned, nor is Esther quoted by any New Testament writer. Though God's name does not appear, His will is in every decision.

Author: Swindoll, Charles R. **1353**
Series: Insight for Living
Title: *Faith That Endures In Times Like These*
Publisher: Word, 1993 ISBN: 0-84998-441-6

Num. Sess.	Group Time	Num. Pgs.	Avg. Qst.	Price	Audience	Format	Bible Study
8	45-60	77	Vary	$4.99	New Christian	Workbk	Topical

Features: Intro to Study, Bibliography, Cassette Avail
★★ Personal Application Preparation Time: Med
★★ Relationship Building Ldr. Guide: No Size: 5.50 x 8.50
Subjects: Faith, Loneliness, Victorious Living
Comments: This 8-lesson study features biblical coaching and encouragement that helps participants firm up their faith and press on to the finish line. The underlining tone of Scripture is one of endurance, not escape. It's refusing to run, not looking for easy ways out. Lessons deal with how not to shrink, taking stands, finishing tasks, dealing with opposition, and living with loneliness.

Author: Swindoll, Charles R. **1354**
Series: Insight for Living
Title: *Following Christ the Man of God: A Study of John 6–14*
Publisher: Word, 1975 ISBN: 0-84998-296-0

Num. Sess.	Group Time	Num. Pgs.	Avg. Qst.	Price	Audience	Format	Bible Study
14	45-60	110	2	$4.99	New Christian	Workbk	Book

Features: Intro to Study, Bibliography, Charts, Cassette Avail
★★ Personal Application Preparation Time: Med
★★ Relationship Building Ldr. Guide: No Size: 5.50 x 8.25
Subjects: Jesus: Life/Teaching, John
Comments: This study of John 6–14 follows Christ through numerous scenes, facing criticism, defending a helpless woman, giving sight to the blind, teaching His disciples, raising the dead, and modeling humility by washing the feet of His closest friends. The more participants know about the Lord, the more they will want to emulate Him. Godly qualities are contagious.

Author: Swindoll, Charles R. **1355**
Series: Insight for Living
Title: *Galatians: Letter of Liberation*
Publisher: Word, 1987 ISBN: 0-84998-294-4

Num. Sess.	Group Time	Num. Pgs.	Avg. Qst.	Price	Audience	Format	Bible Study
20	45-60	157	2	$4.99	New Christian	Book	Book

Features: Intro to Study, Bibliography, Charts, Cassette Avail
★★ Personal Application Preparation Time: Med
★★ Relationship Building Ldr. Guide: No Size: 5.50 x 8.50
Subjects: Galatians, Grace, Holiness
Comments: This study of Galatians promotes rejoicing for freedom in Christ. It is a bold statement of liberation, pointing away from a "Gospel" of works and toward the grace Christ provides His own. Grace is the way to life and the way of life. This study also discusses the experience of being delivered from legalism. A chart divides Galatians into three sections: issues of truth, the nature of salvation, and principles of holiness.

Author: Swindoll, Charles R. **1356**
Series: Insight for Living
Title: *Great Stories From Old Testament Lives*
Publisher: Word, 1992 ISBN: 0-84998-428-9

Num. Sess.	Group Time	Num. Pgs.	Avg. Qst.	Price	Audience	Format	Bible Study
10	45-60	97	Vary	$4.99	New Christian	Workbk	Book

Features: Intro to Study, Bibliography, Cassette Avail
★★ Personal Application Preparation Time: Med
★★ Relationship Building Ldr. Guide: No Size: 5.50 x 8.50
Subjects: Bible Personalities, Old Testament
Comments: This 10-lesson study has 2 objectives: acquaint the uninformed with some of the best Old Testament stories and whet readers' appetites for more. All will read about heroes like David, giants like Goliath, evil kings like Ahab, and conniving queens like Jezebel. And best of all, they'll find truths to help them cope in this world.

Author: Swindoll, Charles R. **1357**
Series: Insight for Living
Title: *Growing Pains*
Publisher: Word, 1989 ISBN: 0-84998-409-2

Num. Sess.	Group Time	Num. Pgs.	Avg. Qst.	Price	Audience	Format	Bible Study
8	45-60	63	2	$4.99	New Christian	Workbk	Topical

Features: Intro to Study, Bibliography, Cassette Avail
★★ Personal Application Preparation Time: Med
★★ Relationship Building Ldr. Guide: No Size: 5.50 x 8.50
Subjects: Christian Living, Emotions, Failure, Hope
Comments: This study elaborates on 8 of life's more difficult and frustrating experiences. It contains neither cliches nor empty promises; rather it offers keys to help Christians through life's more difficult times. Subject matter covered includes growth through waiting, failure, misunderstanding, loss, mistakes, weakness, monotony, and fear. Each lesson brings reassurance and renewed determination to "hang in."

Author: Swindoll, Charles R. **1358**
Series: Insight for Living
Title: *Growth of An Expanding Mission, The*
Publisher: Word, 1992 ISBN: 0-84998-436-X

Num. Sess.	Group Time	Num. Pgs.	Avg. Qst.	Price	Audience	Format	Bible Study
20	45-60	190	Vary	$4.99	New Christian	Workbk	Book

Features: Intro to Study, Bibliography, Charts, Maps, Cassette Avail
★★★ Personal Application Preparation Time: Med
★★ Relationship Building Ldr. Guide: No Size: 5.50 x 8.50
Subjects: Acts
Comments: This 2nd volume of the study of Acts resumes at Chapter 10. Saul of Tarsus, now converted to Christ, emerges as the central figure of significance. Through the study, participants can see the early church blossom into a worldwide outreach, with the Good News of Jesus Christ reaching Thessalonica, Athens, and Corinth. They can even feel the assault of stormy weather and natural enemies.

Author: Swindoll, Charles R. **1359**
Series: Insight for Living
Title: *He Gave Gifts*
Publisher: Word, 1992 ISBN: 0-84998-431-9

Num. Sess.	Group Time	Num. Pgs.	Avg. Qst.	Price	Audience	Format	Bible Study
10	45-60	95	Vary	$4.99	New Christian	Workbk	Topical

Features: Intro to Study, Bibliography, Charts, Cassette Avail
★★★ Personal Application Preparation Time: Med
★★ Relationship Building Ldr. Guide: No Size: 5.50 x 8.50
Subjects: Spiritual Gifts
Comments: This study describes spiritual gifts, discusses why God has given them, and shows how to know which gifts can enhance a participant's walk with Christ as well as their involvement in a local church. It includes 2 helpful charts, 1 listing spiritual gifts found in Corinthians, Romans, Ephesians, and 1 Peter. Another lists spiritual gifts by 1 of 3 categories: support, service, or sign. The final chapter provides guidelines for knowing and using spiritual gifts.

Author: Swindoll, Charles R. **1360**
Series: Insight for Living
Title: *Improving Your Serve: The Art of Unselfish Living*
Publisher: Word, 1993 ISBN: 0-84998-445-9

Num. Sess.	Group Time	Num. Pgs.	Avg. Qst.	Price	Audience	Format	Bible Study
17	45-60	157	Vary	$4.99	New Christian	Workbk	Topical

Features: Intro to Study, Bibliography, Charts, Cassette Avail
★★★ Personal Application Preparation Time: Med
★★ Relationship Building Ldr. Guide: No Size: 5.50 x 8.50
Subjects: Christian Living, Service
Comments: This study offers straight talk and biblical answers on how to live unselfish lives, how to serve rather than be served, and how to give rather than receive and keep. It addresses a "me-first" generation which finds itself in a confused tailspin, smug and preoccupied with its own needs, yet desperately lonely, isolated, and cold. The study encourages participants to "improve their serve."

Author: Swindoll, Charles R. **1361**
Series: Insight for Living
Title: *Issues and Answers in Jesus' Day*
Publisher: Word, 1990 ISBN: 0-84998-413-0

Num. Sess.	Group Time	Num. Pgs.	Avg. Qst.	Price	Audience	Format	Bible Study
18	45-60	157	Vary	$4.99	New Christian	Workbk	Topical

Features: Intro to Study, Bibliography, Charts, Cassette Avail
★★ Personal Application Preparation Time: Med
★★ Relationship Building Ldr. Guide: No Size: 5.50 x 8.50
Subjects: Jesus: Life/Teaching
Comments: This 18-lesson study accomplishes 2 objectives: it makes participants aware that Scriptures are timely, and reinforces Christians' confidence in Christ's counsel. Jesus asked many questions that prompt people to focus on the important issues of life. Some of the questions covered include: Who Do People Say the Son of Man Is? What Then Shall I Do with Jesus? Why Are You So Timid? What Is Your Name? What do You See? and, Shall Not God Bring About Justice?

Author: Swindoll, Charles R. **1362**
Series: Insight for Living
Title: *Jesus, Our Lord*
Publisher: Word, 1981 ISBN: 0-84998-292-8

Num. Sess.	Group Time	Num. Pgs.	Avg. Qst.	Price	Audience	Format	Bible Study
8	45-60	60	2	$4.99	New Christian	Book	Charctr

Features: Intro to Study, Charts, Cassette Avail
★★ Personal Application Preparation Time: Med
★★ Relationship Building Ldr. Guide: No Size: 5.50 x 8.50
Subjects: Jesus: Life/Teaching, New Testament
Comments: This study, responding to the question "Who is Jesus?" can be easily understood by anyone interested in the most unique life ever lived on earth. The study traces Christ's life in chronological order. The journey goes through the New Testament, from His preexistence with the Father to His return to heaven as the ascended Christ. The stories, both interesting and convincing, leave no doubt that Jesus is Lord!

Author: Swindoll, Charles R. **1363**
Series: Insight for Living
Title: *John the Baptizer*
Publisher: Word, 1991 ISBN: 0-84998-425-4

Num. Sess.	Group Time	Num. Pgs.	Avg. Qst.	Price	Audience	Format	Bible Study
8	45-60	77	Vary	$4.99	New Christian	Workbk	Charctr

Features: Intro to Study, Bibliography, Cassette Avail
★★ Personal Application Preparation Time: Med
★★ Relationship Building Ldr. Guide: No Size: 5.50 x 8.50
Subjects: Bible Personalities
Comments: This 8-part series, on the life of John the Baptizer can open participants' eyes to a captivating person, a remarkable man who recklessly rebukes the hypocrites but tenderly baptizes repentant sinners, who audaciously scolds the powerful Herod but humbly bows before the as-yet-unknown Jesus. From his glorious birth to his ignoble death, this man from the desert challenges Christians to more practical devotion to Christ and richer understanding of servant-leadership.

Author: Swindoll, Charles R. **1364**
Series: Insight for Living
Title: *Joseph: From Pit to Pinnacle*
Publisher: Word, 1990 ISBN: 0-84998-421-1

Num. Sess.	Group Time	Num. Pgs.	Avg. Qst.	Price	Audience	Format	Bible Study
12	45-60	113	Vary	$4.99	New Christian	Workbk	Charctr

Features: Intro to Study, Bibliography, Cassette Avail
★★ Personal Application Preparation Time: Med
★★ Relationship Building Ldr. Guide: No Size: 5.50 x 8.50
Subjects: Bible Personalities
Comments: Using 12 segments, this study portrays Joseph's response to broken dreams and impossible circumstances as he rose from the pit of slavery to the pinnacle of respect. He perseveres through mistreatment, false accusations, undeserved punishment, and gross misunderstanding. He exemplifies forgiveness, freedom from bitterness, and a positive attitude toward those who have done him harm.

Author: Swindoll, Charles R. **1365**
Series: Insight for Living
Title: *Laugh Again: Experience Outrageous Joy*
Publisher: Word, 1992 ISBN: 0-84998-434-3

Num. Sess.	Group Time	Num. Pgs.	Avg. Qst.	Price	Audience	Format	Bible Study
14	45-60	127	Vary	$4.99	New Christian	Workbk	Book

Features: Intro to Study, Bibliography, Charts, Cassette Avail
★★ Personal Application Preparation Time: Med
★★ Relationship Building Ldr. Guide: No Size: 5.50 x 8.50
Subjects: Friendships, Hope, Joy, Philippians
Comments: This 14-lesson study helps participants find joy, reminding them how important it is to reflect that joy in their lives and on their faces. Lessons include: "Laughing through Life's Dilemmas"; "The Hidden Secret of a Happy Life"; "Friends Make Life More Fun"; "Happy Hopes for High Achievers"; "Hanging Tough Together...and Loving It"; "Defusing Disharmony"; and "Freeing Yourself Up to Laugh Again."

Author: Swindoll, Charles R. **1366**
Series: Insight for Living
Title: *Living Above The Level of Mediocrity*
Publisher: Word, 1987 ISBN: 0-84998-515-3

Num. Sess.	Group Time	Num. Pgs.	Avg. Qst.	Price	Audience	Format	Bible Study
20	45-60	166	Vary	$4.99	Mature Christian	Workbk	Topical

Features: Intro to Study, Bibliography, Cassette Avail
★★★ Personal Application Preparation Time: Med
★★ Relationship Building Ldr. Guide: No Size: 5.50 x 8.50
Subjects: Accountability, Christian Living, Joy, Obedience, Success
Comments: This study of excellence serves as a powerful motivator that stretches participants' potential and offers new perspectives that can lead to joy and freedom. Breaking out of the rut of mediocrity involves looking at one's mind and the costs, vision, determination, priorities, and accountability involved in living in God's Kingdom. It calls for becoming models of unselfishness, and standing strong when tempted.

Author: Swindoll, Charles R. **1367**
Series: Insight for Living
Title: *Living on the Ragged Edge: Coming to Terms with Reality*
Publisher: Word, 1983 ISBN: 0-84998-212-X

Num. Sess.	Group Time	Num. Pgs.	Avg. Qst.	Price	Audience	Format	Bible Study
24	45-60	134	2	$4.99	Mature Christian	Book	Topical

Features: Intro to Study, Bibliography, Digging Deeper Quest, Charts, Cassette Avail
★★ Personal Application Preparation Time: Med
★★ Relationship Building Ldr. Guide: No Size: 5.50 x 8.50
Subjects: Christian Living, Ecclesiastes, Stress
Comments: This study reveals how empty, disillusioning, and downright depressing life can be. It points out that Solomon, with all his under-the-sun counsel, finally came back to the most foundational of all realities, the living God. As participants study the pages of Ecclesiastes, they will feel as though someone has been looking through their journals.

Author: Swindoll, Charles R. **1368**
Series: Insight for Living
Title: *Look at the Book, A: A Bible Survey*
Publisher: Word, 1994 ISBN: 0-84998-494-7

Num. Sess.	Group Time	Num. Pgs.	Avg. Qst.	Price	Audience	Format	Bible Study
14	45-60	143	Vary	$4.99	New Christian	Workbk	Book

Features: Intro to Study, Prayer Helps, Digging Deeper Quest, Charts
★★★★ Personal Application Preparation Time: Med
★★ Relationship Building Ldr. Guide: No Size: 5.50 x 8.50
Subjects: Bible Study
Comments: One main goal of this 14-lesson study is to gain an overall perspective of the Bible, understanding its flow and how it fits together. A survey chart of Bible books and many other helpful charts provide clarity. Exercises and questions allow participants to apply what they read and study to their own life situation. It's an excellent overview, well organized, and helps clarify new students' questions.

Author: Swindoll, Charles R. **1369**
Series: Insight for Living
Title: *Memorable Scenes From Old Testament Homes*
Publisher: Word, 1992 ISBN: 0-84998-430-0

Num. Sess.	Group Time	Num. Pgs.	Avg. Qst.	Price	Audience	Format	Bible Study
8	45-60	79	Vary	$4.99	New Christian	Workbk	Book

Features: Intro to Study, Bibliography, Cassette Avail
★★★ Personal Application Preparation Time: Med
★★ Relationship Building Ldr. Guide: No Size: 5.50 x 8.50
Subjects: Bible Personalities, Old Testament
Comments: In this 8-lesson study, participants are exposed to memorable scenes of the Old Testament, dramas about real-life people, including impulsive Esau, jealous Cain, resourceful Abigail, and suffering Job, to name a few. As the stories unfold they will enthrall and instruct readers. Many lessons can be learned from each story including timeless lessons on family life.

Author: Swindoll, Charles R. **1370**
Series: Insight for Living
Title: *Minister Everyone Would Respect, A*
Publisher: Word, 1989 ISBN: 0-84998-404-1

Num. Sess.	Group Time	Num. Pgs.	Avg. Qst.	Price	Audience	Format	Bible Study
14	45-60	113	2	$4.99	Mature Christian	Book	Book

Features: Intro to Study, Bibliography, Charts, Cassette Avail
★★ Personal Application Preparation Time: Med
★★ Relationship Building Ldr. Guide: No Size: 5.50 x 8.50
Subjects: Bible Personalities, Church Life, Hope, Integrity, Leadership, Service, Suffering, 2 Corinthians
Comments: In this study of the latter half of his second letter to the Corinthian Christians, Paul spells out the crucial importance of ministering in a way that fosters trust. And by using his own life as an example, the apostle gives participants more than an unforgettable autobiography; he offers a model worth emulating. Paul reminds that confidence in ministry hinges on respect for the minister.

Author: Swindoll, Charles R. **1371**
Series: Insight for Living
Title: *Ministry Anyone Could Trust, A: A Study of 2 Corinthians 1–7*
Publisher: Word, 1989 ISBN: 0-84998-403-3

Num. Sess.	Group Time	Num. Pgs.	Avg. Qst.	Price	Audience	Format	Bible Study
16	45-60	127	2	$4.99	Mature Christian	Book	Book

Features: Intro to Study, Bibliography, Charts, Cassette Avail
★★ Personal Application Preparation Time: Med
★★ Relationship Building Ldr. Guide: No Size: 5.50 x 8.50
Subjects: Church Life, Hope, Integrity, Leadership, Repentance, Service, Suffering, 2 Corinthians
Comments: This study addresses the disappointment and disillusionment found in human ministries, and directs participants to the Word of God for a trustworthy ministry model. The first 7 chapters of 2 Corinthians offer the necessary ingredients: integrity, compassion, dedication, servanthood, realism, hope, and other qualities worth emulating.

Author: Swindoll, Charles R. **1372**
Series: Insight for Living
Title: *Moses: God's Man For a Crisis*
Publisher: Word, 1985 ISBN: 0-84998-217-0

Num. Sess.	Group Time	Num. Pgs.	Avg. Qst.	Price	Audience	Format	Bible Study
20	45-60	110	2	$4.99	New Christian	Book	Charctr

Features: Intro to Study, Bibliography, Charts, Cassette Avail
★★ Personal Application Preparation Time: Med
★★ Relationship Building Ldr. Guide: No Size: 5.50 x 8.50
Subjects: Bible Personalities, Faith, God, Service
Comments: This study uses the books of Exodus, Numbers, and Deuteronomy to present a living portrait of Moses, whose life is traced through 3 40-year segments: from Egyptian Pharaoh-in-the-making, to obscure, forgotten shepherd, to leader of the Exodus. It centers on a man many Christians have never examined in-depth. The study also shows how God prepares people to be used through trust in Him alone.

Author: Swindoll, Charles R. **1373**
Series: Insight for Living
Title: *New Testament Postcards*
Publisher: Word, 1977 ISBN: 0-84998-287-1

Num. Sess.	Group Time	Num. Pgs.	Avg. Qst.	Price	Audience	Format	Bible Study
6	45-60	46	2	$3.99	New Christian	Book	Book

Features: Intro to Study, Bibliography, Digging Deeper Quest, Cassette Avail
★★★ Personal Application Preparation Time: Med
★★ Relationship Building Ldr. Guide: No Size: 5.50 x 8.50
Subjects: Colossians/Philemon, Faith, Love, Marriage, New Testament, 1, 2 & 3 John/Jude
Comments: This 6-lesson study features 6 segments on Philemon, 2 John, 3 John, and Jude. Philemon has a present-day postmark, with modern names on the forwarding address. In 2 John, hospitality is misplaced; it is missing completely in 3 John. The theme of Jude is to "contend earnestly for the faith."

Author: Swindoll, Charles R. **1374**
Series: Insight for Living
Title: *Practical Helps for a Hurting Church: A Study of 1 Corinthians*
Publisher: Word, 1973 ISBN: 0-84998-299-5

Num. Sess.	Group Time	Num. Pgs.	Avg. Qst.	Price	Audience	Format	Bible Study
12	45-60	94	2	$4.99	Mature Christian	Workbk	Book

Features: Intro to Study, Bibliography, Charts, Cassette Avail
★★ Personal Application Preparation Time: Med
★★ Relationship Building Ldr. Guide: No Size: 5.50 x 8.50
Subjects: Church Life, Marriage, Sexual Issues, Singles' Issues, 1 Corinthians
Comments: This study of 1 Corinthians 6:12–11:34 addresses some controversial issues. The study addresses practical problems, such as: "How should I handle my sexual desires?" "Is it OK to remain single?" "How can I handle an unhappy marriage?" "Are there taboos we should shun?" "Does observance of the Lord's Table have certain requirements?"

Author: Swindoll, Charles R. **1375**
Series: Insight for Living
Title: *Practical Life of Faith, The: A Study of Hebrews 11–13*
Publisher: Word, 1989 ISBN: 0-84998-411-4

Num. Sess.	Group Time	Num. Pgs.	Avg. Qst.	Price	Audience	Format	Bible Study
20	45-60	157	Vary	$4.99	New Christian	Workbk	Book

Features: Intro to Study, Bibliography, Cassette Avail
★★ Personal Application Preparation Time: Med
★★ Relationship Building Ldr. Guide: No Size: 5.50 x 8.50
Subjects: Hebrews
Comments: This is the study of the second half of the Book of Hebrews. The first 10 chapters of Hebrews established Christ's preeminence. Walking by faith will be the challenge of these 20 lessons. Participants are exposed to great men and women of faith, and are encouraged to follow their example by walking today as they walked then. These concluding chapters challenge readers to put feet to their beliefs, to become thoroughly Christian in lifestyle and response.

Author: Swindoll, Charles R. **1376**
Series: Insight for Living
Title: *Preeminent Person of Christ, The: A Study of Hebrews 1–10*
Publisher: Word, 1989 ISBN: 0-84998-410-6

Num. Sess.	Group Time	Num. Pgs.	Avg. Qst.	Price	Audience	Format	Bible Study
24	45-60	177	2	$4.99	Mature Christian	Book	Book

Features: Intro to Study, Bibliography, Charts, Cassette Avail
★★ Personal Application Preparation Time: Med
★★ Relationship Building Ldr. Guide: No Size: 5.50 x 8.50
Subjects: Faith, Hebrews, Victorious Living
Comments: This study of the first 10 chapters of Hebrews magnifies the significance of Jesus Christ. He is presented as the Preeminent One, clearly superior to all others—created beings, including men and women in authority. As such, He deserves both highest praise and deepest devotion. This advanced study requires mental energy and spiritual motivation on the part of the participant.

Author: Swindoll, Charles R. **1377**
Series: Insight for Living
Title: *Simple Faith*
Publisher: Word, 1991 ISBN: 0-84998-406-8

Num. Sess.	Group Time	Num. Pgs.	Avg. Qst.	Price	Audience	Format	Bible Study
14	45-60	129	Vary	$4.99	New Christian	Workbk	Topical

Features: Intro to Study, Bibliography, Charts, Cassette Avail
★★★★ Personal Application Preparation Time: Med
★★ Relationship Building Ldr. Guide: No Size: 5.50 x 8.50
Subjects: Faith, Sermon on the Mount
Comments: Matthew 5–7, the real message of the Sermon on the Mount, covers what it means to live authentic, uncomplicated lives. In short, it is a call to simple faith, for Christians whose lives have become exhausting, demanding series of relentless responsibilities. Christians can achieve victory over the tyranny of the urgent, mixed with legalistic demands of modern-day Pharisees.

Author: Swindoll, Charles R. **1378**
Series: Insight for Living
Title: *Steadfast Christianity: A Study of Second Thessalonians*
Publisher: Word, 1986 ISBN: 0-84998-286-3

Num. Sess.	Group Time	Num. Pgs.	Avg. Qst.	Price	Audience	Format	Bible Study
8	45-60	58	2	$4.99	New Christian	Book	Book

Features: Intro to Study, Bibliography, Charts, Cassette Avail
★★ Personal Application Preparation Time: Med
★★ Relationship Building Ldr. Guide: No Size: 5.50 x 8.50
Subjects: Hope, Obedience, 1 & 2 Thessalonians
Comments: This study on 2 Thessalonians, a powerful 3-chapter letter, is packed full of affirmations and encouragement, in spite of hard times endured by Thessalonian Christians. It provides hope for modern Christians who feel persecuted, misunderstood, and "on trial" by others. Through consistency, readiness, determination, and perseverance, participants can find strength and encouragement.

Author: Swindoll, Charles R. **1379**
Series: Insight for Living
Title: *Stones of Remembrance*
Publisher: Word, 1987 ISBN: 0-84998-402-5

Num. Sess.	Group Time	Num. Pgs.	Avg. Qst.	Price	Audience	Format	Bible Study
4	45-60	30	2	$4.99	New Christian	Workbk	Charctr

Features: Intro to Study, Cassette Avail
★★ Personal Application Preparation Time: Med
★★ Relationship Building Ldr. Guide: No Size: 5.50 x 8.50
Subjects: God, Holiness, Theology
Comments: This study recounts God's instructions to Joshua, to leave 12 stones from the Jordan River bed as a remembrance for future generations. When children yet to be born would ask their parents, "What do these stones mean?" they would be told of God's mighty acts and be encouraged to reverence Him forever. The stones stand to remind modern participants of the Lord's sovereignty, mercy, faithfulness, and holiness.

Author: Swindoll, Charles R. **1380**
Series: Insight for Living
Title: *Strengthening Your Grip: Essentials in an Aimless World*
Publisher: Word, 1980 ISBN: 0-84998-407-6

Num. Sess.	Group Time	Num. Pgs.	Avg. Qst.	Price	Audience	Format	Bible Study
16	45-60	127	2	$4.99	New Christian	Workbk	Topical

Features: Intro to Study, Bibliography, Cassette Avail
★★ Personal Application Preparation Time: Med
★★ Relationship Building Ldr. Guide: No Size: 5.50 x 8.50
Subjects: Christian Living, Ethics, Family, Integrity, Morals, Obedience
Comments: This study focuses on certain essentials: keeping priorities straight, staying involved with others, striving for purity of life, maintaining integrity, and cherishing family life. These principles, based on eternal truths, form fixed points that keep the study on track. In order for Christians to live by moral and spiritual absolutes and renew their vigor, they need to "strengthen their grip" on timeless biblical truths.

Author: Swindoll, Charles R. 1381
Series: LifeTopics
Title: *Stress Fractures*
Publisher: David C. Cook Publishing Co., 1991 ISBN: 1-55513-564-1

Num. Sess.	Group Time	Num. Pgs.	Avg. Qst.	Price	Audience	Format	Bible Study
13	45-60	142	Vary	$19.95	Beginner	Workbk	Topical

Features: Intro to Leading a Study, Intro to Study, Objectives, Prayer Helps, Drawings, Handouts, Persnl Study Quest, Publicity Ideas
★★★ Personal Application Preparation Time: None
★★★ Relationship Building Ldr. Guide: Yes Size: 8.50 x 11.0
Subjects: Family, Integrity, Morals, Stress, Time
Comments: This self-contained leader's guide combines learning acitvities for small group interaction and practical application with excerpts and biblical teaching from Swindoll's "Stress Fractures." It helps adults of all ages survive time crunches, family conflicts, and other stresses, stand up to moral pressures without losing integrity, and tap into available anti-stress resources.

Author: Swindoll, Charles R. 1382
Series: LifeTopics
Title: *Strike the Original Match*
Publisher: David C. Cook Publishing Co., 1992 ISBN: 1-55513-571-4

Num. Sess.	Group Time	Num. Pgs.	Avg. Qst.	Price	Audience	Format	Bible Study
13	45-60	134	Vary	$19.95	Beginner	Workbk	Topical

Features: Intro to Leading a Study, Intro to Study, Objectives, Prayer Helps, Drawings, Handouts, Persnl Study Quest, Publicity Ideas
★★★ Personal Application Preparation Time: None
★★★ Relationship Building Ldr. Guide: Yes Size: 8.50 x 11.0
Subjects: Marriage, Relationships
Comments: This self-contained leader's guide combines learning activities for small group interaction and practical application with excerpts and biblical teaching from Swindoll's "Strike the Original Match." It helps couples of all ages keep the spark alive in their marriages, learn how to survive and flex, grow and forgive throughout a lifetime of marriage. It's appropriate for beginners, new, or mature Christians.

Author: Swindoll, Charles R. 1383
Series: LifeTopics
Title: *Strong Family, The*
Publisher: David C. Cook Publishing Co., 1992 ISBN: 0-78149-152-5

Num. Sess.	Group Time	Num. Pgs.	Avg. Qst.	Price	Audience	Format	Bible Study
13	45-60	134	Vary	$19.95	Beginner	Workbk	Topical

Features: Intro to Leading a Study, Intro to Study, Objectives, Prayer Helps, Drawings, Handouts, Persnl Study Quest, Publicity Ideas
★★★ Personal Application Preparation Time: None
★★★ Relationship Building Ldr. Guide: Yes Size: 8.50 x 11.0
Subjects: Family, Relationships
Comments: This self-contained leader's guide combines learning activities for small group interaction and practical application with excerpts and biblical teaching from Swindoll's "The Strong Family." It helps adults of all ages gain wisdom for building strong families, fulfilling God's plan for parents, handling loss and pain biblically, and having fun as a family. Student books are not required.

Author: Swindoll, Charles R. 1384
Series: Insight for Living
Title: *Strong Reproofs for a Scandalous Church*
Publisher: Word, 1973 ISBN: 0-84998-298-7

Num. Sess.	Group Time	Num. Pgs.	Avg. Qst.	Price	Audience	Format	Bible Study
12	45-60	96	2	$4.99	Mature Christian	Workbk	Book

Features: Intro to Study, Bibliography, Charts, Cassette Avail
★★ Personal Application Preparation Time: Med
★★ Relationship Building Ldr. Guide: No Size: 5.50 x 8.50
Subjects: Christian Living, Church Life, Money, Morals, 1 Corinthians
Comments: This study of 1 Corinthians 1:1–6:11 is based on the first part of Paul's first letter to the Corinthian church. Paul's strong words to the Corinthians, a stubborn body of carnal saints, are timely reproofs for Christians living in any modern society. Moral, legal, and carnal disorders are addressed in the study, including Paul's specific comments on domestic, social, ecclesiastical, practical, doctrinal, and financial issues.

Author: Swindoll, Charles R. 1385
Series: Insight for Living
Title: *What It Takes To Win*
Publisher: Word, 1993 ISBN: 0-84998-475-0

Num. Sess.	Group Time	Num. Pgs.	Avg. Qst.	Price	Audience	Format	Bible Study
14	45-60	139	Vary	$4.99	Mature Christian	Workbk	Topical

Features: Intro to Study, Bibliography, Cassette Avail
★★★ Personal Application Preparation Time: Med
★★ Relationship Building Ldr. Guide: No Size: 5.50 x 8.50
Subjects: Victorious Living
Comments: This 14-lesson study explores eternal rewards and what it takes to win them. The rewards are referred to as "crowns" in Scripture, and they are God's way of making all Christian's strain and sacrifice in His service worthwhile. Swindoll hopes that these studies will probe beneath the superficial veneer of mere "religious activity" and force participants to examine not only their actions but also their motives behind them.

Author: Swindoll, Luci 1386
Series:
Title: *Celebrating Life: Catching the Thieves That Steal Your Joy*
Publisher: NavPress, 1989 ISBN: 0-89109-547-0

Num. Sess.	Group Time	Num. Pgs.	Avg. Qst.	Price	Audience	Format	Bible Study
8	60-90	106	20	$6.00	Beginner	Workbk	Topical

Features: Intro to Leading a Study
★★★ Personal Application Preparation Time: Med
★★ Relationship Building Ldr. Guide: No Size: 5.25 x 8.50
Subjects: Emotions, Failure, Joy, Relationships, Stress
Comments: This study is for people who struggle with regret, resentment, disappointment, failure, discontentment, unpleasant relationships, and pressure. It focuses on harnessing these joy-stealers, dwelling on the positive instead of the negative, and counting blessings. Each lesson is divided into six sections: an opening quote, identification of joy-stealers, a Bible Study, quotations and comments from the author, a personal inventory, and putting the new discoveries to work.

Author: Synder, Linda **1387**
Series: Group's Active Bible Curriculum
Title: *Guys & Girls: Understanding Each Other*
Publisher: Group Publishing, 1991 ISBN: 1-55945-110-6

Num. Sess.	Group Time	Num. Pgs.	Avg. Qst.	Price	Audience	Format	Bible Study
4	35-60	48	Vary	$9.99	Beginner	Workbk	Topical

Features: Intro to Leading a Study, Intro to Study, Objectives, Study Overview, Ldr's Notes, Drawings, Handouts, Agenda, Publicity Ideas
★★★★ Personal Application Preparation Time: None
★★★★ Relationship Building Ldr. Guide: No Size: 8.50 x 11.0
Subjects: Teens: Junior High, Teens: Relationships, Teens: Sexuality
Comments: This study helps junior high students unravel the mystery of the oppposite sex. Its 4 lessons help them understand physical and emotional changes, examine how members of the opposite sex express their feelings, explore traditional sex roles and how they're changing, and learn how to relate in a positive way to the opposite sex. No student books are required.

Author: Syrios, Bill **1388**
Series: Christian Character
Title: *Deciding Wisely*
Publisher: InterVarsity, 1992 ISBN: 0-83081-148-6

Num. Sess.	Group Time	Num. Pgs.	Avg. Qst.	Price	Audience	Format	Bible Study
6	30-90	64	22	$4.99	New Christian	Workbk	Topical

Features: Intro to Leading a Study, Intro to Study, Bibliography, Ldr's Notes
★★★★ Personal Application Preparation Time: None
★★★ Relationship Building Ldr. Guide: No Size: 5.50 x 8.25
Subjects: Decision Making
Comments: This study offers 7 options for either individual or group study, ranging from 6–12 weeks and 30″–90″ minutes depending on the number of questions covered. Making tough decisions is part of life. These lessons help participants learn how to pray for God's will, listen to His voice and become wise people. Principles of godly decision making enable them to serve God in the decisions they make.

Author: Syrios, Bill & Teresa **1389**
Series: LifeGuide Bible Study
Title: *Ecclesiastes: Chasing After Meaning*
Publisher: InterVarsity, 1992 ISBN: 0-83081-027-7

Num. Sess.	Group Time	Num. Pgs.	Avg. Qst.	Price	Audience	Format	Bible Study
12	45-60	64	12	$4.99	New Christian	Workbk	Book

Features: Intro to Leading a Study, Intro to Study, Ldr's Notes
★★ Personal Application Preparation Time: Low
★★ Relationship Building Ldr. Guide: No Size: 5.50 x 8.25
Subjects: Ecclesiastes
Comments: This study responds to questions like: Where can I find fulfillment when I seem to be going in circles? Who is really in control when the world looks topsy-turvy? The pessimism of Ecclesiastes helps participants find the hope of a God-centered lifestyle. Ecclesiastes is ultimately an introduction to the One who "came that we might have life abundantly," Jesus Christ Himself.

Author: Syrios, Bill **1390**
Series: The TruthSeed Series
Title: *Knowing Jesus: Our Lord, Our Servant*
Publisher: Victor Books, 1995 ISBN: 1-56476-350-1

Num. Sess.	Group Time	Num. Pgs.	Avg. Qst.	Price	Audience	Format	Bible Study
12	45-60	112	12	$4.99	Beginner	Workbk	Book

Features: Intro to Leading a Study, Intro to Study, Bibliography, Prayer Helps, Follow Up, Ldr's Notes
★★★ Personal Application Preparation Time: None
★★★ Relationship Building Ldr. Guide: No Size: 6.0 x 9.0
Subjects: Jesus: Life/Teaching
Comments: This new series of inductive Bible studies enables men and women to experience community and develop godliness in either discussion group or personal settings. Questions are designed and field-tested for seekers, new believers, and mature Christians. Enrichment material for further study is provided along with a bibliography. Looks at 12 stories of Christ through the eyes of the 4 Gospel writers.

Author: Taylor, Linda Chaffee, et. al. **1391**
Series: Life Application
Title: *Ruth & Esther*
Publisher: Tyndale House, 1989 ISBN: 0-84232-716-9

Num. Sess.	Group Time	Num. Pgs.	Avg. Qst.	Price	Audience	Format	Bible Study
13	60-90	82	11	$4.99	New Christian	Workbk	Book

Features: Intro to Leading a Study, Intro to Study, Study Overview, Digging Deeper Quest, Full Scrpt Printed, Drawings, Charts, Maps, Cross Ref
★★★ Personal Application Preparation Time: Med
★★★ Relationship Building Ldr. Guide: No Size: 6.50 x 9.0
Subjects: Esther, Faith, God, Obedience, Ruth
Comments: This study contains the complete texts of Ruth and Esther. Ruth shows how she, Naomi, and Boaz remained strong in character and true to God. Ruth shows that God is at work in the world. Esther demonstrates God's sovereignty and loving care for His people. Participants will realize that any Christian's life can make a difference.

Author: Taylor, Mark A. **1392**
Series:
Title: *Come to the Party! Celebrate Jesus: Leader's Guide*
Publisher: Standard Publishing, 1994 ISBN: 0-78470-145-8

Num. Sess.	Group Time	Num. Pgs.	Avg. Qst.	Price	Audience	Format	Bible Study
13	30-60	64	9	$4.49	New Christian	Book	Topical

Features: Intro to Study, Objectives, Follow Up
★★★ Personal Application Preparation Time: None
★★★ Relationship Building Ldr. Guide: No Size: 5.50 x 8.50
Subjects: Leader's Guide, Worship
Comments: This leader's guide provides a variety of teaching options. Each session can stand alone, which allows random or selective use, and a variety of learning activities are offered. The main sections in each session include: "Comments on the Text," or Scripture background assigned to each session; "For Your Group's Discussion," questions for groups to answer; and "Lesson Plans," a more detailed teaching plan, with a wider variety of learning activities.

Author: Thatcher, Martha **1393**
Series:
Title: *When the Squeeze Is On: Growing Through Pressure*
Publisher: NavPress, 1987 ISBN: 0-89109-182-3

Num. Sess.	Group Time	Num. Pgs.	Avg. Qst.	Price	Audience	Format	Bible Study
8	60-90	93	10	$5.00	Beginner	Workbk	Topical

Features: Intro to Leading a Study, Intro to Study
★★★ Personal Application Preparation Time: Med
★★ Relationship Building Ldr. Guide: No Size: 5.50 x 8.50
Subjects: Bible Personalities, Christian Living, Decision Making, Money, Relationships, Time
Comments: This practical study on pressure offers Scriptural reinforcement for making the best choices when facing life's pressures. Questions offer new insights about Bible characters like Moses, Samson, David, Daniel, and Peter. Time, relationships, responsibilities, and financial pressures are among topics covered. Participants learn to apply the principles to real-life situations.

Author: Thomas, Mack **1394**
Series:
Title: *Complete Bible Discussion Guide, The: New Testament*
Publisher: Questar Publishers, 1992 ISBN: 0-94556-455-4

Num. Sess.	Group Time	Num. Pgs.	Avg. Qst.	Price	Audience	Format	Bible Study
	—	380	N/A	$21.99	Beginner	Book	Book

Features:
Personal Application Preparation Time:
Relationship Building Ldr. Guide: Size: 6.50 x 9.50
Subjects: New Testament, Small Group Resource
Comments: This book helps readers find God's life-changing answers by including more than 11,000 mind stretching, discussion questions covering every book and chapter in the New Testament in one text. Readers can understand the original meaning for each passage and learn how to apply God's truths to their lives. This resource serves as a good supplement for both group and individual Bible studies.

Author: Thomas, Mack **1395**
Series:
Title: *Complete Bible Discussion Guide, The: Old Testament*
Publisher: Questar Publishers, 1993 ISBN: 0-94556-454-6

Num. Sess.	Group Time	Num. Pgs.	Avg. Qst.	Price	Audience	Format	Bible Study
	—	380	N/A	$21.99	Beginner	Book	Book

Features:
Personal Application Preparation Time:
Relationship Building Ldr. Guide: Size: 6.50 x 9.50
Subjects: Old Testament, Small Group Resource
Comments: This book helps readers find God's life-changing answers, by including more than 11,000 mind-stretching, discussion questions overing every book and chapter in the Old Testament in one text. It helps readers understand the original meaning for each passage, and learn how to apply God's truths to their lives. This resource serves as an effective supplement for both group and individual Bible studies.

Author: Thompson, David A. **1396**
Series:
Title: *Premarital Guide for Couples and Their Counselors, A*
Publisher: Bethany House, 1979 ISBN: 0-87123-465-3

Num. Sess.	Group Time	Num. Pgs.	Avg. Qst.	Price	Audience	Format	Bible Study
6	45-60	80	Vary	$6.99	Beginner	Workbk	Topical

Features: Intro to Study, Bibliography
★★★ Personal Application Preparation Time: Med
★★★ Relationship Building Ldr. Guide: No Size: 8.50 x 11.0
Subjects: Counseling, Ethics, Marriage, Money, Relationships, Sexual Issues
Comments: This premarital guide can be used by couples with the assistance of a counselor or clergy. Subject matter for both prospective bride and groom includes family and dating history; ideas on communication, sex, children, in-laws; values; finances; future employment, home, and friends; and the wedding.

Author: Thompson, Rick and Vernon Grounds **1397**
Series: Christian Lifestyle Series
Title: *Living the Toughest Teachings of Jesus*
Publisher: David C. Cook Publishing Co., 1991 ISBN: 1-55513-380-0

Num. Sess.	Group Time	Num. Pgs.	Avg. Qst.	Price	Audience	Format	Bible Study
7	45-60	96	Vary	$14.95	New Christian	Workbk	Topical

Features: Intro to Study, Prayer Helps, Drawings, Handouts, Persnl Study Quest
★★★ Personal Application Preparation Time: None
★★★ Relationship Building Ldr. Guide: Yes Size: 8.50 x 11.0
Subjects: Christian Living, Jesus: Life/Teaching, Obedience
Comments: This study combines biblical teaching, small group interaction, and practical application. It helps adults of all ages, especially Boomers and younger, interpret and apply such commands as: "Deny yourself, take up your cross, and follow Me" and "Ask Me for anything in My name and I will do it." It's appropriate for singles or marrieds, new or mature Christians.

Author: Tiede, David L. **1398**
Series: Search Weekly Bible
Title: *Unit 1/Acts 1–8*
Publisher: Augsburg Fortress Publishers, 1983

Num. Sess.	Group Time	Num. Pgs.	Avg. Qst.	Price	Audience	Format	Bible Study
8	90-105	64	Vary	$5.50	New Christian	Book	Book

Features: Intro to Study, Objectives, Prayer Helps, Worship Helps, Follow Up, Summary
★★ Personal Application Preparation Time: Med
★★ Relationship Building Ldr. Guide: Yes Size: 8.50 x 11.0
Subjects: Acts
Comments: This review of Acts is 1 of 20 units of a 5-year study titled "Search." The series is divided into 5 themes: Beginnings, Journey, Struggles, Experiences, and Hopes. This study of Acts covers 8 weeks, and 4 sections: "The Commission Is Given"; "The Restoration Begins"; "The Opposition Is Exposed"; and "The Mission Expands."

Author: Tiede, David L. **1399**
Series: Search Weekly Bible
Title: *Unit 2/Acts 9–28*
Publisher: Augsburg Fortress Publishers, 1983

Num. Sess.	Group Time	Num. Pgs.	Avg. Qst.	Price	Audience	Format	Bible Study
8	90-105	64	Vary	$5.50	New Christian	Book	Book

Features: Intro to Study, Objectives, Prayer Helps, Worship Helps, Follow Up, Summary
★★ Personal Application Preparation Time: Med
★★ Relationship Building Ldr. Guide: Yes Size: 8.50 x 11.0
Subjects: Acts
Comments: This review of Acts is 1 of 20 units of a 5-year study titled "Search." The series is divided into 5 themes: Beginnings, Journey, Struggles, Experiences, and Hopes. This study of Acts covers eight weeks, and four sections: "The Commission Is Renewed"; "The Will of God Is Discerned"; "The Witness of Paul Is Tested"; and "The Testimony of the Holy Spirit."

Author: Timmons, Tim **1400**
Series: Video Curriculum Resource
Title: *Maximum Marriage*
Publisher: Word, 1986 ISBN: 8-01940-079-6

Num. Sess.	Group Time	Num. Pgs.	Avg. Qst.	Price	Audience	Format	Bible Study
4	75-105	N/A	Vary	$159.99	Beginner	Video	Topical

Features: Scrpt Memory Helps, Cartoons, Video Study Guide
★★★★ Personal Application Preparation Time: None
★★★ Relationship Building Ldr. Guide: No Size: 10.25 x 12.50
Subjects: Marriage, Young Marrieds
Comments: This 4-session video study is for married people, from newlyweds to "emptynesters," and for those preparing for marriage. Topics include: "Why Marriage When You Can Live Together?" "The Eleven Battlegrounds of Marriage," "Why Are Women So Weird and Men So Strange?" and "How Do You Spell Relief?" The 50″ lessons inspire participants to enter a oneness with their mates, to build strong family units, and to communicate openly.

Author: Towns, Elmer L. **1401**
Series:
Title: *My Father's Names*
Publisher: Regal Books, 1991 ISBN: 0-83071-447-2

Num. Sess.	Group Time	Num. Pgs.	Avg. Qst.	Price	Audience	Format	Bible Study
12	60-90	168	N/A	$9.99	New Christian	Book	Topical

Features: Intro to Study, Appendix
★★★★ Personal Application Preparation Time: Low
★★ Relationship Building Ldr. Guide: Size: 5.50 x 8.50
Subjects: God, Old Testament
Comments: This book explains the meaning of God's names found in the Old Testament. The names chosen for the study are those most discussed in church history, those that give the most significant insights into God's person and nature. Appendix A gives a comprehensive list of God's names in the Old Testament. Also available are a group study guide ($14.99), 2 videos (103″, $29.99), and a package of 2 videos, book, and study guides ($49.99).

Author: Towns, Elmer L. **1402**
Series:
Title: *Names of Jesus, The: Group Study Guide*
Publisher: David C. Cook Publishing Co., 1992 ISBN: 0-89636-289-2

Num. Sess.	Group Time	Num. Pgs.	Avg. Qst.	Price	Audience	Format	Bible Study
12	30-45	92	Vary	$10.95	New Christian	Workbk	Topical

Features: Intro to Study, Objectives, Book Avail
★★★★ Personal Application Preparation Time: Med
★★★ Relationship Building Ldr. Guide: Yes Size: 8.50 x 11.0
Subjects: Jesus: Life/Teaching
Comments: This group study guide and accompanying book "The Names of Jesus" enable anyone to lead a small group Bible study or teach a Sunday School class. It includes study plans, life applications, reproducible handouts, and other resources, to help every member of a group participate as they study more than 700 names of Jesus. The study can be adapted to either an 8- or 12-week study.

Author: Towns, Elmer L. **1403**
Series:
Title: *Names of Jesus, The*
Publisher: David C. Cook Publishing Co., 1987 ISBN: 0-89636-243-4

Num. Sess.	Group Time	Num. Pgs.	Avg. Qst.	Price	Audience	Format	Bible Study
12	30-45	175	N/A	$7.95	New Christian	Book	Topical

Features: Bibliography, Appendix
★★★★ Personal Application Preparation Time: Med
★★★ Relationship Building Ldr. Guide: Yes Size: 5.25 x 8.0
Subjects: Jesus: Life/Teaching
Comments: This book contains over 700 names of Jesus that can help Christians know the Lord they love. The names of God in Scripture are really self-revelations of God in His nature and attributes. An available group study guide (0-89636-289-2) allows anyone to lead a small group Bible study or teach a Sunday School class. This book can be adapted to either an 8- or 12-week study.

Author: Towns, Elmer L. **1404**
Series:
Title: *Names of The Holy Spirit, The*
Publisher: Regal Books, 1994 ISBN: 0-83071-676-9

Num. Sess.	Group Time	Num. Pgs.	Avg. Qst.	Price	Audience	Format	Bible Study
13	60-90	250	N/A	$9.99	New Christian	Book	Topical

Features: Intro to Study, Appendix
★★★★ Personal Application Preparation Time: Low
★★ Relationship Building Ldr. Guide: Size: 5.50 x 8.50
Subjects: Holy Spirit, Victorious Living
Comments: This study of the names of the Holy Spirit goes beyond learning the names to cover His personality and what He does for modern Christians. It is more than a doctrinal study. Multiple appendices provide helpful listings. Also available a group study guide ($14.99). A video package: 2 videos, a book, and study guide ($49.99).

Author: Townsend, John **1405**
Series:
Title: *Hiding from Love*
Publisher: NavPress, 1991 ISBN: 0-89109-645-0

Num. Sess.	Group Time	Num. Pgs.	Avg. Qst.	Price	Audience	Format	Bible Study
8	60-90	96	12	$6.00	New Christian	Workbk	No

Features: Intro to Leading a Study, Prayer Helps, Scrpt Memory Helps, Pre-discussion Quest,Digging Deeper Quest, Follow Up, Ldr's Notes, Persnl Study Quest, Book Avail
★★★★ Personal Application Preparation Time: None
★★★★ Relationship Building Ldr. Guide: No Size: 5.25 x 8.25
Subjects: Counseling, Emotions, Psychology, Relationships
Comments: This companion guide to Townsend's book by the same name can be used without reading the book. Topics include what hiding is and why we hide (we hide from relationships to protect our wounded parts), helpful versus harmful hiding, how to identify ways we hide, and how to come out of harmful hiding.

Author: Traina, Robert A. **1406**
Series:
Title: *Methodical Bible Study*
Publisher: Zondervan, 1952 ISBN: 0-31031-230-2

Num. Sess.	Group Time	Num. Pgs.	Avg. Qst.	Price	Audience	Format	Bible Study
4	—	270	N/A	$19.99	Mature Christian	Book	No

Features: Intro to Study, Bibliography, No Grp Discussion Quest, Summary, Charts, Appendix
Personal Application Preparation Time:
Relationship Building Ldr. Guide: Size: 5.75 x 8.75
Subjects: Bible Study, Small Group Resource
Comments: This guide to inductive Bible study, which involves comparing related Bible texts in order to let the Bible interpret itself. The study is divided into 4 parts: "Observation," "Interpretation," "Evaluation and Application," and "Correlation." Added inductive charts, a word study, outlines, and a teaching manual make this a helpful study aid.

Author: Trenner, Rev. Ed., et. al. **1407**
Series: Life Application
Title: *John*
Publisher: Tyndale House, 1989 ISBN: 0-84232-717-7

Num. Sess.	Group Time	Num. Pgs.	Avg. Qst.	Price	Audience	Format	Bible Study
13	60-90	120	13	$4.99	New Christian	Workbk	Book

Features: Intro to Leading a Study, Intro to Study, Study Overview, Digging Deeper Quest, Full Scrpt Printed, Drawings, Charts, Maps, Cross Ref
★★★ Personal Application Preparation Time: Med
★★★ Relationship Building Ldr. Guide: No Size: 6.50 x 9.0
Subjects: Jesus: Life/Teaching, John
Comments: This study contains a powerful argument for the Incarnation, a conclusive demonstration that Jesus is the Heaven-sent Son of God and the only source of eternal life. The study has 3 main divisions: Jesus' birth and preparation; Jesus' message and ministry; and Jesus' death and resurrection.

Author: Trent, Dr. John **1408**
Series:
Title: *How to Help Your Kids Get Along*
Publisher: Word, 1993 ISBN: 0-84998-457-2

Num. Sess.	Group Time	Num. Pgs.	Avg. Qst.	Price	Audience	Format	Bible Study
2	45-60	N/A	5	$59.99	Beginner	Video	Topical

Features: Intro to Study, Bibliography, Handouts, Book Incl
★★★★ Personal Application Preparation Time: None
★★★★ Relationship Building Ldr. Guide: Yes Size: 10.25 x 12.50
Subjects: Family, Parenting, Self-esteem
Comments: This 2-session (30" each) video resource promotes family harmony and understanding. Before a live audience, Trent proclaims that homes don't have to be battlegrounds, and offers six practical tools to equip parents to understand themselves and one another, provide children with resources that will teach problem solving, and lay foundations for solid self-esteem and close sibling relationships throughout life. This study is ideal for a 1-day workshop.

Author: Trimiew, Anna **1409**
Series: Bible Alive Studies
Title: *Bringing the New Testament to Life*
Publisher: David C. Cook Publishing Co., 1993 ISBN: 0-78145-072-1

Num. Sess.	Group Time	Num. Pgs.	Avg. Qst.	Price	Audience	Format	Bible Study
13	45-60	144	Vary	$19.95	Beginner	Workbk	Book

Features: Intro to Study, Bibliography, Prayer Helps, Drawings, Handouts, Persnl Study Quest, Charts
★★★★ Personal Application Preparation Time: None
★★ Relationship Building Ldr. Guide: Yes Size: 8.50 x 11.0
Subjects: Bible Personalities, Holy Spirit, Jesus: Life/Teaching, New Testament
Comments: This complete leader's guide provides an overview of the entire New Testament. It answers questions such as: "What does the New Testament have to do with me?" "Why do people need to be saved?" "What made the early Christians so bold?" "Who—or what—is the Holy Spirit?" and "Is the world coming to an end?

Author: Truman, Bryan **1410**
Series: Global Issues
Title: *Basic Human Needs*
Publisher: InterVarsity, 1990 ISBN: 0-83084-907-6

Num. Sess.	Group Time	Num. Pgs.	Avg. Qst.	Price	Audience	Format	Bible Study
6	45-60	48	12	$4.99	Beginner	Workbk	Topical

Features: Intro to Leading a Study, Intro to Study, Bibliography, Follow Up
★ Personal Application Preparation Time: Low
★ Relationship Building Ldr. Guide: No Size: 5.50 x 8.25
Subjects: Medical Issues, Social Issues
Comments: This 6-week study discusses the magnitude of unhealthy world living conditions, and identifies ways in which participants can help see that people's needs are met. It describes the following: poverty; poor sanitation; shortage of food, water, and medical supplies; increases in preventable diseases; inadequate housing; illiteracy; population explosion; and insufficient educational facilities.

Author: Van Reken, Ruth E. **1411**
Series: Fisherman Bible Studyguide
Title: *Who Is Jesus? In His Own Words*
Publisher: Shaw, 1993 ISBN: 0-87788-914-7

Num. Sess.	Group Time	Num. Pgs.	Avg. Qst.	Price	Audience	Format	Bible Study
12	45-60	76	12	$4.99	Beginner	Workbk	Charctr

Features: Intro to Leading a Study, Intro to Study, Ldr's Notes
★★★★ Personal Application Preparation Time: None
★★ Relationship Building Ldr. Guide: No Size: 5.25 x 8.25
Subjects: Jesus: Life/Teaching
Comments: This 12-week study answers the question: Who is Jesus? Using His Words it reviews the "I am" statements found in the Gospels. Lessons include: "I Am the Way"; "The Gate"; "The Good Shepherd"; "The Truth"; "The Light"; "The Resurrection"; "The Life"; "The Vine"; and "The Alpha and Omega." Whether this is a participant's 1st or 100th Bible study, they will see more of who God is as Jesus' revelation unfolds in easy-to-understand word pictures.

Author: Varney, Dr. Tom **1412**
Series: IBC Discussion Guide
Title: *Loneliness*
Publisher: NavPress, 1992 ISBN: 0-89109-693-0

Num. Sess.	Group Time	Num. Pgs.	Avg. Qst.	Price	Audience	Format	Bible Study
4	60-90	63	9	$5.00	Beginner	Workbk	Topical

Features: Intro to Leading a Study, Intro to Study, Prayer Helps, Follow Up, Ldr's Notes
★★★★ Personal Application Preparation Time: None
★★★★ Relationship Building Ldr. Guide: No Size: 5.25 x 8.25
Subjects: Counseling, Loneliness, Support
Comments: "Loneliness" is 1 of 6 studies that identify how life struggles affect the way participants relate to themselves, others, and God. Four lessons look at: how to recognize the various dimensions of loneliness, how to profit from facing loneliness, how to respond to loneliness in a way that neither minimizes nor morbidly dwells on it, how to embrace and help others when faced with loneliness.

Author: Vaughn, Joe & Loren L. Nielsen **1413**
Series: Small Group Bible Studies
Title: *Issues That Still Matter*
Publisher: Augsburg Fortress Publishers, 1980

Num. Sess.	Group Time	Num. Pgs.	Avg. Qst.	Price	Audience	Format	Bible Study
6	60-75	24	14	$1.35	New Christian	Book	Book

Features: Intro to Study, Prayer Helps
★★★★ Personal Application Preparation Time: None
★★★★ Relationship Building Ldr. Guide: No Size: 8.50 x 5.50
Subjects: Relationships, 1 Corinthians
Comments: This small pamphlet includes 6 sessions on 1 Corinthians, reviewing advice Paul gave to traveling missionaries who were developing factions among themselves. They were allowing old, ugly problems from their former pagan lives to continue to manifest themselves. He wrote a very practical letter that deals with issues that still matter today.

Author: Veerman, David R. **1414**
Series: Shaw Contemporary Issues
Title: *Holy Ambition*
Publisher: Shaw, 1992 ISBN: 0-87788-363-7

Num. Sess.	Group Time	Num. Pgs.	Avg. Qst.	Price	Audience	Format	Bible Study
8	30-45	48	9	$4.99	New Christian	Workbk	Topical

Features: Intro to Leading a Study, Intro to Study, Objectives, Bibliography, Follow Up, Ldr's Notes
★★★★ Personal Application Preparation Time: Low
★★★ Relationship Building Ldr. Guide: No Size: 5.25 x 8.25
Subjects: Failure, Integrity, Success
Comments: Eight brief lessons help participants explore issues such as competition, recognition, accumulation, and success. Ambition is like a 2-edged sword God doesn't want mankind to be lazy. But there is a dramatic difference between selfish ambition and ambition to know and serve Christ. This study seeks to show participants what it means to have "holy ambition."

Author: Veerman, David R. **1415**
Series: SonPower Youth Sources
Title: *Serious Fun*
Publisher: Victor Books, 1995 ISBN: 1-56476-498-2

Num. Sess.	Group Time	Num. Pgs.	Avg. Qst.	Price	Audience	Format	Bible Study
	—	252	N/A	$14.99			

Features:
Personal Application Preparation Time:
Relationship Building Ldr. Guide: Size: 8.50 x 11.0
Subjects: Teens: Junior High, Teens: Resources, Teens: Senior High
Comments: This revised paperback edition of Veerman's book is a collection of over 1200 "seriously fun activities" for high schoolers, including a variety of games, discussion starters, and icebreakers. Topics discussed include pressure and stress, self-esteem, friendships, love and sex, and salvation. It also uses questions to prompt kids to examine Scripture, and includes outlines for devotional talks.

Author: Veerman, David R. **1416**
Series: SonPower Youth Sources
Title: *Small Group Ministry With Youth*
Publisher: Victor Books, 1992 ISBN: 0-89693-919-7

Num. Sess.	Group Time	Num. Pgs.	Avg. Qst.	Price	Audience	Format	Bible Study
	—	164	N/A	$10.99			

Features:
Personal Application Preparation Time:
Relationship Building Ldr. Guide: Size: 6.0 x 9.0
Subjects: Small Group Resource, Teens: Resources
Comments: Helps youth leaders understand philosophies and strategies of small group ministry. It covers the "hows" and "whys" of effective small group ministries, profiles of successful small groups (including discipleship, Bible study, evangelism, teenage mother support groups, spiritual growth, urban community, evangelism training, and leadership development), enhancing ministry (with worksheets to plan for a small group ministry).

Author: Veerman, Rev. David R., et. al. **1417**
Series: Life Application
Title: *Acts*
Publisher: Tyndale House, 1989 ISBN: 0-84232-730-4

Num. Sess.	Group Time	Num. Pgs.	Avg. Qst.	Price	Audience	Format	Bible Study
13	60-90	136	14	$4.99	New Christian	Workbk	Book

Features: Intro to Leading a Study, Intro to Study, Study Overview, Digging Deeper Quest, Full Scrpt Printed, Drawings, Charts, Maps, Cross Ref
★★★ Personal Application Preparation Time: Med
★★★ Relationship Building Ldr. Guide: No Size: 6.50 x 9.0
Subjects: Acts, Bible Personalities, Church Life
Comments: This study contains the complete text of Acts, which provides an accurate account of the birth and growth of the early Christian Church. It is divided into 2 main sections: Peter's ministry and Paul's ministry. Questions lead to application of biblical truth and action plans.

Author: Virkler, Henry A. **1418**
Series:
Title: *Speaking Your Mind Without Stepping On Toes*
Publisher: Victor Books, 1991 ISBN: 0-89693-399-7

Num. Sess.	Group Time	Num. Pgs.	Avg. Qst.	Price	Audience	Format	Bible Study
10	45-90	200	Vary	$8.99	New Christian	Book	Topical

Features: Summary, Ldr's Notes
★★★★ Personal Application Preparation Time: Med
★★★★ Relationship Building Ldr. Guide: Yes Size: 5.50 x 8.50
Subjects: Conflict, Psychology
Comments: This study offers a corrective to teachings that Christians should be "doormats" while examining the teachings of contemporary assertiveness in light of biblical principles. Step-by-step, this book helps the reader: to "speak the truth with love" through practical exercises that are relevant to life, to be assertive without being aggressive, to build affirmation into assertiveness, and how to remain assertive and positive.

Author: Vogel, Jane & Jay Kesler **1419**
Series: Christian Lifestyle Series
Title: *Finding God's Way in Your World Today*
Publisher: David C. Cook Publishing Co., 1995 ISBN: 0-78145-127-2

Num. Sess.	Group Time	Num. Pgs.	Avg. Qst.	Price	Audience	Format	Bible Study
7	45-60	96	Vary	$14.95	New Christian	Workbk	Topical

Features: Intro to Study, Bibliography, Prayer Helps, Study Overview, Drawings, Handouts, Persnl Study Quest
★★★★ Personal Application Preparation Time: None
★★★★ Relationship Building Ldr. Guide: Yes Size: 8.50 x 11.0
Subjects: Christian Living, God
Comments: This study helps answer questions about God's will and correct misconceptions. Participants will explore the following questions: Does God really have a "knowable" will for our lives? If God has an individual will for each person, how detailed is it? How does God reveal His will? What obstacles keep us from knowing God's will? and How can we tune in to what God wants to tell us?

Author: Wagner, E. Glenn **1420**
Series: Promise Keepers
Title: *Strategies for a Successful Marriage*
Publisher: NavPress, 1994 ISBN: 0-89109-857-7

Num. Sess.	Group Time	Num. Pgs.	Avg. Qst.	Price	Audience	Format	Bible Study
8	45-60	115	Vary	$6.00	Beginner	Book	Topical

Features: Intro to Study, Follow Up
★★★★ Personal Application Preparation Time: Low
★★ Relationship Building Ldr. Guide: No Size: 5.50 x 8.50
Subjects: Marriage, Men's Issues, Relationships
Comments: Part of the Promise Keeper series, this study is designed so men can help each other with accountability, prayer, and encouragement. Using Scripture, personal anecdotes, worksheets, and probing discussion questions, they present workable ways to make marriage more satisfying and fulfilling. In addition to alerting participants to the warning signs, this guide offers practical tips on better communication, romance and fun, and more.

Author: Wald, Oletta **1421**
Series: Small Group Bible Studies
Title: *Ask*
Publisher: Augsburg Fortress Publishers, 1978

Num. Sess.	Group Time	Num. Pgs.	Avg. Qst.	Price	Audience	Format	Bible Study
4	60-75	16	17	$1.15	New Christian	Book	Topical

Features: Intro to Study, Prayer Helps
★★★ Personal Application Preparation Time: None
★★★ Relationship Building Ldr. Guide: No Size: 8.50 x 5.50
Subjects: Forgiveness, Prayer
Comments: This small pamphlet includes 4 sessions on prayer. Session 1, "What Shall I Say?" considers prayers of thanksgiving and praise. Session 2, "What Shall I Say When I Have Needs?" considers prayers of petition, or asking for something. Session 3, "What Shall I Say When Others Have Needs?" considers prayers of intercession. Session 4, "What Shall I Say When I Have Done Wrong?" Considers prayers of confession and forgiveness.

Author: Walker, Catherine B. **1422**
Series:
Title: *Bible Workbook: Volume 2—New Testament*
Publisher: Moody Press, 1994 ISBN: 0-80240-752-8

Num. Sess.	Group Time	Num. Pgs.	Avg. Qst.	Price	Audience	Format	Bible Study
26	60-75	72	Vary	$6.99	Beginner	Workbk	Topical

Features: Intro to Study, Ldr's Notes, Maps
★★★ Personal Application Preparation Time: Med
★★ Relationship Building Ldr. Guide: No Size: 8.0 x 10.50
Subjects: Bible Study, New Testament
Comments: This study, 2nd of a 2-volume series, covers the entire New Testament. It's a systematic, individual study in which participants learn by doing—information is given and questions test their understanding. An introductory section gives a good review of the Bible and how the study is developed, and it shows students how to make the most of the study. The study is appropriate for individuals, or groups of any size.

Author: Walker, Catherine B. 1423
Series:
Title: *Bible Workbook: Volume 1—Old Testament*
Publisher: Moody Press, 1994 ISBN: 0-80240-751-X

Num. Sess.	Group Time	Num. Pgs.	Avg. Qst.	Price	Audience	Format	Bible Study
26	60-75	72	Vary	$6.99	Beginner	Workbk	Topical

Features: Intro to Study, Scrpt Memory Helps, Maps
★★★ Personal Application Preparation Time: Med
★★ Relationship Building Ldr. Guide: No Size: 8.0 x 10.50
Subjects: Bible Study, Old Testament
Comments: This study, first of a two-volume series, covers the entire Old Testament. It's a systematic, individual study in which participants learn by doing—information is given and questions test their understanding. An introductory section gives a good review of the Bible and how the study is developed, and it shows students how to make the most of the study. The study is appropriate for individuals or groups of any size.

Author: Walter, Donna 1424
Series: Discover Your Bible
Title: *Discover: Prayer*
Publisher: Church Development Resources, 1986

Num. Sess.	Group Time	Num. Pgs.	Avg. Qst.	Price	Audience	Format	Bible Study
8	60-75	56	7	$1.60	Beginner	Workbk	Book

Features: Intro to Study, Summary, Full Scrpt Printed
★★★ Personal Application Preparation Time: None
★★ Relationship Building Ldr. Guide: Yes Size: 5.50 x 8.50
Subjects: Faith, God, Obedience, Prayer
Comments: This inductive study on prayer helps participants discover who God is and why it is important to pray to Him. The prayers of Jesus and other Bible characters serve as models. Attitudes and faithfulness in prayer are stressed as well as content. In addition to learning prayer, participants will come to know God, His identity and His relationship with people. A comprehensive leader's guide is available.

Author: Wamberg, Steve & Annie 1425
Series: Group's Active Bible Curriculum
Title: *Building Better Friendships*
Publisher: Group Publishing, 1992 ISBN: 1-55945-138-6

Num. Sess.	Group Time	Num. Pgs.	Avg. Qst.	Price	Audience	Format	Bible Study
4	35-60	48	Vary	$9.99	Beginner	Workbk	Topical

Features: Intro to Leading a Study, Intro to Study, Objectives, Study Overview, Ldr's Notes, Handouts, Agenda, Publicity Ideas
★★★★ Personal Application Preparation Time: None
★★★★ Relationship Building Ldr. Guide: No Size: 8.50 x 11.0
Subjects: Teens: Friends, Teens: Junior High
Comments: In this study, junior highers discover what makes good friendships. Participants learn the elements of a good friendship, know how to respond to conflicts with friends, examine the benefits and risks of having a best friend, and recognize friendship qualities they can apply to their relationships with Jesus. Activity sheets are reproducible.

Author: Wamberg, Steve & Annie 1426
Series: Group's Active Bible Curriculum
Title: *Can Christians Have Fun?*
Publisher: Group Publishing, 1992 ISBN: 1-55945-134-3

Num. Sess.	Group Time	Num. Pgs.	Avg. Qst.	Price	Audience	Format	Bible Study
4	35-60	47	Vary	$9.99	Beginner	Workbk	Topical

Features: Intro to Leading a Study, Intro to Study, Objectives, Study Overview, Ldr's Notes, Handouts, Agenda, Publicity Ideas
★★★★ Personal Application Preparation Time: None
★★★★ Relationship Building Ldr. Guide: No Size: 8.50 x 11.0
Subjects: Teens: Christian Liv, Teens: Junior High
Comments: In this study, junior highers discover God's perspective on having a good time. Participants discover ways to celebrate their faith and illuminate the world with the joy of being a Christian. Plus, they discover ways to find joy in tough times. It can be adapted for a Bible class or youth meeting. Activities sheets are reproducible. Student books not required. The instructions are easy to follow.

Author: Wamberg, Steve & Annie 1427
Series: Group's Active Bible Curriculum
Title: *Christmas: A Fresh Look*
Publisher: Group Publishing, 1991 ISBN: 1-55945-124-6

Num. Sess.	Group Time	Num. Pgs.	Avg. Qst.	Price	Audience	Format	Bible Study
4	35-60	47	Vary	$9.99	Beginner	Workbk	Topical

Features: Intro to Leading a Study, Intro to Study, Objectives, Study Overview, Ldr's Notes, Handouts, Agenda, Publicity Ideas
★★★★ Personal Application Preparation Time: None
★★★★ Relationship Building Ldr. Guide: No Size: 8.50 x 11.0
Subjects: Teens: Christian Liv, Teens: Jesus Life, Teens: Junior High
Comments: Teenagers discover the real meaning of Jesus' birth through this involving course. Participants learn why Christmas should be important to them while they relive the first Christmas, study the feelings of the Bible characters involved, reexamine the "giving" aspect of Christmas, explore their own feelings about Christmas, and discover meaningful ways to celebrate Jesus' birthday.

Author: Wamberg, Steve & Annie 1428
Series: Group's Active Bible Curriculum
Title: *Drugs & Drinking*
Publisher: Group Publishing, 1990 ISBN: 1-55945-118-1

Num. Sess.	Group Time	Num. Pgs.	Avg. Qst.	Price	Audience	Format	Bible Study
4	35-60	48	Vary	$9.99	Beginner	Workbk	Topical

Features: Intro to Leading a Study, Intro to Study, Objectives, Study Overview, Ldr's Notes, Drawings, Handouts, Agenda, Publicity Ideas
★★★★ Personal Application Preparation Time: None
★★★★ Relationship Building Ldr. Guide: No Size: 8.50 x 11.0
Subjects: Teens:Drugs/Drinking, Teens: Junior High
Comments: This 4-lesson study helps young people learn to make Christian decisions about drugs and drinking. Participants will explore the lure of drugs and drinking, weigh the options of having just 1 drink, and learn to avoid drugs and beat the temptation. The studies can be used in a Bible class or youth meeting. Activities and Bible studies are included as separate reproducible sheets.

Author: Wamberg, Steve 1429
Series: Group's Active Bible Curriculum
Title: *Is God Unfair?*
Publisher: Group Publishing, 1990 ISBN: 1-55945-108-4

Num. Sess.	Group Time	Num. Pgs.	Avg. Qst.	Price	Audience	Format	Bible Study
4	35-60	48	Vary	$9.99	New Christian	Workbk	Charctr

Features: Intro to Leading a Study, Intro to Study, Objectives, Study Overview, Ldr's Notes, Drawings, Handouts, Agenda, Publicity Ideas
★★★★ Personal Application Preparation Time: None
★★★★ Relationship Building Ldr. Guide: No Size: 8.50 x 11.0
Subjects: Teens: Emotions, Teens: Junior High, Teens: Theology
Comments: This study prepares junior high youth to answer tough questions about God. The 4 lessons help students grapple with the question: Does God care? They will understand that God loves them no matter how unlovable they feel; learn how to find God's love in the midst of tragedy and suffering; and discover how to turn anger at God into trust in Him. No student books are required.

Author: Warden, Michael 1430
Series:
Title: *Small Church Youth Ministry Programming Ideas*
Publisher: Group Publishing, 1994 ISBN: 1-55945-252-8

Num. Sess.	Group Time	Num. Pgs.	Avg. Qst.	Price	Audience	Format	Bible Study
	—	120	N/A	$12.99			

Features: Intro to Study, Handouts
Personal Application Preparation Time:
Relationship Building Ldr. Guide: Size: 6.0 x 9.0
Subjects: Teens: Resources
Comments: The programming ideas in this book are specifically geared toward enhancing relationships among small group members. Youth leaders using these ideas will require courage and a level of vulnerability. It means taking kids on fun adventures and spending "down time" with them. Help comes in finding tough answers just by asking the right questions, seeing the power of Jesus' teachings by reliving His parables, and teaching kids to seek God in prayer.

Author: Warden, Michael 1431
Series: Projects With a Purpose
Title: *Teaching Teenagers to Pray*
Publisher: Group Publishing, 1994 ISBN: 1-55945-407-5

Num. Sess.	Group Time	Num. Pgs.	Avg. Qst.	Price	Audience	Format	Bible Study
4	45-65	40	Vary	$8.99	New Christian	Workbk	Topical

Features: Intro to Leading a Study, Intro to Study, Objectives, Prayer Helps, Ldr's Notes, Handouts, Agenda
★★★★ Personal Application Preparation Time: Low
★★★★ Relationship Building Ldr. Guide: No Size: 8.50 x 11.0
Subjects: Teens: Prayer, Teens: Senior High
Comments: This 4-week study on prayer helps senior highers explore the depth and excitement of real prayer. Lessons help participants discover the exact nature of prayer and practice keeping a personal prayer journal of their experiences with God. They go on a private excursion with God, pray with people for a special group or person, and design and lead a prayer concert in the congregation.

Author: Ward, Ted 1432
Series:
Title: *Values Begin at Home*
Publisher: Victor Books, 1979 ISBN: 0-89693-646-5

Num. Sess.	Group Time	Num. Pgs.	Avg. Qst.	Price	Audience	Format	Bible Study
13	60-75	144	N/A	$7.99	New Christian	Book	Topical

Features: Intro to Study, Bibliography, Charts, Glossary
★★★★ Personal Application Preparation Time: Med
★★★ Relationship Building Ldr. Guide: Yes Size: 5.50 x 8.0
Subjects: Parenting, Teens: Decisions, Teens: Ethics
Comments: This study concerns the enormous responsibility facing Christian parents of helping their children learn to make positive moral choices. Moral character does not result from building fences around children, but from supervising their interaction with parents, adults, and other children. Participants review children's built-in capability to make decisions about right and wrong, their need for encouragement, discipline, and a foundation of responsible moral conduct.

Author: Warren, Dr. Rick 1433
Series:
Title: *Power to Change Your Life, The*
Publisher: Victor Books, 1990 ISBN: 0-89693-472-1

Num. Sess.	Group Time	Num. Pgs.	Avg. Qst.	Price	Audience	Format	Bible Study
12	60-90	149	N/A	$8.99	New Christian	Book	Topical

Features:
★★★★ Personal Application Preparation Time: Low
★★★ Relationship Building Ldr. Guide: Yes Size: 5.50 x 8.0
Subjects: Christian Life, Discipleship, Fruit of the Spirit
Comments: This book helps readers learn how to cooperate with God, and allow His Holy Spirit to change their bad habits, destructive thoughts, or unpleasant personality traits. Readers will experience the joy of watching God develop in them the fruit of the Spirit. They will learn how to experience peace rather than pressure, joy rather than defeat, patience rather than irritation.

Author: Warren, Ramona 1434
Series: Family Growth Electives
Title: *Parenting Alone: Studies for Single Parents*
Publisher: David C. Cook Publishing Co., 1993 ISBN: 0-78145-024-1

Num. Sess.	Group Time	Num. Pgs.	Avg. Qst.	Price	Audience	Format	Bible Study
13	45-60	128	Vary	$19.95	Beginner	Workbk	Topical

Features: Intro to Study, Objectives, Bibliography, Prayer Helps, Drawings, Handouts, Persnl Study Quest
★★★★ Personal Application Preparation Time: None
★★★★ Relationship Building Ldr. Guide: Yes Size: 8.50 x 11.0
Subjects: Divorce, Family, Loneliness, Parenting, Relationships, Self-esteem, Singles' Issues, Social Issues
Comments: This 13-week study helps single moms and dads face family life without fantasy, deal with loss and broken dreams, handle the day-to-day pressures of parenting alone, develop healthy self-identities, establish trust bonds, and find wholeness as single adults.

Author: Warren, Richard 1435
Series:
Title: *Answers to Life's Difficult Questions*
Publisher: Victor Books, 1985 ISBN: 0-89693-395-4

Num. Sess.	Group Time	Num. Pgs.	Avg. Qst.	Price	Audience	Format	Bible Study
13	60-75	130	N/A	$8.99	Beginner	Book	Topical

Features: Intro to Study
★★★ Personal Application Preparation Time: Low
★★★ Relationship Building Ldr. Guide: Yes Size: 5.50 x 8.0
Subjects: Bible Personalities, Christian Living, Emotions, Friendships, Loneliness, Relationships, Stress, Success, Victorious Living
Comments: This study uses the lives of Bible characters to show how to make the most of difficult circumstances. Difficult questions facing both Christians and non-Christians include stress, discouragement, depression, and loneliness. This study can produce two results: learning God's principles for successful living; and believing God can use anyone in a significant way.

Author: Warren, Romona 1436
Series: Family Growth Electives
Title: *Enjoying Life With Little Ones*
Publisher: David C. Cook Publishing Co., 1993 ISBN: 0-78145-022-5

Num. Sess.	Group Time	Num. Pgs.	Avg. Qst.	Price	Audience	Format	Bible Study
13	45-60	128	Vary	$19.95	Beginner	Workbk	Topical

Features: Intro to Study, Bibliography, Prayer Helps, Drawings, Handouts, Persnl Study Quest
★★★ Personal Application Preparation Time: Low
★★★ Relationship Building Ldr. Guide: Yes Size: 8.50 x 11.0
Subjects: Communication, Family, Parenting, Relationships
Comments: This study helps today's parents of young children understand God's design for the family as they develop their own, unique parenting styles. They'll discover how to establish healthy family communication, build happy memories, and balance career with family responsibilities. It emphasizes successful techniques for transferring biblical values to young children.

Author: Washington, Raleigh and Glen Kehrein 1437
Series:
Title: *Breaking Down Walls*
Publisher: Moody Press, 1993 ISBN: 0-80242-643-3

Num. Sess.	Group Time	Num. Pgs.	Avg. Qst.	Price	Audience	Format	Bible Study
17	60-75	240	N/A	$9.99	New Christian	Book	Topical

Features:
★★★ Personal Application Preparation Time: Low
★ Relationship Building Ldr. Guide: No Size: 6.0 x 9.0
Subjects: Leadership, Social Issues
Comments: This book is about solutions, since the reality of racial strife in society is obvious. Using personal stories the authors lay foundations that underline 8 principles, which have been refined in the crucible of inner city living and ministry and are practical and biblically based. At the conclusion of each chapter, practical applications help readers be reconcilers in their personal lives, work, church, and community.

Author: Webb, Jana L. 1438
Series: Global Issues
Title: *Economic Justice*
Publisher: InterVarsity, 1990 ISBN: 0-83084-906-8

Num. Sess.	Group Time	Num. Pgs.	Avg. Qst.	Price	Audience	Format	Bible Study
6	45-60	48	11	$4.99	Beginner	Workbk	Topical

Features: Intro to Leading a Study, Intro to Study, Bibliography, Follow Up
★★ Personal Application Preparation Time: Low
★★ Relationship Building Ldr. Guide: No Size: 5.50 x 8.25
Subjects: Money, Social Issues
Comments: This 6-week study focuses on global economic injustice. The introduction reinforces its point of reference with statistics, information on "haves" and "have nots," and a recommended response from God's people. Lesson titles include: "An Unjust World," "Money and God's Servants," "The Global Community," "Christians Mobilize," and more. Group leaders should read the introduction before selection.

Author: Weiner, Bob & Rose 1439
Series:
Title: *Bible Studies for a Firm Foundation*
Publisher: Maranatha Publications, 1980 ISBN: 0-93855-800-5

Num. Sess.	Group Time	Num. Pgs.	Avg. Qst.	Price	Audience	Format	Bible Study
22	60-90	128	Vary	$9.95	New Christian	Workbk	Topical

Features:
★★ Personal Application Preparation Time: Med
★★ Relationship Building Ldr. Guide: No Size: 8.50 x 11.0
Subjects: Baptism, Beliefs, Faith, Holy Spirit, Jesus: Life/Teaching, Repentance
Comments: This study deals with the basics—the foundation of Christian belief and faith—and prepares participants for growth once these fundamental issues are dealt with. Beginning with atonement, the study covers repentance, baptism in water and the Holy Spirit, God's provision for healing, the Great Commision, the last days and Christ's return, and more.

Author: Weiner, Bob & Rose 1440
Series:
Title: *Bible Studies for the Life of Excellence: A Study of James*
Publisher: Maranatha Publications, 1981 ISBN: 0-93855-804-8

Num. Sess.	Group Time	Num. Pgs.	Avg. Qst.	Price	Audience	Format	Bible Study
12	60-75	60	20	$7.95	New Christian	Workbk	Book

Features: Intro to Study
★★ Personal Application Preparation Time: Med
★★ Relationship Building Ldr. Guide: No Size: 8.50 x 11.0
Subjects: Faith, Hope, James, Service
Comments: This 12e-lesson study of James, a verse-by-verse exposition, deals with the essence of Christianity—faith, hope, and love. It exhorts, comforts, and encourages participants; and it warns and reproofs as well. It challenges Christians to action, to be "doers" and not just "hearers" of the Word. It demonstrates God's love, and it ends with the hope we share for eternity. Each lesson is composed of a series of questions.

Author: Weiner, Bob & Rose **1441**
Series:
Title: *Bible Studies on the Overcoming Life*
Publisher: Maranatha Publications, 1981 ISBN: 0-93855-801-3

Num. Sess.	Group Time	Num. Pgs.	Avg. Qst.	Price	Audience	Format	Bible Study
20	60-90	113	Vary	$9.95	New Christian	Workbk	Topical

Features:
★★ Personal Application Preparation Time: Med
★★ Relationship Building Ldr. Guide: No Size: 8.50 x 11.0
Subjects: Christian Living, Holy Spirit, Suffering, Victorious Living
Comments: In 20 lessons, this study effectively leads participants through the whole Christian experience. Four series take them from the cross to good works. The first series—"Brokenness"—deals with the path of the cross, personal trial, suffering for others, living in the Spirit, and walking in the resurrection. The second, "Righteousness," deals with becoming new creations and taking on the nature of God. The third and fourth series deal with practical Christian living.

Author: Weiner, Bob & Rose **1442**
Series:
Title: *Bible Studies for the Lovers of God: A Study of Philippians*
Publisher: Maranatha Publications, 1980 ISBN: 0-93855-803-X

Num. Sess.	Group Time	Num. Pgs.	Avg. Qst.	Price	Audience	Format	Bible Study
5	60-90	44	Vary	$7.95	New Christian	Workbk	Topical

Features: Intro to Study, Summary
★★ Personal Application Preparation Time: Med
★★ Relationship Building Ldr. Guide: No Size: 8.50 x 11.0
Subjects: God, Joy, Philippians, Prison Epistles, Relationships, Service, Suffering
Comments: This 5-lesson study of Philippians covers 4 basic areas of the Christian experience. This experience is full of Christ, joy, holy-mindedness, and fellowship. The lesson titles include: "The All-Sufficiency of Christ," "The True Servants of God," "The High Calling of God," and "Our Christian Responsibility." Each lesson comprises a series of questions.

Author: Weiner, Bob & Rose **1443**
Series:
Title: *Bible Studies for the Preparation of the Bride*
Publisher: Maranatha Publications, 1980 ISBN: 0-88270-471-0

Num. Sess.	Group Time	Num. Pgs.	Avg. Qst.	Price	Audience	Format	Bible Study
34	60-90	230	Vary	$14.95	New Christian	Workbk	Book

Features: Intro to Study
★★ Personal Application Preparation Time: Med
★★ Relationship Building Ldr. Guide: No Size: 8.50 x 11.0
Subjects: Love, Marriage, Song of Solomon
Comments: This study, in an effective workbook format, takes participants through the Song of Solomon. It begins with good instructions on how to read the Song of Solomon, then follows with an introduction explaining the book. Thirty-four lessons complete a verse-by-verse, exhaustive study of the entire work, from the initial song of love to the bride making herself ready. Each lesson comprises a series of questions, and all answers are listed together in the back of the book.

Author: Weiner, Bob & Rose **1444**
Series:
Title: *Jesus Brings New Life*
Publisher: Maranatha Publications, 1989 ISBN: 0-93855-824-2

Num. Sess.	Group Time	Num. Pgs.	Avg. Qst.	Price	Audience	Format	Bible Study
7	90-120	31	23	$3.95	Beginner	Workbk	Charctr

Features: Intro to Study, Scrpt Memory Helps, Appendix
★★ Personal Application Preparation Time: Med
★★ Relationship Building Ldr. Guide: No Size: 5.50 x 8.50
Subjects: Baptism, Commitments, Evangelism, Faith, Holy Spirit, Repentance, Youth Life
Comments: This study introduces the Christian faith to college-age adults. A lesson on the authority of God's Word is followed by lessons covering atonement, faith toward God, repentance, baptism in water, baptism in the Holy Spirit, and commitment to Christ. This study can be used either one-on-one or in a group. If used in a group, homework will help facilitate group interaction.

Author: White, Jerry & Mary **1445**
Series:
Title: *Friends & Friendship: The Secrets of Drawing Closer*
Publisher: NavPress, 1982 ISBN: 0-89109-500-4

Num. Sess.	Group Time	Num. Pgs.	Avg. Qst.	Price	Audience	Format	Bible Study
10	60-75	250	13	$9.00	New Christian	Book	Topical

Features: Scrpt Memory Helps, Follow Up, Summary, Charts, Appendix
★★★ Personal Application Preparation Time: Med
★★ Relationship Building Ldr. Guide: No Size: 5.0 x 8.0
Subjects: Christian Living, Family, Friendships, Relationships
Comments: This book discusses friendships, why friends are needed, individual capacities for friendship, right ways to make and keep them, how to heal wounded friendships, closer friendships within the family, and friendships with non-Christians. The book includes a personal test of a participant's friendship potential and Bible study questions for individuals or groups. No leader "helps" are included.

Author: White, John **1446**
Series:
Title: *Fight, The*
Publisher: InterVarsity, 1976 ISBN: 0-87784-777-0

Num. Sess.	Group Time	Num. Pgs.	Avg. Qst.	Price	Audience	Format	Bible Study
11	30-60	230	4	$10.99	New Christian	Book	Topical

Features:
★★★★ Personal Application Preparation Time: Low
★ Relationship Building Ldr. Guide: No Size: 5.50 x 8.25
Subjects: Christian Living
Comments: This book serves as a guide through the basic areas of Christian living: faith, prayer, temptation, evangelism, guidance, Bible study, fellowship, and work. It offers new Christians sound first steps, and mature Christians refreshing insights into the struggles and joys of freedom in Christ. Most chapters close with a summary and a suggested Scripture passage complete with questions. If read prior to a group meeting, more than one chapter could be covered at a time.

Author: White, John 1447
Series: Shaw Contemporary Issues
Title: *Lifestyle Priorities*
Publisher: Shaw, 1990 ISBN: 0-87788-501-X

Num. Sess.	Group Time	Num. Pgs.	Avg. Qst.	Price	Audience	Format	Bible Study
8	30-45	47	5	$4.99	Beginner	Workbk	Topical

Features: Intro to Leading a Study, Intro to Study, Bibliography, Follow Up, Ldr's Notes
★★★★ Personal Application Preparation Time: Low
★★★ Relationship Building Ldr. Guide: No Size: 5.25 x 8.25
Subjects: Christian Living, God, Obedience
Comments: These 8 short studies on worldliness and obedience are designed for people on the move. The course will challenge participants to look beyond traditional "do's and don'ts" that define worldliness for many Christians. Christians are called to radical obedience that will restore priorities and make people stop, take notice, and turn to the living God.

Author: White, John 1448
Series: LifeGuide Bible Study
Title: *Parables: The Greatest Stories Ever Told*
Publisher: InterVarsity, 1988 ISBN: 0-83081-037-4

Num. Sess.	Group Time	Num. Pgs.	Avg. Qst.	Price	Audience	Format	Bible Study
12	45-60	64	11	$4.99	Beginner	Workbk	Topical

Features: Intro to Leading a Study, Intro to Study, Ldr's Notes
★ Personal Application Preparation Time: Low
★ Relationship Building Ldr. Guide: No Size: 5.50 x 8.25
Subjects: Jesus: Life/Teaching, New Testament, Parables
Comments: In this study, 12 parables in Matthew and Luke are introduced, each with a central point, revealing standards and values of the Kingdom that contrast sharply with values in contemporary society. The parables illustrate truths about Christ's Kingdom that demand a response. Included are the parables of the sower, the lost sheep, the lost coin, the lost son, the good Samaritan, the unforgiving servant, the widow and the judge, the wheat and the weeds, the vineyard workers.

Author: White, William A. 1449
Series:
Title: *Single: Understanding and Accepting the Reality of It All*
Publisher: Warner Press, 1990 ISBN: 0-87162-513-X

Num. Sess.	Group Time	Num. Pgs.	Avg. Qst.	Price	Audience	Format	Bible Study
13	60-75	170	Vary	$4.95	Beginner	Book	Topical

Features: Intro to Study, Bibliography
★★★ Personal Application Preparation Time: Low
★★★★ Relationship Building Ldr. Guide: Yes Size: 4.25 x 7.0
Subjects: Singles' Issues
Comments: This 13-week study on being single addresses topics like: the reality of being single, freedom, wholeness, too little self-esteem, loneliness and aloneness, friendship, dating, intimacy, breaking-up, future marriage, single parenting, and growing spiritually. The study is designed to produce in-depth interaction with the text material and achieve informational and behavioral goals. The study doesn't include much Scripture.

Author: Whitney, Donald S. 1450
Series:
Title: *Spiritual Disciplines for the Christian Life*
Publisher: NavPress, 1994 ISBN: 0-89109-759-7

Num. Sess.	Group Time	Num. Pgs.	Avg. Qst.	Price	Audience	Format	Bible Study
10	75-90	95	22	$6.00	New Christian	Workbk	Topical

Features: Prayer Helps, Digging Deeper Quest, Book Avail
★★★ Personal Application Preparation Time: Med
★ Relationship Building Ldr. Guide: No Size: 5.50 x 8.50
Subjects: Christian Life
Comments: This guide, a companion to the book by the same title, leads participants through a variety of disciplines, including Scripture readings, stewardship, prayer, Scripture application, worship, fasting, silence and solitude, Scripture meditation, evangelism, journaling, serving, and learning. This study is for participants who have decided to discipline themselves for godliness, and understanding that waiting for life to "settle down" never comes.

Author: Wichern, Ed & Bo Hoskins 1451
Series:
Title: *Explore the Word*
Publisher: Roper Press, 1988 ISBN: 0-86606-260-2

Num. Sess.	Group Time	Num. Pgs.	Avg. Qst.	Price	Audience	Format	Bible Study
26	45-60	210	Vary	$6.95	New Christian	Book	Book

Features: Intro to Study, Bibliography, Summary, Charts, Maps, Appendix
★★★ Personal Application Preparation Time: Med
★★ Relationship Building Ldr. Guide: Yes Size: 5.50 x 8.50
Subjects: Bible Study, Small Group Resource, Teens: Bible Study
Comments: This book is for those who want to study the Bible but don't have much time. It chronologically takes a reader through the entire Bible and provides a concise grasp of what the Bible says. It features inspirational daily Bible readings, in-depth study of key passages, background material, a summary of each book of the Bible, and practical values for today.

Author: Wichern, Ed & Bo Hoskins 1452
Series:
Title: *Explore the Word: Teacher's Manual*
Publisher: Roper Press, 1988 ISBN: 0-86606-261-0

Num. Sess.	Group Time	Num. Pgs.	Avg. Qst.	Price	Audience	Format	Bible Study
26	45-60	230	Vary	$9.95	New Christian	Book	Book

Features: Intro to Leading a Study, Intro to Study, Objectives, Bibliography, Charts, Maps,Appendix
★★★★ Personal Application Preparation Time: Low
★ Relationship Building Ldr. Guide: No Size: 5.50 x 8.50
Subjects: Bible Study, New Testament, Old Testament
Comments: This manual features "Headings" on each lesson which identify its Bible portion and time period. "Recommended Reading" takes less than 10″ a day, while "For Detailed Study" provides an indepth look at each lesson's passages. "Lesson Capsules" are brief content summaries. "Teaching Plans" provide objectives. "Perspective" is the heart of the lesson and "Value for Today" application.

Author: Wiersbe, Warren W. **1453**
Series: The "Be" Series
Title: *Be Alert*
Publisher: Victor Books, 1984 ISBN: 0-89693-380-6

Num. Sess.	Group Time	Num. Pgs.	Avg. Qst.	Pricc	Audience	Format	Bible Study
13	45-60	168	N/A	$7.99	New Christian	Book	Book

Features: Intro to Study
★★ Personal Application Preparation Time: Low
★★ Relationship Building Ldr. Guide: Yes Size: 5.50 x 8.0
Subjects: Church Life, False Teachers, 1 & 2 Peter, 1, 2 & 3 John/Jude
Comments: This study will help Christians recognize false teachers and know how to fight them. It can also help participants recognize the false doctrines these apostates teach, doctrines that today sometimes pass for Christian truth. The study of the letters of Peter, John, and Jude outline the problems and solutions and sharpen spiritual discernment. A leader's guide, which includes transparency masters, is available.

Author: Wiersbe, Warren W. **1454**
Series: The "Be" Series
Title: *Be Alive*
Publisher: Victor Books, 1986 ISBN: 0-89693-359-8

Num. Sess.	Group Time	Num. Pgs.	Avg. Qst.	Price	Audience	Format	Bible Study
13	45-60	156	N/A	$7.99	Beginner	Book	Book

Features: Intro to Study
★★ Personal Application Preparation Time: Low
★★ Relationship Building Ldr. Guide: Yes Size: 5.50 x 8.0
Subjects: Faith, Jesus: Life/Teaching, John, Miracles
Comments: This study of the first 12 chapters of John focuses on Christ's public ministry, especially His miracles and the messages that grew out of them. The climax of His public ministry was official rejection by the religious rulers of Israel. This is an excellent study for helping Christians strengthen their faith, but is also a good study for those interested in Jesus but not yet committed to Him. A leader's guide, which includes transparency masters, is available.

Author: Wiersbe, Warren W. **1455**
Series: The "Be" Series
Title: *Be Available*
Publisher: Victor Books, 1994 ISBN: 1-56476-319-6

Num. Sess.	Group Time	Num. Pgs.	Avg. Qst.	Price	Audience	Format	Bible Study
13	45-60	168	N/A	$7.99	New Christian	Book	Book

Features:
★★ Personal Application Preparation Time: Low
★★ Relationship Building Ldr. Guide: Yes Size: 5.50 x 8.0
Subjects: Judges
Comments: The modern world and the world of the Judges are similar in many ways. There is greed, sexual immorality, and a disregard for moral absolutes. Even God's people can't seem to work together. This expositional study of the Book of Judges reviews Israel's turning away from God in disobedience, God's chastening and discipline of Israel, and the disorder that consumes the nation when religious confusion, immorality, and civil war break out.

Author: Wiersbe, Warren W. **1456**
Series: The "Be" Series
Title: *Be Comforted*
Publisher: Victor Books, 1992 ISBN: 0-89693-797-6

Num. Sess.	Group Time	Num. Pgs.	Avg. Qst.	Price	Audience	Format	Bible Study
13	45-60	164	N/A	$7.99	New Christian	Book	Book

Features: Intro to Study
★★ Personal Application Preparation Time: Low
★★ Relationship Building Ldr. Guide: Yes Size: 5.50 x 8.0
Subjects: Isaiah/Jeremiah
Comments: "Comfort, comfort My people!" was the good news the prophet Isaiah proclaimed to God's people centuries ago, and his message still applies today. Isaiah not only reveals God's prophetic plan for Israel, but also God's power and peace for all who will trust Him. This study shows participants how God can help them find strength and comfort in times of trial, conquer fear when their worlds are shaking, and experience God's comfort and love.

Author: Wiersbe, Warren W. **1457**
Series: The "Be" Series
Title: *Be Compassionate*
Publisher: Victor Books, 1988 ISBN: 0-89693-591-4

Num. Sess.	Group Time	Num. Pgs.	Avg. Qst.	Price	Audience	Format	Bible Study
13	45-60	156	N/A	$7.99	New Christian	Book	Book

Features: Intro to Study
★★ Personal Application Preparation Time: Low
★★ Relationship Building Ldr. Guide: Yes Size: 5.50 x 8.0
Subjects: Caring, Jesus: Life/Teaching, Luke
Comments: In this study of Dr. Luke's record of Christ, the Great Physician, participants will understand God's compassion. They will be motivated to show more loving concern for others and, with God's power, help others in distress. Jesus showed compassion to all kinds of people: the sinful, rejected, brokenhearted, men, women, and children. Luke exhorts Christians to be more like the Christ, to "be compassionate." A leader's guide is available.

Author: Wiersbe, Warren W. **1458**
Series: The "Be" Series
Title: *Be Complete*
Publisher: Victor Books, 1981 ISBN: 0-89693-726-7

Num. Sess.	Group Time	Num. Pgs.	Avg. Qst.	Price	Audience	Format	Bible Study
13	45-60	159	N/A	$7.99	New Christian	Book	Book

Features: Intro to Study
★★ Personal Application Preparation Time: Low
★★ Relationship Building Ldr. Guide: Yes Size: 5.50 x 8.0
Subjects: Christian Living, Church Life, Colossians/Philemon, False Teachers, Hope, Integrity, Prison Epistles
Comments: This study shows participants how to put Christ first in their lives. Too often, Christians confuse man-made philosophies and legalistic rules with Gospel truth; the Colossians faced that, just as do contemporary believers. Paul corrects erring ways and warns against the temptation to look for spiritual fulfillment from sources other than God. He calls Christians to "be complete" in Christ.

Author: Wiersbe, Warren W. **1459**
Series: The "Be" Series
Title: *Be Confident*
Publisher: Victor Books, 1982 ISBN: 0-89693-728-3

Num. Sess.	Group Time	Num. Pgs.	Avg. Qst.	Price	Audience	Format	Bible Study
13	45-60	157	N/A	$7.99	New Christian	Book	Book

Features: Intro to Study
★★ Personal Application Preparation Time: Low
★★ Relationship Building Ldr. Guide: Yes Size: 5.50 x 8.0
Subjects: Christian Living, Faith, Hebrews
Comments: This study of Hebrews reflects a time when the ages were colliding and everything in society seemed to be shaking. Christians wondered what was going on and what they could do about it. Old stability was passing away, and their faith was wavering. Hebrews' major message is "be confident." God shakes up things so that believers can learn to live by faith, not by sight. A leader's guide, including transparency masters, is available.

Author: Wiersbe, Warren W. **1460**
Series: The "Be" Series
Title: *Be Courageous*
Publisher: Victor Books, 1989 ISBN: 0-89693-665-1

Num. Sess.	Group Time	Num. Pgs.	Avg. Qst.	Price	Audience	Format	Bible Study
13	45-60	151	N/A	$7.99	New Christian	Book	Topical

Features: Intro to Study, Study Overview
★★★ Personal Application Preparation Time: Low
★★★ Relationship Building Ldr. Guide: Yes Size: 5.50 x 8.0
Subjects: Accountability, Christian Living, Discipleship, Jesus: Life/Teaching, Luke, Money, Victorious Living
Comments: This is a study of Luke's account of the Lord's journey to Jerusalem. It reminds participants that the major message for contemporary Christians today is "Be Courageous!" Topics covered include discipleship—its cost and compensation; daily living—wasting, spending, or investing your life; the right and wrong of riches; facing up to Christ's authority; and the power of a joyful life.

Author: Wiersbe, Warren W. **1461**
Series: The "Be" Series
Title: *Be Daring*
Publisher: Victor Books, 1988 ISBN: 0-89693-447-0

Num. Sess.	Group Time	Num. Pgs.	Avg. Qst.	Price	Audience	Format	Bible Study
13	45-60	152	N/A	$7.99	New Christian	Book	Book

Features: Intro to Study
★★ Personal Application Preparation Time: Low
★★ Relationship Building Ldr. Guide: Yes Size: 5.50 x 8.0
Subjects: Acts, Caring, Evangelism, Service
Comments: This practical study of Acts 13–28 explains how God equips and calls ordinary people to perform extraordinary tasks. It deals with questions such as: "What is a call to service?" "How does God equip His servants?" "How can I determine His will for my life?" and "What is God's program for world outreach?" The sin of being a "spectator" is exposed, and Christians are challenged to reach out to others.

Author: Wiersbe, Warren W. **1462**
Series: The "Be" Series
Title: *Be Decisive*
Publisher: Victor Books, 1995 ISBN: 1-56476-489-3

Num. Sess.	Group Time	Num. Pgs.	Avg. Qst.	Price	Audience	Format	Bible Study
13	45-60	168	N/A	$7.99	New Christian	Book	Book

Features: Intro to Study
★★ Personal Application Preparation Time: Low
★★ Relationship Building Ldr. Guide: Yes Size: 5.50 x 8.0
Subjects: Decision Making, Isaiah/Jeremiah
Comments: Wiersbe takes a look at the Book of Jeremiah and the important lessons to be learned from this Old Testament prophet. This study examines what it means to take a stand for the Truth.

Author: Wiersbe, Warren W. **1463**
Series: The "Be" Series
Title: *Be Determined*
Publisher: Victor Books, 1992 ISBN: 0-89693-071-8

Num. Sess.	Group Time	Num. Pgs.	Avg. Qst.	Price	Audience	Format	Bible Study
13	60-75	160	N/A	$7.99	New Christian	Book	Book

Features: Maps
★★★★ Personal Application Preparation Time: Low
★★ Relationship Building Ldr. Guide: Yes Size: 5.50 x 8.0
Subjects: Bible Personalities, Ezra/Nehemiah, Leadership
Comments: Nehemiah was a man of vision, courage, and faith. He was a layman called by God to lead Jerusalem in a new beginning. In spite of opposition, he stayed with the job and saw the holy city restored. Nehemiah was a successful leader who shows participants how to encourage others to serve the Lord, detect and defeat the enemy's tactics, keep going when the going is tough, and make prayer a vital part of everyday life. A leader's guide is available.

Author: Wiersbe, Warren W. **1464**
Series: The "Be" Series
Title: *Be Diligent*
Publisher: Victor Books, 1987 ISBN: 0-89693-356-3

Num. Sess.	Group Time	Num. Pgs.	Avg. Qst.	Price	Audience	Format	Bible Study
13	45-60	156	N/A	$7.99	New Christian	Book	Book

Features: Intro to Study
★★ Personal Application Preparation Time: Low
★★ Relationship Building Ldr. Guide: Yes Size: 5.50 x 8.0
Subjects: Caring, Jesus: Life/Teaching, Mark, Service
Comments: This study of Mark is ideal for busy people who want to use every opportunity to serve God. It presents a Lord "on the move," meeting people's physical and spiritual needs. Mark depicts Christ as God's "suffering servant" who came not to be ministered to, but to minister. The study motivates and encourages believers to reach out to a world filled with hurting people. A leader's guide, which includes transparency masters, is available.

Author: Wiersbe, Warren W. **1465**
Series: The "Be" Series
Title: *Be Dynamic*
Publisher: Victor Books, 1987 ISBN: 0-89693-358-X

Num. Sess.	Group Time	Num. Pgs.	Avg. Qst.	Price	Audience	Format	Bible Study
13	45-60	155	N/A	$7.99	New Christian	Book	Book

Features: Intro to Study
★★ Personal Application Preparation Time: Low
★★ Relationship Building Ldr. Guide: Yes Size: 5.50 x 8.0
Subjects: Acts, Church Life, Holy Spirit
Comments: This exposition of the first 12 chapters of Acts shows how early church history is directly relevant to the modern church. Topics participants cover include: the ministry of the Spirit in the church; how to be an effective witness for Christ; how to turn persecution into blessing; and how to understand and solve church problems. The challenge is for contemporary Christians to claim the power in Acts, to "be dynamic!" A leader's guide is available.

Author: Wiersbe, Warren W. **1466**
Series: The "Be" Series
Title: *Be Encouraged*
Publisher: Victor Books, 1984 ISBN: 0-88207-620-5

Num. Sess.	Group Time	Num. Pgs.	Avg. Qst.	Price	Audience	Format	Bible Study
13	45-60	153	N/A	$7.99	Mature Christian	Book	Book

Features: Intro to Study
★★ Personal Application Preparation Time: Med
★★ Relationship Building Ldr. Guide: Yes Size: 5.50 x 8.0
Subjects: Church Life, Hope, Integrity, Leadership, Repentance, Service, Suffering, 2 Corinthians
Comments: This study of 2 Corinthians shows how God can turn trials into truimphs and sufferings into service. The spiritually young Corinthian church dealt with difficult obstacles; they were confused, defiant, and discouraged. Paul's God-centered perspective serves as the only effective antidote to discouragement, then and now. Participants should read 2 Corinthians twice before beginning the study.

Author: Wiersbe, Warren W. **1467**
Series: The "Be" Series
Title: *Be Faithful*
Publisher: Victor Books, 1981 ISBN: 0-89693-685-6

Num. Sess.	Group Time	Num. Pgs.	Avg. Qst.	Price	Audience	Format	Bible Study
13	45-60	175	N/A	$7.99	New Christian	Book	Topical

Features: Intro to Study, Study Overview
★★★ Personal Application Preparation Time: Low
★★ Relationship Building Ldr. Guide: Yes Size: 5.50 x 8.0
Subjects: Church Life, Colossians/Philemon, Leadership, Service, 1 & 2 Timothy/Titus
Comments: This study helps participants understand a local church's ministry, how to stick with it and be faithful to the Word, their tasks, and other people. If people are faithful to God-given tasks, then His work will prosper and His name will be glorified. A leader's guide with transparency masters is available.

Author: Wiersbe, Warren W. **1468**
Series: The "Be" Series
Title: *Be Free*
Publisher: Victor Books, 1975 ISBN: 0-89693-733-X

Num. Sess.	Group Time	Num. Pgs.	Avg. Qst.	Price	Audience	Format	Bible Study
13	45-60	160	N/A	$7.99	New Christian	Book	Book

Features: Intro to Study
★★ Personal Application Preparation Time: Low
★★ Relationship Building Ldr. Guide: Yes Size: 5.50 x 8.0
Subjects: Christian Living, Church Life, Galatians, Holy Spirit
Comments: This expository study of Galatians helps participants deal with the problem "If I want to be a 'really' good Christian, I must. . . ." It clearly describes one wrong way to do so, as Paul exposes the most popular substitute for spiritual living in churches then and now—legalism. Many people believe themselves "spiritual" because of what they don't do, or a group to which they belong. The correct answer: let the Holy Spirit take over; be free.

Author: Wiersbe, Warren W. **1469**
Series: The "Be" Series
Title: *Be Holy*
Publisher: Victor Books, 1994 ISBN: 1-56476-335-8

Num. Sess.	Group Time	Num. Pgs.	Avg. Qst.	Price	Audience	Format	Bible Study
13	45-60	163	N/A	$7.99	New Christian	Book	Book

Features: Intro to Study
★★★ Personal Application Preparation Time: Low
★★ Relationship Building Ldr. Guide: Yes Size: 5.50 x 8.0
Subjects: Leviticus
Comments: This 13-week study of Leviticus helps participants understand true holiness and the difference it makes, how a holy God deals with sin and provides forgiveness, how believers can grow in personal holiness, the privileges God's people have in worship and service, and the work that Jesus Christ has done for His people. Throughout this study participants are invited to live lives of wholeness and close fellowship with the Lord.

Author: Wiersbe, Warren W. **1470**
Series: The "Be" Series
Title: *Be Hopeful*
Publisher: Victor Books, 1982 ISBN: 0-89693-737-2

Num. Sess.	Group Time	Num. Pgs.	Avg. Qst.	Price	Audience	Format	Bible Study
13	45-60	143	N/A	$7.99	New Christian	Book	Book

Features: Intro to Study
★★ Personal Application Preparation Time: Low
★★ Relationship Building Ldr. Guide: Yes Size: 5.50 x 8.0
Subjects: Grace, Hope, Suffering, 1 & 2 Peter
Comments: This study reviews the people who first read Peter's epistle, people who experienced suffering and persecution because of their loyalty to Christ. Peter warned of a "fiery trial" of persecution; his goal was to prepare believers to be triumphant. Today there is suffering for faith too, but believers should "be hopeful" because God's grace is present for the asking. Participants will prepare for, rather than fear, hatred. A leader's guide is available.

Author: Wiersbe, Warren W. **1471**
Series: The "Be" Series
Title: *Be Joyful*
Publisher: Victor Books, 1974 ISBN: 0-89693-739-9

Num. Sess.	Group Time	Num. Pgs.	Avg. Qst.	Price	Audience	Format	Bible Study
13	45-60	143	N/A	$7.99	New Christian	Book	Book

Features: Intro to Study
★★ Personal Application Preparation Time: Low
★★ Relationship Building Ldr. Guide: Yes Size: 5.50 x 8.0
Subjects: Joy, Obedience, Philippians, Prison Epistles, Suffering, Victorious Living
Comments: Through this study of the joy of Philippians, participants can enjoy a happy Christian life. The lessons identify joy-stealers, put worry in perspective, and outline and define contentment. The four chapters of Philippians identify four attitudes that assist in maintaining joy: the single mind, the submissive mind, the spiritual mind, and the secure mind. They show that joy can be achieved.

Author: Wiersbe, Warren W. **1472**
Series: The "Be" Series
Title: *Be Loyal*
Publisher: Victor Books, 1980 ISBN: 0-89693-313-X

Num. Sess.	Group Time	Num. Pgs.	Avg. Qst.	Price	Audience	Format	Bible Study
26	45-60	220	N/A	$7.99	New Christian	Book	Book

Features: Intro to Study
★★ Personal Application Preparation Time: Low
★★ Relationship Building Ldr. Guide: Yes Size: 5.50 x 8.0
Subjects: Jesus: Life/Teaching, Matthew
Comments: This expository survey of Matthew presents Christ as King and emphasizes Matthew's message to Christians about Christ and His ministry. It leads to a deeper love for, and loyalty to, Christ. Its outline follows the revelation of the King, the rebellion against the King, the retirement of the King, the rejection of the King, and the resurrection of the King. Matthew's material is presented in topical rather than chronological order.

Author: Wiersbe, Warren W. **1473**
Series: The "Be" Series
Title: *Be Mature*
Publisher: Victor Books, 1978 ISBN: 0-89693-754-2

Num. Sess.	Group Time	Num. Pgs.	Avg. Qst.	Price	Audience	Format	Bible Study
13	45-60	176	N/A	$7.99	New Christian	Book	Book

Features: Intro to Study
★★ Personal Application Preparation Time: Low
★★ Relationship Building Ldr. Guide: Yes Size: 5.50 x 8.0
Subjects: Christian Living, Discipleship, Faith, James, Prayer
Comments: The Epistle of James was written to help first-century Christians understand and attain spiritual maturity. This study covers areas of growth such as learning to be patient, overcoming temptation, practicing what the Bible teaches, learning to control the tongue, making peace rather than trouble, and praying and getting results. Many Christian problems are caused by spiritual immaturity. God wants believers to grow up, not just grow old.

Author: Wiersbe, Warren W. **1474**
Series: The "Be" Series
Title: *Be Obedient*
Publisher: Victor Books, 1991 ISBN: 0-89693-875-1

Num. Sess.	Group Time	Num. Pgs.	Avg. Qst.	Price	Audience	Format	Bible Study
12	45-60	137	N/A	$7.99	Beginner	Book	Charctr

Features:
★★ Personal Application Preparation Time: Low
★★ Relationship Building Ldr. Guide: Yes Size: 5.50 x 8.0
Subjects: Bible Personalities, Genesis
Comments: This expository study of Genesis 12–25 focuses on the life and faith of Abraham. It practically and personably explains the 4 tests of true biblical faith: how the life of faith begins, how to have "overcoming faith" while facing life's battles, why and how God tests faith, and what to do when faith fails. A leader's guide, which includes transparency masters, is also available.

Author: Wiersbe, Warren W. **1475**
Series: The "Be" Series
Title: *Be Patient*
Publisher: Victor Books, 1991 ISBN: 0-89693-896-4

Num. Sess.	Group Time	Num. Pgs.	Avg. Qst.	Price	Audience	Format	Bible Study
13	45-60	155	N/A	$7.99	New Christian	Book	Book

Features:
★★ Personal Application Preparation Time: Low
★★ Relationship Building Ldr. Guide: Yes Size: 5.50 x 8.0
Subjects: Bible Personalities, Job, Suffering
Comments: Many people have heard about Job and his trials, but not many have understood what those trials were all about and what God was trying to accomplish through them. Neither did Job, at first. But as he asked hard questions of himself, his friends, and his God; he gained new insights on suffering, patience, and endurance, and he learned how powerful and caring the Lord really is. This study helps those who have suffered or are helping a loved one cope with suffering.

Author: Wiersbe, Warren W. **1476**
Series: The "Be" Series
Title: *Be Ready*
Publisher: Victor Books, 1979 ISBN: 0-89693-773-9

Num. Sess.	Group Time	Num. Pgs.	Avg. Qst.	Price	Audience	Format	Bible Study
13	45-60	178	N/A	$7.99	New Christian	Book	Book

Features: Intro to Study
★★ Personal Application Preparation Time: Low
★★ Relationship Building Ldr. Guide: Yes Size: 5.50 x 8.0
Subjects: Church Life, Holiness, Hope, Suffering, 1 & 2 Thessalonians
Comments: This study focuses on 2 major themes: the return of Christ and the ministry of the local church. Strong emphasis is placed on Christians' need to "be ready," with prepared lives and churches. Utilizing 1 Thessalonians, the study discusses how to walk in holiness, harmony, honesty, hope, and helpfulness. From 2 Thessalonians comes encouragement in suffering, enlightenment in teaching, and enablement in living. A leader's guide is available.

Author: Wiersbe, Warren W. 1477
Series: The "Be" Series
Title: *Be Real*
Publisher: Victor Books, 1972 ISBN: 0-89693-774-7

Num. Sess.	Group Time	Num. Pgs.	Avg. Qst.	Price	Audience	Format	Bible Study
12	45-60	190	N/A	$7.99	New Christian	Book	Book

Features: Intro to Study
★★ Personal Application Preparation Time: Low
★★ Relationship Building Ldr. Guide: Yes Size: 5.50 x 8.0
Subjects: Christian Living, Obedience, 1, 2 & 3 John/Jude
Comments: This study of 1 John emphasizes the truth that "real" living is Christian living as God intended. More than simply being "in" the family of God, it is growing in the Lord, in truth, in obedience, and in love. This through-the-book study deals with a number of subjects. Similar ideas are grouped and only given casual reference when they occur elsewhere. Leaders should be familiar with the entire book prior to beginning the first session.

Author: Wiersbe, Warren W. 1478
Series: The "Be" Series
Title: *Be Rich*
Publisher: Victor Books, 1976 ISBN: 0-89693-775-5

Num. Sess.	Group Time	Num. Pgs.	Avg. Qst.	Price	Audience	Format	Bible Study
13	45-60	175	N/A	$7.99	New Christian	Book	Book

Features: Intro to Study
★★ Personal Application Preparation Time: Low
★★ Relationship Building Ldr. Guide: Yes Size: 5.50 x 8.0
Subjects: Christian Living, Ephesians, Holy Spirit, Satan, Victorious Living
Comments: This study of Ephesians exhorts participants to stop living like paupers when Christ has made them rich. Three points are covered: the Christian home as it relates to the work of the Holy Spirit; Satan's strategy and how Christians can be victorious over him; and each Christian's responsibility in light of his or her great wealth in Christ. A leader's guide is available.

Author: Wiersbe, Warren W. 1479
Series: The "Be" Series
Title: *Be Right*
Publisher: Victor Books, 1977 ISBN: 0-89693-778-X

Num. Sess.	Group Time	Num. Pgs.	Avg. Qst.	Price	Audience	Format	Bible Study
13	45-60	178	N/A	$7.99	New Christian	Book	Book

Features: Intro to Study
★★ Personal Application Preparation Time: Low
★★ Relationship Building Ldr. Guide: Yes Size: 5.50 x 8.0
Subjects: Christian Living, Relationships, Romans, Success
Comments: This study of Romans is not a detailed expository. Rather, it is a survey which helps participants understand the letter's main message and how it applies to their lives today. If participants will commit to concentration as they study this letter, they will better understand the rest of the Bible and the secrets of successful Christian living. Christians can "be right" in the world, with God, and with others. A leader's guide is available.

Author: Wiersbe, Warren W. 1480
Series: The "Be" Series
Title: *Be Satisfied*
Publisher: Victor Books, 1990 ISBN: 0-89693-796-8

Num. Sess.	Group Time	Num. Pgs.	Avg. Qst.	Price	Audience	Format	Bible Study
12	45-60	136	N/A	$7.99	New Christian	Book	Book

Features:
★★ Personal Application Preparation Time: Low
★★ Relationship Building Ldr. Guide: Yes Size: 5.50 x 8.0
Subjects: Ecclesiastes
Comments: This 12-week study of Ecclesiastes provides a search for answers to the meaning of life. Studying King Solomon, readers can see that he had every opportunity to examine life and ponder its mysteries and perplexities. He faced the same daily issues that modern Christians face: the seeming monotony of life, the vanity of wisdom, the futility of wealth, and the certainty of death.

Author: Wiersbe, Warren W. 1481
Series: The "Be" Series
Title: *Be Skillful*
Publisher: Victor Books, 1995 ISBN: 1-56476-430-3

Num. Sess.	Group Time	Num. Pgs.	Avg. Qst.	Price	Audience	Format	Bible Study
13	45-60	168	N/A	$7.99	New Christian	Book	Book

Features: Intro to Study
★★ Personal Application Preparation Time: Low
★★ Relationship Building Ldr. Guide: Yes Size: 5.50 x 8.0
Subjects: Proverbs
Comments: This book takes a look at the Book of Proverbs and important lessons that can be learned from King Solomon. Better than any modern "success manual," Proverbs explores topics such as the nature of wisdom and where to find it, choosing the right path of life, dealing with wrong choices, the best use of time and money, how to make the right kind of friends, and how to build happy home lives.

Author: Wiersbe, Warren W. 1482
Series: The "Be" Series
Title: *Be Strong*
Publisher: Victor Books, 1993 ISBN: 1-56476-122-3

Num. Sess.	Group Time	Num. Pgs.	Avg. Qst.	Price	Audience	Format	Bible Study
13	45-60	168	N/A	$7.99	New Christian	Book	Book

Features: Intro to Study
★★★★ Personal Application Preparation Time: Low
★★ Relationship Building Ldr. Guide: Yes Size: 5.50 x 8.0
Subjects: Joshua, Victorious Living
Comments: God isn't looking for volunteers, because all Christians should be soldiers in the Lord's army. Some are good soldiers while others are AWOL. Joshua was one of God's early soldiers, and was on the winning side. Through his example of putting fear aside and recognizing the Lord as the true source of strength, participants learn the secret of victory over the enemy, how to turn defeat into victory, and how to claim spiritual inheritance.

Author: Wiersbe, Warren W. **1483**
Series: The "Be" Series
Title: *Be Transformed*
Publisher: Victor Books, 1986 ISBN: 0-89693-352-0

Num. Sess.	Group Time	Num. Pgs.	Avg. Qst.	Price	Audience	Format	Bible Study
13	45-60	151	N/A	$7.99	New Christian	Book	Book

Features: Intro to Study
★★ Personal Application Preparation Time: Low
★★ Relationship Building Ldr. Guide: Yes Size: 5.50 x 8.0
Subjects: Holy Spirit, John, Prayer, Relationships, Stress
Comments: This study of John 13–21 covers the private ministry of Christ to His own disciples. He prepared them for future service when the Holy Spirit would empower them. Just as the disciples were transformed, participants will be transformed through lessons with titles like "How Does the Holy Spirit Work in My Life?" "What Are the Secrets of Answered Prayer?" "Why Is Christian Fellowship So Important?" and "How Can I Overcome the Pressures of the World?"

Author: Wiersbe, Warren W. **1484**
Series: The "Be" Series
Title: *Be Victorious*
Publisher: Victor Books, 1985 ISBN: 0-89693-547-7

Num. Sess.	Group Time	Num. Pgs.	Avg. Qst.	Price	Audience	Format	Bible Study
13	45-60	156	N/A	$7.99	New Christian	Book	Book

Features: Intro to Study
★★ Personal Application Preparation Time: Low
★★ Relationship Building Ldr. Guide: Yes Size: 5.50 x 8.0
Subjects: Hope, Revelation, Suffering
Comments: This study of Revelation contains the message of the glorious victory of Christ over all enemies. More than prophecy, Revelation reveals the truth that in Christ all believers can overcome. John wrote this book to encourage 1st-century Christians who were experiencing great suffering. In every age of the church, Revelation brings comfort and hope. Its symbols are timeless and can be understood by believers at any point in history. A leader's guide is available.

Author: Wiersbe, Warren W. **1485**
Series: The "Be" Series
Title: *Be Wise*
Publisher: Victor Books, 1983 ISBN: 0-89693-304-0

Num. Sess.	Group Time	Num. Pgs.	Avg. Qst.	Price	Audience	Format	Bible Study
13	45-60	172	N/A	$7.99	New Christian	Book	Book

Features: Intro to Study
★★ Personal Application Preparation Time: Low
★★ Relationship Building Ldr. Guide: Yes Size: 5.50 x 8.0
Subjects: Church Life, Repentance, Wisdom, 1 Corinthians
Comments: This chapter-by-chapter study of 1 Corinthians explores Paul's letter that confronts Corinthians with their sins and urges them to repent. Christians then and now share problems: overpopulation, pride, and pollution. Church leaders compete with one another. Christians live immorally, and appear proud of it, and so on. Where humankind's knowledge produces problems, God's wisdom provides answers. A leader's guide is available.

Author: Wiersbe, Warren W. **1486**
Series:
Title: *Meet Yourself in the Psalms*
Publisher: Victor Books, 1983 ISBN: 0-88207-740-6

Num. Sess.	Group Time	Num. Pgs.	Avg. Qst.	Price	Audience	Format	Bible Study
13	60-75	140	N/A	$8.99	New Christian	Book	Book

Features: Intro to Study, Full Scrpt Printed
★★★★ Personal Application Preparation Time: Low
★★★ Relationship Building Ldr. Guide: Yes Size: 5.50 x 8.0
Subjects: Failure, Forgiveness, Psalms, Service, Stress
Comments: This 13-week study of selected psalms helps participants find themselves in the Psalms. They will also find the Lord, who waits to give new vision and strength for life and service. The study responds to people who ask why good things happen to bad people, who look for God when the bottom drops out, who face midlife crises with expectations of God's best, and who receive forgiveness and begin again after failure.

Author: Wiersbe, Warren W. **1487**
Series:
Title: *Preaching & Teaching With Imagination*
Publisher: Victor Books, 1994 ISBN: 1-56476-252-1

Num. Sess.	Group Time	Num. Pgs.	Avg. Qst.	Price	Audience	Format	Bible Study
	—	400	N/A	$22.99		Book	

Features: Bibliography, Index, Appendix
Personal Application Preparation Time:
Relationship Building Ldr. Guide: Size: 6.50 x 9.50
Subjects: Small Group Resource
Comments: The author provides communicators of God's Word with keys for doing their tasks with imagination and creativity. Divided into two parts, "Imagination and Life" contains eight chapters which discuss how people think in pictures and respond with their hearts as well as their heads, while "Imagination and Scripture" includes 17 chapters on pictures in the Pentateuch, the Historical books, the Poetical books, the Prophets, as well as the New Testament.

Author: Wiersbe, Warren W. **1488**
Series:
Title: *Wiersbe's Expository Outlines on the New Testament*
Publisher: Victor Books, 1992 ISBN: 0-89693-848-4

Num. Sess.	Group Time	Num. Pgs.	Avg. Qst.	Price	Audience	Format	Bible Study
	—	N/A	N/A	$32.99		Book	

Features:
Personal Application Preparation Time:
Relationship Building Ldr. Guide: Size: 6.50 x 9.75
Subjects: Bible Study, New Testament
Comments: This book, a chapter-by-chapter exposition of the New Testament, gives readers the opportunity to study each Bible book and chapter. It shows how they fit into the total revelation God has given of Christ and His redemptive work. Each study is concise and especially suitable for Sunday School classes and Bible study groups that want to examine God's Word in a systematic manner. It contains material not found in the "Be" series.

Author: Wiersbe, Warren W. **1489**
Series:
Title: *Wiersbe's Expository Outlines on the Old Testament*
Publisher: Victor Books, 1992 ISBN: 0-89693-847-6

Num. Sess.	Group Time	Num. Pgs.	Avg. Qst.	Price	Audience	Format	Bible Study
	—	N/A	N/A	$28.99		Book	

Features:
Personal Application Preparation Time:
Relationship Building Ldr. Guide: Size: 6.50 x 9.75
Subjects: Bible Study, Old Testament
Comments: A companion volume to Wiersbe's Expository Outlines of the New Testament, this unique commentary offers practical expositions of key Old Testament chapters. Each study is concise and especially suitable for Sunday School classes and Bible study groups that want to examine God's Word in a systematic manner. It contains material not found in the "Be" series.

Author: Wiersbe, Warren W. **1490**
Series:
Title: *Window on the Parables*
Publisher: Victor Books, 1979 ISBN: 0-89693-682-1

Num. Sess.	Group Time	Num. Pgs.	Avg. Qst.	Price	Audience	Format	Bible Study
13	60-75	154	N/A	$8.99	New Christian	Book	Topical

Features: Intro to Study
★★★★ Personal Application Preparation Time: Low
★★★ Relationship Building Ldr. Guide: Yes Size: 5.50 x 8.0
Subjects: Forgiveness, Money, Parables, Prayer, Service
Comments: This study offers insights into 13 of Jesus' most beloved parables. In them, Jesus deals with subjects no Christian can afford to treat lightly: salvation, forgiveness of others, love for minorities, right and wrong use of money, prayer, and motives for service. Participants will see themselves in ancient parables and see light shed in their modern lives. The leader's guide includes reproducible response sheets.

Author: Wilcock, Michael **1491**
Series: The Bible Speaks Today
Title: *Message of Revelation, The*
Publisher: InterVarsity, 1975 ISBN: 0-87784-293-0

Num. Sess.	Group Time	Num. Pgs.	Avg. Qst.	Price	Audience	Format	Bible Study
8	60-120	240	Vary	$12.99	New Christian	Book	Book

Features: Intro to Study, Prayer Helps, Follow Up
★★★ Personal Application Preparation Time: Med
★★ Relationship Building Ldr. Guide: No Size: 5.50 x 8.25
Subjects: New Testament, Revelation
Comments: This series of Old and New Testament expositions are characterized by 3 goals: to expound the biblical text with accuracy, relate it to contemporary life, and be readable. Wilcock maintains that God's words, declarations, arguments, and reasonings gave the church "a gorgeous picture book." Wilcox lifts the curtain on Revelation's drama in 8 scenes, helping our imaginations as well as our minds grasp the key concepts of this fascinating and enigmatic book.

Author: Wilcox, Anne **1492**
Series: Building Books
Title: *Building Bible Study Skills*
Publisher: Bethany House, 1985 ISBN: 0-87123-821-7

Num. Sess.	Group Time	Num. Pgs.	Avg. Qst.	Price	Audience	Format	Bible Study
34	45-60	70	Vary	$6.99	New Christian	Workbk	Topical

Features: Intro to Leading a Study, Intro to Study, Scrpt Memory Helps, Charts, Maps
★★★ Personal Application Preparation Time: Low
★★ Relationship Building Ldr. Guide: Yes Size: 8.50 x 11.0
Subjects: Teens: Bible Study, Teens: Discipleship
Comments: This 34-lesson study is divided into 5 sections. Part 1 explores the inspiration of Scripture and the results of careless interpretation. Part 2 is an introduction to Bible reference books. Part 3 gives instructions for using 6 different Bible study methods. Part 4 applies the 6 methods to 1 book of the Bible. Part 5 teaches remembering.

Author: Wilde, Gary A. **1493**
Series: Bible Alive Studies
Title: *Bringing the Christian Faith to Life*
Publisher: David C. Cook Publishing Co., 1993 ISBN: 0-78145-020-9

Num. Sess.	Group Time	Num. Pgs.	Avg. Qst.	Price	Audience	Format	Bible Study
13	45-60	144	Vary	$19.95	Beginner	Workbk	Book

Features: Intro to Study, Bibliography, Prayer Helps, Drawings, Handouts, Persnl Study Quest, Charts
★★★★ Personal Application Preparation Time: None
★★ Relationship Building Ldr. Guide: Yes Size: 8.50 x 11.0
Subjects: Faith, God, Holy Spirit, Jesus: Life/Teaching
Comments: This complete leader's guide provides an overview of the Christian faith. It answers questions such as: "How can I know that God exists?" "Does God love me?" "What will happen when I die?" "Is Jesus really the only way to God?" and "Did Jesus really have to die?" The format provides everything needed for 13 complete sessions. No student book is required.

Author: Wilde, Gary A. **1494**
Series: Group's Active Bible Curriculum
Title: *Dealing with Death*
Publisher: Group Publishing, 1991 ISBN: 1-55945-112-2

Num. Sess.	Group Time	Num. Pgs.	Avg. Qst.	Price	Audience	Format	Bible Study
4	35-60	48	Vary	$9.99	Beginner	Workbk	Topical

Features: Intro to Leading a Study, Intro to Study, Objectives, Study Overview, Ldr's Notes, Drawings, Handouts, Agenda, Publicity Ideas
★★★★ Personal Application Preparation Time: None
★★★★ Relationship Building Ldr. Guide: No Size: 8.50 x 11.0
Subjects: Teens: Emotions, Teens: Friends, Teens: Junior High
Comments: This study helps junior high students answer questions about death. In the 4 lessons participants will explore the Christian response to the idea of reincarnation, learn healthy ways to express feelings when a loved one dies, discover practical ways to help a friend who's mourning, and learn how to reach out to people with terminal illnesses. Instructions are easy to follow.

Author: Wilde, Gary A. **1495**
Series: Encouragers for Men
Title: *Family: My Place to Be*
Publisher: Victor Books, 1996 ISBN: 1-56476-514-8

Num. Sess.	Group Time	Num. Pgs.	Avg. Qst.	Price	Audience	Format	Bible Study
6	45-60	64	6	$3.25	Beginner	Book	Topical

Features: Intro to Leading a Study, Intro to Study, Prayer Helps, Follow Up, Ldr's Notes
★★★★ Personal Application Preparation Time: Low
★★★★ Relationship Building Ldr. Guide: No Size: 4.25 x 7.0
Subjects: Family, Men's Issues
Comments: Each session contains a Check-In/Update where men "report in" on their week. Additional resources include video-night discussions and Fellowship Day Idea Starters. Considers the topics of relating with parents and siblings, becoming a whole man, learning to be playful and tender with children, mentoring the next generation, and discovering your place in the church family.

Author: Wilde, Gary A. **1496**
Series: Encouragers for Men
Title: *Fellowship: Brothers Together*
Publisher: Victor Books, 1996 ISBN: 1-56476-469-9

Num. Sess.	Group Time	Num. Pgs.	Avg. Qst.	Price	Audience	Format	Bible Study
6	45-60	64	6	$3.25	Beginner	Book	Topical

Features: Intro to Leading a Study, Intro to Study, Prayer Helps, Follow Up, Ldr's Notes
★★★★ Personal Application Preparation Time: Low
★★★★ Relationship Building Ldr. Guide: No Size: 4.25 x 7.0
Subjects: Friendships, Men's Issues
Comments: This series is for men from every background and denomination. Each session contains relevant Scripture passages, brief excerpts from a variety of sources, questions, prayer time, and suggestions for practical life-responses. Considers the topics of uniting through shared experience, trust, listening, encouragement, risking realness, and bonding through prayer.

Author: Wilde, Gary A. **1497**
Series: Encouragers for Men
Title: *Fulfillment: Living at Peace*
Publisher: Victor Books, 1996 ISBN: 1-56476-515-6

Num. Sess.	Group Time	Num. Pgs.	Avg. Qst.	Price	Audience	Format	Bible Study
6	45-60	64	6	$3.25	Beginner	Book	Topical

Features: Intro to Leading a Study, Intro to Study, Prayer Helps, Follow Up, Ldr's Notes
★★★★ Personal Application Preparation Time: Low
★★★★ Relationship Building Ldr. Guide: No Size: 4.25 x 7.0
Subjects: Men's Issues
Comments: Each session contains a Check-In/Update where men "report in" on their week, relevant Scripture passages, questions, prayer time, and suggestions for practical life-responses. Considers the topics of healing the father-wound, dealing with frustrated dreams, giving up the rescuer role, pursuing emotional wholeness, learning to be content.

Author: Wilde, Gary A. **1498**
Series: Group's Active Bible Curriculum
Title: *Handling Conflict*
Publisher: Group Publishing, 1991 ISBN: 1-55945-125-4

Num. Sess.	Group Time	Num. Pgs.	Avg. Qst.	Price	Audience	Format	Bible Study
4	35-60	48	Vary	$9.99	Beginner	Workbk	Topical

Features: Intro to Leading a Study, Intro to Study, Objectives, Study Overview, Ldr's Notes, Handouts, Agenda, Publicity Ideas
★★★★ Personal Application Preparation Time: None
★★★★ Relationship Building Ldr. Guide: No Size: 8.50 x 11.0
Subjects: Teens: Christian Liv, Teens: Friends, Teens: Junior High, Teens: Relationships
Comments: In this course, junior highers learn biblical principles for dealing with conflicts with family, friends, and authority. Participants explore natural reactions to specific conflicts, study conflict resolution techniques, and examine biblical examples of people in conflict. It can be adapted for a Bible class or youth meeting.

Author: Wilde, Gary A. **1499**
Series: Group's Active Bible Curriculum
Title: *Heaven & Hell*
Publisher: Group Publishing, 1992 ISBN: 1-55945-131-9

Num. Sess.	Group Time	Num. Pgs.	Avg. Qst.	Price	Audience	Format	Bible Study
4	35-60	46	Vary	$9.99	Beginner	Workbk	Topical

Features: Intro to Leading a Study, Intro to Study, Objectives, Handouts, Agenda, Publicity Ideas
★★★★ Personal Application Preparation Time: None
★★★★ Relationship Building Ldr. Guide: No Size: 8.50 x 11.0
Subjects: Teens: Christian Liv, Teens: Heaven/Hell, Teens: Junior High
Comments: In this course, young teenagers explore biblical perspectives on heaven and hell. Participants uncover what the Bible says about heaven, determine what they believe about hell, discover what it takes to get to heaven, and learn how to live as citizens of heaven while still on earth. It can be adapted for a Bible class or youth meeting. Activity sheets are reproducible. Student books not required.

Author: Wilde, Gary A. **1500**
Series: Encouragers for Men
Title: *Integrity: Character Counts*
Publisher: Victor Books, 1996 ISBN: 1-56476-500-8

Num. Sess.	Group Time	Num. Pgs.	Avg. Qst.	Price	Audience	Format	Bible Study
6	45-60	64	6	$3.25	Beginner	Book	Topical

Features: Intro to Leading a Study, Intro to Study, Prayer Helps, Follow Up, Ldr's Notes
★★★★ Personal Application Preparation Time: Low
★★★★ Relationship Building Ldr. Guide: No Size: 4.25 x 7.0
Subjects: Integrity, Men's Issues
Comments: This series is for men from every background and denomination. Each session contains a Check-In/Update where men "report in" on their week. Resources include video-night discussions and Fellowship Day Idea Starters. Considers the topics of facing the temptation to deceive, moral bravery in confronting evil, spiritual authenticity, sexual purity, and personal accountability.

Author: Wilde, Gary A. **1501**
Series: Encouragers for Men
Title: *Job & Career: Men at Work*
Publisher: Victor Books, 1996 ISBN: 1-56476-478-8

Num. Sess.	Group Time	Num. Pgs.	Avg. Qst.	Price	Audience	Format	Bible Study
6	45-60	64	6	$3.25	Beginner	Book	Topical

Features: Intro to Leading a Study, Intro to Study, Prayer Helps, Follow Up, Ldr's Notes
★★★★ Personal Application Preparation Time: Low
★★★★ Relationship Building Ldr. Guide: No Size: 4.25 x 7.0
Subjects: Men's Issues, Work
Comments: Each session contains a Check-In/Update where men "report in" on their week, relevant Scripture passages, questions, prayer time, and suggestions for practical life-responses. Considers the topics of dealing with the drive to produce, success/failure, pursuing career success, a sense of calling, confronting ethical dilemmas, and controlling the future.

Author: Wilde, Gary A. **1502**
Series: Encouragers for Men
Title: *Spirituality: Loved By God*
Publisher: Victor Books, 1996 ISBN: 1-56476-499-0

Num. Sess.	Group Time	Num. Pgs.	Avg. Qst.	Price	Audience	Format	Bible Study
6	45-60	64	6	$3.25	Beginner	Book	Topical

Features: Intro to Leading a Study, Intro to Study, Prayer Helps, Follow Up, Ldr's Notes
★★★★ Personal Application Preparation Time: Low
★★★★ Relationship Building Ldr. Guide: No Size: 4.25 x 7.0
Subjects: Men's Issues
Comments: Each session contains relevant Scripture passages, questions, prayer time, and suggestions for practical life-responses. Considers the topics of exploring one's God image, experiencing the power of total acceptance, trusting God in the midst of uncertainty, finding purpose in the wounds God allows, making time for a devotional life, and affirming the warrior spirit in kingdom battles.

Author: Wilde, Gary A. **1503**
Series: Group's Active Bible Curriculum
Title: *Suicide: The Silent Epidemic*
Publisher: Group Publishing, 1992 ISBN: 1-55945-145-9

Num. Sess.	Group Time	Num. Pgs.	Avg. Qst.	Price	Audience	Format	Bible Study
4	35-60	45	Vary	$9.99	Beginner	Workbk	Topical

Features: Intro to Leading a Study, Intro to Study, Objectives, Study Overview, Ldr's Notes, Handouts, Agenda, Publicity Ideas
★★★★ Personal Application Preparation Time: None
★★★★ Relationship Building Ldr. Guide: No Size: 8.50 x 11.0
Subjects: Teens: Christian Liv, Teens: Emotions, Teens: Junior High, Teens: Self-esteem
Comments: This course helps junior highers understand the dangers of suicide while exploring painful feelings and discovering God's redeeming love. Plus, participants learn to deal effectively with depression. It can be adapted for a Bible class or youth meeting. Activity sheets are reproducible. Student books not required.

Author: Wilde, Gary A. **1504**
Series: Lay Action Ministry
Title: *Your Ministry of Prayer*
Publisher: Lay Action Ministry Program, 1990 ISBN: 0-89191-490-0

Num. Sess.	Group Time	Num. Pgs.	Avg. Qst.	Price	Audience	Format	Bible Study
12	60-90	143	Vary	$6.95	New Christian	Workbk	Topical

Features: Prayer Helps, Ldr's Notes
★★★ Personal Application Preparation Time: Low
★★★ Relationship Building Ldr. Guide: Yes Size: 5.25 x 8.25
Subjects: God, Prayer
Comments: This practical study helps participants grow in understanding and practicing prayer, while showing them how to organize with others in the church an ongoing prayer ministry. They will become familiar with the names and attributes of God, deal with the tough questions concerning God's will, and grapple with what it means to truly worship God in prayer. Examples of Jesus and other biblical pray-ers provide insights to apply to one's own prayer life.

Author: Wilger, Jennifer Root **1505**
Series: Group's Active Bible Curriculum
Title: *Real People, Real Faith*
Publisher: Group Publishing, 1994 ISBN: 1-55945-238-2

Num. Sess.	Group Time	Num. Pgs.	Avg. Qst.	Price	Audience	Format	Bible Study
4	35-60	52	Vary	$9.99	Beginner	Workbk	Topical

Features: Intro to Leading a Study, Intro to Study, Objectives, Study Overview, Ldr's Notes, Handouts, Agenda, Publicity Ideas
★★★★ Personal Application Preparation Time: None
★★★★ Relationship Building Ldr. Guide: No Size: 8.50 x 11.0
Subjects: Teens: Christian Liv, Teens: Emotions, Teens: Missions, Teens: Senior High
Comments: In this course, teenagers meet positive Christian role models to follow. Amy Grant, Joni Eareckson Tada, Dave Dravecky, and Terry Anderson. Teenagers learn to express their Christian faith, rely on God's power when weak, identify their dreams, and trust God when their lives seem out of control.

Author: Williams, Dan **1506**
Series:
Title: *Seven Myths About Small Groups*
Publisher: InterVarsity, 1991 ISBN: 0-83081-721-2

Num. Sess.	Group Time	Num. Pgs.	Avg. Qst.	Price	Audience	Format	Bible Study
7	—	144	N/A	$7.99			

Features: Bibliography, Cartoons
Personal Application Preparation Time:
Relationship Building Ldr. Guide: Size: 5.50 x 8.25
Subjects: Small Group Resource
Comments: This book is for small group leaders, pastors, and participants who want to see groups revitalized. Each chapter addresses 1 of 7 key myths and shows how they can be harmful. It offers suggestions and creative ideas for moving a group from the doldrums. Myths addressed include: "Groups Should Last Forever"; "Bigger is Better"; "Groups Need Strong Leaders"; "More Members Should Lead"; "Good Groups are Polite"; and "Mission Must Wait."

Author: Williams, Michael 1507
Series: Bible Study for Christian
Title: *Acts—Volumes 1 & 2*
Publisher: Cokesbury, 1990 ISBN: 0-68776-155-7

Num. Sess.	Group Time	Num. Pgs.	Avg. Qst.	Price	Audience	Format	Bible Study
7	45-60	N/A	Vary	$25.00	New Christian	Video	Book

Features: Intro to Leading a Study, Intro to Study, Summary, Video Study Guide
★★★ Personal Application Preparation Time: Low
★★★ Relationship Building Ldr. Guide: Yes Size: 4.75 x 8.0
Subjects: Acts, Bible Personalities, Church Life, Faith
Comments: This 2-volume video lecture series on Acts includes 7 20″ lessons. It introduces participants to early Church members, shows them growing in faith and understanding, and follows them as they begin to carry out the Great Commission. Lessons cover "The New Community," "Pentecost," "Stephen," "Paul," "Peter and Cornelius," "Barnabas," and "The Acts."

Author: Williamson, David 1508
Series: Serendipity Support Group
Title: *Unemployed Unfulfilled: Down but Not Out*
Publisher: Serendipity House, 1990 ISBN: 1-88341-960-3

Num. Sess.	Group Time	Num. Pgs.	Avg. Qst.	Price	Audience	Format	Bible Study
7	60-90	80	Vary	$5.45	Beginner	Workbk	Topical

Features: Intro to Leading a Study, Objectives, Bibliography, Prayer Helps, Full Scrpt Printed, Cartoons, Agenda
★★★★ Personal Application Preparation Time: None
★★★★ Relationship Building Ldr. Guide: No Size: 6.50 x 9.25
Subjects: Emotions, Hope, Support, Work
Comments: This study, for the unemployed and underemployed, surveys interests and career options, and helps participants focus on the "right" job. Lessons are entitled "The Toughest Job," "Emotion Control," "Discovering the Real You," "The Meaning of Work," "The Hunt Begins," "Coming Up Empty," and "Keeping Hope Alive." The format includes icebreakers, Bible study, and prayer.

Author: Willis, Wes and Elaine 1509
Series: Accent On Truth
Title: *Fanning the Flames of Light*
Publisher: David C. Cook Publishing Co., 1993 ISBN: 0-89636-298-1

Num. Sess.	Group Time	Num. Pgs.	Avg. Qst.	Price	Audience	Format	Bible Study
12	60-90	96	18	$5.49	New Christian	Workbk	Book

Features: Intro to Study, Digging Deeper Quest, Cartoons
★★★★ Personal Application Preparation Time: Med
★★ Relationship Building Ldr. Guide: No Size: 6.0 x 9.0
Subjects: Ephesians
Comments: This study of Ephesians was written to remind Christians of things they might take for granted. Written to non-Jewish believers in the 1st century, Ephesians is a message for modern churches. Paul reminds Christians that spiritual blessings hold center court and that inheritance is given freely because of their position in Christ. Participants are reminded to be spiritual lights in a dark world, count blessings daily and exercise godly resources.

Author: Willis, Wes and Elaine 1510
Series: Accent On Truth
Title: *Living Life to the Fullest*
Publisher: David C. Cook Publishing Co., 1992 ISBN: 0-89636-290-6

Num. Sess.	Group Time	Num. Pgs.	Avg. Qst.	Price	Audience	Format	Bible Study
12	60-90	111	18	$5.49	New Christian	Workbk	Book

Features: Intro to Study, Digging Deeper Quest, Cartoons
★★★★ Personal Application Preparation Time: Med
★★ Relationship Building Ldr. Guide: No Size: 6.0 x 9.0
Subjects: Colossians/Philemon, Philippians
Comments: Paul, confined to a Roman dungeon, urges the Philippians to stand fast, be careful for nothing, and rejoice. He warns the Colossians against the powers of darkness, deceivers, and empty religion. Paul asks Philemon for mercy, not for himself but a runaway slave. These pictures of love at work study practical Christian behavior and relationships. These 3 letters issue wake-up calls for extraordinary levels of commitment and ministry.

Author: Willis, Wes and Elaine 1511
Series: Accent On Truth
Title: *Loving God in a Hostile World*
Publisher: David C. Cook Publishing Co., 1993 ISBN: 0-89636-293-0

Num. Sess.	Group Time	Num. Pgs.	Avg. Qst.	Price	Audience	Format	Bible Study
12	60-90	112	18	$5.49	New Christian	Workbk	Book

Features: Intro to Study, Digging Deeper Quest, Cartoons
★★★★ Personal Application Preparation Time: Med
★★ Relationship Building Ldr. Guide: No Size: 6.0 x 9.0
Subjects: 1 Corinthians
Comments: This study of 1 Corinthians exposes openly-flaunted evil perversion, factionalism, sin, and sexual looseness. The first 6 chapters address specific sins, factionalism, and rivalry within the church. Chapter 7 begins Paul's answers to specific questions from the house of Chloe. In the midst of answers to questions about Christian living, he inserted a poetic masterpiece on love, the ultimate standard by which we should live.

Author: Willis, Wes and Elaine 1512
Series: Accent On Truth
Title: *Revealing the Heart of a Servant: A Study of Mark*
Publisher: David C. Cook Publishing Co., 1994 ISBN: 0-89636-308-2

Num. Sess.	Group Time	Num. Pgs.	Avg. Qst.	Price	Audience	Format	Bible Study
12	60-90	112	18	$5.49	New Christian	Workbk	Book

Features: Intro to Study, Digging Deeper Quest, Cartoons
★★★★ Personal Application Preparation Time: Med
★★ Relationship Building Ldr. Guide: No Size: 6.0 x 9.0
Subjects: Mark
Comments: This study of Mark takes participants on an intimate journey with the Servant-Savior who can change their lives if they're brave enough to become like Him. The life of a servant isn't easy. He has no background, except that given him by his Master. He has no rights, no position. That's what Christ expects of those who answer His call to "follow me."

Author: Willis, Wes and Elaine **1513**
Series: Accent On Truth
Title: *Thriving in the Midst of Chaos*
Publisher: David C. Cook Publishing Co., 1992 ISBN: 0-89636-287-6

Num. Sess.	Group Time	Num. Pgs.	Avg. Qst.	Price	Audience	Format	Bible Study
12	60-90	112	19	$5.49	New Christian	Workbk	Book

Features: Intro to Study, Digging Deeper Quest, Cartoons
★★★★ Personal Application Preparation Time: Med
★★ Relationship Building Ldr. Guide: No Size: 6.0 x 9.0
Subjects: James
Comments: This interactive Bible study takes a fresh look at life-related and practical applications of biblical principles and truths. Its hands-on approach lets participants discover God's availability for whatever they face. Participants delve into what commitment to God means in the "ordinary" moments of life. God's sovereignty, patience, the tongue, and material possessions are part of the Bible study guide. Participants weave these truths into daily decisions, actions, and words.

Author: Willmington, Harold L. **1514**
Series:
Title: *Introduction to Theology*
Publisher: Tyndale House, 1990 ISBN: 0-84238-166-X

Num. Sess.	Group Time	Num. Pgs.	Avg. Qst.	Price	Audience	Format	Bible Study
	—	660	N/A	$24.99		Book	

Features: Bibliography
Personal Application Preparation Time:
Relationship Building Ldr. Guide: Size: 7.25 x 9.25
Subjects: Bible Study, Small Group Resource, Theology
Comments: This book is written for serious Bible students seeking quick and concise answers about Christian theology. From angels to the Trinity, 12 major doctrines are presented in easy-to-read format, including Scriptural and historical proofs for why Christians believe what they believe. An extended table of contents helps readers find specific theological points. Other doctrines include: the church, the deity of Christ, the ministry of the Holy Spirit, sin, and more.

Author: Willmington, Harold L. **1515**
Series:
Title: *Life of Christ, The: Willmington's Complete Guide to Bible Knowledge*
Publisher: Tyndale House, 1991 ISBN: 0-84238-163-5

Num. Sess.	Group Time	Num. Pgs.	Avg. Qst.	Price	Audience	Format	Bible Study
	—	290	N/A	$24.99		Book	

Features:
Personal Application Preparation Time:
Relationship Building Ldr. Guide: Size: 7.25 x 9.25
Subjects: Bible Study, Jesus: Life/Teaching, Small Group Resource
Comments: This book includes: statistics on the life of Christ in full detail; a summary of the life of Christ, sharing the details of His genealogies, His miracles, and teachings, precisely stated; a chronological overview, a harmonized treatment of the teaching and events of Christ's life and ministry; an overview of the ministry of Christ, His teachings, parables, miracles and their purpose; and more.

Author: Willmington, Harold L. **1516**
Series:
Title: *New Testament Survey*
Publisher: Tyndale House, 1990 ISBN: 0-84238-164-3

Num. Sess.	Group Time	Num. Pgs.	Avg. Qst.	Price	Audience	Format	Bible Study
	—	500	N/A	$24.99		Book	

Features: Bibliography
Personal Application Preparation Time:
Relationship Building Ldr. Guide: Size: 7.25 x 9.25
Subjects: Bible Study, New Testament, Small Group Resource
Comments: This book provides easy-to-read guides to the books of the New Testament, including author information and historical background of each book in a clear outline format. It provides verse-by-verse explanations of New Testament books; a harmonized outline of the life of Christ; the specifics concerning Christ's suffering and death; and the prophecies fulfilled by Christ's coming.

Author: Willmington, Harold L. **1517**
Series:
Title: *New Testament People*
Publisher: Tyndale House, 1990 ISBN: 0-84238-162-7

Num. Sess.	Group Time	Num. Pgs.	Avg. Qst.	Price	Audience	Format	Bible Study
	—	260	N/A	$24.99		Book	

Features:
Personal Application Preparation Time:
Relationship Building Ldr. Guide: Size: 7.25 x 9.25
Subjects: Bible Personalities, Bible Study, Small Group Resource
Comments: This book is written for serious Bible students seeking quick and concise answers about New Testament people. It includes: an alphabetical list of every significant person mentioned in the New Testament; a chronological summary of every name with Scripture reference and a summary of the significance of the event; a theological summary for important characters; the theological issues raised by their lives, their teachings, and Old Testament references.

Author: Willmington, Harold L. **1518**
Series:
Title: *Old Testament Survey*
Publisher: Tyndale House, 1992 ISBN: 0-84238-165-1

Num. Sess.	Group Time	Num. Pgs.	Avg. Qst.	Price	Audience	Format	Bible Study
	—	550	N/A	$24.99		Book	

Features:
Personal Application Preparation Time:
Relationship Building Ldr. Guide: Size: 7.25 x 9.25
Subjects: Bible Study, Old Testament, Small Group Resource
Comments: This book is written for serious Bible students seeking quick and concise answers about the Old Testament. From Genesis to Malachi, an easy-to-read guide to all the books of the Old Testament includes author information and historical background of each book, presented in a clear outline format. It provides verse-be-verse explanations of Old Testament books with a summary of each author's life and the most important verses in each book.

Author: Willmington, Harold L. **1519**
Series:
Title: *Old Testament People*
Publisher: Tyndale House, 1990 ISBN: 0-84238-161-9

Num. Sess.	Group Time	Num. Pgs.	Avg. Qst.	Price	Audience	Format	Bible Study
	—	370	N/A	$24.99		Book	

Features:
Personal Application Preparation Time:
Relationship Building Ldr. Guide: Size: 7.25 x 9.25
Subjects: Bible Personalities, Bible Study, Small Group Resource
Comments: This book includes: an alphabetical list of every significant person mentioned in the Old Testament; a chronological summary of every mention of the name with Scripture reference and a summary of the significance of the event; a theological summary for important characters; the theological issues raised by their lives; their teachings; and New Testament references to them.

Author: Wilson, Rev. Neil S., et al. **1520**
Series: Life Application
Title: *Genesis*
Publisher: Tyndale House, 1989 ISBN: 0-84232-714-2

Num. Sess.	Group Time	Num. Pgs.	Avg. Qst.	Price	Audience	Format	Bible Study
13	60-90	146	13	$4.99	New Christian	Workbk	Book

Features: Intro to Leading a Study, Intro to Study, Study Overview, Digging Deeper Quest, Full Scrpt Printed, Drawings, Charts, Maps, Cross Ref
★★★ Personal Application Preparation Time: Med
★★★ Relationship Building Ldr. Guide: No Size: 6.50 x 9.0
Subjects: Bible Personalities, Faith, Genesis, God, God's Promises, Obedience, Success
Comments: This study covers God's creation of the world and His desire to have a people set apart to worship Him. Key people include Adam, Eve, Noah, Isaac, Jacob, and Joseph. Themes include: beginnings, disobedience, sin, promises, obedience, prosperity, and Israel.

Author: Wilson, Rev. Neil S., et al. **1521**
Series: Life Application
Title: *Joshua*
Publisher: Tyndale House, 1989 ISBN: 0-84232-723-1

Num. Sess.	Group Time	Num. Pgs.	Avg. Qst.	Price	Audience	Format	Bible Study
13	60-90	96	15	$4.99	New Christian	Workbk	Book

Features: Intro to Leading a Study, Intro to Study, Study Overview, Digging Deeper Quest, Full Scrpt Printed, Drawings, Charts, Maps, Cross Ref
★★★ Personal Application Preparation Time: Med
★★★ Relationship Building Ldr. Guide: No Size: 6.50 x 9.0
Subjects: Failure, Joshua, Leadership, Obedience, Success
Comments: In this study, complete with the full text of the book, Joshua outlines the history of Israel's conquest of the Promised Land. It is presented in 3 parts: entering the Promised Land, conquering the Promised Land, and dividing the Promised Land. Themes include success, faith, guidance, leadership, and conquest.

Author: Wimber, John & Kevin Springer **1522**
Series:
Title: *Way To Maturity, The*
Publisher: Regal Books, 1993 ISBN: 0-83071-579-7

Num. Sess.	Group Time	Num. Pgs.	Avg. Qst.	Price	Audience	Format	Bible Study
13	60-90	147	Vary	$9.99	New Christian	Workbk	Topical

Features: Intro to Leading a Study, Intro to Study, Scrpt Memory Helps, Digging Deeper Quest, Charts
★★★★ Personal Application Preparation Time: Low
★★★★ Relationship Building Ldr. Guide: No Size: 6.0 x 9.0
Subjects: Discipleship
Comments: Written for both leader and student, each of thirteen lessons can be used in either 60″ or 90″ time frames. The study can be compressed into 8 sessions (an overview gives the details). Lessons include: "A Changed Life"; "The Way to Maturity"; "Knowing God's Word"; "Hearing God's Voice"; "Knowing God"; "Intimacy With The Father"; "Who Do You Say I Am?" and more.

Author: Wingeier, Douglas E. & David Lowes Watson **1523**
Series:
Title: *Troublesome Bible Passages*
Publisher: Abingdon Press, 1994 ISBN: 0-68778-377-1

Num. Sess.	Group Time	Num. Pgs.	Avg. Qst.	Price	Audience	Format	Bible Study
23	45-60	112	N/A	$2.95	Beginner	Book	Book

Features:
★★★ Personal Application Preparation Time: Low
★★ Relationship Building Ldr. Guide: Yes Size: 5.25 x 8.50
Subjects: Bible Study
Comments: The Bible has many passages that are not fully understood, which Christians often ignore or overlook. This study addresses 23 Scriptures in a way that brings out the transforming message in each passage. It deals with theological, ethical, and practical issues. The study is ideal for classes that seek short-term flexible resources, since units can be studied in any order and class members can rotate teaching.

Author: Wingeier, Douglas E. & David Lowes Watson **1524**
Series:
Title: *Troublesome Bible Passages: Leader's Guide*
Publisher: Abingdon Press, 1994 ISBN: 0-68778-378-X

Num. Sess.	Group Time	Num. Pgs.	Avg. Qst.	Price	Audience	Format	Bible Study
23	45-60	64	Vary	$4.95	Beginner	Book	Book

Features: Prayer Helps
Personal Application Preparation Time:
Relationship Building Ldr. Guide: Size: 8.50 x 11.0
Subjects: Bible Study, Leader's Guide
Comments: The Bible has many passages that are not fully understood, which Christians often ignore or overlook. This study addresses 23 Scriptures in a way that brings out the transforming message in each passage. These troublesome passages deal with theological, ethical, and practical issues. This leader's guide carries step-by-step teaching methods with questions and instructions for other exercises. Homework is encouraged.

Author: Wisner, Don **1525**
Series: Faith Horizons
Title: *Faith & Freedom*
Publisher: Augsburg Fortress Publishers, 1993

Num. Sess.	Group Time	Num. Pgs.	Avg. Qst.	Price	Audience	Format	Bible Study
6	60-75	40	9	$4.95	Beginner	Workbk	Topical

Features: Intro to Study, Prayer Helps, Worship Helps, Follow Up, Photos
★★ Personal Application Preparation Time: Low
★★ Relationship Building Ldr. Guide: No Size: 5.50 x 8.50
Subjects: Teens: Values
Comments: Each book in the Faith Horizons series explores a theme through a topical essay, Bible study, personal reflection and response, and worship. Each offers suggestions for using media (TV, movies, books, music, etc.) to enhance interaction. This study celebrates freedom given in Christ Jesus, and responds to a central question: How does faith lead to true personal freedom?

Author: Wohlrabe, Lawrence R. **1526**
Series: Youth Talk
Title: *Religion*
Publisher: Augsburg Fortress Publishers, 1994

Num. Sess.	Group Time	Num. Pgs.	Avg. Qst.	Price	Audience	Format	Bible Study
5	45-60	46	N/A	$4.95	Beginner	Book	Topical

Features: Prayer Helps, Worship Helps, Photos
★★★★ Personal Application Preparation Time: Low
★★★★ Relationship Building Ldr. Guide: Yes Size: 8.0 x 11.0
Subjects: Teens: Junior High, Teens: Theology
Comments: An alternative to the "textbook approach," these studies are energetic, contemporary, and modeled after popular teen magazines. Advice columns, fiction, poetry, and other features are mostly written by youth. Young people can better respond to conflicting attitudes and beliefs if they know more about their theology. This course helps youth recognize the role of religion in society and appreciate the role of religion in their lives.

Author: Wold, Margaret **1527**
Series: Small Group Bible Studies
Title: *Miracles*
Publisher: Augsburg Fortress Publishers, 1980

Num. Sess.	Group Time	Num. Pgs.	Avg. Qst.	Price	Audience	Format	Bible Study
6	60-75	16	6	$1.35	New Christian	Book	Topical

Features: Intro to Study, Prayer Helps
★★★ Personal Application Preparation Time: None
★★ Relationship Building Ldr. Guide: No Size: 8.50 x 5.50
Subjects: Faith, Jesus: Life/Teaching, Miracles
Comments: This small pamphlet includes 6 sessions on miracles. It is not designed to argue whether or not the miracles actually occurred. That is a matter of faith. However, throughout history many different ways of interpreting miracles have developed, all worthy of discussion. Sessions discuss Jesus' miracles of healing, of feeding, of casting out demons, of faith, and of challenging nature.

Author: Wood, Randy **1528**
Series: Spiritual Development Work
Title: *God, I Need To Talk!*
Publisher: Woman's Missionary Union, 1993 ISBN: 1-56309-066-X

Num. Sess.	Group Time	Num. Pgs.	Avg. Qst.	Price	Audience	Format	Bible Study
5	—	26	N/A	$4.95		Workbk	Topical

Features: Intro to Study, Prayer Helps, Ldr's Notes
Personal Application Preparation Time:
Relationship Building Ldr. Guide: Size: 8.50 x 11.0
Subjects: Teens: Discipleship, Teens: Prayer
Comments: Youths can develop meaningful prayer lives by following these guidelines for public and private prayer, keeping prayer journals and praying for missions. The SDW series is 3 workbooks containing Bible study material that will strengthen youth's prayerlife, stretch their involvement in peer ministry, and exercise youth's personal witnessing skills. Included in this book are ideas, suggestions, and reproducible learning activities for group and individual study.

Author: Woods, Len **1529**
Series: SonPower Youth Sources
Title: *Getting Kids To Mix*
Publisher: Victor Books, 1993 ISBN: 1-56476-115-0

Num. Sess.	Group Time	Num. Pgs.	Avg. Qst.	Price	Audience	Format	Bible Study
	—	127	N/A	$12.99			

Features: Appendix
Personal Application Preparation Time:
Relationship Building Ldr. Guide: Size: 8.50 x 11.0
Subjects: Teens: Resources
Comments: This resource for youth leaders helps youth deepen their relationships with others. The book has 101 events that can get group members to talk and discover more about one another. Each mixer fits on a single page making it easy to copy and distribute to group members. Mixers are included for meeting and greeting, mixing and mingling, and listening and learning. Also included are tips for dividing into small groups, and 101 questions and discussion starters.

Author: Woods, Paul **1530**
Series: Group's Active Bible Curriculum
Title: *Advice to Young Christians: Exploring Paul's Letters*
Publisher: Group Publishing, 1992 ISBN: 1-55945-146-7

Num. Sess.	Group Time	Num. Pgs.	Avg. Qst.	Price	Audience	Format	Bible Study
4	35-60	41	Vary	$9.99	Beginner	Workbk	Topical

Features: Intro to Leading a Study, Intro to Study, Objectives, Study Overview, Ldr's Notes, Handouts, Agenda, Publicity Ideas
★★★★ Personal Application Preparation Time: None
★★★★ Relationship Building Ldr. Guide: No Size: 8.50 x 11.0
Subjects: Teens: Bible Study, Teens: Christian Liv, Teens: Decisions, Teens: Junior High
Comments: In this course, junior highers learn to look to God's Word for answers to life's questions. Drawing from Paul's letters, these lessons help participants grow more thankful for their relationship with God, strive to be humble like Jesus, learn to accept God's protections, and begin to let the Holy Spirit work through them.

Author: Woods, Paul 1531
Series: Group's Active Bible Curriculum
Title: *Applying the Bible to Life*
Publisher: Group Publishing, 1991 ISBN: 1-55945-116-5

Num. Sess.	Group Time	Num. Pgs.	Avg. Qst.	Price	Audience	Format	Bible Study
4	35-60	48	Vary	$9.99	New Christian	Workbk	Topical

Features: Intro to Leading a Study, Intro to Study, Objectives, Study Overview, Ldr's Notes, Drawings, Handouts, Agenda, Publicity Ideas
★★★★ Personal Application Preparation Time: None
★★★★ Relationship Building Ldr. Guide: No Size: 8.50 x 11.0
Subjects: Teens: Bible Study, Teens: Junior High
Comments: This study helps junior high students get excited about reading the Bible. Its 4 lessons allow students to see how the Bible helps them overcome everyday problems and worries; learn an easy-to-use method for personal Bible study; discover how study tools can make reading the Bible fun; examine how Bible study is critical to knowing God; and show how the Bible is a guide to life.

Author: Woods, Paul 1532
Series: Group's Active Bible Curriculum
Title: *Bible Heroes: Joseph, Esther, Mary & Peter*
Publisher: Group Publishing, 1991 ISBN: 1-55945-137-8

Num. Sess.	Group Time	Num. Pgs.	Avg. Qst.	Price	Audience	Format	Bible Study
4	35-60	48	Vary	$9.99	Beginner	Workbk	Charctr

Features: Intro to Leading a Study, Intro to Study, Objectives, Study Overview, Ldr's Notes, Handouts, Agenda, Publicity Ideas
★★★★ Personal Application Preparation Time: None
★★★★ Relationship Building Ldr. Guide: No Size: 8.50 x 11.0
Subjects: Teens: Bible/Pers., Teens: Bible Study, Teens: Junior High
Comments: These lessons help junior highers get excited about reading the Bible. Through this course, participants see how the Bible can help them overcome everyday problems and worries, learn an easy-to-use method for personal Bible study, discover how Bible study tools can make reading it fun, and explore how the Bible can be a guide for life. It can be adapted for a Bible class or youth meeting.

Author: Woods, Paul 1533
Series: Group's Active Bible Curriculum
Title: *Miracles!*
Publisher: Group Publishing, 1991 ISBN: 1-55945-117-3

Num. Sess.	Group Time	Num. Pgs.	Avg. Qst.	Price	Audience	Format	Bible Study
4	35-60	43	Vary	$9.99	Beginner	Workbk	Topical

Features: Intro to Leading a Study, Intro to Study, Objectives, Study Overview, Handouts, Agenda, Publicity Ideas
★★★★ Personal Application Preparation Time: None
★★★★ Relationship Building Ldr. Guide: No Size: 8.50 x 11.0
Subjects: Teens: Junior High, Teens: Miracles
Comments: In this course, junior highers discover the wonder and meaning of Jesus' miracles and learn how He used miracles to meet people's needs and draw them closer to God. Participants learn what a "true" miracle is, discover the miracle of God's power, explore Jesus' miracles and what they mean for today, and learn to recognize the miracles of everyday life. Activity sheets are reproducible.

Author: Woods, Paul 1534
Series: Group's Active Bible Curriculum
Title: *Ten Commandments, The*
Publisher: Group Publishing, 1992 ISBN: 1-55945-127-0

Num. Sess.	Group Time	Num. Pgs.	Avg. Qst.	Price	Audience	Format	Bible Study
4	35-60	44	Vary	$9.99	Beginner	Workbk	Topical

Features: Intro to Leading a Study, Intro to Study, Objectives, Study Overview, Ldr's Notes, Handouts, Agenda, Publicity Ideas
★★★★ Personal Application Preparation Time: None
★★★★ Relationship Building Ldr. Guide: No Size: 8.50 x 11.0
Subjects: Teens: Bible Study, Teens: Christian Liv, Teens: Junior High, Teens: Old Testament
Comments: This course helps junior highers understand the laws that God made and the forgiveness Jesus brought. Participants examine the Ten Commandments as gifts of God's love, understand what Jesus meant when He said loving God is the most important law of all, and discover why thoughts mean as much as deeds.

Author: Woods, Paul 1535
Series: Group's Active Bible Curriculum
Title: *What's a Christian?*
Publisher: Group Publishing, 1990 ISBN: 1-55945-105-X

Num. Sess.	Group Time	Num. Pgs.	Avg. Qst.	Price	Audience	Format	Bible Study
4	35-60	46	Vary	$9.99	Beginner	Workbk	Topical

Features: Intro to Leading a Study, Intro to Study, Objectives, Study Overview, Ldr's Notes, Handouts, Agenda, Publicity Ideas
★★★ Personal Application Preparation Time: None
★★★ Relationship Building Ldr. Guide: No Size: 8.50 x 11.0
Subjects: Teens: Evangelism, Teens: Junior High
Comments: In this study, the basics of Christianity are taught to help teenagers learn to live out their faith in Christ. Four lessons cover the rich history of Christian faith, the meaning and significance of salvation, putting faith into action, and building faith on true hope in Jesus Christ. It can be adapted for use in a Bible class or youth meeting. Activities and Bible studies are included as separate sheets.

Author: Worthington, Dr. Everett 1536
Series:
Title: *I Care About Your Marriage*
Publisher: Moody Press, 1994 ISBN: 0-80241-575-X

Num. Sess.	Group Time	Num. Pgs.	Avg. Qst.	Price	Audience	Format	Bible Study
6	90-120	290	N/A	$9.99	Mature Christian	Book	Topical

Features: No Grp Discussion Quest, Appendix
★★★★ Personal Application Preparation Time: High
★ Relationship Building Ldr. Guide: No Size: 5.50 x 8.50
Subjects: Counseling, Marriage, Self-help, Support
Comments: This manual is for Christians who care enough to get involved in the lives of friends and family with marital problems. It is built on 5 convictions: single or married you can help; you can help more effectively if you know more about both helping and marriage; most important are listening, supporting, know- ing your limits and strengths, and depending on the Lord; understanding God's description of marriage; finally, the realization that a helper is an agent of hope.

Author: Wright, H. Norman **1537**
Series:
Title: *Communication: Key To Your Marriage*
Publisher: Regal Books, 1974 ISBN: 0-83070-726-3

Num. Sess.	Group Time	Num. Pgs.	Avg. Qst.	Price	Audience	Format	Bible Study
10	60-90	190	Vary	$7.99	New Christian	Workbk	Topical

Features: Intro to Study, Bibliography, Drawings
★★★★ Personal Application Preparation Time: Low
★★★★ Relationship Building Ldr. Guide: Yes Size: 5.25 x 7.75
Subjects: Communication
Comments: Based on the premise that effective communication with Christ and one another is the key to marriage, this book helps readers avoid typical pitfalls that trap couples. It explores ways to cope with marital conflict, practical principles for building partner's self-esteem through understanding and respect, methods for handling angry feelings, and steps to avoid the high cost of anxiety and worry. Leader's guide $16.99. A 60"–75" video for $19.99 includes a leader's guide.

Author: Wright, H. Norman **1538**
Series:
Title: *More Communication Keys for Your Marriage*
Publisher: Regal Books, 1983 ISBN: 0-83070-904-5

Num. Sess.	Group Time	Num. Pgs.	Avg. Qst.	Price	Audience	Format	Bible Study
11	60-90	200	Vary	$9.99	Beginner	Workbk	Topical

Features:
★★★★ Personal Application Preparation Time: Low
★★★★ Relationship Building Ldr. Guide: Yes Size: 5.0 x 8.0
Subjects: Emotions, Marriage, Relationships
Comments: Personal involvement is the key feature of 11 sessions designed to involve couples in thinking, interacting, and communicating to build successful marriage relationships. Areas covered include: mutual servanthood, self-talk and how it affects one's emotions, the significance of the past, passive/active coping. The leader's guide includes preparation notes, session guidelines, recommended books, time frames and overhead transparencies. A video is available.

Author: Wright, H. Norman & Gary J. Oliver **1539**
Series:
Title: *Raising Emotionally Healthy Kids*
Publisher: Victor Books, 1995 ISBN: 1-56476-451-6

Num. Sess.	Group Time	Num. Pgs.	Avg. Qst.	Price	Audience	Format	Bible Study
	60-90	240	N/A	$9.99	New Christian	Book	Topical

Features: Intro to Study, Follow Up, Handouts
Personal Application Preparation Time:
Relationship Building Ldr. Guide: Yes Size: 6.0 x 9.0
Subjects: Counseling, Family, Parenting
Comments: Raising emotionally healthy kids may not be easy, but it is possible. Parents can help children understand their God-given emotional natures, and teach them appropriate emotional responses that enable them to develop healthy self-images and relate to God in more meaningful ways. In a paperback edition, available for the first time with a leader's guide, the authors share their combined 50 years of experience counseling Christian families.

Author: Wright, Vinita Hampton **1540**
Series: Fisherman Bible Studyguide
Title: *Angels and Other Spiritual Beings*
Publisher: Shaw, 1995 ISBN: 0-87788-013-1

Num. Sess.	Group Time	Num. Pgs.	Avg. Qst.	Price	Audience	Format	Bible Study
8	4-60	64	12	$4.99	Beginner	Workbk	Topical

Features: Intro to Leading a Study, Intro to Study, Ldr's Notes
★★★ Personal Application Preparation Time: None
★★★ Relationship Building Ldr. Guide: No Size: 5.0 x 8.25
Subjects: Angels
Comments: Using biblical stories this study looks at various ways angels minister and work as messengers, protectors, and providers.

Author: Wright, Vinita Hampton **1541**
Series: Fisherman Bible Studyguide
Title: *Doing Justice, Showing Mercy*
Publisher: Shaw, 1993 ISBN: 0-87788-180-4

Num. Sess.	Group Time	Num. Pgs.	Avg. Qst.	Price	Audience	Format	Bible Study
13	45-60	94	12	$4.99	New Christian	Workbk	Topical

Features: Intro to Leading a Study, Intro to Study, Prayer Helps, Follow Up, Ldr's Notes
★★★★ Personal Application Preparation Time: Low
★★★ Relationship Building Ldr. Guide: No Size: 5.25 x 8.25
Subjects: Old Testament, Prophecy
Comments: This 13-week study explores biblical principles concerning power, leadership, our response to the poor, mercy, and the role of Christ in bringing about justice. Christians aware of injustices will find answers to questions such as, "How are we to respond?" and "Can one person make a difference?" Many of the passages used in the study come from Old Testament law and prophecy.

Author: Wright, Vinita Hampton **1542**
Series: Fisherman Bible Studyguide
Title: *Prophets, The: God's Truth Tellers*
Publisher: Shaw, 1994 ISBN: 0-87788-665-2

Num. Sess.	Group Time	Num. Pgs.	Avg. Qst.	Price	Audience	Format	Bible Study
13	45-60	87	13	$4.99	New Christian	Workbk	Charctr

Features: Intro to Leading a Study, Intro to Study, Prayer Helps, Ldr's Notes
★★★★ Personal Application Preparation Time: Low
★★ Relationship Building Ldr. Guide: No Size: 5.25 x 8.25
Subjects: Old Testament, Prophecy
Comments: This study helps participants understand God's truth anew through the lives and messages of 13 prophets from Elijah to John the Baptist. The study reveals a variety of personalities' poignant life stories, wisdom about life, relationships with one another and with God. The prophets spoke with courage about things that were both fascinating and frightening to hear.

Author: Wright, Vinita Hampton **1543**
Series: Fisherman Bible Studyguide
Title: *Proverbs: Wisdom That Works*
Publisher: Shaw, 1995 ISBN: 0-87788-668-7

Num. Sess.	Group Time	Num. Pgs.	Avg. Qst.	Price	Audience	Format	Bible Study
12	45-50	80	12	$4.99	Beginner	Workbk	Book

Features: Intro to Leading a Study, Intro to Study, Ldr's Notes
★★★ Personal Application Preparation Time: None
★★ Relationship Building Ldr. Guide: No Size: 5.0 x 8.25
Subjects: Proverbs, Wisdom
Comments: The world keeps changing, yet certain life issues remain the same: a need for work and discipline, perspective in good and bad times, the ability to think through words and actions, and the practice of moral character with integrity, wisdom, and kindness. The sayings collected in the book of Proverbs gave practical handles to these matters thousands of years ago, and their wisdom is as refreshing and helpful today as ever.

Author: Wunder, Jerry, et al. **1544**
Series: HomeBuilders Couples
Title: *Expressing Love in Your Marriage*
Publisher: Gospel Light Publications, 1994 ISBN: 0-83071-668-8

Num. Sess.	Group Time	Num. Pgs.	Avg. Qst.	Price	Audience	Format	Bible Study
6	60-90	140	Vary	$9.99	Beginner	Workbk	Topical

Features: Intro to Study, Appendix
★★★★ Personal Application Preparation Time: Low
★★★★ Relationship Building Ldr. Guide: Yes Size: 5.75 x 8.50
Subjects: Family, Marriage
Comments: This study recognizes that at times it's painfully difficult to express love for one's mate. Couples can rejoice when they learn how to consistently express love, why patience and kindness are essential, and ways to discover true oneness in marriage by considering the needs of a spouse. It teaches how to solve conflict constructively, how to open the channels for love, and how living biblically can strengthen and secure marriage.

Author: Yancey, Philip & Tim Stafford **1545**
Series:
Title: *Students Guide to the Bible, The*
Publisher: Zondervan, 1988 ISBN: 0-31058-961-4

Num. Sess.	Group Time	Num. Pgs.	Avg. Qst.	Price	Audience	Format	Bible Study
	—	96	N/A	$4.95	Beginner	Workbk	No

Features: Intro to Study, Study Overview
Personal Application Preparation Time:
Relationship Building Ldr. Guide: Size: 7.0 x 9.0
Subjects: Bible Study, Teens: Bible Study
Comments: This guide for students introduces each Bible book, giving keen insight into the story line, eliminating much of the mystery, and enhancing its wonderment and sense of adventure. Written in magazine style, the guide is especially helpful for those reading the Bible for the first time. Blanks for taking notes follow the introduction to each lesson, and enhance the guide's use in study groups.

Author: Yandala, Deborah S. **1546**
Series: Youth Talk
Title: *Relationships*
Publisher: Augsburg Fortress Publishers, 1994

Num. Sess.	Group Time	Num. Pgs.	Avg. Qst.	Price	Audience	Format	Bible Study
5	45-60	46	7	$4.95	Beginner	Book	Topical

Features: Prayer Helps, Worship Helps, Photos
★★★★ Personal Application Preparation Time: Low
★★★★ Relationship Building Ldr. Guide: Yes Size: 8.0 x 11.0
Subjects: Teens: Discipleship, Teens: Family, Teens: Friends, Teens: Junior High
Comments: These studies are modeled after popular teen magazines. Advice columns, fiction, poetry, and other features are mostly written by youth. This course helps youth use the example of God's relationship with creation to examine their relationships with family and friends. Topics: Somebody worth knowing, Families at work, Being a friend, In place of prejudice, Differing abilities.

Author: Yernberg, Ralph **1547**
Series: Youth Talk
Title: *Voices & Messages*
Publisher: Augsburg Fortress Publishers, 1994

Num. Sess.	Group Time	Num. Pgs.	Avg. Qst.	Price	Audience	Format	Bible Study
5	45-60	46	N/A	$4.95	Beginner	Book	Topical

Features: Prayer Helps, Worship Helps, Photos
★★★★ Personal Application Preparation Time: Low
★★★★ Relationship Building Ldr. Guide: Yes Size: 8.0 x 11.0
Subjects: Teens: Decisions, Teens: Junior High, Teens: Media, Teens: Music
Comments: These studies are modeled after popular teen magazines. Advice columns, fiction, poetry, and other features are mostly written by youth. This course helps youth explore and discern the messages they receive, and respond in ways that affirm their faith. Topics: Media madness, Its got rhythm, TV time, Film fans, and Conscience and choice.

Author: Yoder, George and Virginia Knueppel **1548**
Series: Cross Signs
Title: *Where in the World? Called to Be a Community of Faith*
Publisher: Augsburg Fortress Publishers, 1992

Num. Sess.	Group Time	Num. Pgs.	Avg. Qst.	Price	Audience	Format	Bible Study
7	90-105	48	5	$3.75	New Christian	Book	Topical

Features: Intro to Study, Prayer Helps, Worship Helps
★★★ Personal Application Preparation Time: Low
★★ Relationship Building Ldr. Guide: Yes Size: 5.50 x 8.50
Subjects: Christian Living, Faith
Comments: In this study a number of "call" narratives from the Bible focus on how community of faith is created through God's calling. The texts that form the basis for this unit are, in many respects, like familiar places in people's lives. They include some of the Bible's grand, pivotal texts. The texts review the identity and purpose of God's people, which in turn have shaped people's sense of identity and purpose over many centuries.

Author: Yohn, Rick 1549
Series: Living Studies
Title: *Discover Your Spiritual Gift and Use It*
Publisher: Tyndale House, 1974 ISBN: 0-84230-626-9

Num. Sess.	Group Time	Num. Pgs.	Avg. Qst.	Price	Audience	Format	Bible Study
13	60-90	154	N/A	$7.99	Mature Christian	Book	Topical

Features: Bibliography, No Grp Discussion Quest
★★ Personal Application Preparation Time: Low
★★ Relationship Building Ldr. Guide: No Size: 5.0 x 8.0
Subjects: Discipleship, Spiritual Gifts
Comments: This book argues that God gives every believer gifts for maximum service, and examines the relevancy and necessity of spiritual gifts for contemporary Christians. It outlines New Testament gifts, discusses their biblical meaning, and describes contemporary ways they can be used. It makes the case that these gifts are not to be exercised only within church walls, but wherever there is need. Study questions are not provided.

Author: Younger, Carol 1550
Series: Group's Active Bible Curriculum
Title: *Overcoming Insecurities*
Publisher: Group Publishing, 1991 ISBN: 1-55945-221-8

Num. Sess.	Group Time	Num. Pgs.	Avg. Qst.	Price	Audience	Format	Bible Study
4	35-60	48	Vary	$9.99	Beginner	Workbk	Topical

Features: Intro to Leading a Study, Intro to Study, Objectives, Study Overview, Ldr's Notes, Handouts, Agenda, Publicity Ideas
★★★★ Personal Application Preparation Time: None
★★★★ Relationship Building Ldr. Guide: No Size: 8.50 x 11.0
Subjects: Teens: Christian Liv, Teens: Self-esteem, Teens: Senior High
Comments: Four participatory sessions show senior highers how to find self-esteem in their relationship with God. Participants discover their unique talents and skills, explore how to be confident without being arrogant, examine the value of humility, and learn that God has a purpose for each person's life. It can be adapted for a Bible class or youth meeting. Activity sheets are reproducible.

Author: Yount, Christine 1551
Series: Group's Active Bible Curriculum
Title: *Responding to Injustice*
Publisher: Group Publishing, 1991 ISBN: 1-55945-214-5

Num. Sess.	Group Time	Num. Pgs.	Avg. Qst.	Price	Audience	Format	Bible Study
4	35-60	48	Vary	$9.99	New Christian	Workbk	Topical

Features: Intro to Leading a Study, Intro to Study, Objectives, Study Overview, Ldr's Notes, Drawings, Handouts, Agenda, Publicity Ideas
★★★★ Personal Application Preparation Time: None
★★★★ Relationship Building Ldr. Guide: No Size: 8.50 x 11.0
Subjects: Teens: Ethics, Teens: Relationships, Teens: Senior High
Comments: This 4-lesson study helps senior highs learn to recognize injustice and respond with Christian love, commit themselves toward eliminating prejudice, examine what the Bible says about personal rights, discover why some people play favorites and learn practical ways to confront favoritism, and learn how they can make a positive difference in the world.

Author: Yount, Christine 1552
Series: Group's Active Bible Curriculum
Title: *Telling Your Friends About Christ*
Publisher: Group Publishing, 1991 ISBN: 1-55945-114-9

Num. Sess.	Group Time	Num. Pgs.	Avg. Qst.	Price	Audience	Format	Bible Study
4	35-60	48	Vary	$9.99	New Christian	Workbk	Topical

Features: Intro to Leading a Study, Intro to Study, Objectives, Study Overview, Ldr's Notes, Drawings, Handouts, Agenda, Publicity Ideas
★★★★ Personal Application Preparation Time: None
★★★★ Relationship Building Ldr. Guide: No Size: 8.50 x 11.0
Subjects: Teens: Evangelism, Teens: Junior High
Comments: This 4-lesson study helps youth learn practical skills for sharing their faith. Teens will understand their friends' need for Christ, how to reach out, how to tell others, and how to develop their own method for telling others about their relationship with God. They can be used in a Bible class or youth meeting. Instructions are easy to follow and provide multiple options for teachers.

Author: Youssef, Michael 1553
Series:
Title: *Leadership Style of Jesus, The*
Publisher: Victor Books, 1986 ISBN: 0-89693-168-4

Num. Sess.	Group Time	Num. Pgs.	Avg. Qst.	Price	Audience	Format	Bible Study
13	60-90	168	N/A	$7.99	New Christian	Book	Topical

Features:
★★★ Personal Application Preparation Time: Med
★★★ Relationship Building Ldr. Guide: Yes Size: 5.50 x 8.0
Subjects: Gospels, Leadership, Loneliness, Stress
Comments: This study outlines Jesus' style of leadership, as derived from the Gospel accounts. It uses 18 principles to suggest Christlike qualities every leader needs. It also considers how to deal with the temptations and pressures leaders face, including ego, anger, loneliness, doubters, criticism, the use of power, and passing the leadership torch to others. A leader's guide with transparency masters is available.

PERSONAL GROWTH BOOKSHELF

$3 OFF PURCHASE OF SINGLE TITLE

ATTENTION CUSTOMER:
Offer expires 12/31/96. No Cash Value. Coupon is redeemable at time of purchase. No photocopies will be accepted.

ATTENTION DEALER:
Mail coupons directly to Publisher at:
Victor Books
1825 College Ave.
Wheaton, IL 60187
Credits will be posted directly to your account by Publisher.

VICTOR BOOKS

TRUTHSEED SERIES

$1 OFF EACH COPY (SINGLE OR ASSORTED TITLES)
-LIMIT $5 MAXIMUM

ATTENTION CUSTOMER:
Offer expires 12/31/96. No Cash Value. Coupon is redeemable at time of purchase. No photocopies will be accepted.

ATTENTION DEALER:
Mail coupons directly to Publisher at:
Victor Books
1825 College Ave.
Wheaton, IL 60187
Credits will be posted directly to your account by Publisher.

VICTOR BOOKS

MOVING TOWARD MATURITY SERIES

$2 OFF ANY ONE TITLE ($5.99 +)

ATTENTION CUSTOMER:
Offer expires 12/31/96. No Cash Value. Coupon is redeemable at time of purchase. No photocopies will be accepted.

ATTENTION DEALER:
Mail coupons directly to Publisher at:
Victor Books
1825 College Ave.
Wheaton, IL 60187
Credits will be posted directly to your account by Publisher.

VICTOR BOOKS

SONPOWER BIBLELOG SERIES

$2 OFF PURCHASE OF SINGLE TITLE

ATTENTION CUSTOMER:
Offer expires 12/31/96. No Cash Value. Coupon is redeemable at time of purchase. No photocopies will be accepted.

ATTENTION DEALER:
Mail coupons directly to Publisher at:
Victor Books
1825 College Ave
Wheaton, IL 60187
Credits will be posted directly to your account by Publisher.

VICTOR BOOKS

EVELYN CHRISTENSON

$2 OFF ANY ONE TITLE:
Battling the Prince of Darkness
Journey Into Prayer
Lord Change Me
What Happens When God Answers Prayer
What Happens When We Pray for Our Families
What Happens When Women Pray

ATTENTION CUSTOMER:
Offer expires 12/31/96. No Cash Value. Coupon is redeemable at time of purchase. No photocopies will be accepted.

ATTENTION DEALER:
Mail coupons directly to Publisher at:
Victor Books
1825 College Ave.
Wheaton, IL 60187
Credits will be posted directly to your account by Publisher.

VICTOR BOOKS